D0116947

UNIVERSITY OF WASHINGTON PUBLICATIONS
IN
LANGUAGE AND LITERATURE

Volume 10                                                   May, 1938

# A REFERENCE GUIDE TO THE LITERATURE OF TRAVEL

Including Voyages, Geographical Descriptions, Adventures, Shipwrecks and Expeditions

BY

EDWARD GODFREY COX

VOLUME TWO
## THE NEW WORLD

GREENWOOD PRESS, PUBLISHERS
NEW YORK

Originally published in 1938 and reprinted
with the permission of the University of Washington Press

First Greenwood Reprinting 1969

Library of Congress Catalogue Card Number 70-90492

SBN 8371-2162-0

PRINTED IN UNITED STATES OF AMERICA

## Preface

It will be noticed that in these two volumes I have included no items dealing with travel in Great Britain and Eire. It has been my intention to make a third volume of such references, either separately or in connection with a projected work on travel in England in the eighteenth century. The accomplishment of such a project, however, lies concealed in the future. But toward this end I have already accumulated a large amount of material.

Edward Godfrey Cox
University of Washington

Seattle, Washington
May 13, 1938

# Contents of Volume Two

# I

## Northwest Passage

1576 GILBERT, SIR HUMPHREY. A Discourse of a Discoverie for a Newe Passage to Cataia, and the East Indies. 4to. London.

This tract expresses Gilbert's view that the continent of America was an island, representing the Atlantis of Plato and other writers of antiquity. Written several years before publication it is among the most notable contributions to the subject of exploration preceding the monumental work of Hakluyt.—*Camb. Hist. Eng. Lit.*, IV, v. He argues with much plausibility the existence of ocean currents which starting from the Cape of Good Hope, moved across the Atlantic to the Strait of Magellan, whence the surplus flowed north and through the Northwest Passage and down to China, the Moluccas, and back to their starting point at the Cape. Richard Willes, in his enlarged edition of Eden (See Eden below under 1577), wrote a discourse sustaining Gilbert's views. Frobisher was probably the first to put these theories to a test.—Gilbert used a variety of sources, some of them second-hand. His knowledge of English attempts at western discovery was really very meagre.—Taylor. For a Latin poem on the voyage see below.

1582 PARMENIUS, STEPHANUS, BUDAEUS. De Navigatione Humfredi Gilberte Carmen. London.

So cited by Taylor, who adds that the author had been brought to London by Hakluyt of Oxford to meet the principal adventurers and friends of this voyage.

1577 EDEN, RICHARD. For Willes' Discourse on the Northwest Passage see Eden's *History of Travayle in the West and East Indies,* under COLLECTIONS.

SETTLE, DIONYSE. A True Report of the last Voyage into the West and Northwest Regions, . . . 1517, worthily atchieued by Capteine Frobisher of the sayde Voyage the First Finder and Generall. With a Description of the People there inhabiting, and other Circumstances notable. Written by Dionyse Settle, one of the Companie in the sayde Voyage, and seruant to the Right Honourable the Earle of Cumberland. 8vo. London. (24 leaves.)

There were two editions the same year, with some slight differences.—Lowndes. Reprinted in Pinkerton XII, 494-503. Translated into French, 1578. This version was turned into German, Gerlachen, 1580; into Latin, Nürnberg, 1580. Another Latin edition, Hamburg, 1675, and an Italian version, Naples, 1582. See below and also under Best and Churchyard under 1578, this section.
This is an account of Frobisher's second voyage in 1577, and is the rarest of all Frobisher material and one of the rarest of books in the English portion of Americana. Both Settle and Best accompanied Frobisher on this voyage, but there are a number of variations between the accounts of the two.—From Waldman. Frobisher made three voyages to the Northwest,—in 1576, 1577, and 1578. The first had the interest and support of Queen Elizabeth, the Earls of Warwick, Leicester, and Pembroke, the merchant Michael Lok, Richard Willes, and others. The new land discovered, which was the southeast part of Baffin Island, received

the name of Meta Incognita. Greenland may also be said to have been rediscovered. But what was of most consequence was the finding of the "peece of blacke stone," which excited the gold fever. The second voyage concerned itself less with discoveries than with ore, of which 200 tons were brought back and found to be of no value. The third voyage had for its object establishing a colony in Meta Incognita. Storms and disasters pursued the attempt, which was as futile as it was ill-advised. The pioneer work of Frobisher was carried on by John Davis (see Davis under 1595-98 below).

1578    (In French.)   La Navigation dv Capitaine Martin Frobisher Anglois, en regions de west et Nordwest, en l'année M.D.LXXVII. Contenant les moeurs et facons de viure des Peuples, et habitants d'icelles, auec le portraict de leur habits et armes, et autres choses memorables et singulières, du tout incognues par deca. 8vo. Geneva.

   So cited in the John Carter Brown catalogue.

1580    (In German.)   Beschreibung seiner Schiffahrt aus Engellandt in die Gegendt West und Nordwest im Jahre 1577. Aus dem Französische ins Teutsche gebracht.   Nürnberg.

1580    (In Latin.)   De Martini Forbisseri Anglii Navigatione in Regiones Occidentis et Septentrionis Narratio historica, ex Gallico sermone in Latinum translata per J. T. Freigium.   Folding woodcut frontispiece of Greenlanders with canoe spearing fish, etc.   Gerlachen.

   This, the first Latin edition of Frobisher's second voyage, was translated from the French edition. The name of the translator appears also as Joan. Tho. Fruhium or Frugium.

1582    (In Italian.)   Lo scoprimento della Artico et di Meta incognita retrovato nel anno 1577 e 1588 (*sic*) dal Capitano Martino Forbisero inglese, posto nel italiano.   Naples.

   So cited in Lowndes. In the Hakluyt Society edition of Frobisher's voyages the name of the translator is given as Geo. Lor. Anania.

1675    (In Latin.)   Historia Navigationis Martini Forbisseri Angli Praetoris sive Capitanei A.D. 1577 . . . jussu Reginae Elisabethae . . . in Septentrionis et Occidentis tractum susceptae . . . a Joh. Freigio translata.   Engraved frontispiece, with a compartment showing a small map of Frobisher's Strait.   Hamburg.

   This edition contains much that is not found in the earlier edition. —Robinson, No. 20.


1578   BEST, GEORGE.   A Trve Discovrse of the late Voyage of Discouerie, for the finding of a Passage to Cathaya, by the Northvvest, vnder the Conduct of Martin Frobisher Generall: Deuided into three Bookes. In the first whereof is shewed, his first Voyage, wherein also by the vvay is sette out a Geographicall Description of the Worlde, and what partes thereof haue bin discouered by the Nauigations of the Englishmen. Also, there are annexed certayne Reasons, to proue all partes of the Worlde habitable, with a generall Mappe adioyned. In the second, is set out his second Voyage, vvith the Aduentures and Accidents thereof. In the thirde, is declared the strange Fortunes which hapned in the thirde Voyage, with a seuerall Description of the Countrey and the People there inhabiting. VVith a particular Card therevnto adioyned of Meta Incognita, so farre forth as the Secretes of the Voyage may permit. 4to. London.

These three voyages, taken from Hakluyt's edition, were reprinted by the Hakluyt Society, London 1867. Three other accounts of them appeared in Pinkerton XII, 490 ff., made up of Christopher Hall's account of the first voyage, of the second Settle's, of the third Thomas Ellis's, etc. The three, presumably Best's account, translated into Dutch, Leyden, 1706, Pieter van der Aa's Collection. See below.

The most comprehensive of the half dozen accounts written and printed in 1577-78 which have survived to us is that of Captain George Best. It contains one of the most important world maps of the time.—Waldman.

1867 FROBISHER, MARTIN. The three Voyages of Sir Martin Frobisher, In search of a Passage to Cathaia and India by the North-West, A.D. 1576-78. By George Best. Reprinted from the First Edition of Hakluyt's Voyages. With Selections from MS. Documents in the British Museum and State Paper Office. Edited by Admiral Sir Richard Collinson, K.C.B. 2 maps and 1 illus. Hak. Soc., ser. I, vol. 38. London.

1706 (In Dutch.) Drie seldsame scheeps-togten van Martin Frobisher. De eerste na China in het jaar 1576; de tweede na Cataya, China en Oost-Indien in het jaar 1577; de derda na Cataya in het jaar 1578. Door een der reysigers in het Engels beschreeven, en nu aldereerst vertalt. Leyden.

CHURCHYARD, THOMAS. A Prayse and Reporte of Maister Martyne Frobisher's Voyage to Meta Incognita. 16mo. London.

This has to do with the second voyage. It casts a number of interesting lights on current opinion in England, as, for instance, the assertion, based on Eden, that Cabot explored the coast from 67 to 36 degrees latitude.—Waldman.

CHURCHYARD, THOMAS. A Welcome home to M. Martin Frobisher, and all those Gentlemen and Souldiers that have bene with him this last Journey in the Countrey, called Meta Incognita; whiche welcome was written since this Booke was put to the Printing, and ioyned to the same Book for a true Testimony of Churchyarde's good will for the furtherance of Mayster Frobisher's fame. London.

ELLIS, THOMAS. A True Report of Martin Frobisher, his third and last voyage written by Thomas Ellis, sailor and one of the Company. London.

Cited as by John Ellis under date of 1577 by Parks.

1595 DAVIS, JOHN. Account of his second Voyage to discover a Northwest Passage in 1586. London.

Davis made three voyages in search of the Northwest Passage—in 1585, 1586, and 1587. The account of the second he wrote himself; the other two were written by John James. All three were reprinted by the Hakluyt Society, London,

1878. See below. For his dealings with the problem of the Northwest Passage see his *The Worldes Hydrographical Description* under 1595, GEOGRAPHY.

Davis carried the work of exploration in the northwest further ahead than any navigator had hitherto done, and added materially to the geographical knowledge of what was known of Greenland. Besides he penetrated farther towards the real Northwest Passage, in whose existence he firmly believed. His log of the third voyage alone is preserved.

1878  DAVIS, JOHN. The Voyages and Works of John Davis the Navigator. Edited by Capt. Albert Hastings Markham, R.N. 2 maps, 15 illus., bibliography, and index. Hak. Soc., ser. I, vol. 59. London.

1596  DAVIS, JOHN. A Traverse Book made by John Davis in his third Voyage for the Discoverie of the North-west Passage in 1587. London.

1612  The Circumference of the Earth or a Relacon on the North-west Passage. London.

So entered in the *Stationers' Register*.

1622  BRIGGS, HENRY. Treatise on the North-West Passage to the South Sea, through the Continent of Virginia, and by Fretum Hudson. 4to. London.

The author was a mathematician of some fame, who published various works on mathematics, arithmetic, navigation, etc. The above work was signed with his initials only, and appeared as an Appendix to the second edition of Edward Waterhouse's *Declaration of the Colony and Affaires in Virginia*, London, 1622. It was reprinted in full by Purchas. It is full of erroneous and amusingly absurd speculations.—From Hakluyt Society volume for 1893.

1633  JAMES, THOMAS. The Strange and Dangerous Voyage of Captaine Thomas Iames, in his intended Discouery of the Northwest Passage into the South Sea . . . To which are added, A Plat or Card for the Sayling in those Seas. Diuers little Tables of the Authors, of the Variation of the Compasse, &c. With an Appendix concerning Longitude, by Master Henry Gellibrand . . . Large folding map of the region from Labrador to Greenland. 4to. London.

2nd edit., revised and corrected, 8vo, London, 1740 (said to be inferior to the original); reprinted in Churchill II, 428-488; in Harris II, 406-436; in Daniel Coxe's Collection, 1741; see also the Hakluyt Society edition of Luke Foxe, 1893, under Foxe, 1635, below.

James, a Bristol man of Welsh origin, started in May, 1631, and returned home in September, 1632, having met Luke Foxe somewhere in Button's Bay. His record is full of hardships and perils, and is said to have supplied Coleridge with some of the matter of his "Ancient Mariner." As a good Welshman, James named the region south of Hudson's Bay New South Wales, while Foxe, who was from Hull, called it New Yorkshire.—Quaritch. James was forced by exceptionally bad weather into Hudson's Bay and wintered in the southern portion now called James Bay. His voyage was due solely to a wholesome feeling of rivalry between the merchants of Bristol and those of London. His account was printed by King

Charles' I command. It contains some remarkable physical observations respecting the intensity of the cold and the accumulation of ice in northern latitudes.— Lowndes. In many respects the voyage was a failure and nearly put an end to Northwest explorations, but it has left its mark in our Atlas of North America.— Maggs, No. 465. James represents the new spirit of science in the nautical world. He was sensible of the proper knowledge of navigation, and of the need of proper instruments. Before putting to sea he had endeavored to extend his former studies by obtaining journals, charts, descriptions, etc., and set skilful craftsmen to work making quadrants, staves, semi-circles, and compass needles. The school of experience was represented by Foxe.—*Cam. Hist. Eng. Lit.* IV, v.

1744-48  JAMES, THOMAS. The accurate and admirable Voyage of Captain Thomas James, for the Discovery of a Passage into the South Sea, by the North-West; his Wintering in Charlton Island, and wonderful Return with his Ship, and most of the Crew, into England. Extracted from his own Account and delivered in his own Words. In Harris II, 406-436.

1635  FOX, LUKE (Captain). North-VVest Fox, or Fox from the Northwest Passage, Beginning with King Arthur, Malga, Octhur, the Two Zeni's of Iseland, Estotiland and Dorgia: Following with Briefe Abstracts of the Voyages of Cabot, Frobisher, Davis, Weymouth, Knight, Hudson, Button, Gibbons, Bylot, Baffin, Hawkridge . . . Mr. Iames Hall's Three Voyages to Groynland . . . With the Author His Owne Voyage, being the XVI . . . By Capitaine Lvke Foxe of Kingstone Vpon Hull, Captain and Pylot for the Voyage, in His Majesties Pinnace the Charles. London.

Reprinted, with James' Voyage, by the Hakluyt Society, London, 1893. See below.

Foxe sailed on May 5, 1631, and returned home within six months, having in the meantime explored the western part of Hudson's Bay. In leading up to his own voyage through those of his predecessors, he was merely following the precedent of other writers, notably John Smith, whose *General History* had only just dropped from the best seller class . . . He gives a great deal of valuable information on ice, tides, bearings and northern phenomena.—From Waldman. Foxe belonged to the old school of seamen who had learned in the practical business of the sea. He derides the "mathematicall sea-man," who, he avers, would fail in contest with the "ruffe and boisterous Ocean."—*Camb. Hist. Eng. Lit.* IV, v. Early voyagers to the Northwest did not seem to have published in separate form detailed accounts of their explorations, though there are narratives of most of them in Hakluyt and Purchas. Foxe and James were almost the first to issue separately published works describing voyages in search of the Northwest Passage. These two companion volumes are noteworthy in that both record voyages that were made in the same year (1631), to the same place, and with the same object. The two captains met by accident at the scene of their explorations and exchanged information. See the Introduction to the Hakluyt Society volume cited below. These voyages closed this phase of exploration.

1893  FOXE, CAPTAIN LUKE, and JAMES, CAPTAIN THOMAS. The Voyages of Captain Luke Foxe, of Hull, and Captain Thomas James, of Bristol, In Search of a North-West Passage, 1631-32; with Narratives of the Earlier North-West Voyages of Frobisher, Davis, Weymouth, Hall, etc. Edited with Notes and Introduction, by Miller Christy, F.L.S. Maps and illus. 2 vols. Hak. Soc., ser. I, vols. 88-89.

1674  MOXON, JOSEPH.  A Brief Discourse of a Passage by the North Pole to Japon.  London.

> Issued again in 1675 and 1697.

1732  MONCK, JOHN (Captain).  An account of a most Dangerous Voyage Performed by the Famous Capt. J. Monck in the Yeares 1619 and 1620, by the special Command of Christian IV, King of Denmark, Norway, . . . to Hudson's Straits, in order to discover a Passage on that Side, betwixt Greenland and America to the East Indies.  With a Description of Old and New Greenland, for the better Elucidation of the said Treatise.  Translated from the High Dutch Original.  In Churchill II, 422-426.

> This "High Dutch Original" was really the first German version of Isaac de la Peyrère's *Relation. du Groênland,* a fact of which the editors of Churchill's Collection were ignorant.  See La Peyrère under 1732, ARCTIC REGIONS.  The first English translation of Munk's own journal was done for the Hakluyt Society, vol. II, 1897 (see this date under ARCTIC REGIONS).  An edition, 2 vols., London, 1748-49, is cited in Chavanne.  Danish original, Copenhagen, 1624.  See below.
>
> Captain Jens Munk was a much travelled and experienced officer in the Danish navy.  When the newly formed Danish East India Company planned to send an expedition to India they selected Munk, with the consent of the King, for the command of the vessels.  Munk chose to go by the Northwest Passage, which was supposed to exist though yet to be discovered.  He wintered on the west coast of Hudson's Bay at the mouth of Churchill River, where he and his crew suffered so severely from scurvy that only himself and two others escaped the ravages of the disease.  The survivors managed finally to return to Denmark in the smaller of the two ships, leaving the Danish East India Company probably wiser but undoubtedly sadder at the loss of a ship and the money invested.

>> 1624  MUNK JENS.  Navigatio Septentrionalis.  Det er: Relation Eller Beschriffuelse, om Seiglade oc Reyse, paa denne Nord vestiske Passagie, som nu kaldes Nova Dania . . . 4to.  Copenhagen.
>>
>> This work was known at second hand through Lyschander's *Chronica,* a popular piece in verse, based on the accounts of voyagers to Greenland, and La Peyrère's *Relation du Groênland,* Paris, 1647.  This latter was translated into German, Frankfort, 1650, and thence into English by the Churchills for their 1704 Collection.

1743  MIDDLETON, CHRISTOPHER.  A Vindication of the Conduct of Captain Christopher Middleton, in a late Voyage on board His Majesty's Ship the Furnace, for discovering a North-West Passage to the Western American Ocean.  In answer to certain Objections and Aspersions of Arthur Dobbs, Esq.  8vo.  London.

> Reprinted, Dublin, 1744.  An account of Middleton's voyage in Harris II, 437-451.  Extracts from his log printed in the Hakluyt Society volume for 1852.  See below.
>
> The charter of the Hudson's Bay Company enjoined on its directors the duty of undertaking exploration as well as engaging in trade.  In answer to the criticisms that they had neglected their obligations, they sent Captain Middleton in 1742 to find a passage west of Southampton Island.  Considerable controversy arose over this voyage, some of which is listed below.  The doubt thrown on Mid-

dleton's account of his voyage sent to Dobbs may well have been written by John Wygate, clerk to the *Furnace* on this expedition. The latter seems to have had a decided grudge against Middleton because of this officer's attitude toward his men. In the MS. record he kept of the trip, he writes: "He (the captain) treated all on board as blockheads and fools, thro' his Vanity, Ostentation, and superiority of Post. Nobody dared speak their minds freely, tho' never so reasonably or modestly, but what they said was always turned to ridicule, or answer'd with an angry countenance and sharp words." Middleton, in his account given to the Admiralty, on his part complained that more might have been done had not the ships been "pestered with such a set of rogues, most of them having deserved hanging before they entered with me." It seems quite evident from this Manuscript of Wygate's that Middleton did not do all in his power toward effecting the discovery of the Northwest Passage during this expedition.—From Maggs, No. 549.

1744-48 MIDDLETON, CHRISTOPHER. The late Attempts made for the discovery of a Passage to the South Sea, from Hudson's Bay, more particularly that of Capt. Christopher Middleton, Commander of His Majesty's Sloop the *Furnace*, Interspersed with original Papers. In Harris II, 437-451.

The rational and philosophical Motives for seeking a Passage into the South Seas by the North-west examined and explained; together with the History of the Attempts made with that View for the Space of 130 years. In Harris II, 399-405.

1744 DOBBS, ARTHUR. Remarks on Capt. Middleton's Defence, wherein his Conduct during a Passage from Hudson's Bay to the South Sea is impartially considered. London.

Dobbs was the chief promoter of an expedition in 1741 to discover the Northwest Passage through Hudson's Straits. Middleton had announced on his return from his voyage of that same year that what had at one time been thought to be the passage was only a large river. Dobbs at first accepted this statement, but some one sent him an anonymous letter suggesting that Middleton was in connivance with the Hudson's Bay Company. Hence the series of controversial pamphlets that ensued. Finally another expedition was sent out and Middleton was proved to be correct. See Dobbs under 1744, NORTH AMERICA; under 1754, NORTH PACIFIC; Ellis and Swindrage under 1748 below; Swindrage under 1768 below; and the Hakluyt Society volume under 1852 below.

1744 Reply to the Remarks of Arthur Dobbs on Capt. Middleton's Vindication of his Conduct on board H.M.S. Furnace when Sent in Search of a North-west Passage, by Hudson's Bay to the Western American Ocean. 8vo. London.

1745 DOBBS, ARTHUR. A Reply to Capt. Middleton's Answer to the Remarks on Vindication of his Conduct on a Voyage for a North-West Passage. London.

1745 MIDDLETON, CHRISTOPHER. Forgery Detected, by which it is evidenced, how groundless are all the Calumnies cast upon the Editor, in a Pamphlet published under the name of Arthur Dobbs. 8vo. London.

1746 Articles of Agreement, for carrying on an Expedition by Hudson's Straights, for the Discovery of a N.W. Passage to the Western and Southern Ocean of America. 8vo. Dublin. (16 pp.)

1748  ELLIS, HENRY.  A Voyage to Hudson's Bay, in the year 1746-47, for Discovering a North-West Passage, and an Account of a Voyage for the Discovery of a North-West Passage by Hudson's Straits to the Western and Southern Ocean of America, in the year 1746-47 on the Ship California.  Maps and cuts.  3 vols.  8vo.  London.

> Reprinted, Dublin, 1749. For Ellis' account alone see item following. Note also Swindrage's account under this date below.

1748  ELLIS, HENRY.  Voyage to Hudson's Bay, by the Dobbs Galley and California, in the years 1746-47, for discovering a North-West Passage. 8vo.  London.

> Translated into French, Paris, 1749; into Dutch, Leyden, 1750; into German, Göttingen, 1750. See below.

> This expedition was sent out at the suggestion of Arthur Dobbs. It put a definite end to the supposition that the Northwest Passage lay through Hudson's Bay. It also contains interesting descriptions of the Eskimos.

1749  (In French.)  Voyage de la Baye Hudson, fait en 1746 et 1747, pour la découverte du Passage de Nord-Ouest.  Folding map and 10 plates.  2 vols.  8vo.  Paris.

1750  (In Dutch.)  Reize naar de Baai van Hudson, Ter ontdekkinge van eenen Noord-wester Doortogt, Gedaan in de Jaaren 1746 en 1747, met de Schepen de Dobbs-Galley en de California, . . . Folding map and plates. 8vo.  Leyden.

1750  (In German.)  Reise nach der Hudsonbay, aus dem Englischen von J. Ph. Murray.  Maps.  Göttingen.

SWINDRAGE, THEODORE.  An Account of a Voyage for the Discovery of a North-West Passage by Hudson's Streights, to the Western and Southern Ocean of America.  Performed in the years 1745 and 1747, in the Ship California, Capt. Francis Smith, Commander. By the Clerk of the California.  6 folding maps and 4 plates.  2 vols. 8vo.  London.

> This was the voyage that vindicated Middleton's veracity and disposed of the charge that he had been influenced by the Hudson's Bay Company into making false statements.

1750  ELLIS, HENRY.  Considerations on the great Advantages which would arise of the North-West Passage and a clear Account of the most practicable Method of attempting that Discovery.  London.

1761  MÜLLER, SAMUEL.  For one of the most important works relating to the discoveries on the Northwest Passage, see his *Voyages from Asia to America,* under NORTH PACIFIC.

1768 SWINDRAGE, THEODORE. The Great Probability of a North West Passage: deduced from the Observations on the Letter of Admiral de Fonte (or Fuentes), who sailed from the Callao of Lima on the Discovery of a Communication between the South Sea and the Atlantic Ocean; and to intercept some Navigators from Boston in New England, whom he met with, then in search of a North West Passage. Proving the Authenticity of the Admiral's Letter. With an Appendix. Containing the Account of a Discovery of Part of the Coast and Inland Country of Labrador, made in 1753. The whole intended for the Advancement of Trade and Commerce. 3 folding maps comprising a general map of Admiral Fonte's supposed discoveries in the North West; an old Spanish map of America of 1608; discoveries made in Hudson's Bay in 1746-47 by Captain Smith. 4to. London.

> An extremely interesting and curious work in the history of the search for the Northwest Passage, discussing the possibility of a passage through to Hudson's Bay or Baffin Bay via the Strait of Juan de Fuca or at about the latitude of Queen Charlotte Island. . . . If Fuentes' account is based on the truth, the probability is that he sailed among the numerous islands north of Queen Charlotte Island and mistook the straits as rivers and the wider stretches as lakes, and that if he met there a vessel from Boston, that vessel had sailed around by way of South America.—Maggs, No. 465. Admiral Bartholomew de Fonte or Fuentes, a Spanish or Portuguese navigator, is supposed to have sailed from Callao on April 3, 1640, with four vessels up the coast to California and thence northwards to about latitude 53 degrees, where he found numerous islands . . . and where he entered a great river or strait running toward the east. . . . He came across an English vessel belonging to Major General Gibbons of Massachusetts in charge of Captain Shapley, which had come from Boston, presumably from the east. Having taken over Captain Shapley's charts, he returned to Lima and wrote a long letter detailing his explorations and discoveries. Various long discussions took place among savants as to whether Admiral Fuentes' accounts were true.—From Maggs, No. 549. This work is sometimes listed under the name of Thomas Jefferys, who, however, was rather the publisher and not the author. Swindrage's name is sometimes found spelled Dragge.

1776 TRAVERS, VAL. Summary Observations and Facts Collected from late and authentic Accounts of Russian and other Navigators to show the Practicability and good Prospect of Success in Enterprises to discover a Northern Passage for Vessels by Sea, between the Atlantic and Pacific Oceans, or nearly to approach the North Pole. In Büsching, *Nachrichten,* IV, p. 401. Berlin.

1780 COOK, JAMES (Captain). For an attempt to make the Northwest Passage from the Pacific, see his third and last voyage under this and later dates, NORTH PACIFIC.

1782 PICKERSGILL, RICHARD. For his account of voyages for the discovery of a Northwest Passage, see this date under COLLECTIONS.

1786   FORSTER, JOHANN REINHOLD.  History of the Voyages and Discoveries in the North, dealing largely with the Travels of Cabot, Frobisher, Davis, Baffin, Henry Hudson, and others in North America. See under COLLECTIONS.

1790   MEARES, JOHN.  For conjectures on the probability of a Northwest Passage, see his *Voyages . . . from China to the Northwest Coast of America,* under NORTH PACIFIC.

1793   GOLDSON, WILLIAM.  Observations on the Passage between the Atlantic and Pacific Oceans, in two Memoirs on the Straits of Anian, and the Discoveries of De Fonte, elucidated by a new and original map: to which is prefixed, An Historical Abridgement of Discoveries in the North of America.  Portsmouth.

## ADDENDA

1849   Narratives of Voyages towards the North-West, In Search of a Passage to Cathay and India, 1496 to 1631.  With Selections from the early Records of . . . the East India Company and from MSS. in the British Museum.  Edited by Thomas Rundall.  2 maps.  Hak. Soc., ser. I, vol. 5.  London.

1852   COATS, W. (Captain).  The Geography of Hudson's Bay, Being the Remarks of Captain W. Coats, in many Voyages to that Locality, between the years 1727 and 1751.  With an Appendix containing Extracts from the Log of Captain Middleton on his Voyage for the Discovery of the North-west Passage, in H.M.S. *Furnace,* in 1741-43.  Edited by John Barrow, F.R.S., F.S.A.  Hak. Soc., ser. I, vol. 11.  London.

1860   HUDSON, HENRY.  Henry Hudson, the Navigator, 1607-1613.  The Original Documents in which his Career is recorded.  Collected, partly translated and annotated, with an introduction by George Michael Asher, LL.D.  2 maps and bibliography.  Hak. Soc., ser. I, vol. 27.  London.

   One would think that the tragic death of Henry Hudson in the Arctic wastes of the Hudson's Bay region would have stimulated English curiosity and sympathy to some contemporary record.  But according to Maggs, No. 479, the first printed account of his discoveries in the Northwest was the following item:

   1612  HUDSON, HENRY. Descriptio ac delineatio Geographica Detectionis Freti, sive, Transitus ad Oceanum, supra terras Americanas, in Chinam atque Japonem ducturi. Recens investigati ab M. Henrico Hudsono Anglo. 5 large folding maps. 4to. Amsterdam.

1877  KNIGHT, JOHN (Captain).  The Voyage of Capt. John Knight, 1606, to seek the North-West Passage.  See Lancaster, Sir James:  The Voyages of . . . to the East Indies,  Hak. Soc., ser. I, vol. 56,  London, under EAST INDIES.

1880  BAFFIN, WILLIAM.  The Voyages of William Baffin, 1612-1622.  Edited, with Notes and an Introduction, by Clements R. Markham, C.B., F.R.S., ex-Pres. R.G.S.  Maps and illus.  Hak. Soc., ser. I, vol. 63. London.

1886  For Weymouth's voyage in search of the Northwest Passage, see *The Dawn of British Trade to the East Indies,* under EAST INDIES.

# II

## Northeast Passage

1577 CABOTA, SEBASTIANO. Voyages to the North-east frosty Seas, and to the Kingdoms lying that way. London.

> So cited in Chavanne. No other notice of such a work has come to the attention of the editor. The date suggests that it might belong to Eden's *The History of Travayle in the West and East Indies.* See this date under COLLECTIONS.

1609 VEER, GERRIT DE. The True and perfect Description of three Voyages, so strange and wonderfull, that the like hath neuer been heard before; Done and performed three yeares, one after the other, by the Ships of Holland and Zeland, on the North sides of Norway, Muscouia and Tartaria, towards the Kingdomes of Cathaia and China; shewing the discouerie of the Straights of Weigates, Noua Zembla, and the Countrie lying vnder 80 degrees; which is thought to be Greenland: whereneuer any man had bin before: with the cruell Beares, and other Monsters of the Sea, and the unsupportable and extreme cold that is found to be in those Places, and how in the last Voyage, the Shippe was so inclosed by the Ice, that it was left there for ten months, the great danger and Miseries of the Navigators, . . . and how . . . they were constrained to sayle above 1000 miles English, in open Boates. Translated (from the Dutch) by William Phillip. 4to. London.

> A very brief summary of the three voyages in Harris I, 550-564; in Pinkerton I, 81-127. Reprinted by the Hakluyt Society, London, 1853, and again 1876. Dutch original, Amsterdam, 1598. See below.
> Phillip states in his dedication that he translated this work at the suggestion of Richard Hakluyt. According to the editor of the Hakluyt Society reprint, the translation is full of errors in consequence of an inadequate knowledge of the Dutch language. This account relates the fortunes of the three expeditions sent out in 1594, 1595, and 1596, by the Dutch in their search for a northern passage to China. The outstanding figure in these voyages was Barents, who proved to be almost as indomitable as the icy barrier blocking his way round Nova Zembla. It was on the third voyage that he reached Spitsbergen Islands, thus bringing them for the first time into European contact. He also succeeded in rounding the northern tip of Nova Zembla, where he was forced to winter. Since the summer ice failed to break up and release his ship, he and his survivors were forced to attempt the return in open boats. Before they were succored Barents died. Three centuries later the hut in which the crew lived during this unprecedented experience was found intact together with a number of relics. The bad fortune of these voyages led the Dutch to drop the project for some time. For the earlier English attempts see Hakluyt's *Principal Navigations.*

>> 1808-1814 First Voyage of the Dutch and Zealanders by the North along the Coasts of Norway, Moscovy and Tartary, in order to Seek a Passage to the Kingdoms of Cathay and China. Second and Third Voyages of the Same. In Pinkerton I, 81-127.

>> Newly translated from the *Recueil des Voyages qui ont servi à l'établissement et aux progres de la Compagnie des Indes Orientales,* Amsterdam, 1702.

1853  A True Description of Three Voyages by the North-East Towards Cathay and China, undertaken by the Dutch in the years 1594, 1595, and 1596, with their Discovery of Spitzbergen, their residence of ten months in Novaya Zemlya, and their safe return in two open boats. By Gerrit de Veer. Translated into English by William Philip in 1609. Edited by Charles Tilstone Beke, Ph.D., F.S.A. 4 maps and 12 illus. Hak. Soc., ser. I, vol. 13. London.

> Reprinted as vol. 54, 1876, under the editorship of Lieut. Koolemans Beynen.

1598  VEER, GERRIT DE. Waerachtige Beschryvinghe van Drie Seylagen, ter werelt noyt soo vreemt ghehoort, drie jaaren achter mal aandered deur de Hollandtsche end Zeilandtsche schepen by noorden Noorveghen, Moskovia ende Tartaria, na de Coninckrijcken van Catthay ende China, so mede vande Weygats, Nova Sembla, en van't landt op de 80 graden dat men acht Groenlandt tezijn . . . Gedaen deur Gerrit de Veer van Amsterredam. 4to. Amsterdam.

1612  Of the Circumference of the Earth, or a Treatise of the North-East Passage. 12mo. London.

1615  DIGGES, DUDLEY. Of the North-East Passage, 1611. (*Bibliog. Misc.*) London.

> So cited by Chavanne. Digges formed a company to trade with the East by way of the supposed Northern routes.

1692  EDGE, THOMAS. The English and Dutch Discoveries in the North-East. London.

> A supplement was added in 1694. So cited by Chavanne. Edge commanded a vessel in an expedition sent out by the Muscovy Company in 1610-12 to explore the west coast of Spitsbergen.

1694  WOOD, JOHN (Captain). An Account of his attempt to make the Northeast Passage is to be found in Robinson's Collection. See Robinson under COLLECTIONS. See also Astley I, 252-254; Kerr, VII.

> Wood had a theory, based on his own studies and on the reports and experiences of earlier voyagers, that a passage to Japan could be found about midway between Nova Zembla and Spitsbergen. With the support of King Charles II and other important personages, he set out in 1676 with two ships. But the ice so completely blocked his way everywhere that he made little headway and was himself wrecked off the coast of Nova Zembla. He was rescued by the other ship and managed to get safely back home, a thoroughly disillusioned navigator.

1699  ALLISON, THOMAS (Captain). An Account of a Voyage from Archangel, in Russia, in the Year 1697, by Thomas Allison, Commander of the Ship. 8vo. London.

> In Pinkerton I, 491-521.
> This journal is rare and has escaped collectors.—Pinkerton.

**1744-48**  A Succinct Account of the Grounds upon which a North-East Passage into the Sea of Japan has been expected and sought for. The Attempts of the English and Dutch on that side, with the Reasons why all Thoughts of a Passage that way have been for many Years given up. Collected from the Dutch as well as English Authors. In Harris II, 452-456.

**1744**  PHIPPS, CONSTANTINE JOHN (Commodore). For an account of voyages in search of a Northeast Passage, see his *Journal of a Voyage undertaken by order of his present Majesty*, under ARCTIC REGIONS.

## ADDENDA

**1808-1814**  PONTANUS, JOHN ISAAC. Dissertation of the Learned John Isaac Pontanus, in which he answers the Objections of those who consider the Search of a Northern Passage as a Task of Too Great Difficulty; and in which he proposes the most probable Means of Accomplishing this Design. In Pinkerton I, 127-130.

Translated from the *Recueil des Voyages qui ont servi à l'établissement et aux progres de la Compagnie des Indes Orientales*, Amsterdam, 1702.

**1869**  HUDSON, HENRY. Sailing Directions of Henry Hudson prepared for his use in 1608, from the Old Danish of Ivar Bardsen. With introduction and notes; also A Dissertation on the Discovery of the Hudson River, By B. F. DeCosta. 8vo. Albany.

The voyage of 1608 was Hudson's second and was made "For finding a passage to the East Indies by the North-east." He tried for a way between Nova Zembla and Spitsbergen but was stopped by the ice. This failure convinced him that such a route was impracticable.

# III

## Arctic Regions

1631 PELHAM, EDWARD. God's Power and Providence, shewed in the miraculous Preservation and Deliverance of eight Englishmen; left by Mischance in Greenland, anno 1630, nine months and twelve dayes. With a true Relation of all their Miseries, their Shifts and Hardships they were put to, their food, . . . such as neither Heathen nor Christian Men ever before endured. With a Description of the Chief Places and Rarities of that barren and cold Country. Faithfully reported by Edw. Pelham, one of the eight men aforesaid. As also with a map of Greenland. London.

> Reprinted in Churchill IV, 750-761. Included also in the Hakluyt Society volume on Spitsbergen and Greenland. See below under Martens, 1694.
> The eight Englishmen, left by negligence on one of the islands of the Spitsbergen group, faced a hard prospect, but by preparing against the winter they pulled through in fine shape. This was the first time an Arctic winter was successfully braved on the shores of Spitsbergen. Pelham's account of the feat attracted great attention. Holland profited by it as well as England. See also the Hakluyt Society volume for 1902 below.

1694 MARTENS, FREDERICK. Observations on his Voyage to Spitzbergen and Greenland; printed in an account of Several Late Voyages to the South and North (i. e., in Robinson's Collection), translated from the High Dutch. London.

> Included in the Hakluyt Society volume for 1856. German original, Hamburg, 1675. See below.
> This is the first published work in English on Spitsbergen, and its description of the ice and the animals of that region seems to be very correct and graphic. It gives a very good account of the mode pursued by the Dutch in the capture of the whale and walrus at that time.—From Hakluyt Society edition. Martens, who was a German surgeon, visited Spitsbergen in 1671.

> 1856 A Collection of Documents on Spitzbergen and Greenland, Comprising a Translation from F. Martens' Voyage to Spitzbergen, 1671; a Translation from Isaac de la Peyrère's *Histoire du Groênland*, 1663, and *God's Power and Providence in the Preservation of Eight Men in Greenland Nine Moneths and Twelve Dayes*, 1630. Edited by Adam White, of the British Museum. 2 maps. Hak. Soc., ser. I, vol. 18. London.

> 1675 MARTENS, FRIEDRICH. Spitzbergische und Grönländische Reisebeschreibung, im Jahr 1671. Mit Figuren. 4to. Hamburg.

1711 Description of John Mayens Island. In the second edition of Robinson's Collection.

1725 ZORDRAGER, CORNELIUS GISBERT. A View of the Greenland Trade and Whale Fishery. With the National and Private Advantages thereof.

> So cited in Pinkerton XVII, where what appears to be the Dutch original is also given. See below. This same work has come to notice as having been written by H. Elking (also E. C. King), with the date 1722. Perhaps this is the name of the translator.

> 1646 ZORDRAGER, CORNELIUS GISBERT. Groenlandische Vischerey en walvischvangst. 4to. Delft.

1732 GATONBE, JOHN. A Voyage into the North-west Passage undertaken in the year 1612 by the Merchant Adventurers of London. Map. In Churchill VI, 241-256.

> This is the title given in Churchill; it may be Gatonbe's or the eaitors'. Another title reads: An Account of the English Expedition to Greenland under the Command of Captain James Hall, in 1612. By John Gatonbe, Quartermaster. Baffin went as chief pilot in one of the ships and wrote an account of the voyage, of which Purchas has included a portion. Outside of Purchas there is no contemporary account of any of Baffin's seven voyages. Captain Hall had acted as pilot to the Danish expeditions of 1605 and 1606. His report to the King of Denmark on these voyages was printed for the first time by the Hakluyt Society, vol. I, 1897, as well as his voyage of 1612 related by Gatonbe. See below under 1896. The object of the voyage is in doubt. On his earlier expeditions Hall thought he had discovered a body of silver ore. Apparently he had in mind not the discovery of the Northwest Passage but the profitable working of his silver mine. Commercially the voyage was a failure, though it added to the geographical knowledge of the southwest coast of Greenland. Hall died at the hands of the Eskimos.

PEYRERE, ISAAC DE LA. An Account of Greenland sent to Monsieur de la Mothe de Vayer. (Dated from the Hague, Jan. 18, 1646.) In Churchill II, 396-427.

> Translated by the Hakluyt Society, 1896. See under this date below. French original published anonymously at Paris, 1647. See below.

> 1647 PEYRERE, ISAAC DE LA. Relation du Groênland. 8vo. Paris. 1647.

> > About one half of this work was an abstract of Lyschander's *Den Grønlandske Chronica*, a popular composition in verse based on the accounts of those who had taken part in the three Danish voyages of 1605-07. Owing to La Peyrère's ignorance of Danish, his work is full of errors.—From Introduction to the Hakluyt Society volume, 1896. The author had made the journey to Copenhagen in 1644 in company with the French Ambassador, M. de la Thuillerie, and during his stay there collected many curious and interesting particulars on the northern countries.

A True and Short Account of 42 Persons who perished by Shipwreck near Spitzbergen, in the year 1646. In Churchill II, 381-382.

> Reprinted in Pinkerton I, 537.

Two Journals: The First Kept by Seven Sailors in the Isle of St. Maurice, in Greenland, in the years 1633, 1634; Who pass'd the Winter there, and all died in the said Island. The Second Kept by seven other Sailors, who in the years 1633 and 1634, wintered at Spitzbergen; with An account of their Adventures and sufferings from the Bears and Whales, insupportable cold and storms, . . . Done out of Low Dutch. In Churchill II, 367-380.

> The first seven were picked men left by their choice in Greenland to satisfy the desire of the Greenland Company to find out what the winter was like in those parts. The second seven were likewise left on Spitsbergen for the same purpose. The first seven were found dead in their cabins by the relief ship. One was in a coffin. The second group was also found dead shut up close in their tent to secure their bodies from the bears and other ravenous beasts. Three of these were in coffins.

1744-48  The History of the Countries lying round the North Pole; their Climate, Soil, and Produce; together with an Account of the Customs, Manners, and Trade of their Inhabitants.   In Harris II, 377-398.

1745  EGEDE, HANS.  A Description of Greenland, shewing the Natural History, Boundaries and Face of the Country, Rise and Progress of the Old Norwegian Colonies, Ancient and Modern Inhabitants, . . . Translated by Richard Norcliffe.  Maps and plates.  8vo.  London.

> Danish original, Copenhagen, 1729. See below.
> The author was an ingenious merchant at Frederckshauld in Norway. He sent over to the Gentlemen's Society at Spaulding specimens of all the minerals of that country with a great variety of fossil fish-shells, etc., and a manuscript translation of the above work, with an index, etc.—From Nichols, *Literary Anecdotes.* Egede was a missionary and superintendent in Greenland for his Danish Majesty. He induced the Danes to reestablish their settlements there. His account (see also that of Crantz under 1767 below) gives an authentic description of that region.

> 1729  EGEDE, HANS.  De gamle Grønlandes nye perlustrations, eller en kort beskrivelse om de gamle Nordske coloniers begyndelse og undergang, . . . først anno 1724 forfattet af H. Egede, og nu anno 1729 efter seet . . . af een der paa nogen tiid har vaaret in Grønland. 4to. Copenhagen.

1754  MYLIUS, CHRISTLOB.  Translation from the High German of his Account of a New-Zoophite, or Animal Plant from Greenland, in a Letter to Dr. Haller.  London.

> German original, Hanover, 1753.

1766  GAMBOLD, JOHN (Rev.).  The History of Greenland.  London.

> The author, who was consecrated as a bishop in 1754, was connected with the Brethren of the Moravian Church. "He was a singular, overzealous, but innocent enthusiast. He has not quite fire enough in him to form a second Simon Stylites." —From Nichols, *Literary Anecdotes.*

1767   CRANTZ, DAVID.   The History of Greenland containing a Description
of the Country and its Inhabitants and particularly a Relation of the
Mission carried on for above these 30 years by the Unitas Fratrum at
New Herrnhuth and Lichtenfels in that Country. Translated from the
High Dutch.  Maps and copperplates.  2 vols.  8vo.  London.

>      Another edition, with a slightly different title, London, 1780. German original,
> Barby, 1765. See below.
>      In speaking of this work, Dr. Johnson declared that very few books had ever
> affected him so deeply, and that the man who did not relish the first part was no
> philosopher, and he who did not enjoy the second part, no Christian.—Maggs, No.
> 442. There is a section devoted to whaling, consisting of a description of the
> Greenland black whale and an account of its habits; the Jupiter whale, the hump-
> back whale, the knotted whale, whales of Bermuda, the cachelot and its store of
> spermaceti, the white whale, and the whaling industry in general.

>      1780   CRANTZ, DAVID.   The Antient and Modern History of the (United)
>           Brethren in the Remote Ages and particularly in the present Century.
>           Translated from the German, with additional Notes, by Benjamin la
>           Trobe.  London.

>      1765   CRANTZ, DAVID.   Historie von Grönland, enthaltend die Beschreibung
>           des Landes und der Einwohner, . . . inbesondere die Geschichte der
>           dortigen Missionen der Evangelischen Bruder.  Folding maps and plates.
>           8vo.  Barby.

1768-69   Official Documents from the Resolutions of the States of Holland concerning the whalefishing, the Navigations to Greenland, the Straits of
Davis, . . . London.

1774   HORSLEY, SAMUEL (Bishop).   Remarks on the Observations made
in the last Voyage towards the North Pole, for discovering the Accel-
eration of the Pendulum, in Latitude 70°50'; in a Letter to the Hon.
Constantine John Phipps.  4to.  London.

>      For Phipps' voyage toward the North Pole see this date below. There is a
> brief sketch of Bishop Horsley in Nichols' *Literary Anecdotes* IV, 674.

LE ROY, PIERRE LOUIS.   A Narrative of the Adventures of four
Russian Sailors, who were cast away on the desert Island of East
Spitzbergen on which they lived for six years and three months, as
related by themselves; with some Observations on the Productions of
that Island, . . . Translated from the German by C. Heydinger.  8vo.
London.

>      In Jacob von Stählin's *An Account of the New Northern Archipelago* (see
> this date under NORTH PACIFIC). Reprinted in Pinkerton I, 595-613. The
> English version (of which there must be an earlier one) translated into French,
> Amsterdam and Paris, 1767. A German version, Riga and Mietau, 1768. See below.

>      1767   (In French.)   Récit des Aventures singulières de quatre Voyageurs russes
>           qui feront jétés dans l'île déserte du Spitzberg oriental, auquel sont

jointes quelques Observations sur les productions de cette île. Traduit de l'original allemand en anglais, et de l'anglais en francais. 8vo. Amsterdam and Paris.

1768 LE ROY, PIERRE LOUIS. Erzählung der Begebenheiten vier russischer Matrosen die durch einen Sturm bis zur wüsten Ostspitzenbergen verschlagen worden. Nebst einigen Anmerkungen über verschiedene im Russland eingeführten Gewohnheiten. 8vo. Riga and Mietau.

PHIPPS, CONSTANTINE JOHN (Commodore), and LUTWIDGE, —— (Captain). The Journal of a Voyage undertaken by order of His Present Majesty, for making Discoveries towards the North Pole, by the Hon. Commodore Phipps and Captain Lutwidge, in His Majesty's Sloops Racehorse and Carcase. To which is prefixed, An Account of the several Voyages undertaken for the Discovery of the North-East Passage to China and Japan. View of the whale fishery and 2 folding maps. 4to. London.

Another issue, London, 1774.
This narrative is by some member of the expedition and contains particulars not mentioned in the official account.—Maggs, No. 465.

PHIPPS, CONSTANTINE JOHN (Hon. Captain). A Voyage from June 4 to September 24, 1773, to determine how far Navigation was practicable to the North Pole. 4to. London.

An edition, Dublin, 1775. Reprinted in Anderson, 314-335, to which is prefixed A Genuine Account of the several Voyages undertaken for the Discovery of the North East Passage to China and Japan; in Pinkerton I, 538-594. Translated into German, Berlin, 1774; into French, Paris, 1775. See below. Noticed, with an extract, in the *Journal des Scavans*, 1774, VII, 481.
"While the book was in the Press, I believe, nearly the whole of the ship's crew, in their turn visited my Printing-Office."—Nichols, *Literary Anecdotes*. This expedition was undertaken for the purpose of discovering a route to India through the Polar Regions. North of Spitsbergen the sea was absolutely blocked with ice and the vessels had to return . . . Lord Nelson, then fourteen years old, accompanied it as a midshipman.—Maggs, No. 502. It made an important addition to the science of navigation and to the knowledge of the natural productions of Spitsbergen. Phipps afterwards became Lord Mulgrave.

1774 (In German.) Tagebuch einer Reise nach Spitzbergen. In Büsching, *Nachrichten* II, 273. Berlin.

1775 (In French.) Voyage au pôle boréal fait en 1773 par ordre du roi d'Angleterre par Constantin-Jean Phipps, traduit de l'anglois. 12 plates, 3 maps, and numerous illus. 4to. Paris.

1774-75 BARRINGTON, DAINES. The Probability of reaching the North Pole discussed. Additional Proofs that the Polar Seas are Open. Read at a Meeting of the Royal Society, Dec. 22, 1774. Thoughts on the Probability, Expediency and Utility of Discovering a Passage by the North Pole. (Supplement: Additional Instances of Navigators, who have reached High Northern Latitudes, lately received from Holland. Second Supplement: Observations on the Floating Ice which is found in High Northern and Southern Latitudes. To which are added Experiments on the Freezing of Sea Water. By B. Higgins, M.D.). 3 vols. in 1. 4to. London.

A new edition with an Appendix containing papers on the same subject and on a North-West Passage by Col. Beaufoy, F.R.S., with a map of the North Pole, London, 1780. Translated into French, London, 1775. See below.

These are Barrington's celebrated "Tracts on the Possibility of approaching the North Pole" (which contain five parts), and the two supplements, but the pagination was continued throughout the three . . . The Tracts were reissued in a large collection of curious papers known as his "Miscellanies," published in 1781. The original issues are very scarce.—Maggs, No. 502. Barrington's interest in the project was instrumental in moving the Royal Society to apply to the Admiralty for an Arctic expedition. The request was granted and Phipps was sent out in 1773. The farthest north reached was latitude 80° 5′. See also Barrington under 1781, NORTH PACIFIC.

1775   (In French.)   Discussion sur la Possibilité du passage près le pôle du Nord. Londres.

1776   Summary Observations and Facts collected from late and authentic Accounts of Russian and other Navigators to show the Practicability and good Prospect of Success in Enterprises to discover a northern Passage between the Atlantic and Pacific Oceans, or nearly to approach the North Pole.   London.

1784   COOK, JAMES (Captain).   For accounts of his attempts to get into the high latitudes by way of the Bering Sea, see his Third Voyage, under NORTH PACIFIC.

1784-87   PENNANT, THOMAS.   Arctic Zoology; with the Introduction. Plates, supplement, and 2 maps.   2 vols.   London.

Vol. I, 1784; vol. II, 1785; supplement, 1787. 2nd edit., 2 vols., London, 1792. Translated into German, Leipzig, 1787. See below.

This work relates to the Kurile Islands, Alaska, British America, California, the Polar Seas of America, Greenland, Baffin's Bay, Hudson's Bay, Canada, and Nova Scotia, etc.—Maggs, No. 442.

1787   (In German.)   Thiergeschichte der nördlichen Polarländer. Aus dem Englischen von Jacob Heinrich Wittekop und Hoffman (1786) mit Anmerkungen und Zusätzen von E. A. W. Zimmerman. 24 original English copperplates. 2 parts. Leipzig.

1786   FORSTER, JOHANN REINHOLD.   For voyages and discoveries in the Polar Regions, see his *History and Discoveries made in the North*, under COLLECTIONS.

1789 EGEDE, HANS. An Account of his Mission to Greenland. London.

> See under 1745 above.

1792-93 PAGES, PIERRE MARIE FRANCOIS. For an account of a voyage towards the North Pole, see his *Travels round the World in 1767-1771*, under CIRCUMNAVIGATIONS.

1799 BACSTROM, JOHN. An Account of a Voyage to Spitzbergen in 1780. Communicated by the Author to the Philosophical Magazine, July, 1799, extracted from a Journal kept at the time.

> Reprinted in Pinkerton I, 614-620.
> Bacstrom's career was one of vicissitudes and misfortunes. He visited Iceland with Banks, sailed in the *Adventure* with Captain Cook on his second circumnavigation, and knocked about the world as surgeon on several ships. He was interested in agricultural experiments, especially such as increasing the yield of plants, vines, corn, wheat, and rye by means of "proper Natural Magneta."

## ADDENDA

1808-1814 KERGUELEN, TREMAIREC. Relation of a Voyage in the North Sea, along the Coasts of Iceland, Greenland, Ferro, Shetland, the Orcades,. and Norway, made in the years 1767 and 1768 by M. de Kerguelen Tremaria, of the Royal Marine Academy in France, Lieut. Commander of the Frigates La Folle and L'Hirondelle. In Pinkerton I, 735-803.

> French original, Paris, 1771. See below.
> The preface states that the purpose of the voyage was to give protection and encouragement to the cod fishermen on the coast of Iceland, and to preserve order among the French fishermen.

> 1771 KERGUELEN, TREMAIREC DE. Relation d'un Voyage dans la Mer du Nord, Aux Côtes d'Islande, du Groênland, de Ferro, de Schettland, des Orcades et de Norwège; fait en 1767 et 1768. 13 maps and plans and 4 other plates. 4to. Paris.

1873 ZENO, NICOLO and ANTONIO. The Voyages of the Venetian Brothers Nicolo and Antonio Zeno to the Northern Seas in the Fourteenth Century. Comprising the latest known Accounts of the Lost Colony of Greenland, and of the Northmen in America before Columbus. Translated and Edited, with Notes and Introduction, by Richard Henry Major, F.S.A., Keeper of Maps, Brit. Mus., Sec. R.G.S. Maps. Hak. Soc., ser. I, vol. 50. London.

> These voyages are now believed to be largely fictitious.

1876  VEER, GERRIT DE.  For Barents' voyages to the Arctic regions see under 1609, NORTHEAST PASSAGE.

1896  Danish Arctic Expeditions, 1605 to 1620.  Book I, The Danish Expeditions to Greenland, 1605-07; to which is added Captain James Hall's Voyage to Greenland in 1612.  Edited by Christian Carl August Gosch. Maps.  Book II.  The Expedition of Captain Jens Munk to Hudson's Bay in search of a North-West Passage in 1619-1620.  Edited by Christian Carl August Gosch.  Maps, illus.  Hak. Soc., ser. I, vols. 96-97. London.

     See Gatonbe, under 1732 above, and Monck under 1732, NORTHWEST PASSAGE.

1902  Early Dutch and English Voyages to Spitzbergen in the Seventeenth Century, Including Hessel Gerritsz, *Histoire du Pays nommé Spitsberghe,* 1613, translated by Basil H. Soulsby, F.S.A.; and Jacob Segersz. van der Brugge, *Journael of Dagh Register,* Amsterdam, 1634, translated by J. A. J. de Villiers.  Edited by Sir W. Martin Conway.  3 maps and 3 illus.  Hak. Soc., ser. II, vol. 11.  London.

# IV

# North Pacific

**1744-48** BERING, VITUS. For a generalized account of Bering's voyages see this date, under SIBERIA, and for a translation of his journal see Coxe under 1780, and also Müller under 1761 below.

Interest in furthering the exploration of the unknown area between Asia and America led to several expeditions. That which was to carry on the work east of Kamtschatka was entrusted to the command of Bering as Commodore. The ships *St. Paul* and *St. Peter* left port June 4, 1741. The vessels got separated in a storm never to rejoin. Bering sighted Mt. St. Elias, Kodiak Island, and a portion of the Aleutian Peninsula, the Shumagin Islands, and passed along the Aleutian Islands to the south. Being attacked by scurvy Bering was removed to the island that still bears his name, where he died, Dec. 19, 1742.

> **1922-25** BERING, VITUS. Bering's Voyages (vol. I). An Account of the Efforts of the Russians to determine the Relation of Asia and America (vol. II). By F. A. Colder. 2 vols. Amer. Geog. Research Series, No. 2. New York.
>
> The first volume of this scholarly work contains the Log Books of the First and Second Expeditions of 1725-1730 and 1733-1742. The second contains the journal of Georg Wilhelm Steller (now first turned into English), the scientist aboard Bering's vessel the *St. Peter,* and other matter. The American Geographical Society announces a new edition of this work.

**1754** A Letter from a Russian Sea-Officer, to a person of Distinction at the Court of St. Petersburg: Containing His Remarks upon Mr. de l'Isle's Chart and Memoir, relative to the New Discoveries Northward and Eastward from Kamtschatka. Together with Some Observations on that Letter, By Arthur Dobbs, Esq., Governor of North Carolina. To which is added, Mr. de l'Isle's Explanatory Memoir on his Chart Published at Paris, and now translated from the original French. London.

"This pamphlet relates chiefly to the attempts that have been so worthily made by Mr. Dobbs, and other Gentlemen, associated for the patriotic purpose of discovering a N. W. Passage to the South Sea."—*Monthly Review,* X, 320, quoted by Sabin.

**1761** MÜLLER, SAMUEL Voyages from Asia to America, to complete the Discoveries of the North-West Coast of America; to which is prefixed a Summary of the Voyage of the Russians on the Frozen-Sea: translated from the German by Thomas Jefferys. 3 new maps. 4to. London.

2nd edition, London, 1764. See under COLLECTIONS.
This contains the original account of Captain Behring's Polar Expedition, and the discovery of the Strait which bears his name, and the western limits of North America. Since the rapid development of British Columbia and Alaska this important book is becoming indispensable for the history of discovery and exploration in the Northern Pacific.—Quoted by Maggs, No. 465.

1768 SWINDRAGE, THEODORE. For reference to the supposed discoveries of Admiral de Fuentes on the Northwest coast of America, see his *The Great Probability of a North-West Passage,* under NORTHWEST PASSAGE.

1774 STÄHLIN, JACOB VON. An Account of the New Northern Archipelago lately discovered by the Russians in the Seas of Kamtschatka and Anadir. To which is added, a Narrative of the Adventures of Four Russian Sailors, who were cast away on the desert Island of East-Spitzbergen: together with some Observations on the Productions of that Island . . . Translated from the German Originals at the desire of several Members of the Royal Society. Engraved folding map, outlined in color, of the Aleutian Islands, with Kamtschatka, parts of Alaska, etc. 8vo. London.

> German original, Stuttgart, 1774. See below.
> An important work in the history of the exploration of the Aleutian Archipelago and Northeast Asia. The map marks the route followed by various Russian expeditions, including that of the Russian ships which were supposed to have sailed right through the Behring Straits in 1728, and of St. Sindo in 1764-68. The map shows the Peninsula of Alaska as an island.—Maggs, No. 502.

> 1774 STÄHLIN, JACOB VON. Von den Russen, in den Jahren 1765, 1766 und 1767 entdecktes nordisches Inselmeer, zwischen Kamtschatka und Nordamerika. Stuttgart.

1778 TRUSLER, JOHN (Rev.). For an account of Kamtschatka see his *Descriptive Account of the Islands lately discovered in the South Seas,* under SOUTH SEAS.

1780 COOK, JAMES (Captain). Remarks and Conjectures on the Voyage of the Ships Resolution and Discovery, in Search of a northerly Passage from Kamtschatka to England, after the Death of Captain James Cook: with Reasons to imagine that these Ships have wintered in Siberia, Nova Zembla, or Lapland. To which is added, An Eulogium, or Tribute of Gratitude to the Memory of that celebrated Navigator. Intended as a Prelude or Introduction to a future Publication on the Subject of a Northeast Passage. 8vo. London.

> According to Halkett and Laing, the author was Robert Brooke.

COXE, WILLIAM. An Account of the Russian Discoveries between Asia and America, to which are added, the Conquest of Siberia and History of the Transactions and Commerce between Russia and China. Maps and a view of the Chinese frontier town of Maimatschin. 4to. London.

Later editions, London, 1781 and 1787. Translated into French, Paris, 1781; into German, Frankfort a. Main and Leipzig, 1784. See below. Noticed in the *Journal des Scavans,* 1780, VII, 191.

This work contains translations of Bering's voyages, with those of his predecessors and followers, to the Aleutian or Fox Islands, an account of their inhabitants and their language, observations on the fur trade, etc. Coxe made the suggestions which led the Russians to prosecute expeditions of discovery to the northern parts of Siberia. See Billings under 1800, SIBERIA.

1781 (In French.) Découvertes nouvelles des Russes, entre l'Asie et l'Amérique, avec l'Histoire des conquête de la Sibérie. Traduit de l'anglois par M. Demeunier. Maps. 4to. Paris.

1784 (In German.) Die neuen Entdeckungen der Russen zwischen Asien und Amerika, nebst der Geschichte der Eroberung Siberiens und des Handels der Russen und Chinesen. Aus dem Englischen übersetzt. Frankfort a. Main und Leipzig.

PERIPLUS. A Summary Account of the Voyage undertaken by order of Government in His Majesty's Ships, the Resolution and Discovery. Compiled from authentic Papers, and revised . . . Chart. 8vo. London.

Extract from the *London Magazine,* issued as an extra half sheet. It is a republication, with corrections to both account and chart, from the July, 1780, number of the magazine.—*Cook Bibliography.*

1781 BARRINGTON, DAINES. Miscellanies. Engraved map of the coast of California, portrait of Mozart at the age of seven, another portrait, map and five tables. 4to. London.

The last section, occupying ninety pages, is especially valuable, as it contains the "Journal of a Voyage in 1775, to explore the Coast of America, Northward of California, by the Second Pilot of the Fleet, Don Francisco Antonio Maurelle, in the King's Schooner, called the Sonora, and commanded by Don Juan Francisco de la Bodega." This comprises Maurelle's Diary, which he claimed "served as the only record for later navigators."—Maggs, No. 502. This work contains also the tracts on the possibility of reaching the North Pole. See under 1774-75, ARCTIC REGIONS.

COOK, JAMES (Captain). For the *Journal of Captain Cook's Last Voyage* see under CIRCUMNAVIGATIONS, and also under Ledyard, 1785, below.

FORSTER, JOHANN REINHOLD. For his *Tagebuch einer Entdeckungsreise nach der Südsee,* see under CIRCUMNAVIGATIONS.

MAURELLE, DON FRANCISCO ANTONIO. For his *Journal of a Voyage Northward of California* see Barrington under 1781 above.

1782   BAYLY, WILLIAM.   Astronomical Observations made in a Voyage to the North Pacific Ocean in 1776, 1777, 1778, 1779 and 1780.   1 plate. 4to.   London.

> Bayly was with Captain Cook on his third voyage.

ELLIS, WILLIAM.   An Authentic Narrative of a Voyage performed by Captain Cook and Captain Clerke, in His Majesty's Ships Resolution and Discovery during 1776-1780; in search of a North-West Passage between the Continents of Asia and America; including a faithful account of their Discoveries, and the unfortunate Death of Captain Cook.   Folding chart and 21 engravings.   2 vols.   London.

> 3rd edition, London, 1784. Translated into German, Frankfurt and Leipzig, 1783. See below.
> Ellis was the assistant surgeon during Cook's third voyage, and gives quite a good history of this expedition.—Maggs, No. 491.

> 1783   (In German.)   Zuverlässige Nachricht von der dritten und letzten Reise der Capt. Cook und Clerke 1776-1780. Aus dem Englischen.   Map.   Frankfurt und Leipzig.

1784   COOK, JAMES (Captain).   For the official account (in three volumes) of Cook's third and last voyage, see under CIRCUMNAVIGATIONS. Vols. I and II were written by Cook and Vol. III by Clerke.

> Cook sailed from Plymouth July 11, 1776, and reached the coast of western North America in March, 1778, at about latitude 44 degrees north. He sighted Cape Flattery but saw nothing of the Straits of Juan de Fuca, whose existence he believed to be imaginary. He beached his boats in Nootka Sound on Vancouver Island, and then made land again in the Alaskan regions where the Russians had already made contact. He visited Prince William Sound and Cook's Inlet and sailed into the Bering Sea as far as Cape Prince of Wales, Icy Cape, and East Cape before the ice made him return for wintering in the Hawaiian Islands, where he met his death. His explorations were continued in the northern latitudes by Captain Clerke, who coasted Kamtschatka and made the high latitude of 70 degrees north. After his death at Petrapavlovsk the command fell to Captain Gore, of the *Discovery*. His journal supplies further matter for this voyage. Numerous editions, versions, compendiums, and translations followed. See below as well as under CIRCUMNAVIGATIONS.

> 1784   COOK, JAMES (Captain).   Voyage to the Pacific Ocean by Command of His Majesty for making Discoveries in the Northern Hemisphere; performed under the Direction of Captains Cook, Clerke and Gore, in the years 1776-1780.   Being a copious, comprehensive and satisfactory abridgement of the Voyage written by Captain James Cook and Captain J. King.   Maps and 40 plates.   4 vols.   8vo.   London.

> 1785-87   COOK, JAMES (Captain).   A Voyage to the Pacific Ocean . . . under the directions of Captains Cook, Clerke and Gore, 1776-1780.   Portraits and numerous plates, including plate of the death of Cook.   4 vols. 12mo.   Perth.

> This may be a reissue of the preceding item.

1788   COOK, JAMES. Cook's Voyage to the Pacific Ocean. In the *Lady's Magazine*. London.

1794   COOK, JAMES (Captain). An Abridgement of Captain Cook's last Voyage . . . for making Discoveries in the Northern Hemisphere. Engraved frontispiece of Cook's death, and other engraved plates. London.

1787-88   (In German.) Dritte Entdeckungsreise in der Südsee und nach dem Nordpol während der Jahre 1776-1780. Aus dem Tagebüchern der Schiffsbefehlshaber Cook, Clerke, King und Anderson's vollständlich beschrieben. Aus dem Englischen mit Zusätzen und mit einer Einleitung über Cook's Verdienste und Charakter, und über Entdeckungsreisen überhaupt von G. Forster. Maps and plates. 2 vols. 4to. Berlin.

1788   (In German.) Dritte und letzte Reise, oder Geschichte einer Entdeckungsreise nach dem Stillen Ocean, welche zu genauerer Erforschung der nördlicher Halbkugel unternommen unter der Anführung der Capt. Cook, Clerke und Gore während der Jahre 1776-1780 ausgefuhrt worden ist. Aus dem Tagebüchern der Capt. James Cook und James King. Eine Übersetzung nach der 2. grossen englischen Ausgaben, mit einigen Anmerkungen von J. L. Wetzel. Maps. 2 vols. Berlin.

1797   (In French.) Abrégé de la relation d'un voyage entrepris . . . 1776-79 par le capitaine Cook et le capitaine Clerke. In Parkinson, Voyage autour du Monde, tome 2, 235-309.

This is to be found in the French edition of 1797 of Parkinson's *Voyage round the World*. See Parkinson under 1773, CIRCUMNAVIGATIONS.

1785   LEDYARD, JOHN. Journal of Captain Cook's last Voyage to the Pacific Ocean, on Discovery; performed in the years 1776-1780. Large folding chart and 10 engraved plates, one representing the death of Cook at Owhyee. London.

This is described as a new edition, compared with and corrected from the voyage published by authority. Published earlier in 1783 at Hartford, Conn. There is a French translation, Paris, 1782, which was probably made from the surreptitious account put out in 1781. See the *Journal of Captain Cook's last Voyage* under 1781 above.
The details of Cook's death given here differ considerably from those found in other accounts. Ledyard pretended that his private journal had been seized by those in authority along with other journals, but he managed to anticipate the official account of the voyage. He was an adventurous American of some education. While on a visit to England he entered as corporal of marines under Cook, then about to sail on his third voyage. He was later promoted to sergeant of marines. After his return he undertook to carry on exploration in Africa in behalf of the African Association, but he died at Cairo on the eve of this enterprise. His memoirs and travels were written up by Jared Sparks, London, 1828.

1787   COXE, WILLIAM. Comparative View of the Russian Voyages, with those made by Captain Cook and Captain Clerke; and a Sketch of what remains to be ascertained by future Navigators. 8vo. London.

1789   PORTLOCK, NATHANIEL, and DIXON, GEORGE. Voyage round the World, but more particularly to the North-West Coast of America, performed in 1785-88, in the "King George" and "Queen Charlotte." 6 folding charts and 20 plates of views, birds, etc. 4to. London.

> 2nd edit., 4to, London, 1789. An abridgement, 8vo, London, 1789. Translated into French, Paris, 1789; into German, Berlin, 1789; into Dutch, Amsterdam, 1796. See below.
>
> The above item really represents two separate works, for each captain wrote his own account of the voyage and used precisely the same wording for his title as did the other. According to Maggs, No. 491, Dixon's volume was written by his supercargo, William Beresford. Both men were employed by the "King George's Sound Company" to secure furs on the Northwest coast of North America, i. e., Alaska, British Columbia, Vancouver and Queen Charlotte Islands, which were to be sold in the China market.—From Robinson, No. 46. In the furtherance of the trade the ships separated and worked independently of each other. Their voyages were important for the supplementary detail to be added to the geographical explorations of Cook. For Dixon's remarks on the voyages of Meares see under 1790 and 1791 below.

1789 PORTLOCK, NATHANIEL, and DIXON, GEORGE. An Abridgement of Portlock's and Dixon's Voyage round the World, performed in 1785-88. Large folding map and portrait. 8vo. London.

> This edition is very uncommon and much scarcer than the original quarto edition.—Maggs, No. 502.

1789 (In French.) Voyage autour du monde et principalement à la côte Nord-Ouest de l'Amérique fait en 1785-88 par les Capitaines Portlock et Dixon. Traduit de l'anglais par M. Lebas. Folding map and 21 plates. 2 vols. 4to. Paris.

1789 (In German.) Reise um die Welt besonders nach der Nordwest-Küste von Amerika 1785-88. Herausgegeben von G. Dixon. Aus dem Englischen übersetzt und mit Anmerkungen erläutert von J. R. Forster. Map and plates. Berlin.

1795 (In Dutch.) Reis naar de Noord-West Kust van Amerika. 10 plates and charts. 4to. Amsterdam.

> This is based on the two English narratives.—Maggs, No. 562.

1790 BENYOWSKY, MAURITIUS AUGUSTUS, COUNTE DE. For his voyage through the North Pacific, see under SIBERIA.

> This work includes a description of the Aleutian Islands.

DIXON, GEORGE. Remarks on the Voyages of John Meares, in a Letter to that Gentleman. 4to. London.

1791 DIXON, GEORGE. Further Remarks on the Voyages of John Meares. 4to. London.

LESSEPS, J. B. B. DE. For the portion of his voyage relating to the North Pacific see under SIBERIA.

MEARES, JOHN (Captain). Voyages made in the years 1788 and 1789 from China to the North-West Coast of America; To which are prefixed an introductory Narrative of a Voyage performed in 1786, from Bengal, in the Ship Nootka; to which are annexed, Observations on the Probable Existence of a North West Passage, and some account of the Trade between the North West Coast of America and China; and the latter Country and Great Britain. Portrait, 10 maps, and 17 plates. 4to. London.

Another edition 2 vols., 8vo, London, 1791. Translated into French, Paris, 1794; into German, Berlin, 1796; into Italian, Florence, 1796. See below.
"This narrative is a most important work. It was on these discoveries by Meares that the claims of Great Britain to Oregon mainly depended. In the treaty between England and Spain which followed the Nootka affair the Spanish claims were disallowed, and the Spaniards withdrew (see Vancouver, under 1798 below). Subsequently in the arbitration on the Oregon question, England finally yielded to the United States much territory claimed under the discoveries by Meares." Meares had been engaged in the fur trade between British Columbia and China. His vessels were seized at Nootka Sound by the Spaniards, who claimed all that coast as Spanish territory. War nearly broke out over the question and Spain had to give way. Meares also stayed for a month, August, 1788, at Hawaii and gives a long account of the Islands and the inhabitants.—Maggs, No. 491. This important voyage gives an excellent account of the Indian Nations on the North-West Coast of America.—Robinson, No. 46.

1794   (In French.) Voyage de la Chine à la côte Nord-Ouest d'Amérique, fait dans les années 1778-89. Précédes de la relation d'un autre voyage exécuté en 1786 sur le vaisseau *Le Nootka* parti du Bengale. D'un recueil d'observations sur la probabilité d'un passage Nord-Ouest, et d'un traité abrégé du commerce entre la côte Nord-Ouest et la Chine par John Meares. Traduit de l'anglais par J.-B.-L. Billecocq. 3 vols. in 8vo and atlas in 4to consisting of 28 maps, maritime views, plans, and portraits. Paris.

1796   (In German.) Reisen nach der Nordwestküste von Amerika 1786-89. Aus dem Englischen und mit Anmerkungen von G. Forster. Nebst einer Abhandlung desselben über die Nordwest Küste von Amerika. 2 maps. Berlin.

1796   (In Italian.) Viaggi dalla China alla costa Nord-Ouest d'America. Fatti negli anni 1788 e 1789. Plates and maps. 4 vols. 8vo. Florence.

MEARES, JOHN. An authentic Copy of his Memorial; containing every particular respecting the capture of his Vessels in Nootka Sound. London.

An authentic Statement of all the Facts relative to Nootka Sound. 8vo. London.

In this tract the high claims of the Spaniards to a monopoly of almost half the globe are exposed with great spirit, and treated with the utmost contempt.— Puttick and Simpson, *Bibliotheca Americana.* It is signed "Argonaut."

1791 MEARES, JOHN. In Answer to George Dixon, late Commander of the Queen Charlotte, in the review of Messrs. Etchee and Company. . . . In which the remarks of Mr. Dixon on the Voyage to the N.W. Coast of America, etc., lately published, are carefully considered and refuted. 4to. London. (32 pp.)

DIXON, GEORGE. Further remarks on the Voyages of John Meares, Esq.; in which several important facts, misrepresented in the said Voyages, relative to Geography and Commerce, are fully substantiated. To which is added, A Letter from Captain Duncan, containing a decisive Refutation of several unfounded Assertions of Mr. Meares; and a final reply to his answer. 4to. London.

1792-93 PAGES, PIERRE MARIE FRANCOIS DE. For his reputed voyage towards the North Pole, see under CIRCUMNAVIGATIONS.

1793 GOLDSON, WILLIAM. For his memoirs on the Straits of Anian see under NORTHWEST PASSAGE.

1798 LA PEROUSE, JOHN FRANCIS GALAUP. A Voyage round the World, in the years 1785-88, with the Nautical Tables. Arranged by M. A. Milet Mureau. To which is prefixed, a Narrative of an Interesting Voyage from Manilla to St. Blaise. And annexed, Travels over the Continent, with the Dispatches of La Pérouse in 1787 and 1788, by M. de Lesseps. Engraved portrait and 50 engraved portraits and maps. 2 vols. 8vo. London.

> For a description of the various editions of La Pérouse's voyage and his discoveries, see under CIRCUMNAVIGATIONS. The work of Captain Cook in the North Pacific and on the northwest coast of America had impressed European governments with an idea of what remained to be done in that region. La Pérouse had already distinguished himself in his encounters at sea with English fleets and in particular with his capture of the English forts at the southern end of Hudson's Bay. His voyage was replete with misfortunes. After leaving the Hawaiian Islands he next sighted the American coast near Cape St. Elias in Alaska. In this vicinity he lost twenty-one men, who were drowned when their boats were caught in the strong current at the entrance to Lituya Bay. He examined much of the fringe of islands lying off the Alaskan coast south, and continued his explorations down to Monterey Bay in California. His labors furnished geographers with results whereby they could check the charts of Russian, English, and Spanish navigators. From California he sailed across the Pacific and explored numerous island groups in the South Seas. His ships were lost after sailing from Botany Bay and were never heard of again.

VANCOUVER, GEORGE (Captain). A Voyage of Discovery to the North Pacific Ocean and round the World, in which the Coast of North-West America has been carefully examined and accurately surveyed principally with a View to ascertain the Existence of any navigable Communication between the North Pacific and North Atlantic Oceans, performed in 1790-95 in the Discovery Sloop-of-War, and armed Tender Chatham, under his Command. 18 engraved views. 3 vols. in 4to and 1 vol. fol., containing an atlas of maps and charts. London.

2nd edition, with corrections, 19 views and charts, 6 vols., 8vo, London, 1801. A modern reprint of the portions dealing with waters of the Strait of Juan de Fuca, Puget Sound, and British Columbia, edited by Professor Edmond Meany, of the University of Washington, New York, 1907. See Menzie's Journal, Victoria, 1923. Translated into Danish, Copenhagen, 1799; into German, Halle, 1799, 1800, and Berlin, 1799-1800; into French, Paris, 1800. See below.

This is one of the most important voyages ever made in the interests of geographical knowledge. Vancouver put an end to the delusion that the subarctic seas in the direction of Greenland could be reached from Nootka Sound or any of the inlets in its vicinity, and his description of the Port of San Francisco and the coasts of California in Spanish hands is most interesting.—From Quaritch. Vancouver was appointed in command of the Discovery with the tender Chatham under Lieut. Broughten, "to receive back in form the territory which the Spaniards had seized." He was also to make an accurate survey of the coast northward from the 30th degree latitude. Proceeding by way of the Cape of Good Hope, he touched at various places in the South Seas, and finally on April 18, 1792, he sighted the west coast of North America. He then sailed to the north, and carried out the formalities of taking over from the Spaniards at Nootka Sound the disputed territory. He examined the Straits of Juan de Fuca, discovered the Gulf of Georgia, and circumnavigated the island known by his name—Vancouver Island. (He also did exploration in Puget Sound.) In 1793 he examined the coast of North America northwards from San Francisco, which for the first time was accurately delineated. This work ranks with the voyages of Cook and La Pérouse among the most important of the 18th and 19th centuries.—From Maggs, No. 491. On his return to England he busied himself with preparing his volumes for the press, but before completing volume III he died. His brother John finished the task.

1907 VANCOUVER, GEORGE (Captain). Description of Puget Sound. Portraits and Biographies of the Men Honored in the Naming of Geographical Features of Northwestern America, by (the late) Professor Edmond Meany. 8vo. New York.

In addition to the interesting biographical accounts, this book reproduces that portion of Vancouver's Diary relating to the Puget Sound and British Columbia regions, taken from the original journal. The editing of the text is done with painstaking scholarship. It was reprinted in 1915.

1923 Menzie's Journal of Vancouver's Voyage, April to October, 1792, edited by C. F. Newcombe. Maps and illus. 8vo. Archives of British Columbia, No. 5 Victoria, B. C.

1799 (In Danish.) Opdagelsesreise i de nordlige Dele af Sydhavet fra 1790-95. Oversat af Brun Juul. Copenhagen.

1799 (In German.) Entdeckungsreise in den nördlichen Gewässern der Südsee und längs den westlichen Küsten von America von 1790-95. Aus dem Englischen von M. C. Sprengel. Halle.

1799 (In German.) Reisen nach dem nördlichen Theile der Südsee 1790-95. Aus dem Englischen von J. Fr. Herbst. Map. 2 vols. Berlin.

Volumes XVIII and XIX of *Merkwürdige neuen Reisebeschreibungen.*

1800 (In French.) Voyage de découvertes à l'Océan Pacifique du Nord et autour du monde, dans lequel la côte Nord-Ouest de l'Amérique a été soigneusement reconnue et exactement relevée. Ordonné par le roi d'Angleterre, principalement dans la vue de constater s'il existe, à travers le continent de l'Amérique, un passage pour les vaisseaux de l'Océan Pacifique du Nord à l'Océan Atlantique septentrional et exécuté en 1790, 1791, 1792, 1793, 1794 et 1795. Traduit de l'anglais, par Demeunier et Morelet. 3 vols. in 4to and an atlas in fol., with the original maps. Paris.

1800 BILLINGS, JOSEPH (Commodore). For his voyage along the coasts of southwestern and central Alaska see under SIBERIA.

## ADDENDA

1804 BROUGHTEN, WILLIAM ROBERT. A Voyage of Discovery to the North Pacific Ocean in which the Coast of Asia, from Latitude of 35 degrees North to Latitude of 52 North, the Island of Insu (commonly known under the Name of the Land of Jeddo), the North South and East Coasts of Japan, the Lieuchieux and adjacent Isles, as well as the Coast of Corea, have been examined and surveyed. Performed in His Majesty's Sloop Providence, and her Tender, in the years 1795-98, by William Robert Broughten. 3 folding maps and plates. 4to. London.

A German edition, Weimar, 1805. See below.
Capt. Broughton saw much important service along the coast of North-West America, in the East Indies, and along the coast of N.E. Asia. In 1790 he was appointed to accompany Vancouver in his famous Voyage, but was for some time employed in the survey of the Columbia River and the adjacent coast. He returned to England with despatches, and on Oct. 3, 1793, was made Commander of the "Providence" (Capt. Bligh's old ship), and again sent out to the N. W. Coast of America to join Vancouver. He sailed to Rio de Janeiro, thence to Australia, Tahiti, the Hawaiian Islands and so to Nootka Sound, in Vancouver Island. Finding that Capt. Vancouver had left he sailed down to Monterrey in California, and then across the Pacific again to the Hawaiian Islands and on to Japan. For four years he carried out a close survey of the Coast of Asia and the Islands of Japan. The "Providence" was lost off Formosa, but the crew were all saved, and the work continued in the tender. He arrived back in England in February, 1799, and until his death in 1821 saw much further important service for most part in the Far East.—Maggs, No. 491. This voyage was one of the most important ever made to the North-West Coast of America. It is on this document that Great Britain based her claim to the Oregon Territory in 1846.—Robinson, No. 45.

1805 (In German.) Entdeckungsreise in das Stille Meer, und vorzüglich nach der Nordostküste von Asien, gethan in den Jahren 1795-98. Maps. 8vo. Weimar.

1929 STRANGE, JAMES. Journal and Narrative of the Commercial Expedition from Bombay to the North-West Coast of America. Together with a Chart showing the track of the Expedition. With an Introduction by A. V. Venkatarama Ayyar, M.A., L.T. Fol. Madras.

This is the first published account of this voyage. James Strange was the eldest son of Sir Robt. Strange, and was inspired to undertake this voyage to Nootka Sound by the account of Cook's last voyage, which had recently appeared. Its object was to establish the fur trade between China and America, and it was sent out by David Scott of Bombay, 1785-87.—Maggs, No. 562.

1930 A Spanish Voyage to Vancouver and the North-West Coast of America. Being the Narrative of the Voyage made in the year 1792 by the Schooner Sutil and Mexicana to explore the Strait of Fuca. Translated from the Spanish with an Introduction by Cecil Jane. Folding map and 6 illus. 4to. Argonaut Press. London.

> Spanish original, Madrid, 1802. See below.
> An important voyage undertaken for the purpose of exploring the Strait of Juan de Fuca, between Vancouver Island and the Mainland. About half of the volume of text gives a record of various Spanish voyages which had been undertaken for the purpose of Northwest exploration and the discovery of the Northwest passage.—Maggs, No. 562. This account was printed by Martin Fernandez de Navarrete, but has not previously been translated into English. It contains an interesting and lucid description of the districts visited and gives an excellent account of the manners and customs of the natives of those districts. It is essentially the account of a naval officer whose primary aim was to extend geographical, scientific, and ethnographical knowledge.—Quoted from Publishers' Notice.

> 1802 "Sutil and Mexicana." Relacion del Viage hecho por las Goletas Sutil y Mexicana en el Ano de 1792, para reconocer el Estrecho de Fuca: con una Introduccion en que se da noticia de las Expediciones executadas Anteriormente por los Espanoles en busca del paso del Noroeste de la America. Atlas of 9 charts and 8 views and plates. 4 vols. 4to. Madrid.

# V

## North America

1563 RIBAUT, JEAN (Captain). The Whole and true Discouerye of Terra
Florida (englished the Flourishing lande). Conteyning as well the
wonderfull straunge Natures and Maners of the People, with the mer-
veylous Commodities and Treasures of the Country: As also the pleas-
unt Portes, Hauens, and wayes therevnto Neuer founde out before
the last yere 1562. Written in French by Captaine Ribauld . . . And
newly set forthe in Englishe the XXX of May, 1563. 8vo. London.
(23 leaves.)

> The translator was probably Thomas Hackitt, for whom this version was
> published. His name is attached to the account included by Hakluyt in his *Divers
> Voyages*, 1582. For other accounts see Le Challeux under 1566, Vezarianus un-
> der 1582, and Laudonnière under 1587 below. French original, London, 1563. See
> below.

> 1582 RIBAULT, JOHN. The true Discovery, by Captain John Ribault, in the
> yeare 1563. Translated into English by one Thomas Hackitt. 4to.
> London.
>
> > A portion of "Divers Voyages touching the Discovery of Ameri-
> > ca."—Lowndes. See Hakluyt this date, under COLLECTIONS.

> 1563 RIBAUT, JEAN. Histoire de l'Expeditione Francaise en Floride. Lon-
> don.

SEALE, ROBERT. A Commendation of the Adventurous Voyage of
Thomas Stukeley and others towards the land called Terra Florida.
London.

> So cited by Taylor, who notes that this is a unique copy in the Henry Hunt-
> ington Library.

1566 LE CHALLEUX, NICOLAS. A True and Perfect Description of the
last Voyage or Nauigation, attempted by Capitaine John Rybaut, depu-
tie and Generall for the French Men, into Terra Florida, this year past,
1565 (1563?). Truely set forth by those that returned from thence,
wherein are contayned things as lamentable to heare as they haue bene
cruelly executed. London.

> French original, Dieppe, 1566. See below.
> This is the only record of French Florida until Hakluyt published the Lau-
> donnière narratives in 1586.—Parks. It is introduced by an epistle "from the Au-
> thor to his Friend,—Deepe the xxv day of May, 1566. Your louing Brother and
> friend, N. le Shalleux." The running title is "The last voyage to Terra Florida."
> —Lowndes.

1566  LE CHALLEUX, NICOLAS. Discovrs et Histoire de la Floride, con-
      tenant las Cruauté des Espagnols contre les subiets du Roy, en l' an
      mil cinq cens soixante cinq. Redigé au vray par ceux qui en sont
      restez. Chose autant lamentable à ouir, qu'elle a este proditoirement &
      cruellement exécutée par lesdits Espagnols : Contre l autorité du Roy
      nostre Sire, à la perte & dommage de tout ce Royaume. Item, vne
      Reqveste av Roy, faite en forme de complainte par les femmes vefues,
      petit enfans orphelins & autres leurs amis, parens & alliez de ceux qui
      ont esté cruellement envahis par les Espagnols, en la France anthar-
      tique, dite la Floride. 12mo. Dieppe.

          Another French account, Lyons, 1566. See below. The second por-
      tion or 'requests' mentioned in the title is not in the work. The work
      is extracted from G. Benzoni.—Sabin quoted by Bradford.

1566  LE CHALLEUX, NICOLAS. Histoire memorable dv dernier Voyage
      avx Indes, Lieu appelé la Floride, fait par le Captaine Iean Ribaut, &
      entrepris par la commandement du Roy, en l'an MDLXV. 12mo.
      Lyons.

1578  THEVET, ANDRE. For some chapters on Canada see his *The New
      found VVorlde,* under SOUTH AMERICA.

1576  GILBERT, SIR HUMPHREY. For Sebastian Cabot's first voyage see
      *A Discourse of a Discoverie for a Newe Passage to Cataia,* under
      NORTHWEST PASSAGE. Other items under this section likewise
      relate to North America. For more detail concerning the Cabots see
      Columbus under 1892, WEST INDIES, and Williamson under 1929
      below.

1580  CARTIER, JACQUES. A Shorte and Briefe Narration of the two Nau-
      igations and Discoueries to the Northwest Partes called Newe Fraunce :
      First translated out of French into Italian, by that famous learned
      man Gio. Bapt. Ramusius, and now turned into English by Iohn Florio :
      Worthy the reading of all Venturers, Trauellers, and Discouerers.
      London.

          This is an account of Cartier's first two voyages (those of 1534 and 1535)
      up the St. Lawrence. The translation and publication were arranged by Hakluyt
      from his copy of Ramusio's Navigationi, vol. III. It was reprinted, with a frag-
      mentary account of Cartier's last voyage, in Hakluyt, 1600.—From Parks. The
      title page of Florio's book tells us that he made his translation from Ramusio,
      but it is possible that this applies only to the first voyage, and that he made the
      second direct. . . . Cartier made four voyages in all, the first in 1534. This took
      him up the Gulf of St. Lawrence, which he persisted in believing was the short
      route to India, the much-sought-for North-west Passage, even after he got well
      into fresh water ; his second, the next year, took him to the site of Montreal. . . .
      Very little material survives of the Cartier voyages. Ramusio published an ac-
      count in 1556, which remained unquestioned until the discovery in Paris (in the
      middle of the nineteenth century), of an ancient manuscript which seems to be
      not only Cartier's own account of it, but even partially in his own hand ; the
      latter contradicts Ramusio at many points. The original description of the sec-
      ond voyage, the Brief Recit & Succincte Narration, survives in only one copy.—
      Waldman. According to other authorities Cartier seems to have written none of
      the journals recording his voyages. The first account that was printed was that

of the second voyage in 1535, at Paris, 1545. In 1598 appeared a published account of the first voyage. The journal of the third can be found in Hakluyt, 1600. Relations of the first three voyages, taken from Hakluyt, appear in Pinkerton XII, 629-674. A modern reprint, New York, 1906. For this and the modern French accounts see below.

1906  BAXTER, J.P.  A Memoir of Jacques Cartier, Sieur De Limoilou. His Voyage to the St. Lawrence. A Bibliography and a Facsimile of the Manuscript of 1534 with Annotations, etc.  Illus.  4to.  New York.

1863-67  CARTIER, JACQUES.  Bref récit et succincte narration de la navigation faite en 1535 et 1536 par le capitaine Jacques Cartier aux iles de Canada, Hochelaga, Saguenay, et autres.  Reimpression figurée de l'édition originale rarissime de 1545 avec les varientes des manuscrits de la Bibliothéque imperiale, précédée d'une breve et succincte introduction historique par M. d'Avezac.—RELATION originale du voyage de Jacques Cartier au Canada en 1534. Documents inédits sur Jacques Cartier et le Canada, publiés par H. Michelant et A. Rame, accompagnes de deux portraits de Cartier et de deux vues de son manoir. 2 vols. 8vo. Paris.

1931  GUEGAN, B. (Publisher).  Trois Voyages au Canada publiés par Bertrand Guegan. Illus.  4to.  Paris.

Among the contents is the following: Cartier (Jacques) Voyages faits en la Nouvelle France en 1534 et 1536.

1581  CARLEILL, CHRISTOPHER.  A Discourse vpon the entended Voyage to the hethermoste partes of America: written by Captaine Carleill, for the better Inducement to satisfie suche Marchauntes, as in disburcing their money towardes the Furniture of the present Charge; doe demaunde forthwith a present Returne of Gaine: albeit their saied perticular disburcementes are in such slender sommes, as are not worth the speakyng of.  London.

These are the "Articles set downe by the Comitties appointed in the behalfe of the Companie of Moscuian Marchauntes, to conferre with Maister Carleill vpon his entended discoueries and attempt into the hethermost parties of America."—From John Carter Brown.

1582  VEZARIANUS, JOHN.  To the King of Fraunce, Francis the first: The Relation of John Vezarianus, a Florentine, of the Land discouered in the Name of his Maiestie. Written in Dieppe 1524. The true Discovery by Captain John Ribault, in the Yeare 1563. Translated into English by one Thomas Hackitt.  4to.  London.

A portion of the *Divers Voyages touching the Discovery of America.*—Lowndes.

1583  PECKHAM, SIR GEORGE.  A true Reporte of the late Discoveries . . . of the Newfound Landes.  London.

Reprinted in Hakluyt, 1600. A full reprint is to be found in the *Magazine of History*, ex. ser., no. 68, Tarrytown, N. Y., 1920.—Parks.
Peckham was a merchant adventurer associated with Gilbert, Grenville, and Carleill in American exploration.—D.N.B.

1584 LLOYD, HUMPHREY. The Historie of Cambria, now called Wales:
A part of the most famous Yland of Brytaine, written in the Brytish
Language aboue two hundreth yeares past: translated into English by
H. Lloyd Gentleman: Corrected, augmented, and continued out of
Records and best approued Authors, by David Powel, Doctor in divini-
tie. Numerous woodcuts in the text. London.

> Dedicated to Sir Philip Sidney. . . . "This work is of special interest to the
> collector of Americana, as it relates to the discoveries made by David, the son of
> Owen Gwyneth. . . . 'Sailing west . . . he came to a land unknown, where he saw
> manie strange things . . . this land . . . must needs be some part of Nova His-
> pania or Florida. Whereupon it is manifest that that countrie was long before
> by Brytaines discovered, afore either Columbus or Americua Vesputius lead
> anie Spaniards thither.' "—Quoted by Maggs, No. 465.

1587 ESPEJO, ANTONIO DE. New-Mexico, otherwise the Voyage of Anthony of Espeio, who in the yeare 1583, with his Company, discovered
a Lande of 15 Provinces, replenished with Townes and Villages,
with Houses of four or five stories Height. It lieth northward, and
some suppose that the same way, by Places inhabited, go the Land
termed the Labrador. Translated out of the Spanish. 12mo. London.

> Entered in the *Stationers' Register* 1587. Modern reprint, New York, 1928.
> Another account, London, 1929. A French translation, by Basanier, Paris, 1586.
> See below. Spanish original, 1586.
> The French translation was undertaken by Basanier at the suggestion of
> Hakluyt, who himself printed the Spanish edition in Paris in 1586. That edition
> is now unfortunately unprocurable, for it is represented by only one copy which
> is in the British Museum. Antonio de Espejo, a Spanish soldier with the army
> in Mexico, having acquired considerable wealth, led an expedition into New
> Mexico in 1582 and explored well into the interior. He later applied to the
> King for permission to settle those parts, but died before his project could be
> realized.—Quaritch.

> 1928 ESPEJO, ANTONIO DE. New Mexico. Otherwise the Voiage of An-
> thony of Espejo in 1583. London (1587). With foreword by F. W.
> Hodge. 8vo. New York. (Privately printed.)

> 1929 ESPEJO, ANTONIO DE. Expedition into New Mexico, 1582-1583. As
> revealed in the Journal of Diego Perez de Luxan. Translated by
> George P. Hammond and Agapito Rey. Illus. 8vo. London.

> This is vol. I of the Publications of the Quivira Society and the
> key volume to a complete set.—Bookseller's Note.

LAUDONNIERE, RENE GOULAINE DE. A Notable Historie, Containing foure voyages made by Certayne French Captaynes vnto Florida; Wherein the great riches and fruitfulness of the Countrey with
the maners of the people, hitherto concealed, are brought to light, written all, sauing the last, by Monsieur Laudonniere who remained there
himself, as the French Kings Lieutenant a yere and a quarter; Newly
translated out of French into English, by R. H. In the end is added a

large table for the better finding out the principall matters contayned in this worke. Table. 4to. London.

The French edition was published at Paris (1586) at the expense of Hakluyt, and dedicated to Sir Walter Raleigh.—Lowndes. See below. A Latin version in De Bry; translated into Dutch.

This is the history of the Huguenots' colony in Florida and its fate. It is based on three letters of Rene de Laudonnière, the commandant. It covers the two expeditions of Ribault, made in 1562 and 1563, Laudonnière's of 1564, and the futile revenge expedition of Gourgues' in 1567. . . . The last part is probably the work of the editor and compiler of the book. After Cabeca de Vaca this work gives the earliest description of Florida, a name which, by the way, covered a vastly larger amount of territory than it does now.—Waldman. Hakluyt added some entertaining matter to the French edition. It is also far rarer than the other, being one of the scarcest of Hakluyt's books.—Waldman.

1586  LAUDONNIERE, RENE DE.  L'Histoire Notable de la Floride sitvée ès Indes Occidentales, contenant les trois voyages faits en icelle par certain Capitaines & Pilotes Francois, descrits par le Capitaine Laudonniere, qui y a commandé l'espace d'vn an trois moys; à laquelle a esté adiousté vn quatriesme voyage fait par le Capitaine Gourgues. Mise en lumière par M. Basanier. . . . 8vo. Paris.

1588  HARIOT, THOMAS.  A briefe and true report of the new found land of Virginia: of the commodities there found and to be raysed, as well marchantable, as others for victuall, building and other necessarie vses for those that are and shalbe the planters there; and of the nature and manners of the naturall inhabitants: Discouered by the English Colony there seated by Sir Richard Greinuile Knight in the yeere 1585. . . . 4to. London.

Reprinted in Hakluyt, 1589 and 1600. It forms Part I of the *Grands Voyages* of De Bry in all four languages. For the English and the French versions from De Bry (1590) see below. A facsimile reprint of the 1590 edition, New York, 1903. See below.

The author was a member of the first colony planted by Sir Walter Raleigh at Roanoke, which was rescued by Drake in July, 1586. His Virginia, as it is commonly known, is only a small tract of 24 leaves, but the amount of information he managed to compress in them is astonishing. As Henry Stevens, the well known bookseller-bibliographer says, "This book of Hariot's, with Laudonnière's Florida, . . . affords at this day more authentic materials for the early history of the Atlantic coast of North America, from the River of May to the Chesapeake, than any other portion of the New World, Spanish or English, can boast of."—Waldman.

1590  HARIOT, THOMAS.  A briefe and true Report of the New Found Land of Virginia, of the Commodities and of the Nature and Manners of the Naturall Inhabitants. Discouered by the English Colony there seated by Sir Richard Greinuile Knight In the yeare 1585. Which Remained Vnder the gouernment of the twelue monethes, At the speciall charge and direction of the Honourable Sir Walter Raleigh Knight lord Warden of the stanneries who therein hath beene fauored and authorised by her Maiestie and her letter patents: This fore Books is made in English By Thomas Hariot seruant to the aboue named Sir Walter, a member of the Colony, and there imployed in discouering . . . Translated out of Latin into English by Richard Hacklvit. . . . Diligentlye collected and drawne by Iohn White who was sent thither speciallye and for the same purpose by the said Sir Walter Ralegh the year abouesaid 1585, and also the year 1588. Now cut in copper and first published by Theodore De Bry.

A photolitho facsimile issued at Manchester, 1888.

1590 (In French.) Merveilleux et estrange Rapport toutesfois fidele des com-
moditez qui se trouvent en Virginia, des facons des natureles habitants d'icelle, la quelle a esté nouvellement descouverte par les Anglois
que Messire Richard Greinville Chevalier y mena en Colonie L'an
1585, à la charge principale de Messire Walter Raleigh, Chevalier Sur-
intendant des Mines d'Estain, favorisé par la Reyne d'Angleterre, et
autorisé par ses Lettres Patentes. Par Thomas Hariot, Serviteur du
Sus-dit Messire Walter, l'un de Ceux de la dite Colonie, et qui a été
employé à descouvrir. Traduit nouvellement d'Anglois en Francois
avec Privilege du Roy pour quatre ans. Franckfurt.

This is the first and only edition in French and the first issue of
the plates, which were used later in the English, Latin, and German
issues. All the plates were engraved by De Bry. . . . This French
translation is of the greatest rarity. It is the only part of De Bry's
Collection that was published in French, which from the date of its
dedication, "24 de Mars 1590," appears to have been published before
the English Virginia, dated "the first of Apprill, 1590," the Latin Virginia, dated "KL, Aprilis MDXC," and the German Virginia, dated
"den 3 Aprill im funffsehen hundert und neuntzigsten."—From Maggs,
No. 479.

1893 HARIOT, THOMAS. Narrative of the First English Plantation of Virginia. Illus. 4to. London.

A scarce reprint from the excessively rare edition of 1590. With
De Bry's engravings. The illustrations were designed in Virginia in
1585 by John White.—Bookseller's Note.

1903 HARIOT, THOMAS. A Briefe and True Report of the New Found
Land of Virginia. Reproduced in facsimile from the first edition of
1588. 8vo. New York.

"A Facsimile reprint of the first edition of Hariot, was published
in 'The Bibliographer,' Jan., Feb., March, 1902. This was issued . .
in book form, in 1903."—Bradford. See this date, under WEST IN-
DIES.

1598 LINSCHOTEN, JAN HUIGHEN VAN. For descriptions of New
France, Florida, and the Antilles see his *Discours of Voyages into ye
Easte and West Indies,* under EAST INDIES.

1602 BRERETON, JOHN. A Briefe and true Relation of the Discouerie of
the North part of Virginia; being a most pleasant, fruitfull and com-
modious soile: Made this present yeere 1602, by Captaine Bartholomew
Gosnold, Captaine Bartholomew Gilbert, and diuers other gentlemen
their associates, by the permission of the honourable knight, Sir Walter
Raleigh, . . . Written by M. John Brereton, one of the voyage. Whereunto is annexed a Treatise, conteining important inducements for the
planting in those parts, and finding a Passage that way to the South
sea, and China. Written by M. Edward Hayes, a gentleman long since
imploied in the like action. 4to. London.

2nd edit., with added matter, London, 1602. A modern reprint, New York
1903. See below.
The story of Gosnold's expedition. Without any color of authority Gosnold
set out on a journey in March, 1602, to see what he could find. . . . He established a settlement on Cuttyhunk Island near Cape Cod, the first English col-

ony in New England, and the second in America. Returning in July he ran into Raleigh, the patentee, upon whose preserves he had been poaching, and his cargo, chiefly of sassafras, was confiscated. . . . But he gained the good graces of Raleigh and was taken into his employ. He went also on the Jamestown expedition.—From Waldman. The second edition is very nearly as rare as the first, and from an historical point of view is much more interesting. It has twelve more leaves made up of "diuers instructions of speciall moment." These consist of "Inducements to the liking of the voyage intended towards Virginia . . . written in 1585 by M. Richard Hakluyt the elder. . . ."—"A briefe note on the corne, fowles, fruits and beasts of the Island of Florida on the backside of Virginia . . . begun by Fernando de Soto gouernor of Cuba, in the yeere of our Lord 1539."—"A Note of such commodities as are found in Florida . . . by Mounsieur Rene Laudonnière. . . ."—"A briefe extracte of the merchantable commodities found in the South part of Virginia, ann. 1585. and 1586. Gathered out of the learned work of Master Thomas Herriot . . ." and "Certaine briefe testimonies touching sundry rich mines of Gold, Siluer, and Copper, in part found and in part constantly heard of, in North Florida, and the Island of the Maine of Virginia . . ."—From Quaritch.

1903  BRERETON, JOHN.  A Briefe and True Relation of the Discoverie of the North Part of Virginia. Reproduced in facsimile from the first edition of 1602. 8vo. New York.

1604  WATSON, THOMAS.  A Trve Relation of such Occurences and Accidents of Noate as hath hapned in Virginia since the first Planting of that Colony which is now resident in the South Part thereof, till the last Returne from thence.  Written by Thomas Watson, Gent. one of the said Collony, to a worshipfull Friend of his in England. 4to. London.

It appears from the printer's address that Capt. J. Smith was the real author and that the name of Watson was inserted by mistake.—Lowndes. See Smith under 1608 below and note the similarity of title.

1605  ROSIER, JAMES.  A trve Relation of the most prosperous Voyage made this present yeere 1605 by Captaine George Waymouth, in the Discouery of the land of Virginia: Where he discouered 60 miles vp a most excellent Riuer: together with a most fertile Land. Written by James Rosier, a Gentleman employed in the Voyage. 4to. London.

Later editions: Bath, 1860; printed for the Gorges Society, Portland, 1887 See below.
A narrative of the voyage of Captain George Weymouth up to Kennebec River. Although he planted no colony, his expedition was far-reaching in its results on New England's future, since it stimulated a group of influential men in London to a series of further efforts. Weymouth also led the way for Luke Foxe (see Foxe under 1635, NORTHWEST PASSAGE). The author, James Rosier, had accompanied both Gosnold and Weymouth.—From Waldman.

1860  ROSIER, JAMES.  Rosier's Narrative of Waymouth's Voyage to the Coast of Maine, in 1605. Complete, with Remarks by George Prince shewing the river explored to have been the George River; Together with a Map of the same and adjacent Islands. . . . 8vo. Bath.

1606 CANNER, THOMAS. Scheeps-togt van M. Pringe gedaan in't jaar 1603, van Bristol na't noorder gedeelte van Virginien. Mitsgaders een tweede reys in't selve jaar 1603 naar Virginien gedaan van B. Gilbert. Beschreven door Thomas Canner. Nu aldereerst uyt het Engelsch vertaald. 8vo. Leyden.

> The English original is unknown to the editor.

1607 GORGES, SIR FERDINANDO. Relation of a Voyage Into New England. London.

> 1607 is the date given in John Carter Brown. Waldman thinks it is later. This is an account of Capt. Popham's voyage in 1607 based on papers left by Gorges. Popham was a brother of the Chief Justice who was Gorges' associate. Gorges was governor of Plymouth, who became interested in colonization. He formed two companies which received grants of land in the colonies and established the settlement of New Plymouth, 1628. He became Lord Proprietary of Maine in 1639. See Gorges under 1654 and Johnson under 1657 below.

1608 POWELL, NATHANIEL. The Diarie of the Second Voyage in discovering the (Chesapeake) Bay. London (?).

> Cited in D. N. B.
> The author was one of the early settlers of Virginia to which he came in 1607. He did some exploring work with Captain John Smith.

SMITH, JOHN (Captain). A True Relation of suche Occurrences and Accidents of Noate as Hath Happened in Virginia Synce the first Plantynge of that Colonye which is nowe resident in the South Parte of Virginia till Master Nelsons comminge away from them. . . . Map. 4to. London.

> An edition issued in 1866, with full bibliographical details by Charles Deane. Another edition in the *Amer. Colon. Tracts*, vol. 2, no. 1, May 1, 1898, Rochester, N. Y. See also Smith under dates 1612, 1616, 1624, and 1631 below and under 1630, GENERAL TRAVELS AND DESCRIPTIONS.
> This constitutes the earliest printed account of the Jamestown settlement, from April, 1607, to June, 1608. It was written by Smith in the form of a letter to a friend in England, who had it printed. The work was issued with four different title pages, the first stating merely that it was written by a Gentleman of the said colony; the second that Thomas Watson was the author; the third and fourth state that he was Captain Smith and "Captaine Smith colonell of the said Collony, respectively."—Waldman. If the item listed above under 1604 refers to the Colony at Jamestown, then the date of that item is wrong, as the plantation was not made until 1607.

1609 DE SOTO, DON FERDINANDO. Virginia richly valued, By the Description of the maine land of Florida, her next Neighbour: Out of the foure yeers continuall Trauell and Discouerie, for about one thousand miles East and West, of Don Ferdinando de Soto, and six hundred able men in his Companie. Wherein are truly observed the Riches and Fertilitie of those Parts, abounding with things necessarie, pleas-

ant, and profitable for the life of man: with the Nature and Dispositions of the Inhabitants. Written by a Portugall gentleman of Eluas,
emploied in all the action, and translated out of Portuguese by Richard
Haklvyt. 4to. London.

2nd edit., with a different title, London, 1611; reprinted, with added matter,
London, 1686. The 1611 edition reprinted, with the addition of Biedma's account,
Hakluyt Society, London, 1851. A new translation, Bradford Club, N. Y., 1866.
Re-edited with the addition of other matter, Trailmakers Series, New York,
1904 and 1922. Portuguese original, Evora, 1557. For a modern text and translation of this see under 1933 below. Other sources dealing with De Soto's expedition are Garcilaso de la Vega's *La Florida del Inca* (never translated in full
into English), Lisbon, 1605, Oviedo's *Historia General y Natural de las Indias,*
and Biedma's account included in the Hakluyt Society edition. For the relation
and significance of these various editions see Professor Bourne's introduction to
the edition in the Trailmakers Series. See also L'Estrange under 1896 below.

In his preface Hakluyt states that his purpose in bringing this work to the
attention of the public was to encourage the young colony in Virginia. See
Parks, pp. 220-221.—De Soto landed on the west coast of Florida, at Espiritu
Bay, in May, 1539, with 600 Spaniards, and wandered about the country for
nearly four years. Much of his route is difficult to identify, but he seems to
have passed north through Florida and Georgia, to the neighborhood of Mobile,
and then Northwest towards the Mississippi, which was reached early in 1541.
The following winter was spent on the Washita. Finally De Soto "sickened and
died," and his body was sunk in the river in a lead coffin. The remnant of the
Spaniards under Luis de Moscoso succeeded in getting out by drifting down the
Mississippi to its mouth and reaching Christian communit es.—From Maggs, No.
549. According to Professor Bourne, "The expeditions of De Soto and Coronado
were the most elaborate efforts made by the Spaniards to explore the interior of
North America, and in some respects they have never been surpassed. Between
them they nearly spanned the continent from Georgia to California." Furthermore they give us early valuable accounts of many Indian tribes, such as the
Choctaws, the Cherokees, the Creeks, and the Seminoles.

1686  DE SOTO, FERNANDO. A Relation of the Invasion and Conquest of
       Florida by the Spaniards, under the command of Fernando de Soto.
       Written in Portuguese by a Gentleman of the Town of Elvas, now
       Englished: to which is subjoyned, Two Journeys of the present Em-
       perour of China into Tartary, in the years 1682 and 1683, with some
       Discoveries made by the Spaniards in the Island of California, 1683.
       8vo. London.

            According to Maggs, No. 549, this is the first printed account in
       English of the settlement of Lower California.

1851  DE SOTO, DON FERDINANDO. The Discovery and Conquest of
       Terra Florida, by Don Ferdinando de Soto, and Six Hundred Span-
       iards his followers. Written by a Gentleman of Elvas, employed in all
       the action, and translated out of Portuguese by Richard Hakluyt.
       Reprinted from the edition of 1611. Edited with Notes and an In-
       troduction, and a Translation of a Narrative of the Expedition by
       Luis Hernandez de Biedma, Factor to the same, by William Brenchley
       Rye, Keeper of Printed Books, Brit. Mus. Map. Hak. Soc., ser. I, vol.
       9. London.

            Biedma's account is the official narrative of the expedition, which
       was drawn up in 1544.—Bourne.

1866  DE SOTO, HERNANDO. Narratives of the Career of Hernando De
       Soto in the Conquest of Florida as told by a Knight of Elvas and in a
       Relation of Luys Hernandes de Biedma, a Factor of the Expedition.
       Translated by Buckingham Smith. 8vo. Bradford Club. New York.

1922 De Soto, Hernando. Narratives of the career of Hernando de Soto in the Conquest of Florida, as told by a Knight of Elvas and in a relation by Luys Hernandez de Biedma, factor of the Expedition. Translated by Buckingham Smith together with an account of De Soto's Expedition Based on the Diary of Rodrigo Ranjel, his Private Secretary translated from Oviedo's Historia General y Natural de las Indias. Edited with an Introduction by Edward Gaylord Bourne, Professor of History in Yale University. 2 vols. 8vo. Trailmakers Series. New York.

1933 DE SOTO, DON FERDINANDO. True Relation of the Hardships suffered by Governor De Soto and Certain Portuguese Gentlemen during the Discovery of the Province of Florida. By a Gentleman of Elvas. 2 vols. 8vo. The Florida State Historical Society. Deland, Fla.

>Vol. I is a facsimile of the original Portuguese edition of 1557. Vol. II is a translation, with annotations by James Alexander Robertson.—Bookseller's Note.

1557 DE SOTO, FERNANDO. Relacam veridadei ra dos trabalhos que ho guernador do Fernado d' Souto e certos fidal gos portugueses passarom no d'scomrimento da prouincia da Florida. Agora neuamete feita por hu fidalgo Deluas. Foy vista por ho senor inquisidor. (Colophon) Foy impressa esta relacam do descoubrimento da Frolida em casa de anfree de Burgos impressor caulleiro da casa do senhor Cardeal iffante. acabouse aos des dias de Febrero do anno de mil & quinbentos & cincoenta & sete annos. no nobre & sempre leal cidad e de Euora. 8vo. Evora.

>A volume of the greatest rarity. . . . It is reprinted in facsimile in Vol. 1 of Collecao de opusculos reimpressos relitavos a historia das navigacoes. Lisbon, 1844.—Sabin.

## GRAY, ROBERT. Good Speed to Virginia. 4to. London.

>A tract which contains the earliest statement in print of the "White Man's Burden." . . . "Oh how happy were the man which could reduce this people (the Indians) from brutishness to civilitie, to religion, to Christianitie, to the saving of their souls. . . . Farre be it from the hearts of the English, they should give any cause to the world to say that they sought the wealth of that country, above or before the glorie of God, and the propagation of his Kingdom." The author then goes on to refute any objections, on moral grounds, against invading the Indians.—Waldman. This is one of the rarest of tracts relating to Virginia. It is dedicated to "the Noblemen, Merchants, and Gentlemen Adventurers to the Plantation of Virginia."—Sabin.

## JOHNSON, ROBERT. Noua Britannia. Offering most excellent fruites by Planting in Virginia. Exciting all such as be well affected to further the same. 4to. London.

>A second part, London, 1612. See below. A modern reprint, Rochester, N. Y., 1897.
>After Smith's 'True Relation' of 1608, the 'Nova Britannia' is the first printed book relating to the English settlement in Virginia. In making this statement no account is taken of Raleigh's abortive attempt to found a colony on the coast of North Carolina.—quoted by Bradford.

1612 JOHNSON, ROBERT. The New Life of Virginia: declaring the former svccesse and present estate of that Plantation, being the second part of Noua Britannia. Published by the authoritie of his Maiesties Counsell of Virginia. 4to. London.

>The author, in his preface, complains that nothing in his day, except it be the name of God, was so depraved, traduced, and derided as

the name of Virginia.—Puttick and Simpson. The dedication to Sir Thomas Smith of London is signed R. I.—Lowndes.

LESCARBOT, MARC. Nova Francia Or the Description of that Part of Nevv France which is one continent with Virginia. Described in the three late Voyages and Plantation made by Monsieur de Monts, Monsieur du Pont-Graue, and Monsieur de Pontriucourt, into the countries called by the Frenchmen La Cadie, lying to the Southwest of Cape Breton. Together with an excellent seuerall Treatie of all the commodities of the said Countries, and Manners of the naturall Inhabitants of the same. Translated out of French into English by P. E. London.

> 2nd and 3rd editions the same year. In Osborne II, 795-914. Modern reprint, London, 1928. French original, Paris, 1609. See below.
> Lescarbot spent a year in the colony, from 1606 to 1607, and on his return completed this elaborate undertaking. The original is in three parts, devoted respectively to the voyages of Verrazano, Laudonnière, Gourgues, etc.; of Cartier, Roberval, Pontricourt (whom Lescarbot accompanied), and the earlier voyages of Champlain; the last concerns itself with Indian customs and manners. It is a first-class history. . . . Much the best part of his work is in the English version. —From Waldman. It was turned into English at Hakluyt's suggestion by Pierre Erondelle, a French schoolmaster in London and a stockholder in the Virginia Company. Hakluyt aimed thereby to encourage Englishmen to settle in the more equitable climate of Virginia.

> 1928 LESCARBOT, MARC. Nova Francia. A Description of Acadia, 1606. Translated by P. Erondelle, 1609, with an Introduction by H. P. Biggar. 2 maps. 8vo. Broadway Travellers. London.

> 1609 LESCARBOT, MARC. Histoire de la Nouvelle France. Contenant les navigations, découvertes, & habitations faites par les Francois sous l'avoeu & authorité de noz Rois Tres-Chrétiens, & les diverses fortunes d'iceux en l'exécution de ces choses, depuis cent ans jusques à hui. En quoy est compris l'Histoire Morale, Naturelle, & Géographique de ladite province. Avec les Tables & Figures d'icelle. Paris.

1610 RICH, ROBERT. Nevves from Virginia. The lost Flocke triumphant. With the happy Arriual of that famous and worthy knight, Sir Thomas Gates and the well reputed and valiant Captaine Newporte, and others into England. With the maner of their distresse in the Iland of Deuils (otherwise called Bermoothawes) where they remayned 42 weekes, and builded two Pynaces, in which they returned to Virginia. Vignettes, 4to. London.

> Reprinted London, 1865, 1874. See below.
> This is a tract in verse. Only one original copy is known. The author, a brother of Sir Nathaniel Rich, was a settler in the Bermudas and died there in 1620.—John Carter Brown. In his address "To the Reader" he says: "Reader, thou dost peradventure imagine that I . . . write for money (as your moderne Poets vse) . . . to flatter the world: No, I disclaime it, I haue knowne the Voyage, past the danger, seen that honorable work of Virginia, & I thanke God am arriued here to tell thee what I haue seene, don, & past . . . : I am a Soldier, blunt and plaine, and so is the phrase of my newes. . . . If thou aske me why I put it in verse? I prithee knowe, it was onely to feed my owne humour."—Sabin.

"In all probability Shakespeare read this or some other account of the Bermudas before writing 'The Tempest,' where in I. ii. he refers to 'The still vexed Bermoothes.' A fleet of nine vessels under command of Sir Thomas Gates sailed for Virginia in May, 1609, and Gates' own ship was separated from the others by a storm and driven ashore on Bermuda. After nine months there, the party sailed for Virginia in two pinnaces which they had built on the island."—Bartlett *Shakespeare Source Books.* Quoted by Robinson.

1865 Newes from Virginia. (1610). A Poetical Tract, describing the Adventures supposed to be referred to in Shakespeare's Tempest. Reprinted from a copy believed to be unique. Edited by J. O. Hallowell, Esq. 16mo. London. (22 pages.)

A Trve Declaration of the Estate of the Colonie in Virginia, With a confutation of such scandalous reports as haue tended to the disgrace of so worthy an enterprise. Published by aduise and direction of the Councell of Virginia. 4to. London.

Reprinted in Force's *Tracts,* III, No. 1.
Extremely rare. This narrative was issued at a time when the fortunes of the little colony of Virginia seemed to be sinking, just as Raleigh's first settlement had done. Many were in favor of abandoning it, and this pamphlet is a strong argument for its continuation.—From Robinson. It deals with the expedition of Sir Thomas Gates cited in the notes to the item just above. This may have been the pamphlet Shakespeare is thought to have read before writing *The Tempest.* See Rich above.

1611 SERRES, JEAN DE. A Generall Historie of France. Written by Iohn de Serres vnto the yeare 1598. Much augmented and continued vnto this present, out of the most approued authors that haue written of that subject. By Edward Grimeston, Esquire. Numerous woodcut portraits in the text. Fol. London.

This is the 2nd edit. The 1st appeared in 1607, and contained the first account in the English language of the French expedition to Canada in 1603, commanded by the Sieur Du Pont, and accompanied by Samuel de Champlain. The expedition left Honfleur on March 15, 1603, and after a tempestuous voyage of 40 days reached Tadoussac. From this point Champlain explored the Saguenay for about 30 or 40 miles, and then the St. Lawrence as far as the falls above the present site of Montreal. Returning to Tadoussac he explored the shores of the Gulf, secured a valuable cargo of furs, and returned to France, which he reached on September 20, 1603. In this edition the account begins on page 1163.—From Robinson.

WEST, THOMAS, LORD DELAWARE. Relation to the Counsell of Virginia. 4to. London.

Thomas West, Baron of Delaware, Captain General of the Colony, was a member of the Virginia Company, 1609; he took out fresh colonists in 1610, and on his return published this Relation, in which he gives a favorable account of the colony. He died in Virginia on a second visit in 1618.

1612 The Lottaryes best prize declaring the former successe and present estate of Virginias plantation.

So entered in the *Stationers' Register.*

SMITH, JOHN (Captain). A Map of Virginia. VVith a Description of the Countrey, the Commodities, People, Government and Religion. VVritten by Captaine Smith, sometimes Governour of the Countrey. Wherevnto is annexed the proceedings of those Colonies, since their first departure from England, with the discourses, Orations, and relations of the Salvages, and the accidents that befell them in all their Iournies and discoveries. Taken faithfvlly as they were written out of the writings of Dr. Rvssell, Tho. Stvdley, Anas Todkill, Ieffra Abot, Richard Wiefin, Will Phettiplace, Nathaniel Povvell, Richard Pots. And the relations of divers other diligent observers there present then, and now many of them in England. By VV. S. Map of Virginia. Oxford. (Followed by Wm. Symonds, The Proceedings of the English Colonie, see Symonds below.)

The original map of Virginia, with the tall standing Indian Chief in the corner, was first engraved for this work in 1612, but was afterwards much changed and used in the several issues of Smith's Virginia, and in Purchas' *Pilgrimes,* vol. 4. This early map is scarcely known to bibliographers, the subsequent issues of it being almost always inserted in this edition.—Puttick and Simpson. This work had the Oxford instead of the usual London imprint because the book did not suit the purposes of the Virginia Company, which was able, by means of its interlocking members of the Stationers' Company, to prevent its license. . . . It is often referred to as the Oxford Tract. . . . The content is divided into two parts—the first is Smith's description of the topography, products, climate, and aborigines of Virginia; the second contains a chronicle of the Colony until 1612 by W. S. (William Symonds). By far the most interesting feature of the pamphlet is the map which gives it its title. This map is one of Smith's most important contributions to cartography, although it has been said that he merely copied it from previous charts by Gosnold, Waymouth and others. . . . The entire content of this work was introduced by Smith, with changes and additions into his General History (see below under 1624). Purchas used it in an abridged form.—From Waldman.

STRACHEY, WILLIAM. For The Colony in Virginea Britannia. Lavve Diuine, Morall and Martiall, &c. Alget qui non Ardet. Res nostrae subinde non sunt, quales quis optaret, sed quales esse possunt. London.

Reprinted in Force's *Tracts,* III, No. 2.
The laws were drawn up by Strachey, Sir Thomas Gates, and Sir Thomas Dale, in the colony and are said to have been brought home by Strachey in the autumn of 1611. . . . See C. M. Andrews' "Colonial Period," vol. 1, 1934, p. 114, as to the fact that they were probably not modeled after Dutch law or translated from the martial law of the Netherlands, as has been stated. See the Report of the Director of the Folger Shakespeare Library for 1934, pp. 18-22, as to the possibility of contacts between Strachey and Shakespeare, and a summary of research as to the letter of Strachey which is supposed to have been one of his sources of the "Tempest," the similar use of Florio's Montaigne by Strachey in his preface to the Lawes, and by Shakespeare in the play, etc.—Sabin.

SYMONDS, WILLIAM. The Proceedings of the English Colony in Virginia since their first beginning in the yeare of our Lord 1606, till this present 1612, with all their accidents that befell them in their Iournies and Discoveries. Also the Salvages discourses, orations and relations of the Bordering neighbours, and how they became subject to the English. Vnfolding even the fundamentall causes from whence haue sprang so many miseries to the vndertakers, and the scandals to the businesses taken faithfully as they were written out of the Writings of Thomas Studley the first provant maister, Anas Todkill, Walter Russell Doctor of Phisicke, Nathaniel Powell, William Phettyplace, Richard Wyffin, Thomas Abbey, Tho. Hope, Rich. Pots and the labours of divers other diligent observers, that were residents·in Virginia. And pervsed and confirmed by diverse now resident in England that were actors in this business. By W. S. Oxford.

> The first portion of this tract was written by Smith (see Smith this date above) as he states in his 'Generall Historie,' 'with his owne hand.' It consists of a description of the country, its soil and productions, with a full account of the native inhabitants. This part ends at page 39. The second part has a separate title, Proceedings, &c., pp. 110. This tract was reprinted in Smith's *Generall Historie of Virginia* with some changes and the introduction of new matter. It also appears in Purchas' *Pilgrimes*, Vol. 4, pp. 1691.—Murphy, quoted by Bradford.

1613. WHITAKER, ALEXANDER. Good Newes from Virginia. Sent to the Covnsell and Company of Virginia, resident in England. From Alexander Whitaker, the Minister of Henrico in Virginia. Wherein also is a Narration of the present State of that Countrey, and our Colonies there. Perused and published by direction from that Counsell. And a Preface prefixed of some matters touching that Plantation, very requisite to be made knowne. London.

> Modern reprint, 1936, New York (Scholars' Facsimiles and Reprints).
> In this work the history of the colony is carried forward to 1613 by the author, who went to Virginia in 1611, and became preacher to the parish at Henrico. . . . He officiated at the first Anglo-American wedding, that of Pocohontas with John Rolfe.—Waldman.

1614 BREREWOOD, EDWARD. Enqviries Touching the Diversity of Langvages and Religions, through the Chiefe Parts of the World. 4to. London.

> The author devotes a portion of the work to the first peopling of America, claiming the Tartars as their forefathers. His account of religion in America is very curious, especially the part where he describes an old priest who baptised 700,000. Chapter XXII relates to the idolatrous practices in America.—Robinson, No. 41.

1615 HAMOR, RALPH. A Trve Discovrse of the present Estate of Virginia, and the success of the affairs there till the 18 of Iune, 1614. Together, With a Relation of the seuerall English Townes and forts, the assured hopes of that countrie and the peace concluded with the Indians. The Christening of Powhatans daughter and her marriage with an Englishman. 4to. London.

There are two issues of Hamor's Virginia, a fact apparently not recorded by any American bibliographer, till Mr. H. N. Stevens pointed it out in 1898. . . . —Leffert's Catalog, 1902, quoted by Bradford. Translated into German in Hulsius' Collection, 1617. See below.

This contains the most authentic and certainly the best known early account of the christening and marriage of Pocohontas. Hamor was a former secretary of the colony. His book brings the story down to June 18, 1614; its primary object was, like most of the others, to draw so optimistic a picture of the state of affairs in Virginia as to induce people to venture money, their personal cooperation, or both in the colony.—From Waldman.

1617  (In German.)  Virginien Tochter Pocahuntas genant Christlichen getaufft vnd mit einen Engelischen verheurhtet (verheiratet?) worden sehr anmutig zu lesen. . . . Gedruckt zu Hanaw In Verlegung der Hulsischen. 4to. Plates. See Hulsius under 1598-1660, COLLECTIONS.

1616  SMITH, JOHN (Captain).  A Description of New England: or the Observations, and discoueries, of Captain Iohn Smith (Admirall of that Country) in the North of America, in the year of our Lord 1614: with the successe of sixe Ships, that went the next yeare 1615; and the accidents that befell him among the French men of warre: with the proofe of the present benefit this Countrey affoords: whither this present yeare 1616, eight voluntary Ships are gone to make further tryall. London.

Reprinted in Pinkerton XIII, 206-253.

This is the literary fruit of the author's voyage of exploration of the New England coast in 1614. It was this voyage that gave him the title of Admiral of New-England, which he ever after employed. It was written while Smith was a prisoner of some French pirates. This pamphlet was one of the author's favorite works and has generally been exempted from the violent attacks his other productions have sustained. It is an unpretentious, yet roughly quite accurate, description of the salient features of what he saw on his hasty visit. He considers also the possible advantages offered by New England to adventurers, a theme he reworked 1629 in an almost unknown eight-page tract, New England's Trials (see under 1620 below). Among other distinctions, the title page of the Description is the first ever to bear the name New England, which had previously been known simply as North Virginia. . . . Smith describes it as " that part of America in the Ocean sea opposite to Noua Albyon (California): discovered by the most memorable Sir Francis Drake in his voyage about the worlde." The accompanying map has been called by Justin Winsor "the earliest thoroughly accurate map of Massachusetts Bay," . . . even in Smith's time its quality was widely recognized. It was dedicated to Prince Charles (later Charles I) with the request that he change the barbarous native names to good English ones, which His Royal Highness obligingly did.—Waldman.

The State of the Colony and Affairs in Virginia.  (With other tracts.) London.

1620  MASON, JOHN.  A Briefe Discovrse of the Nevv-found-land, with the situation, temperature, and commodities thereof, inciting our Nation to goe forward in that hopefull Plantation begunne. . . . Edinburgh.

This tract of seven leaves, like Whitbourne's Discourse and Discovery (see this date below), was intended to obtain adventurers in the settlement of Newfoundland. Mason's tract was supplanted by Sir William Alexander's Encouragement to Colonies, 1624.

Observations to be followed, for the Making of Fit Roomes, to keepe Silk-Worms in: As also, for the Best Manner of Planting Mulberry Trees, to feed them. Published by Authority for the Benefit of the Noble Plantation in Virginia. 4to. London.

> An exceedingly rare tract. The last four pages are occupied with "A Valuation of the Commodities growing and to·be had in Virginia rated as they are there worthe." Wild cats are rated as eight pence a piece; fox skins at six pence a piece; Pearles of all sorts you can find; Ambergreece as much as you can get," etc.—Quoted from Bookseller's Note.

SMITH, JOHN (Captain). New England's Trials. Declaring the Successe of 26 Ships employed thither within these sixe yeares: with the Benefit of that Countrey by Sea and Land: and how to build three-score sayle of good Ships, to make a little Navie Royall. London.

> 2nd edition, London, 1622, which states that 80 ships were employed within eight years and includes "the present State of that happie Plantation begun by 60 weake men in the yeare 1620." Facsimile printed in *Trans. Mass. Hist. Soc.*, Feb., 1873. In Force, *Tracts*, II, No. 2.

WHITBOURNE, SIR RICHARD. A Discourse and Discovery of Nevvfoundland, With many reasons to proove how worthy and beneficiall a Plantation may there be made, after a far better manner than now it is. . . . London.

> See Whitbourne under 1622 below. This work was written for the encouragement of colonists. It gives a general description of Newfoundland and invites settlers to the country. The author has been called the "Father of New-foundland." He was a Devonshire man and served against the Armada in 1588 in a ship of his own. He had already made a voyage to Newfoundland in 1580. He met Sir Humphrey Gilbert at St. John's a few years later, and frequently returned to the same shores afterwards. His work bears the same relation to that colony that the works of Champlain do to New France.—From Maggs, Nos. 429 and 479. There was a reissue of this pamphlet with a Loving Invitation, a Reference from the King and letters from Bishops, circulated in England, and the anonymous Short Discourse was designed for Ireland.—John Carter Brown. Another issue appeared in 1623.

1622 BONOEIL, JOHN. His Maiesties graciovs Letter to the Earle of Sovth Hampton, Treasurer, and to the Councell and Company of Virginia heere: commanding the present setting vp of Silke works, and planting of Vines in Virginia. And the Letter of the Treasurer, Councell, and Company, to the Gouernour and Councell of State there, for the strict execution of his Maiesties Royall Commands herein. Also, a Treatise of the Art of making Silke: or, Directions for the making of lodgings, and the breeding, nourishing, and ordering of Silke-wormes, and for the planting of Mulbery trees, and all other things belonging to the Silke Art. Together with instructions how to plant and dresse Vines, and to make Wine, and how to dry Raisins, Figs, and other Fruits, and to set Oliues, Oranges, Lemons, Pomegranates, Almonds, and many other Fruits, . . . And in the end, a Conclusion, with sundry profitable Remonstrances to the Colonies. Set foorth for the benefit of the two renowned and most hopefull Sisters, Virginia, and the Summers-Ilands. By John Bonoeil Frenchman, seruant in these imployments to his most Excellent Maiesty of Great Britaine, France, Ireland, Virginia, and the Summer-Ilands. 4to. London.

> Efforts were early made in the Virginia Company to encourage the breeding of silkworms. So great was the interest taken in the subject by the Virginia Company at home that on Nov. 9, 1621, the Court recommended the translation and printing of the treatise on making silk written by Boneill, the French master of the King's silk-works at Oatland, that it might be sent to the governor, council, and colonists in Virginia. This is one of the earliest publications relating to the subject. The work is of great rarity.—Robinson, No. 41.

A briefe Relation of the Discovery and Plantation of Nevv England: and of svndry Accidents therein occvrring, from the yeere of our Lord M.DC.VII. to this present M.DC.XXII. Together with the State thereof as now it standeth, the generall Form of Gouernment intended; and the Diuision of the whole Territorie into Counties, Baronies, . . . 4to. London.

> This is the official publication of the Council for New England.—Waldman. Reprinted in *Mass. Hist. Soc. Coll.*, 2nd ser., vol. 8.

JAMES I. Letter to the Governor of Virginia on Cultivating the Silkworm. London.

> Cited by Sabin as taken from Ternaux.

LOCHINVAR, ——. Encouragements for such as shall have Intention to bee Vndertakers in the new Plantation of Cape Breton, near New Galloway, in America, by Mr. Lochinvar. 4to. Edinburgh.

MOURT (or MORTON), GEORGE. A Relation or Iournall of the beginning and proceedings of the English Plantation setled at Plimouth in New England, by certaine English Aduenturers both Merchants and others. With their difficult passage, their safe ariuall, their ioyfull building of, and the comfortable planting themselves in the now well defended Towne of New Plimoth. As Also A Relation Of Fovre seuerall discoueries since made by some of the same English Planters there resident. . . . 4to. London.

> The preface is signed "G. Mourt" (i.e., George Morton). It is not definitely known by whom the work was written, but it is generally accepted that Bradford and Winslow were the authors, and that the manuscript, having come into Morton's hands, was seen by him through the press in London. It is the first work published in Great Britain to give an account of the planting of the Plymouth colony, and this together with Winslow's Good Newes, 1624, gives the earliest account of the voyage of the Pilgrims in the Mayflower, their settlement

at Plymouth, and of the neighbouring Indians, who had been nearly exterminated by a recent plague. The work is an authority even at the present day. It was no doubt this work which suggested to Longfellow at least the name of his hero "Miles Standish, the Puritan Captain."—Quaritch.

WATERHOUSE, EDWARD. A Declaration of the State of the Colony and Affaires in Virginia. With a Relation of the Barbarous Massacre in the time of peace and League, treacherously executed by the Naytiue Infidels vpon the English, the 22 of March last. Together with the names of those that were then massacred; their lawfull heyres, by this notice giuen, may take order for the inheriting of their lands and estates in Virginia. And a Treatise annexed Written by that learned Mathematician Mr. Henry Briggs, of the Northwest passage to the South Sea through the Continent of Virginia, and by Fretum Hudson. Also a Commemoration of such worthy Benefactors as haue contributed their Christian Charitie towards the aduancement of the Colony. And a Note of the charges of necessary prouisions fit for euery man that intends to goe to Virginia. 4to. London.

WATERHOUSE, EDWARD. The Inconveniences that have happened to some Persons which have transported themselves from England to Virginia, vvithout prouisions necessary to sustaine themselues, hath greatly hindered the Progresse of that noble Plantation: For preuention of the like disorders heereafter, that no man suffer through ignorance or misinformation; it is thought requisite to publish this short Declaration: wherein is contained a particular of such necessaries, as either priuate families or single persons shall haue cause to furnish themselues with, for their better support at their first landing in Virginia; whereby also greater numbers may receive in part Directions how to prouide themselues. London.

WHITBOURNE, SIR RICHARD. A Discourse Containing a Loving Invitation both Honourable, and profitable to all such as shall be Aduenturers, either in Person, or purse, for the aduancement of his Maiesties most hopeful Plantation in the Nevv-found-land, latele vndertaken. London.

WYNNE, EDWARD (Captain). A Letter from Captaine Edward Wynne, Gouernor of the Colony at Ferryland, within the Prouince of Aualon, in New-found-land, vnto . . . Sir George Caluert Knight, his Maiesties Principall Secretary, Iuly 1622. (and other letters from Wynne, Captain Daniel Powell and N. H.). London.

1623 SCOTT, THOMAS. An Experimentall Discoverie of Spanish Practices, or the Counsell of a well-wishing Souldier, for the good of his Prince and State. Wherein is manifested from known experience, both the Cruelty and Policy of the Spaniard, to effect his own ends. Chiefly swelling with multiplicity of glorious titles, as one of the greatest Monarchs of the earth, that being admired of all his greatnesse might amaze all, and so by degrees seeking covertly to tyrannize over all. When as indeed and truth, the greatest part of his pretended Greatnesse, is but a windy crack of an ambitious minde. London.

> A curious and interesting work, endeavoring to stir up popular feeling against Spain, shewing how much England had to fear from the increasing wealth Spain was obtaining from the Indies, and proving that England had prior rights to the Mainland of America, owing to Sebastian Cabot having, with his English companions, reached the mainland of America a year earlier than Columbus and shewing the fallacy of the Spanish claims to that Continent. . . . In speaking of Florida, the author refers to the undiscovered land to the North, and states that its "infiniteness is such, as no mortall tongue can expresse, nor eye hath seen," and that the inland inhabitants do not even dream of the existence of any other land than their own, and that the natives on the coast believe the English, French, Dutch, and Spaniards to be all one people.—Maggs, No. 502.

A Short Discovrse of the New-Found-Land: Contayning diverse Reasons and inducements for the planting of that Countrey. Published for the satisfaction of all such as shall be willing to be Adventurers in the said Plantation. Woodcut. Dublin.

> The epistle is signed "T. C. B."—John Carver Brown.

1624 ALEXANDER, SIR WILLIAM. An Encouragement to Colonies. Engraved folding map of Nova Scotia and surrounding parts of New England, Newfoundland and Canada. London.

> Reprinted with the title, The Mapp and Description of New England, London, 1630.
> This is a record of the Earl of Stirling's (Sir William Alexander) unsuccessful attempt to found a Scotch Colony in Nova Scotia, to which he gave its name. It gives some account of the French Settlement in New France. Some copies bear the date of 1625. The unsold sheets were reissued without the dedication in 1630, with a new title, as The Mapp and Description of New England. . . . Sir William Alexander was a celebrated Scotch poet and statesman, and friend of Charles I. . . . In 1621 he was given a grant of Nova Scotia, then known as New Scotland, and (practically) of Canada.—From Maggs, No. 502.

SMITH, JOHN (Captain). The Generall Historie of Virginia, New-England, and the Summer Isles: with the names of the Adventurers, Planters, and Governours from their first beginning An: 1584 to this present 1624. With the Procedings of those Severall Colonies and the Accidents that befell them in all their Iournyes and Discoveries. Also the Maps and Descriptions of all those Countryes, their Commodities, people, Government, Customes, and Religion yet knowne. Divided into

sixe Bookes. By Captaine John Smith sometymes Governor in those
Countryes & Admirall of New England. Portrait of Duchess of Richmond and maps. Fol. London.

> Other issues, London imprints, are dated 1625, 1626, 1627, 1632. Reprinted in
> Pinkerton XIII, 1-205. The same, together with the *True Travels,* 2 vols., Glas-
> gow, 1907 (the MacLehose edition) ; an edition of the Travels and Works, edit.
> by Arber, London, 1895, and again in 1910. A German account of Smith's travels
> in German, Berlin, 1782. See below.
> Smith's whole being had been mastered by the enthusiasm for planting new
> states in America, and in the early days of Virginia, that colony depended for its
> life and preservation on his firmness and courage.—*Camb. Hist. Eng. Lit.,* IV, v.
> In 1624 Smith completed a project he had had in mind a long time since, the in-
> clusion of his previous writings, revised and expanded, into one volume known as
> the Generall Historie of Virginia. This, his chef-d'oeuvre, contains the materials
> whereby he is to be judged as man and historian. . . . It is one of the half a dozen
> principal ornaments of Americana. . . . The faults and virtues of the work may
> be stated concisely as exaggeration, invention, praise of self and dispraise of oth-
> ers on the one hand, keen personal observation, humor, imagination and a rare
> faculty of writing on the other. . . . Into this book Smith interpolated for the first
> time the story of his rescue by Pocohontas, which he had not mentioned in the
> account of 1608, so much nearer the event. The story is an embellishment con-
> ceived by Smith years later. The original edition of the Generall Historie was so
> popular that it was reissued frequently.—Waldman (who goes into detail on the
> variations in the reissues). See also Smith under 1630, GENERAL TRAVELS
> AND DESCRIPTIONS.

1895  SMITH, JOHN. Travels and Works of Captain John Smith. Edited by
      Edward Arber. Facsimiles. 2 vols. 8vo. London.

> New edition, 2 vols., Edinburgh, 1910.

1907  SMITH, JOHN. The Generall Historie of Virginia, New England, and
      the Summer Isles; together with the True Travels, Adventures, and
      Observations, and a Sea Grammar. Facsimile illustrations from the
      original edition and maps. 2 vols. 8vo. Glasgow.

1782  SMITH, JOHN. Reisen, Entdeckungen, und Untersuchungen des Schiff-
      Capitains, J. Smith, in Virginien, von C. F. Scheibler. Berlin.

WINSLOW, EDWARD. Good Nevves from New England: or a true
Relation of things very remarkable at the Plantation of Plimoth in
Nevv-England. Shewing the wondrous providence and goodness of
God, in their preservation and continuance, being delivered from many
apparent deaths and dangers. Together with a Relation of such religious and civill Lawes and Customes, as are practised among the Indians, adjoyning to them at this day. As also what Commodities are
there to be raysed for the maintenance of that and other Plantations in
the said Country. Written by E. W. who hath borne a part in the fore-
named troubles, and there liued since their first Arrivall. 4to. London.

> Winslow was probably the most cultivated of the first Pilgrim settlers. . . .
> His work is a mine of information on the voyage of the Mayflower, the first set-
> tlement, relations with the Indians, etc., as well as being the first book to recount
> the exploits of the doughty Miles Standish.—Waldman.

1625 MORRELL, WILLIAM. New England. Or a briefe enarration of the ayre, earth, water, fish and fowles of that Country. 4to. London.

> In Latin and English verse. Cited in *Short Title Catalogue*. In *Mass. Hist. Soc. Coll.* 1st ser., vol. 1.

1626 VAUGHAN, SIR WILLIAM. The Golden Fleece. Diuided into three Parts. Vnder which are discouered the Errours of Religion, the Vices and Decayes of the Kingdome, and lastly the wayes to get wealth and to restore Trading so much complayned of. Transported from Cambrioll Colchos, out of the Southermost Part of the Iland commonly called the Newfoundland. By Orpheus Junior. For the generall and perpetuall Good of Great Britaine. With extremely rare folding map of "Newfound Land described by Captaine Iohn Mason, an industrious Gent; who spent seuen years in the Countrey"; . . . London.

> The author planted Newfoundland with Welshmen, spent several years as owner of a large tract of land, and wrote this curious book partly in verse, partly in prose, to encourage fresh emigration. More than half of the work is a fantastic discussion on manners and customs, in which a number of Shakespearean illustrations will be found. . . . "This work ranks among the earliest contributions to English literature from America."—Quoted from D. N. B. by Robinson, No. 19.

1627 An Historicall Discoverie and Relation of the English Plantation in New England. 4to. London.

> Cited in *Short Title Catalogue*.

1628 LEVETT, CHRISTOPHER. A Voyage into Nevv England Begun in 1623, and ended in 1624. Performed by Christopher Levett, his Maiesties Woodward of Somerset-shire, and one of the Councell of New-England. Woodcut of ship. 4to. London.

> A tract of greatest rarity . . . reprinted in *Mass. Hist. Soc. Coll.,* 3rd ser., vol. 8, and in *Maine Hist. Soc. Coll.,* vol. 2, p. 36.—Sabin.

1630 ALEXANDER, SIR WILLIAM. The Mapp and Description of New-England: Together with a Discourse of Plantation, and Collonies: Also, A Relation of the nature of the Climate, and how it agrees with our owne Country England. How neere it lyes to Newfound-Land, Virginia, Noua Francia, Canada, and other Parts of the West-Indies. Map. 4to. London.

> See Alexander under 1624 above.

HIGGINSON, FRANCIS. New England's Plantation. Or, A Short and trve Description of the Commodities and Discommodities of that Countrey. Written by a reuerend Diuine now there resident. Woodcut. 4to. London.

> 2nd edit., London, 1630; 3rd edit., enlarged with the addition of a Letter, sent by Mr. Graues an Enginere, out of New-England, London, 1630. In Force's *Tracts* I.

A Proportion of Provisions needfull for such as intend to plant themselves in New England. 4to. London.

WHITE, JOHN. The Planters Plea. Or the Grounds of Plantations Examined, and vsuall Objections answered. Together with a manifestation of the causes mooving such as have lately vndertaken a Plantation in New-England: For the satisfaction of those that question the lawfulnesse of the Action . . . 4to. London.

> Very rare. "This work, unknown to Cotton Mather, Prince, Hutchinson, and Bancroft, historians of New England, contains the earliest trustworthy information on the planting of the colony."—D. N. B., quoted by Quaritch, who adds that White was the chief promoter of the colonization of Massachusetts, although he himself never set foot there.—This is an answer to critics of colonial policy.— Waldman.

1631 SMITH, JOHN (Captain). Advertisements for the unexperienced Planters of New-England, or any where. Or, the Path-way to experience to erect a Plantation. With the yearely proceedings of this Country in Fishing and Planting, since the yeare 1614 to the yeare 1630 and their present estate. Also how to prevent the greatest inconveniences, by their proceedings in Virginia, and other Plantations, by approved examples. With the Countries Armes, a description of the Coast, Harbours, Habitations, Land-markes, Latitude and Longitude: with the Map, allowed by our Royall King Charles. Woodcuts. London.

> The woodcuts on p. 1 are the blocks used in Smith's *True Travels*, 1630.— John Carter Brown.

1634 A Relation of the sucessefull beginnings of the Lord Baltimore's Plantation in Mary-land. Being an extract of certaine Letters written from thence, by some of the Aduenturers, to their friends in England. To which is added, The Conditions of plantation propounded by his Lordship for the second voyage intended this present yeere, 1634. 4to. London. (14 pages.)

> This is the earliest publication relating to Maryland, and one of the rarest of Anglo-American books. The authorship has been attributed to Father Andrew White, and also to Cecilius Calvert, Lord Baltimore.—Sabin.

A History of New-England, from the English Planting in the year 1608 until the year 1630; declaring the form of their government, civil, military, and ecclesiastic. London.

WOOD, WILLIAM. New England's Prospect. A true, lively, and experimental Description of that part of America, commonly called New England: discovering the state of that Countrie, both as it now stands to our new-come English Planters; and to the old Native Inhabitants. Laying downe that which may both enrich the knowledge of the mind-travelling Reader, or benefit the future Voyager. Folding woodcut map, "The South part of New-England." London.

> 2nd edit., with folding woodcut map of "The South part of New England, as it is Planted this Yeare, 1635," London, 1635; a later edition, 4to, London, 1639.
> This, "the first detailed account of Massachusetts, gives a topographical account of the Massachusetts colony as far as it then extended, and also a full description of its fauna and flora. The second part treats 'Of the Indians, their persons, cloathings, diet, natures, customs, lawes, mariages, worships, conjurations, warres, games, hunting, fishings, sports, language, death and burials.' An Indian vocabulary of five pages is placed at the end, earlier than the works of Roger Williams and John Eliot. In the compilation of this vocabulary Wood may have been assisted by Roger Williams, who before he lived at Salem had made considerable progress in the Indian language. It is possible that he may also have had the co-operation of John Eliot, who came to New England in 1631, the same year as Roger Williams. Wood, according to his own account, lived four years in New England." —Quoted by Maggs, No. 625.

1635 A Relation of Maryland; Together With A Map of the Countrey, The Conditions of Plantation, His Maiesties Charter to the Lord Baltimore, translated into English. Folding lithographic map. 4to. London.

> Reprinted with a Prefatory Note and Appendix by Francis L. Hawks, 4to, New York, 1865.

1637 MORTON, THOMAS. New English Canaan or New Canaan. Containing an Abstract of New England, Composed in three Bookes. The first Booke setting forth the originall of the Natives, their Manners and Customes, together with their tractable Nature and Love towards the English. The second Booke setting forth the naturall Indowments of the Country, and what staple Commodities it yealdeth. The third Booke setting forth, what people are planted there, their prosperity, what remarkable accidents have happened since the first planting of it, together with their Tenents and practice of their Church. Written by Thomas Morton of Cliffords Inne gent, upon tenne yeares knowledge and experiment of the Country. 4to. Amsterdam.

> The book was entered in the *Stationers' Register,* 1633, bearing the imprint and name of Charles Greene. The original title seems to be unknown. The first two parts of the book, Morton's account of the country and its native inhabitants, are of great interest and value. The third part is more or less a satire on the Puritan inhabi-

tants of Plymouth and Massachusetts, who regarded him and his friends as little better than pirates. The Plymouth community twice contrived to get him sent back to England, where he wrote this book prior to his final return and settlement at Acomenticus.—Quaritch. The author came over to New England to enjoy himself in a manner more suited to the reign of Charles II than to that of his father, and speedily found himself superlatively unpopular amidst his Puritan neighbors. . . . Though a great pretension as an historian, the author has a sense of humor which makes his work distinctly amusing. The book is prized as a sort of freak among the sober early chronicles of the colony. It was printed at Amsterdam, as probably the friends of the colony were powerful enough to prevent its licensing or circulation in London. It may be that the Amsterdam imprint was a blind.—From Waldman. A number of poetical pieces are interspersed through this curious work; among others one entitled "Of the Bacanall Triumphe of the nine Worthies of New Canaan," by Ben Jonson, which is not included in any edition of his Works. —Lowndes.

1638 UNDERHILL, JOHN (CAPTAIN). Nevves from America; A New and Experimentall Discoverie of New England; Containing, A Trve Relation of Their War-like proceedings these two yeares last past, with a Figure of the Indian Fort, or Palizado. Also a discovery of these places, that as yet have very few or no inhabitants which would yeeld speciall accomodation to such as will Plant there. Viz. . . . Hudsons River. Long Island. . . . Pequet. Naransett Bay. Elizabeth Islands. . . . 4to. London. (44 pages.)

> Reprinted in *Mass. Hist. Soc. Coll.,* 3rd ser. vol. 6.
> This is an early narrative of the first serious trouble with the Indians, in 1637, the Pequot War. Captain Underhill was commander of the Massachusetts forces at the storming of the fort. He was one of the three deputies from Boston to the General Court, and was one of the earliest officers of the Ancient and Honorable Artillery Co.—Deane Catalog, quoted by Bradford.

VINCENT, PHILIP. A True Relation of the late Battell fought in New England, between the English, and the Pequet Salvages: In which was slaine and taken prisoners about 700 Salvages; and those who escaped, had their heads cutt off by the Mohocks; With the present state of things there. 4to. London.

> Reprinted in *Mass. Hist. Soc. Coll.,* 3rd ser., vol. 6.
> Extremely rare. It contains an extremely interesting account of the War against the Pequot Indians in 1637, especially of the expedition commanded by Captain John Underhill. The narrative bears all marks of having been written by an eyewitness of the occurrences and even minor details connected with the fighting are given.—Quaritch. The authorship of this exceedingly rare pamphlet has been attributed to Vincent by the Publishing Committee of the Massachusetts Historical Society in their note to the reprint of the Relation, in the third volume of their Collections. It . . . was . . . printed in 1638 under the title of "News from America." Vincent's Relation is of even greater rarity than Underhill's. This is attested by the fact that the reprint named was made from a mutilated copy, the imperfections of which were uncorrected in the reprint, from the impossibility of finding a perfect copy for comparison.—Field's *Indian Bibliography,* Deane Catalog, quoted by Bradford.

1642  LECHFORD, THOMAS.  Plain Dealing: or Nevves from New-England.
. . . A Short View of New Englands present Government, both Ec-
clesiasticall and Civil, compared with the Anciently-received and established Government of England, in some materiall points; fit for the
gravest consideration in these times. . . .  4to.  London.

> Reprinted, edit. by J. H. Trumbull, Boston, 1867.
> The author, a lawyer, came to Boston in 1638, where he lived until 1641, and
> wrote this book, one of the most interesting and authentic of the early narratives
> relating to the colony. It is full of valuable information respecting the manners
> and customs of the colony, and is written by an able and impartial hand.—
> Maggs, No. 549. For an account of the work and its author, see Hutchinson's
> *History of Massachusetts Bay*, I, 451.—Sabin.

Newes, True Newes, Laudable Newes, Citie Newes, Court Newes, Countrey Newes: The World is Mad, or it is a mad World my Masters,
especially now when in the Antipodes these things are come to passe.
4to.  London.  (8 pp.)

> Chiefly about the antipodes, of which there is a most ridiculous woodcut on
> the title page. Thomas Thorpe catalogues this work under Americana, but it
> can only be so by assuming that the author is satirising the first settlers in New
> England. It is a very amusing performance.—Sabin.

1643  Nevv England's first Fruits; in Respect, First of the Conversion of some,
Conviction of divers, Preparation of sundry of the Indians. 2. Of
the Progress of Learning, in the Colledge at Cambridge in Massachusets Bay. With Divers other speciall Matter concerning that Countrey.
Published by the instant request of sundry Friends, who desire to be
satisfied in these points by many New-England Men who are here present, and were eye or eare-witnesses of the same.  4to.  London.

WILLIAMS, ROGER.  A Key into the Language of America; or, An help
to the Language of the Natives in that part of America, called New-
England.  Together, with briefe Observations of the Customs, Manners and Worships, &c. of the aforesaid Natives, in Peace and Warre,
in Life and Death . . . 8vo.  London.

> Very rare. The first printed book by Roger Williams, the founder of the
> colony of Rhode Island. It is the earliest attempt to record a vocabulary of the
> language of the Indians in the neighborhood of Massachusetts (but see Wood
> under 1634 above). Scattered through the work are explanatory observations on
> the language and contributions in verse.—Quaritch. The licenser, John Langley,
> asserts that he had "read over these thirty chapters of the American Language,
> to me wholly unknowne, and the Observations, these I conceive inoffensive; and
> that the Worke may conduce to the happy end intended by the Author."—John
> Carter Brown.

1643-1671  ELIOT, JOHN.  The Eliot Indian Tracts.  4to.  London.

> (For title of 1671 edition see below).
> These make up a series of eleven little quartos, printed most of them at the
> direction of the Corporation for the "propagation of the Gospel among the In-
> dians of New England," to whom Eliot and several co-workers addressed these
> reports of the progress of their mission. Although they were intended primarily
> to enlighten the Corporation as to the work for which it was providing funds,
> they contain an abundance of general contemporary information, even to the ex-
> tent of preserving the content of other documents which have perished.—
> Waldman. The first and one of the rarest of the series of reports from New
> England relative to the conversion of the aborigines. Pages 18-20 contain the
> Commencement theses at the graduation of the first class in 1642.—Sabin.

> 1671  ELIOT, JOHN.  A Brief Narrative of the Progress of the Gospel
>       amongst the Indians in New England, in the Year 1670. Given in By
>       Reverend John Eliot, Minister of the Gospel there, In a Letter by him
>       directed to the Right Worshipfull the Commissioners under his Majes-
>       ties Great-Seal for Propagation of the Gospel amongst the poor Blind
>       Natives in those United Colonies.  4to.  London.
>
>> Eliot learned the Natick dialect of the Algonquin tongue, which
>> he reduced to grammar and syntax. His Indian Bible, which was done
>> in 1661-63, was the first Bible printed in the New World.

1644  CASTELL, WILLIAM.  A Short Discovery of the Coast and Continent
of America, from the Equinoctial Northward; and the Adjacent
Islands. Whereunto is added the Author's Petition to the Parliament,
for the Propagation of the Gospel in America. . . . And an Ordnance
of Parliament for that Purpose, and for the better Government of the
English Plantations there. Together with Sir Benjamin Rudyer's
Speech in Parliament, Jan. 21, 1644, concerning America.  4to.  London.

> Reprinted in Osborne II, 733-781, London.
> The author was a minister of the Gospel at Courtenhall in Northampton-
> shire. The description extends from Newfoundland down to the Spanish pos-
> sessions in South America as far as Guiana.

1645  COTTON, JOHN.  The Way of the Churches of Christ in New England.
4to.  London.

> This answer to Baylie's "Disswasive" is one of Cotton's rarest and most
> important works. It contains a mass of historical matter relating to New Eng-
> land, Rhode Island, Plymouth Colony, Mistress Hutchinson, John Winthrop,
> Thomas Lechford, John Davenport, John Eliot, Roger Williams, and the work
> of the latter among the Indians.—Robinson, No. 41. See Baylie following.

1646  BAYLIE, ROBERT.  A Dissuasive From the Errours Of the Time:
Wherein the Tenets of the principall Sects, especially of the Independ-
ents, are drawn together in one map. . . .  London.

> This book relates almost wholly to New England, and is an important docu-
> ment in the history of that district. Baylie was a personal friend of Roger Wil-
> liams, whose writings he here discusses, together with those of Cotton, Rath-
> band, Winthrop, and many others connected with the early history of the

American Colonies.—Bookseller's Note. It would seem from the date of Cotton's reply that this is either a second edition of Baylie's book or that Cotton's should be dated a year later.

HILTON, WILLIAM. A Relation of A Discovery lately made on the Coast Of Florida, (from Lat. 31 to 33 Deg. 45 Min. North-Lat.) By William Hilton Commander and Commissioner with Capt. Anthony Long, and Peter Fabian, in the Ship Adventure, which set sayl from Spikes Bay, Aug. 10, 1663, and was set forth by several Gentlemen and Merchants of the Island of Barbadoes. Giving an Account of the nature and temperature of the Soyl, the Manners and disposition of the Natives and whatsoever else is remarkable therein. Together with Proposals made by the Commissioners of the Lords Proprietors, to all such persons as shall become the first Setlers on the Rivers, Harbors, and Creeks there. 4to. London.

Another edition, London, 1664. Reprinted in Force's *Tracts*, III.

1647 WARD, NATHANIEL. The Simple Cobbler of Aggavvam (now Ipswich, Mass.) in America, willing to help mend his native Country, lamentably tattered, both in the upper-leather and sole, with all honest stitches he can take. . . . By Theodore de la Guard. 4to. London.

The "Simple Cobbler" will keep for its author a perpetual place in American literature. It is a droll and pungent satire on the times—the frivolity of women —the long hair of men. The author was a minister in Massachusetts.—Robinson, No. 57.

1648 PLANTAGENET, BEAUCHAMP. A Description of the Province of New Albion. And a Direction for Adventurers with small stock to get two for one, and good land freely: And for Gentlemen, and all Servants, Labourers and Artificers to live plentifully. And a former Description reprinted of the healthiest, pleasantest, and richest Plantation of New Albion in North Virginia, proved by thirteen witnesses. Together with a Letter from Master Robert Evelin, that lived there many years, shewing the particularities, and excellency thereof. With a briefe of the charge of victuall, and necessaries, to transport and buy stock for each Planter, or Labourer, there to get his Master 50 1. (pound) per Annum, or more in twelve trades, at 10 1. charges only a man. 4to. London.

Another edition, London, 1650.—This edition of 1650 is believed to be unique, the two or three copies, all that are known, being a different edition throughout, and bearing the date 1648.—Puttick and Simpson. Included in Force's *Tracts*, II, No. 7.

The country described includes portions of Delaware, New Jersey, and Long Island. In the dedication of this extremely rare tract Plantagenet refers to 'the two former books printed of Albion, 1637 and 1642.' No copy has been found of the former, and even the title seems to be unknown; but the latter is undoubtedly the 'former Description reprinted,' mentioned in Plantagenet's title page, and comprising Chapter 3, 'The Description of Master Robert Evelin and 13 witnesses, printed 7 years since and now reprinted.'—Sabin.

Good News from Nevv-England: with An exact relation of the first planting that Country: A description of the profits accruing by the Worke. Together with a briefe, but true discovery of their Order both in Church and Commonwealth, and maintenance allowed the painfull Labourer's in that Vineyard of the Lord. With the names of severall Towns, and who be Preachers to Them. 4to. London. (25 pp.)

> Reprinted in *Mass. Hist. Soc. Coll.,* 4th ser., vol. I.

1649 BULLOCK, WILLIAM. Virginia Impartially examined, and left to pub lick view, to be considered by all Iudicious and honest men. Under which Title, is comprehended the Degrees from 34 to 39, wherein lyes the rich and healthful Countries of Roanock, the now Plantations of Virginia and Maryland. Looke not upon this Booke, as those that are set out by private men for private ends; for being read, you'l find, the publick good is the Authors onely aime. For this Piece is no other than the Adventurers or Planters faithfull Steward, disposing the Adventure for the best advantage, advising people of all degrees, from the highest Master to the meanest Servant, how suddenly to raise their fortunes. Peruse the Table, and you shall finde the way plainely layd downe. 4to. London.

> Reprinted in Force's *Tracts,* III.—Sabin.
> This pamphlet endeavors to discover the reason of the slow progress in the development of Virginia. The author makes a study of the food and sport of the country, its economic necessities, how it might be recovered, how money might be disposed to advantage there, etc. He had known the pioneers and captains in the trade, his father had lived in the colony twelve years, and he himself had had extensive commerce with it.—From *Camb. Hist. Eng. Lit.,* IV, v. This work, though but a compilation, is replete with valuable information. The author states that it was composed in six nights.—Puttick and Simpson.

A Perfect Description of Virginia: being a full and true Relation of the present State of the Plantation, their Health, Peace and Plenty: the number of people, with their abundance of Cattell, Fowl, Fish, &c. with severall sorts of rich and good Commodities, which may there be had, either Naturally, or by Art and Labour. Which we are fain to procure from Spain, France, Denmark, Swedeland, Germany, Poland, yea, from the East-Indies. There having been nothing related of the true estate of the Plantation these 25 years. Being sent from Virginia, at the request of a Gentleman of worthy note, who desired to know the true state of Virginia as it now stands. Also, A Narration of the Country, within a few dayes journey of Virginia, West and by South, where People come to trade: being related to the Governor, Sir William

Berckley, who is to go himself to discover it, with 30 horse and 50 foot, and other things needful for his enterprize. With the manner how the Emperor Nichotawance came to Sir William Berckley, attended with five petty Kings, to doe Homage and bring Tribute to King Charles with his solemne Protestation, that the Sun and Moon should loose their lights, before he (or his people in that Country), should prove disloyal, but ever to keepe Faith and Allegiance to King Charles. 4to. London.

> Reprinted in Force's *Tracts*, II, No. 8.

1650 FARRER, JOHN. Virginia's Discovery of Silke Wormes, with their Benefit and the Implanting of Mulberry Trees. Also the Dressing and Keeping of Vines for the Rich Trade of Making Wines there, together with the Making of the Saw Mill, very useful in Virginia for Cutting of Timber and Clapboard to build withal, and its conversion to other as profitable uses, illustrated with curious woodcuts. 4to. London.

THOROWGOOD, THOMAS. Jewes in America, or, Probabilities that the Americans are of that Race. With the removall of some contrary reasonings, and earliest desires for effectual endeavours to make them Christian. (Also contains: an Epistolicall Discourse of Mr. John Dury, to Mr. Thorowgood. Concerning his conjecture that the Americans are descended from the Israelites. With the History of a Portugall Jew, Antonie Monterinos, attested by Manasseh Ben Israel, to the same effect.) 4to. London.

> For Manasseh Ben Israel's account see below. This is one of the best known briefs in the debate that continued through most of the seventeenth and eighteenth centuries on the question, Were the red men the lost ten tribes of Israel.— Waldman. For a reply see L'Estrange under 1652 below.

> 1650 MANNASEH, BEN ISRAEL. The Hope of Israel newly extant and printed in Amsterdam. Dedicated by the Author to the High Court, the Parliament of England, and the Council of State: with the strange relation of Anthony Montezinus, a Jew, of what befell him as he travelled over the "Mountaines Cordilliere," in America. 8vo. London. (?).

>> Spanish original, Amsterdam, 1649. See below.
>> Manasseh, born at La Rochelle, settled in Holland where he distinguished himself as one of the best orators of the Amsterdam pulpit, and where he founded the first Hebrew printing press in Holland. He was profoundly interested in Messianic prophecy and came to believe that the North American Indians were the lost ten tribes. Convinced also that the Jews would never regain the Holy Land until they had spread to all parts of the earth, he wrote the *Hope of Israel* to further their admittance into England.—From Maggs, No. 479.

> 1649 MANASSEH, BEN ISRAEL. Esperanca de Israel. Obra con suma curiosidad compuesta por Menassem Ben Israel Theologico, y Philosopho Hebreo. Trata del admirable esparzimiemto de los diez Tribus,

y su infalible reduccion con losdemas, a la patria: con muchos puntos, y Historias curiosas, y declaracion de varias Prophecias por el Author rectamente interpredas, Dirigido a los senores Parnassim del K. K. de Talmud Tora. 12mo. Amsterdam.

WILLIAMS, EDWARD. Virginia: More Especially the South Part thereof, richly and truly Valued, viz. The Fertile Carolina, and no less excellent Isle Roanoak, of latitude 31 to 37 degrees relating the meanes of raysing infinite profits to the Adventurers and Planters, the Second edition, with addition of the Discovery of Silk Worms. Large copperplate map of Virginia. 4to. London.

1651 BLAND, EDWARD (and Others). The Discovery of Nevv Brittaine, Began August 27 Anno Dom. 1650. By Edward Bland, Merchant. Abraham Woode, Captaine. Sackford Brewster, Elias Pannant, Gentleman. From Fort Henry, at the head of Appamatuck River in Virginia, to the Falls of Blandina, first River in New Brittaine, which runneth West; being 120 Mile Southwest, between 35 and 37 degrees (a pleasant Country), of temperate Ayre, and fertile Soyle. Map and plate of Indian wheat and an Indian jay. 4to. London. (8 pp.)

GARDYNER, GEORGE. A Description of the New World. Or, America Islands and Continent: and by what people those Regions are now inhabited. And what places are there desolate and without Inhabitants. And the Bays, Rivers, Capes, Forts, Cities and their Latitudes, the Seas on their Coasts: the Trade, Winds, the North-west Passage, and the Commerce of the English Nation, as they were all in the year 1649. Faithfully described for information of such of his Countrey as desire Intelligence of these Particulars. London.

Virginia. For a description of Virginia see *Copy of a Petition from the Governor and Company of the Sommer Islands, under* WEST INDIES.

1652 ELIOT, JOHN (and Others). Strength out of Weakness. Or a Glorious Manifestation of ... the Gospel Amongst the Indians in New England, ... 12mo. London.

There are at least 3 editions with 5 variations of title-page published in 1652. —Bookseller's Note.

HARTLIB, SAMUEL. Glory be to God on high, Peace on Earth, Good Will amongst men. A Rare and New Discovery of a speedy way, and easie means, found out by a young Lady in England, she having

made full proofe thereof in May, Anno 1652, For the feeding of Silk-
worms in the Woods, on the Mulberry-Tree-leaves in Virginia: Who
after fourty days time present there most rich golden-coloured silken
Fleece, to the instant wonderfull enriching of all the Planters, requir-
ing from them neither cost, labour, or hindrance in any of their other
employments whatsoever. And also to the good hopes that the Indians,
Seeing and finding that there is neither Art, Skill or Pains in the
Thing: they will readily set upon it, being by the benefit thereof inabled to buy of the English (in way of Truck for their Silk-bottomes)
all those things that they most desire. So that not only their Civilizing
will follow, thereupon, but by the most infinite mercie of God, their
Conversion to the Christian Faith, the Glory of our Nation, which is
the daily humble prayer of Virginia. With two Propositions tending
to England's and the Colonies infinite advantage. 4to. London.

> Reprinted, London, 1655. Reprinted with title: The Reformed Common-
> wealth of Bees and the reformed Silk Worm. London. 1855. See also Force's
> *Tracts,* III, No. 13.
> The young lady was Virginia Ferrar, daughter of John Ferrar, of Little
> Gidding, Huntingdonshire, both of whose names are connected with the map
> of Virginia in Williams and Bland (see under 1650 and 1651 above).—From
> John Carter Brown.

L'ESTRANGE, SIR HAMOR.   Americans no Jewes or Improbabilities
that, . . .   London.

> This is a reply to Thomas Thorowgood's *Jewes in America.* See Thorow-
> good under 1650 above. D.N.B. gives Hamon as the first name of this theolo-
> gian.

1654   JOHNSON, EDWARD.   A History of New-England. From the English
Planting in the Yeere 1628, untill the Yeere 1652. Declaring the form
of their Government, civill, Military, and Ecclesiastique. Their Wars
with the Indians, their Troubles with the Gortonists and other Her-
etiques. . . .   4to.   London.

> Reprinted Andover, 1867.
> This was thought for a long time to be the work of Thomas Hooker owing
> to the fact that the preface is signed T. H. It is now, however, generally agreed
> to have been the work of Edward Johnson of Woburn. It is the first published
> narrative which treats of Massachusetts. . . . The running title by which the
> book is often cited is "Wonder-working Providence of Sions Saviour, in New
> England."—Quaritch. "Four years after its publication, Brooke, the same pub-
> lisher, issued Gorges' America Painted to the Life, incorporating Johnson's book
> with it. . . . Johnson's book belonged to Brooke, and, not being swift of sale,
> after four years, when publishing Gorges' book, he took upon himself the re-
> sponsibility of working in and off his dead stock. As soon as Gorges found out
> this trick . . . he inserted in the Mercurius Publicus, newspaper of the 13th
> September, 1660, the following: "ADVERTISEMENT:—I, Ferdinando Gorges,
> the entituled Author of a late book, called America Painted to the Life, am in-
> jured in that additional part called Sion's Saviour in New England (as writ-
> ten by Sir Ferdinando Gorges), that being none of his and formerly printed in
> another name, the true owner."—Stevens, quoted by Bradford. On the title page
> the book is called "A History of New England" (which is erroneous, as it limits

itself to Massachusetts), but it was registered under the other name, which is preserved in the headlines. It was, of course, the author who chose the more theological title, while his publisher naturally preferred the one more likely to sell the book. The publication is anonymous. See Gorges under 1658-59 below. The following title seems to be a Latin version of this work.

H., T.   Historia Novae-Engliae a Primordiis Colonae Anglicanae, scilicet, 1628 ad annum 1652, a T. H.   London.

> So cited by Pinkerton XVII.

H., T.   Historical Relation of the first planting of the English in New-England in the year 1653, and all the materiall passages happening there Exactly performed . . . above. With the names of all their Governours, Magistrates, and eminent Ministers. By T. H.   4to.   London.

> This seems to be identical with the Latin title cited just above. It was reprinted as Wonder-working Providence of Sions Saviour this same year and is ascribed to Edward Johnson. It was also included in America Painted to the Life. See Gorges under 1659 below. Reprinted with an Historical Introduction and an Index by William Frederick Poole, 1867, *Mass. Hist. Soc. Coll.*, 2nd ser., vol. 7.

1656   HAMMOND, JOHN.   Leah and Rachel, or, the Two Fruitfull Sisters Virginia, and Maryland: Their Present Condition Impartially stated and related.   4to.   London.

> A volume of extreme rarity. . . . —Sabin.   In Force's *Tracts,* III.

1657   PEAKE, THOMAS.   For a description of the mainland coast regions of America see his *America; Or an Exact Description of the West Indies,* under WEST INDIES.

1658-59   GORGES, SIR FERDINANDO.   America Painted to the Life. The true History of the Spaniards Proceedings in the Conquests of the Indians, and of their Civil Wars among themselves, from Columbus his first Discovery, to these later Times. As also of the Original Undertakings of the Advancement of Plantations into those Parts; With a perfect Relation of Our English Discoveries, shewing their beginning, progress, and Continuance, from the Year 1628 to 1658. Declaring the forms of their Government, Policies, Religions, manners, Customs, Military Discipline, Wars with the Indians, the Commodities of their Countries, a Description of their Towns and Havens, the Increase of their Trading, with the Names of their Governors and Magistrates. More especially, an absolute Narrative of the North parts of America, and of the Discoveries and Plantations of our English in Virginia, New England and Barbadoes. Publisht by Ferdinando Gorges, Esq.; A

Work now at last exposed for the Publick good, to stir up the Heroick and Active Spirits of these times, to benefit their Countrey, and Eternize their Names by such Honourable Attempts. . . . Portrait and Map. London, . . . 1659. Part II. A Briefe Narration of the Originall Undertakings of the Advancement of Plantations Into the parts of America. . . . Written by the right Worshipfull, Sir Ferdinando Gorges . . . 1658. Part III. America painted to the Life. A True History of the Originall Undertakings of the advancement of Plantations into those parts . . . Written by Sir Ferdinando Gorges. . . . Publisht into his decease, by his Grandchild, Ferdinando Gorges, Esquire, who hath much enlarged it and added severall accurate Descriptions of his owne . . . 1658. Part IV. America Painted to the Life. The History of the Spaniards Proceedings in America, their Conquests of the Indians . . . by Ferdinand Gorges, Esq.; . . . Table. London. 1659.

Part II of this was printed in the *Maine Hist. Soc. Coll.,* vol. 2; also in the *Mass. Hist. Soc. Coll.,* 3rd ser., vol. 6. These four works were all printed separately (the 2nd and 3rd in 1658), but I believe are always found together . . . —Rich, Cat. No. 314, quoted by Sabin.

This is a compilation of papers by Sir Ferdinando Gorges' grandson and namesake, bound together under a new title-page bearing Sir Ferdinando's name. The younger Gorges disclaimed the attribution. Edward Johnson is seemingly responsible for the compilation. See Waldman. See also Johnson under 1654 above.

1659 FOWLER, ROBERT. A Quaker's Sea-Journal: being a True Relation of a Voyage to New-England. Performed by Robert Fowler of the town of Burlington, in Yorkshire, in the year 1658. 4to. London. (8 pp.)

1659 ROUS, JOHN. New-England A Degenerate Plant. Who having forgot their former Sufferings, and lost their ancient tenderness, are now become famous among the Nations in bringing forth the fruits of cruelty, wherein they have far outstript their Persecutors the Bishops, as by these their ensuing Laws you may plainly see. Published for the information of all sober People, who desire to know how the state of New-England now stands, and upon what foundation the New-England Churches are built, and by whose strength they are upholden now they are degenerated and have forsaken the Lord. . . . Whereunto is annexed a Copy of a Letter which came from . . . a Magistrate among them, to a friend . . . in London, wherein he gives an account of some of the cruel suffering of the people of God in those parts under the Rulers of New-England, and their unrighteous Laws. 4to. London. (20 pp.)

Extremely rare. It contains the Laws and Proceedings of the General Courts of Massachusetts, Plymouth and New Haven against the Quakers 1656-59; followed by . . . the letter of Captain James Cudworth, of Scituate, for writing of which he was disfranchised by the Plymouth Court. It was reprinted by Bishop, in New England Judged, pp. 168-176.—Sabin. See Bishop under 1661 below.

1661 BISHOP, GEORGE. New England Judged . . . And the Summe sealed up of New-England's Persecutions. Being a Brief Relation of the Sufferings of the People called Quakers in those Parts of America, from the beginning of the Fifth Moneth 1656. (the time of the first Arrival at Boston from England) to the later end of the Tenth Moneth, 1660 . . . 4to. London.

> Reprinted somewhat abbreviated, London, 1703.
> A full account of the persecution of the Quakers in New England from the time of their first appearance in the colony. It was written "In Answer to a Certain Printed Paper, Intituled, A Declaration of the General Court of Massachusetts holden at Boston, the 18. October, 1658." The paper, addressed to King Charles II, constituted the colony's defense of its hanging of three Quakers. This is a striking contribution to New England history. Bishop afterwards wrote an Appendix and a second part (London, 1667), but this is the main work and is now a very rare book.—Quaritch.

BERKLEY, SIR WILLIAM. A Discourse and View of Virginia. 4to. London. (12 pp.)

> Watts mentions "A Description of Virginia" in Francis Moryson's edition of the Laws of Virginia, London, 1662, and states that Berkeley was the author of the greater part and the best laws of that province.

1663 HOWGILL, ——. The Testimony concerning the Life, Death, Trials, Travels, and Labours of Edward Burroughs, that worthy Prophet of the Lord, who died a Prisoner. 4to. London.

> Burroughs is the author of a pamphlet (1660) dealing with the persecution of the Quakers in New England.

1666 ALSOP, GEORGE. A Character of the Province of Maryland, wherein is Described in four distinct Parts (viz.) I. The Scituation, and Plenty of the Province. II. The Laws, Customs, and natural Demeanour of the Inhabitants. III. The worst and best Usage of a *Mary-Land* Servant, opened in view. IV. The Traffique and vendable Commodities of the Countrey. Also A small Treatise on the Wilde and Naked *Indians* (or Susquehanokes) of Mary-Land, their Customs, Manners, Absurdities, & Religion. Together with a Collection of Historical Letters. By George Alsop. 8vo. Portrait and map. London.

> Reprinted, Cleveland, 1902. See below.
> One of the rarest of books.—Sabin.

> 1902 ALSOP, GEORGE. A Character of the Province of Maryland. . . . Reprinted from the original edition. . . . With Introduction and Notes by Newton D. Mereness, Ph. D., Acting Professor of History and Economics in the College of Charleston, Author of "Maryland as a Proprietary Province." 8vo. Cleveland.

HORNE, ROBERT.  A Brief Description of The Province of Carolina on the Coasts of Floreda; And More particularly of a New Plantation begun by the English at Cape Feare, on that River now by them called Charles-River, the 29th of May, 1664. . . . Also, Directions and Advice to such as shall go thither. . . . Map  4to.  London.

> The first printed work relating to Carolina. . . —Quaritch. Barlow questions if the author be not Sir Peter Collaton.—Bradford.

1667  Strange Newes from Virginia being a true Relation of a Great Tempest in Virginia, by which many people lost their Lives, great numbers of Cattle destroyed, and in many places whole Plantations overturned, and whole Woods torn up by the Roots. As a further addition to this calamity the sea exceeded its usual height above twelve Foot, overflowing all the Plaine Country, carrying away much Corn and Tobacco, with many Cattle, forcing the Inhabitants into the Mountains for the security of their Lives.  London.

1669  ELIOT, JOHN.  The Indian Primer.  Or, the way of training up our Indian Youth in the good knowledge of God.  London.

> Reprinted, Edinburgh, 1877.
> "The Indian Primer, now reprinted, is one of the works of the pious and worthy John Eliot, familiarly known as the apostle of the Indians of New England, whose labours may be regarded as the morning star of modern missionary enterprise. It is interesting as being a work of its distinguished author, of which no perfect copy is known, except the one preserved in the Library of the University of Edinburgh; it is also valuable as bringing into notice an additional specimen of the now obsolete language of the aborigines of North America."—From Bookseller's Note.

SHRIGLY, NATHANIEL.  True Relation of Virginia and Maryland; With the Commodities therein, which in part the Author saw; the rest he had from knowing and Credible persons in the Moneths of February, March, April and May.  4to.  London.  (4 leaves.)

> Reprinted in Force's *Tracts*, III.

1670  CLARKE, SAMUEL.  A True, and Faithful Account of the Four Chiefest Plantations of the English in America. To wit, Of Virginia, New England, Bermvdvs, Barbados. With the Temperature of the Air: The nature of the Soil: The Rivers, Mountains, Beasts, Fowls, Birds, Fishes, Trees, Plants, Fruits, etc. As also, Of the Natives of Virginia, and New England, their Religion, Customs, Fishing, Huntings, etc. Collected by Samuel Clarke, sometimes Pastor in Saint Bennet-Fink, London.  Fol.  London.

> Also included in Clarke's Geographical Description of all the Countries in the Knowne Worlde. London: 1670-71.—From Bradford. See Clarke under 1657, GEOGRAPHY.

DENTON, DANIEL. A Brief Description Of New York: Formerly Called New-Netherlands. With the Places thereunto Adjoyning. Together with the Manner of its Scituation, Fertility of the Soyle, Healthfulness of the Climate, and the Commodities thence produced. Also Some Directions and Advice to such as shall go thither: An Account of what Commodities they shall take with them: The Profit and Pleasure that may accrew to them thereby. Likewise A Brief Relation of the Customs of the Indians there. 4to. London.

> Modern reprint, Cleveland, 1902. See below.
> The first book in English that gives a description of New York. The author tells us that at this date it was "built of Brick and Stone, and covered with red and black Tile, and the Land being high, it gives at a distance a pleasing Aspect to the spectators."—Quaritch.

> 1902 DENTON, DANIEL. A Brief Description of New York; formerly called the New Netherlands. Also a brief relation of the customs of the Indians there. With a bibliographical introduction. Reprinted from the edition of 1670. 8vo. Cleveland.

1671 OGILBY, JOHN. America: Being the Latest, and most Accurate Description of the New World; containing the Original of the Inhabitants, and the Remarkable Voyages thither. The conquest of the Vast Empires of Mexico and Peru, and other large Provinces and Territories, with the several European Plantations in those Parts, . . . Collected from the most authentic Authors. Maps, numerous folding and other copper-plates (over 100), and views of New Amsterdam, New York, Maryland, Virginia, Havana, Florida, Porto Rico, the Bermudas, the Barbadoes, Yucatan, Chili, Peru, Brazil, etc. Also portraits of Columbus, Vespucius, Montezuma, and Pizarro. Fol. London.

> In reality this is a translation from the work by Arnoldus Montanus, *De Nieuwe en Onbekende Weereld*. Ogilby may be considered as the English De Bry, his works are similar in their objects, compilation, and mode of illustration. —Maggs, No. 549. It contains accounts of Canada, Nova Scotia, New England, New York, Virginia, etc.

1672 BLOME, RICHARD. For a description of the colonies on the mainland of America see his *A Description of the Island of Jamaica*, under WEST INDIES.

DOWNING, SIR GEORGE. A Discourse written by Sir George Downing, the King of Great Britain's Envoy Extraordinary to the States of the United Provinces. 12mo. London.

> This book contains important and interesting details regarding New Netherlands and the Dutch claims to that part of America. . . . Sir George Downing was one of the most remarkable men that New England ever produced. He was the son of Emanuel Downing and Lucy, sister of Gov. John Winthrop, who emigrated to Salem, Mass., in 1638, when George was fourteen years old. He

was in the first class that graduated from Harvard University in 1642, and his name stands second on the list of the 7,000 alumni of that institution. It was chiefly through the agency of Downing, in the war between England and Holland, that New Netherland was wrested from the Dutch.—From Maggs, No. 549.

HUGHES, WILLIAM. The American Physician, or a Treatise of the Roots, etc., growing in the English Plantations. 12mo. London.

JOSSELYN, JOHN. New-Englands Rarities Discovered: In Birds, Beasts, Fishes, Serpents, and Plants of that Country. Together with The . . . Remedies wherewith the Natives constantly use to Cure their Distempers . . . Also A perfect Description of an Indian Sqva . . . with a Poem. . . . Lastly A Chronological Table of the most remarkable Passages in that Country amongst the English . . . Woodcuts. Plate. 8vo. London.

> Reprinted, Boston, 1865. See below.
> The earliest work on the Natural History of New England.—Rich. Josselyn first sailed for New England in 1638, and stayed there a little over a year. During this period he visited John Winthrop and John Cotton, to the latter of whom he delivered from Francis Quarles a metrical version of six of the Psalms for his approbation. His next stay, of which this book was one of the fruits, commenced in July 1663, and lasted nearly eight years and a half. A brief account of Boston and New England generally is followed by the interesting description of the fauna and flora; and the "Chronological Table," which occupies over twelve pages at the end, is not the least valuable feature of the book.—Quaritch. For an account of his two voyages to New England see under 1674 below.

> 1865   JOSSELYN, JOHN. New-Englands Rarities discovered in Birds, Beasts, Fishes, Serpents and Plants of that Country. . . . With an Introduction and Notes, By Edward Tuckerman, M. A. 4to. Boston.
>
> > Not merely reprints. The copious, interesting and valuable annotations lend a new value to the work.—Menzies Cat., quoted by Bradford.

LEDERER, JOHN. The Discoveries Of John Lederer, In three several Marches from Virginia, To the West of Carolina, And other parts of the Continent: Begun in March, 1669, and ended in September, 1670. Together with A General Map of the whole Territory which he traversed. Collected and Translated out of Latine from his Discourse and Writings, By Sir William Talbot, Baronet. Map. 4to. London.

> Modern edition, Rochester, N. Y., 1902.
> Extraordinarily rare. Sir William Talbot wrote: "From this discourse it is clear, that the long looked-for discovery of the Indian Sea does nearly approach and that . . . Carolina presumes that the accomplishment of this glorious Designe is reserved for her." Lederer, who was a German, travelled far into the interior of Virginia, and imagined that he had nearly approached the shores of the South Sea. He had made himself obnoxious to the people of Virginia, and sought refuge in Maryland, where he was well received by Sir William Talbot, who, finding him "a modest ingenious person, & a pretty Scholar," says in the preface: "I thought it common Justice to give him an occasion of vindicating himself from what I had heard of him; which truly he did with so convincing

Reason and circumstance, as quite abolished those former impressions in me, and made me desire this Account of his Travels, which here you have faithfully rendred out of Latine from his owne Writings and Discourse, with an entire Map of the Territory he traversed."—Quaritch. Lederer was sent out in 1669 by one of Virginia's governors to discover the Pacific. . . .His book advances the theory, based on investigation, that the distance from the Atlantic to the Pacific was certainly more than eight or ten days' journey, contrary to popular belief. The author admits nevertheless that the Western Ocean may stretch an arm as far east as some point in the Appalachian range!—Waldman. Prof. Cyrus Thomas, of the Bureau of Ethnology, has within a few years declared that this book is largely a literary fake. In examining the original copy of the book he discovered many mistakes. "Lederer was an engineer or surveyor, he could read and write English, Spanish, German and Latin, was something of a poetaster and litterateur, danced well, and was a scholar." Lederer had many quarrels with his party while making a survey of the York River and the Roanoke River. Captain Harris and his soldiers finally refused to go any further . . . and when later Lederer arrived at Jamestown with tales of the marvels he had seen, the colonists drove him out of the colony. He then met William Talbot, who befriended him.—Bradford.

1673 BLOME, RICHARD. Britannia; or, a Geographical Description of the Kingdoms of England, Scotland, and Ireland (and Wales; also the Isles and Territories belonging to His Majesty in America). Maps, folding and double-page. London.

1674 JOSSELYN, JOHN. An Account Of Two Voyages to New England. Wherein you have the setting out of a Ship, with the charges; The price of all necessaries for furnishing a Planter and his Family at his first coming; A Description of the Countrey, Natives and Creatures, with their Merchantil and Physical use; the Government of the Countrey as it is now posessed by the English, &c. A large Chronological Table of the most remarkable passages, from the first discovering of the Continent of America to the year 1673. . . . 8vo. London.

In the first of these there is little besides the sea-journal and common observations, unless it be an account of the necessaries for planters. The second is a very particular description of all the country, its beasts, fowls, fish, trees, the manners and customs of the English inhabitants, the time of their settling there. . . . Of the Indians he has very little or nothing . . . in many places where the author makes his own remarks, there are the oddest uncouth expressions imaginable, which look very conceited, but that is only as to his style.—Churchill, *Introduction.* His own observations are valuable. The work contains many curious particulars regarding medicine and surgery.—Quoted by Maggs, No. 429.

REYNAL, CAREW. The True English Interest: Or An Account Of The Chief National Improvements; In Some Political Observations, Demonstrating an Infallible Advance of this Nation to Infinite Wealth and Greatness, Trade and Populacy, with Imployment, and Preferment for all Persons. 8vo. London.

The last three chapters are "Of Navigation and Sea Affairs"; "Of New Inventions and Discoveries" (referring to American matters, the settling of New York and Carolina, the discovery of the Magellan Straits and Hudson's Bay, etc.); "Of Plantations" (concerning the West Indies, Hispaniola, Cuba, Florida, etc.).—From Quaritch.

1675    A Brief and True Narration of the Late Wars risen in New England: Occasioned by the Quarrelsome disposition, and Perfidious Carriage of the Barbarous, Savage and Heathenish Natives There.  4to.  London. (8 pp.)

1675-76    A Farther Brief and True Narrative of the Late Wars risen in New England, Occasioned by the quarrelsome Disposition and perfidious Carriage of the Barbarous and Savage Indian Natives there; with an Account of the Fight the 19th of December, 1675.  4to.  London. (12 pp.)

> See Drake's *Indian Chronicle,* Boston, 1836 and 1867.
> Nineteen of these war pamphlets were published, of which this is the first. It is an account of the "Great Swamp Fight" in Rhode Island.—Bradford.

1675-77    KING PHILIP'S WAR TRACTS. (Complete Set.)

I.    The Present State of New-England, with Respect to the Indian VVar, Wherein is an Account of the True Reason thereof (as far as can be judged by Men).  Together with most of the Remarkable Passages that have happened from the 20th of June till the 10th of November, 1675.  Faithfully composed by a Merchant of Boston, and communicated to his friend in London.  Folio.  London.  (19 pp.)

> Reprinted in Drake's *Indian Chronicle.*
> This is one of the scarcest documents in New England historical literature. The first edition of the work may be distinguished from the second (with the same date) by the fact that in the former the word New England in the title is in capitals, and in lower case in the latter. This pamphlet gives an account of the growing friction between the Indians and the English and of the atrocious massacres at Swanzey and other places, of the missionary activities of John Eliot, including a specimen of his translation of the Bible into the languages of the Massachusetts Indians.

II.    A Continuation of the State of New-England, being a further Account of the Indian Warr, and of the Engagement betwixt the Joynt Forces of the United English Collonies and the Indians, on the 19th December, 1675, with the True Number of the Slain and Wounded, and the Transactions of the English Army since the said fight.  With all other Passages that have happened from the 10th of November, 1675, to the 8th of February, 1675-6.  Together with an account of the intended Rebellion of the Negroes in the Barbadoes.  Fol.  London. (20 pp.)

> To be found also in Drake's *Indian Chronicle,* pp. 39-69.
> This tract opens with an account of the Indian plot to exterminate the English, as revealed by Sausamon, who was an Indian convert and native preacher employed by Philip (Matacon) as a sort of private secretary. The writer tells of an expedition under Captain Prentice against Seamonck in which ten Indians were killed and fifty-five taken prisoners and 150 wigwams burnt. There is a list of the English killed and wounded in the battle of Nov. 19, 1675.

III. A New and Further Narrative of the State of New-England, being a Continued Account of the Bloudy Indian War, from March till August, 1676. Giving a Perfect Relation of the Several Devastations, Engagements, and Transactions there; as also the Great Successes lately obtained against the Barbarous Indians, the Reducing of King Philip, and the Killing of one of the Queens, etc. Together with a Catalogue of the Losses in the Whole, sustained on either side, since the said War began, as near as can be collected. Fol. London (1676). (14 pp.)

This tract opens with "dolefull tidings of new massacres, slaughters and devastations committed by the brutish heathens." One of these incidents was the murder of two travellers by a horde of Indian women, with unusually revolting details. This is followed by an account of the killing of an English woman in an atrocious manner, of children being dashed against rocks before their mothers' eyes, etc. This rare and interesting tract is reprinted in Drake's *Indian Chronicle;* the first in the series, but should be the third in order of time. This is probably the Narrative mentioned by Increase Mather (*War with the Indians* (—Address to the Reader) as having been written by a "Quaker in Road-Island." (See *Present State of New-England* under Hubbard, 1677 below.) Of this work there is another edition with the same title-page, but with the woodcut of the Royal Arms on the title.—Sabin.

IV. A True Account of the Most Considerable Occurrences that have hapned in the Warre between the English and the Indians in New England, from the Fifth of May, 1676, to the Fourth of August last; as also of the Successes it hath pleased God to give the English against them. As it hath been communicated by Letters to a Friend in London. The most exact Account yet printed. Fol. London. (6 pp.)

The present tract is not by the same hand as the three preceding ones. The author states that the war "hath not been represented so exactly as it might have been." He seeks to remedy the defect.

V. The Warr in New-England Visibly Ended, King Philip, that Barbarous Indian now beheaded, and most of his bloudy Adherents submitted to Mercy, the rest fled far up into the Countrey, which hath given the Inhabitants encouragement to prepare their Settlement. Being a true and perfect Account brought in by Caleb More, Master of a Vessel newly arrived from Rhode Island, and published for general satisfaction. Fol. London (1677).

This tract is chiefly devoted to an account of the death of King Philip (Metacom).—From Robinson, No. 41 (as are the notes to the preceding four).

1676 A Further Account of New Jersey, in an Abstract of Letters lately writ from thence, by several inhabitants there resident. Printed in the Year 1676. 4to. (n.p.)

2nd edit., the same year (though no date is given), 4to, London.
One of the earliest accounts of New Jersey. It is signed by Richard Hartshorne, Martha S———, Robert Wade, Ester Huckens and Roger Paederick, all being among the first settlers in the province.—Sabin.

MATHER, INCREASE.   A Briefe History of the War with the Indians in New England.  From June 24, 1675, (when the first English-man was Murdered by the Indians) to August 12, 1676, when Philip, alias Metacomet, the Principal Author and Beginner of the War, was slain. Wherein the Grounds, Beginning, and Progress of the War, is summarily expressed.  Together with a serious Exhortation to Inhabitants of that Land. . . .  4to.  London.

> Printed first at Boston, 1676.
> Of this exceedingly rare book two copies only are known, Mr. Brinley's copy and one in England.—Sabin, quoted by Bradford. The 'Serious Exhortation,' though named in the title, is not given in this edition (i. e., London). The Preface refers to John Eliot as 'this now aged servant of the Lord.' . . .—*Ibid.* In the eyes of collectors this is the most prized relic of King Philip's War. This book was long listed among the *introuvables* of American historical literature; known only by hearsay, it was omitted from standard bibliographies until Mr. Brinley's copy came on the market about fifty years ago. The first edition of 1676 was printed by John Foster, who set up the first press in Boston; an English edition of the same year is commoner.—Waldman.

New England's Tears for her present miseries; or a late and true relation of the calamities of New England since April last past.  With an account of the Battel between the English and Indians upon Seaconk Plain, and of the Indians burning and destroying Marlbury, Rehoboth, Chelmsford, Sudbury and Providence; with the death of the Antononies, the Grand Indian Sachem, and a relation of a Fortification began by women on Boston Neck, Together with an Elegy on the Death of John Winthrop, Esq., late Governor of Connecticott, and Fellow of the Royal Society.  Written by an Inhabitant of Boston in New England, to his friend in London.  4to.  London.

News from New England, Being A True and last Account of the present Bloody Wars carried on betwixt the Infidels, Natives, and the English Christians, and Converted Indians of New-England, declaring the many Dreadful Battles Fought betwixt them: As also the many Towns and Villages burnt by the merciless Heathens.  And also the true Number of all Christians slain since the beginning of that War, as it was sent over by a Factor of New-England to a Merchant in London.  4to.  London.  (6 pp.)

> This short tract is of extreme rarity. Reprinted with a variation in the title, London, the same year.—Sabin.

1677   HUBBARD, WILLIAM (Rev.).  The Present State of New-England. Being a Narrative of the Troubles with the Indians in New-England, from the first planting thereof in the year 1607, to this present year 1677; but chiefly of the late troubles in the two last years 1675, and 1676.  To which is added a Discourse about the War with the Pequods in the year 1637. Folding woodcut map of New England. 4to. London.

> An important authoritative work on the early Indian Wars in New England. The author went out to New England in 1635, and was a member of the first class to graduate from Harvard College in 1642.—Maggs, No. 502.

Strange News from Virginia: being a full and true Account of the Life and Death of Nathaniel Bacon, Esquire, who was the only Cause and Original of all the late Troubles in that country. With a full Relation of all the accidents which have happened in the late War there between the Christians and the Indians. London.

> It will be remembered that Bacon led colonists against the Susquehannocks in 1675-76, in which he acted against Governor Berkeley's orders. The rebellion he started subsided after his death in 1676.

1680 GODWYN, MORGAN. The Negro's and Indians Advocate, Suing for their Admission into the Church: or A Persuasive to the Instructing and Baptising of the Negro's and Indians in our Plantations (in America). . . . To which is added, A Brief Account of Religion in Virginia. . . . 8vo. London.

> Very rare. It contains at the end: "The State of Religion in Virginia, as it was some time before the late Rebellion; represented in a letter to Sir W. B., then Governour thereof."—Robinson, No. 26.

1681 An Abstract, or Abbreviation of Some Few of the Many (Later and Former) Testimonys from the Inhabitants of New-Jersey, and other Eminent Persons, who have Wrote particularly concerning that place. 4to. London.

PENN, WILLIAM. Some Account of The Province of Pennsilvania In America; Lately Granted under the Great Seal Of England To William Penn, &c. Together with Privileges and Powers necessary to the well-governing thereof. Made publick for the Information of such as are or may be disposed to Transport themselves of Servants into these Parts. Fol. London.

> Translated into Dutch, Rotterdam, 1681. See below.
> This is the first publication relating to the province after the grant to William Penn. This brochure was published . . . before Penn's departure for the province. It contains a preface arguing at length the advantage of the country with a view to encouraging emigration. There is also information given for intending emigrants, extracts from the charter, and a description of the country with an outline of the conditions under which it was to be governed.—Robinson, No. 41.

> 1681 (In Dutch.) Een kort Bericht Van de Provintie often Landschap Pennsylvania genaemt, leggende in America; Nu onlangs onder het groote Zegel van Engeland gegeven aan William Penn, &c. Mitsgaders Van

de Priviligien, ende Macht om het selve wel te Regeeren. Uyt het Engels overgeset na de Copye tot Londen gedrukt by Benjamin Clark, Bockverkooper in George Yard Lombardstreet. 1681. Waer by nu gevoegt is de Notificatie van s'Konings Plaacaet, in date van den 2 April 1681. waar inne de tegenwoordige Inwoonders van Penn-Sylvania, belast word Willem Penn en zijn Erfgenamen, als volkomene Eygenaars en Gouverneurs, te gehoorsamen. Als mede, De Copye van een Brief by den selven W. P. geschreven aan zekere Regeeringe Anno 1675, tegens de Vervolginge en voor de Vryheyt van Conscientie, aan alle &c. 4to. Rotterdam.

The first Dutch translation. . . .—Sabin.

1682    ASHE, THOMAS. Carolina; or, A Description of the Present State of that Country, and the Natural Excellencies thereof. 4to. London.

A Description of New England in general; with a Description of the Town of Boston in particular. 4to. London.

F., R. The Present State of Carolina, with Advice to the Settlers. 4to. London.

FOX, ——. An Epistle to all Planters, and such who are transporting themselves into Foreign Plantations in America, . . . Fol. London. (2 pp.)

GIBBON, JOHN. Introductio ad Blasoniam, or Essay to a more correct Blason than hath formerly been used. 8vo. London.

A curious book, by an ancestor of the great historian (see his Autobiography for an account of it). The author passed a year in Virginia, 1659, "being most hospitably entertained by the Hon. Col. Richard Lee, Secretary of State there," and gives a singular account of the war dances, etc., of the Indians, which he saw in America.—Sabin.

LODDINGTON, WILLIAM. Plantation work the work of this Generation, written in true love to all such as are weightily inclined to Transport themselves and Families to any of the English Plantations in America. 4to. London. (20 pp.)

PENN, WILLIAM. A Brief Account of The Province Of Pennsilvania. Lately Granted by the King, Under the Great Seal of England, To William Penn, And His Heirs And Assigns. 4to. London. (16 pp.)

Translated into Dutch, Amsterdam, 1685. See below.
Excessively rare. . . . It differs widely in its contents from Penn's *Some Account Of The Province Of Pennsilvania* printed in the preceding year, and it contains King Charles' *Declaration to the Inhabitants and Planters of the*

*Province of Pensilvania* dated 1681, which is not found in the earlier tract. It is one of the earliest writings on Pennsylvania and one of the chief sources of information.—Quaritch.

1685   (In Dutch.)   Tweede Bericht ofte Relaas Van William Penn. Eygenaar en Gouverneur van de Provintie van Pennsylvania, In America. Behelsende een korte Beschrijvinge van den tegenwoordige toestand en gelegentheid van die Colonie. Mitsgaders, een aanwijsinge op wat voor Conditien, die gene die onmachtig zijin, om haar selven te konner transporteeren daarheenen souden konnen worden gebracht, met voordeel tot de gene, die daer Penningen toe souden verschieten, Uyt het Engels overgeset. t'Amsterdam. By Jacob Claus, Boekverkoper in de Prince-straat. 4to. (20 pp.)

The second account of Pennsylvania is as rare as the other Dutch translations of the first account.—Sabin.

## ROWLANDSON, MARY.   A True History Of The Captivity & Restoration Of Mrs. Mary Rowlandson, A Minister's Wife in New-England. Wherein is set forth, The Cruel and Inhumane Usage she underwent amongst the Heathens, for Eleven Weeks time: And her Deliverance from them. Written by her own Hand, for her Private Use. . . . Whereunto is annexed, A Sermon. . . . Preached by Mr. Joseph Rowlandson. . . . 4to. London.

This was first printed "at New-England." Modern reprint, Boston, 1930.
One of the earliest narratives of Indian captivities; it is written by a very observant woman who had a keen regard to the smallest details of the attack on the settlement, the firing of the houses, the fierce and bloody fighting, and the eventual capture of the twenty-four survivors. She also describes the march and her varying fortunes during her stay with the savages, and gives a very entertaining account of the habits and customs of the Indians. An Indian messenger who was of service in the negotiations for her release is called "James, the Printer": this may well be an Indian assistant to a New England printing house. —Robinson.

## W., J.   A Letter from New England, concerning their Customs, Manners, and Religion. Written upon occasion of a Report about a Quo Warranto brought against that Government.   Fol.   London.   (9 pp.)

This remarkable letter, written with a free flowing and gossiping pen, is signed "J. W." "It is a most extraordinary production, both for the matter it contains and its extreme rarity. The tone of it is anything but complimentary to the Bostonians, especially those belonging to the Independent Church. The writer remarks 'For lying and cheating they outvie Judas, and all false Merchants in Hell; and the worst Drunkards may here find pot-companions enough for all their pretense to sobriety. They make a sport of cheating and look upon it as a commendable piece of ingenuity, and brag of those vile actions which others are ashamed of, commending him that has the most skill to commit a piece of roguery.' Many of the stories related of particular persons, whose initials the author gives, are not such as could be quoted. . . . "—Brinley Catalogue.

## WILSON, SAMUEL.   An account of the Province of Carolina in America, Together with an Abstract of the Patent, and several other Necessary and Useful Particulars, to such as have thoughts of Transporting themselves thither.   Map.   4to.   London.

"Wilson was secretary to the Proprietors of Carolina. His work relates particularly to the southern settlement in that province, and contains much useful and necessary information concerning the natural history of the country, together with its laws and government."—Church Catalogue, quoted by Robinson, No. 58.

1683 A Brief Account of the Province of East New Jersey in America: Published by the Scots Proprietors Having Interest there. For the Information of such, as may have a Desire to Transport themselves, or their Families thither. Wherein The Nature and Advantage of, and Interest in a Forraign Plantation to this Country is Demonstrated. 4to. London. (8 pp.)

Mr. S. L. M. Barlow, of New York, possesses the only known copy. It was reprinted in the "Historical Magazine," Vol. I, Second Series, and twenty-five copies were issued.—Quoted.

Britanniae Speculum; or, A Short View of the Ancient and Modern State of Great Britain, and the Adjacent Isles, and of all other Dominions and Territories now in actual possession of His present Sacred Majesty, King Charles II. 12mo. London.

CLARKE, SAMUEL (Rev.) Lives of Sundry Eminent Persons, in the latter age. Fol. London.

Contains the life, voyage, and settlement in America, of Richard Mather, father of Increase Mather.—Sabin.

CRAFFORD, JOHN. A New and Most Exact Account of the Fertile and Famous Colony of Carolina (on the Continent of America) whose Latitude is from 36 Deg. of North Latitude, to 29 Deg. Together with a Maritine (*sic*) Account of its Rivers, Barrs, Soundings and Harbours; also of the Natives, their Religion, Traffick and Commodities. Likewise the Advantages accrewing to all Adventurers by the Customs of the Countrey; Being the most Healthful and Fertile of his Majesties Territories on the said Continent. As also an Account of the Islands of Bermudas, the Harbours, Situation, People, Commodities, &c., belong to said Islands; the whole being a Compendious Account of a Voyage made by the Ingenious Person for a full discovery of the above-said places. . . . 4to. Dublin.

The two last lines read: 'Taken by John Crafford, who was Super cargo of the good Ship the James of Erwin, burthen about 50 Tuns.'—Sabin.

HOLME, THOMAS. A Portraiture of the City of Philadelphia in the Province of Pennsylvania in America by Thomas Holme Surveyor General. London.

> A folding plan measuring 11¾ by 17½ inches. This plan was issued with Penn's *A letter from William Penn to the Free Society of Traders* 1683, and is the first depicting the City of Philadelphia. It shows admirably that the far-seeing mind of Penn fully grasped the probability of an enormous increase of population, and provides the first instance of an adequate and scientific town-planning in the United States.—Quaritch.

PENN, WILLIAM. A Letter from William Penn, Proprietary and Governour of Pennsylvania in America to the Committee of the Free Society of Traders of that Province residing in London. Containing a General Description of the Said Province, . . . of the Natives, . . . their Languages, Customs and Manners. . . . Of the first Planters, the Dutch, . . . and the Present Condition and Settlement of the said Province. . . . To which is added An Account of the City of Philadelphia, newly laid out, its Scituation between two Navigable Rivers, . . . with a Portraicture thereof, wherein the Purchasers Lots are distinguished. Folding map of Philadelphia (see under Holme above). Fol. London.

> The first edition of this tract, of which there are four, is excessively rare. In the other three it reads Poprietary (for Proprietary). A few copies have an appendix of 4 pp. containing a list of lot-holders. Justin Winsor describes it as "the most important of the series."—From Robinson, No. 41.

1684 Carolina described more fully than heretofore, being an impartial Collection from the several Relations of that place, since its first planting by the English, and before under the Denomination of Florida, from Divers Letters from the Irish Settled there, and Relations of those who have been there several years, whereunto is added the Charter, with the Fundamental Constitutions of that Province, . . . 4to. Dublin.

> This is "one of the most interesting and rare volumes relating to the Province."—Quoted by Sabin.

PENN, WILLIAM. Information and Direction to such Persons as are inclined to America, More Especially Those related to the Province of Pennsylvania. Fol. London. (4 pp.)

> This tract is of interest as exhibiting the terms upon which Penn disposed of his lands.—From Sabin.

1685 BUDD, THOMAS. Good Order Established in Pennsilvania & New-Jersey in America, Being a true Account of the Country; With its Produce and commodities there made. And the great Improvements that may be made by means of Publick Store-houses for Hemp, Flax, and

Linnen-Cloth; also, the Advantages of a Publick-School, the Profits of a Publick-Bank, and the Probability of its arising, those directions here laid down are followed. With the advantages of Publick Granaries. Likewise, several other things needful to be understood by those that are or do intend to be concerned in planting in the said Countries. All which is laid down very plain, in this small Treatise; it being easie to be understood by any ordinary Capacity. To which the Reader is referred for his further satisfaction. . . .  4to.  London.

Modern edition, Cleveland, 1902. See below.

1902  BUDD, THOMAS.  Good Order Established in Pennsylvania and New Jersey. Reprinted from the original edition of 1685. With Introduction and Notes by Frederick J. Shepard, of the Buffalo Public Library. 8vo.  Cleveland.

BURTON, ROBERT.  The English Empire in America: Or a Prospect of His Majestes Dominions in the West-Indies.  Namely Newfoundland; New England, New York, Pennsylvania, New Jersey, Maryland, Virginia, Carolina, Bermuda's, Barbada, Anguilla, Montserrat, Dominica, St. Vincent, Antego, Mevis, Or Nevis, S. Christophers, Barbadoes, Jamaica, with an account of the Discovery, Situation, Product, and other Excellencies of these Countries. To which is prefixed a Relation of the first Discovery of the New World called America, by the Spaniards, And of the Remarkable Voyages of several Englishmen to divers places therein. Maps and pictures.  12mo.  London.

2nd edit., London, 1692; 6th in 18mo, London, 1728; 7th, Dublin, 1729; another 7th, London, 1739.
It has been suggested that the name Robert Burton was a non-de-plume of the bookseller Nathaniel Crouch (for whom it was printed).—Maggs, No. 502. Crouch was a writer of miscellaneous works, who was apprenticed to a London Stationer and who made free use of the Stationers' Company.—D. N. B.

PENN, WILLIAM.  A Further Account of the Province of Pennsylvania and its improvements. For the Satisfaction of those that are Adventurers, and enclined to be so.  4to.  London.  (20 pp.)

An extremely interesting work in the history of Pennsylvania and Philadelphia. In regard to Philadelphia, Penn states that it is two miles long and a mile broad, . . . (its street names) mostly taken from the things that spontaneously grow in the country, as Vine-Street, Mulberry-Street, Chestnut-Street, Wallnut-Street, Strawberry-Street, Cranberry-Street, . . . and that in the past year (1684?) the town had advanced to three hundred and fifty-seven houses. . . . Later on in his narrative, under date of 3d. of August, 1685, he remarks, ". . . and there are about 600 Houses in three years time."—From Maggs, No. 465.

SCOT, GEORGE.  The Model of Government of the Province of East-New-Jersey in America. And Encouragement for such as Design to be concerned there. Published for Information of such as are desirous to be Interested in that place.  8vo.  Edinburgh.

It appears that Scot, by whom the Preface is signed, came to America and examined the coast 'from the River of Canada, Northerly, to the River of May, Southerly, in that part of Florida, now called Caralina. . . . ' About one-third of the volume is taken up with contemporary letters from persons living in New Jersey, to their friends in Scotland. . . . —Murphy, quoted by Bradford. The effect of the publication of this book was highly beneficial to the province in promoting its settlement, "particularly as the author added example to precept by embarking himself and family for East Jersey. He was accompanied by nearly two hundred persons, and sailed from Scotland in September, 1685, but himself and wife died on the passage."—Quoted by Sabin. The work was reprinted in W. Whitehead's *East Jersey under Proprietary Governments*, New York, 1846:

1686 BLOME, RICHARD. The present State of His Majesties Isles and Territories in America, viz. Jamaica, Barabadoes, St. Christophers, Mevis, Antegos, St. Vincent, Dominica, New Jersey, Pennsylvania, Montserrat, Anguilla, Bermudas, Carolina, Virginia, New-England, Tobago, Newfoundland, Maryland, New York; with new Maps of every place: Together with Astronomical Tables, which will serve as a constant Diary for the use of the English Inhabitants in those Islands, from 1686 to 1700. Also a Table by which, at any time in England, you may know what hour it is in any of those parts; and how to make Sun-Dials for any of those places, . . . 8vo. London.

Translated into French, Amsterdam, 1688. See below.

1688 (In French.) L'Amérique Angloise: ou Description des Isles et Terres du Roi d'Angleterre dans L'Amérique. Avec de nouvelles Cartes de Chaque Isle et Terre. Traduit de l'Anglois. 7 folding maps by Morden. Amsterdam.

1688 WIDDERS, ROBERT. Life and Death, Travels and Sufferings of Robert Widders of Kellet, in Lancashire. 4to. London.

A "Testimonie" by G. F(ox), says that Widders "about 1670, Travelled with me into America, Barbados, Jamaica, Virginia, and Maryland."—Bookseller's Note.

1689 BYFIELD, NATHANIEL. An Account of the late Revolution in New England. Together with the Declaration of the Gentlemen, Merchants, and Inhabitants of Boston, and the Country adjacent. April 18, 1689. Written by Mr. Nathaniel Byfield, A merchant of Bristol in New England, to his Friends in London. 4to. London.

An edition appeared at Edinburgh, 1689. Reprinted in Force's *Tracts*, IV, No. 10, and in the *Andros Tracts*, 1865.—Sabin.
This tells of the rebellion against Sir Edmund Andros, whom James II had made governor of the consolidated colonies of New York and New England. The uprising in Boston and the imprisonment of Andros was a momentous event in colonial history.—From Waldman.

MATHER, INCREASE.  A Brief Relation of the State of New England, From the Beginning of that Plantation To this Present Year, 1689. In a Letter to a Person of Quality.  4to.  London.  (18 pp.)

> Reprinted in the *Mass. Hist. Soc. Coll.*, XXI, 93; Force's *Tracts* IV, No. 11; and *Andros Tracts*, II, 149.—Sabin. The history of the colony was published by Mather as part of the propaganda to obtain from William and Mary the charters which had been cancelled by James II.—Quaritch.

MATHER, INCREASE.  The Present State of New England impartially considered in a Letter to the Clergy.  4to.  London.  (44 pp.)

1690  PALMER, JOHN.  An Impartial Account of the State of New England, or, The late Government there, Vindicated.  In answer to the Declaration Which the Faction set forth when they Overturn'd that Government.  With a Relation Of the horrible Usage they treated the Governour with, and his Council. . . .  4to.  London.

> Palmer was a colonial official who went from the Barbadoes to New York, where he attained to some judicial position.

1691  BURNYEAT, JOHN.  The Truth Exalted in the writings of John Burnyeat, collected into this volume as a Memorial to his faithful Labours and for the Truth.  4to.  London.

> This contains the Journal of Burnyeat's travels in Maryland, Virginia, New York, Rhode Island, Connecticut, New England, and Long Island, with an account of a dispute he had with Roger Williams, and of cruelties inflicted upon the Quakers in New England.—Robinson, No. 41.

MATHER, COTTON.  Late Memorable Providences Relating to Witchcrafts and Possessions. . . The Second Impression.  Recommended by the Reverend Mr. Richard Baxter in London, and by the Ministers of Boston and Charlestown in New England. . . .  12mo.  London.

> 1st impression, Boston, 1689; 3rd, Edinburgh, 1697.
> The latest Witchcraft frenzy was in New England in 1692, when the execution of witches became a calamity more dreadful than the sword or the pestilence.—Robinson's *Theological Dictionary*.

MATHER, COTTON.  The Life and Death of the Renown'd Mr. John Eliot, who was the First Preacher of the Gospel to the Indians in America.  With an Account of the wonderful success which the Gospel has had amongst the Heathen in that part of the World: and of the many strange customs of the Pagan Indians in New-England.  The 2nd edition carefully corrected. 1st edition English.  12mo.  London.

> This was first published in Boston under the title, "The Triumphs of the Reformed Religion," 1691. 3rd edit., 8vo, London, 1694.

Some Letters and an Abstract of Letters from Pennsylvania, concerning The State and Improvement of that Province. Published to Prevent Mis-Reports. 4to. London. (12 pp.)

1692 BOYLE, R. General Heads for the Natural History of a country Great or Small; Drawn for the use of Travellers and Navigators. 12mo. London.

> Ch. VIII relates to Virginia; IX to Guiana and Brazil; X to the Antilles and Carribbe Islands.—Sabin.

1694 CRISP, STEPHEN. A Memorable Account of the Gospel Labours, Travels and Sufferings of that ancient servant of Christ, Stephen Crisp in his Books and writings herein Collected. London.

> Stephen Crisp was a Quaker, a Separatist, then a Baptist, then a Quaker again. He visited Holland in 1661 and Germany in 1667 as a missionary. He was fined for infringing the Conventicle Act of 1670.—D.N.B.

FOX, GEORGE. A Journal, or Historical Account of the Life, Travels, Sufferings, Christian Experiences, and Labour of Love, in the work of the Ministry, of that Ancient, Eminent, and Faithful Servant of Jesus Christ, George Fox, who departed this Life in great Peace with the Lord the 13th of the 11th Month 1690. Fol. London.

> 2nd edit., 2 vols., 8vo, London, 1709; 3rd edit., fol., London, 1765, and many later editions in America. See below.
> Fox, the celebrated founder of the Society of Friends, made several missionary journies to America, and endured much persecution for his practises and beliefs. His journal was revised by William Penn.

> 1911 FOX, GEORGE. The Journal of George Fox, edited from the MSS., by Norman Penney, with an Introduction, by T. E. Harvey. 2 portraits and 3 facsimiles. 2 vols. 8vo. Cambridge.

1695 P., L. Two Essays sent in a Letter from Oxford to a Nobleman in London. 8vo. London.

> Pages 15-28 contain "Peopling and Planting the New World."—Sabin.

1696 CROESE, GERARD. The General History of the Quakers: containing the Lives, Tendents, Sufferings, Tryals, Speeches, and Letters of all the most eminent Quakers, both Men and Women; Collected from the first Rise of that Sect, down to the present Time. Collected from Manuscripts, etc., a Work never attempted before in English. Being written originally in Latin by Gerard Croese. To which is added, a Letter writ by George Keith, and sent by him to the Author of this Book.

Containing a Vindication of himself, and several Remarks on this History. 8vo. London.

Translated into German, Berlin, 1696.
This work contains some particulars of the Quakers in Pennsylvania.

1698  HENNEPIN, LOUIS.  A New Discovery of a Vast Country in America, extending above Four Thousand Miles between New France and New Mexico, with a Description of the Great Lakes, Cataracts, Rivers, Plants, and Animals; also the Manners, Customs, and Languages of the several Native Indians, and the advantage of Commerce with those different Nations.  With a Continuation, giving an account of the Attempt of the Sieur La Salle upon the Mines of St. Barbe, . . . the Taking of Quebec by the English; with the advantages of a shorter cut to China and Japan.  Both parts illustrated with Maps and Figures . . . to which is added, Several new discoveries in North America not published in the French Edition.  8vo.  London.

Two editions of this work appeared in English the same year. The one (see above) which has the first line of the imprint ending in Bon/ (i.e., Bonwick) is considered to be the earlier. The other is known as the Tonson edition from the fact that the first line of its imprint ends in this name. The two differ in set-up, pagination, and in some of the illustrations. In this edition the title to the second part reads: "A New Voyage into the North-west Parts of America; describing a country larger than Europe, inhabited by 200 different Nations; situate between the Frozen-Sea and New Mexico. . . ." A variant of the Tonson edition appeared the same year, with a slightly different title.—From Maggs, No. 502. The Bonwick edition was reprinted, London, 1699. An abstract of Hennepin's discoveries was printed about 1720 to raise the credit of the South Sea stock.—From Sabin. Modern edition, Chicago, 1903. French original, Utrecht, 1697, and another edition, Amsterdam and Utrecht, 1698. See below.
Following upon the discovery of the Mississippi by Marquette and Joliet, La Salle set out in 1678 to open up this fertile basin. The chronicler of his expedition was Father Louis Hennepin, who explored the upper reaches of the Mississippi while La Salle was retracing his way to raise funds for renewing his voyage, after its disastrous experience on the Illinois river. Hennepin may have touched the site of the future city of Minneapolis. After La Salle's death in 1687, Hennepin, in the second edition of his work, claimed to have made the discovery of the Father of Waters its whole length to the sea, a claim that is easily disproved. "In Le Clercq's 'Premier Etablissement de la Foy,' had appeared an account by Hennepin's colleague, Father Zenobe Membré, giving an account of La Salle's expedition to the mouth of the Mississippi, in which Membré took part. This account, owing to its rarity, was little known at the time, and Hennepin boldly appropriated it with such verbal changes as to make it appear to be a narrative drawn from his own journal of 1680, . . ."—From Maggs, No. 502. But Hennepin can rightfully lay claim to have been the first to have described Niagara Falls, to which he gives the height of 600 feet. He also notes the building of Fort Crevecouer, whose Indian name was Checagou. The Account of the New Discoveries not in the French were added by the English editor. They deal with the voyages of Joliet, Marquette and La Salle.

1720(?)  A Discovery of a Large, Rich and Plentiful Country in the North America, extending about 4000 Leagues. Wherein by a very short passage, lately found out, through the Mer-Bermejo into the South Sea, by which a considerable Trade might be carried on, as well in the northern as the southern parts of America. 8vo. London.

1903 HENNEPIN, FATHER LOUIS. A New Discovery of a Vast Country in America. Reprinted from edition of 1698. Notes and index by Reuben Gold Thwaites. Maps and illustrations. 2 vols. 8vo. Chicago.

1697 HENNEPIN, LOUIS. Nouvelle Découverte d'un très Grand Pays situé dans l'Amérique entre Le Nouveau Mexique et La Mer Glaciale, avec les Cartes, & les Figures necessaires, & de plus l'Histoire Naturelle & Morale, & les avantages, qu'on en peut tirer par établissement des Colonies. Large folding map of the Mississippi basin with parts of Canada and the United States. Large folding map of North America, with California, and an inset map of the land between California and Japan; engraving of a buffalo; and the first engraved view of Niagara Falls. 12mo. Utrecht.

This is the first edition of the second part; it includes the substance of his first book, but gives, before the account of his voyage up the Mississippi, an account of a voyage he here claims to have made down to the mouth and up again. . . . —Sabin.

1698 HENNEPIN, LOUIS. Nouveau voyage d'un Pais plus grand que l'Europe avec les reflections des entreprises du Sieur de la Salle, sur les mines de Ste. Barbe, . . . Map and 4 plates. 12mo. Utrecht, chez Ernestus Voskuyl, Imprimeur.

This is the first issue to bear the printer's name in the imprint, and is all but unknown to bibliographers. The first eight chapters give a description of the adventures of La Salle. There are also some remarks on the Indians and the history of the siege of Quebec by the English in 1628.—Hiersemann Catalogue.

LA SALLE, ROBERT CAVALIER DE. An Account of Monsieur De La Salle's last Expedition and Discoveries in North America; also the Adventures of the Sieur de Montavban, Captain of the French Buccaneers on the Coast of Guinea, in the year 1695. 8vo. London.

A much rarer work than the ordinary Relation of La Salle.—Puttick and Simpson. For a collected account of the journies of La Salle see the volume edited by Professor I. J. Cox, following under 1922 below. One should also consult Joutel under 1714 below.

1922 The Journals of Rene Robert Cavalier, Sieur de la Salle, 1668-1687, as related by his followers, Tonty, Hennepin, Joutel, etc. Edited with an Introduction by Prof. Isaac Joslin Cox. 2 vols. 12mo. London.

The complete story of La Salle's eventful and dramatic career forms the most striking chapter of French exploration of North America. The original narratives of Tonty and others, which have been practically inaccessible, are here presented under Professor Cox's careful editorship. They are of intense interest as stories of thrilling adventure and of peculiar consequence, showing as they do the origin of the French claim to the Mississippi valley.—Publisher's Notice.

Tonty was an Italian officer whom La Salle attached to his service and he proved to be a faithful assistant among a jealous and treacherous lot of associates. After several laborious journies to the region of the Illinois River, La Salle finally entered the Mississippi in February, 1682. On April 6 they came to the mouth of the great river, and dividing into parties they passed through the three main channels of the delta and united on the outside, where they ceremoniously took possession of the territory of the Mississippi basin in the name of the French King. The return journey was difficult and hazardous, but it was successfully completed. Circumvented by enemies in Canada,

La Salle returned to France and obtained from the King approval of an expedition by way of the Gulf to the mouth of the river. This expedition was pursued by ill fortune from the start and culminated in the explorer's death by murder. Joutel led the remnants of the voyagers to the Illinois River. His account of this journey is the best remaining, while the memoirs published by Tonty are a chief source of historical information on these enterprises. See Joutel under 1714 below. For Tonty's account see the following item.

1697 TONTI, LE CHEVALIER. Dernières Découvertes dans l'Amérique Septentrionale de M. de la Sale; mises au jour par M. le Chevalier Tonti, Gouverneur du Fort Saint Loüis, aux Islinois. 12mo. Paris.

A New Account of North America, as it was lately presented to the French King; containing a more particular account of that vast country, and of the manners and customs of the Inhabitants, than has been hitherto published. 8vo. London.

We have here a French account of those countries, but more particularly what belongs to them, more exact than any other that has been delivered.—Churchill, *Introduction.*

THOMAS, GABRIEL. An Historical and Geographical Account Of The Province and Country Of Pensilvania; And Of West-New-Jersey In America. The Richness of the Soil, the Sweetness of the Situation, the Wholesomeness of the Air, the Navigable Rivers, and others, the prodigious Encrease of Corn, the flourishing Condition of the City of Philadelphia. . . . Folding map of Pennsylvania and West Jersey. 8vo. London.

A modern edition (no date), Cleveland. See below.

(n.d.) THOMAS, GABRIEL. An account of Pennsylvania and West New Jersey. . . . Reprinted from the original edition of 1698 With Introduction by Cyrus Townsend Brady, LL. D. Cleveland.

1699 WARD, NED. A Trip to New-England. With a Character of the Country and People, Both English and Indians. Fol. London.

2nd edit. (with other matter), London, 1704. Modern reprint, Providence, 1905. See below.
A scurrilous, though very amusing tract. The author, whose trip was made to Boston, is very severe on the Puritans. Among other disparaging statements, he says: "Many of the leading Puritans may (without Injustice) be thus characteris'd. They are saints without religion, traders without honesty, Christians without charity, magistrates without mercy, subjects without loyalty, neighbours without amity, faithless friends, implacable enemies, and rich men without money."—Quaritch. He gives an interesting account of the Indians.—*Ibid.* This tract is by the well known author of the *London Spy.*

1704 WARD, NED. Writings of the Author of the London Spy including "A Trip to Jamaica with a true Character of the People and Island"; and "A Trip to New England, with a Character of the Country and People, both English and Indians." The Second Edition. 8vo. London.

1905 WARD, NED. Boston in 1682 and 1699. A Trip to New England by Edward Ward and a Letter from New England by J. W. Providence.

1700 DICKINSON, JONATHAN. God's Protecting Providence Man's Surest Help and Defence. . . . Evidenced in the Remarkable Deliverence Of divers Persons (among them Robert Barrow), From the devouring Waves of the Sea, amongst which they Suffered Shipwrack. And also From the more cruelly devouring jawes of the inhumane Canibals of Florida. London.

> First printed at Philadelphia 1699. 3rd edit., London, 1720; 4th, London, 1759; and again, London, 1787, 1790.
> Dickenson was a native of Jamaica, who, with his wife, had joined the Society of Friends a short time before embarking on the voyage, the misfortunes of which are the subject of this book: His vessel was wrecked on Sept. 23, 1696, on the coast of Florida, and he lived among the Indians for some time. He later settled in Philadelphia and became one of the most extensive and successful merchants of his time.—Maggs, No. 479. He also became Speaker of the Assembly and Chief Justice of the Province of Pennsylvania. He died in 1722.

1701 An Essay upon the Government of The Plantations on the Continent of America; Together with some Remarks upon the Discourse on the Plantation Trade, written by the Author of the Essay on Ways and Means, and Published in the Second Part of His Discourses, on the Publick Revenues and on the Trade of England. By an American. 8vo. London.

WOLLEY, CHARLES. A Two Years' Journal in New York. London.

> Modern edition edited by E. G. Bourne, Cleveland, 1902.
> The author was chaplain to Governor Andros from 1678 until his return in 1680 to England. He states that he waited so long before publishing in the hope that a more competent account would be brought out; but not having heard of any, and being at the moment idle, decided that since "I would not do what I ought, I ought to do what I would." A curious piece of information imparted by Wolley is the fact that during his residence land could be bought at twopence or threepence an acre, a valid deed from the governor included.—Waldman.

1702 MATHER, COTTON. Magnalia, Christi Americana: or, the Ecclesiastical History of New-England, from its First Planting in the Year 1620, unto the Year of our Lord, 1698. In Seven Books. . . . By the Reverend and Learned Cotton Mather, M.A. And Pastor of the North Church in Boston, New-England. Map of New England and New York. Fol. London.

> Mather, in this huge record of the first seventy years of American national life, has given us a marvellous insight into the lines of thought of the earliest English-speaking colonists, their records, the history of the foundation and rise of Harvard College, biographies of leading men, and a thousand and one other details of the common life of the period. Admittedly it contains many inaccuracies, but nevertheless our knowledge of the beginnings of the American nation is largely founded on this imperishable work. . . . This book is the first collected edition of an American Author.—Robinson, No. 20.

1703　BUGG, FRANCIS. News from Pensilvania, or a Brief Narrative of Several Remarkable Passages in the Government of the Quakers of that Province. Touching their Proceedings in their Pretended Courts of Justice, their Way of Trade and Commerce; with Remarks and Observations upon the whole. Published by the Author of Pilgrim's Progress. Together with a Postscript. 8vo. London.

　　LAHONTAN, LOUIS ARMAND DE LOM D'ARCE, BARON DE. New voyages to North-America. Containing an Account of the Several Nations of that Vast Continent: their Customs, Commerce, and Way of Navigation, upon the Lakes and Rivers; the Several Attempts of the English and French to dispossess one another; with the Reasons of the Miscarriage of the Former; and the Various Adventures between the French and the Iroquese Confederates of England, from 1683 to 1694. A geographical Description of Canada, and a Natural History of the Country, with Remarks upon their Government, and the Interest of the English and French in their Commerce. Also a Dialogue between the Author and a General of the Savages, giving a Full View of the Religion and Strange Opinions of those People . . . and his Remarks on those Courts. To which is added, A Dictionary of the Algonkine Language, which is generally spoken in North-America. . . . Done into English. Numerous maps and plates. 2 vols. 8vo. London.

　　　This is a translation of the French original published at the Hague, 1703. But Arber says a great part of it was never printed in the original. 2nd edit., 2 vols., London, 1735; reprinted in Pinkerton XIII, 336-373; a modern reprint, 2 vols., Chicago, 1905. See below.
　　　La Hontan was born in Gascony in 1666 and went out to Canada at the age of sixteen. . . . He commanded various forts in the interior, and journeyed to the western extremity of the Great Lakes. In 1685 he set out with several soldiers and five Indians from Michillimakinac, reached the Mississippi via Wisconsin, and on Nov. 7 of that year came across a river which from its size must have been the Minnesota. He tells us that he went up this river, coming across various tribes of Indians. There has been much controversy as to the truth of La Hontan's statements concerning this part of the journey.—From Maggs, No. 465. La Hontan's book is more purely a work of the imagination than Hennepin's; there is very little basis of fact in it, but it is the expression of a gay, caustic and skeptical soul, qualities every decent charlatan should have. There is almost no malice in it, and the borrowing is quite harmless. Like his contemporary, La Hontan was quickly and completely discredited. . . . His book went through various editions all over Europe, and has been reprinted in recent years.—Waldman. Part of the attack on La Hontan's Narrative is due to the fact that he was a freethinker and in consequence was out of favor with the French clergy and others, and writers of a later date were apt to copy their opinions. The author was in England at the time of the publication of his work in English and, to some extent, supervised it.—Maggs, No. 549.

　　1735　LA HONTAN, BARON DE. New Voyages to North America, . . . With an Account of the Author's Retreat to Portugal and Denmark, and his Remarks on those Courts. 2 vols. 8vo. London.

　　1905　LA HONTAN, BARON DE. New Voyages to North America. Reprinted from the edition of 1703, with notes by Reuben Gold Thwaites. Maps and plates. 2 vols. 8vo. Chicago.

1703  LA HONTAN, BARON DE.  Nouveaux Voyages dans l'Amérique Septentrionale qui contiennent une relation des différens peuples qui y habitent, la nature de leur gouvernement, leur commerce, leurs coutûmes,
leur religion, et leur manière de faire la guerre. L'intérêt des Francois
et des Anglois dans le commerce qu'ils font avec ces nations, l'avantage
que l'Angleterre peut retirer de ce pais, etant en guerre avec la France.
2 vols. in 1. 12mo.  3 cartes et 22 planches gravées hors texte.  The
Hague.

1705  BEVERLEY, ROBERT.  The History and Present State of Virginia; In
Four Parts. I. The History of the First Settlement of Virginia, and
the Government thereof, to the Present Time. II. The Natural Productions and Conveniences of the Country, suited to Trade and Improvement. III. The Native Indians, their Religion, Laws, and Customs in War and Peace. IV. The Present State of the Country, . . . By
a Native and Inhabitant of the Place.  14 folding copper plates (after
de Bry) of Indians.  8vo.  London.

   2nd edit., with omission of dedication, change in preface, and many suppres-
sions and additions, London, 1722. Translated into French, Paris, 1707. See below.
   "This is the earliest history of Virginia after Capt. John Smith's, and was
written primarily to correct Oldmixon."—Quoted by Maggs, No. 442. Beverley
is the best authority concerning the particular subjects delineated in his quaint and
agreeable pages; and his work affords the most vivid, comprehensive, instructive,
and entertaining picture of Virginia at the date of his writing that is to be found,
being most useful for the period following the Restoration, and especially important for its interesting particulars relative to the numerous Indian tribes. He was
a native of Virginia and Clerk of the Council about 1697 when Andros was governor, and so obtained considerable experience in the public records of the Colony.
—From Robinson, No. 27.

   1707  (In French.)  Histoire de la Virginie, contenant l'Histoire du premier établissement dans la Virginie et de son gouvernement jusques à présent, les
productions naturelles et les commodités du Pais, avant que les Anglais
y négociassent et l'améliorassent. La Religion, les lois et les coutûmes
des Indiens Naturels. L'Etat présent du pays. Par un auteur natif et
habitant du Pais, traduite de l'anglois. 8 planches. 12mo. Paris.

DUNTON, JOHN.  The Life and Errors of John Dunton Late Citizen of
London; written by Himself in Solitude.  With an Idea of a New Life;
Wherein is Shewn How he'd Think, Speak, and Act, might he Live
over his Days again: Intermix'd with the New Discoveries the Author
has made in his Travels Abroad, And in his Private Conversation at
Home.  Together with the Lives and Characters of a Thousand Per-
sons now Living in London, . . . Digested into Seven Stages with their
Respective Ideas.  8vo.  London.

   "This curious work abounds with interesting literary history, anecdotes of
Bostonian's, etc."—*Blackwood's Magazine,* VI, 26. Lowndes mentions a portrait, but
it is evident, from the lines preceding the title page, "The Author's Speaking Picture," that more was published with the volume. Eighty-four pages are occupied
with the account of his visit to New England, his opening a bookstore in Boston;
intercourse with the Mathers, John Cotton, Eliot, Hubbard, Indian sachems, and
several ladies of Boston, of some of whom he relates very curious particulars.—
Sabin. See Dunton under 1867 below.

WILLIAMS, GRIFFITH (Captain).  An account of the Island of Newfoundland, its Trade and Fishery.  8vo.  London.  (35 pp.)

1706  ASH, JOHN.   Charters of Carolina, and appendix of documents. Numbered from No. 1 to No. 14, forming 67 pp.   4to.   London.

> "The above tract, now rare, is said by Oldmixon (who wrote contemporaneously) to have been drawn up by John Ash, on his mission to the proprietary government of Carolina in London. It is usually found appended to 'the Case of the Protestant Dissenters in Carolina,' London, 1706, and is on the same subject. Sometimes it is found separately, but without title page."—Sabin.

KEITH, GEORGE.   A Journal of Travels from New Hampshire to Caratuck on the Continent of North America.   4to.   London.

> Keith was a missionary of the Society for the Propagation of the Gospel in Foreign Parts.—He had a continuous series of theological disputes with the stubborn inhabitants, which he is more concerned with than his actual travels. He states that he has given an entire Journal of his two years missionary travel and service, on the Continent of North America, "betwixt Piscataway-River in New England and Coretuck in North Carolina; . . ."—From Maggs, No. 625.

LANGFORD, JONAS.   A Brief Account of the Suffering of the Servants of the Lord, called Quakers: from their first Arrival in the Island of Antegoa, under the several Governours; from the years 1660, to 1695.   4to.   London.   (28 pp.)

1707  ARCHDALE, JOHN (Governor).   A New Description of that Fertile and Pleasant Province of Carolina: with a Brief Account of its Discovery, Settling, and the Government Thereof to this Time.   4to. London.   (32 pp.)

> Reprinted, Charleston, S. C., 1822; also included in Carroll's Collection, vol. II.
>
> Archdale introduced the cultivation of rice into Carolina.—Rich.

The Monthly Miscellany, or Memoirs for the Curious.   4to.   London.

> Contains articles on Virginia, Jamaica, American Botany, etc.

1708  COOK, EBEN.   The Sot-weed Factor: or, a Voyage to Maryland. A Satyr.   In which is described The Laws, Government, Courts and Constitution of the Country; and also the Buildings, Feats, Frolics, Entertainments and Drunken Humors of the Inhabitants of that Part of America.   In Burlesque Verse.   4to.   London.

> Reprinted with a glossary, as No. II of Shea's *Reprints of Southern Tracts*, New York, 1865, with an introduction by Brantz Mayer of Baltimore. Mayer says this was reprinted with a poem on "Bacon's Rebellion," by a Mr. Green, at Anapolis, in 1731. Green warns the reader to remember that this description was written twenty-three years before, and did "not agree with the condition of Anapolis at the time of its publication." Sotweed is another name for tobacco.—From Sabin.

OLDMIXON, JOHN. The British Empire in America; Containing the History of the Discovery, Settlement, Progress, and present State, of all the British Colonies on the Continent and Islands of America. Being an Account of the Country, Soil, Climate, Product, and Trades, of them. Viz. Vol. I. Newfoundland, New Scotland, New England, New York, New Jersey, Pensilvania, Maryland, Virginia, Carolina, and Hudson's Bay. II. Barbadoes, St. Lucar, St. Vincent, Domingo, Antigo, Montserrat, Nevis, St. Christopher's, Bermudas, Anguilla, Jamaica, and the Bahama Islands. Maps by Herman Moll. 2 vols. 8vo. London.

> 2nd edit., corrected and amended and brought down to date, 2 vols., 8vo, London, 1741.
> This work is often attributed to Herman Moll, but he probably did no more than prepare the maps. The second edition is considered the best as bringing the account down to a later date and as containing the story of William Penn and the Indian Princess, which was related to the author by Penn himself.

1709  LAWSON, JOHN. The History of Carolina; containing the exact description and natural history of that Country, together with the present State thereof; and a Journal of a thousand Miles Travels through several Nations of the Indians, giving a particular Account of their Customs, Manners, . . . Map and plates. 4to. London.

> Other editions: London, 1714; 1718; again, Dublin, 1738, an edition which was doubtless intended for Brickell's plagiarism (see Brickell under 1737 below). Translated into German, Hamburg, 1712. See below.
> It was first issued as a part of Steven's *Collection of Voyages,* 1708. Title reads in Bradford: A New Voyage to Carolina; etc. "It is the relation of a man of acute habits of observation, some intelligence, and entire veracity." Lawson was a land surveyor in the employment of the government and because of his death at the hands of the Tuscarora Indians was the cause of the exile of this tribe to New York state and its incorporation into the Iroquois Confederacy, by which the name of the latter was changed to the Six Nations.—From Sabin. See also Field, *An Essay towards an Indian Bibliography.*

> 1712  (In German.) Allerneueste Beschreibung der Provintz Carolina in West-Indien. Samt einem Reise-Journal von mehr als Tausend Meilen unter allerhand Indianischen Nationen. . . . Übersetzt durch M. Vischer. Large folding map of North and South Carolina. Hamburg.

The Present State of the Tobacco Plantations in America. Fol. London. (1 leaf.)

1710  The Four Kings of Canada. Being A Succinct Account of the Four Indian Princes lately arriv'd from North America, with A particular Description of their Country, their strange and Remarkable Religion, Feasts, Marriages, Burials, Remedies for their sick, Customs, Manners, Constitution, Habits, Sports, War, Peace, Policy, Hunting, Fishing, Utensils belonging to the Savages, with several other Extraordinary

Things worthy of Observation, as to the natural or curious Productions, Beauty or Fertility of that Part of the World. 12mo. London.

> The purported speech made by the four Indian Kings to Queen Anne was translated into verse by J. S. Here is a specimen of the verse:
>
> "Great Queen!
> A tedious voyage from near Canada,
> On that vast continent, America,
> A voyage our predecessors ne'er did make,
> Nor could prevailed with to undertake."
>
> The Indian chiefs went to England with Colonel Schuyler of New York, and attracted great attention throughout the kingdom. Their visit is commemorated in the *Spectator Papers*, No. 50; and they are mentioned by Swift in one of his letters to Stella.—From Sabin.

Hudson's Bay. A General Collection of Treatys, Declarations of War, Manifestos, and other Public Papers relating to Peace and War . . . To which is added, an Historical Account of the French King's Breach of the most solemn Treatys. 8vo. London.

> This contains valuable matter relative to North America, including "A Deduction of the Right and Title of the Crown of Great Britain to all Straits, Bays, Seas, Rivers, Lakes, etc., etc., and Places whatsoever within Hudson's Bay, and of the Right and Property of the Hudson's Bay Company," etc. . . .—Bookseller's Note.

NAIRN, THOMAS. A Letter from South-Carolina; giving an Account of the Soil, Air, Productions, Trade, Government, Laws, Religion, Inhabitants, Military Strength, . . . of this Province. Written by a Swiss Gentleman to his Friend at Bern. London.

> The recipient of this report is believed to have been Jean Pierre Purry, who was interested in Swiss emigration to South Carolina.—Maggs, No. 625.

SANSOM, OLIVER. Account of many remarkable passages of the Life of, shewing his Trials and sufferings, etc., also relating some of his Travels and Labour in the Work of the Ministry. 8vo. London.

TAYLOR, JOHN. An account of some of the Labours, Exercises, Travels and Perils by Sea and Land, of John Taylor, of York; and also, his Deliverances by way of Journal. 12mo. London.

> Taylor was a celebrated Quaker. The period covered by his journal is from 1656 to 1705. The first half of the volume relates to his travels among the West Indian Islands and in New England and Newfoundland. Once he narrowly escaped capture by French pirates off Cuba.—Maggs, No. 534.

1711   SETTLE, ELKANAH.   A Pindaric Poem on the Propagation of the
       Gospel in Foreign Parts.   A Work of Piety so Zealously Recommended
       and Promoted by Her Most Gracious Majesty.   Fol.   London.

>   This poem relates almost entirely to America, and makes several references
> to the visit to England of the three (or four?) North American Indian Kings of
> the Five Nations. These chiefs were brought to England by Col. Nicholson, Gov-
> ernor of Maryland, in 1710, and on April 19 were received in audience by Queen
> Anne.—Quoted.

       THOMPSON, THOMAS.   Considerations on the Trade to Newfound-
       land.   Fol.   London.   (4 pp.)

1712   A Letter from a West Indian Merchant to a Gentleman at Tunbridg,
       concerning that part of the French Proposals which relates to North
       America and particularly Newfoundland.   With some Thoughts on
       their Offers about our Trade to Spain and the West Indies, and an Ab-
       stract of the Assiento.   8vo.   London.

>   An interesting work, being an analysis of the position between England and
> France in regard to North America, particularly Nova Scotia, Hudson's Bay,
> the West Indies, and the fishing rights of Newfoundland. This letter was reprinted
> 1762 by Joseph Massie to help elucidate his pamphlet "An Historical account
> of the Naval Power of France."—From Bookseller's Note.

       NORRIS, JOHN.   Profitable Advice for Rich and Poor.   In a Dialogue,
       or Discourse between James Freeman, a Carolina Planter, Simon
       Question, a West-Country Farmer, containing A Description, or true
       Relation of South Carolina, an English Plantation, or Colony, in Amer-
       ica: with Propositions for the Advantageous Settlement of People, in
       General, but especially the Laborious Poor, in that Fruitful, Pleasant,
       and Profitable Country, for its Inhabitants.   12mo.   London.

1713   EDMUNDSON, WILLIAM.   A Journal of the Life, Travels, Sufferings,
       and a Labour of Love in the Work of the Ministry, of that worthy
       Elder, and Faithful Servant of Jesus Christ, William Edmundson, who
       Departed this Life, the 31st of the 6th Month, 1712.   4to.   London.

>   Reprinted, Dublin, and London, 1715; 3rd edition, London, 1774. Reprinted
> in the "Friends' Library," 1838, Philadelphia, and Lindfield, 1833.
>   Edmundson was a distinguished preacher of the Society of Friends, and made
> three voyages to America previous to the year 1700. In 1671 "he had movings of
> the spirit" to come to America, and sailed in company with George Fox. He visited
> the West Indies, Virginia, Maryland, New Jersey, New York, and New England.
> —Sabin.

       KENNETT, WHITE.   Bibliotheca Americana Primordia.   An Attempt
       Towards laying the Foundation of an American Library, In several
       Books, Papers, and Writings, Humbly given to the Society for the

Propagation of the Gospel in Foreign Parts, For the Perpetual Use and Benefit of their Members, their Missionaries, Friends, Correspondents, and Others concern'd in the Good Design of Planting and Promoting Christianity within Her Majesties Colonies and Plantations in the West-Indies. By a Member of the said Society. 4to. London.

> "In this short catalogue will be found about twenty original tracts relating to Newfoundland; about fifty concerning Virginia, a hundred or more of New England; and so on in proportion to the colonies."—Preface. "This, as far as it goes, is the best catalogue of books relating to America extant, the title being copied at full length with the greatest exactness, together with name of the printer, and the number of pages in each volume. It unfortunately contains only the books given to the Society by White Kennett, Bishop of Peterborough. It is rich in tracts relating to New England."—Rich. This collection has disappeared—some scattered and neglected remains were found a few years since among the archives of the Society at Lambeth.—From Sabin.

1714   JOUTEL, HENRI.   A Journal of the Last Voyage perform'd by the Monsr. de la Sale, To the Gulph of Mexico, To Find out the Mouth of the Mississipi River; Containing An Account of the Settlements he endeavour'd to Make on the Coast of the Aforesaid Bay, his unfortunate Death, and Travels of his Companions for the Space of Eight Hundred Leagues across . . . Louisiana . . . till they came into Canada. Written in French by Monsieur Joutel, a Commander in that Expedition; And Translated. . . . Folding map of North America with a view of Niagara Falls and a figure of a buffalo (these probably taken from Hennepin). 8vo. London.

> Reprinted, with a new title, London, 1715, and again in London, 1719. Modern editions, Caxton Club, Chicago, 1896; Albany, 1906; and London, 1922. French original, Paris, 1713. See below.
> Parkman says that of the three accounts of this expedition, written by Joutel, Cavelier, and Douay, this is by far the best.—Quoted by Quaritch. For further details of this voyage see Hennepin and La Salle under 1698 above. It is usually stated that Joutel complained about the publication of this book, stating that it was not authorized by him, and further, that it was not his work. Nevertheless, those who have compared this book with his own narrative state that it must have been taken from the narrative which still exists in the Department of Marine, in Paris. —Maggs, No. 610. Joutel . . . was an honest burgher of Rouen. His family had close and honorable relations with the family of La Salle . . . He was not a hero, . . . ; when La Salle was murdered he followed the prudent course and saved his skin. But there was no obvious reason why he should have taken a needless risk when La Salle's blood was already shed, and we can feel a wise and proper gratitude that he ran away, not to fight another day, but to write his admirable account of the hero's voyage. . . ."—The *Spectator,* quoted by Bradford.

> 1719   JOUTEL, HENRI.   Mr. Joutel's Journal of his Voyage to Mexico: His Travels Eight hundred Leagues through Forty Nations of Indians in Louisiana to Canada: His Account of the great River of Missasipi. To which is added, a Map of that Country; with a Description of the great Water-Falls in the River Misouris. Engraved folding map with view of Niagara Falls. 8vo. London.

>> The map is important in the history of American Cartography, as it was designed by Joutel, and is the first map to show the results of the last two journeys of La Salle, and gives a very accurate delineation of the course of the Mississippi as far as its mouth.—Maggs, No. 502.

1906 JOUTEL, HENRI. Joutel's "Journal" of La Salle's Last Voyage into North America, 1684-87. Historical and biographical Notes by Dr. H. R. Stiles. 4to. Albany.

1922 LA SALLE, RENE ROBERT CAVELIER, SIEUR DE. The Journeys of . . . 1668-1687, as related by his followers, Tonty, Hennepin, Joutel, etc. Edited with an Introduction by Prof. Isaac Joslin Cox, Ph.D. 2 vols. 12mo. London.

> The original narratives of Tonty and others have been hitherto quite inaccessible.

1713 JOUTEL, HENRI.. Journal historique du Dernier Voyage que feu M. de la Sale fit dans le Golfe de Mexique, pour trouver l'embouchure & le cours de la Rivière de Missicipi, nommé à présent le Rivière de Saint Louis, qui traverse la Louisiane. Où l'on voit l'Histoire tragique de sa more, & plûsiers choses curieuses du nouveau monde. Par Monsieur Jovtel l'un des campagnons de ce voyage, redigé & mis en ordre par Monsieur De Michel. 12mo. Map. Paris.

**1715** BANISTER. Letter to the Right Hon. the Lords Commissioners of Trade and Plantations; or an Essay on the Principal Branches of Trade in New-England. 8vo. London. (19 pp.)

Observations on the Report of the Committee of Secrecy. 4to. Dublin.

> Interesting economic tract relating to the affairs and Trade of Spain, New-foundland Fishery, Yielding of Cape Breton, etc.—Bookseller's Note.

**1717** MONTGOMERY, SIR ROBERT. A Discourse concerning the design'd Establishment of a New Colony to the South of Carolina, in the most delightful Country of the Universe. Large folding "plan representing the Form of Settling the Districts or County Divisions in the Margravate of Azilia." 8vo. London.

> "Sir Robert Montgomery obtained a grant of all the Land between the rivers Altamaha and Savanah, now a part of Georgia. This territory he called Azilia, and issued these proposals for settling it. Although extensively advertised his scheme failed to meet with public favor and ended in disappointment."—Quoted by Maggs, No. 479. Reprinted in Force's *Tracts,* I. See Barnwell under 1720 below.

**1719** PARKER, GEORGE. For accounts of New England or Virginia (all the English Dominions south of Canada) see his *The West-India Almanack for the Year 1719,* under WEST INDIES.

**1720** BARNWELL, JOHN. An Account of the Foundation, and Establishment of a design, now on Foot, for a Settlement on the Golden Islands, To the South of Port Royal in Carolina. By Authority of a Royal Charter. 4to. London. (8 pp.)

> This relates to the project of Sir Robert Montgomery. See Montgomery under 1719 above, and the following item.

A Description of the Golden Islands, with an Account of the undertaking now on Foot for making a Settlement there: Explaining. 1st. The Nature of that Design in General. 2dly. The Measures already taken. And 3dly. Those intended to be taken hereafter. 8vo. London.

>     This likewise refers to Sir Robert Montgomery's project. The Golden Islands were called by Sir Robert St. Symon, Sapella, Santa Catrina, and Ogeche, afterwards changed to Montgomerie. They are described to "lie within a day's rowing of the English habitations of South Carolina."—Bartlett, quoted by Sabin.

A Full and Impartial Account of the Company of Mississippi otherwise called the French East-India Company, Projected and Settled by Mr. (John) Law (founder of the Mississippi scheme and connected with the South Sea Bubble). Wherein the Nature of that Establishment and the almost incredible Advantages thereby accruing to the French King, and a great Number of his Subjects, are clearly explain'd and made out. . . . To which are added, A Description of the country of the Mississippi, and a Relation of the Discovery of it, in Two Letters from a Gentleman to his Friend. 8vo. London.

>     Printed in French and English on opposite pages. This is one of the tracts that induced so many to embark in the famous "Mississippi Bubble." The Company "had the sole privilege of the trade of the Mississippi. Mr. Law, a Scotch gentleman, whose genius always carried him to the study of trade and money, contrived the plan of this establishment, of which he was appointed the principal director." —Quoted by Sabin. It gives the history of the discovery of the Mississippi by Joliet, La Salle, and Hennepin, and a description of the country from the mouth of the great river.—Robinson, No. 20. See Law under 1721 below.

LOCKE, JOHN. A Collection of several Pieces never before printed or not extant in his works. 8vo. London.

>     This includes "The Fundamental Constitutions of Carolina," containing some interesting information relative to the state of Carolina at that Period.—Bookseller's Note.

NEAL, DANIEL. The History of New-England, Containing an Impartial Account of the Civil and Ecclesiastical Affairs of the Country to the Year of our Lord, 1700. To which is added, the Present State of New-England. With a new and accurate Map of the Country, and an Appendix Containing their Present Charter, their Ecclesiastical Discipline, and their Municipal Laws. Engraved folding map of the New England States, with Insert maps of Nova Scotia and Boston Harbor. 2 vols. 8vo. London.

>     2nd and best edition, 2 vols., 8vo, London, 1747.—Puttick and Simpson. It contains "many additions by the author."
>     "Governor Hutchinson says this is little more than an abridgement of Mather's *Magnalia*. Thomas Prince says: '. . . yet considering the materials this worthy writer was confined to, and that he was never here; it seems to me scarce possible, that any, under his disadvantages, should form a better.' "—Quoted by Maggs, No. 502.

1721  KING, ARTHUR.  The British Merchant: a collection of papers . . . by Sir Theodore Janssen, Bart., Sir Charles Cooke, . . . and others.  3 vols.  8vo.  London.

> This first appeared in weekly numbers and was issued in a collected edition as listed above. It contains an account of the Assiento Contract, the Newfoundland Fishery, Brazil Mines, etc. There is a long note relative to this work in McCulloch's *Literature of Political Economy*, 142-4.—From Sabin.

LAW, JOHN.  The Memoirs, Life, and Character of the Great Mr. Law and his Brother at Paris . . . with an Accurate and Particular Account of the Establishment of the Missippi *(sic)* Company in France, . . . Written by a Scots Gentleman.  8vo.  London.

TROTT, NICHOLAS (Chief Justice of South Carolina).  The Laws of the British Plantations in America relating to the Church and Clergy, Religion and Learning.  Collected in one volume.  London (?).

> Extremely rare. A later edition, London, 1725.

1722  COXE, DANIEL.  A Description of the English Province of Carolina, By the Spaniards call'd Florida, and by the French La Louisiane.  As also of the Great and Famous River Meschacebe or Mississippi, The Five vast Navigable Lakes of Fresh Water, and the Parts Adjacent.  Folding map.  8vo.  London.

> Later editions, with change in title page, London, 1727 and 1741. It was also reprinted in St. Louis, 8vo, 1840, and included in French's *Historical Collections of Louisiana*, vol. II.—Sabin.
> "A compilation from various journals to impress the public with the great importance of the region described, and to make them jealous of its occupation by the French. The whole of this territory was claimed by Dr. Coxe, the father of the author, as proprietor under the Crown. The author explored a great part of it, and lived there fourteen years."– Quoted by Quaritch.

1724  JONES, HUGH.  The Present State of Virginia.  Giving A particular and short Account of Indian, English, and Negroe Inhabitants of that Colony.  Shewing their Religion, Manners, Government, Trade, Way of Living, &c., with a Description of the Country.  From whence is inferred a short View of Maryland and North Carolina.  To which are added, Schemes and Propositions for the better Promotion of Learning, Religion, Inventions, Manufactures, and Trade in Virginia, and other Plantations.  For the information of the Curious, and for the Service of such as are engaged in the Propagation of the Gospel and Advancement of Learning, and for the Use of all Persons concerned in the Virginia Trade and Plantation. . . . By Hvgh Jones, A. M. Chaplain to the Honourable Assembly, and lately Minister of James-Town, &c., in Virginia. 8vo. London.

> The author thinks that the settlement of America by the Europeans is a ful-fillment of the scriptural text, Japhet being the English, Shem the Indians, and Canaan the Negroes.—From Rich.

PURRY, JEAN PIERRE. Mémoire Presenté à Sa Gr. Mylord Duc de Newcastle, . . . Sur l état présent de la Caroline & sur les moyens de l'améliorer: Par Jean Pierre Purry. 4to. London. (11 pp.)

> English version, 2nd edit., London, 1732. See below.

> 1732 (In English.) A Letter from South Carolina giving an Account of the Soil, Air, Product, &c, of that Province. 2d edit. 8vo. London.

1725  BERKELEY, GEORGE (Bishop). Proposals for the better supplying of Churches in our Foreign Plantations and for converting the savage Americans to Christianity. 8vo. London.

1726  CHETWOOD, W. R. For a description of Philadelphia and Pennsylvania see *Voyages and Adventures of Capt. Robert Boyle,* under FICTITIOUS VOYAGES AND TRAVELS.

KER, JOHN. The Memoirs of John Ker of Kersland, in North Britain, Esq., containing his Secret Transactions and Negotiations, with an Account of the Rise and Progress of the Ostend Company in the Austrian Netherlands. Portrait and map of Louisiana and the Mississippi. 2 vols. 8vo. London.

> John Ker, a Government spy in the pay of both the Government and the Jacobites, was sent in 1713 on a private mission to the Emperor of Austria in connection with a scheme for employing buccaneers to harass the trade of France and Spain. Vol. II deals in large part with America, giving some curious details respecting Louisiana and the consequences of the French settling Colonies on the Mississippi, French encroachments, the settling and fortifying of Nova Scotia, etc.—Bookseller's Note. Great importance seems to be attached to the possibility of the French becoming masters of the Gulf of Mexico and ruining trade with Jamaica.—From Maggs, No. 502. Although the printer, the notorious Curll, did not put his name on the imprint, he was prosecuted for publishing the work and put in the pillory. —Robinson, No. 26.

1726-27  Miscellanea Curiosa. Containing a Collection of some of the principal Phaenomena in Nature, accounted for by the greatest Philosophers of this Age . . . to which is added, a Discourse of the Influence of the Sun and Moon on human Bodies, . . . By R. Mead, etc. Frontispiece, folding map and folding plates. 3 vols. 8vo. London.

> Vol. III gives an account of Virginia and the Scots Colony at Darien.—Maggs, No. 502.

1727 HARTWELL, HENRY; BLAIR, JAMES; and CHILTON, EDWARD. The Present State of Virginia, and the College (of William and Mary) by . . . To which is added, The Charter for Erecting the said College, granted by their late Majesties King William and Queen Mary of Ever Glorious and Pious Memory. 8vo. London.

> Hartwell belonged to the Royal Council of Virginia, Blair was President of the College, and Chilton was Attorney General of Virginia. "None of the (tracts relating to Virginia) is of greater significance or fuller of material of permanent historical value than 'The Present State of Virginia and the College,' an invaluable exposition of the state of affairs in the colony as presented by the President of William and Mary College, and two of his close friends in 1727."—W. L. Clements' *Library of Americana*, quoted by Bookseller.

MATHER, EXPERIENCE (Preacher of the Gospel to the Indians). Indian Converts, or Some Account of the Lives and Dying Speeches of a considerable number of the Christianized Indians of Martha's Vineyard in New England . . . to which is added, Some Account of those English Ministers who have successfully presided over the Indian Work in that and adjacent Islands, by Mr. Prince. 8vo. London.

1727-1739 MOLL, HERMAN. Modern History: or the Present State of All Nations, including a Dissertation on the first Peopling of America; the Discovery . . . by Columbus; the Conquest by Cortez; an Account of Florida, and of the British Plantations. . . . Maps and Plates. 6 vols. 4to. Dublin.

> Vols. V and VI relate to America.

1729 The Historical Register, Containing an Impartial Relation of all Transactions, Foreign and Domestick. . . . With a Chronological Diary of all the remarkable Occurrences. . . . Vol. XIV. For the Year 1729. London.

> This volume contains letters from Charleston, South Carolina, giving accounts of the ravages and assaults committed by pirates.—Gosse, *The Pirate's Who's Who*.

1730 HUMPHREYS, DAVID. An Historical Account of the Incorporated Society for the Propagation of the Gospel in Foreign Parts, containing their Foundation, Proceedings and the Success of their Missionaries in the British Colonies to the year 1728. 2 large folding maps. 8vo. London.

> This account deals entirely with America and is compiled from papers transmitted to the Society of Governors of the Colonies. It contains detailed accounts of the travels, hardships and adventures of missionaries sent to New York City, Westchester County, Albany, Staten-Island, Pennsylvania, North and South Carolina, etc. It offers accounts of the Iroquois Indians bordering on New York and New England, "the genius of the Northern Indians, and the conditions of their Countries"; account of the people and churches at Boston, in Rhode Island, Narragansett, Newbury, etc., etc.—From Robinson, No. 41.

1731   HALL, F.   The Importance of the British Plantations in America to this Kingdom; with the State of their Trade, and Methods for Improving it; As Also A Description of the several Colonies there.   8vo.   London.

Observations on the Trade between Ireland and the English and Foreign Colonies in America. . . . 8vo.   London.

1732   Britannia Major: the New Scheme, or Essay for Discharging the Debts, Improving the Lands, and Enlarging the Trade, of the British Dominions in Europe and America.   8vo.   London.

A Comparison between the British Sugar Colonies and New England, with some Observations on the State of the Case of New England.   8vo. London.

NORWOOD, —— (Colonel).   A Voyage to Virginia.   In Churchill VI, 143-170.

> The author, with two others, sailed to Virginia on Sept. 15, 1649, to make their fortunes. After storms and shipwrecks they finally made Jamestown, where they were well received by Royalist friends. Norwood became treasurer to Virginia.

OGLETHORPE, JAMES-EDWARD.   An Account of the Colony in Georgia; and an Essay on Plantations; or, Tracts relating to the Colonies.   London.

> Reissued, London, 1733. See also the following item.
> This is the well known humanitarian in prison reforms and the founder of the colony in Georgia, to which he made his first trip in 1732. On this enterprise of assisting debtors to become colonists, he spent huge sums of his private fortune, which, it is believed, were never repaid. On his second voyage in 1735 he took with him the two Wesleys, John and Charles, who went out with the pious intention of converting the Indians. On his third voyage in 1738 he carried over a regiment of soldiers for the service of the colonies, every man of whom was permitted to take a wife with him. In 1737 he was made general of the forces in South Carolina and Georgia. He finally returned to England in 1743, and was the recipient of successive military honors. He appears frequently in the pages of Boswell with every expression of esteem. He died in 1785.

OGLETHORPE, JAMES-EDWARD.   A New and Accurate Account of the Provinces of South Carolina and Georgia: With many curious and Useful Observations on the Trade, Navigation and Plantations of Great Britain, compared with her most Powerful Maritime Neighbours in Antient and Modern Times.   12mo.   London.

> Reprinted, London, 1733. Reprinted in the *Georgia Hist. Soc., Coll*, I.—Sabin.

1733 MARTYN, BENJAMIN. Reasons for the Establishing the Colony of Georgia, with regard to the Trade of Great Britain, the Increase of our People, and the Employment and Support it will afford to great Numbers of our own Poor . . . with some Account of the Country, and the Design of the Trustees. Map of Carolina, Georgia, Florida, and the Mississippi. 4to. London.

> 2nd edit., London, the same year.
> This is the earliest tract relating to the founding of the colony of Georgia. The writer was Secretary to the Trustees; he represents the promising prospects of Georgia becoming a great Silk-producing Colony; a haven of employment and prosperity for the needy, for poor prisoners for debt; for the persecuted German refugees, a suitable land for the establishment of new branches of trade, previously in the hands of other nations; . . . and above all, a means of weakening the growing dangers of French rivalry.—Robinson, No. 20. See Martyn under 1741 below.

1734 CATESBY, MARK. The Natural History of Carolina, Florida, and the Bahama Islands: containing the Figures of Birds, Beasts, Fishes, Serpents, Insects, and Plants, together with their Descriptions in English and French; to which are added, Observations on the Air, Soil, and Water, with Remarks upon Agriculture, Grain, Pulse, Roots, . . . 2 vols. London.

> Another edition, 2 vols., London, 1743; again with Appendix to the Natural History of Carolina, London, 1748. The same with the Appendix, corrected and augmented by George Edwards, with colored plates, 2 vols., fol., London, 1764 and 1771.
> "Catesby, after having lived in Virginia from 1712-19, principally engaged in the study of its natural history, returned to England, when he was induced by Dr. Sherard and others, to undertake another voyage to America, for the express purpose of collecting and describing its natural productions. This work was the fruit of his voyage. It does great honor to him and to his native country, and is perhaps the most curious and elegant performance of its kind that has appeared anywhere in Europe."—Peter Collinson. Laurens also remarks that it is the best natural history of this country.—The work contains 100 plates to each volume, and 20 plates to the Supplement. At the end of vol. 2 is a 44-page "Account of Carolina and the Bahama Islands."—Maggs, No. 442.

A Description of the famous New Colony of Georgia in South Carolina. Dublin.

VON RECK, BARON P. G. F., and BOLZIUS, JOHN MARTIN. An Extract of the Journals of Mr. Commissary Von Reck, Who Conducted the First Transport of Saltzburgers to Georgia: And of the Reverend Mr. Bolzius, One of their Ministers. Giving an Account of their Voyage to, and happy Settlement in that Province. London.

1735 HALL, —— (Captain). Account of the Settlement of Virginia. London.

> So cited in Nichols, *Literary Anecdotes,* II.

A New Voyage to Georgia. By a Young Gentleman, Giving an Account of his Travels to South Carolina, and part of North Carolina. To which is added, a Curious Account of the Indians, By an Honourable Person. And a Poem to James Oglethorpe, Esq. On his Arrival from Georgia. 8vo. London.

> 2nd edit., 8vo, London, 1737 (with merely a new title-page). Reprinted in *Georgia Hist. Soc. Coll.*, II.—Sabin.

A Short Account of the final Settlement of Virginia, Maryland, New York, New Jersey, and Pennsylvania by the English. Map of Maryland. 4to. London.

> Facsimile reprint, with large folding map, New York, 1922.

1736 The Case of the Planters of Tobacco in Virginia as represented by themselves. 8vo. London.

PRINCE, THOMAS. A Briefe History of the Pequot War. London.

> This is the best account of the Pequot war, which ended in 1637. It was undertaken by Prince from material left by Major John Mason, commander of Connecticut's troops.—Waldman.

PRINCE, THOMAS. A Chronological History of New-England in the Form of Annals: being A summary and exact Account of the most material Transactions and Occurrences relating to This Country, in the Order of Time wherein they happened, from the Discovery by Capt. Gosnold in 1602, to the Arrival of Governor Belcher, 1730. With an Introduction, Containing a brief Epitome of the most remarkable Transactions and Events Abroad, from the Creation: Including . . . the gradual Discoveries of America. . . . Boston (and London). 8vo. Vol. 1.

> "Prince spent seven years in the preparation of this work, which he intended to bring down to 1730. It begins, as was customary with writers of those times, with the creation of the World, and approaches modern times with such fulness of detail that it embraces only a few years of New England history. Had he confined himself to New England, and finished the work, it would have been of incalculable value, as it was carefully compiled from a large number of authentic records and relations. It was continued nearly twenty years later, as a portion of a second volume, consisting of 96 pages, but breaking off in the middle of a sentence, being printed. The whole was published in 1826."—Quoted by Maggs, No. 479. The second volume was called "Annals of New England," and was printed at Boston.

1737 BRICKELL, JOHN (M. D.). The Natural History of North-Carolina. With an Account of the Trade, Manners, and Customs of the Christian and Indian Inhabitants. Illustrated with Copper-Plates whereon are curiously engraved the Map of the Country, several strange Beasts, Birds, Fishes, Snakes, Insects, Trees and Plants. . . . Folding map and plates. 8vo. Dublin.

The material for this work was stolen from Lawson's *New Voyage to Carolina* (see under 1709 above).

1738 KEITH, SIR WILLIAM. The History of the British Plantations in America. With a Chronological Account of the most remarkable Things which happen'd to the first Adventurers in their several Discoveries of that New World. Part I (all published). Containing the History of Virginia with Remarks on the Trade and Commerce of that Colony. Large folding map of America, and folding map of Virginia. 4to. London.

This History of Virginia was to have been one of a series of the English Plantations. This is the only one of the series ever published. It was undertaken at the instance of the Society for the Encouragement of Learning, and printed at its expense. Keith depended almost entirely for his information upon Beverley, and brings his narrative down to 1723. The author was Governor of Virginia from 1717 to 1726.—Maggs, No. 429.

The Merchant's Complaint against Spain, containing their Behaviour towards England in the Peaceable Reign of King James I., a Letter from a Gentleman in the West Indies to a Merchant in London concerning Trade; the Pretensions of Spain to Georgia; the Depredations and Cruelties committed by their Guarda Costa's on the English Merchants and Sailors, etc. 8vo. London.

WHITEFIELD, GEORGE. A Journal of a Voyage from London to Savannah in Georgia. In Two Parts. Part I. from London to Gibraltar. Part II. from Gibraltar to Savannah. With a short Preface shewing the reasons for its publications. 8vo. London.

A spurious edition had been advertised by T. Cox, with an assurance that *his* edition was *genuine*.—Nichols, *Literary Anecdotes*. Of this journal there were a number of successive editions, the sixth of which appeared in 1743. There were also Continuations to the number of at least six. These are sometimes found all combined in one volume. The various Continuations are listed below.

Whitefield was the celebrated preacher long associated with John Wesley in evangelical work. His Calvinistic doctrine, however, led to a separation of the two.

1739 Continuation from his Arrival at Savannah to his return to England. London.

2nd edition, London, 1739.

1739 A Continuation of Mr. Whitefield's Journal from his Arrival in London to his Departure on his Way to Georgia. London.

2nd edit., London, 1744.

1739   A Continuation of Mr. Whitefield's Journal during the Time he was detained in London by the Embargo.  London.

>  4th edit., London, 1739.

1739   A Continuation of Mr. Whitefield's Journal from his Embarking after the Embargo to his Arrival in Savannah.  London.

>  2nd edit., London, 1740.

1741   A Continuation of Mr. Whitefield's Journal after his Arrival at Georgia, to a few days after his second Return thither from Philadelphia.  London.

1744   A Continuation of the Reverend Mr. Whitefield's Journal, from a few Days after his Return to Georgia to his Arrival at Falmouth, on the 11th of March, 1741.  Containing an Account of the Work of God at Georgia, Rhode-Island, New-England, New-York, Pennsylvania and South Carolina.  (2nd edit.)  8vo.  London.

1739   Farther Considerations on the present State of Affairs at Home and Abroad, as affected by the late Convention, in a Letter to the Minister; with an Appendix containing a true State of the South-Sea Company's Affairs in 1718.  8vo.  London.

>  Largely concerned with the rivalry of the English and Spanish merchantmen and their trade in America and the West Indies.—Bookseller's Note.

MARCHMONT, (H. H. Campbell), EARL OF.  A State of the Rise and Progress of our Disputes with Spain, and of the Conduct of our Ministers relating thereunto.  8vo.  London.

>  A very important tract relating to the new British Colony of Georgia, British trade to America, and the free navigation of American Seas.—Robinson, No. 20.

ROBINS, BENJAMIN.  Observations on the Present Convention with Spain.  8vo.  London.

>  A rare and important tract dealing with the boundaries of Georgia, Carolina, and Florida.  Robins was a well-known military engineer.—Robinson, No. 20.

WILSON, HENRY.  Description of America, etc.  London.

>  So cited by Pinkerton XVII.

1740   MITCHELL, ——.  The Present State of Carolina.  London.

>  So cited by Pinkerton XVII.

PERRIN, WILLIAM.  The Present State of the British and French Sugar Colonies, and our own Northern Colonies, considered.  Together with some Remarks on the Decay of our Trade, and the Improvements made of Late Years by the French in theirs.  8vo.  London.

>  This relates to Virginia and other colonies.

For some observations on the colonies on the mainland see *The Present State of the Revenues and Forces by Sea and Land,* under WEST INDIES.

SEWARD, WILLIAM. Journal of a Voyage from Savannah to Philadelphia and from Philadelphia to England, 1740. 8vo. London.

> The author was the travelling companion of the Reverend George Whitefield.

1741 CAMPBELL, JOHN. For a description of California and Florida and New Mexico see his *History of the Spanish America,* under WEST INDIES.

A Description of Georgia, by a Gentleman who has resided there upwards of seven years and was one of the first settlers. London.

> Reprinted in Force's *Tracts* II.

MARTYN, BENJAMIN. An Account showing the Progress of the Colony of Georgia from its first establishment. Fol. London.

> "The rarest of Martyn's Georgian tracts. . . ."—Winsor, quoted by Robinson, No. 58.

MARTYN, BENJAMIN. An Impartial Enquiry into the State and Utility of the Province of Georgia. 8vo. London.

> "A well-written tract, defending the colony from the malignant reports that had been circulated. It includes an account of South Carolina. Its authorship has also been attributed to Lord John Percival." Martyn was the first promoter of the design for erecting a monument to Shakespeare at Westminster Abbey.—Maggs, No. 465.

1742 BLUMEAN, JONATHAN. Remarks on several Acts of Parliament Relating more especially to the Colonies abroad: As also on diverse Acts of Assemblies there: Together with a comparison of the Practice of the Courts of Law in some of the Plantations, with those of Westminister-Hall: And a modest Apology for the former: so far as they materially differ from the latter. Wherein is likewise contained, A discourse concerning the 4½ per Cent. Duty paid in Barbadoes, and the Leeward Islands . . . 8vo. London.

> Attributed to Jonathan Blumean, Attorney General of Barbadoes.—Sabin.

MACKAY, HUGH.   A Letter from Lieut. Hugh Mackay, of General Oglethorpe's Regiment, to John Mackay, Esq. in the Shire of Sutherland in Scotland.  8vo.  London.  (39 pp.)

> This relates to the miscarriage of the siege of St. Augustine. It was printed with a view to correct some misstatements that had appeared in London newspapers. This was followed by a number of replies and countercharges. See following item.

OGLETHORPE, JAMES EDWARD.   An Impartial Account of the late Expedition Against St. Augustine under General Oglethorpe. Occasioned by The Suppression of the Report, made by a Committee of the General Assembly in South-Carolina, transmitted, under the Great Seal of that Province, to their Agent in England, in order to be printed. With an Exact Plan of the Town, Castle and Harbour of St. Augustine, and the adjacent Coast of Florida; shewing the Disposition of our Forces on that Enterprize . . . Plan.  8vo.  London.

A State of the Province of Georgia attested upon Oath in the Court of Savannah, November 10, 1740.  8vo.  London.

> The first 24 pages contain a general account of Georgia, its settlement, rivers, and coast line; details regarding the Indians' natural products, etc. This signed by 25 of the early settlers. . . . Two letters from the Rev. Boltzius of Ebenezer, Georgia, concerning the fruitfulness of the ground in Georgia for various crops, etc.— Maggs, No. 465. This tract gives much information relating to the exploits of General Oglethorpe in Georgia. . . .—From Robinson, No. 26. "The tract was prepared by William Stephens, the secretary of the province, at the suggestion of the trustees. Intended to counteract the agitation of the malcontent Patrick Tailfer and his associates, it was read by Stephens in court on the November 10, 1740, and signed at that time by him and seventeen others under oath. . . ."—Sabin. Tailfer's account, entitled "A True and Historical Narrative of the Colony of Georgia in America," etc., was printed at Charleston, 1741. It is highly praised by Tyler the historian.

STEPHENS, WILLIAM.   A Journal of the Proceedings in Georgia beginning October 20, 1737, to which is added a State of the Province, as attested upon Oath in the City of Savannah, November 10, 1740. 2 vols.  8vo.  London.

> See Thomas Stephens, under 1743 below.

1743  BRAINERD, JOHN.   A Genuine Letter from Mr. John Brainerd, Employed by the Scotch Society for the Propagating the Gospel, A Missionary to the Indians in America, and Minister to a Congregation Of Indians, at Bethel in East Jersey. To his Friend in England. Giving an account of the Success of his Labours, as well as the Difficulties and Discouragements that attend his Mission among the Savages.  8vo. London.  (16 pp.)

> There is an abridgement of a Mr. David Brainerd's Journal among the Indians printed at Edinburgh, 1748. Except for the first name the item corresponds to the one here listed. See also Brainerd under 1765 below.

BURRINGTON, GEORGE.   Seasonable Considerations; or the Expediency of a War with France. . . . To which are added, a Postscript on
the French Army, a Short Comparison between the British and French
Dominions. . . . 8vo.   London.

> This discusses the comparative trading and militant power of the English and
> French possessions in Canada, the West Indies, etc.—Bookseller's Note.

MORALEY, WILLIAM.   The Infortunate: or, the Voyage and Adventures of William Moraley of Moraley, in the County of Northumberland, Gent.   From his Birth, to the Present Time.   Containing whatever is curious and remarkable in the Provinces of Pensilvania and
New Jersey; an Account of the Laws and Customs of the Inhabitants;
the Product, Soil and Climate; also the Author's several Adventures
through divers Parts of America, and his surprising Return to Newcastle.   To which is added, His Case, recommended to the Gentlemen of the Law.   Newcastle

> An extremely rare and interesting record.  Being obliged to seek his fortune,
> Moraley sold himself for a period of five years as a voluntary slave into the Amer-
> ican Plantations.  In 1729 he reached Philadelphia . . . and stopped there three
> weeks, being sold to one Mr. Isaac Pearson clockmaker, of Burlington, N. J., for
> eleven pounds. . . . After his time of indenture had expired, he wandered about
> mending and cleaning clocks, and doing odd jobs.  Before returning to England he
> made a short visit to Maryland.  There are interesting descriptions of rivers, an-
> imals, places, customs, etc.—From Maggs, No. 465.

For the travels of the Jesuits in North America see Lockman under 1743,
COLLECTIONS, and Shea under 1858-1868 below.

STEPHENS, THOMAS.   A Brief Account of the Causes That have re-
tarded the Progress of the Colony of Georgia, in America; Attested
upon Oath, being a proper Contrast to, A State of the Province of
Georgia.   Attested upon Oath, and some Misrepresentations on the
Same Subject.   8vo.   London.

1744   DOBBS, ARTHUR.   An Account of the Countries adjoining to Hudson's
Bay, in the North-west Part of America, showing the Benefit to be
made by settling Colonies and opening Trade in these Parts, whereby
the French will be deprived in a great Measure of their Traffick in
Furs, and the Communication between Canada and Mississippi be cut
off, with Abstract of Captain Middleton's Journal.   To which are added: A Letter from Bartholomew de Fonte; giving an Account of his
Voyage to prevent any ships that should attempt to find a North-west
Passage to the South-Sea; an Abstract of all the Discoveries which
have been published of the Islands and Countries adjoining to the
Great Western Ocean; the Hudson's Bay Company's Charter; the

Standard of Trade in those Parts of America; and the Vocabularies of several Indian Nations adjoining to Hudson's Bay; with a drawn map of North America as described by Joseph La France, a French Canadian Indian. Large folding map. 4to. London.

> Another edition, 4to, London, 1764.
> This work was published soon after the commencement of the controversy between Dobbs and Middleton (see Middleton under 1743, NORTHWEST PASSAGE). "Apart from the controversial portions, the work contains much valuable and interesting information. The author states that it was compiled from accounts published by the French and communications received from persons who had resided there and been employed in the trade, and particularly from Joseph de la France, a French Canadian half-breed, who came over to England in 1742. Dobbs strongly urged that the trade should be thrown open, alleging that the rapacity of the Hudson's Bay Company in dealing with the Indians had thrown the fur trade into the hands of the French in Canada."—Quoted by Maggs, No. 549. There were charges made that the Company had failed to live up to its charter, which enjoined them to carry on exploration.

MOORE, FRANCIS.  A Voyage to Georgia. Begun in the Year 1735. Containing, an Account of the Settling of the Town of Frederica in the Southern Part of the Province; and a Description of the Soil, Birds, Beasts, Trees, Rivers, Islands, . . . also a Description of the Town and Country of Savannah in the Northern Part . . . the manner of dividing and granting the Lands and the Improvements there. . . . 8vo. London.

> For Moore's account of his experiences in the service of the Royal African Company see under 1738, AFRICA. In 1736 he was employed by the Trustees for establishing the Colony of Georgia, as a storekeeper, and accompanied General Oglethorpe until July, 1736. He visited Georgia again in 1738 and remained until 1743. It is his first journey that is here published. He intended to publish his second journey but did not meet with sufficient encouragement to do so.—From Maggs, No. 625.

The Present State of Louisiana, containing the Garrisons, Forts and Forces, Price of all Manner of Provisions and Liquors, . . . also an Account of their drunken lewd Lives, which lead them to Excesses of Debauchery and Villany. To which is added, Letters from the Governor of that Province on the Trade of the French and English with the Natives. Also Proposals to them to put an end to their Traffick with the English. Annual Presents to the Savages; a list of the Country goods, and those proper to be sent to them. . . . Translated from the French originals, taken in the Golden Lyon, Prize, . . . by the Hon. Capt. Aylmer, Commander of his Majesty's Ship the Portmahon, and by him sent to the Admiralty Office. 8vo. London.

> The Louisiana of this book included Alabama, the whole of the Mississippi Valley, the Great West, the Ohio Valley, and the country of the Illinois as far as Canada. The letters referred to are from M. de Yandreil, Governor of New Orleans.—Sabin.

1744-48   The Discoveries, Conquests, Settlements and Present State of the Dutch
Colonies in America; the Nature and Value of their Commerce with
the Spaniards, and the Manner in which their Returns are made to
Europe; to which is added an Account of the Danish Settlements; the
whole collected chiefly from the Dutch Writers.   In Harris II, 365-
376.

The Discoveries and Settlements made by the English in different Parts of
America, from the Reign of Henry VII, to the Close of that of Queen
Elizabeth; interspersed with various Remarks on the Progress of our
Trade, Naval Power, and the Difficulties which the Nation had to
struggle with in their first Attempts. From the Accession of James I
to the Restoration. From the Restoration of King Charles II to the
Revolution.   In Harris II, 189-322.

The History of the Rise, Progress, and Present State of the Colony of
Georgia; with the Attempts made upon it by the Spaniards, and their
total Defeat. Interspersed with Original Papers.   In Harris II, 323-
347.

A Succinct History of the Discoveries, Settlements and Conquests, made
by the French in America; A View of their Policy, Numbers, Commerce, and Strength, in that Part of the World, and some Conjectures
as to the Event of their Designs; extracted chiefly from their own Authors.   In Harris II, 348-364.

1745   The Case of the British Northern Colonies. (No place of printing or date
but probably London, c. 1745.)

> An extremely scarce document, containing a long series of statements concern-
> ing the special merits of the English North American Colonies as compared with
> those of the West Indian, and particularly concerning the Sugar trade. At this
> period there was evidently a movement on foot for granting the West Indies or
> the "sugar plantations" some special trading facilities with respect to their sugar
> industry, and this document was drawn up to point out the superior merits of the
> American colonies on the mainland, and the harm that would be caused to their
> shipping industry.—From Maggs, No. 465.

Considerations on the Trade to Newfoundland.   In Osborne II, 693-794.

> Written in William III's reign.

DICKINSON, JAMES.   A Journal of the Life, Travels, and Labour of
Love in the Work of the Ministry, of that worthy Elder, and Faithful
Servant of Jesus Christ, James Dickinson.   8vo.   London.

> Reprinted with *The Journal of Thomas Wilson*, London, 1847, and in "The
> Friends Library," Philadelphia, 1848.—Sabin.

DURELL, PHILLIP.   A Particular Account of the Taking Cape Breton From the French, by Admiral Warren, and Sir William Pepperell, The 17th of June 1745, With a Description of the Place and Fortification; the Loss it will be to the French Trade, and the Advantage it will be to Great Britain and Ireland: With the Articles of Capitulation of Fort Louisbourg. . . . To which is added, A Letter from the Officer of Marines to his friend in London, giving an Account of the Siege of Louisbourg and a Description of the Town, Harbour, Batteries, Number of Guns, etc. Also the Happy Situation of that Country; and an Account of M. Chambon, Governor of Louisbourg, being laid in Irons for surrendering it: In a Letter from a Gentleman in London, to a Merchant in the West of England.   Fol.   London.   (8 pp.)

1746 BOLLAN, WILLIAM.   The Importance and Advantage of Cape Breton truly stated and impartially considered.   2 folding maps.   London.

> This is said to have been written by Wm. Bollan for Charlevoix's *Nouvelle France.*—Puttick and Simpson. The British Museum Catalogue ascribes the authorship to Lt.-Gen. Sir William Pepperell, "the hero of Louisbourg," but the work is not mentioned as being his by D.N.B. or Allibone.—Sotheran. Bollan was Agent of Massachusetts in Great Britain. See Pepperell this date under MILITARY EXPEDITIONS.

The Great Importance of Cape Breton Demonstrated and Exemplified, by Extracts from the best writers, French and English, who have treated of that Colony. The Whole containing, besides the most accurate Descriptions of the Place, a Series of the Arguments that induced the French Court to settle and fortify it; the Plan laid down for making the Establishment, and the great Progress made in the Execution of that Plan: With the Reasons that induced the People of New England to subdue this formidable and dangerous Rival, and that should determine the British Nation never to part with it again, on any Consideration whatever. In this pamphlet is included all that Father Charlevoix says of this Island in his celebrated History of New France, etc. . . . 2 maps.   8vo.   London.

> Cape Breton, at the eastern extremity of Nova Scotia, was taken from the French in 1745, as a retaliation for French depredations, acting from their base at Louisbourg, but subsequently restored. .It was captured again in 1758, and in 1819 became part of the province of Nova Scotia. It was the fortress of Louisbourg which Gen. Pepperell and the colonial militia captured with so much daring. —Sotheran.

Two Letters, concerning some Farther Advantages and Improvements that may seem Necessary to be made on the Taking and Keeping of Cape Breton.   8vo.   London.   (12 pp.)

1747 The Importance of Cape Breton consider'd; in a Letter to a member of Parliament, From an Inhabitant of New England.   8vo.   London.

COLDEN, CADWALLADER. The History of the Five Nations of Canada, which are dependent on the Province of New York in America, and are the Barrier between the English and French in that part of the World. With Accounts of their Religion, Manners, Customs, Laws, and Forms of Government; their several Battles and Treaties with the European Nations; . . . In which are shewn the great Advantage of their Trade and Alliance to the British Nation, and the Intrigues and Attempts of the French to engage them from us; . . . To which are added, Accounts of several other Nations of Indians in North America, their Numbers, Strength, etc., and the Treaties which have been lately made with them. A work highly entertaining to all and particularly useful to Persons who have any Trade or Concern in that Part of the World. Folding map. 8vo. London.

1st issued New York, 1727; 2nd edit., 8vo, London, 1750; 3rd edit., 2 vols., 8vo, London, 1755. A modern reprint, 2 vols., New York, 1904. See below.
Colden dedicated his work to Gov. Burnet, and his dedication explains itself; in the London edition, Burnet gives place to Gen. Oglethorpe, and the dedication becomes nonsense. The English editor also shows an antipathy to Indian names, suppressing them habitually, striking out important passages and, instead of the speeches which Colden gives at length substitutes meagre abridgments. In fact, the whole work is so cut up and altered, that the reader of the English edition cannot be sure that he is quoting Colden at all. Still this edition is desirable, as it contains many public documents.—Sabin. A most accurate and intelligent piece of work, written with sincerity and candor. Colden points out bluntly how the aborigines had been degraded by their intercourse with the white invaders. It has value as being the first historical work printed in New York.—Waldman. Colden became Surveyor-General for the Province of New York in 1718. A few years later he visited and studied the Mohawks and was adopted into their tribe. . . . The History of the Five Nations contains . . . political considerations, intrigues of the French, etc., which were of great significance to the American Colonies and far-reaching in their results.—Dauber and Pine.

1904 COLDEN, CADWALLADER. The History of the Five Indian Nations of Canada; Which Are Dependent on the Province of New York, and Are A Barrier Between the English and the French in that Part of the World. Portrait, map. 2 vols. 12mo. New York.

NILES, SAMUEL. A Brief and Plain Essay on God's Wonderworking Providence for New-England, In the Reduction of Louisburg, and Fortresses thereto belonging on Cape Breton. With A short hint in the Beginning, on the French Taking & Plundering the People of Canso, which led the several Governments to Unite and Pursue that Expedition. With the names of the Leading Officers in the Army and the several Regiments to which they belonged. 8vo. London. (34 pp.)

STORY, THOMAS. A Journal of the Life of Thomas Story; Containing an Account of his Remarkable Convincement of, and Embracing the Principles as held by the People called Quakers. As also of his

Travels and Labours in the Service of the Gospel. With many other Occurrences and Observations. Fol. Newcastle-upon-Tyne..

> The author was the first Recorder of the City of Philadelphia, 1701, . . . and in 1703 was elected mayor. During his residence in Pennsylvania, Story travelled about preaching, and his journal contained an account of these journies, and of some remarkable interviews with persons of rank.—Robinson, No. 20.

1748  BICKHAM, GEORGE. The British Monarchy, or a New Chorographical Description of all the Dominions including A Short Description of the American Colonies. Engraved vignettes. Fol. London.

> According to Sabin the first edition of this work was printed in 1743, with some copies bearing dates of 1747 and 1748. He also notes a separate issue of the Short Description dated 1749.

JEFFERYS, THOMAS. For matter relating to Labrador see his *The Great Probability of a North-west Passage,* under NORTHWEST PASSAGE. Other items under this section should be consulted, as the great majority of them deal with the northern parts of North America.

LITTLE, OTIS. The State of Trade in the Northern Colonies considered; with an Account of their Produce, and a particular Description of Nova Scotia. London.

> An important tract, pointing out the value of the North American Colonies to Great Britain, and the necessity of encouraging the trade between them and the Mother Country. It also refers to the settling of the new colony of Nova-Scotia.—Robinson, No. 20.

WALCOT, JAMES. The New Pilgrim's Progress; or, The Pious Indian Convert, containing a Faithful Account of Hattain Gelashmin, who was baptis'd by the name of George James, together with a Narrative of his laborious and dangerous Travels among the Savage Indians for their Conversion; his many Sufferings and miraculous Deliverances, and the wonderful Things which he saw in a Vision. 12mo. London.

> Another edition, London, 1763.
> An account of experiences in Carolina, and in particular at Charles-Town. Together with the Journal of George James in his Pilgrimage amongst the Inland Natives of the Countries adjoining to South Carolina, and among the Checkbatoe Indians, etc.—Bookseller's Note.

1749  A Geographical History of Nova Scotia. 8vo. London.

> Translated into French, London, 1755. See below.

> 1755  (In French.) Histoire géographique de la Nouvelle-Ecosse. Traduit de l'anglais (by Lafargue). 12mo. London.

GOADBY, ROBERT. An Apology for the Life of Mr. Bampfylde-Moor Carew . . . For the Full account of this rogue and his adventures in England and America see Carew under 1745, ADVENTURES, DISASTERS, SHIPWRECKS.

Report from the Committee Appointed to Inquire into the State and Condition of the Countries Adjoining to Hudson's Bay, and of the Trade Carried on there . . . (Also an Appendix containing His Majesty's Royal Charter to the Governor and Company of Hudson's Bay.) Fol. London.

> An interesting volume on account of the information given of the northern parts of the province of Quebec. It also contains narratives of travellers hitherto unpublished, notably that of Joseph La France.—Bookseller's Note. At this period certain people in London were endeavoring to form a new Company in rivalry to the old Hudson's Bay Company. Both sent petitions to Parliament, and this forms the Parliamentary Committee's Report on the whole matter. It entirely relates to the Hudson's Bay districts and to the Indians and their trade with the Company. The Appendix is in two parts, . . . the second contains a report by a French Canadian half-breed hunter and trader named Joseph la France. He describes visits into French Canada, to Quebec and Montreal, and the state of the French fortresses there, and their trade with the Indians. He gives many particulars regarding the Indians, and the Geography of the Country. His report occupies 16 pages.—Maggs, No. 479.

1750 America. Translated from the French. 2 vols. 8vo. London.

> A scarce and interesting privately printed book, chiefly relating to the Aborigines.—Quoted.

A Genuine Account of Nova Scotia: Containing a Description of its Situation, Air, Climate, Soil and its Produce; also Rivers, Bays, Harbours, and Fish, with which they abound in very great Plenty. To which is added, His Majesty's Proposals, as an Encouragement to those who are willing to settle there. 8vo. London. (16 pp.)

> Reprinted, Dublin, 1750.

LOCKMAN, JOHN. The Vast Importance of the Herring Fishery, . . . to those Kingdoms as respecting the National Wealth, our Naval Strength, and the Highlanders. 2nd edit. 8vo. London.

> This refers to the settlements in North America.—Sabin.

1751 BARTRAM, JOHN. Observations on the Inhabitants, Climate, Soil, Rivers, Productions, Animals, and other matters worthy of Notice. Made by Mr. John Bartram in his Travels from Pensilvania to Onondago, Oswego, and the Lake Ontario . . . To which is annex'd, a curious Account of the Cataracts at Niagara. By Mr. Peter Kalm . . . Plan of Oswego. 8vo. London.

> "A very reliable work by two of the most eminent . . . naturalists of their day . . . Kalm's account is the first scientific description, in English, of Niagara Falls." —Church Catalogue, quoted by Quaritch. The Swedish original of Kalm's travels appeared at Stockholm, 1753-1761. See Kalm under 1770-1771 below, and also Fagin, *William Bartram, Interpreter of the American Landscape,* under Fagin, GENERAL REFERENCE.

CHALKLEY, THOMAS.  A Journal or Historical Account of the Life, Travels and Christian Experiences of that ancient, faithful servant of Jesus Christ, Thomas Chalkley, who departed this Life in the Island of Tortola, the fourth Day of the ninth Month, 1741.  2nd edit.  8vo. London.

> Reprinted in Collected Works, London, 1766. Fifth edition, Philadelphia and London, 1790.
>
> Thomas Chalkley, a Quaker preacher, came to America in the year 1700, and settled at Philadelphia. He travelled and preached in all the British Colonies from New England to North Carolina. He also visited the West Indies, and the Bermudas. "Some of the New England Priests," he says, "were so bitter against Friends, that, instead of being humbled, under the mighty hand of God upon them in suffering the Indians to destroy them, they expressed their enmity against the poor Quakers. In a sermon preached by one of their priests, he divided it into these heads, viz.: That the Judgments of God were upon them, in letting the savage Indians upon them. Secondly, In that he withheld the fruits of the earth from them. Thirdly, That the Quakers prevailed and were suffered to increase so much among them the which was worse than the Indians destroying of them."—From Sabin.

The Importance of Settling and Fortifying Nova Scotia; with a particular Account of the Climate, Soil, and Native Inhabitants of the Country. By a Gentleman lately arrived from that Colony.  8vo.  London.

> "We find very little, if anything, worth notice in this piece."—*Monthly Review,* V, 397.—Quoted.

UZTARIZ, DON GERONYMO DE.  The Theory and Practice of Commerce and Maritime Affairs. Written originally in Spanish . . . Translated by John Kippax.  2 vols.  8vo.  London.

> This is a treatise upon the trade and manufactures of the Spanish Monarchy, and naturally deals extensively with America.—Robinson, No. 26.

1752 FENNINGS, S.  Description of the European Colonies in America.  London.

> So cited by Pinkerton XVII.

ROBSON, JOSEPH.  An Account of Six Years Residence in Hudson's Bay, From 1733 to 1736, and 1744 to 1747. . . . Containing a Variety of Facts, Observations and Discoveries, tending to shew, I. The vast Importance of the Countries about Hudson's Bay to Great Britain, on account of the Extensive Improvements that may be made there in many beneficial Articles of Commerce, particularly in the Furs and the Whale and Seal Fisheries. And II. The interested Views of the Hudson's Bay Company; and the absolute Necessity of laying open the Trade, and making it the Object of National Encouragement, as the only Method of keeping it out of the Hands of the French. To which is added an Appendix; containing, I. A Short History of the Discovery of Hudson's Bay; and of the Proceedings of the English there since the Grant of the Hudson's Bay Charter. II. An Estimate of the Expense of building the Stone Fort, called Prince of Wales'-fort, at the entrance of Churchill-River. III. Soundings of Nelson-River. IV. A Survey of the Course of Nelson-River. V. A Survey of the Seal and Gillam's Island. And, VI. A Journal of the Winds and Tides at Churchill-river, for Part of the Years 1746 and 1747. 3 folding maps and plans. 8vo. London.

> This is one of the earliest, and certainly the fullest, work that had hitherto been published on the Hudson Bay territory. The author (who was surveyor and supervisor of the buildings to the Company) mentions in his preface that he had been "six years in the countries adjoining to Hudson's Bay." The territory was not properly opened up until after 1763, when Canada passed from French into British possession, and British adventurers from the great lakes began to penetrate the country.—Sotheran. "A very severe arraignment of the narrow measures and selfishness of the Hudson's Bay Company."—Winslow, quoted by Quaritch.

1753 Candid Narrative of the Rise and Progress of the Herrnhuters. 8vo. London.

> A Supplement to the Candid Narrative appeared, London, 1775. See also Frey just below.

FOTHERGILL, JOHN. An Account of the Life and Travels in the Work of the Ministry, of John Fothergill. To which are added, Divers Epistles to Friends in Great Britain and America, on various Occasions. 8vo. London.

> 2nd edit., London, 1773; reprinted also in Philadelphia, 1754.

FREY, ANDREW. A True and Authentic Account of Andrew Frey, containing the Occasion of his coming among the Herrnhuters or Moravians, his Observations on their Conferences, Casting Lots, Marriages, Festivals, Merriments, . . . faithfully translated from the German. 8vo. London.

> The Herrnhuters were a religious sect, resembling the Moravians; some of them emigrated to America.

HOLME, BENJAMIN.   A Collection of the Epistles and Works of Benjamin Holme. To which is prefix'd an Account of his Life and Travels through several parts of Europe and America, written by himself. 8vo.   London.

> "Chapters IV and V give an account of his travels in America from 1715 to 1720. Holme visited, 'scattering the truth and confounding the priests,' various parts of New England, particularly Rhode Island and Connecticut, thence to Long Island, New York, New Jersey, Pennsylvania, Virginia and Carolina."—Quoted by Hiersemann.

MACSPARRAN, JAMES.   America Dissected, being a Full and True Account of all the American Colonies: shewing the Intemperance of the Climates; excessive Heat and Cold, and sudden violent Changes of Weather; terrible and mischievous Thunder and Lightning; bad and unwholesome Air, destructive to Human Bodies; Badness of Money; Danger from Enemies; but, above all, the Danger to the Souls of the Poor People that remove thither, from multifarious wicked and pestilent Heresies that prevail in those Parts. In Several Letters, From a Rev. Divine of the Church of England, Missionary to America and Doctor of Divinity. Published as a Caution to Unsteady People who may be tempted to leave their Native Country.   8vo.   Dublin.

> Reprinted in Updike's *History of the Narragansett Church*, with notes.
> Very rare. These letters are signed James Macsparran, and addressed to the Hon. Col. Henry Cary, Esq. The author resided in the Narragansett country as missionary for upwards of thirty years.—Sabin.

PALAIRET, JOHN.   Concise Description of the English and French Possessions in North-America, for the better explaining of the map published under that title.   8vo.   London.

STITH, WILLIAM.   The History of the First Discovery and Settlement of Virginia. Together with an Appendix to the First Part of the History of Virginia. Containing a Collection of such ancient Charters or Letters Patent, as relate to that Period of Time, and are still extant in our publick Offices in the Capitol, or in any other authentick Papers and Records.   London.

> There were two editions printed at Williamsburg in 1747, one of which was printed on poorer paper than the other and always has sheets X of the text and Cc, Dd of the Appendix discoloured.—Quaritch. "This work only brings the History of Virginia down to 1624. The early charters contained in the Appendix give this work its chief value at the present day. . . . Notwithstanding his diffuseness and lack of literary style, his book has become a high authority to later writers."—Quoted by Maggs, No. 465.

1754 ANDERSON, ——. The History of the Life and Adventures of Mr. Anderson, containing his strange varieties of fortune in Europe and America. Compiled from his own papers. 12mo. London.

> Reprinted, Dublin, 1754; Berwick, 1782.
> The author was kidnapped in London, taken to America, and sold to a planter in Maryland for £10, and afterwards joined the Virginia Rangers against the French Indians.—From Sabin.

ANSTED, D. I. Scenery, Science, and Art, being extracts from the notebook of a Geologist and Mining Engineer, by Prof. D. I. Ansted. 8vo. London.

> Pages 241 to 311 relate to America.—Sabin.

Essays and Observations Physical and Literary, published by a Society in Edinburgh. Plates. 2 vols. 8vo. Edinburgh.

> This contains papers on the "Natural History of America," etc., by Dr. J. Lining and Dr. Alex. Gorden, of Charleston, etc.

JEFFERYS, THOMAS. The Conduct of the French with regard to Nova Scotia, Virginia, and other parts of the Continent of North America. From its First Settlement to the Present Time. . . . In a Letter to a Member of Parliament. 8vo. London.

> Translated into French, London, 1755. See below.

> 1755 (In French.) Conduite des Francais par rapport à la Nouvelle-Ecosse. Traduit de l'anglais avec des notes, par Georges Marie Butel-Dumont. 12mo. London.

Some Account of the North-American Indians, their Genius, Characters, Customs, and Dispositions, towards the French and English Nations. To which are added, Indian Miscellanies, viz. 1. The Speech of a Creek Indian. . . . 2. A Letter from Yariza, an Indian Maid. . . . 3. Indian Songs of Peace. 4. An American Fable, Collected by a learned and ingenious Gentleman in the Province of Pensylvania. . . . 8vo. London.

1755 BRADDOCK, EDWARD (General). The Expedition of Major General Braddock to Virginia; with The Two Regiments of Hackett and Dunbar. Being Extracts of Letters from an Officer in one of those Regiments to his Friend in London, describing the March and Engagement in the Woods. Together With many little Incidents, giving A lively Idea of the Nature of the Country, Climate, and Manner in which the Officers and Soldiers lived; also the Difficulties they went through in the Wilderness. 8vo. London.

A rare tract and a vile misrepresentation of everything that the worthless, unknown scribbler undertakes to describe.—Sabin.

BUTEL-DUMONT, GEORGES MARIE. Histoire et Commerce des Colonies Angloises dans l'Amérique Septentrionale. Où l'on trouve l'état actuel de leur population, et des détails curieux sur la constitution de leur gouvernement, principalement sur celue de la Nouvelle Angleterre, de la Pensilvanie, de la Caroline, et de la Georgie. 2 vols. Plates. 12mo. Londres, et se vend à Paris.

CLARKE, WILLIAM. Observations on the late and present Conduct of the French, with regard to their Encroachments on the British Colonies in North-America. Boston and London.

CROSS. An Answer To an invidious Pamphlet, intituled A Brief State of the Province of Pennsylvania, Wherein are exposed The many false Assertions of the Author or Authors, of the said Pamphlet, with a view to render the Quakers of Pennsylvania and their Government obnoxious to the British Parliament and Ministry; and the Several Transactions, most grossly misrepresented therein, set in their true light. 8vo. London.

"This answer is said to be the production of one Cross, formerly an attorney's clerk. He was convicted of forgery, sentenced to be hanged, but after some time obtained the favour of transportation; and did us the honor to take up his residence in the Province."—*Brief View*, p. 13, quoted by Bradford.

A Description of the English and French Territories in North America: being, An Explanation of a New Map of the Same. Shewing all the Encroachments of the French, with their Forts, and Usurpations on the English Settlements; and the Fortifications of the Latter. And compared with Dr. Mitchell's F. R. S. and every Omission carefully supplied from it. Plan. 8vo. Dublin.

DOUGLASS, WILLIAM.—A Summary, Historical and Political, of the First Planting, Progressive Improvements, and the Present State of the British Settlements in North America. Containing some General Account of the Colonies, the Hudson's Bay Company's Fur and Skin Trade, the several Grants of Sagadahock, Main, Massachusetts and New Plymouth, commonly called New England. Large folding map. 2 vols. 8vo. London.

An exact reprint of the Boston edition of 1749. 2nd edit., with a different map, and few alterations and corrections, London, 1760. (The Boston edition did not contain the map.)

EVANS, LEWIS.  Geographical, Historical, Philosophical and Mechanical Essays. The First, containing an Analysis of a General Map of the Middle British Colonies in America; And of the Country of the Confederate Indians: A Description of the Face of the Country; the Boundaries of the Confederates; and the Maritime and Inland Navigations of the several Rivers and Lakes contained therein. Large folding colored map engraved by James Turner in Philadelphia. Philadelphia, sold by Dodsley, London.

> The map was far in advance of anything that had hitherto been attempted.—Robinson, No. 20.

French Policy Defeated.  Being, an Account of all the Hostile Proceedings of the French, Against the Inhabitants of the British Colonies in North America, For the last Seven Years. Also, The Vigorous Measures pursued both in England and America, to vindicate the Rights of British Subjects, and the Honour of the Crown, from the Insults and Invasions of their perfidious Enemies. With an Authentic Account of the Naval Engagements off Newfoundland, and the Taking of the Forts in the Bay of Fundy. Embellished with Two curious Maps, Describing all the Coasts, Bays, Lakes, Rivers, Soundings, principal Towns and Forts, confining on the British Plantations in America. 2 maps. 8vo. London.

> Reprinted, with a new title page, London, 1760.

GREEN, JOHN.  Explanation for the New Map of Nova Scotia and Cape Breton, with the Adjacent Parts of New England and Canada. 4to. London.  (22 pp.)

HASKE, JOHN.  The Present State of North America. I. The Discoveries, Rights and Possessions of Great Britain. II. The Discoveries, Rights and Possessions of France. III. The Encroachments and Depredations of the French upon His Majesty's Territories in North America in Times when Peace subsisted in Europe between the Two Crowns, . . .  4to.  London.

> 2nd edit., with emendations, London, 1755. Also printed at Boston, 8vo, 1755. Principally taken from Dumont's *Histoire et Commerce des Colonies Angloises* (see Butel-Dumont this date above).—Sabin. It is an interesting work, proposing measures for the conquest of Canada from the French, and the destruction of the French line of forts lying on the Western frontiers of the colonies.—Bookseller's Note.

The Memorials of the English and French Commissaries concerning the Limits of Nova Scotia or Acadia.—The Memorials . . . concerning St. Lucia.  Large folding map.  2 vols.  4to.  London.

In French, 2 vols., 4to, London. See below.

"Some of the memorials which have been respectively delivered by the English and French Commissaries, concerning the limits of Acadia or Nova Scotia, and the Right to St. Lucia, having been printed in Paris, it has been thought necessary to print at London this edition of all the memorials upon these points, in the form in which they were delivered." . . . "This work, containing the various papers drawn up by the English and French Commissaries, respecting the history and geography of Eastern Canada, Maine, New Brunswick, Nova Scotia, the Gulf of St. Lawrence, etc., is of the utmost importance to the historian of these districts. It was drawn up by Charles Townsend, and published by order of the Lords of Trade as a full exhibit to the English title of that part of America."—From Sabin.

1755   (In French.)   Mémoires des commissaires de roi de France et d'Angleterre sur les anciennes limites de l'Acadie, . . . 4 vols. 4to. London.

SMITH, WILLIAM (Dr).   A Brief State of the Province of Pennsylvania, in which The Conduct of their Assemblies for several Years past is impartially examined, and the true Cause of the continual Encroachments of the French displayed, more especially the secret Design of their late unwarrantable Invasion and Settlement upon the River Ohio. To which is annexed, An easy Plan for restoring Quiet in the public Measures of that Province, and defeating the ambitious Views of the French in time to come. In a Letter from a Gentleman who has resided many Years in Pennsylvania to his Friend in London. 8vo. 2nd edit. London.

3rd edit., London, 1756. See Smith under 1756 below.

The work related to the French invasion in Ohio.—Rich. It has been conjectured that Benjamin Franklin assisted in the authorship.

The State of the British and French Colonies in North America, with respect to Number of People, Forces, Forts, Indians, Trade, and other Advantages. In two letters to a friend, In which are considered: I., The defenceless Condition of our Plantations . . . II., Pernicious Tendency of the French Encroachments . . . III., What it was occasioned their present Invasions . . . With a Proper Expedient proposed for preventing future Disputes. 8vo. London.

1756   An Account of the Present State of Nova-Scotia; In Two Letters to a Noble Lord: One from a Gentleman in the Navy lately arrived thence. The other from a Gentleman who long resided there. Made publick by his Lordship's Desire. 8vo. London. (31 pp.)

The letters are signed respectively "J. B." and "W. M."—Sabin.

All the Memorials of the Courts of Great Britain and France since the peace of Aix la Chapelle, relative to the Limits of the territories of both Crowns in North America, and the Right to the Neutral Islands in the West Indies. To which are annexed Two maps, one delineating the Right of Great Britain and the other the Claim of France. The French Memorials are Translated and the whole is printed in English. 4to. London. (See *Memorials* under 1755 above.)

BOWNAS, SAMUEL. An Account of the Life, Travels and Christian Experiences in the work of the Ministry of Samuel Bownas. Edited by J. Besse. 8vo. London.

> 2nd edit., London, 1761; again, London, 1795. Reprinted in the *Friends Library*, vol. XII, London, 1836, and vol. III, Philadelphia, 1839.
> Bownas landed in Maryland, 1702. Soon after he arrived he held a dispute with George Keith; also with William Bradford, and suffered imprisonment for his belief. His account of the Labadies, a community resembling the Shakers, is very amusing. A statement on page 58 of the first edition conveys the idea that his answer to George Keith was printed at Philadelphia.—Sabin. See also Richardson under 1758 below.

The French Encroachments Exposed; or, Britain's original Right to all that part of the American Continent claimed by France fully asserted; wherein it appears, that the Honour and Interest of Great Britain are equally concerned, from the Conduct of the French, for more than a Century past, to Vindicate her Rights ... In Two Letters from a Merchant retired from Business, to his Friend in London. ... 8vo. London. (44 pp.)

An Humble Apology for the Quakers, Addressed to Great and Small. Occasioned by certain gross Abuses and Imperfect Vindications of that People, relative to the late Pamphlet, intituled A Brief View of the Conduct of Pennsylvania For the Year 1755. So far as to show the real Spirit and Design, of that Angry Writer. And also A much Fairer Method pointed out, than that contained in a Brief State of Pennsylvania, to prevent the Incroachments of the French, and restore Quiet to the Province. 12mo. London. (38 pp.)

> The "angry writer" is doubtless William Smith. See Smith this date below.

JOHNSON, SIR WILLIAM. An Account of the Conferences held, and Treaties made, Between Major-general Sir William Johnson, Bart. and the chief Sachems and warriors of the Mohawks, Oneidas, Onondagas, Cayugas, Senekas, Tuskaroras, ... Indian Nations in North America, At their Meetings, on different Occasions at Fort Johnson in the County of Albany, in the Colony of New York, in the years 1755 and 56. With a Letter from the Rev. Mr. Hawley to Sir William Johnson, written at the Desire of the Delaware Indians. And a Preface, Giving a short Account of the Six Nations, some Anecdotes of the Life of Sir William, and Notes illustrating the Whole; Also an Appendix contain-

ing an Account of conferences between several Quakers in Philadelphia, and some of the Heads of the Six Nations, in April 1756. 8vo.
London.

A Letter from New Jersey in America giving some Account and Description of that Province, By a Gentleman late of Christs College, Cambridge. 8vo. London. (26 pp.)

> Belongs to the "catch-penny class."—*Monthly Review,* XV, 427. It is as rare
> as it is worthless; but would sell for a good price. The author's initials are J. T.
> —Sabin.

A New and Complete History of the British Empire in America. Maps
and plates. 3 vols. 8vo. London.

> This contains an account of Hudson's Bay, Newfoundland, Nova Scotia, New
> England, New York, New Jersey, Pennsylvania, Maryland, Virginia and North
> Carolina, ending abruptly at page 272 of volume III.—Quoted.

POSTLETHWAYT, MALACHY. A Short State of the Progress of the
French Trade and Navigation, wherein is shewn the great Foundation
that France has laid by dint of Commerce . . . to a pitch equal if not
superior to that of Great-Britain, . . . 8vo. London.

> Treats for the main part of the French Colonies and Plantations in America
> and the trade and commerce in America and Canada.—Bookseller's Note.

Remarks on the French Memorials concerning the Limits of Acadia;
Printed at the Royal Printing-house at Paris, and distributed by the
French Ministers at all the Foreign Courts of Europe. With Two
Maps, Exhibiting the Limits: One according to the System of the
French, as inserted in the said Memorials; the other conformable to
the English Rights, as supported by the Authority of Treaties, contin-
ual Grants of the French Kings, and express Passages of the best
French Authors. To which is added, An Answer to the Summary Dis-
cussion, . . . 2 maps. List of books. 8vo. London.

> "This volume surpasses all others for valuable historical, geographical and
> bibliographical information respecting Nova Scotia or Acadia and part of Canada.
> The two maps on the same scale show clearly what is claimed by both parties,
> French and English. . . . The text well illustrates and explains these two maps."—
> H. Stevens, quoted by Sabin.

SMITH, WILLIAM (Dr.) A Brief View of the Conduct of Pennsylvania, For the Year 1755: So far as it affected the General Service of
the British Colonies, particularly the Expedition under the late General
Braddock, With an Account of the shocking Inhumanities committed
by Incursions of the Indians upon the Province in October and No-

vember; . . . and the Passing of a Law for the Defence of the Country. Interspers'd with several interesting Anecdotes and original Papers relating to the Politics and Principles of the People called Quakers; Being a Sequel to a late well-known Pamphlet, entitled, A Brief State of Pennsylvania. In a Second Letter to a Friend in London. 8vo. London.

> A French edition was published in 8vo, Paris, 1756.
> This is one of the Paxson Boy pamphlets. Written anonymously by Dr. Wm. Smith, it is a continuation of his *Brief State*. See *Monthly Review,* xii, 192; xiv, 208.

1756-57 SHEBBEARE, JOHN. (Letters to the People of England.) A First Letter to the People of England, on the Present Situation and Conduct of National Affairs. 4th edit., 1756. A Second Letter . . . on Foreign Subsidies, Subsidiary Armies, and their Consequences to the Nation. 4th edit., 1756. A Third Letter . . . On Liberty, Taxes, and the Application of Public Money, 4th edit., 1756. A Fourth Letter . . . on the Conduct of the M—rs in Alliances, Fleets and Armies, since the first differences on the Ohio, 1st edit., 1756. A Fifth Letter . . . in the Subversion of the Constitution, 2nd edit., 1757. A Sixth Letter . . . on the Progress of National Ruin, 2nd edit., 1757. In 1 vol. 8vo. London.

> This makes up a complete set of these important letters relating to American affairs. Upon the publication of the sixth letter, Shebbeare was fined, imprisoned, and pilloried for political libel. In 1792 he received a pension from the Government, and in return defended the American policy of George III. against the attacks of Burke and Price, thereby bringing his name into conjunction with Dr. Johnson as a Government hireling.—Robinson, No. 31.

1757 DUPLESSIS, ——. Duplessis's Memoirs, or a Variety of Adventures in England and America, interspersed with Characters and Reflections, and a Description of some Strolling Players, with whom he travelled. 2 vols. London.

> This relates to South Carolina, Georgia, etc.—Quoted.

A Letter from a Merchant of the City of London to the R-t H-ble W-P-, Esq., upon the Affairs and Commerce of North America and the West Indies; Our African Trade; The Destination of our Squadrons and Convoys; New Taxes . . . 8vo. London.

> An important pamphlet. It emphasizes the great importance of the American colonies to Great Britain and the measure that should be taken for the protection of North American and West Indian Trade, the Boundaries of the Colonies, the Newfoundland Fishery, the Indian Nations, etc.—Robinson, No. 41.

LIVINGSTON, ——. A Review of the Military Operations in North America; from the Commencement of the French Hostilities on the Frontiers of Virginia in 1753, to the Surrender of Oswego, on the 14th of August, 1756. Interspersed with various Observations, Characters, and Anecdotes; necessary to give Light into the Conduct of American Transactions in general; and more especially into the political Management of Affairs in New York. In a Letter to a Nobleman. 4to. London.

> Reprinted, Dublin, 1757, with additions. See below.
> "The author's chief design is to vindicate Governor Sherley, and to asperse the characters of those who opposed his measures."—*Monthly Review,* XVI, 524.— Quoted by Sabin.

> 1757 LIVINGSTON, ——. A Review of the Military Operations . . . To which are added, Colonel Washington's Journal of his Expedition to the Ohio, in 1754, and several Letters and other Papers of Consequence, found in the Cabinet of Major-General Braddock, after his defeat near Fort DuQuesne; and since published by the French Court. None of these Papers are contained in the English edition. 8vo. Dublin.
>
>> The latter part of this work is a translation of the "Mémoire contenant le Précis des Faits," printed by the French Court, charging Washington with the assassination of Jumonville. The authorship has been attributed to William Smith, of New York, who perhaps aided the author as did also J. M. Scott. The facts were supplied by W. Alexander, afterwards the soi-disant Earl of Stirling, brother-in-law of Livingston. . . . It was reprinted in the *Mass. Hist. Soc. Coll.,* vol. VII.—Sabin.

MITCHELL, JOHN. The Contest in America between Great Britain and France, with its Consequences and Importance; giving. . . the Situation of all the British and French Colonies in all parts of America . . . By an impartial Hand. 8vo. London.

> "The Monthly Review allows '. . . this work abounds with truths . . . and with observations and proposals that indicate the author's knowledge of the subject . . . and his ardent zeal for the interests of Britain.' "—Rich, quoted by Quaritch. This work has been attributed to Dr. Oliver Goldsmith, but it is practically certain the work of the distinguished botanist Dr. John Mitchell, who emigrated to America about 1700, and lived in Virginia for some time. His work shows considerable knowledge of Geography of America as well as the affairs of the French on the Lakes, along the Ohio, on the Western slopes of the Alleghanies, and in Western Virginia. . . .—Maggs, No. 465.

RICHARDSON, JOHN. An Account of the Life of that Ancient Servant of Jesus Christ, John Richardson, giving a Relation of many of his Trials and Exercises in his Youth, and his Services in the Work of the Ministry, in England, Ireland, America, etc. 8vo. London.

> 2nd edit., London, 1758; 3rd edit., London, 1774.
> During his tour of America he stayed with William Penn.

SMITH, WILLIAM. The History of the Province of New-York From the First Discovery to the year M. D. CC. XXXII. To which is annexed, A Description of the Country, with a short Account of the Inhabitants, their Trade, Religious and Political State, and the Constitution of the Courts of Justice in that Colony . . . Folding frontispiece view of Oswego. 4to. London.

Reprinted, London, 1776. Translated into French, London, 1767. See below.
The first history of New York. The author was-graduated from Yale College in 1745, became a distinguished lawyer, and later chief Justice of the Province. Being a loyalist during the Revolutionary War, after the contest was over, he moved to Canada . . . The work as published only brought the history of the colony down to 1736.—Maggs, No. 502.

1767 (In French.) Histoire de la Nouvelle York, Depuis La Découverte de cette Province Jusqu'à notre siècle. Dans laquelle on rapporte les démêlés qu'elle a eus avec les Canadiens & les Indiens; les Guerres qu'elle a Soutenues contre ces Peuples; les Traités & les Alliances qu'elle a faits avec eux, &c. On y a Joint Une Description Géographique du Pays, & une Histoire Abrégée de ses Habitans, de leur Religion, de leur Gouvernement Civil & Ecclésiastique, &c. . . . Traduite de l'Anglois par M. E. 16mo. Londres.

"M. E." stands for M. Eidous.

1758 An Account of the Customs and Manners of the Mickmakis and Maricheets Savage Nations, now dependent on the government of Cape-Breton, from an Original French Manuscript letter, never published, written by a French Abbot, who resided many years, in quality of Missionary, among them. To which are annexed, Several Pieces, relative to the Savages, to Novia-Scotia, and to North America in general. 8vo. London.

This was a translation from the French.—Lowndes.

BURKE, EDMUND (or WILLIAM). An Account of the European Settlements in America, in Six Parts, I. A Short History of the Discovery of that Part of the World; II. The Manners and Customs of the Original Inhabitants; III. Of the Spanish Settlements; IV. Of the Portuguese; V. Of the French, Dutch and Danish; VI. Of the English . . . ; each part containing a Description of the Settlements in it, the interests of the Powers of Europe with respect to those Settlements and their political and commercial views with regard to each other. 2 vols. 8vo. London.

2nd edit., 2 vols., 1758; 3rd edit., 2 vols., London, 1760; an edition, 2 vols. 12mo, Dublin; 4th, London, 1765; 5th, London, 1770; 6th, London, 1777. Translated into German, Leipzig, 1758; into French, Paris, 1767, and later. These later editions have "improvements" and maps. See below.
"A celebrated and somewhat singular work. I would recommend its perusal before the histories of Robertson, Raynal, and Marshall."—Prof. Smyth, quoted by Sotheran. As regards the authorship, Burke told Boswell, "I did not write it. I will not deny that a friend did and I revised it." "Malone tells me," adds Boswell, "that it was written by William Burke, the cousin of Edmund, but it was everywhere evident that Burke himself has contributed a great deal to it."—D. N. B., quoted by Sotheran. It was immensely popular and was translated into va-

rious foreign languages. According to Maggs, No. 442, it is now decided to be mainly the work of Edmund Burke himself, assisted by his brother Richard, and his friend Wm. Bourke. In some listings the author's name is given as William Burke. At any rate, while it was included in at least one American edition of his works, it is not to be found in any English edition.

1767   (In French.)   Histoire des colonies européennes dans l'Amérique en six parties. Traduite de l'anglais de M. W. Burk, par M. E. 3 vols. 12mo. Paris.

>   According to Guerard, W. Burk was a pseudonym of Soame Jenyns, and the translator was Eidous.—Barringer.

THOMPSON, THOMAS.   An Account of Two Missionary Voyages by the Appointment of the Society for the Propagation of the Gospel in Foreign Parts, the one to New Jersey in North America, the other from America to the Coast of Guiney. 8vo. London.

WILLIAMSON, PETER.   French and Indian Cruelty Exemplified in the Life of Peter Williamson, during his Captivity among the Indians. 8vo. London (?).

>   2nd edit., 12mo, York, 1758; 8vo, London, 1759; 8vo, Dublin, 1766; 12mo, Edinburgh, 1792. The London edition of 1759 is cited by Robinson, No. 32, as the fourth edition and the first London edition. It contains "considerable improvements." See below.
>   Williamson, at eight years of age, was kidnapped in Aberdeen, shipped to America, and sold as a slave in Pennsylvania. He afterwards married and settled as a planter, but during an Indian raid his home was burnt and he was carried off into captivity. Making his escape he served in many expeditions against the Indians. This work is important for the history of the French and Indian War, giving an accurate detail of the operations of the French and Indian forces at the siege of Oswego, etc.—Robinson, No. 32.

1759   WILLIAMSON, PETER.   French and Indian Cruelty; exemplified in the Life and various Vicissitudes of Fortune of Peter Williamson. Containing a particular Account of the Manners, Customs and Dress of the Savages; of their Scalping, Burning, and other Barbarities committed on the English in North America . . . his being carried off as a captive . . . comprehending a Summary of the Transactions of the several Provinces in America, particularly those relative to the intended attack on Crown-Point and Niagara . . . Written by Himself. Portrait of Williamson in the dress of a Delaware Indian. 8vo. London.

1759   Considerations on the Importance of Canada, and the Bay and River of St. Lawrence; and of the American Fisheries dependent on the Islands of Cape Breton, St. John's, Newfoundland, and the Seas adjacent. Address'd to the Right Hon. William Pitt. 8vo. London.

FRANKLIN, BENJAMIN.   An Historical Review of the Constitution and Government of Pennsylvania, From its Origin; So far as regards the several Points of Controversy, which have, from Time to Time, arisen between the several Governors of that Province, and their several Assemblies. Founded on Authentic Documents. 8vo. London.

"This volume was not written by me ... except the remarks in the Proprietor's estimate of his estate, and some of the inserted messages and reports of the Assembly which I wrote when at home."—Franklin. See Spark's *Works of Franklin,* 7, 208.—Quoted by Bradford.

A Letter to the Right Hon. William Pitt, Esq.; from an Officer at Fort Frontenac. 8vo. London. (38 pp.)

"Fort Frontenac was a French fort at the entrance to the St. Lawrence from Lake Ontario, on the site of the present town of Kingston. The writer gives a description of the fort and its surroundings, which he considers one of the most important positions in Canada. . . ."—*Monthly Review,* XX, 185, quoted by Sabin. The author at the beginning makes a plea for a changed attitude on the part of British settlers towards the Indians and gives an instance of the brutality of a group of Colonials towards them, and the subsequent retaliation of the Indians on the innocent members of a settlement.—From John Grant Catalogue.

THOMSON, CHARLES. An Enquiry into the Causes of the Alienation of the Delaware and Shawanese Indians from the British Interest, and into the Measures taken for Recovering their Friendship. Extracted from the Public Treaties and other Authentic Papers Relating to the Transactions of the Government of Pensilvania and the said Indians, for near Forty Years; and Explained by a Map of the Country. Together with the Remarkable Journal of Christian Frederic Post, by whose Negotiations among the Indians of Ohio, they were Withdrawn from the Interest of the French, who thereupon Abandoned the Fort and Country. With Notes, by the Editor, explaining Sundry Indian Customs, etc. Written in Pensilvania. Map. 12mo. London.

VENEGAS, (Father) MIGUEL. A Natural and Civil History of California, containing an Accurate Description of that Country. Its Soil, Mountains, Harbors, Lakes, Rivers, and Seas; its Animals, Vegetables, Minerals, and Famous Fishery for Pearls; the Customs of the Inhabitants, their Religion, Government and Manner of Living before their Conversion to the Christian Religion by the Missionary Jesuits. Together with Copper Plates and an accurate Map of the Country and the adjacent Seas. Translated from the Original Spanish of Miguel Venegas, a Mexican Jesuit. . . . In 2 vols. Illustrated. Map and 3 plates. 8vo. London.

The English version translated into French, Paris, 1766; into German, Lemgo, 1769. Spanish original, Madrid, 1757. See below.
"The best book on California history."—Quoted by Maggs, No. 532. This is the first judicious account published relative to California.—Pinkerton XVII. This famous book is one of the earliest and most important contributions to the historical literature of California. At the end are five appendices with an introduction. In this introduction is a recommendation to the Spanish Government for the col-

onization of California on the grounds that any other country's efforts there would be a menace to the existing Spanish colonies.—Robinson, No. 54.

1766 (In French.) Histoire naturelle et civile de la Californie Contenant une description exacte de ce Pays, de son Sol, de ses Montagnes, Lacs, Rivières, & Mers, . . . les Moeurs de ses Habitans, leur Religion, leur Gouvernement, & leur facon de vivre avant leur conversion au Christianisme; un détail des différens Voyages, & Tentatives qu'on a faites pour s'y établir, & reconnoitre son Golf & la Côte de la Mer de Sud. Enrichée de la Carte du Pays & des Mers adjacentes. Traduite de l'Anglais par M. E. (Eidous). 3 vols. Map. 12mo. Paris.

> The French and German translations are made from the English version.—Sabin.

1769 (In German.) Natürliche und bürgerliche Geschichte von Californien nebst einer neuen Charte dieses Landes und der benachbarten Meere, Aus dem Englischen . . . vom John Christoph Adelung. . . . Maps. 3 vols. 4to. Lemgo.

1757 VENEGAS, MIGUEL. Noticia de la California, y de su Conquista Temporal, y Espirital Hasta el Tiempo Presente. Sacada de la Historia Manuscrita, formada en Mexico año de 1739, por el Padre Miguel Venegas, de la Compania de Hesus; y de otras Noticias, y Relaciones antiguas, y modernas . . . An Adida de algunos mapas particulares; y uno general de la America Septentrional, Asia Oriental, y Mar del Sur intermedio, formados sobre las Memorias mas recientes, y exactas, que se publican juntamente. . . . 3 vols. 4to. Madrid.

> There is one map in the first volume; none in the second; three folding maps in the third volume.—Bradford. "This work, compiled in 1739 by the Jesuit Venegas, was, after his death, recast, completed, augmented and corrected by Marcus Antonio Buniel. The name of the latter does not appear in the book."—Quaritch.

1759-1764 MARTIN, BENJAMIN. Miscellaneous Correspondence, 1755-63, including, Account of North America, Historical and Geographical; Description of Cape Breton; Naval Activities in the West Indies, etc. Maps of the British and French settlements in North America, plans of Louisbourg, New York, etc. 4 vols. Also A System of Philology, with a Geographical and Natural History of America, Asia, etc. 2 vols. And, A Philosophical Survey of Nature. 2 vols. 8 vols. in all. 8vo. London.

1760 FRANKLIN, BENJAMIN. The Interest of Great Britain considered, with regard to her Colonies, and the acquisitions of Canada and Guadeloupe. To which are added, Observations concerning the Increase of Mankind, Peopling of Countries, . . . 8vo. London.

> 2nd edit., London, 1761.
> An important pamphlet, written by Franklin when in London as Agent for Pennsylvania, . . . until recently this pamphlet was ascribed to Richard Jackson, Law Officer to the Board of Trade. . . . Extracts from the Export Account follow the Introductory remarks.—From Robinson, No. 41.

A Genuine Letter from a Volunteer, in the British Service, at Quebec. 8vo. London. (39 pp.)

> The date is problematical but belongs to this decade. See *Monthly Review*, XXI, 367.—Sabin.

The Importance of Canada considered, in two Letters to a Nobleman. London.

JEFFERYS, THOMAS. The Natural and Civil History of the French Dominions in North and South America. Giving a particular Account of the Climate, Soil, Minerals, Animals, Trade, Commerce, and Languages; together with the Religion, Government, Character, Manners, and Customs, of the Indians, and other Inhabitants. 2 parts in 1. 18 folding maps and plans. Fol. London.

> The first part of this work describes Canada and Louisiana, and the second the West Indies and South America. It is an interesting work and important for its contemporary relation of the successes against Canada and the capture of Quebec, being one of the earliest accounts of that victory. This narration of the operations against Quebec is contained in 12 "starred" pages, which were added after most of the volume had been printed.—From Maggs, No. 442 and 479.

Letter to the People of England on the Necessity of putting an immediate End to the War. 8vo. London.

> Has six pages on the respective merits of Canada and Guadaloupe.—Bookseller's Note.

Lettres et Mémoires pour servir à l'Histoire naturelle et civile du Cap-Breton, jusqu' à la réprise de cette île par les Anglais, en 1758. London.

> So cited by Pinkerton XVII.

PICHON, T. Genuine Letters and Memoirs, relating to the . . . History of the Islands of Cape Breton, and Saint John, from the first Settlement there, to the Taking of Louisbourg by the English, in 1758. Translated from the Author's original Manuscript. 8vo. London.

> An important work, including a general description of Cape Breton and the Island of St. John; an account of the French Government at Louisbourg; the trade to New England, etc.—Robinson, No. 20.

1761 CALCOTT, ALEXANDER. Treatise on the Deluge. 8vo. London.

> 2nd edit., enlarged, London, 1768.
> The time, when, and the manner how, America was peopled, occupies thirty-one pages of the second edition.—Sabin.

CHARLEVOIX, PIERRE FRANCOIS XAVIER DE. Journal of a Voyage to North-America. Undertaken by Order of the French King. Containing the Geographical Description and Natural History of that Country, particularly Canada. Together with an Account of the Customs, Characters, Manners, and Traditions of the Original Inhabitants. . . . Translated from the French. Folding Map.  2 vols.  8vo.  London.

Another edition, with a different title, 1 vol., London, 1763; another in 2 vols., Dublin, 1766 (said to be superior to others in English). A modern reprint, 6 vols., New York (?), 1900; another, 2 vols., Chicago, 1923. French original, Paris, 1744. See below.

"This translation betrays, by numerous Scotticisms and misrepresentations, the hand of a North Briton, too little acquainted with the French and English languages to read or write either with propriety."—Quoted by Maggs, No. 502. In spite of the above criticism of the translator, the work is an extremely valuable one for the study of the history of Canada, and also for Louisiana.—Maggs, No. 549. The lure of the Great Western Ocean, which constantly retreated before advancing exploration, led to a desire to investigate the truth of Indian reports and the possibility of discovering the way to the sea, and Father Charlevoix was sent out in 1720 to test these reports and to find a feasible route. He reported that, "I saw only two practical routes to discover this sea: that the first was to ascend the Missouri whose source is certainly not far from the sea . . . that the second is to establish a mission with the Sioux, . . . The missionaries will have . . . all the information they wish."—Quoted by Baker from N. M. Crouse. The second plan was adopted but the mission established in 1727 on the Mississippi led to no results of this kind.

1763 CHARLEVOIX, P. DE. Letters to the Dutchess of Lesdiguieres; Giving an Account of a Voyage to Canada, and Travels through that Vast Country, and Louisiana, to the Gulf of Mexico. Undertaken by Order of the present King of France. . . . Being a more full and accurate Description of Canada and the neighboring Countries than has been before published . . . 8vo. London.

1900 CHARLEVOIX, REV. P. F. X. DE. History and General Description of New France. Translated by Dr. John Gilmary Shea. 6 vols. 8vo. New York.

The only complete edition in English almost impossible to find.— Bookseller's Note.

1923 CHARLEVOIX, PIERRE FRANCOIS XAVIER DE. Journal of a Voyage to North America. The Geographical Description and Natural History of that Country, particularly Canada. Translated from the French of . . . Edited with Historical Introduction, Notes and Index, by Louise Phelps Kellogg, Ph. D. Maps. 2 vols. 8vo. Caxton Club edition. Chicago.

1744 CHARLEVOIX, P. Histoire et Description générale de la Nouvelle-France; avec le journal historique d'un voyage fait par ordre du Roi, dans l'Amérique Septentrionale. Maps. 6 vols. in 16mo and 4 vols. in 4to. Paris.

GLEN, JAMES (Dr.). A Description of South Carolina; Containing many Curious and Interesting Particulars relating to the Civil, Natural, and Commercial History of that Colony, viz. The Succession of European Settlers there; Grants of English Charters; Boundaries; Constitution of the Government; Taxes; Number of Inhabitants, and of the neighboring Indian Nations, . . . The Culture and Product of Rice, Indian Corn and Indigo; The Process of extracting Tar and Turpentine; . . . To which is added a very particular Account of their Rice Trade for twenty years, with their Exports of Raw Silk and Imports of British Silk Manufacturers for twenty-five years. 8vo. London.

> Reprinted in the *South Carolina Hist. Coll.* vol. II, 1836. This work has been attributed to Governor Glenn of South Carolina. "With the exception of Hewett's history, it is the most complete early history of the State we have."— Preface to *South Carolina Hist. Coll.*, quoted by Sabin.

MASSIE, J. Brief Observations on the Management of the War and the means to Prevent the Ruin of Great Britain, with notices of the Gold Mines of Peru and Mexico, the Possessions of the French in America, 1761. Fol. London.

RUTHERFORD, JOHN. The Importance of the Colonies to Great Britain. With some Hints towards making Improvements to their mutual Advantage: And upon Trade in General. 8vo. London. (46 pp.)

1762 The American Gazetteer. Containing a distinct Account of all the parts of the New World: their Situation, Climate, Soil, Produce, Former and present Condition; Commodities, Manufacturers, and Commerce. Together with an accurate Account of the Cities, Towns, Ports, Bays, Rivers, Lakes, Mountains, Passes, and Fortifications. The whole intended to exhibit the Present State of Things in that Part of the Globe, and the Views and Interests of the several Powers who have Possessions in America. Maps. 3 vols. 12mo. London.

> Translated into Italian, Livorno, 1763. See below.

> 1763 (In Italian.) Il Gazzettiere Americano. Contenente un distinto ragguaglio di tutte le parti del Nuovo Mondo, della loro situazione, clima, terreno, prodotti, stati antico e moderno, merci, manifatture, e commercio, con una estata descrizione della città, piazze, porti, baji, fiumi, laghi, montagne, passi e fortificazione, . . . Tradotto dall' Inglese e arricchito di Aggiunte, Note, Carte e Rami. 78 maps. 3 vols. 4to. Livorno.

BOLLAN, WILLIAM. Coloniae Anglicanae Illustratae; Or, the Acquest of Dominion, and the Plantation of Colonies made by the English in America, with the Rights of the Colonists, Examined, stated and illustrated. Part I. Containing I. The Plan of the whole Work, including the Proposition, asserting the Rights of the Colonists, intended to be established. II. A Brief History of the Wars, Revolutions, and

Events which gave rise to all the marine Discoveries and foreign Acquisitions made by the modern Europeans. III. A Survey of the Knowledge and the Opinions which the Europeans had of the Earth in Times preceding these Discoveries; with other matters relating to this subject. IV. The Particulars of the Progress made by the Portuguese, from their beginning these Discoveries, to the Death of King John II, and an Account of the Grants made to the kings of Portugal of the Countries that were or might be discovered, by the Bulls of several Popes, with one of them set forth at large . . . 4to. London.

> A very learned work, but of which, unfortunately, no more was published. The author was the Massachusetts Agent in England from 1745 to 1762. See also Bollan under 1746 above.

Comparative Importance of our Acquisitions from France in America, with Remarks on a pamphlet Examination of the Commercial Principles of the late Negociation, 1761. 8vo. London.

> A comparative view of the value of the Imports and Exports of Canada and the West Indies, etc.—Bookseller's Note.

An Impartial Enquiry into the Right of the French King to the Territory West of the Great River Mississippi, in North America, not ceded by the Preliminaries, including a Summary Account of that River, and the Country adjacent; with a short Detail of the Advantages it possesses, its Native Commodities, and how they might be improved to the Advantage of the British Commerce. Comprehending a Vindication of the English Claim to that whole Continent, from the Authentic Records, and indisputable Historical Facts; and Particular Directions to Navigators for entering the several Mouths of that important River. 8vo. London.

JEFFERYS, THOMAS.  For an account of Florida see his *Account of the Spanish Settlements in America,* under WEST INDIES.

1762-1785.  Society for the Propagation of the Gospel in Foreign Parts—Collection of 10 Sermons published under the Society's auspices by the Bishops of Chester, Rochester, Glocester, etc., 1762, 1766-68, 1780-85, each sermon complete with the scarce Abstracts of the Society's Proceedings. 2 vols. 4to. London.

> The Abstracts are of particular interest as they consist of records of activities among the Indians of Newfoundland, Nova Scotia, New England, New Jersey, Carolina, Pennsylvania, Bahama Islands, etc. . . . The fact that the Sermons were often issued without the Abstracts has rendered the latter very difficult to obtain.—Bookseller's Note.

1763 An Account of the late Attempts by the Correspondents of the Society for propagating Christian Knowledge, To Christianize the North American Indians. 8vo. Edinburgh. (12 pp.)

> Includes Letters from Mather, Chauncey, Bostwick, also Accounts of the Mohawks and Oneida Indians.—Sabin.

The Advantages of a Settlement upon the Ohio in North America. 8vo. London. (44 pp.)

> Extremely scarce. See *Monthly Review,* XLVIII, 63.—Sabin.

The Expediency of Securing our American Colonies by Settling the Country adjoining the River Mississippi, and the Country upon the Ohio Considered. 12mo. Edinburgh.

An Impartial History of the late Glorious War in Europe, Asia, Africa, and America, with an Account of the Places ceded to Great Britain. Manchester.

LE PAGE DU PRATZ. The History of Louisiana, or of the Western Parts of Virginia and Carolina: Containing A Description of the Countries that lye on both Sides of the River Missippi (*sic*); With An Account of the Settlements, Inhabitants, Soil, Climate, and Products. Translated from the French, . . . with some Notes and Observations relating to our Colonies . . . Folding maps of the Mississippi basin and its mouth. 2 vols. 12mo. London.

> Reprinted, 8vo, London, 1774. French original, Paris, 1758. See below.
> "The author lived in Louisiana for fifteen years, and it is from his relations that most of the details of the life of the Natchez and other Mississippi tribes have been derived."—Quoted by Maggs, No. 465. The author arrived in Louisiana in 1718 and remained there sixteen years. He had ample opportunities as official physician to exercise his powers of observation on men and events. His book is one of the most valuable for the history of the Colony. He gives minute descriptions of the different Indian tribes, particularly the Natchez, with accounts of their wars, manners, customs, language, government, religion, etc.—Bookseller's Note. The work is important as showing the French claims to the Southern territory now occupied by several states but claimed also by the English under the name of "Carolina." . . . The long preface is the work of the English editor, who informs us that he "has left out many things that appeared to be trifling, and abridged some parts of it." . . .—Sabin.

> 1758 LE PAGE DU PRATZ. Histoire de la Louisiane, contenant la Découverte de ce vaste Pays: sa Description géographique; un Voyage dans les Terres; l'Histoire Naturelle; les Moeurs, Coûtumes & Religion des Naturels, avec leur Origines; deux Voyages dans le nord du nouveau Mexique, dont un jusqu'à la Mer du Sud. 2 maps and 40 plates. 3 vols. 12mo. Paris.

MASSIE, J.   An Historical Account of the Naval Power of France, . . .
with a State of the English Fisheries at Newfoundland, for a hundred
and fifty years past . . . To which is added, A Narrative of the Proceedings of the French at Newfoundland, from the Reign of King
Charles the First, to the Reign of Queen Anne, shewing what Measures were taken on the Part of England, during that Interval, in relation to the said French Proceedings, . . . First printed in the year
1712, and now Reprinted for general Information.   4to.   London.

> Sabin says that he has never seen the first edition. See *Monthly Review*,
> XXVII, 461. It is probably the Narrative of the Proceedings of the French that
> was printed in 1712. See also Massie under 1761 above.

ROBERTS, WM.   An Account of the First Discovery and Natural History of Florida, with a particular Detail of the several Expeditions and
Descents made on that Coast. Collected from the best Authorities. Illustrated by a general Map, and some particular Plans, together with a
Geographical Description of that Country, by T. Jefferys, Geographer
to his Majesty.   7 maps and 1 plate.   4to.   London.

> After belonging alternately to France and Spain, Florida was finally ceded
> to England in this year, and Roberts' book was in response to the awakened in-
> terest in the colony.—Robinson, No. 35. Contains view and plan of Pensacola,
> plan of Town, Harbor, of St. Augustine.

1764   BOLLAN, WILLIAM.   The Ancient Right of the English Nation to the
American Fishery; and its Various Diminutions; examined and stated.
With a Map of the Lakes, Islands, Gulfs, Seas, Fishing Banks, com-
prising the whole. Humbly inscribed to sincere Friends of the British
Naval Empire.   Map.   4to.   London.

HUTCHINSON, THOMAS (Governor).   The History of the Colony of
Massachusetts-Bay, from the First Settlement thereof in 1628 until its
Incorporation with the Colony of Plimouth . . . in 1691.   8vo.   Lon-
don.

> 2nd edit., 2 vols., London, 1765-68. The second edition was issued in Lon-
> don at first with the date 1760 in error for 1765, but the title was cancelled, and
> the date corrected. Vol. II of this set has the date 1760.—Puttick and Simpson.
> The first edition was printed at Boston, 1764.

1765   BRAINERD, DAVID.   An Account of the Life of the late Reverend Mr.
David Brainerd, Minister of the Gospel, Missionary to the Indians,
from the Honourable Society in Scotland for the Propagation of Christian Knowledge, and Pastor of a Church of Christian Indians in New
Jersey. Who died at Northampton in New England, Oct. 9, 1747. To

which is annexed Mr. Brainerd's Journal while among the Indians, etc. With an Appendix relative to Indian Affairs. 8vo. Edinburgh.

An abridged version of his Journal printed, Edinburgh, 1748; another edition, Edinburgh, 1798. A modern editioin of his Journal, London, 1902. See below. The Journal was translated into Dutch.—Sabin. See also Brainerd under 1743 above.

1798 BRAINERD, DAVID. An Account of the Life of Mr. David Brainerd, ... Published by Jonathan Edwards, M. A. With Mr. Brainerd's Public Journal, To which is added Mr. Beatty's Mission to the Westward of the Alleghany Mountains. 8vo. Edinburgh.

Beatty's Journal is sometimes found separately published. See Beatty under 1768 below.

1902 BRAINERD, DAVID. Diary and Journal of Life and Missionary Work among Red Indians. With Introduction. 2 vols. 8vo. London.

CAMPBELL, JOHN. View of the European Settlements in America. London.

So cited by Pinkerton XVII.

FOTHERGILL, JOHN. Considerations relative to the North American Colonies. 8vo. London. (48 pp.)

"One of the most important pamphlets published at this important period." —Rich. Reprinted in the Works of John Fothergill, M.D., 3 vols., 8vo, London, 1783-84; and 4to, 1784. See *Monthly Review,* XLIII, 249.—Sabin.

POWNALL, THOMAS. The Administration of the British Colonies, wherein their Rights and Constitution are discussed. London.

2nd edit., revised and corrected and enlarged, 8vo, London, 1765; 3rd edit., to which is added an Appendix, London, 1766; 4th, London, 1768; 5th and "best," 2 vols., 8vo, London, 1774.
A very celebrated production, frequently reprinted.—Puttick and Simpson. Pownall had considerable experience in administrative work in the colonies, having been lieutenant governor of New Jersey and governor of Massachusetts. Later he was transferred to South Carolina. He returned to England in 1760. In the above work he projected the union of all the American possessions in one dominion, and drew attention to the reluctance of the colonists to be taxed without their consent.—D.N.B.

RAY, NICHOLAS. The Importance of the Colonies of North America considered, ... 4to. London.

ROGERS, ROBERT (Major). A Concise Account of North America, containing a Description of the several British Colonies, including the Islands of Newfoundland, Cape Breton, also of the Interior, or Westerly Parts of the Country, upon the rivers St. Lawrence, the Mississippi, Christine, and the Great Lakes, to which is subjoined an Account of the Several Nations and Tribes of Indians. 8vo. London.

Reprinted in *A New Collection of Voyages*, London, 1767 (see Knox under 1767, COLLECTIONS). Noticed in the *Journal des Scavans*, 1766, II, 426, also in the *Monthly Review*, Jan., 1766. For his Journals see this date under MILITARY EXPEDITIONS.

The author was born in New Hampshire, where his father, James Rogers, was one of the first settlers. He gained great celebrity as commander of "Rogers' Rangers" in the war with the French in North America, 1755-60, and a precipice near Lake George is named "Rogers' Slide," after his escape down the precipice from the Indians. In 1765 he was appointed governor of Mackinaw, Michigan, and was later accused of intriguing with the Spaniards, and sent in irons to Montreal and tried by court-martial. Subsequently he became a colonel in the British army in America and raised the "Queen's Rangers." His printed circular to recruits promised them "their proportion of all rebel lands."—Robinson, No. 41.

TIMBERLAKE, HENRY (Lieut.). The Memoirs of Lieut. Henry Timberlake (who accompanied the Three Cherokee Indians to England in the Year 1762). Containing whatever he observed remarkable, or worthy of public Notice, during his Travels to and from that Nation; wherein the Country, Government, Genius and Customs of the Inhabitants are authentically described. Also the Principal Occurrences during their Residence in London. Illustrated with an Accurate Map of their Over-hill Settlement, and a curious Secret Journal, taken by the Indians out of the Pocket of a Frenchman they had killed. 8vo. London.

Translated into French, Paris, 1797. See below. Noticed in the *Journal des Scavans*, 1766, V, 131.

The author was a native of Virginia, who was engaged in subduing the Cherokees. He took three chiefs over to England to see King George III.

1797 TIMBERLAKE, HENRI. Voyages du lieutenant H. Timberlake qui fut chargé dans l'année 1760 de conduire en Angleterre trois Sauvages de la Tribu des Cherokes. Traduits de l'anglais par J. -B. -L. -J. Billecocq. 18mo. Paris.

1766 BARTRAM, JOHN. See under William Stork below.

HANWAY, JONAS. The Soldier's Faithful Friend: political, moral, and religious Monitions to Officers and Private Men in the Army and Militia. 2 vols. 8vo. London.

Pp. 129-156 contain a chapter on North America: Observations relating to the present State of North America, respecting the Jurisdiction of the British Legislation. Hanway is better known for his *Historical Account of the British Trade over the Caspian Sea* (see under 1753, CENTRAL ASIA).

POWNALL, THOMAS. A Topographical Description of Some Parts of North America as are contained in the (annexed) Map of the middle British Colonies, . . . of North America. Map. Fol. London.

The appendix contains an account of Gordon's Expedition to Illinois in 1766, and Gist's journey to North Carolina.—Robinson, No. 48.

ROLLE, DENYS. To the Right Honourable the Lords of His Majesty's Most Honourable Privy Council. The Humble Petition of Denys Rolle, Esq.: setting forth the Hardships, Inconveniences, and Grevances, which have attended him in his Attempts to make a Settlement in East Florida, humbly praying such Relief, as in their Lordships Wisdom shall seem meet. 8vo. London. (47 pp.)

This is a privately printed volume, of which very few were taken off, with the maps drawn by the author in blanks left for the purpose in the text. "In 1766 Rolle purchased a whole district in Florida, whither he proceeded with 1000 persons to people his new possessions, but, through the unhealthiness of climate and the desertion of those who escaped disease, he soon found himself without colonists and without money, and was compelled to work his passage back to England in an American vessel."—Drake, quoted by Sabin. See second Stork item this date below.

SMITH, WILLIAM (Dr.) An Historical Account of the Expedition against the Ohio Indians, in the Year 1764. Under the command of Henry Bouquet, Esq. Colonel of Foot, and now Brigadier General in America. Including his Transactions with the Indians, Relative to the Delivery of their Prisoners, And the Preliminaries of Peace. With an Introductory Account of the Preceding Campaign, and the Battle at Bushy-Run, To which are annexed Military Papers, Containing Reflections on the Settlements; some Account of the Indian Country; with a List of Nations, Fighting Men, Towns, Distances, and different Routs. The whole illustrated with a Map and Copper-Plates. Published from authentic Documents, by a Lover of his Country. Map, plans, 2 plates. 4to. London. (Reprint of the Philadelphia edition.)

Translated into French, Amsterdam, 1769. See below.
In this edition the three plans are on a reduced scale, but it contains in addition two fine historical plates engraved by Grignon from the earliest drawings of Benjamin West, to one of which his autograph signature is attached.—Barlow. The Bradford edition contains four appendices. . . . The Jefferies edition has an additional appendix, making five. . . .—Bradford.

1769 (In French.) Relation Historique de l'Expédition, contre les Indiens de l'Ohio en 1764. Commandée par le Chevalier Henry Bouquet, Colonel d'Infanterie, et ensuite Brigadier-Général en Amérique; contenant ses Transactions avec les Indiens, relativement à la délivrance des Prisonniers et aux Préliminaires de la Paix; avec un Récit introductoire de la Campagne précédente de l'an 1763, et de la Bataille de Bushy-Run. 4 engraved folding maps and plans and 2 engraved plates. 8vo. Amsterdam.

The French edition contains some biographical notices of Bouquet not to be found in any of the Editions in English.—Puttick and Simpson. This book gives an account of the first victory gained by the

English over the Indians after the latter had learned the use of fire-arms. General Wayne adopted Bouquet's Strategy in his western campaign. The author states, in a letter to Sir William Johnson, that his narrative was based on papers supplied by Bouquet himself. Bouquet also contributed some or all of the essays in the appendix, viz.: Indian warfare, the construction of forts in Louisiana ceded by France to Great Britain, the route from Philadelphia to Fort Pitt, Indian towns on, or near the Ohio River, the names of the Indian tribes of North America. . . . Justin Winsor thinks that the seated figure at the left of plate at page 49 represents Bouquet.—From Robinson, No. 41.

STORK, WILLIAM, and BARTRAM, JOHN. An Account of East-Florida, with a Journal, kept by John Bartram, of Philadelphia, Botanist to His Majesty for the Floridas; upon a Journey from St. Augustine up the River St. Johns, as far as the Lakes. 8vo. London.

3rd and "best" edit., notes, maps, 4to, London, 1769.
Bartram was the father of the more celebrated traveller and botanist, William Bartram. For the latter see under 1792 below, and also John Bartram under 1751 above.

STORK, WILLIAM. An Extract from the Account of East Florida, published by Dr. Stork, who resided a considerable time in Augustine, the Metropolis of that Province. With the Observations of Denys Rolle, Who formed a Settlement on St. John's river, in the same Province. 8vo. London. (39 pp.)

WHEELOCK, ELEAZAR. A Brief Narrative of the Indian Charity-School in Lebanon in Connecticut, New England, founded and carried on by Eleazar Wheelock. 8vo. London.

This contains Letters and Extracts of Letters from American Indians, Missionaries to the Indians and Indian Teachers.—The particulars of missionary work among the "six Nations" are of much interest. One man tells "there is a good deal wavering" and his "going" has the approval of Sir Wm. Johnson, who thinks "it may be the means of securing them before the French renew and strengthen their interests among them."—Bookseller's Notes.

1767 MITCHELL, JOHN (Dr.). The Present State of Great Britain and North America, with regard to Agriculture, Population, Trade, and Manufacturers impartially considered. 8vo. London.

A valuable compilation of facts regarding the critical situation of the colonies in North America. The advantages of extending the settlements in Canada and the territories of the Ohio and Mississippi, the trade of the plantations, the impropriety of the famous Stamp Act, with reference to other taxes, the fur trade of North America and the fisheries.—Bookseller's Note. See also Mitchell under 1757 above.

1768 BEATTY, CHARLES. The Journal of a Two-Months Tour; with a view of Promoting Religion among the Frontier Inhabitants of Pennsylvania and of Introducing Christianity among the Indians to the

Westward of the Alegh-geny Mountains, with Remarks on the Language and Customs of some particular Tribes among the Indians. 8vo. London.

> "This journal, though mostly of a religious cast, is enlivened with many agreeable notes and circumstances relating to the manners and customs of the Delaware Indians, who, from certain similar customs and some traditions among them, the author conjectures to be the descendants of the ten tribes of Israel."— Quoted by Maggs, No. 465. See Brainerd under 1765 above.

CANNING, GEORGE. A Letter to the Right Honourable Wills Earl of Hillsborough, on the Connection between Great Britain and her American Colonies . . . 8vo. London. (47 pp.)

> Appeared also in Dublin, 1768.

The Present State of the British Empire in Europe, America, Africa, and Asia, containing a concise Account of our Possessions in every part of the Globe. 8vo. London.

> The American portion occupies some 150 pages, with general summary and separate articles on Maryland, Carolina, Nova Scotia, Hudson's Bay, Florida, West Florida, and the West Indies.—Bookseller's Note.

SANDBY, PAUL. Twenty-seven Views in North America and the West Indies, with Descriptions in English and French. Oblong fol. London.

> Sandby deserves the thanks of posterity for his numerous volumes of "Views of Gentlemen's Seats" in England, many of which have since been pulled down. He was the first to introduce the aqua-tint process into England.

SWINDRAGE, THEODORE. For an account of exploration in Labrador see his *The Great Probability of a North-West Passage,* under NORTHWEST PASSAGE.

WILLIAMSON, PETER. The Travels of . . . among the different Nations and Tribes of savage Indians in America; with an Account of their Principles, religious, civil, and Military; their Genius, strength, ideas of Deity, and notions of Creations. Frontispiece and plates. 12mo. Edinburgh.

1769 CHEVALIER DE, ***. Voyages et avantures due chevalier de ***. 4 vols. 12 mo. London.

> Cet ouvrage très rare contient des documents intéressants sur l'Amérique Septentrionale, les Isles Caraibes, de St.-Vincent, Sainte Lucie, l'Isle de Cuba, Porto-Rico, Cayenne, la Havane, ancien et nouveau Mexique, la Louisiane, le Canada, etc.—From Bookseller's Note.

CLUNY, ALEXANDER. The American Traveller: or, Observations on the Present State, Culture and Commerce of the British Colonies in America, and further Improvements of which they are capable; with an Account of the Exports, Imports, and Returns of each Colony respectively—and of the Numbers of British Ships and Seamen, Merchants, Traders and Manufactures employed by all collectively; together with the Amount of the Revenue arising to Great-Britain therefrom. In a series of Letters written originally to the Right Honourable the Earl of * * * *. By an Old and Experienced Trader. Engraved plate and large folding map. 4to. London.

> Translated into French, Amsterdam, 1782 (date of 1783 also given). See below.
> "The author was the first to give accurate intelligence of Hudson's Bay, and to institute an enquiry about a more successful commerce with the Americans. The book is said to have been published under the auspices of Lord Chatham, and both the English and Americans, at that crisis, were so eager to possess it, that it was bought and read by one party with the avidity that it was bought and destroyed by the other."—Dibdin's *Library Companion*, II, 65, quoted by Maggs, No. 465.

> 1782 (In French.) Le Voyageur Américain ou observations sur l'état actuel, le commerce des colonies britanniques en Amérique, les exportations et importations respectives entre elles et la Grande Bretagne, avec un état des revenus que cette dernière en retire, . . . Adressées par un négociant expérimenté, en forme de lettres. Traduit de l'anglois (par Mandrillon); augmentée d'un précis sur l'Amérique septentrionale et la République des Treize-Etats-Unis. 8vo. Amsterdam.

KNOX, JOHN (Captain). An Historical Journal of the Campaigns in North America, for the Years 1757-1760; containing the most Remarkable Occurrences of the Period; particularly the Two Sieges of Quebec, under the orders of the Admiral and General Officers, Description of the Countries where the Author has served, with their Forts and Garrisons, their Climate, Soil and Produce, and a regular Diary of the Weather; also several Manifestoes, a Mandate of the Bishop of Canada, the French Order and Dispositions for that Colony. Engraved portraits of Amherst and Wolfe, and large folding map. 2 vols. 4to. London.

> "A very valuable collection of materials towards a history of the Canadian war, as well as for a description and natural history of the country, in which this attentive and industrious author personally served, and the best original authority for the death of Wolfe and the conquest of Canada."—Quoted by Maggs, No. 479.

A Letter to a Friend; in which some Account is given of the Brethren's Society for the Furtherance of the Gospel among the Heathen. 8vo. London. (12 pp.)

> An extremely rare Moravian tract, relative to the Indians.—Sabin.

MAUDIT, ISRAEL. A Short View of the History of the Colony of Massachusetts Bay, with respect to their Original Charter and Constitution. 8vo. London.

> 3rd edit., London, 1774; 4th edit., both with additions, London, 1776.
> The author states that in all the later American disturbances, and in every attempt against the authority of the British government the people of Massachusetts have taken the lead.—Quaritch.

Private Letter from an American in England to his Friends in America. 8vo. London.

1770 JOHNSTON, GEORGE MILLIGEN (M. D.) A Short Description of the Province of South Carolina, written in the year 1763. London.

PITTMAN, PHILIP (Captain). The Present State of the European Settlements on the Mississippi; with a geographical Description of that River. Plans and draughts. 4to. London.

> "The author resided several years in the countries he describes, and was employed in surveying and exploring the inner parts."—Quoted by Maggs, No. 429.

ROBERT, T. A Narrative of the Life of the Reverend Mr. George Whitefield, Late Chaplain to the Right Honourable The Countess of Huntingdon. With the History of his Travels through England, Scotland, and Ireland; his Voyages to, and Travels through America, Pensylvania, Maryland, South-Carolina, Virginia, Georgia, Bermudas, and the Jerseys; and his Voyage to Lisbon. Faithfully published by T. Robert, A. M. To which is added, A particular Account of his Death and Funeral, with Extracts from several Sermons, preached on that Occasion, both in England and America. Also, His last Will and Testament; and an exact Description of his Person. 12mo. London.

WYNNE, JOHN H. A General History of the British Empire in America: containing, An Historical, Political, and Commercial View of the English Settlements: including all the Countries in North America and the West Indies, ceded by the Peace of Paris. Large folding map of the British Empire in America. 2 vols. 8vo. London.

1770-71 KALM, PETER. Travels into North America; Containing its Natural History, and a circumstantial Account of its Plantations and Agriculture in general, with the Civil, Ecclesiastical State of the Country, the Manners of the Inhabitants and several curious and Important Remarks on various subjects. . . . Translated into English by John Reinhold Forster, F.A.S. Maps, illustrations of natural history, and some additional notes. 3 vols. 8vo. London.

2nd edit., slightly abridged, 2 vols., 8vo. London, 1772; reprinted in Pinkerton XIII, 374-700. Modern reprint, New York, 1937. Swedish original, Stockholm, 1753-1761. See below.
This voyage of the Swedish naturalist was undertaken for the purpose of discovering whether any North American plants could be introduced advantageously into Sweden.—Maggs, No. 549. His expenses were defrayed by the Universities of Upsala and Abo. He sailed from Gotenborg Dec. 11, 1747, stayed in England from Feb. 17 to Aug. 15, 1748, and arrived in Philadelphia Sept. 26 of that year. He remained in America until 1751, travelling through the central provinces and sending much material back to Sweden. His account of his visit to England appeared in English under the title of *Kalm's Account of his Visit to England on his Way to America in 1748,* London, 1892. See *American-Scandinavian Review,* June, 1922.

1937  KALM, PETER. The America of 1750: Peter Kalm's Travels in North America. A reprint of the English version of 1770 revised from the original Swedish and edited by Dr. Adolph B. Benson. With a translation of new material from Kalm's notes. New York.

1753-1761  KALM, PETER. En Resa til Norra America, paa Kongl. Swenska Wetenskaps Academiens befallning, och publici kostnad, förrättad af Pehr Kalm, Professor i Abo. 3 vols. 4to. Stockholm.

1771  BLACKFORT, DOMINIQUE. Précis de l'état actuel des Colonies Anglaises dans l'Amérique-Septentrionale, par Dominique Blackfort, avec la response de M. Franklin á l'Interrogatoire qu'il a subi devant la chambre des communes, au mois Février 1766, lorsque la resolution de l'édit du timbre y fut mise en délibération: traduit de l'Anglais. Milan.

Cited by Pinkerton. The original has not come to the notice of the editor.

BOSSU, NICOLAS. Travels through that part of North America formerly called Louisiana, translated from the French by J. Reinhold Forster, illustrated with Notes relative chiefly to Natural History, to which is added by the translator, a systematic Catalogue of all the known Plants of English North America, or a Flora Americae Septentrionalis, together with an Abstract of the most useful and necessary articles contained in Peter Loefling's Travels through Spain and Cumana in South America. 2 vols. 8vo. London.

French original, Paris, 1768. 3rd voyage, Amsterdam, 1777. See below.
This work forms a portion of the Linnean Voyages.—Lowndes. "His account of his first two voyages to Louisiana were printed in 1768, after which he made a third voyage, which, not having been reprinted nor translated into any other language, is a much scarcer work than the former."—Quoted by Maggs, No. 465.

1768  BOSSU, NICOLAS. Nouveaux voyages aux Indes Occidentales; contenant une relation des différens peuples qui habitent les environs du Grand Fleuve Saint-Louis, appellé vulgairement le Mississippi; leur religion; leur gouvernement; leur moeurs; leur guerres et leur commerce. 2 parts in 1 vol. 12mo. Paris.

Le chevalier Bossu est un de ceux qui ont le mieux fait connaitre la Louisiane et les peuples sauvages qui l'habitaient. Il fut envoyé dans ce pays en 1750. Ayant eu l'occasion de faire plusieurs voyages dans l'intérieur, il fut à portée de connaître les moeurs et les habitants de l'Illinois, de l'Arkansas, des Allimabous et autres peuplades de sauvages qui habitent les bords du Mississippi.—Bookseller's Note. The French edition of 1777 has a slightly different title. See below.

1777 BOSSU, MONS. N. Nouveaux Voyages dans l'Amérique Septentrionale, contenant une Collection de Lettres écrites sur les lieux par l'Auteur à son ami M. Douin, ci-devant son camarade dans le Nouveau Monde. 4 plates. 8vo. Amsterdam.

FORSTER, JOHN REINHOLD. Catalogue of Animals of North America, containing an Enumeration of the known Quadrupeds, Birds, Fish, Insects, crustaceous and testaceous Animals, many . . . never described before, with Directions for Collecting, Preserving, and Transporting all Kinds of Natural History Curiosities. Engraved frontispiece of the Little Falcon. London.

PENN, WILLIAM. Select Works: Journal; Travels in Holland; Description of Pennsylvania; Letters to Friends in Maryland; No Cross, No Crown; Reflections and Maxims, etc. Fol. London.

TAYLOR, G. (of Sheffield). A voyage to North America performed by G. Taylor of Sheffield in the years 1768 and 1769, . . . the Author's Manner of trading with the Indians, a Concise History of their Manners,· Diversions, and barbarous Customs, with his Journey by land from New-York to Quebec in Canada by way of Albany, Saratoga, Fort Edward, Lake George, Ticonderago, Crown Point, Lake Champlain and Montreal; his Passage from Quebec down the River St. Laurence to Boston, . . . from Philadelphia to New Orleans . . . up the River Mississippi to the Illinois and down from Fort Chartres, over the Ohio River, through the Cherokee, Chicsaw and Chactaw Indian Settlements to Pensacola . . . Georgia . . . Virginia . . . Maryland, etc., with a particular Account of the Climate, Soil and disposition of the Inhabitants in each Settlement, . . . 8vo. Nottingham.

WILKINSON, T. R. Holiday Rambles. Illus. 8vo. Manchester. Pp. 1-67, A Month in America.—Bookseller's Note.

1772 BAILEY, W. The Advancement of Arts, Manufactures and Commerce; together with an Account of the several Discoveries and Improvements in Agriculture, Mechanics, . . . and also in the British Colonies in America. 4to. London.

MASERES, BARON FRANCIS. A Collection of several Commissions and other Public Instruments, Proceeding from His Majesty's Royal Authority, and other Papers, Relating to the State of the Province of Quebec in North America, since the Conquest of it by the British Arms in 1760. Collected by Francis Masères, Esquire, His Majesty's Attorney General in the said Province. 4to. London.

> The author published "Additional Papers concerning the Province of Quebec," 8vo. London, 1776. See also under 1775 below.

The History of the British Dominions in North America, from the first discovery of that vast Continent by Sebastian Cabot, in 1497, to the present glorious Establishment as confirmed by the late Treaty of Peace in 1763. . . . Map by Peter Bell. 4to. London.

> Reprinted, London, 1788. Translated into German, Leipzig, 1777, 2nd edit. See below.

> 1777 (In German.) Geschichte der englischen Colonien in Nord-Amerika von der Entdeckung durch Sebastian Cabot bis 1763. Aus dem Englischen (by E. E. von Klausing). 2 Thiele. Leipzig. (2nd edit.)

Mexican Letters, Containing Satirical Observations on the Manners, Customs, Religion, and Policy of the English, French, Spaniards ,and Americans. Interspersed with a Great Variety of Interesting and Entertaining Anecdotes, Illustrated by Moral and other suitable Reflections. 2 vols. 12mo. London.

Scotus Americanus. Information concerning the Province of North Carolina, addressed to the Emigrants from the Highlands and Western Isles of Scotland. . . . 8vo. Glasgow.

> A pamphlet of 32 pp. signed "Scotus Americanus."—Puttick and Simpson.

1774 BERNARD, FRANCIS (Governor). Select Letters on the Trade and Government of America; and the Principles of Law and Polity applied to the American Colonies. Written by Governor Bernard at Boston, 1763-68. . . . To which are added the Petition of the Assembly of Massachuset's-Bay against the Governor. . . . 8vo. London.

A Brief Account of the Mission established among the Esquimaux Indians, on the Coast of Labrador, by the Church of the Brethren or Unitas Fratrum. 8vo. London.

> An interesting pamphlet describing the foundation of the Moravian Settlement in Labrador and of their early work among the Esquimaux.—Maggs, No. 549.

A Brief Review of the Rise and Progress, Services and Sufferings, of New England, especially the Province of Massachuset's Bay. Humbly submitted to the consideration of both Houses of Parliament. 8vo. London. (32 pp.)

> Printed also at Norwich, 1774.
> "Contains a very decent, and, to all appearances, a very fair and impartial statement of facts that ought to have due attention paid to them."—*Monthly Review*, L, 324.—Quoted by Sabin.

LEIGH, SIR EGERTON. Considerations on certain Political Transactions of the Province of South Carolina; containing a View of the Colony Legislatures (under the Description of That of Carolina in particular). With Observations, Shewing their Resemblances to the British Model. London.

> This shrewd and dispassionate examination of the internal disputes of the colony of South Carolina, containing a detail of curious and interesting transactions. See *Monthly Review*, L, 288, 486.—Sabin.

ROBINSON, JOHN, and RISPIN, THOMAS. A Journey through Nova Scotia, containing a particular account of the Country and its Inhabitants; with Observations on their Management in Husbandry; the Breed of Horses and other Cattle, and everything material relating to Farming. To which is added an Account of several Estates for sale in different Townships of Nova Scotia, with their number of acres, and the price at which each is set. By John Robinson, Farmer at Bewholm, in Holderness, and Thomas Rispin, Farmer at Fangfoss, County of York, who sailed for Nova Scotia the 8th of April 1774, from Scarborough, on Board the Ship Prince George. 12mo. London. (48 pp.)

A Short Account of the Province of New England, in North America, From the First Discovery thereof; selected from Various Authors, with Additional Remarks. 8vo. London. (32 pp.)

SMETHURST, GAMALIEL. A Narrative of an Extraordinary Escape out of the Hands of the Indians, in the Gulph of St. Lawrence; interspersed with a Description of the Coast, and Remarks on the Customs and Manners of the Savages there: Also A Providential Escape after a Shipwreck, in coming from the Island St. John, in said Gulph; with an Account of the Fisheries round that Island. Likewise, A Plan for reconciling the Differences between Great Britain and her colonies. ... 4to. London. (48 pp.)

> Smethurst was a member of the Assembly in the province of Nova Scotia and comptroller of his Majesty's customs. He was with Capt. McKenzie, who was charged with the removal of the Acadians, from about the Bay of Chaleurs, in 1761.—Quoted by Sabin.

1775   ADAIR, JAMES.  The History of the American Indians; particularly
those Nations adjoining to the Mississippi, East and West Florida,
Georgia, South and North Carolina, and Virginia; containing an Account of their Origin, Language, Manners, Religions, Laws, Forms of
Government. Punishments, Conduct in War and Domestic Life, Habits,
Diet, Agriculture, Manufactures, Diseases and Method of Cure, and
other particulars, sufficient to render it a Complete Indian System, with
Observations on former Historians, the Conduct of our Colony Governors, Superintendents, Missionaries, . . . also an Appendix, containing a Description of the Floridas and the Mississippi Lands. . . . Folding map. 4to. London.

> A modern edition, edited by S. C. Williams, Johnson City, Tenn., 1930.
> The first considerable work to appear on the North American Indians. Adair
> espouses the theory first put forward by the early Spanish missionaries that the
> Indians had a Hebrew origin.—Quaritch. This work has long been recognized
> as an outstanding authority on the southern Indians and the English traders. He
> himself resided about forty years among the aborigines of the region.

BURNABY, ANDREW.  Travels through the Middle Settlements in
North America in the years 1759-1760, with Observations upon the
State of the Colonies.  4to.  London.

> 2nd edit., 8vo, London, 1775; a pirated edition, 12mo, Dublin, 1775; 3rd
> edit., 4to, London, 1798. This edition, which contains nearly double the mate-
> rial of the original, being largely rewritten, and containing many references to
> events of the war, is considered the best.—Maggs, No. 549. Reprinted in Pink-
> erton XIII, 701-752. Reprinted from the 3rd edition, New York, 1904. Trans-
> lated into German, Hamburg, 1776; into French, Lausanne, 1778. See below.
> The first two editions, which appeared in close succession, were published
> in the hopes of preventing the rupture between the colonies and England then
> threatening. Even in 1798 Burnaby believed that the colonies would be unable to
> remain one, but would break up.—"Valuable as exhibiting a view of the colonies
> immediately preceding the Revolution."—Quoted by Maggs, No. 429. The au-
> thor was Archbishop of Leicester and Vicar of Greenwich.

> 1776   (In German.) Reisen durch die Mittlern Kolonien der Engländer in
> Nord-America, nebst Anmerkungen über der Zustand der Kolonien.
> 8vo. Hamburg.

> 1778   (In French.) Voyages dans les colonies du milieu de l'Amérique Sep-
> tentrionale, fait en 1759 et 1760. Avec observations sur l'état des col-
> onies. Tr. par M. Wild. 8vo. Lausanne.

MASERES, FRANCIS (Baron).  An Account of the Proceedings of the
British and other Protestant Inhabitants of the Province of Quebec,
. . . 8vo.  London.

> See Masères further under 1777-79 below. The author was Attorney-General
> of Quebec.

A Pocket Mirror for North America.  12mo.  London ( ? ).

WOOLMAN, JOHN.   The Works of John Woolman, in two Parts: I. A Journal of his Life and Travels, in the Service of the Gospel; II. Considerations on the True Harmony of Mankind, and how it is to be Maintained.   8vo.   London.

> Later editions: Dublin, 1778; again Dublin, 1794. See below.
> Woolman was a Quaker born in America, and one of the earliest preachers against slavery.

> 1778   WOOLMAN, JOHN.   A Journal of the Life, Gospel Labours and Christian Experiences of the Faithful Minister of Jesus Christ. 8vo. Dublin.

1775-1784   ALMON, JOHN.   Almon's Remembrancer.   London.

> The most valuable historically of all the publications, English or American, on the Revolutionary War. This is a series of 17 octavo volumes, published first by John Almon, later by his successor Debrett. Almon's purpose was "to select from all the Public Prints the best account of every material Public Event." He included every authentic paper of the British Ministry of the American Congress.—Waldman.

1776   An authentic Account of the Rise and Progress of the present Contest in America.   To which is added the Discovery of America by Columbus.   8vo.   London.

BOWRIE, THOMAS.   A Dictionary of the Hudson's Bay Indian Language.   Fol.   London.   (8 pp.)

> Allibone gives the author's name as Bowrey and the date 1701.—From Sabin.

CHALMERS, LIONEL.   An account of the Storms and Diseases of South Carolina.   London.

A Compendious Account of the British Colonies in North America, with Map of the Theatre of War in North America.   Fol.   London.

> See Sayer and Bennett under MAPS AND ATLASES.

The Discovery of America, with an Enquiry into the Rise and Progress of the Contest there.   8vo.   London.

The History of North America. Containing an Exact Account of their first Settlement; Their Situation, Climate, Soil, Produce, Beasts, Birds, Fishes, Commodities, Manufactures, Commerce, Religion, Charters, Laws, Governments, Cities, Towns, Ports, Rivers, Lakes, Mountains, and Fortifications. With the Present State of the Different Colonies; and A large Introduction. Map. 12mo. London.

> A capital book. The singular speech on page 82 was composed by Dr. Franklin.—Sabin.

The History of North and South America, Containing, An Account of the first Discoveries of the New World, the Customs, Genius, and Persons of the original Inhabitants, and a particular Description of the Air, Soil, natural Productions, Manufactures and Commerce of each Settlement. Including a Geographical, Commercial, and Historical Survey of the British Settlements, From the earliest Times to the present Period. With an Account of the West Indies and the American Islands. To which is added an Impartial Enquiry into the present American Disputes. 2 vols. Frontispiece. 12mo. London.

> First published in 16 parts.—Sabin.

JEFFERYS, THOMAS. For a geographical description of the whole continent of North America see his *American Atlas,* under MAPS AND ATLASES.

The Lottery Magazine; or, Compleat Fund of Literary, Political and Commercial Knowledge. For August and September, 1776. 8vo. London.

> The number for August contains the Declaration of Independence, probably the earliest publication of it in England. The September number has a description of the City of New York, with a plan.—Sabin.

JEFFERYS, THOMAS. The North-American and the West-Indian Gazetteer, containing An Authentic Description of the Colonies and Islands in That Part of the Globe, shewing their Situation, Climate, Soil, Produce and Trade; with their Former and Present Condition, also An Exact Account of the Cities, Towns, Harbours, Ports, Bays, Rivers, Lakes, Mountains, Number of Inhabitants, . . . Folding map of North-America, with tables of distances of towns and forts, and with folding map of the West Indies. 12mo. London.

> Another edition, 12mo. London, 1778.
> Published towards the commencement of hostilities between America and England, this little volume was designed to enlighten the inhabitants of Great Britain as to the extent, power, and situation of the American Colonies.—Bookseller's Note.

M'ROBERT, PATRICK. A Tour through part of the North Provinces of America: . . . a Series of Letters wrote in . . . 1774 & 1775 . . . 8vo. Edinburgh.

POWNALL, THOMAS (Governor). A Topographical Description of such Parts of North America as are contained in the annexed Map of the Middle British Colonies in North America. Fol. London.

> Reprinted London, 1800.
> This is a republication of the *Map* and *Analysis,* issued by Lewis Evans in 1755; the present having considerable improvements and additions.—Rich, quoted by Puttick and Simpson. Contains interesting accounts of New England and the Southern Colonies.—Bradford.

PUNDERSON, EBENEZER. The Narrative of Mr. Ebenezer Punderson Merchant: Who was drove away by the Rebels in America from his Family and a very considerable fortune in Norwich, in Connecticut. Together with some Letters and Clauses of Letters, wrote to his Family during his absence: Taken from his epistolary Journal. London.

> No copy of this, so far as can be learned, has ever appeared in a catalogue in this country. It was unknown to Sabin and other bibliographers, and is undoubtedly unique.—Bradford.

RAYNAL, GUILLAUME THOMAS (Abbé). For descriptions of English Colonies in North America see his *History of the Settlements and Trade of the Europeans in the East and West Indies,* under WEST INDIES.

RECKITT, WILLIAM. Some Account of the Life and Gospel Labours of John Reckitt. 16mo. London.

> An uncommon little volume of Quaker travels. The author came to America in 1758 and travelled through New England, New Jersey, and spent some time in North Carolina.—Bookseller's Note.

WEIN, PAUL. A Concise Historical Account of all the British Colonies in North America, comprehending their Rise, Progress, and Modern State, particularly of the Massachusets Bay (the Seat of the Present Civil War); together with the other Provinces of New England. Folding map. 8vo. Dublin.

1777 BARROW, WILLIAM. History of the Colonization of the Free States of Antiquity, applied to the present Contest between Great Britain and her American Colonies, with Reflections concerning the Future Settlement of these Colonies. 4to. London.

> Translated into French, Utrecht, 1778. See below.

> 1778 (In French.) Histoire de la Fondation des Colonies des Anciennes Républiques, adaptée à la Dispute présent de la Grande Bretagne avec des colonies Américaines, traduits de l'Anglais. Utrecht.

> The translator was Antoine Marie Cerisier, according to Sabin.

A Compendious Description of the Thirteen Colonies in British America. 12mo. London.

HUTCHINS, THOMAS. Topographical Description of Virginia, Pennsylvania, Maryland, and North-Carolina; containing the Rivers of Ohio, Konhawa, Scioto, Cherokees, Wabash, Illinois, Mississippi. 2 plans and a table of distances. 8vo. London.

> Cited in Bradford as of 1778. Modern edition, Cleveland, 1904. See below. Translated into French, Paris, 1781.
> "The greater part," says Hutchins, "done from my own Surveys preceding and during the last War, and, since in many reconnoitering tours between 1764 and 1770."—Quoted by Sabin. Thomas Hutchins, the author, occupies a unique place in the history of American cartography, being the only incumbent of the civil office of "Geographer of the United States," the position ceasing to exist after his death in 1789.—Burrows Bros. Cat.

> 1904 HUTCHINS, THOMAS. A Topographical Description of Virginia, etc. Edited by Frederick Charles Hicks. Folding maps. Portrait and plates. Cleveland.

MONTCALM, MARQUIS DE. Lettres de Le Marquis de Montcalm; à Messieurs de Berryer et de la Mole, écrites dans les années 1757, 1758, et 1759. Avec une version Angloise. 8vo. London.

PLOTT, ROBERT. An Account of the Discovery of America by the Welsh, more than 300 years before the Voyage of Columbus . . . (in Rev. N. Owen's *British Remains*). 8vo. London.

ROBERTSON, WILLIAM. The History of America (with Notes, Catalogue of Spanish Books and Manuscripts, etc.). Large folding map of South America, the Gulf of Mexico, and the countries of the South Sea. 2 vols. 4to. London.

> 2nd edit., 2 vols., 4to, London, 1778; an edition. 2 vols., 8vo, Cork, 1778; 9th edit., 3 vols., London, 1800. Translated into Italian, Florence, 1777-78; into French, Paris, 1778; into Polish, Warsaw, 1789. See below.
> A popular work which was reprinted several times and translated into many languages. A Spanish translation was stopped by the authorities after two volumes had appeared. Its vivid descriptions and philosophical disquisitions on aboriginal society captivated the literary world, while the outbreak of the American War lent the book pertinent public interest and rendered it more popular than either of the author's previous works.—From Bookseller's Note. The work is said to account for some of the matter found in Keats' sonnet "On Looking into Chapman's Homer." Robertson, with Hume and Gibbon, made up the great triumvirate of historians of the eighteenth century.

> 1800 ROBERTSON, WILLIAM. History of America, containing the History of Virginia and the History of New England. 4 vols. 8vo. London.

> 1777-78 (In Italian.) Storia de America del dottore Robertson, Tradotta dall' originale inglese dall' abbate Antonio Pillori, . . . 4 vols. 12mo. Florence.

1778 (In French.) Histoire de l'Amérique, par Robertson. Traduit de l'anglais par M. E. . . . 4 vols. 12mo. Paris.

> According to Barbier the translator was M. Eidoux.—Barringer.

1789 (In Polish.) Historya Odkrycia Ameryki przez Kolomba, wynafezienia i podbicia Mexyku przez Korteza, podbicia Peru przez Pizarra. Napisana w Francuzkim Jezyku przez Robertsona, a na Polski przelozona i skrocona przez J. J. Jezierskiego Kastelana Lukowskiego. 12mo. Warsaw.

1777-79 MASERES, FRANCIS (Baron). The Canadian Freeholder. 3 vols. 8vo. London.

1778 BARCLAY, JAMES. The Voyages and Travels of . . . containing many surprising Adventures and interesting Narratives, printed for the Author. 8vo. London.

> This contains an interesting description of South Carolina.—Bookseller's Note.

CARVER, JONATHAN. Travels through the Interior Parts of North America in the Years 1766, 1767 and 1768, by Jonathan Carver, Esq., Captain of a Company of Provincial Troops during the late War with France. 2 large folding tinted maps and 4 copperplates. 8vo. London.

> 2nd edit., with an extra plate of the tobacco plant, London, 1779; 8vo, Dublin, 1779; 3rd edit., London, 1781; Edinburgh, 1798; and several reprints in the United States. For fuller title, see the Philadelphia edition, 1796, below. This edition had a second issue the same year. Translated into German, Altenburg and Hamburg, 1780; into French (from the 3rd edition), Paris, 1784; into Dutch, Leyden, 1796. Noticed in the *Monthly Review,* Feb. and April, 1779; in the *Journal des Scavans,* VII, 222; 1780, II, 446. See below.
> The 3rd edition is considered the best. To this is prefixed some account of the author by Dr. Lettsom, a portrait and a colored engraving of the tobacco plant. This valuable work has lately (*i.e.* about 1862) attracted much attention from its description of parts near to the supposed North-west Passage.—Lowndes. After serving in five campaigns against the French in Canada, and narrowly escaping massacre whilst commanding a regiment at Fort William Henry, Carver determined to explore out beyond the Mississippi, and to find an overland route to the Pacific Ocean. He started from Boston in June, 1766, travelled 1300 miles to the most remote British post, surveyed the bays and rivers of Lake Superior, and proceeded as far as the sources of the River St. Pierre. He returned to Boston October, 1768, having travelled 7000 miles.—From Maggs, No. 549. On his projected second expedition he hoped to reach a "river of the west," which may have been the Columbia, called "Oregon." But he was unable to carry out his plan. Modern geographers do not regard his work as wholly reliable, in that some of it may have been made up from other accounts. His journey may have had some influence in moving Jefferson to encourage the Lewis and Clark expedition of 1814. His is said to be the earliest mention of the name Oregon.

> 1796 CARVER, JONATHAN (Capt.). Three Travels through the Interior Parts of North America for more than Five Thousand Miles; containing an Account of the Great Lakes, and all the Lakes, Islands and Rivers, Cataracts, Mountains, Minerals, Soil, and Vegetable Productions of the North West Regions of that Vast Continent, with a De-

scription of the Birds, Beasts, Reptiles, Insects and Fishes Peculiar to the Country, together with a Concise History of the Genius, Manners and Customs of the Indians inhabiting the Lands that lie adjacent to the Heads and to the Westward of the Great River Mississippi; and an Appendix Describing the Uncultivated Parts of America that are the most proper for forming Settlements. 8vo. Philadelphia.

Other editions: 12mo, 1797, Boston; 8vo, 1798, Edinburgh; 12mo, 1802, Charleston; 8vo, 1807, Edinburgh; 8vo, 1808, Edinburgh; 12mo, 1813, Walpole, N. H.; 12mo, 1838, Walpole, N. H.

1780    (In German.)  Reisen durch die inneren Gegenden von Nord-amerika in den Jahren 1766-1768 mit einer Landkarte. Aus dem Englischen. 8vo. Altenburgh; Hamburgh.

1784    (In French.)  Voyage dans les parties intérieures de l'Amérique Septentrionale pendant les années 1766, 1767 et 1768. Ouvrage traduit sur la troisième édition angloise de M. de C., avec des remarques et quelques additions du traducteur. 8vo. Paris.

According to Barbier the translator was M. de Montucla.—Barringer.

1796    (In Dutch.)  Reize door de binnenlanden van Noord-Amerika, door. . . . —Naar den derden Druk uit het Engelsch vertaald door J. D. Pasteur. 2 vols. Met plaaten. 8vo. Leyden.

CASSINI, —— DE.  A Voyage to Newfoundland and Sallee to make Experiments on Mr. LeRoy's Time Keepers (in Chappe d'Auteroche, see below).

CHAPPE D'AUTEROCHE, JEAN.  A Voyage to California to observe the Transit of Venus. With an Historical Description of the Author's Route through Mexico, and the Natural History of that Province. Also, a Voyage to Newfoundland and Sallee, to make Experiments on Mr. Le Roy's Time Keepers. By Monsieur De Cassini. Plan. 8vo. London.

French original, Paris, 1772.  See below.
"At page 104 is the following note: 'We are farther obliged to Don Alzate for a ·ery accurate map of Mexico, which he has delineated from the best accounts of such travellers as he is within reach of consulting in that country. He has also sent us a map, drawn up in Cortes's life time, by which it is evident that in those early times they already knew California to be a peninsula, and the extent of it was as well ascertained as it has since been by later discoveries. Had this map been published in his time, it would have saved many disputes about California.' "—From the Bibliography to the Hakluyt Society edition of Diaz del Castillo (see Diaz del Castillo under 1800, MEXICO). With reference to this error it may be pointed out that Cortes sent out an expedition in 1533 under Jiminez, who first discovered Lower California near the present bay of La Paz. The first to discover its peninsular character was Francesco de Ulloa, who sailed up the Gulf of California in 1539. And the first Spaniard to reach Upper California was Juan Rodriguez Cabrillo. These voyages are recorded in Gomara (see under 1553, MEXICO).

1772    CHAPPE D'AUTEROCHE, JEAN.  Voyage en Californie pour l'Observation du Passage de Vénus sur le Disque du Soleil, le 3 Juin, 1769. Contenant les observations de ce phénomène, & la description historique de la route de l'Auteur à travers le Mexique . . . 4to. Paris.

KELLET, ALEXANDER   A Packet of Prose and Verse: being a Selection from the Literary Productions of Alexander Kellet, Esq. 18mo. London.

> The first thirty-three pages treat of the North American Indians.—Sabin.

Narrative of the Revival of Religion in Virginia, in a Letter to a Friend. 8vo. London. (26 pp.)

RUSSELL, WILLIAM.   The History of America, from its Discovery by Columbus to the Conclusion of the late War, with an Appendix, containing an Account of the Rise and Progress of the Present Unhappy Contest between Great Britain and her Colonies. Numerous plates and maps. 2 vols. 4to. London.

1779   A Brief Account of the Mission established among the Esquimaux Indians, on the Coast of Labrador, by the Church of the Brethren, or Unitas Fratrum. 8vo. London. (33 pp.)

> See same title under 1774 above.

GRIFFITH, JOHN.   A Journal of the Life, Travels, and Labours in the Work of the Ministry of John Griffith. 8vo. London.

> Griffith, a Welsh youth, sailed for America in 1726. The passage took eight weeks. He returned to England in 1766. The time in between was a record of innumerable Quaker meetings in the central sea-board and New England provinces.

HEWATT, ALEXANDER.   An Historical Account of the Rise and Progress of the Colonies of South Carolina and Georgia. 2 vols. 8vo. London.

> The author was sometime resident at Charlestown.—Rich. "Dr. Hewatt's work, published in the third year of America, was evidently written some time prior to the revolutionary period, as it is only in the last chapter that he refers to the colonial claims for Independence. He gives an account of the war with the Yemassee Indians."—Field, quoted by Bradford.

MILES, WILLIAM AUGUSTUS.   Remarks on An Act of Parliament, . . . intituled, "An Act for the Encouragement of the Fisheries" carried on from Great Britain, Ireland, etc., to Newfoundland, etc. For the Repeal or Amendment of which, A Petition . . . has . . . been presented . . . (With the) State of the Fishery in 1771. . . 4to. London. (15 pp.)

1780 CHALMERS, GEORGE. Political Annals of the present United Colonies, from their Settlement to the Peace of 1763; compiled chiefly from records, and authorised often by the insertion of State-Papers. Book I, all published. 4to. London.

> A history of the English-American Colonies prior to 1689 from the materials in the British Public Record Office. The author was an authority of first importance on points of Colonial public law.—Bookseller's Note.

COOPER, ——— (Rev.). The History of North America, Containing, A Review of the Customs and Manners of the Original Inhabitants; The first Settlement of the British Colonies, their Rise and Progress, from the earliest Period to the Time of their becoming United, free and Independent States. Copperplates. 12mo. London.

> Reprinted, 12mo, London, 1789. And frequently printed in the States. See below.

> 1789 COOPER, (Rev. Mr.). The History of North America. Containing a Review of the Customs and Manners of the Original Inhabitants; the First Settlement of the British Colonies, their Rise and Progress, from the earliest period to the Time of their becoming United, free and independent States. Together with, The History of South America. Containing the Discoveries of Columbus, the Conquest of Mexico and Peru, and the other transactions of the Spaniards of the New World. Plates. 2 vols. in 1. 12mo. London.

1781 BARRINGTON, DAINES. For an account of a voyage to explore the coast north of California see his *Miscellanies*, under NORTH PACIFIC.

PETERS, SAMUEL A. (Rev.). A General History of Connecticut, From its First Settlement under George Fenwick, Esq. To its Latest Period of Amity with Great Britain; Including A Description of the Country. And many curious and interesting Anecdotes. To which is added, An Appendix, wherein new and true Sources of the present Rebellion in America are pointed out; together with the particular Part taken by the People of Connecticut in its Promotion. By a Gentleman of the Province. 8vo. London.

> 2nd edit., 8vo, London, 1782. To which is added a Supplement verifying many important statements made by the Author. Illustrated with 8 Engravings. 8 Woodcuts. 12mo. New Haven. " . . . The so-called second edition differs only in the substitution of a new title page."—Sabin.
> Dr. Peters, like most of the Church of England Clergy in America, at the breaking out of the Revolution, espoused the Tory side, and rendering himself, as many thought, too conspicuous in his opposition to the popular cause, was presented with a coat of tar and feathers by the good people of his parish in Connecticut, and compelled to evacuate his living. He came to England and published this book in ridicule of Connecticut. It is often by foreigners regarded as a true history, but is about as much entitled to that character as Knickerbocker's *History of New York*.—Puttick and Simpson.

RAYNAL, GUILLAUME THOMAS (Abbé). The Revolution of America. 8vo. London.

French original, London, 1781. See below.

1781 RAYNAL, GUILLAUME THOMAS (Abbé). Révolution d'Amérique. 12mo. Londres.

1782 ANDERSON, DAVID. Canada, or a View of the Importance of the British American Colonies. 8vo. London.

ARNOLD, C. H. The New and Impartial Universal History of North and South America, and of the Present Trans-Atlantic War . . . 12mo. London.

Reprinted, London, 1790 and 1798.

Considerations on the Sovereignty, Independence, Trade and Fisheries of New-Ireland (formerly known by the name Nova-Scotia) and the Adjacent Islands. 18mo. London.

CREVECOEUR, MICHEL GUILLAUME ST. JEAN DE. Letters from an American Farmer; describing certain provincial Situations, Manners, and Customs, not generally known; and conveying some Idea of the late and present Interior Circumstances of the British Colonies in North America, written for the Information of a Friend in England. Folding maps. 8vo. London.

Other editions: 12mo, Dublin, 1782; a new edition, 8vo, London, 1783; 8vo, Belfast, 1783. Modern editions, New York, 1904; London, 1913; New Haven, 1925. In Everyman's Library, London, 1912, 1926. Translated into French, Paris, 1784; into German, Leignits and Leipzig, 1784. See below.
A writer in the Edinburgh Review (said to be Hazlitt) allows this to be one of the few well-written books produced by American authors.—Puttick and Simpson. "The author was a native of Normandy, of noble birth, and came to the British colonies at the age of 16. Having established himself on a farm near the frontier, he became one of the first victims of the War of Independence, the Indian allies of Great Britain having set fire to and destroyed his property. He wrote his letters during the different epochs of the war, in English. Returning to France, he translated them into French."—Rich. His work is a most pleasing report of the resources and charms of the country when it was far more isolated and exclusively rural than at present. Somewhat like a prose idyl is this record; Hazlitt delighted in its naive innocence, and commended it to Charles Lamb, as well as in the "Quarterly," . . .—Tuckerman, *America and her Commentators,* quoted by Sabin. He came to New York in 1759, served with Montcalm, became naturalized in 1764, and served as French consul from 1783 to 1790, when he went back to France. His pictures of American life induced many colonists to emigrate to the New World. They also provoked hostile commentaries from the British.

1904 CREVECOEUR, HECTOR ST. JOHN DE. Letters from an American Farmer, Reprinted from the original edition. 8vo. New York.

1925 CREVECOEUR, ST. JOHN DE. Sketches of Eighteenth Century America. More "Letters from an American Farmer." Edited by H. L. Bourdin, R. H. Gabriel, and S. T. Williams. 8vo. New Haven.

1784　(In French.) Lettres d'un cultivateur américain, écrites à W. S. (William Seton.) Ecuyer, depuis l'année 1770 jusqu'à 1781, traduites de l'anglois par—(Crevecoeur himself). 2 vols. 8vo. Paris.

1784　(In German.) Sittliche Schilderungen von Amerika, in Briefen eines Amerikanischen Guthbesitzers an einer Freund in England. Aus dem Englischen. 12mo. Leignitz and Leipzig.

> The following item is inserted here for its relation to the foregoing work.

1801　CREVECOEUR, HECTOR SAINT-JOHN DE. Voyage dans la Haute Pensylvanie et dans l'Etat de New-York, par un membre adoptif de la Nation Oneida. Traduit et publié par l'auteur des lettres d'un cultivateur américain. 3 vols. 8vo. Paris.

> This is not, as the title says, a translation but the original work itself, which can be regarded as a continuation of the *Letters from an American Farmer.*

Remarks on the letters from an American Farmer; or, a Detection of the Errors of Mr. J. Hector St. John, pointing out the pernicious Tendency of these Letters to Great Britain. 8vo. London.

KELLET, ALEXANDER. The Mental Novelist, and amusing comparisons; a collection of Histories, Essays, & Novels; containing Historical Description of the Indians in North America, . . . unheard of sufferings of David Menzies amongst the Cherokees and his Surprising Deliverance. . . . 12mo. London.

> The accurate local references indicate this to be a true relation.—Sabin. See also Kellet, under 1778 above.

PAINE, THOMAS. A Letter addressed to the Abbé Raynal, on the Affairs of North America, in which the Mistakes in the Abbé's Account of the Revolution of America are corrected and cleared up. Dublin (reprinted from the Philadelphia edition).

> Another edition, London, 1791 (with *Rights of Man* and *Common Sense*). For this French work see Raynal under 1781 above.

The Polite Traveller: being a Modern View of the Thirteen United States of America. . . . With a short View of the Independent State of Vermont, and of East and West Florida. . . British North America . . . and West Indian Islands. Map. 12mo. London.

STOKES, ANTHONY. View of the Constitution of the British Colonies in North America and the West Indies, at the Time the Civil War broke out on the Continent of America. In which Notice is taken of such Alterations as have happened since that time, down to the Present. With a Variety of Colony Precedents adapted to the British West Indies. 8vo. London.

1783 SHEFFIELD, JOHN BAKER HOLROYD (Lord). Observations on the Commerce of the American States. London.

> Another edit., much enlarged, Dublin, 1784; 6th edit., London, 1784. See below.
>
> This was written in opposition to the bill introduced in 1783 by Pitt proposing to relax the navigation laws in favor of the United States. It was the beginning of a long controversy and finally led to the abandonment of the proposal.—D.N.B. Lord Sheffield was one of the leading authorities of the time in matters relating to commerce and agriculture. He is probably better known as the editor of Gibbon's *Miscellaneous Works and Memoirs.*

> 1784 SHEFFIELD, JOHN (Lord). Observations on the Commerce of the American States, with Appendix containing Tables of Imports and Exports of Great Britain to and from all parts from 1700 to 1782, also Exports of America, . . . 8vo. Dublin.
>
> > This edition contains answers to three pamphlets which appeared after the first publication of the work.—Bookseller's Note.

1784 CHAMPION, RICHARD. Considerations on the Present Situation of Great Britain and the United States of North America, with a view of their future Commercial Connections . . . with Observations on the State of Canada, Nova Scotia, and the Fisheries, with various accounts to shew the State of the Shipping and Trade of this Country and the United States. . . . 8vo. London.

> "If there is any Englishman who does not regret the loss of America, he does not deserve that name; but to suppose, as we have been seriously told, that independence must prove ruinous to America, requires more belief than even Englishmen themselves possess."—Quoted by Quaritch.

FRANKLIN, BENJAMIN. Internal Estate of America. Being a True Description of the Interest and Policy of that vast Continent. 8vo. London ( ?).

> Sabin says that he infers the title of this pamphlet from Sparks' *Franklin*, II, 453, where it is said to be reprinted in Dilly's edition of Franklin's works.

FRANKLIN, BENJAMIN. Two Tracts: Information to those who would remove to America. And, Remarks concerning the Savages of North America. 8vo. London.

> 3rd edit., London, Dublin, 1784. See under 1794 below.
>
> The first of these tracts was written by Dr. Franklin, on account of numerous applications made to him by persons desirous of emigrating to America, with a sanguine expectation, in order that they might not be disappointed on their arrival. The second is a reprint of first item under Franklin above.—Sabin.

FRANKLIN, JAMES. The Philosophical and Political History of the Thirteen United States of America . . . containing a concise Account of their first Settlements, principal Cities, and Towns, Air, Soil, Produce, Manufactures, and Commerce . . . also a General Survey of the Remains of British North America and of the British American and West Indian Islands; to which is prefixed an Account of Persons, Singular Customs and Manners of the Original Inhabitants of America. 8vo. London.

Remarks on the Climate, Produce, and Natural Advantages of Nova Scotia. In a Letter to the Right Hon. the Earl of Macclesfield. Map. 8vo. London. (28 pp.)

SMYTH, J. F. D. A Tour in the United States of America, containing an Account of the Present Situation of the Country, the Population, Agriculture, Commerce, Customs and Manners of the Congress and General Officers in the American Army, and many other very singular and interesting Occurrences. 2 vols. 8vo. London.

> Translated into French, Paris, 1791. See below.
> This is a very important work containing many interesting details concerning Virginia, Maryland, the two Carolinas, Louisiana, Florida, etc.; and many particulars concerning the towns and settlements of Jamestown, Williamsburg, Richmond, etc.; with remarks on the results of the War of Independence.— From Maggs, No. 442. The author, who was a zealous loyalist, lost his property during the war; and his work is said to have been written to gain favor with the Government, by abusing the Americans and magnifying his own losses.— Puttick and Simpson.

> 1791   (In French.) Voyage dans les Etat-unis de l'Amérique, fait en 1784; contenant une description présente de sa Population, Agriculture, Commerce, Coûtumes et Moeurs de ses Habitants, des Nations indiennes, et des principales Villes et Rivières, avec quelques Anecdotes sur plusieurs Membres du Congres et Officiers Généraux de l'armée Américainne. Traduit de l'Anglois par M. de Barentin Monchal. 2 vols. in 1. Paris.

1784-87  PENNANT, THOMAS. Arctic Zoology, etc.

> Portions of this relate to California, Nootka Sound, British Columbia, Canda, Hudson's Bay, Nova Scotia, etc. See under ARCTIC REGIONS.

1785  A Short Account of the First Settlement of the Provinces of Virginia, Maryland, New-York, New-Jersey, and Pennsylvania, by the English. To which is annexed, a Map of Maryland, according to the bounds mentioned in the Charter, and also of the adjacent Country, Anno 1630. 4to. London. (20 pp.)

1786  The American Spy; Letters written in London 1764-65. 12mo. London.

> See also same title under 1791 below.

HOLLINGSWORTH, S. The Present State of Nova Scotia. With a Brief Account of Canada, and the British Islands on the Coast of North America. Map. Edinburgh.

2nd edit., enlarged and corrected, Edinburgh, 1787. Translated into French, Paris, 1787. See below.

1787 (In French.) Etat actuel de la Nouvelle Ecosse. Traduit de l'anglais. 8vo. Paris.

1787 BARTON, BENJAMIN SMITH. Observations on Some Parts of Natural History, To which is Prefixed an Account of Several Remarkable Vestiges of an Ancient Date Which have been discovered in Different Parts of North America. Part I (all published). Folding plate. 8vo. London.

From some remains on the Ohio, resembling the Danish camps in Great Britain, the author conjectures, rather precipitately, that this was the part of America which the Scandinavians discovered in the eleventh century, and named Vinland.—Pinkerton XVII.

CHASTELLUX, FRANCOIS JEAN, MARQUIS DE. Travels in North America, in the years 1780, 1781, and 1782, translated from the French by an English Gentleman, with Notes. 2 maps and 3 plates. 2 vols. 8vo. London.

2nd edit., 2 vols., 8vo. London, 1787; 2 vols., 8vo, Dublin, 1787. French original, Paris, 1786. See below.
The translator was George Greive or Grieve (*Mass. Hist. Soc. Proc.*, 1869, 79, 5-9). The author travelled through the States of Virginia, Pennsylvania, Connecticut, Massachusetts, and New Hampshire, and kept a journal of his expeditions. "His work abounds not only with observations which are of importance, but with details of even the most trifling incidents that roads, inconvenient inns and distracted times usually afford."—Quoted by Maggs, No. 465. See also Brissot de Warville, *Examen*, following just below.

1786 CHASTELLUX, FRANCOIS JEAN, MARQUIS DE. Voyage de M. le Marquis de Chastellux dans l'Amérique Septentrionale dans les années 1780, 1781, & 1782. Map. 2 vols. 8vo. Paris.

1786 BRISSOT DE WARVILLE, JACQUES PIERRE. Examen critique des Voyages dans L'Amérique septentrionale de M. le marquis de Chastellux, ou Lettre à M. le marquis de Chastellux, dans laquelle on réfute principalement ses opinions sur les quakers, sur les nègres, sur le peuple et sur l'homme. 8vo. London.

Remarks on the Travels of the Marquis de Chastellux, in North America. 8vo. London.

The authorship has been attributed to Benedict Arnold. See the *Gentleman's Magazine* for 1787, p. 605; *Monthly Review*, LXXVIII, 43. Referred to by Sabin.

JEFFERSON, THOMAS.  Notes on the State of Virginia. Large folding map of Virginia, Maryland, Delaware, and Pennsylvania, engraved by Neele.  8vo.  London.

> Privately printed edition, Paris, 1784 (?).  Modern reprint of the 1784 edition, Brooklyn, 1894.  Translated into French, Paris, 1786.  See below.
> The English edition was the reproduction of the limited edition, privately printed in Paris about 1784.  The French translation, which is the first published issue, was made by Abbé Morellet, and was in part revised by the author himself.  In it is found the map engraved by Neele which appeared in the edition of 1784.  This map is about two feet square and embraces the country between Albemarle Sound and Lake Erie, comprehending the whole of Virginia, Maryland, etc.  Jefferson went to Paris in 1784 as Minister Plenipotentiary to assist Franklin, and printed the private edition at his own expense to give certain important men in France an adequate conception of the United States.—From Maggs, No. 465.

> 1784 (?)  JEFFERSON, THOMAS.  Notes on the State of Virginia; written in the Year 1781, somewhat corrected and enlarged in the winter of 1782, for the use of a Foreigner of distinction, in answer to certain queries proposed by him respecting 1. Its Boundaries. 2. Rivers. 3. Seaports. 4. Mountains. 5. Cascades and Caverns; 6. Productions—Mineral, Vegetable and Animal; 7. Climate. 8. Population, 9. Military Force, 10. Marine Force, 11. Aborigines, 12. Counties and Towns; 13. Constitution, 14. Laws, 15. Colleges, Buildings and Roads; 16. Proceedings as to Tories; 17. Religion, 18. Manners, 19. Manufactures; 20. Subjects of Commerce; 21. Weights, Measures and Money; 22. Public Revenue and Expences; 23. Histories, Memorials and State Papers.  8vo.  Paris.

> Another edition of the above, Paris, 1785.

> 1894  JEFFERSON, THOMAS.  Reprint of above 1784 edition, " . . . with the Additions, Corrections and Illustrations . . . by the Author . . . together with Notes from other Sources and an Introduction.  Edited by Paul L. Ford.  Map and Plates.  8vo.  Brooklyn.

> 1786  JEFFERSON, THOMAS.  Observations sur la Virginie, par M. J——.  Traduites de l'Anglois.  Map and engravings.  8vo.  Paris.

1787  TARLETON, SIR BANASTRE (General).  For Tarleton's campaigns in the southern provinces see his *History of the Campaigns of 1780-81,* under MILITARY EXPEDITIONS.

THICKNESSE, PHILIP.  Memoirs and Ancedotes by the Lieutenant Governor of Land Guard Fort and unfortunately Father to George Rouchet.  8vo.  (place?)

> This is in fact only the first of three volumes.  Two complete sets are known.  The Georgia matter is complete in the first volume.  He describes life in "Savanha" the building of Savannah on the site of Tom Chachi's Palace, etc.  For his travels in Europe see under 1777, 1784, 1788, WEST EUROPE.

1788 BRISSOT DE WARVILLE, JAMES PETER, and CLAVIERE, ETIENNE. Considerations on the relative Situation of France and the United States of America: shewing the Importance of the American Revolution to the Welfare of France. . . . 8vo. London.

> French original, London, 1787. See below.

> 1787 BRISSOT DE WARVILLE, JACQUES PIERRE, et CLAVIERE, ETIENNE. De la France et des Etats-Unis, ou De l'importance de la Révolution d'Amérique pour le bonheur de la France, des rapports de ce royaume et des Etats-Unis, des avantages réciproques qu'ils peuvent retirer de leur liaisons de commerce, et enfin de la situation actuelle des Etats-Unis. 8vo. London.
>
> > This was later included as vol. 3 of his *Nouveau voyage dans les Etats-Unis*. See under 1792 below.

GORDON, WILLIAM. The History of the Rise, Progress, Establishment of the Independence of the United States of America: including an Account of the late War; and of the Thirteen Colonies, from their origin to that period. Folding maps and plates. 4 vols. 8vo. London.

> Another edition, 3 vols., 8vo, London, 1789.
> This work, the major part of which was written in America, is said to be distinguished by great fidelity.—Puttick and Simpson.

A Review of the Government and Grievances of the Province of Quebec, since the Conquest of it by the British Arms, with Appendix containing extracts from Authentic Papers (bound together with other pamphlets in 1 vol.). 8vo. London.

1789 ANBUREY, THOMAS. Travels through the Interior Parts of America; in a Series of Letters. By an Officer. Maps and Plates. 2 vols. 8vo. London.

> 2nd edit., 2 vols., London, 1791. "This edition is rather better produced than the first." The next edition is of 1792 and bore the author's name. A modern reprint, Boston and New York, 1923. Translated into French, Paris, 1790. See below.
> "Mr. Thos. Anburey, the author of these travels, was an officer under Gen. Burgoyne, whose conduct, in his unfortunate campaign, one object of this publication appears to have been to vindicate. The *Monthly Review* states: 'He sometimes diverts us with anecdotes concerning the speeches, customs, or manners of the people, as he passed among them, which, though droll, or even ridiculous enough, are of that kind to which something similar may be met with in all countries.'" Anburey obtained some of his information from Burgoyne's Narrative, also from Burnaby, Peters, and Smyth.—Maggs, No. 465.

> 1791 ANBUREY, THOMAS. Travels through the Interior Parts of America: In a Series of Letters. By an Officer. A New Edition. Large engraved map of the United States of America, 6 engraved plates, some folding; and a folding plate of eight examples of American paper money. 2 vols. London.

1923 ANBUREY, THOMAS. Travels through the Interior Parts of America with a Foreword by Major-General W. H. Carter. Folding map. 2 vols. Boston and New York.

1790 (In French.) Voyages dans les parties intérieures de l'Amérique, pendant le cours de la dernière guerre, par un officier de l'armée royal. Traduit de l'anglais. Folding map of the United States. 2 vols. 8vo. Paris.

> The translation is attributed to P. L. Lebas.—Maggs, No. 442.

COKE, THOMAS (Rev. Dr.). For tour on the mainland of North America see, under WEST INDIES, this date and also 1791-92; see also under 1793 below.

Emigration to America candidly considered in a Series of Letters from a Gentleman, resident there to his Friend in England. 8vo. London.

An Historical Review of North America, containing a Geographical, Political, and natural History of the British and other European Settlements, By a Gentleman immediately returned from a Tour of that Continent. . . . 2 vols. 18mo. Dublin.

PAUW, M. DE. Selections from "Les Recherches Philosophiques sur les Américains," by Mr. *** (Webb). 8vo. Bath.

> Fifty copies of this work were printed and given to the author's friends.— Puttick and Simpson. French original, Berlin, 1770. See below.

1770 PAUW, M. DE. Recherches Philosophiques sur les Américains. Avec une Dissertation sur l'Amérique et les Américains, par Don Pernetty. Et las Defense de l'Auteur des Recherches contre cette Dissertation. 3 vols. 8vo. Berlin.

The State of the Present Form of Government of the Province of Quebec. With a large Appendix containing Extracts from the Minutes of an Investigation into the past Administration of Justice in that Province. 8vo. London.

1790 COSTANSO,——. An Historical Journal of the Expedition by Sea and Land to the North of California: in 1768, 1769, and 1770; when Spanish Establishments were first made at San Diego and Monte Rey. From a Spanish MS., translated by William Revely, Esq. 2 maps. 4to. London.

> According to Rich, this is a translation of a Spanish manuscript presented to Dr. Dalrymple by Dr. Robertson. The rarity of the original may have rendered it necessary to cause a transcript to be made; according to the *Monthly Review*, the translator has enriched it with notes and two maps.—Sabin.

GAULD, GEORGE.  An Account of the Surveys of Florida, . . . with Directions for Sailing from Jamaica or the West Indies, by the West End of Cuba, and through the Gulf of Florida. To accompany Mr. Gauld's Charts. 4to. London.  (27 pp.)

UMFREVILLE, EDWARD.  The Present State of Hudson's Bay; containing a full Description of that Settlement and the adjacent Country, and a Journal of a Journey from Montreal to New York. 8vo. London.

> Translated into German, Helmstadt, 1791 (by A. W. Zimmermann).
> At page 202 is a "Specimen of Indian Languages spoken in the Inland parts of Hudson's Bay, and between that Coast and the Coast of California."—Puttick and Simpson.

WALTON, WILLIAM.  A Narrative of the Captivity and Sufferings of Benjamin Gilbert and his Family; who were surprised by the Indians, and taken from their Farms, on the Frontiers of Pennsylvania. In the Spring, 1780. 8vo. London.

> First printed at Philadelphia, 1790.
> "Benjamin Gilbert and his family, with that of a neighbour, in all fifteen persons, were captured on the 25th of April, 1780, and did not reach their homes again until the 28th of September, 1782. The Gilberts were a very well known family, especially among the Quakers of Eastern Pennsylvania, and their captivity attracted wide attention. The narrative, published soon after their return, was written by William Walton, a brother of Mrs. Gilbert, from the verbal relations of Gilbert and his family."—Quoted by Maggs, No. 502.

1791  The American Spy: a Collection of 34 Letters written to various persons resident in the Sister Land. 12mo. London.

BOWLES, WILLIAM AUGUSTUS.  Authentic Memoirs of William Augustus Bowles, Esquire, Ambassador From the United Nations of Creeks and Cherokees, to the Court of London. 12mo. London.

> "Mr. Bowles was a native of Maryland; and, being of an unsettled, roving, and enterprising disposition, attached himself to one of the Indian nations, became enamoured of savage life, and married a savage girl; then settled among her friends, and became by adoption an Indian warrior."—Rich. The pamphlet does not state the object of his errand to England.—Sabin.

LONG, JOHN.  Voyages and Travels of an Indian Interpreter and Trader, describing the Manners and Customs of the North American Indians; with an Account of the Posts situated on the River Saint Laurence, Lake Ontario, . . . To which is added, a Vocabulary of the Chippeway Language, names of Furs and Skins, in English and French, a List of words in the Iroquois, Mohegan, Shawnee, and Esquimaux Tongues, and a Table, shewing the Analogy between the Algonkin and Chippeway Languages. Engraved map, "Sketch of the Western Countries of Canada, 1791." 4to. London.

> A modern reprint, Chicago, 1922. Translated into German, Hamburg, 1791; into French, Paris, 1802 (stated by Maggs, No. 465, to be the first French edition). See below.
> The author was in the service of the Hudson's Bay Company in 1768, and journeyed as a fur trader among the Indians of Canada for 19 years. "A most faithful picture of the life and manners of the Indian and Canadian traders. It is also linguistically valuable. He gives a candid account of the injustices perpetrated on the Indians by the British."—Quoted by Maggs, No. 479.

1922    LONG, JOHN.  Voyages and Travels in the Years 1768-1788. Edited . . . with Notes by Milo M. Quaife. Map. Lakeside Classics. Chicago.

1791    (In German.)  See- und Landreisen oder Beschreibung der Sitten und Gewohnheiten der Nordamerikanischen Wilden, ferner ein umständliches Wörterbuch der Chippewaischen und anderen nordamerikanischen Sprachen. Aus dem Englischen mit einer kurzen Einleitung über Canada. Karte von Ebh. A. W. Zimmermann. Band der See- und Landreisen. Hamburg.

1802    (In French.)  Voyages chez différentes nations sauvages de l'Amérique Septentrionale. Traduit de l'Anglois avec des notes et additions intéressantes par J. B. L. Billecocq. 8vo. Paris.


PAGES, PIERRE MARIE FRANCOIS. DE.   For an account of a journey up the Mississippi from New Orleans to Nachitoches, thence overland to Acapulco through Texas and New Mexico, see his *Travels round the World,* under 1792-93, CIRCUMNAVIGATIONS. (The date 1791 is given in Sabin for the first two volumes.)


WILLIAMS, JOHN.   An Inquiry into the Truth of the Tradition concerning the Discovery of America by Prince Madog ab Owen Gwynedd about the year 1170. London.

> For a further discussion of this theme see also Williams under 1792 below.


1792    BARTRAM, WILLIAM.   Travels through North & South Carolina, Georgia, East & West Florida, the Cherokee Country, the Extensive Territories of the Muscogulges, or Creek Confederacy, and the Country of the Choctaws: containing an Account of the Soil and Natural Productions of those Regions, together with Observations on the Manners of the Indians.  Map and plates. 8vo. London.

> First published, Philadelphia, 1791. An edition, Dublin, 1793; 2nd London edit., 1794. A modern reprint, The American Bookshelf series, edited by Mark Van Doren, New York, 1928. Translated into German, Berlin, 1793; into Dutch, Haarlem, 1794-97; into French, Paris, 1799-1801. See below.
> This book of travels is famous both for its intrinsic worth and for its associations with Wordsworth and Coleridge. Bartram presented the American landscape, especially in its tropical aspects, to the earlier romanticists, as Chateaubriand did to the succeeding generation. While Bartram loved to parade his knowledge of botanical nomenclature, he leaves plenty of room for a fasci-

nating narrative of his journies and a valuable description of Indian life. He embarked for Charleston, South Carolina, in April, 1773, and returned to Philadelphia in January, 1778, but he makes no mention of the Revolutionary war then under way. For a study of Bartram as "Interpreter of the American Landscape" see Fagin, under GENERAL REFERENCE.

1793 (In German.) Reisen durch Nord- und Süd-Karolina, Georgien, Ost- und West-Florida, das Gebiet der Tskerokesen, Krihks und Tschaktahs. Aus dem Englischen mit Anmerkungen von E. A. W. Zimmermann. Plate. 8vo. Berlin.

1794-97 (In Dutch.) Reizen door Noord- en Zuid-Carolina, Georgie, Oost- en West-Florida; de Landen der Cherokees, des Muscogulges, of het Creek londgenootschap en het land der Chactaws. Uit het Engelsch vertaald, door J. D. Pasteur. 8 vols. Haarlem.

1799-1801 (In French.) Voyage dans les parties sud de l'Amérique septentrionale; Savoir: les Carolines septentrionale et méridionale la Georgie, les Florides orientale et occidentale, le pays des Cherokées, le vast territoire des Muscogulges, ou de la confédération Creek, et le pays des Chactaws. Contenant de détails sur le sol et les productions naturelles de ces contrées, et des observations sur les moeurs des Sauvages qui les habitent. . . . trad. de l'ang. par P. V. Benoist. Portrait, map and 4 plates. 2 vols. 8vo. Paris.

BRISSOT DE WARVILLE, JAMES PETER. New Travels in the United States of America, performed in 1788. Translated from the French. 8vo. London.

2nd edit., 2 vols., 8vo, London, 1794. French original, 3 vols., 8vo, Paris, 1791. See below. American editions: New York, 1792; Boston, 1797.

In 1787 Brissot was threatened with the Bastile and fled to England, where he came in contact with the Society for the Abolition of Slavery. On his return to France in Feb., 1788, he founded the "Société des amis de noire," and determined to visit the United States to investigate the slavery system there. This work is the result of his visit. Among other matters he gives a long account of Benjamin Franklin, interesting personal details regarding Washington, and also a curious account of how he witnessed Mr. Fitch's experiments on the Delaware with his newly invented steamship, and in a footnote mentions that in England Mr. Rumsey was planning a steam vessel to cross the Atlantic in fifteen days.— Maggs, No. 549. Brissot has been the subject of a number of studies. See Monoghan, *French Travellers in the United States,* under BIBLIOGRAPHIES. See also under 1788 above and 1794 below.

1791 BRISSOT DE WARVILLE, JACQUES PIERRE. Nouveau voyage dans les Etats-Unis de l'Amérique Septentrionale, fait en 1788. 3 vols. vols. 8vo. Paris.

A Description of Kentucky in North America, to which are prefixed Miscellaneous Observations respecting the United States. 8vo. London.

CARTWRIGHT, GEORGE. A Journal of Transactions and Events during a Residence of nearly Sixteen Years on the Coast of Labrador, containing most interesting particulars both of the Country and its Inhabitants not hitherto known. Portrait and charts. 3 vols. 4to. Newark.

A modern account by Wendell Townsend, Boston, 1911. See below. "This journal is written with care and fidelity; the style of the author is plain and manly; . . . and asserts only those circumstances which, from his own observations he knows to be facts. . . . Coleridge highly commended the work." —Quoted by Maggs, No. 502. The work contains interesting accounts of his struggles to make himself an independent trader, as well as of the hunting, fishing, the berries, the natives, his fatal attempt to educate some natives in England for service in his trading with the Eskimos, and the raids on his property by American privateers.

1911 CARTWRIGHT, GEORGE (Captain). Cartwright and his Labrador Journal, edited by C. Wendell Townsend, with Introduction by Dr. Wilfred Grenfell. Illustrations from old engravings, etc., and a map. 8vo. Boston.

EDDIS, WILLIAM. Letters from America, Historical and Descriptive; comprising Occurrences from 1769, to 1777, inclusive. By William Eddis, late Surveyor of the Customs, etc., at Anapolis, in Maryland. 8vo. London.

Valuable as indicating the state of public feeling anterior to the Revolution. "Mr. Eddis's letters are forty in number. The first contains an account of the country, the government, trade, manners, and customs of the inhabitants, followed by others, giving an account of the progress of the war till his departure from New York. The concluding letters narrate the difficulties and dangers which the author experienced, in consequence of his refusing to take the oath tendered him by the Americans."—*Monthly Review*, VIII, 124, quoted by Sabin.

FILSON, JOHN. The Discovery, Settlement, and Present State of Kentucky. And an Introduction to the Topography and Natural History of that Rich and Important Country; also, Colonel Daniel Boon's Narrative of the Wars of Kentucky: with An Account of the Indian Nations within the Limits of the United States, their Manners, Customs, Religion, and their Origin; and the Stages and Distances between Philadelphia and the Falls of the Ohio; from Pittsburgh to Pensacola, and several other Places. . . . Illustrated with a large whole sheet Map of Kentucky from actual Surveys, and a Plan with a Description of the Rapids of Ohio. By Captain Thomas Hutchins, Geographer to the Congress. 8vo. London.

The name of the author is spelled Filsen by Bradford. The above is the first London edition. First printed at Wilmington, 1784: this version translated into French, 8vo, Paris, 1785, with additions, according to Sabin; into German, Leipzig, 1790. See below.
This is also included in Imlay's *Topographical Description*, second and third editions. See Imlay this date below. Filson believed in the existence of a Welsh settlement in this colony under Prince Madoc, in 1170. See *Monthly Review*, XIV, 148.—From Sabin. "The map mentioned in the title seems never to have been published with the book; when found it is supplied from the French version of the book."—Ives' Catalog, quoted by Bradford.

1785 (In French.) Histoire De Kentucke, Nouvelle Colonie à L'Ouest De La Virginie Contenant, 1. La Découverte, l'Acquisition, l'Establissement, la Description topographique, l'Histoire Naturelle, &c. du Territoire: 2. la Relation historique du Colonel Boon, un des premiers Colons, sur les guerres contre les Naturels: 3. l'Assemblée des Piankashaws au Poste Saint-Vincent: 4. un Exposé succinct des Nations Indiennes qui habitent dans les limites des Treize Etats-Unis, de leurs Moeurs et Coûtumes, & des Réflexions sur les Origine; & autres Pièces: Avec une Carte. Ouvrage pour servir de suite aux Lettres d'un Cultivateur Américain. Traduit de l'Anglois de M. John Filson; Par M. Parraud de l'Académie des Arcades de Rome. 8vo. Paris.

> The translator has made some additions; but the map is often deficient—being extracted for insertion as a substitute in the Wilmington edition.—Sabin.

1790    (In German.) Riese nach Kentucke, &c.  24mo.  Leipzig. (This edition is also minus a map.)

IMLAY, GILBERT. A Topographical Description of the Western Territory of North America; containing a succinct account of its Climate, Natural History, Population, Agriculture, Manners and Customs; with an ample description of the several divisions into which the country is partitioned. And an accurate Statement of the various Tribes of Indians that Inhabit the Frontier Country. To which is annexed, a delineation of the Laws and Government of the State of Kentucky. Tending to shew the probable rise and Grandeur of the American Empire. In a Series of Letters to a Friend in England. . . . 8vo.  London.

> 2nd edit., with additions, London, 1793; 12mo, Dublin, 1793. This edition translated into German, Berlin, 1793. Another German version is included in J. G. Forster's *Magazine.*—Sabin. 3rd edit., greatly enlarged, London, 1797. See below.
> This work is in the form of eleven long letters written from Kentucky by one of the early witnesses to the settlement of that State, and describes the conditions of life there, and gives a general account of the now Middle States and the Mississippi basin at the period of the admission of Kentucky into the federal government.—Maggs, No. 465. In the enlarged shape which the work took in the third and last edition, it comprises a most valuable mass of material for the early history of the Western Country, embodying the entire works of Filson, Hutchins, and various other tracts and original narratives. The author's Christian name varies in the title pages.—Sabin. Imlay was a captain in the American army during the Revolutionary War, and commissioner for laying out lands in the backwoods settlements. He was also the ci-devant husband of Mary Wollestonecraft.

1793    IMLAY, GILBERT. A Topographical Description of the Western Territory: to which are added, The Discovery, Settlement and Present State of Kentucky by John Filson, the Adventures of Daniel Boone, the Minutes of the Piankashaw Council, . . . Maps. 8vo. London.

1797    IMLAY, GILBERT. A Topographical Description of the Western Territory . . . To which are added, I. The Discovery, Settlement, and Present State of Kentucky, . . . II. The Indian Nations, . . . III. The Culture of the Indian Corn, . . . IV. Ancient Works, native Inhabitants of the Western Country, by Major J. Hart, . . . V. Louisiana and West Florida, . . . VI. Soil and Timber, . . . VII. Remarks to Settlers, by Dr. Franklin, . . . VIII. Virginia, Pennsylvania, Maryland, and North Carolina, . . . IX. Mr. Patrick Kennedy's Journey up the Illinois River, . . . X. Tenasee, . . . XI. Act for establishing Knoxville, . . . XII. Treaty for free Navigation of the Mississippi, . . . XIII. North American Land Co. . . . Engraved folding maps. 8vo. London.

MORSE, JEDIDIAH. The American Geography; or, a View of the Present Situation of the United States of America. . . . With a particular Description of Kentucky, the Western Territory and Vermont . . . To which is added, an Abridgement of the Geography of the British, Spanish, French, and Dutch Dominions in America and the West Indies. . . . Large folding maps. 8vo. London.

Another edition, Dublin, 1792; a new edition, revised, corrected, and greatly enlarged by the author, and illustrated with 25 maps, including John Filson's large and important map of Kentucky, 4to, London, 1794; reprinted, London, 1798.

Included in the volume is a short account of new discoveries in the South Seas.—From Maggs, No. 429. The plan of Washington, shewing the "town lots," is one of the earliest printed maps of the city; that of the "Tennessee Government," dated 1794, is, possibly, the earliest.—Robinson, No. 56.

PHILLIPS, J. A General History of Inland Navigation, Foreign and Domestic: containing a Complete Account of the Canals executed in England, with considerations of those projected. Map and 4 plates. 4to. London.

Another edition, London, 1794.
This contains an account of the canals of North and South America.—Sabin.

Some Transactions between the Indians and Friends in Pennsylvania, in 1791-2. 8vo. London.

State of the Newfoundland Fishery in the years 1699, 1700, 1701, 1714, 1715, 1716, 1749, 1750, 1751, 1764 to 1774, 1784 to 1791, taken from the Returns of the Admirals who commanded on that Station. Large folio. (n.p. given by bookseller.)

VARLO, CHARLES. A Twelve Month's Tour of Observation through America, by an English Gentleman. In *Miscellany of Knowledge;* a new work by several English Gentlemen. 8vo. London.

2nd edit., London, 1792.
Varlo was an agriculturist who visited America in 1784 to establish his claim to the governorship of New Jersey under the charter granted to his ancestor, Sir Edmund Plowden, by Charles I. He writes "Business . . . brought me up to . . . America . . . Having a claim . . . to a province therein called New Albion, but corruptly . . . known by the name of East and West Jerseys, being 120 miles square." Varlo's remarkable claim was disallowed (see Winsor III, 476).—Quaritch.

WILLIAMS, JOHN. Further Observations on the Discovery of America, by Prince Madog ab Owen Gwynedd about the Year 1170, containing the Account given by General Bowes, the Creek or Cheroke Indian, lately in London, and by several others, of a Welsh Tribe or

Tribes of Indians, now living in the Western parts of North America. 8vo. London.

See Bowles under 1791 above.

1793 CAMPBELL, P. Travels in the Interior Inhabited Parts of North America, in the years 1791 and 1792. In which is given an account of the Manners and Customs of the Indians, and the present War between them and the Federal States, the Mode of Life and System of Farming among the new Settlers of both Canadas, New York, New England, New Brunswick, and Nova Scotia; interspersed with anecdotes of People, Observations on the Soil, Natural Productions, and political Situation of these Countries. Copperplates. 8vo. Edinburgh.

A curious and entertaining book. "The author set out from the Highlands of Scotland, with the intention to explore the interior inhabited parts of North America, attended with an old faithful servant, a dog and a gun. Only, as he travelled much in wilderness and in birch bark canoes, through lakes and rapid streams, where the mind could not at all times be inattentive to safety, he wrote on canoes and on the stumps of trees occasionally, as he went along."—Preface, quoted by Sabin.

COKE, THOMAS (Rev. Dr.). Extracts of the Journals of the Rev. Dr. Coke's Three Visits to America, 1790. And Extracts of the Journals of the Rev. Dr. Coke's Five Visits to America. 12mo. London.

"Dr. Coke was an eminent Wesleyan missionary, educated at Oxford. In 1784 he visited America, and made altogether nine visits to the United States."— Allibone, quoted by Sabin.

GOLDSON, WILLIAM. For an historical Abridgement of Discoveries in the North of America, see his *Observations on the Passage between the Atlantic and Pacific Oceans,* under NORTHWEST PASSAGE.

RAMSAY, DAVID. The History of the Revolution of South Carolina from a British Province to an Independent State. 2 vols. 8vo. London.

This is a new edition of a work published at Trenton, N. J., 1785.

REEVES, JOHN. History of the Government of the Island of Newfoundland, with an Appendix, containing the Acts of Parliament made respecting the Trade and Fishery, by J. Reeves, Chief Justice of the Island. 8vo. London.

The author gave the profits arising from the publication for the suffering clergy of France, refugees in the British Dominions. The preface states that the history was written from information derived from the Board of Trade and from the Registers of the Committee of Council for Trade and Plantations.— Bookseller's Note. Reeves was the Chief Justice of Newfoundland.

1794　BRISSOT DE WARVILLE, JACQUES PIERRE, AND CLAVIERE, ETIENNE. The commerce of America with Europe; particularly with France and Great Britain, . . . Shewing the Importance of the American Revolution to the Interests of France. . . . Translated from the last French edition, revised by Brissot, and called the 2nd volume of his View of America. 8vo. London.

COGHLAN, MARGARET. Memoirs of Mrs. Coghlan (Daughter of the late Major Moncrieffe), written by Herself. . . . Being interspersed with anecdotes of the Late American and present French War. 12mo. Dublin. (a reprint).

 This book is of particular interest, as it contains information relative to Washington's early life. Margaret Coghlan, nee Moncrieff, was, according to her own account, married at New York to an American army officer at the age of fourteen. She was at one time intimate with Aaron Burr and at another formed part of George Washington's family circle. In view of this latter connection it is difficult to credit a remark made concerning her in the "Gentleman's Magazine"——that she was "celebrated in the annals of gallantry."—Robinson, No. 56, quoted by Bradford.

COOPER, THOMAS. Some Information respecting America, collected by Thomas Cooper, late of Manchester. Folding map of the Middle States of America by T. Conder. 8vo. London.

 2nd edit., London, 1795. Translated into French, Hamburg, 1795. See below. The author was afterwards president of the College of South Carolina.

 1795　(In French.) Renseignements sur l'Amérique, rassemblés par Thomas Cooper, . . . traduits de l'Anglais avec une carte. 8vo. Hamburg.

FRANKLIN, BENJAMIN. Information for those who would remove to America. By Dr. Benjamin Franklin. 8vo. London.

 Another edition, 4to, London, 1796.
 Sparks says it was first published in England in 1784, and afterwards in 1787 included in Dilly's edition of Franklin's works. See Sparks's Franklin, II, 450. Sabin. See under 1784 above.

HODGKINSON, ——. Letters on Emigration, By a Gentleman, lately returned from America. 8vo. London.

 The chief interest in this work lies in the Account of the Inland State of Kentucky, contained in the last of a series of five letters. The first four relate to the emigrants' voyage out to America, various particulars concerning emigration to the Southern States, etc., and accounts of New York and Philadelphia. The author was no friend to emigration.—Maggs, No. 465.

LOSKIEL, G. H. History of the Mission of the United Brethren among the Indians in North America, in 3 parts, translated from the German by Christian Ignatius La Trobe. Map. 8vo. London.

> German original, Barby and Leipzig, 1789. See below.
> The labours of this mission lay chiefly among the Delawares, the Nauti-kokes, the Shawanese, and other tribes in Pennsylvania and New York, upon which it is the best authority, both as to tradition and facts, having been drawn up from the accounts furnished by Gottlieb Spangenburg and David Zeisberger, missionaries among the Indian tribes during 40 years. Among the subjects nar-rated is that of the massacre of Gnadenhutten and Salem. The translator has omitted some matter relative to former enemies of the mission.—Bookseller's Note.

> 1789 LOSKIEL, G. H. Geschichte der Mission der Evangelischen unter den Indianern in Nordamerika. 8vo. Barby and Leipzig.

Thoughts on Emigration in a Letter from a Gentleman in Philadelphia to his Friend in England. 8vo. London.

1795 COXE, TENCH. View of the United-States of America, in a Series of Papers, written at various Times between the Years 1787 and 1794. With Authentic Documents, exhibiting Exports, Imports, Fisheries, Navigation, Ship-Building, Manufactures and General Improvement. 8vo. London.

> Originally printed at Philadelphia, 1794.

CROOKSHANKS, JOHN. For matter relating to various parts of America see *The Conduct and Treatment of John Crookshanks,* under NAVAL EXPEDITIONS.

HEARNE, SAMUEL. A Journey from Prince of Wales Fort, in Hud-son's Bay, to the Northern Ocean, undertaken by order of the Hud-son's Bay Company for the Discovery of Copper Mines, a North-West Passage, . . . in 1769-1772. Maps and plates. 4to. London.

> Another edition, Dublin, 1796. Translated into Dutch, the Hague, 1797; into German, Halle, 1797; into French, Paris, 1798; into Swedish, Stockholm, 1798. See below.
> A very important work. "It was the first of a long series of Arctic voyages and travels which reflect so much credit on the British Press. Its publication is due to the celebrated navigator La Pérouse, who captured Fort Albany, Hudson's Bay, and found the Manuscript of Hearne. The fort was afterward surrendered to the British, but La Pérouse stipulated for the publication of this work by the Hudson's Bay Company, which stipulation was honorably fulfilled in this beautiful vol-ume. The author will be remembered as the first white man that ever gazed on the dreary expanse of the Arctic or Frozen Ocean from the Northern shores of the Continent of America."—Quoted by Maggs, No. 549. The Hudson's Bay Company had long been interested in investigating the reports of copper mines to the north, and somewhat in the possibility of the Northwest Passage. Hearne made three starts, the last of which led to the mouth of the Coppermine River on the shore of the Arctic Ocean. These covered the years 1769-1772. On his

return he discovered what has been decided to be the Great Slave Lake. No further efforts were made in this direction for some time by the Company. Students of literature will remember this account for its connection with Wordsworth's "Complaint of a Forsaken Indian Woman."

1797    (In Dutch.)  Landreis van 't Prins van Wallis Fort aan Hudsons-Baii naar den Noorder Oceaan. Uit het Engelsch vertaalt met aanmerkungen van J. R. Forster. Maps. 2 vols. 8vo. The Hague.

1797    (In German.)  Reise von Fort Prinz Wallis in der Hudsonbai nach dem nördlichen Weltmeer. Aus dem Englischen von M. Chr. Sprengel. 8vo. Halle.

1798    (In French.)  Voyage de Samuel Hearne, du Fort du Prince de Galles, dans le Baie de Hudson, à l'Océan Nord, entrepris par ordre de la Compagnie de la Baie de Hudson, dans les années 1769, 1770, 1771 et 1772 et exécuté par terre pour la découverte d'un passage au nord-ouest. Traduit de l'anglais (by A. J. N. Lallemand). 2 vols. 8vo. Paris.

1798    (In Swedish.)  Resa til Norra Americas Ishaf samt En obesant Engelsman, samt Resor Bland Canadas Wildar, utgivne af Le Long Jamte Edvard Umfrevilles Bestrisning um Hudsons Baie och tilgränsande Wildar. 8vo. Stockholm.

A Letter descriptive of the different Settlements in the Province of Upper Canada. 12mo. London.

"This pamphlet gives a very advantageous account of the country of Upper Canada, and of the Settlers there, subjects to the British Government; it also contains some particulars relative to the American Indians."—*Monthly Review,* XX, 479, quoted by Sabin.

WINTERBOTHAM, WILLIAM.  Historical, Geographical, Commercial and Philosophical View of the American United States, and of the European Settlements in America and the West Indies. Portraits and Maps. 4 vols. 8vo. London.

This was written while the author was a prisoner in Newgate.—Puttick and Simpson.

1796   EUSTACE, J. S.  (Major-General).  Official and Private Correspondence of Major General J. S. Eustace, . . . Colonel and Adjutant-General in the Service of Georgia during the American War and Marechal-de-Camp in the Armies of the Republic of France . . . 8vo.  Paris.

GAULD, GEORGE.  Observations on the Florida Kays, Reef, and Gulf; Also, a Description of the Coast of West Florida between the Bay of Spiritu Santo and Cape Sable. 4to. London. (28 pp.)

HILLS, JOHN.  Plan of Philadelphia. 4to. London.

HULL, JOHN SIMPSON. Remarks on the United States of America, drawn up from his own Observations, and from the Observations of other Travellers. 8vo. Dublin.

The date is in the neighborhood of 1796.

LA ROCHEFOUCAULD-LIANCOURT, FRANCOIS ALEXANDRE FREDERIC, DUC DE. A comparative View of mild and sanguinary Laws; and the good Effects of the former exhibited in the Present Economy of the Prisons of Philadelphia. 12mo. London. (48 pp.)

A reprint of the Philadelphia edition of 1796. The same author also wrote *Des Prisons de Philadelphie,* printed at this same city in the same year. He was an enlightened Frenchman much interested in the improvement of agricultural economy, and gave Arthur Young every facility for studying his farming methods on his estates in France (see Young under 1792, WEST EUROPE). See also La Rochefoucauld-Liancourt under 1799 below.

PAYNE, JOHN. Geographical Extracts, forming a General View of Earth and Nature. In Four Parts. . . . Maps. 8vo. London.

This contains many interesting notifications on the physical and geographical positions of North America.—Sabin.

WANSEY, HENRY. The Journal of an Excursion to the United States of North America in the Summer of 1794. Profile view of Washington and aqua-tint view of the State House at Philadelphia. 8vo. Salisbury.

2nd edit., with additions, Salisbury, 1798.

1797  ABBOT, JOHN, and SMITH, SIR JAMES EDWARD. The Natural History of the Rarer Lepidopterous Insects of Georgia. Including their Systematic Characters, the Particulars of their Several Metamorphoses, and the Plants on which they feed. 104 colored plates. 4 vols. 4to. London.

Sir James Edward Smith was founder of the Linnaean Society.

BURDER, GEORGE. The Welch Indians; or, a Collation of Papers, respecting a people whose Ancestors emigrated from Wales to America, in the year 1170, with Prince Madoc, . . . And who are now said to inhabit a beautiful Country on the West side of the Mississippi. Dedicated to the Missionary Society by George Burder. 8vo. London. (35 pp.)

No date on the title, but the dedication bears the date of March 10, 1797.—Sabin.
There are Irish claims to the discovery of America by St. Brendan in the fifth century, which make later pretenders to the honor mere upstarts. But the

Irish never fathered themselves upon any tribe of Indians. To be on the safe side, however, one should offer his congratulations to these Welsh Indians. For still earlier pretensions to the discovery of America, this time by the Chinese, see Leland under 1875 below.

CRESPEL, EMANUEL. Travels in North America, . . . with a Narrative of His Shipwreck, and Extraordinary Hardships and Sufferings on the Island of Anticosti; and an Account of that Island, and of the Shipwreck of his Majesty's Ship Active, and Others. 12mo. London.

GRAHAM, J. A. A Descriptive Sketch of the Present State of Vermont, one of the United States of America. 8vo. London.

> The author at the time of publication of this work was in England, as agent of the Episcopal Church of Vermont to the Society for Propagating the Gospel in Foreign Parts.—Quoted by Maggs, No. 625.

PHILLIPS, CATHERINE. Memoirs of the Life of Catherine Phillips; to which are added some of her Epistles. 8vo. London.

> Chapter IV contains minutes of her travels, labors, and sufferings in America, etc.—Sabin.

TURNBULL, ROBERT J. A Visit to the Philadelphia Prison . . . containing also an Account of the Gradual Reformation and Present State of the Penal Laws of Pennsylvania, with Observations on . . . Capital Punishments. Appendix of Tables. 8vo. London.

1798 ALLEN, IRA. The Natural and Political History of the State of Vermont. To which is added, An Appendix, containing Answers to Sundry Queries, addressed to the author. Map of the State. 8vo. London.

> See *Monthly Review,* XXIX, New Series, p. 260.—Sabin. The author was Major-General of the Militia in the State of Vermont.

BEATTY, —— (Rev.). For an account of his mission westward of the Alleghany Mountains see Brainerd under 1765, the 1798 edition.

A Description of the Island of St. John, in the Gulf of St. Lawrence, North America; with a map of the Island, and a few cursory Observations respecting the Climate, Natural Productions and Advantages of its Situation, in regard to Agriculture and Commerce. By a Person many years resident there. Map. 8vo. London.

> The date of publication is problematical.

The Present State of Nova Scotia and Canada. 8vo. London.

SCOTT, JOB. Journal of the Life, Travels, and Gospel Labours. 8vo. Warrington.

1799 HOMER, ARTHUR. Proposals for Printing by Subscription a new work for the benefit of a Public Institution, entitled Bibliotheca Universalis Americana, or an universal American Library; containing a General Catalogue of Publications relating to America and the West Indies, from the first Discovery of those Countries by Columbus in 1492 to the end of the present Century. Fol. London. (4 pp.)

> "This promising project of a General Bibliotheca Americana in two quarto Volumes of 500 pages each, price two pounds two shillings, or $16.00 in America, was never carried out although Mr. Homer prints the names of above 200 subscribers, a respectable list headed by Rufus King, the American Minister, and including Gov. Franklin of New Jersey, Richard Penrose, etc."—Stevens. If the reader will consult the preface to Stevens' *American Bibliographer* he will perhaps be inclined to run a parallel. The original MS. of this work is now at Harvard College.—Sabin.

LA ROCHEFOUCAULT-LIANCOURT, FRANCOIS ALEXANDRE FREDERIC, DUC DE. Travels through the United States of America, the Country of the Iroquois, and Upper Canada, in the years 1795, 1796, and 1797; with an Authentic Account of Lower Canada. . . . (translated by H. Newman), 4 large maps and several tables. 2 vols. 4to. London.

> 2nd edit, 4 vols., 8vo, London. French original, Paris, 1799. See below.
> This contains a description of the Senecas, and other Indians in the vicinity of Buffalo, and a narrative of the captivity of "Mr. Johnson, of Virginia," among the Shawnees in 1794, dictated to the author by the captive himself.—Robinson, No. 56, quoted by Bradford. The author was an exiled French nobleman, and his work is one of the source books for American history at the close of the eighteenth century. The first volume was originally intended as the complete work and bears no reference to volume number. The second volume is called "Vol. II, containing the tour through Virginia, Pennsylvania, the Jerseys, and New York."—Maggs, No. 562. This gives a tolerably fair picture of America at this period, with respect to agriculture, national and domestic habits. —Lowndes. The translator appears to have executed his task faithfully, and to be well acquainted with the country described. His notes frequently increase the information, and sometimes correct the errors of the original.—Rich, quoted by Sabin.

> 1799 LA ROCHEFOUCAULT-LIANCOURT, DUC DE. Voyage dans les Etats-Unis d'Amérique, fait en 1795, 1796 et 1797. Folding maps and tables. 8 vols. 8vo. Paris.

LAWSON, JAMES. Private Case before the House of Lords, between James Lawson and Jno. Tait, relative to Estates in the Province of Maryland, and to tracts of Land on the Potomack and Occoquan in Virginia, held by John Sempill, with full descriptions of the Estates which were purchased by Col. Ewell. Privately printed. Fol. London. (40 pp.)

A Short State of the Countries and Trade of North America. Claimed by the Hudson's Bay Company, under Pretense of a Charter for Ever, of Lands without Bounds or Limits, and an exclusive Trade to those un-bounded Seas and Countries; Shewing the Illegality of the said Grant, and the Abuse they have made of it; and the Great Benefit Britain may obtain by settling those Countries, and extending the Trade amongst the Natives by civilizing and incorporating with them, and laying a Foundation for their becoming Christians and industrious Subjects of Great-Britain; . . . 8vo. London. (44 pp.)

SMYTH, DANIEL WILLIAM. A Short Topographical Description of His Majesty's province of Upper Canada, in North America. To which is annexed a Provincial Gazetteer. Folding table of distances. 8vo. London.

STANTON, DANIEL. A Journal of the Life, Travels, and Gospel La-bours of a faithful Minister of Jesus Christ, Daniel Stanton, late of Philadelphia . . . with the testimony of the Monthly Meeting of Friends in that City concerning him. London.

WELD, ISAAC. Travels through the States of North America and the Provinces of Upper and Lower Canada, 1795-97. 16 plates and maps. 4to. London.

> 2nd edit., 2 vols., 8vo, London, 1799; 3rd edit., 2 vols., 8vo, London, 1800; 4th, London, 1800. Translated into French, Paris, 1799; into German, Berlin, 1800. See below.
> Weld arrived in America Nov., 1795, and "accompanied by a faithful serv-ant, sometimes on horseback, sometimes on foot or in a canoe, he made his way (often under the guidance of Indians) through the vast forests and along the great rivers. He narrowly escaped shipwreck on Lake Erie and experienced all the adventures incident to passing through an unsettled country. While in the towns he mixed in the best society, and had the privilege of meeting George Washington. He paid a visit to Mt. Vernon, and meditated upon the slaves' cabins that disfigured the prospect. . . ."—From Maggs, No. 442.

> 1799　(In French.) Voyage au Canada, pendant les années 1795-97. Large folding map of the East United States and Canada, and 11 engraved plates, including views of Niagara Falls, Mohawk Falls, River Pa-towmac, Town of Bethlehem, etc. 3 vols. Paris.

> 1800　(In German.) Reisen durch die vereinigten Staaten von Nord-Amerika und durch die Provinzien Ober- und Unter-Kanada, 1795-97. 4 fold-ing plates in aquatint. 2 vols. Berlin.

1800 BARRY, THOMAS. Narrative of the Singular Adventures and Captivity of Mr. Thomas Barry among the Munsipi Indians, in the unexplored regions of North America, during the years 1797, 1798, and 1799; including the Manners, Customs, etc., of that Tribe; also a particular Account of his Escape, accompanied by an American Female; the extraordinary Hardships they encountered, and their safe Arrival in London. Written by himself. Colored plate. 12mo. London.

The Happy Negro, being a true Account of a very extraordinary Negro, in North America, and of an interesting Conversation he had with a very respectable Gentleman from England. 8vo. London.

> The negro was a slave of a Quaker master.—Maggs. No. 502.

OLIPHANT, EDWARD. The History of North America and its United States. Including also, a Distinct History of each Individual State; the Manners and Customs, Trade, Commerce, Religion, and Government; Manufactures and Agriculture, Climate, Soil, and Produce with new Tables of the whole of their Imports and Exports, Revenue, Debt, Expenditure, Currency of Coins, . . . To which is annexed, An Account of New Discoveries. Map. 8vo. London.

> 2nd edit., London, 1801.
> Extracted from Jedidiah Morse's *History of America,* without acknowledgement.—Sabin.

WASHINGTON, GEORGE. Letters from His Excellency George Washington, President of the United States, to Sir John Sinclair, on Agricultural and other Interesting Topics, engraved from the Original Letters so as to be an Exact Facsimile. London.

> Sir John Sinclair was the famous British agriculturist, president of the Board of Agriculture, who initiated sheep-shearing, introduced improved methods of tillage and new breeds of live stock in northern Scotland. He carried out a "Statistical Account of Scotland (1791-99)" and a system of county reports for Great Britain. He also superintended the publication of Macpherson's Ossianic transcripts.—D.N.B.

## ADDENDA

1801 MACKENZIE, ALEXANDER. Voyages from Montreal through the Continent of North America to the Frozen and Pacific Oceans in the years 1789 and 1793. Portrait and 3 folding maps. 4to. London.

> Modern reprint with Introduction and footnotes by Milo M. Quaife, New York, 1931. Translated into French, Paris, 1802; into German, Berlin, 1802. See below.

This is a fascinating account of the descent of the river named after this intrepid explorer, who was the first white man to navigate its length from its source in the Great Slave Lake to its mouth. This part of the journey took from the last of June, 1789, to July 16, when he began the arduous return trip. On the way back he heard reports of the western sea and of another great river, likely the Yukon, and of white traders, who may have been those exploring the coast. His trip from Fort Chipewyan to the Arctic and return lasted about three months and a half. Having resolved to continue exploration to the west, he returned to England to purchase instruments in preparation for the difficult task ahead of him. He left Fort Chipewyan on October 12, 1792. Working his way up the Peace River he finally established winter quarters. In the spring he continued up across the Rocky Mountain Divide, and after many hazardous experiences reached the Pacific Ocean by way of the Bella Coola river. The vast region of the Rocky Mountains and the coastal zone was thus opened up at last and Mackenzie won to the top rank of explorers on the American continent.

1931   MACKENZIE, ALEXANDER.  Voyage to the Pacific Ocean in 1793. Introduction and Notes by Milo M. Quaife. Frontispiece and map. New York.

1802   (In French.)  Voyages d'Alexandre Mackenzie, dans l'Intérieur de l'Amérique Septentrionale, faits en 1789, 1792, et 1793 . . . Précédés d'un Tableau historique et politique sur le commerce des Pelleteries, dans le Canada. Traduit de l'anglais, par J. Castéra, avec des Notes et un Itinéraire, tirés en partie des papiers du vice-amiral Bougainville. Portrait and a large folding map. 3 vols. 8vo. Paris.

1802   PRIEST, WILLIAM.  Travels in the United States, 1793-97, with his Journals of Two Voyages across the Atlantic. 8vo. London.

An interesting account of nearly four years' travel in the United States of America. The author was a musician attached to a theatrical company.—Maggs, No. 549.

1803   DAVIS, JOHN.  Travels of Four Years and a Half in the United States of America; During the Years 1798, 1799, 1800, and 1802. 8vo. London.

Two modern editions, New York, 1909; Boston, 1910. See below.

1909   DAVIS, JOHN.  Travels of Four Years and a Half in the United States of America during 1798, 1799, 1800, 1801, and 1802, with an introduction and notes by A. J. Morrison.  New York.

1910   DAVIS, JOHN.  Travels of John Davis in the United States of America, 1798 to 1802. Edited by John Vance Cheney (privately printed and sold by subscription to members of the Bibliophile Society). 2 vols. 8vo. Boston.

1805   PARKINSON, RICHARD.  Tour in America, 1798-1800: Exhibiting Sketches of Society and Manners and the American System of Agriculture. 2 vols. 8vo. London.

Parkinson was acquainted with Washington, and makes interesting observations on his handling of negroes and estate management at Mt. Vernon. His book contains also lengthy accounts of the murder of Col. Crawford by the Indians, near the Sandusky River, the difficulties of emigrants, conditions of labor, etc.— Bookseller's Note.

1806 TALLEYRAND-PERIGORD, CHARLES MAURICE CAMILLE, MARQUIS DE. Memoir concerning the Commercial Relations of the United States with England . . . to which is added An Essay upon the Advantages to be derived from new Colonies in the existing Circumstances. . . . 8vo. London.

> French original, Paris, 1799. See below.

> 1799 TALLEYRAND-PERIGORD, C. M. C., MARQUIS DE. Mémoir sur les relations commerciales des Etats-Unis avec l'Angleterre, par le citoyen Talleyrand. Lu le 15 germinal an 5. (Institut national des sciences et arts. Mémoires. Sciences morales et politiques. tome 2.) 4to. Paris.

> Reprinted, London, 1808.

1807 HERIOT, GEORGE. Travels through the Canadas, containing a Description of the Picturesque Scenery on some of the Rivers and Lakes with an Account of the Productions, Commerce, and Inhabitants of those Provinces. To which is subjoined a comparative View of the Manners and Customs of several of the Indian Nations of North and South America. Map and 27 aquatint plates. 4to. London.

> Part Second contains a minute description of various nations of American aborigines. The last thirty-one pages are filled with Father Raslé's Vocabulary of the Algonquin language. An extended review, amounting to an abridgement of the book, is in Phillips' Voyages Vol. vii. See also *Edinburgh Review*, xi. 212 —Bookseller's Note. Heriot was postmaster-general of upper Canada. As he took his orders from London, he was frequently at variance with Governor Sir George Drummond.

1808-1814 LA ROCHE, JOHN FRANCIS DE. Voyage of . . . to the Countries of Canada, Saguenay, etc. Begun in 1542. In Pinkerton XII, 675-677.

ROBERVAL, ——. Voyage of . . . into Saguenay in 1543. In Pinkerton XII, 677-678. (A fragment.)

The Voyages and Navigations of the English Nation to Virginia and Several Descriptions thereof. Chiefly at the Charges of the Hon. Sir Walter Raleigh, etc. In Pinkerton XII, 560-628. (Taken from Hakluyt.)

> This includes the voyage of Philip Amadas and Arthur Barlow in 1584; Sir Richard Grenville, 1585; Relief Ship to Raleigh's Colony, 1586; Voyage to transport the second colony, 1587; John White into the West Indies, 1590.

1809 HENRY, ALEXANDER. Travels and Adventures in Canada and the Indian Territories, between the years 1760 and 1776. New York.

> Modern editions: Boston, 1901; Lakeside Classics, Chicago, 1921. There is also an abridged edition in the Lakeside Classics. See below.
> The author escaped from the massacre at Detroit in the war occasioned by the conspiracy of Pontiac. But he had a long experience of captivity with the Northern Indians.

> 1901 HENRY, ALEXANDER. Travels and Adventures in Canada and the Indian Territories, 1760-1776. New edition edited by James Bain. 8vo. Boston.
>
> > Of this important volume—the original edition is of great rarity —only this well edited reprint, which is also scarce, and the abridged edition in the Lakeside Classics can be had. Only 250 copies were printed.—Bookseller's Note. The work has much to do with fur-hunting.

1813 GERROUD, JOHN. Poetical Works, with his Life and Travels in America and Nova Scotia, written by himself, with a portrait of the author shooting in a wood, by John Kay, engraved by R. Scott. 8vo. Leith.

> Gerroud, blacksmith, born near Dumfries, 1765, was an eccentric character. His work includes two poems on Burns.—From Bookseller's Note.

1827 JOHNSTON, CHARLES. A Narrative of the Incidents Attending the Capture, Detension and Ransom of Charles Johnston of Botetourt, W. Va., who was made prisoner by the Indians, on the River Ohio, in the year 1790. New York.

1842 VAN SCHAACK, H. C. The Life of Peter Van Schaack ,embracing selections from his Correspondence and other Writings, during the American Revolution, and His Exile in England. 8vo. London (?).

1843 MILLER, JOHN. A Description of the Province and City of New York with plans of the city and several forts as they existed in the year 1695. Now first printed from the original MS. 8vo. London.

> An edition edited by J. G. Shea, New York (?), 1862.

1847 SEAVER, JAMES E. Deh-He-Wa-Mis: or, A Narrative of the Life of Mary Jemison; otherwise called the White Woman, who was taken captive by the Indians in 1755, and who continued with them seventy-eight years. Containing an Account of the Murder of her Father and his Family, her Marriage and Sufferings, Indian Barbarities, Customs and Traditions. Carefully taken from her own words. . . . Also Historical Sketches of the Six Nations, the Genesee Country, etc., by Ebenezer Mix. 12mo. Shebbear, Devon.

Modern reprint, New York, 1929.

This story of the first white woman to see the Ohio River is one of the most important sources of our knowledge of the Iroquois, and especially of the Indian campaigns of the Revolution.—Robinson, No. 41.

1849 STRACHEY, WILLIAM. The Historie of Travaile into Virginia Britannia, Expressing the Cosmographie and Commodities of the Country, together with the manners and customs of the people, gathered and observed as well by those who went first thither as collected by William Strachey, Gent., the first Secretary of the Colony. Now first edited from the original MS. in the British Museum by Richard Henry Major, F.S.A., Keeper of Maps, British Museum, Sec. R.G.S. 1 map, 6 illus., Glossary, Index. Hak. Soc., ser. I, vol. 6. London.

See Strachey under 1612 above.

1852 COATS, WILLIAM (Captain). The Geography of Hudson's Bay, being the Remarks of Captain W. Coats, in many Voyages to that locality, between the years 1727 and 1751. With an Appendix containing Extracts from the Log of Captain Middleton on his Voyage for the Discovery of the North-west Passage, in H. M. S. "Furnace," in 1741-3. Edited by John Barrow, F.R.S., F.S.A. Hak. Soc., ser. I, vol. 11. London.

1853 DE VRIES, DAVID PETERSON. Voyages from Holland to America, 1632-1644. From the Dutch by H. C. Murphy. 4to. New York.

Dutch original, Horn, 1655. See below.
Une introduction très intéressante sur la vie de de Vries et plusieurs notes augmentent la valeur de cette traduction.—Bookseller's Note.

1655 DE VRIES, DAVID P. Korte Historiael Ende Journaels aenteyckeninge, Van verscheyden Voyagiens in de vier deelen des Wereldes-Ronde, als Europa, Africa, Asia, ende Amerika gedaen, Door . . . Waer in verhaelt werd wat Batailjes hy te Water gedaen heeft: Oder Landtschap zigjn Gedierte, Gevogelt, wat soozte van Dissen, ende wat wilde Menschen naer 't leben gecontersaeyt, ende van de Bosschen ende Kavieren met haer Dzuchten. 4to. t'Hoorn.

Short history and notes of a journal, kept during several Voyages undertaken in the four parts of the World, viz.: Europe, Africa, Asia, and America, by D. D. de Vries, Artillery Master of their noble and Mighty Lordships, the Commissioned Counsellors of West Friesland and North Holland. In which there are described the different battles he has fought at sea, The Animals, the Birds, the different sorts of Fishes and some savages drawn from life: and of the forests and rivers with the fruits.—Asher. Besides Hudson no navigator except De Vries published a narrative of his voyages to New Netherland during the Dutch possession.—Murphy Catalog, quoted by Bradford.

SHEA, JOHN GILMARY. Discovery and Exploration of the Mississippi Valley: With the Original Narratives of Marquette, Allouez, Membré, Hennepin, and Anastase Douay. Map. 8vo. Redfield.

1854 FONTANEDA, HERNANDO DE. Memoir respecting Florida, written in Spain, about the Year 1575, &c. Translated by Buckingham Smith. Map. Folio. Washington.

VAN DER DONCK, ——. Vertoogh van Nieu Nederland;... and Breeden Raedt aende vereeniche Nederlandsche Provintien. Two Rare Tracts, Printed in 1649-50, relating to the Administration of Affairs in New-Netherland. Translated from the Dutch (the Hague, 1650) by Henry C. Murphy, New York, 1854. 4to. Reprinted in New York, 1854.

1856 BAILY, FRANCIS. Journal of a Tour in unsettled Parts of North America in 1796 and 1797. . . . With a Memoir of the Author (by Sir J. Herschel). 8vo. London.

1857 BENZONI, GIROLAMO. History of the New World, by . . . of Milan. Showing his Travels in America, from A. D. 1541 to 1556: with some particulars of the Island of Canary. Now first translated, and Edited by Rear-Admiral W. H. Smythe. 8vo. London.

See also *Purchas His Pilgrimes,* IV, 1445.—Sabin.

1858-1868 SHEA, JOHN GILMARY (Editor). The Jesuit Relations—Cramoisy Series. 25 vols. (Various sizes and bindings.) Quebec.

Two volumes were added to this series later. The first Quebec edition of 1858 consisted of three volumes and was published by the Canadian government. In 1894 the Quebec edition was republished at Cleveland with page for page translations. Then soon after Reuben Gold Thwaites, secretary of the State Historical Society of Wisconsin, edited documents from 1610 to 1791. By 1901 73 volumes had appeared as *The Jesuit Relations and Allied Documents,* which included all the Relations as well as related documents and translations. A Selection, edited by Edna Kenton, with an Introduction by R. G. Thwaites, appeared at New York, 1925 (London, 1926), in the American Library Series. These volumes comprise the reports of the Jesuit Missionaries to their superior at Quebec or to the provincial of the Order in France. They include travel, letters, journals, adventures, accounts of the Indians, captivities, tortures, and martyrdoms, running in date from 1611 to 1678. From 1632 to 1673 these Relations were published annually in Paris by Sebastian Cramoisy. But after 1673 they sank into obscurity until their reappearance in print at Quebec in 1858. The value of these reports, which is one of the most difficult of all sets to procure at any price, for the early history of North America, particularly for New France, is incalculable. The Jesuits played an important role in the history of New France in the seventeenth century, as they were constantly in the thick of all the religious and political developments of that colony. Parkman says that "with regard to the condition and character of the primitive inhabitants of North

America it is impossible to exaggerate the value of the Jesuit Relations as an authority." See also under COLLECTIONS for the following related items: *Annuae Litterae Societatis Jesu* (Foreign-Addenda II), 1580-1661 (Contents of this collection listed in Maggs, No. 429); *The Travels of Several Learned Missioners of the Society of Jesus,* 1714; Lockman, 1743; *Lettres édifiantes et curieuses,* 1819-1854 (Addenda II). A complete set of the Cramoisy series is to be found in the New York Public Library.

1858 SHEA, JOHN GILMARY. Relations des jésuites contenant ce qui s'est passé de plus remarquable dans les Missions des Pères de la Compagnie de Jésus dans la Nouvelle France. 3 vols. 8vo. Quebec.

1862 MILLER, JOHN. A Description of the Province and City of New York with plans of the city and several forts as they existed in the year 1695. Edited by J. G. Shea. 8vo. New York.

1865 JONES, DAVID (Rev.). A Journal of two Visits made to some Nations of Indians on the West Side of the River Ohio, in 1772 and 1773, with a biographical notice of the author. 8vo. Sabin's Reprint. New York.

> An interesting account of the manners and customs among some Indian tribes now nearly extinct.

1866 POUCHOT, ——. Memoir of the late War in North America between the French and English, 1755-1760, followed by Observations upon the Theatre of Actual War and by New Details concerning the Manners and Customs of the Indians. Translated and edited by Franklin B. Hough. 2 vols. 8vo. London.

1867 DANKERS, JASPAR, and SLUYTER, PETER (of Wiewerd in Friesland). Journal of a Voyage to New York and Tour in Several of the American Colonies in 1679-1680. Translated from the original MS. in Dutch by H. C. Murphy. Folding colored views and tinted maps. 8vo. Memoirs of the Long Island Historical Society, vol. I. Brooklyn.

> Another edition, New York, 1913.

DUNTON, JOHN. Letters written from New England, A.D. 1686. . . . In which are described his Voyages by Sea, his Travels on Land, and the Characters of his Friends and Acquaintances. . . . from the Original Manuscript, In the Bodleian Library, Oxford, with Notes and an Appendix, by W. H. Whitmore. 4to. Boston.

> See also Dunton under 1705 above.

1871  CABECA DE VACA, ALVAR NUNEZ.   Relation of Alvar Nunez Cabeca de Vaca.  Translated from the Spanish by Buckingham Smith.
Portraits.  8vo.  New York.  (Privately printed.)

> A new edition based on this translation, San Francisco, 1929. See this and
> Bishop's account below. Spanish original, Valladolid, 1555. See below.
> Cabeca de Vaca landed in Florida in 1528 and crossed overland, reaching
> Mexico in 1536. He told some tall tales of immense stores of wealth to be had
> in the unexplored countries to the north. Expeditions sent out to investigate the
> truth of these seemed to confirm his reports. One result was the dispatch of an
> expedition under Coronado (see Coronado under 1896 below).

1929  CABECA DE VACA.   Relation that Alvar Nunez Cabeca de Vaca gave
of what befell the armament in the Indies whither Panphilo de Nar-
vaez went for Governor (from the years 1527 to 1537) when with
three comrades he returned and came to Sevilla.  Printed from the
Buckingham Smith translation of 1871.  8vo.  San Francisco.

1933  BISHOP, MORRIS.   The Odyssey of Cabeza de Vaca.  Illus. and Maps.
12mo.  New York.

1555  CABECA DE VACA, ALVAR NUNEZ.   La relacion y commentarios
del governador Aluar Nunez Cabeca de Vaca, de lo acaescido en las
dos jornadas que hizo a las Indias.  2 parts in 1 vol.  4to.  Valladolid.

> The first part gives an account of Cabeca de Vaca's journey
> through the Southern parts of the United States, from Tampa Bay to
> old Mexico. It is a thrilling story of adventure, and describes the Au-
> thor's wanderings with the survivors of Narvaez' expedition, which
> set out in 1527 for the conquest of Florida, or all the regions after-
> wards known as Florida and Louisiana. It is the record of the first
> journey made by Europeans through any part of the country now in-
> cluded within the boundaries of the United States. The second part
> contains a contemporary account of his journey to the River Plate in
> South America, after his appointment as Governor. He explored the
> regions around the Paraguay and Parana, conciliated the Indian tribes,
> and discovered the route towards Peru. On the complaint of his lieu-
> tenant Domingo de Irala he was arrested and sent back to Spain in
> 1545, where he spent several years freeing himself from the charges
> made against him. The first part was first published in 1542, and the
> second in 1555, and is the first printed account of the La Plata regions.
> —From Maggs, No. 479.

1875  LELAND, C. G.   Fusang; or the Discovery of America by Chinese Budd-
hist Priests in the Fifth Century.  8vo.  Oriental Series.  London.

> This contains the Narrative of Hoei-Syin, with comments by Prof. C. F.
> Neumann, with subsequent discussion and correspondence.—Heffer and Sons.

LE MOYNE, ——.   Narrative of Le Moyne, an Artist who accompanied
the French Expedition to Florida under Laudonnière, 1564.  Translated
from the Latin of De Bry.  Illustrated with heliotypes of engravings
taken from the artist's original drawings.  4to.  Boston.

1877 BROGLIE, VICTOR CLAUDE, PRINCE DE. Narrative of the Prince de Broglie. *Magazine of American History,* vol. I. New York.

> See the following item.
>
> 1903 Deux Français aux Etats-Unis et dans la Nouvelle Espagne en 1782. Journal de voyage du prince de Broglie et Lettres du comte de Ségur . . . (Mélanges publiés par la Société des bibliophiles françois). 8vo. Paris.
>
> Cited by Monoghan.

HAKLUYT, RICHARD. A Discourse concerning Western Planting, written in the Year 1584, now first printed from a contemporary Manuscript. With a Preface and Introduction by Leonard Woods. Edited, with Notes in the Appendix. 8vo. Cambridge.

1878-1882 SEWELL, S. Diary: 1674-1729. *Maine Hist. Soc. Coll.,* 5th ser., vols. V-VII. 8vo. Boston.

> The diary expresses 17th century New England just as that of Pepys does the England of the Restoration.—Davies, *Bibliography of British History.*

1881 PENN, WILLIAM. Coleman's Reprint of Mr. Penn's original Proposal and Plan for the Founding and Building of Philadelphia in Pennsylvania, in 1683. Fol. London.

1883 M'ALPINE, J. Genuine Narratives and Concise Memoirs of his Adventures in America, 1773-79. 8vo. Greenock.

> A reprint of the 1780 edition.

1885 ARBER, EDWARD (Editor). The First Three Books on America, being chiefly translations and compilations by Richard Eden from the writings, maps, etc., of Pietro Martire (1455-1526); Sebastian Munster (1489-1552); Sebastian Cabot (1474-1557) and Spanish, Italian and German writers of the times. 4to. Birmingham.

> See Eden under 1553, COLLECTIONS.

STIRLING, WILLIAM ALEXANDER (Earl of). Register of Royal Letters, relative to affairs of Scotland and Nova Scotia from 1615 to 1635. Expenses of Nova Scotia; Colonisation of America; trade; taxation; Newfoundland, etc. Edited with very complete index. 2 vols. 4to. Edinburgh. (Privately printed.)

1887 BAXTER, J. PHINNEY. The British Invasion from the North: The Campaigns of Generals Carleton and Burgoyne from Canada, 1776-77, with the Journal of Lieut. William Digby. Illus*/* with historical notes. 4 plates. 4to. Albany.

1892 CABOT, JOHN. For voyages of John Cabot and Gaspar Corte Real and documents relating to them, see *Christopher Columbus* under 1892, WEST INDIES.

QUESNAY DE BEAUREPAIRE, ALEXANDRE MARIE. Memoir concerning the Academy of the Arts and Sciences of the United States of America at Richmond, Virginia . . . Translated by Rosewell Page. 8vo. Richmond. (Published as part of the report of the Virginia State Library for 1920-21.)

French original, Paris, 1788. See below.

1788 QUESNAY DE BEAUREPAIRE, ALEXANDRE MARIE. Mémoire, statuts et prospectus, concernant l'Académie des sciences et beaux arts des Etats-Unis de l'Amérique, établié à Richemond, capitale de la Virginie; présenté au Roi, par le chevalier Quesnay de Beaurepaire. 12mo. Paris.

Cited by Monoghan.

WASHINGTON, GEORGE (Major). The Daily Journal of Major George Washington, in 1751-1752, kept while on a Tour of Virginia to the Island of Barbadoes, with his invalid Brother, Major Lawrence Washington, Proprietor of Mount Vernon on the Potomac. Copied from the original with literal exactness and edited with notes by J. M. Toner, M.D. Frontispiece. 4to. Albany.

1893 GIST, CHRISTOPHER. Christopher Gist's Journals; with Historical, Geographical, and Ethnological Notes, and Biographies of his Contemporaries. By William M. Darlington. 4to. Pittsburgh.

"One of the three journals of Christopher Gist was never before published; three are now published together for the first time. They cover the periods of 1750-51, 1751-52, and 1753, the first two giving an account of his travels and discoveries down the river Ohio and its branches for the Ohio Company, together with his transactions with the Indians and his return home; the third is an account of a journey in attendance upon Major George Washington, to the commandant of the French Fort on the Ohio River. Gist's explorations of the region now included within the boundaries of Ohio, Ky., W. Va., and parts of Western Maryland and S. W. Penn., were the earliest made so far west for the single object of examining the country, as they are the first also of which a regular journal was kept. As they were in the interests of a great land company, their results were not generally made known. In 1776 the first journal was published in London, but few copies came to America. . . ."—*Publ. Weekly,* quoted by Bradford.

1896 CORONADO, FRANCISCO VASQUEZ DE. The Coronado Expedition 1540-1542. Edited by George Parker Winship. Maps and illus. 8vo. Washington.

> This, "the best of all editions," is to be found in Part I, Vol. 14, Bureau of Ethnology. Reprinted for the Trail Makers Series, 16mo, 1904; again New York, 1922. See below.
>
> The Coronado expedition was of far-reaching importance from a geographical point of view for it combined with the journey of de Soto in giving to the world an insight into the hitherto unknown vast interior of the northern continent and formed the basis of the cartography of that region. It was the means also of making known the sedentary Pueblo tribes of the south-west and the hunting tribes of the great plains, the Grand Canon of the Colorado and the lower reaches of that stream, and the teeming herds of bison and the absolute dependence on them by the hunting Indians for every want.—Hodge and Lewis, *Spanish Explorers in the Southern United States* (1925), quoted by Baker, *Geographical Discovery*. Inasmuch as the expected gold and silver failed to materialize, Coronado lost favor as an explorer. This edition of Winship's includes all the known documents bearing on the expedition printed in Spanish and English with copious notes and annotated bibliography. The original documents appear for the first time in English.

> 1922 CORONADO, FRANCISCO VASQUEZ DE. The Journey of Coronado, 1540-1542, from the City of Mexico to the Grand Canyon of the Colorado and the Buffalo Plains of Texas, Kansas and Nebraska: as told by Himself and His Followers. Map. 12mo. American Explorers Series. New York.

POTE, WILLIAM (Jr.). Journal during his Captivity in the French and Indian War from May, 1745, to August, 1747. Edited by J. F. Hurst. Map. 2 vols. 8vo. New York.

> Important journal that appears in no other form, only 350 copies having been printed.—Bookseller's Note.

1897 LINCKLAEN, JOHN. Travels in the years 1791 and 1792 in Pennsylvania, New York and Vermont of John Lincklaen, agent of the Holland Land Company. With biographical sketch and notes. 8vo. New York.

MILET, PIERRE (Father). Captivity among the Oneidas in 1690-91 of Father Pierre Milet of the Society of Jesus. Edited in French by J. M. Shea. Translated with notes by Mrs. Edward Ayer. 16mo. Chicago.

1898 HUMPHREY, GEORGE P. (Publisher). Reprints of Rare, Early Tracts containing: Capt. John Smith, A Description of New England, 1717; New England Trials, 1622; The Planters' Plea, 1630; Gov. Thomas Dudley's Letter, 1631; Extract from a manuscript Collection of Annals relative to Virginia, 1634; Description of the Province of New Albion, 1648. 8vo. Rochester.

1900    GARCES, FRANCISCO.   On the Trail of a Spanish Pioneer. The Diary
and Itinerary of Francisco Garces, in His Travels Through Sonora,
Arizona, and California, 1775-1776.   Edited by Elliott Coues.   Maps,
views, and Facsimiles.   2 vols.   8vo.   London and New York.

> One of the great source books for the history of the Southwest. Only a
> limited number were issued, now quite scarce.—Bookseller's Note. Translation
> from the Spanish MS. of the Diary with notes from the MS. belonging to Dr.
> Leon and from the only printed copy heretofore in existence. This diary de-
> scribes the fifth and last journey of Garces as a missionary priest among the
> wild tribes from his station near Tucson, Ariz. He accompanied the expedition
> of Lt. Col. Anza to the San Gabriel Mission near Los Angeles, and thence jour-
> neyed eastward as far as Zuni.—Bookseller's Note.

HAKLUYT, RICHARD.   Divers Voyages touching the discoveries of
America and Islands adjacent unto the same, made first of all by our
Englishmen, and afterwards by the Frenchmen and Britons.   Photo-
lithographic reprint.   2 maps.   Original edition 1582.   (Reprint made
around 1900.)   8vo.   London.

> 300 copies of this reprint were made by Sir John Evans but never put in
> circulation. The first map was sent by Robert Thorne to Dr. Ley in 1527. The
> second was made by Michael Lok in 1582. The original is one of the rarest of
> all English books relating to America.—Bookseller's Note. See Hakluyt under
> 1582, COLLECTIONS.

1901    HEMPSTEAD, JOSHUA.   Diary covering a period of forty-seven years
(in New London) from 1711 to 1758.   8vo.   New London Historical
Society.

1902    Early Voyages Up and Down the Mississippi, by Chevalier, St. Cosme, Le
Sueur, Gravier, and Guignas.   Introduction and notes by J. G. Shea.
4to.   Albany.

1904    GLOVER, THOMAS.   An Account of Virginia, its Situation, Temperature, Productions, Inhabitants and their Manner of Planting and Ordering Tobacco, etc. . . . Reprinted from the *Phi. Trans. Roy. Soc.*
June 20, 1676.   8vo.   Oxford.

> Only 250 copies printed from the type that is contemporary with the tract,
> having been cast under the direction of Bishop Fell in 1675 and presented by him
> to Oxford University. Printed by the University of Oxford Press.—Bradford.

MICHAELIUS, JONAS.   Manhattan in 1628, as described in the recently discovered authograph letter of Jonas Michaelius, written from
the settlement on the 8th of August of that year and now first published. With a review of the letter and an Historical Sketch of New
Netherland in 1628 by Dingman Versteeg.   4to.   New York.

MICHAUX, ANDRE. Travels into Kentucky, 1793-96; also, Travels West of the Alleghany Mountains, 1802; also T. M. Harris' Journal of a Tour Northwest of the Alleghany Mountains, 1803. Reprinted 3 vols. in 1. 8vo. Cleveland.

1904-07 THWAITES, REUBEN GOLD. Early Western Travels 1748-1846. Edited with Notes, Introductions, index, and 1 vol. of plates. Illus. 32 vols. 8vo (one vol. fol.). Cleveland.

> A series of annotated reprints of some of the best and rarest contemporary volumes of travels, descriptive of the aborigines and social and economic conditions in the Middle and Far West, during the period of Early American Settlement. Vol. XXV (in folio) comprises reproductions of the series of original paintings, by Charles Bodmer, to illustrate Maximilian, Prince of Wiedls, Travels in the Interior of North America, 1832-34.—Bookseller's Note.

1905 LATROBE, BENJAMIN H. The Journal of Latrobe. The notes and sketches of an Architect, Naturalist and Traveller in the U. S., 1796-1820. Illus. 8vo. New York.

WINSHIP, G. P. Sailors' Narratives of Voyages along the New England Coast, 1524-1624. 8vo. Boston.

> Portions of these narratives are printed here, some of which are not to be found in Hakluyt.—From Read, *Bibliography of British History*.

1906 HERVEY, HON. WILLIAM. Journals of. In North America and Europe, from 1755 to 1814. With order books at Montreal, 1760-1763. With Memoir and Notes. Suffolk Green Books. Portraits, views and folding map. 4to. London.

OLSON, J. E., and BOURNE, E. G. (Editors). The Voyages of the Northmen. The Voyages of Columbus and of John Cabot. Maps. 8vo. Original Narratives Series. New York.

Pre-Columbian Discovery of America. The Flateley Book and Recently Discovered Vatican Manuscripts Concerning America as Early as the Tenth Century. Reproductions of the Original Manuscripts together with English Translations. 4to. The Norroena Society. London.

> Documents now published for the first time showing that North America was settled by Norsemen 500 years before the time of Columbus. Together with Sagas that describe the voyage to, and character of, the new country, and letters from several Popes directing Bishops in their government of the church in the western world. A valuable and interesting work.—Bookseller's Note.

1907  Apperson, G. L. (Editor).  Gleanings after Time.  Chapters in Social and Domestic History.  29 illus.  8vo.  London.

> This contains "First Parliament in America, 1619"; "The Cromwells of America"; "A Visit to America 1774."—Bookseller's Note.

DYOTT, WILLIAM (General).  For matter relating to Nova Scotia see his *Diary,* under WEST INDIES.

HAMILTON, ALEXANDER (Dr.).  Hamilton's Itinerarium.  Being a Narrative of a Journey from Annapolis through Delaware, Pennsylvania, New York, New Jersey, Connecticut, Rhode Island, Massachusetts, & New Hampshire from May to December, 1744.  By Dr. Alexander Hamilton.  Edit. by A. H. Hart.  Map and illus.  4to.  St. Louis.

> Few of the numerous journals and narratives of travels in the Colonial Period are so lively and full of good humored comment on people and customs as the Itinerarium of Dr. Hamilton.—Dauber and Pine.

HODGE, F. W., and LEWIS, T. H. (Editors).  Spanish Explorers in the Southern United States.  Original Narratives Series.  New York.

TYLER, L. G. (Editor).  Narratives of Early Virginia.  Original Narratives Series.  New York.

1908  WINTHROP, JOHN.  Journal.  "History of New England," 1636-1649.  2 vols.  Original Narratives Series.  New York.

1909  JAMESON, J. FRANKLIN (Editor).  Narratives of New Netherland, 1609-1664.  Maps and facsimiles.  Original Narratives Series.  New York.

> Among other things it contains reprints of Hudson's Voyage; "New World" by J. de Laet; Johannes' "Account of Mohawk Indians."

1910  HALL, C. C. (Editor).  Narratives of early Maryland.  Original Narratives Series.  New York.

1911  JEYES, S. H.  The Russells of Birmingham in the French Revolution and in America, 1791-1814.  8vo.  London.

> The Russells came to America in 1795 and spent five years here.—Bookseller's Note.

SALLEY, A. S. (Editor).  Narratives of early Carolina, 1650-1708.  Original Narratives Series.  New York.

SCHOEPF, JOHANN DAVID. Travels in the Confederation, 1783-1784. Translated by Alfred J. Morrison. 2 vols. 12mo. London.

1912 ALVORD, CLARENCE W., and BIDGOOD, LEE. First Explorations of the Trans-Alleghany Region by the Virginians, 1650-1674. With bibliography, analytical index, facsimiles and maps. 8vo. London.

> Herein is recorded the hitherto inaccessible original accounts of the first explorers —Englishmen who were in the region almost as early as the French were on the Mississippi waters; for, two years before Joliet and Marquette made their famous journey down the Mississippi River, Thomas Batts and Robert Fallam camped by the side of the new River, a branch of the Great Kanawha.—Bookseller's Note. "This carefully edited collection of original documents relating the adventures and discoveries of the English explorers prominent in the early expeditions to the Ohio and Mississippi valleys is the first authoritative work on the subject, and, in view of the fact for the first time presented, should prove an important contribution to the history of western exploration." —A.L.A.

CHAMPLAIN, SAMUEL DE. The Voyages and Explorations of Samuel de Champlain, 1604-1616, Narrated by Himself. Translated by Annie Nettleton Bourne, together with The Voyage of 1603 Reprinted from Purchas His Pilgrimes. Edited with Introduction and Notes by Edward Gaylord Bourne. Illus. 2 vols. 12mo. American Explorers Series. New York.

> Outside of the Purchas version of the 1603 voyage, there was no English translation of Champlain's voyages until 1878 when the Prince Society undertook to translate and edit all the narratives that had to do with the New England coast down to 1617. Being a limited edition and scarce, this work is practically inaccessible. A popular edition in English was prepared in 1904 from the final edition of 1632 for the Trail Makers Series. This was reprinted as listed above in 1922. Vol. I of his works, extending from 1599 to 1607, was published by the Champlain Society, Toronto, 1922. The voyage of 1603 appeared in French, Paris, 1604, and the complete narrative of all the voyages, revised by Champlain himself, was printed, Paris, 1632. See below.
>
> Champlain made eight voyages to the St. Lawrence region: 1st in 1603—exploration of the St. Lawrence as far as the rapids above Montreal; 2nd of 1604—exploration of the coasts of Nova Scotia, Maine, Massachusetts and attempts to found a settlement south of St. Lawrence; 3rd of 1608—further explorations on the St. Lawrence and the foundation of Quebec; 4th of 1610—no new exploration but cementing more firmly friendship with the Algonquins; 5th of 1611—journey up the St. Lawrence to meet the Algonquins with whom he had left one of his men; 6th of 1613—the important expedition up the Ottawa river; 7th of 1615—return with Recollet missionaries and the discovery of Lake Huron, war on the Iroquois, and wintering with the Algonquins; 8th of 1633—return to Canada as Governor. He died in 1635. Champlain stands at the top of the list of explorers in America in that he combined with the leadership requisite for such enterprises the abilities of an historian and of a colonizer.

1604 CHAMPLAIN, SAMUEL DE. Des Sauvages, ou Voyage de Sammuel Champlain de Brouage faict en la France Nouvelle, l'an mil six cens trois. Paris.

1632 CHAMPLAIN, SAMUEL DE. Les Voyages de la Nouvelle France Occidentale, dicte Canada, faits par le Sr. de Champlain Xainctongeois, Capitaine pour le Roy en la Marine du Ponant, et toutes les Descouvertes qu'il a faites en ce païs depuis l'an 1603 jusques en l'an 1629. Ou se voit comme ce pays a esté premièrement descouvert par les Francois . . . avec un traitté des qualités et conditions requises à un bon et parfaict Navigateur . . . Folding map and copperplates. 4to. Paris.

This is the best edition of Champlain's voyages, as it contains a collective account of all preceding French expeditions to the New World, some of which had not been embodied in the earlier editions.

LEVERMORE, CHARLES HERBERT (Editor). Forerunners and Competitors of the Pilgrims and Puritans or Narratives of Voyages made by persons other than the Pilgrims and Puritans to the Shores of New England, 1601-1625. 2 vols. 8vo. Brooklyn. (Privately printed.)

This contains the voyages of Pring, Waymouth, Argall and Somers, etc.

TRUDEAU, JEAN BAPTISTE. Journal of Jean Baptiste Trudeau among the Arikara Indians in 1795. 8vo. *Missouri Hist. Soc. Coll.,* vol. 4, 9-14. St. Louis.

Translated by Mrs. H. T. Beauregard.—Monoghan.

1912-13 MATHER, COTTON. Diary. Edited by W. C. Ford. *Mass. Hist. Soc. Coll.,* 7th ser., vols. VI-VIII. Boston.

This supplements the Diary of Judge Sewell (see Sewell under 1878-1882 above) and throws much light upon the social conditions in Boston during a period of change and unrest.—Davies, *Bibliography of British History.*

1913 LINCOLN, C. H. (Dr.). Narratives of the Indian Wars, edit. by Dr. C. H. Lincoln: Easton's Relacion, Mrs. Rowlandson's Captivity, . . . 8vo. London.

MYERS, A. C. (Editor). Narratives of early Pennsylvania, Delaware, and West New Jersey, 1630-1700. Original Narratives Series. New York.

1914 TRUDEAU, JEAN BAPTISTE. Journal of Jean Baptiste Trudeau on the upper Missouri, "Première Partie," June 7, 1794-March 26, 1795. 8vo. *Amer. Hist. Rev.,* vol. 19, 299-333. Lancaster, Pa.

TRUDEAU, JEAN BAPTISTE. Trudeau's Journal. 8vo. *South Dakota Hist. Coll.,* vol. 7, 403-474. Pierre, S. D.

1915 BENAVIDES, ALONSO DE. Memorial of, 1630. Translated by Mrs. Edward E. Ayer. Annotated by Frederick W. Hodge and Charles F. Lummis. Illus. 8vo. Chicago. (Privately printed.)

SHERRILL, CHARLES H. (Editor). French Memories of Eighteenth Century America. Illus. 8vo. London.

> This contains selections from famous French travellers in America before 1800.—Bookseller's Note.

WRAXALL, P. An Abridgement of the Indian Affairs contained in four folio volumes transacted in the Colony of New York, from the year 1678 to the year 1751. Edited by C. McIlwain. 8vo. Cambridge.

1917 KELLOGG, LOUISE PHELPS (Editor). Early Narratives of the Northwest, 1634-1699. Facsimile and 2 maps. Original Narratives Series. New York.

1919 SAILLY, PIERRE DE. Diary of Peter Sailly on a Journey in America in the year 1784. 8vo. Albany. (In George S. Bixby, Peter Sailly, 1754-1826, a pioneer of the Champlain Valley, with extracts from his diary and letters.)

> This was issued as Bulletin 680 of the University of the State of New York, State Library, Historical Bulletin 12.—Monoghan.

1921 DOYSIE, ABEL (Editor). Journal of a French Traveller in the Colonies, 1765. 4to. *Amer. Hist. Rev.,* vol. 26, 726-747; vol. 27, 70-89. New York.

TRUDEAU, JEAN BAPTISTE. Trudeau's Description of the Upper Missouri. 8vo. *Miss. Valley Hist. Rev.,* vol. 8, 149-179. Cedar Rapids, Ia.

1922 CAZENOVE, THEOPHILE. Cazenove's Journal, 1794. A Record of the Journey of Theophile Cazenove through New Jersey and Pennsylvania. Translated from the French. Edited by R. W. Kelsey. 8vo. The Pennsylvania History Press. Haverford, Pa. (*Haverford College Studies,* No. 13.)

> The author was the first agent for the Holland Land Company in the United States.—From Monoghan.

HARMON, DANIEL. A Journal of Voyages and Travels in the Interior of North America between the 47th and 58th degree of North latitude, extending from Montreal nearly to the Pacific Ocean, a distance of about 5000 miles, including an account of the Principal occurrences during a residence of nearly nineteen years in different parts of that country. To which are added A Concise Description of the face of the Country, Its Inhabitants, their manners, customs, laws, etc. Illus. 12mo. American Explorers Series. New York.

> This is a fascinating account of the experiences of a man who as a youth left his native state of Vermont to enter the service of the Northwest Fur Company at a time when the competition between this enterprising but unscrupulous concern and the moribund Hudson's Bay Company was at its height. He remained in the Far Northwest from 1800 to 1819, when he returned home and had his journals prepared for the press by the Rev. Daniel Haskel.

MORRISON, ALFRED J. Travels in Virginia in Revolutionary Times. Richmond.

1925 BOUCHER, JONATHAN. Reminiscences of an American Loyalist, 1738-1789. The Autobiography of Rev. Jonathan Boucher. Edited by his Grandson Jonathan Boucher. 8vo. Boston.

CRESSWELL, NICHOLAS. The Journal of Nicholas Cresswell of Edale Parish in the Peak of Derby-shire, 1774-77, now newly discovered and for the first time printed, containing the Adventures and Observations of the said Nicholas during a Trip to His Majesty's late Colonies in North America. 8vo. London.

> He was a Derbyshire squire's son; went to America, stayed at Mount Vernon, wandered alone to the Ohio; saw the unburied bodies of Braddock's men, watched Washington's battles and describes the General; also describes New York in 1777. —Bookseller's Note. The mystery of his disgrace that sent him to America remains a mystery even after his return home. The trials of a Britisher in the colonies during the early period of the Revolution are vividly related, as well as those of a man trying to swear off drinking.

WAGNER, HENRY R. (Editor). California Voyages 1539-1541. 8vo. New York.

1926 JEREMIE, ——. Twenty Years of York Factory, 1694-1714: Jérémie's Account of Hudson Strait and Bay, translated (for the first time) by R. Douglas and J. N. Wallace. 7 maps of Port Nelson (Thornton, 1685, Robson, 1745) and Hudson Bay and air views of York Factory. 8vo. Ottawa.

> The best first hand record of the events of the time.—Bookseller's Note.

1927 MACKENZIE, FRED (Lieut.). A British Fusilier in Revolutionary Boston; a Diary, January 5th to April 30th, 1775, with a Letter describing his Voyage to America. 8vo. Oxford.

SHAW, "JEN." For matter relating to North Carolina see her *Journal of a Lady of Quality,* under WEST INDIES.

1928 PRIESTLEY, H. I. The Luna Papers, documents relating to the Expedition of Don Tristan de Luna y Arellano 'for the Conquest. of La Florida in 1559-61. 2 vols. 8vo. Deland.

1929 A Declaration of the Lord Baltimore's Plantation in Mary-land. Wherein is set forth how Englishmen may become Angels, the King's Dominions be extended and the adventurers attain Land and Gear; together with other advantages of that Sweet Land. A facsimile of the original text of 1633 made by permission from the only known copy in the possession of his Eminence the Cardinal Archbishop of Westminster. With an Introduction by Lawrence C. Wroth. 4to. Baltimore.

WILLIAMSON, JAMES A. (Editor). The Voyages of the Cabots and the English Discovery of America under Henry VII. and Henry VIII. 13 maps. Argonaut Press. Cambridge.

> Of John Cabot and his son Sebastian very little is known to general readers. The reason of this neglect is not that there is nothing more to be told, but that the Cabot adventures are not enshrined in any single narrative which might have become, like the Journal or Letters of Columbus, a classic of discovery. John Cabot wrote nothing, Sebastian wrote little, that has survived; nor did any faithful admirer describe their achievements in detail. A mass of evidence has been gathered together with infinite care and labor—contemporary news-letters, letters patent and commissions, administrative documents, quotations from historians and geographers of the sixteenth century—eighty-one pieces in all, a varied assortment of all the categories of historical raw material. . . . The world map of Juan de la Cosa forms the frontispiece. It has a double interest, as the earliest map drawn after crossing of the Atlantic and Indian Oceans by Europeans, and as the only map which indicates the discoveries of John Cabot. Nine other maps of the early period are also included, together with sketch-maps for the elucidation of debatable points.—Publisher's Note. For materials used hitherto to form our knowledge of John Cabot see Chas. Deane Winsor's *Narrative and Critical History of America,* III, 1-58.

1930 BOLTON, HERBERT EUGENE (Editor). Spanish Exploration in the Southwest, 1542-1706. Original Narratives Series. 8vo. New York.

> Many of the documents have never before been published and some only in Spanish.

1931 LAWRENCE, A. W., and YOUNG, J. For narratives of the discovery of America see their work with this title, under COLLECTIONS.

1933 DIEREVILLE, SIEUR DE. Relation of the Voyage to Port Royal in Acadia or New France, translated by Mrs. C. Webster. Maps and illus. 8vo. The Champlain Society. Toronto.

HADFIELD, JOSEPH. An Englishman in America. A Journal of Joseph Hadfield's Travels in America and his excellent Comments on the Life and Customs of the People with whom he came in Contact (1784-5). 8vo. Toronto.

This is the travel diary of an English merchant in America.

1934    DURAND, —— (Of Dauphine). A Huguenot Exile in Virginia or Voyages of a Frenchman Exiled for His Religion with a Description of Virginia and Maryland from the London edition of 1687. Introduction and Notes by Gilbert Chinard. Illus. 8vo. London.

Translated for the first time. The author was known as "Durand of Dauphine." This is the only complete edition in English.—Bookseller's Note.

HEARNE, SAMUEL, and TURNOR, PHILIP. Journals of Samuel Hearne and Philip Turnor, between the Years 1774 and 1792, edited with Introduction and Notes by J. B. Tyrrell. Maps. 8vo. The Champlain Society. Toronto.

1935    CALDER, ISABEL M. Colonial Captivities, Marches and Journeys, Edited under the auspices of the National Society of Colonial Dames of America. New York.

This contains selections from unpublished journals and letters of pre-revolutionary America.

JANSON, CHARLES WILLIAM. The Stranger in America, 1793-1806. Introduction and Notes by Dr. Carl S. Driver. 8vo. New York.

An Englishman's impressions of the United States in the early days of the Republic. Reprinted from the London edition of 1807.—Bookseller's Note.

M'ROBERT, PATRICK. A Tour through Part of the North Provinces of America. 8vo. The Historical Society of Pennsylvania. Philadelphia.

These are the letters of a visiting Scotchman, 1774-75.—Bookseller's Note.

MORSE, WILLIAM INGLIS. Acadiensia Nova (1598-1779). New and unpublished Documents and other Data relating to Acadia. The Actors: Sir William Alexander, Jacques de Meulles Gargas, Vincent de Saccardy, Marquis de la Roche, Delabat and J. F. W. des Barres. Collected and edited by William Inglis Morse. 2 vols. 8vo. London.

This book covers entirely new ground, and therefore will be eagerly welcomed by scholars and antiquaries interested in the subject and period. It contains original unpublished documents hitherto mostly unknown to historical students. The MSS. discovered do not exist either in copies or abstracts in the great repositories of such material, as for example the Bibliothèque Nationale in Paris, the British Museum, the Library of Congress at Washington, and the Public Archives at Ottawa. The acquisition of the manuscripts has occupied Dr. Morse, who is a well-known author and enthusiastic student in the field of Acadian history, over a decade.— Quaritch.

1937 CORRY, JOHN PITTS. Indian Affairs in Georgia. 1732-1756. 8vo. Huntington, Pa.

> The role of the Indians in the struggle among England, France, and Spain for control of the Southeast.—From notice of the work.

New Castle on the Delaware. 8vo. New Castle Historical Society, Richard S. Rodney, Secretary. New Castle, Del.

> History and description of the town, compiled by the Delaware Federal Writters' Project.—From notice of the work.

# VI

## West Indies

(In early Spanish and English writings the term West Indies is frequently made to include the mainland of Mexico and the adjacent parts of South America.)

1553 EDEN, RICHARD. For voyages of Columbus and his followers and a cosmography see *A Treatyse of the Newe India* (Sebastian Munster), under COLLECTIONS.

1555 EDEN, RICHARD. For the navigation and conquests of the Spaniards in the West Indies see *The Decades of the Newe Worlde or West India* (Peter Martyr), under COLLECTIONS.

1569 HAWKINS, SIR JOHN. A true Declaration of the troublesome Voyage of Mr. John Hawkins to the Partes of Guynea and the West Indies, in the years of our Lord 1567 and 1568. London.

> Reprinted in Beazley I, 1903. See under 1903 below for this and succeeding voyages.
> This is one of the rarest gems of Americana. It is the earliest book written and printed in the English language that pertains to the adventures of an Englishman in the Western World; all other English books on the subject were translations from other languages. It contains the only account of important events of which we should never have known otherwise and in no period of American history is there a greater dearth of exact information. It is from nearly every point of view a key-book.—Waldman. For the two preceding voyages of Hawkins see Hawkins under 1903 below. This third voyage so marked by disaster to the adventurers and ill consequences for the Spaniards was like the other two a slaving expedition. But as Beazley remarks, far from being a discouragement to English seamen, it only stung them to a manifold revenge; and the baptism of blood at San Juan de Ulua ("the port which serveth the city of Mexico") was afterwards expiated in the plunder of many an unfortunate Spanish ship. Hawkins's concluding words may be quoted again: "If all the miseries and troublesome affaires of this sorrowful voyage should be perfectly and thoroughly written there should neede a paynfull man with his penne as great a time as hee had that wrote the lives and deaths of the martirs." See also Hortop under 1591 below.

1577 EDEN, RICHARD. See also *The History of Travayle in the West and East Indies,* under COLLECTIONS.

MONARDES, NICOLAS. Joyfull Newes out of the New-Found Worlde. Wherein are declared the rare and singuler Vertues of diuers Herbs, Trees, Plantes, Oyles, and Stones, with their applications, as well to the use of Phisicke, as of Chirurgery: which being well applyed, bring such present remedie for all diseases, as may seeme altogether incredible: notwithstanding by practice found out to be true. Also the portrature of the said Hearbs, verie aptly described: Englished by John Frampton Merchant. London.

2nd edit., enlarged, 4to, London, 1580; 3rd edit., complete translation, London, 1596. A modern reprint, Tudor Translations. London, 1925. Spanish original, 1574, Seville. See below.

The author was a very noted Spanish physician living in Seville. In this work he describes the medicines and herbs carried back to Europe from the West Indies and the Spanish possessions in America, and the quaint uses to which they were put by the Indians. It contains a long account of tobacco and is the earliest notice of its use in Spain or elsewhere. This is supplemented by Frampton's story of its introduction into France by Jean Nicot, French ambassador at Lisbon. The editor of the edition in the Tudor Translations suggests that this account paved the way for its first use in England, for nine years after the translation had appeared Ralph Lane and Francis Drake brought to England the first smoking implements and a supply of tobacco.

1596 MONARDES, NICOLAS. Ioyfull Newes Out of the New-found VVorlde, Wherein are declared, the rare and singular vertues of diuers Herbs, Trees, Plantes, . . . Englished by John Frampton Merchant. Newly corrected as by conference with the olde copies may appeare. Where-vnto are added three other bookes treating of the Bezaar stone, the herb Escuerconora, the properties of Iron and Steele in Medicine, and the benefit of Snow. The Second parte of this Booke is of the things that are brought from our Occidental Indias, which serue for the use of Medicine, wherein is treated of the Tabaco, and of the Sassafras, and of the Carlo Sancto, and of many other hearbes and plantes, seedes and licours, etc. Written by Doctor Monardus Phisition of Seuill. The third Parte of the Medicinal Historie, which treateth of the thinges that are brought from our Occidentall Indias, seruing for the vse of Medicine. Wherein is there mention made of many things Medicinall, that haue great secretes and vertues. Nowe newely set foorth by the sayde Doctor Monardus, after that he made the first and second partes. A Booke which treateth of two medicines most excellent against all venome, which are the Bezaar stone, . . . and the hearbe Escuerconera. Wherein are declared their maruellous effectes and great vertues, with the manner how to cure the sayde venoms, . . . Newly compiled by Doctor Monardus of Seuill, 1574. Translated out of Spanish into English by Iohn Frampton. 1580. The Dialogve of Yron, which treateth of the greatnesse thereof, and how it is the most excellent metall of all others, and the thing most necessarie for the seruice of man: and of the greate medicinall vertues which it hath an Eccho for the Doctor Monardus Phisition of Seuill. In Seuill in the House of Escriuano. The Boke which treateth of the Snow, and of the properties and vertues thereof: And of the maner that should be vsed to make the drinke cold therewith, and of other waies wherewith is to be made cold: Where-of is shewed partly, in the latter part of the second Dialogue of Iron. With other curiosities which will giue contentment by other ancient thinges worthy to bee known, which in this treatise shall be declared. Written by Doctor Monardus Phisition of Seuill. 1574. London.

1925 MONARDES, NICHOLAS. Joyfull Newes out of the Newe Founde Worlde, written in Spanish . . . and Englished by John Frampton, Merchant, 1577, with an Introduction by Stephen Gaselee. 2 vols. 4to. Tudor Translations, Nos. 9-10. London.

1574 MONARDES, NICHOLAS. Primera Y Segunda Y Tercera Partes Dela Historia Medicinal delas que se traen de neustras Indias Occidentales, que sirven en Medinica. Tratado dela Piedra Bezaar, y dela yerba Escuerconera. Dialogo delas grandezas del Hierro, y de sus Virtudes Medicinales. Tratado dela Nieve, y del bever Frio. 4to. Seville.

1578   ENCISCO, MARTIN FERNANDEZ DE.  A briefe Description of the portes . . . of the Weast India.  Translated by John Frampton.  4to. London.

>   Spanish original Seville, 1519.  See below.  See also Barlow under 1931, GEOGRAPHY.
>   This account of the West Indies is but a section from Encisco's work, which was translated fairly completely with modifications by Roger Barlow in 1540-41. Barlow's work was presented to Henry VIII but remained in manuscript until the Hakluyt Society issued it in 1931.  For an account of Barlow see Taylor's *Tudor Geography* pp. 45-58 and the introduction to the Hakluyt Society volume.—Encisco wrote the *Suma de geographia* to aid pilots and mariners in accomplishing discoveries, and also for the instruction of Charles V.  He spent some time in America and wrote his descriptions from his own observations.  He records a curious conversation with two chiefs of Zenu, in which he informed them that the Pope had bestowed all those regions upon the King of Spain; they replied "that the Pope must have been drunk and that the King was an idiot."—From Maggs, No. 479.

>   1519   ENCISCO, MARTIN FERNANDEZ DE.  Suma de geographia que trata de todas las partidas y provincias del mundo; en especial de las Indias y trata largamente del arte del marear; Juntamente con la esphera en romance; con el regimiento del Sol y del Norte; nuevamente hecha. Fol.  Seville.
>
>>   This is the 1st edition of the 1st book printed in Spain and in Spanish on America.—Maggs, No. 496.

1583   LAS CASAS, BARTHOLOMEW DE.  The Spanish Colonie, Or Briefe Chronicle of the Acts and gestes of Spaniardes in the West Indies, called the newe World, for the space of xl. yeeres: written in the Castilian tongue by the reuerend Bishop Bartholomew de las Casas or Casaus . . . And nowe first translated into English, by M. M. S.  4to. London.

>   This is a translation of the first of the nine tracts (Seville, 1552-53).  For the Spanish original see below.  For translations of other tracts see Las Casas under 1656, 1689, and 1699 below.  Reprinted in *Purchas His Pilgrimes,* 1625.
>   This work is incomplete, and is translated not from the Spanish, but from the French of Miggrode, which name is misspelled Allegrodo in the "To the Reader" portion, which goes on to say that the book was "to serve as a President and a warning to the XII provinces of the lowe Countries"—history reversing itself rapidly.—Waldman.  The volume contains an account of the inhuman cruelties practiced by the Spaniards in Peru and Mexico from the time of their landing in 1493.—Quaritch.  Las Casas, the Apostle to the Indians and their great defender against Spanish cruelty, was born at Seville in 1474, and died at the great age of ninety-two at Madrid.  In 1502 he went out and settled in the West Indies and soon became the advocate of the Indians against the terrible wrongs committed by their conquerors.  This drew on him the animosity of his countrymen and was not successful in stopping the atrocities.  He returned to Spain in 1515 and appealed to his Sovereign, whose untimely death upset his endeavours.  Wearied out by his fruitless efforts he retired to a Monastery in Santo Domingo and spent eight years in study and writing.  Publication of his books was at first forbidden, but after a lapse of twelve years these tracts, which form one of the most gruesome books ever written, were finally published.—Maggs, No. 612.  The number of Indians destroyed—forty millions—was halved by Phillips.  Modern critics are inclined to decrease it still further.—Waldman.  For a summary of each of the nine tracts see Maggs, No. 479.

>   1552   LAS CASAS, BARTOLOME DE.  Breuissima relacion de la destruycion de las Indias.  Seville.

NICHOLS, THOMAS.   A pleasant Description of the fortunate Ilandes. London.

1589   DRAKE, SIR FRANCIS.   A Summarie and True Discourse of Sir Francis Drake's VVest Indian Voyage, Wherein were taken the Townes of Saint Jago, Sancto Domingo, Cartagena & Saint Augustin.   London.

>   According to Waldman, the *Expeditio Francisco Draki* (Leyden, 1588—see below) was the first account of this plundering voyage of Drake's. But according to John Carter Brown, the Leyden version was a translation of the *Summarie,* which, he says, was written by Walter Bigges, and edited by Thomas Cates, London. The respective dates, however seem to preclude this supposition. Another edition, 4to, London, 1589. A French account, 1590. See below and also Drake under 1626 and following items, CIRCUMNAVIGATIONS.
>   The first part of the above work was written by Bigges, an officer under Drake, and finished, after his suicide, by his lieutenant Crofts. The editor, Thomas Cates, vouches for the truth of this report from personal knowledge.—From Waldman. This expedition was sanctioned by a commission from Queen Elizabeth and letters of marque. On his return Drake brought back to England the unfortunate colonists left by Sir Richard Grenville in Virginia.

>   1588   DRAKE, SIR FRANCIS.   Expeditio Francisco Draki Eqvitis Anli in Indias Occidentales M.D.LXXXV. Qua vrbes, Fanum D. Iacobi, D. Dominici, D. Augustini & Carthagena captae fuere. Additis passim regionum locorumque omnium tabulis Geographicis quam accuratissimis. 4 maps.   Leyden.

>   1590   DRAKE, SIR FRANCIS.   Le premier recueil contenant les choses les plus memorables advenues sous la Ligue. Tant en France, Angleterre qu'autres lieux.   8vo.   (Place?)
>
>>   A la fin de ce volume, pages 771-805, se trove le texte suivant: "Le Voyage de Messire Francois Drake, chevalier, aux Indes Occidentales l'an 1585, auquel les villes de S. Iago, S. Domingo, S. Augustino et Cartageno ont esté prises." 35 pp. La premier édition du voyage de Drake, publiée en France par de Louvencourt étant de 1613, celleci l'a précédée de onze ans. Nous avons donc là la veritable édition originale française.—From Emile Nourry, Catalogue No. 248, 1933.

1591   HORTOP, JOB.   The Rare Travailes of Job Hortop, an Englishman, who was not heard of, in three and twenty years' space. Where is declared the dangers he escaped in his Voyage to Guinea; where, after he was set on shore, in a wilderness near to Panuco (Tampico), he endured much slavery and bondage in the Spanish Galleys. . . . London.

>   This narrative was rewritten in Hakluyt, 1600. Another edition the same year. Reprinted in Beazley I, 1903, London.
>   Hortop was one of the company that begged to be set ashore rather than endure longer the miseries of starvation on board Hawkins's ship, which had just escaped from the treacherous attack of the Spaniards at San Juan de Ulua in Mexico. With others he managed to make his way back to Mexico, where he was seized and sent to Spain. There he was sentenced to the galleys and served thus twelve years. A few more years of hardship was his lot before he reached England again.

1598   LINSCHOTEN, JOHN HUYGHEN VAN.   For his voyages into the West Indies see his *Discours of Voyages into ye Easte and West Indies,* under EAST INDIES.

1600  HAKLUYT, RICHARD.  The historie of the West Indies, containing the actes and adventures of the Spaniards, which have conquered and peopled those Countries, inriched with Varietie of pleasant relations of the Manners, Ceremonies, Lawes, Governments, and Warres of the Indians. Published in Latin by Mr. Hakluyt, and translated into English by M. Lok, Gent.  4to.  London.

> The date of this item is unsettled.

1604  ACOSTA, JOSEPH.  The Naturall and Morall Historie of the East and West Indies, . . . 4to.  London.

> This famous work is chiefly concerned with South America. See under that section.

1610  JOURDAN, SILVESTER.  A Discovery of the Barmudas, otherwise called the Ile of Divels.  London.

> Reprinted London, 1613. See below.
> Jourdan had suffered shipwreck on this island. His work is supposed to have been known to Shakespeare.

> 1613  JOURDAN, SILVESTER.  A plaine Description of the Barmvdas, now called Sommer Ilands. With the Manner of their Discouerie Anno 1609, by the shipwrack and admirable deliuerance of Sir Thomas Gates, and Sir George Sommers, wherein are truly set forth the commodities and profits of that rich, pleasant and healthfull covntrie. With an Addition, or more ample relation of diuers other remarkeable matters concerning those Ilands, since then experienced, lately sent from thence by one of the Colonie now there resident. . . . Ecclesiastes 3:11. God hath made euery thing beautiful in his time.  4to.  London.

> The dedication is signed "W. C." (Castell?).—Sabin.

1620-24  SCOTT, THOMAS.  Vox Populi, or News from Spayne (A-D2 in fours, no preface, errata corrected), 1620; the Second Part of Vox Populi, 2 engravings in text.  4to.  Printed at Goricum by Asherus Jans.  1624 (new style).

> This work is cited here on account of its numerous references to the West Indies and America.

1625  HAGTHORPE, JOHN (Captain).  England's Exchequer, or A Discovrse of the Sea and Navigation, with some things thereto coincident concerning Plantations. Likewise Some Particular Remonstrances, how a Sea-force might be profitably imployed. Wherein by the way, is likewise set down the great Commodities and Victories the Portingalls, Spaniards, Dutch, and others have gotten by Navigation and Plantations in the West Indies, and elsewhere. Written as an incouragement to our English Nation, to affect the like, who are better provided than any of those.  4to.  London.  (49 pp.)

> Hagthorpe took part in the Cadiz expedition, 1625.

1635 BURTON, ROBERT. The English Empire in America, Or, A Prospect of His Majesties Dominions in the West Indies . . . With an account of the Discovery, Scituation, Product, and other Excellencies of these Countries. To which is prefixed a Relation of the first Discovery of the New World called America, by the Spaniards. And of the Remarkable Voyages of several Englishmen to divers places therein. . . . Maps and plates. 12mo. London.

> 2nd edit., London, 1692; 3rd edit., London, 1698; 7th, Dublin, 1729; (second 7th) Dublin, 1735; another, London, 1739.

1648 GOLDING, WILLIAM. Servants on Horse-Back: or, A Free-People bestrided in their persons, and Liberties, by worthlesse men: Being A Representation of the dejected state of the Inhabitants of Summer Islands. Containing Short Illustrations upon a Petition presented to the High Court of Parliament for Redresse. Published by Will. Golding Master of Arts, and Teacher to the Congregation in that Island. 4to. London. (24 pp.)

> This writer complains bitterly of the Governor's tyranny manifested towards himself and "other poor plantours."—Sabin. He was a "Teacher to the Congregation in that Island."

1650 Newes from Sea, concerning Prince Rupert, Capt. Pluncket, Capt. Munckel, and others, with some transactions betwixt the King of Portingal and them, together with the taking of certain ships, and a Relation touching the Strange Newes of Barbadoes. 4to. London. (6 pp.)

> Barbadoes is referred to as "a plantation belonging to the Commonwealth of England."—Bookseller's Note.

1651 Copy of a Petition from the Governor and Company of the Sommer Islands, With annexed Papers, presented to the Right Honorable The Councel of State July the 18th, 1651. Other Copies of several Letters from Captain Josias Forster Governor of the said Islands, and from the said Governor and Councel there: with a Petition from the Inhabitants . . . As also An occasional Letter written to Sir John Danvers, Governor of the said Company. With a Short Collection of the most remarkable Passages from the Original to the Dissolution of the Virginia Company. And a large Description of Virginia, with the several Commodities thereof, wherein the general Company of the Sommer Islands, as many of their Members have considerable Interest. London.

> The letter to Danvers was written by George Wither, and ends the tract. The "Short Collection" was issued separately.—From John Carter Brown.

1655   PEAKE, THOMAS.   America: or, An Exact Description of the West
       Indies. More especially of those Provinces which are under the Do-
       minion of the King of Spain. Faithfully represented by N. N. Gent.
       Map. 8vo. London.

> Reprinted, 8vo, London, 1657; again, London, 1665.
> Who the author was, is uncertain. On the title he is given as N. N. Gent., and
> the Dedicatory Epistle is signed N. N.; but the book was entered at Stationers'
> Hall, July 6, 1655, as by Thomas Peake. The book is divided into two parts, the
> first of which gives a description of the discovery of America and accounts of va-
> rious navigators. The second contains descriptions of Canada, New Spain, Peru,
> Chili, Brazil, Guiana, the West Indies, etc.—Quaritch. This work was evidently
> written with a view to instigating the English to conquer the Spanish dominions
> in America, though the author or publisher disclaimed any such intention in his ad-
> vertisement "To the Reader."—Rich.

1656   LAS CASAS, BARTHOLOMEW DE.   The Tears of the Indians: being
       an Historical and true Account of the Cruel Massacres and Slaughters
       of above Twenty Millions of innocent People: Committed by the Span-
       iards in the Islands of Hispaniola, Cuba, Jamaica, &c. As also, in the
       Continent of Mexico, Peru, & other Places of the West-Indies, To the
       total destruction of those Countries. Written in Spanish by Casaus, an
       Eye-witness of those things: and made English by J. P. . . . London.

> This was the work of John Phillips, a nephew of the poet Milton. It is dedi-
> cated to Oliver Cromwell, and reminds the English of their preeminent position in
> liberty, civil and religious, denounces the Spanish nation . . . and appeals for aid
> to the Protector in the conquest of the West Indies. This 1656 translation omits,
> unfortunately, the Sepulcoda controversy, though it contains accounts of cruelty
> committed.—From Waldman. See Las Casas under 1583 above.

1657   For a description of Jamaica see *A Book of the Continuation of Foreign
       Passages,* under NAVAL EXPEDITIONS.

       LIGON, RICHARD.   A True and Exact History of the Island of Bar-
       badoes, illustrated with a Mapp of the Island as also the Principall
       Trees and Plants there set forth in their due Proportions and Shapes,
       drawn out by their severall and respective Scales. Together with the
       Ingenio that makes the Sugar, with the Plots of the Severall Houses,
       Roomes, and other places, that are used in the whole processe of sugar-
       making, . . . 9 engraved plates. Fol. London.

> Later editions: Folio, London, 1673; and London, 1695, and 1750.
> This volume is of especial importance for its account of the early modes of
> sugar-making in the West Indies. At page 55 occurs the original account on which
> was based the story of Inkle and Yarico. "The book is amusing and with the ex-
> ception of a fib or two, as 'sauce piquante,' is a very accurate account of Barba-
> does." On it are depicted various small engravings of runaway slaves, galleons, sea-
> monsters, camels, and other animals, etc.—Maggs. No. 479.

1661 HICKERINGILL, EDWARD. Jamaica Viewed; With all the Ports, Harbours, and their several Soundings, Towns, and Settlements thereunto belonging. Together with the nature of its Climate, fruitfulnesses of the Soile, and its suitablenesse to English Complexions. With several other collateral Observations and Reflexions upon the Island. Folding map. 8vo. London.

> 2nd edit., 16mo, London, 1661; 3rd edit., 4to, London, 1705.
> The author, who was an eccentric man, after having been an officer in the army, took orders and became a priest, when he gave much offence to his brethren by his wild and often scurrilous attacks upon the church, in a variety of pamphlets. —Chalmers, quoted by Sabin. Barcia says that "this work is a paraphrase of all that had been previously written on the subject,"—Sabin. The work is divided into two parts, the first is devoted to a poetical description of the Island of Jamaica; the second, Reflections upon Jamaica . . . and contains much interesting matter relating to the Indians. There is a long poem describing the Indian methods of hunting, their superstitions, customs, etc.—From Robinson, No. 31. The map is often wanting and was probably not issued with all copies of the book.— Maggs, No. 502.

1666 ROCHEFORT, ——. The History of the Carriby-Islands. Viz. Barbados, St. Christophers, St. Vincents, Martinico, Domenico, Barbouthos, Monserrat, Mevis, Antego, &c. in all XXVIII. I. The Natural; II. The Moral History of those Islands illustrated with several pieces of sculpture representing rarities, with a Caribbian Vocabulary. Rendered into English by John Davies of Kidwelly. Plates. Fol. London.

> French original, Rotterdam, 1660. See below.
> A considerable part of the impression was destroyed in the Great Fire of London; hence its rarity.—Puttick and Simpson.

> 1660 ROCHEFORT, ——. Histoire Naturelle et Morale des Antilles; enrichie d'un grand nombre de belle figures en tailledouce, des places et des raretés les plus considérables qui y font décrites; avec un vocabulaire Caraibe. Rotterdam.

1670 CLARKE, SAMUEL. For a description of the Bermudas and Barbadoes see his *A True, and Faithful Account of the Four Chiefest Plantations of the English in America,* under NORTH AMERICA.

1671 ANDERSON, WILLIAM WEMYSS. A Description and History of the Island of Jamaica. London.

> Jamaica, which had been captured in 1655 by Admiral Penn, became of increasing interest to the English and called forth many books, tracts, and pamphlets in the years to come.

CLARKE, SAMUEL. The Life and Death of the Valiant and Renowned Sir Francis Drake, his Voyages and Discoveries in the West Indies. London.

HARDY, JOHN.   A Description of the Last Voyage to Bermudas, In the Ship Marygold, S. P. Commander. . . . Begun in November the twelfth, 1670. And ending May the third, 1671, with Allowance.   4to.   London.   (24 pp.)

> This is written in verse. Ternaux quotes it under date of 1661.—Sabin.

1672   BLOME, RICHARD.   A Description of the Island of Jamaica; with the other Isles and Territories in America, to which the English are Related, *viz.*, Barbadoes, St. Christophers, Nievis, or Mevis, Antego, St. Vincent, Dominica, Montserrat, Anguilla, Barbada, Bermudes, Carolina, Virginia, Maryland, New-York, New-England, New-Found-Land. Taken from the papers of Sr. Thomas Linch Knight, Governour of Jamaica; and other Experienced Persons in the said Place.   Folding maps of Carolina and Virginia.   16mo.   London.

> 2nd edit., with additions, 8vo, London, 1678; again, 8vo, London, 1687. Translated into French, Amsterdam, 1688. See below.

> 1678   BLOME, RICHARD.   A Description of the Island of Jamaica; . . . Together with the Present State of Algiers. Portrait of Admiral de Ruyter, and 4 folding maps.   8vo.   London.
>
> > The portrait appears for the first time in this edition. The maps are said to have special value.

> 1688   (In French.)   L'Amérique Angloise: ou, Description des Isles et Terres du Roi d'Angleterre dans l'Amérique. Avec de nouvelles Cartes de Chaque Isle et Terre. Traduit de l'Anglois. 7 folding maps by Morden. 8vo.   Amsterdam.

1679   TRAPHAM, THOMAS.   A Discourse of the State of Health in the Island of Jamaica, with a provision therefore Calculated from the Air, the Place, and the Water: The Customs and Manners of Living, . . . 8vo.   London.

> The work includes a long description of the island.—Robinson, No. 20. A scarce medical work. The author treats of the Flux, Fevers, Dropsy, Worms, Venereal Diseases, Dry Belly Ache, etc.—Maggs, No. 549.

1683   POYNTZ, JOHN (Captain).   The Present Prospect of the Famous and Fertile Island of Tobago: with a Description of the Scituation, Growth, Fertility, and Manufacture, of the said Island. To which is added, Proposals for the Encouragement of all those that are minded to settle there.   4to.   London.

> 2nd edit., 4to, London, 1695.
> Poyntz's project for the settling of Tobago, an outlying island of the Lesser Antilles, situated 20 miles N. E. of Trinidad, was unsuccessful.—Quaritch.

The Present State of Jamaica, with the Life of the Great Columbus the first Discoverer: To which is added An Exact Account of Sir Henry Morgan's Voyage to, and famous Siege and taking of Panama from the Spaniards. 12mo. London.

> This is probably one of the books connected with the libel upon Sir Henry Morgan, for which he recovered the sum of 200 pounds, in an action against the publisher, T. Malthus. See *London Gazette,* June eighth, 1685. Rich says that this work was published in order to create a favorable impression of Morgan.— Puttick and Simpson. When one reads Esquemeling (see 1684-85 below) one wonders how it could be possible to say anything libellous about Sir Henry Morgan.

1684-85 ESQUEMELING, JOHN. The Bucaniers of America: Or, a true Account Of The Most remarkable Assaults Committed of late years upon the Coasts of The West-Indies, By the Bucaniers of Jamaica and Tortuga, Both English and French. Wherein are contained more especially, The unparallel'd Exploits of Sir Henry Morgan, our English Jamaican Hero, who sack'd Puerto Velo, burnt Panama, . . . written originally in Dutch by John Esquemeling, one of the Bucaniers, who was present at these Tragedies; and thence translated into Spanish, by Alonso de Bonne-maison, Doctor of Physick, and Practitioner at Amsterdam. Now faithfully rendered into English, London, 1684. The Second Volume. Containing The Dangerous Voyage and Bold Attempts of Captain Bartholomew Sharp, and others, . . . Written by Mr. Basil Ringrose. . . . 4 portraits, 3 maps, and 4 other plates. 2 vols. 4to. London. 1685.

> Vol. I, which consists of three parts, is sometimes found alone. 2nd edit. of the composite version, 8vo, London, 1699; 3rd edit. (said by Quaritch to be really the 4th), with added matter, 8vo, London, 1704; 4th, 2 vols, 12mo, London, 1741; 5th, 2 vols. (without plates), London, 1771; a chapbook version, Glasgow, 1757. Modern editions: Edited by H. Powell, London, 1898; edited for the Broadway Travellers by W. S. Stallybrass, London, 1928. Dutch original, Amsterdam, 1678. The first French edition was translated also from the Spanish (Cologne, 1681), Paris, 1686. See below.
> This work became the inspiration of a vast number of novels, plays, imaginary voyages, and doubtless inspired many an adventurous spirit to turn sea-rover.— Maggs, No. 465. It has well been called the classic of buccaneering books. It is an account which needs to be taken in small doses. Evidently Esquemeling was made of softer stuff than his brother pirates, for he does not always approve of the relish with which the infamous L'Ollonois would tear out the hearts from victims still living. Nor did he applaud the duplicity of Sir Henry Morgan, who violated the honor of a pirate and absconded without dividing the booty obtained in the sack of Panama. He saw the error of his ways and withdrew from the profession and so lived to tell the story. His career as buccaneer ran from 1666 to 1672.

> 1699 ESQUEMELING, JOHN. The History of the Bucaniers of America; From their First Original down to this Time; written in Several Languages; and now collected into one Volume. . . . The Whole newly Translated into English, and illustrated with 25 Copper Plates. 8vo. London.

> > To the contents of the first complete edition are here added "The Journal of Sieur Raveneau de Lussan," and "A Relation of the Voyage of the Sieur de Montauban, the Captain of the Freebooters in Guinea." The editor, name not given, explains his reasons for altering

this edition from the original one: "For whereas the Style before was loose and uncouth in divers parts thereof, the same is now Rectified, and made more correct throughout the whole Body of it; which cannot but add a new life and relish thereunto."—From Gosse. Raveneau de Lussan's account was written originally in French. This was issued separately in 1689. See de Lussan under 1741, SOUTH AMERICA.

1757 ESQUEMELING, JOHN. The History of the Bucaniers of America: Being an Entertaining Narrative of the Exploits, Cruelties and Sufferings of the following noted Commanders. Viz. Joseph Esquemeling, Bat the Portugese, Pierre le Grand, Capt. Sharp, Lolonois, Capt. Watling, Roche Brasiliano, Capt. Cook, . . . Together with a curious Description of the Manners, Customs, Dress, and Ceremonies of the Indians inhabiting near Cape Gracias a Dios. Published for the Improvement and Entertainment of the British Youth of both Sexes. Glasgow.

A very scarce little book.—Gosse.

1928 ESQUEMELING, JOHN. The Buccaneers of America; the translation of 1684-85, revised and edited by W. S. Stallybrass, and with Introduction by Andrew Lang. Illus. 8vo. Broadway Travellers. London.

1678 ESQUEMELING, JOHN. De Americaensche Zeerovers. Amsterdam.

1681 (In Spanish.) Piratas de la America, Y luz a la defensa de las costas de Indias Occidentales. 4 engraved portraits, 5 plates (some folding), folding map and some woodcuts. 4to. Cologne.

This version was the original of the English and French translations.

The Laws of Jamaica, Passed by the Assembly, and Confirmed by His Majesty April 17, 1684. To which is added The State of Jamaica as it is now under the Government of Sir Thomas Lynch. Fol. London.

1685 BURTON, ROBERT. For a description of the West Indies see his *The English Empire in America,* under NORTH AMERICA.

CRAFFORD, JOHN. For a description of the Bermudas see his *A New and Most Exact Account of the Fertile and Famous Colony of Carolina,* under NORTH AMERICA.

1686 BLOME, RICHARD. For a description of the West Indies see his *The present State of His Majesty's Isles and Territories in America,* under NORTH AMERICA.

1689 LAS CASAS, BARTHOLOMEW DE. Popery Truly Display'd in its Bloody Colours: Or a Faithful Narrative of the Horrid and Unexampled Massacres, Butcheries, and all Manner of Cruelties, that Hell and Malice could invent, committed by the Popish Spanish Party on the Inhabitants of the West-Indies: together with the Devastations of several Kingdoms in America by Fire and Sword, for the space of Forty and Two Years, from the time of its first discovery by them. Composed first in Spanish by Bartholomew de las Casas, a Bishop there, and an Eye-Witness of most of these Barbarous Cruelties; afterwards Translated by him into Latin, then by other hands into High-Dutch, Low-Dutch, French, and now Taught to speak Modern English. 4to. London.

> See Las Casas under 1583 and 1656 above.

LITTLETON, EDWARD. The Groans of the Plantations: or a True Account of their Grievous and Extreme Sufferings by the Heavy Impositions upon Sugar, and other hardships. Relating more particularly to the Island of Barbadoes. 4to. London.

> "As the Old Duties upon Sugar did fleece us, so the Addition of the New doth flea us." The high price of Negroes, through the monopoly of the London Company, so affects the planters that "one of the great Burdens of our Lives is the going to buy Negroes. But we must have them. . . . Our Miseries make us savage: they make us forget all Rules of Decency."—Quoted by Robinson, No. 20.

1690 THOMAS, DALBY. An Historical Account of the Rise and Growth of the West-India Colonies, and of the Great Advantages they are to England in respect to Trade. 4to. London.

1692 TUTCHIN, ——. The Earthquake of Jamaica, Described in a Pindarick Poem. Fol. London. (8 pp.)

1693 An Account of the Late Earthquake in Jamaica, June 7th, 1692. Written by a Reverend Divine there to his Friend in London. With some Improvement thereof by another Hand. . . . 4to. London. (26 pp.)

> According to Sabin there is a Dutch translation of this item.
> On June 7th, 1692, Port Royal—then the finest town in the West Indies, and one of the richest places in the world, by reason of the treasures brought in by the buccaneers, whose headquarters it was and the centre of much debauchery—was almost totally destroyed by earthquake, which event led to the development of the town of Kingston.—Cundall, quoted by Maggs, No. 549.

GORDON, PATRICK. The Present State of the European Plantations in the East and West Indies. Subjoined to *Geography Anatomized.* See this date under GEOGRAPHY.

1696 MOQUET, JOHN. For his voyage to the West Indies see his *Travels and Voyages into Asia, Africa, and America,* under GENERAL TRAVELS AND DESCRIPTIONS.

1697   DAMPIER, WILLIAM (Captain).   For descriptions of the islands of
       the West Indies see his *New Voyage round the World,* under CIR-
       CUMNAVIGATIONS.

1699   LAS CASAS, BARTHOLOMEW DE.   An Account of the First Voyages
       and Discoveries made by the Spaniards in America. Containing the
       most Exact Relation hitherto publish'd, of their unparallel'd Cruelties
       on the Indians, in the destruction of above Forty Millions of People.
       Together with the Propositions offer'd to the King of Spain, to pre-
       vent further Ruin of the West-Indies. . . . Illus. with cuts. To which is
       added, The Art of Travelling, shewing how a man may dispose his
       Travels to the best Advantage.   2 plates.   4to.   London.

> A translation of six of the nine Spanish tracts written in 1552. The two
> plates are usually lacking.—From Quaritch. See Las Casas under 1583, 1656, and
> 1689 above.

       MARIANO, JOHN DE.   For references to discoveries and conquests in
       the West Indies see his *General History of Spain,* under WEST EUR-
       OPE.

       WARD, NED.   A trip to Jamaica, with a True Character of the People
       and Island.   Fol.   London.

> Interspersed with poetry, and written in the ordinary style of the "facetious
> author," who is very severe in his observations especially on the people of Port
> Royal, whom he describes as scare-crows, and says: "They have this pleasure in
> drinking that what they put into their bellies, they soon stroke out at their finger
> ends."—Quoted by Sabin. T. Brown's name has also been associated with this
> work. See Ward's *Trip to New England* under this date, NORTH AMERICA.

1702   VEITIA LINAGE, JOSEPH DE.   The Spanish Rule of Trade to the
       West Indies. Written in Spanish. Made English by Capt. John Stev-
       ens.   London.

1707   SLOANE, SIR HANS.   A Voyage to the Islands of Madera, Barbados,
       Nieves (Nevis), St. Christophers, and Jamaica; with the Natural His-
       tory of the Herbs and Trees, Fourfooted Beasts, Fishes, Birds, Insects,
       Reptiles, . . . of the last of these Islands. To which is prefixed, An
       Introduction; wherein is an Account of the Inhabitants, Air, Waters,
       Diseases, Trade, etc., of that place; with some Relations concerning the
       Neighbouring Continent and Islands of America.   160 large Copper
       Plates as big as Life.   2 vols.   Fol.   London.

> Another edition, 2 vols., London, 1725. Noticed in the *Journal des Scavans,*
> 1708, II, 283; 1728, III, 543. (The number of plates is also given as 274.)
> Sir Hans Sloane will be remembered for his famous collection which became
> the foundation of the British Museum.

1708 An Account of Jamaica and its Inhabitants, by a Gentleman long resident in the West Indies. 8vo. London.

GRAVES, JOHN. A Memorial: or a Short Account of the Bahama Islands; Of their Situation, Product, Conveniency of Trading with the Spaniards; The Benefit that ariseth by the great Quantities of Salt that is made by the Sun; and the Safety of all Ships that are in distress near those parts do find, by having so good a Harbour as Providence to bare away to for Succour. Delivered to the Hon. Commissioners of Her Majesty's Customs. By John Graves, Collector of Customs in those Islands, and now Humbly Presented to both Houses of Parliament. 4to. London. (8 pp.)

OLDMIXON, JOHN. For an account of the present state of the British colonies in the West Indies see his *British Empire in America,* under NORTH AMERICA.

1709 SLONENBERGH, JASPER VAN. Useful Transactions for the Months of May-September, 1709, containing a Voyage to the Island of Cajamai in America. 12mo. London.

> Cajamai is an anagram for Jamaica. William King's name is also associated with this item.

1712 For reference to the West Indies see *A Letter from a West India Merchant to a Gentleman at Tunbridge,* under NORTH AMERICA.

1714 The Assiento Contract Consider'd: as also the Advantages and Decay of the Trade of Jamaica and the Plantations . . . . 12mo. London.

> This was the arrangement between Great Britain and Spain whereby the former was allowed to send one trading ship a year to the Spanish colonies. The West Indian colonies were opposed to the arrangement.

The Present State of the Sugar Plantations considered; but more especially that of the Island of Barbadoes. 8vo. London. (30 pp.)

1716 FRENCH, G. History of Col. Parke's Administration whilst . . . Governor of Leeward Islands, with Account of the Rebellion in Antegoa, wherein he, with several others, were Murther'd. Portrait. 8vo. London.

> This includes the articles of complaint exhibited against Parke.—Bookseller's Note.

1719   PARKER, GEORGE.   The West-India Almanack for the Year 1719.
       18mo.   London.

> This contains an account of America, particularly of "New England or Vir-
> ginia (all of the English dominions south of Canada, etc.), and the West Indies;
> a Jamaica Chronology from 1494, and a list of governors of the West India
> Islands.—Sabin.

1721   The Case of the Present Possessors of the French Lands in the Island of
       St. Christophers . . . 8vo.   London.

1722   M., R.   A General Survey of that part of the Island of St. Christopher's
       which formerly belonged to France; and now was yielded up to Great
       Britain forever by the late Treaty of Utrecht. Together with an esti-
       mate of the value of those Lands, and a Proposal and Scheme for rais-
       ing a very considerable Sum of Money, for the use of the Publick, on
       the Produce thereof . . . 8vo.   London.   (48 pp.)

1725   A Relation of the late intended Settlement of the Islands of St. Lucia and
       St. Vincent in America, in the year 1722.   London.

1725-26   HERRERA, ANTONIO DE.   The General History of the Vast Con-
       tinent and Islands of America, commonly call'd The West Indies, from
       the First Discovery thereof: with the Best Accounts the People could
       give of their Antiquities. Collected from the original Relations sent to
       the Kings of Spain. . . . 2 maps and 16 plates, and portraits of Columbus
       and Cortez. Translated into English by Capt. John Stevens. 6 vols.
       8vo.   London.

> Spanish original, Madrid, 1601-1615. See below.
> One of the greatest historical works ever written, and the most valuable and
> accurate work on the early history of America. Herrera was born in 1559. He
> became official historian to Philip II, III, and IV. He had free access to many
> documentary sources which have since been lost or destroyed.—Maggs, No. 549.
> "His work is a perfect treasure-house of the most valuable details, regarding the
> original state of the religion and manners of the Indians."—Field, *Indian Bibli-
> ography*, quoted. Though possessing some defects, this is the best translation of
> the whole of Herrera.—Bookseller's Note.

> 1601-1615   HERRERA Y TORDESILLAS, ANTONIO DE. Historia de los
>       Hechos de los Castellanos en las islas i tierra firme del mar oceano.
>       Plates. 8 vols. in 4. 4to. Madrid.

1726   The State of the Island of Jamaica. Chiefly in Relation to its Commerce,
       and the Conduct of the Spaniards in the West-Indies. Addressed to
       a Member of Parliament, By a Person who resided several years at
       Jamaica. 8vo.   London.

TOWNE, R.   A Treatise of the Diseases most frequent in the West Indies, and herein more particularly of those which occur in Barbadoes.
8vo.   London.

1727   Some Modern Observations on Jamaica, its Natural History, Improvements, Trade and Manner of Living.   London.

> This is to be found at the end of vol. 2 of WHARTONIA: or, Miscellanies
> in Verse and Prose, by the Wharton Family, and Several other Persons of Dis-
> tinction, 2 vols., 12mo. It is a collection of poems, ballads, letters, and prose writ-
> ings. These two volumes were published by Curll ("the Unspeakable") without
> his imprint, and it is presumed they were intended to accompany Curll's two vol-
> umes of Pope's *Miscellanies,* published in 1727.—Bookseller's Note. The Obser-
> vations are dated from Port Royal, 1726.

1729   A Letter to Caleb D'Anvers, Esq.: occasioned by the Depredations committed by the Spaniards in the West Indies.   With some Observations
on the Trade carried on from Jamaica to the Spanish Coast.   8vo.
London.   (32 pp.)

1730   ROBERTSON, —— (Rev. Mr. of Mavis).   A Letter to the Right Reverend the Lord Bishop of London, from an Inhabitant of His Majesty's Leeward-Caribbee-Islands.   Containing some Considerations on his
Lordship's Two Letters of May 19, 1727.   The first to the Masters
and Mistresses of Families in the English Plantations abroad; The
Second to the Missionaries there.   In which is Inserted, A Short Essay
concerning the Conversion of the Negro-Slaves in our Sugar Colonies: Written in the Month of June, 1727, by the same Inhabitant.
4to.   London.

1731   Remarks upon a Book, entitled The Present State of the Sugar Colonies
Consider'd.   Wherein some of the Consequences and Effects of Re-
straining our Trade are Examined.   8vo.   London.

> Relating to the sugar and rum trade between Barbadoes, Jamaica, the Eng-
> lish and French West Indian Islands, and the English and French North Amer-
> ican Colonies and Great Britain.—Maggs, No. 502. See under 1714 above.

1732   COLUMBUS, CHRISTOPHER.   The History of the Life and Actions
of Admiral Christopher Colon, and of his Discovery of the West Indies Called the New World.   Written by his own Son Don Ferdinand
Colon.   In Churchill II, 501-628.

> Reprinted in Pinkerton XII, 1-155. For other items concerning Columbus
> see under the following dates below: 1744-48, 1799, 1847, 1870, 1892, 1900, 1902,
> 1929, and 1930.

PULLEN, JOHN. The Original Plan, Progress and Present State of the South-Sea Company: Or, Some Occasional Thoughts upon the State of the British Trade in the West Indies, . . . 8vo. London.

1734 CATESBY, MARK. For a description of the Bahama Islands see his *The Natural History of Carolina, Florida, and the Bahama Islands,* under NORTH AMERICA.

A Letter From one of the Leeward Islands, Tending to show the immediate Necessity of a further Inspection into the State of the British Sugar Colonies and Trade. 8vo. London. (15 pp.)

1735 ATKINS, JOHN. For an account of the West Indies see his *A Voyage to Guinea, Brasil, and the West Indies,* under GENERAL TRAVELS AND DESCRIPTIONS.

1738 BENNETT, JOHN. Two Letters and several Calculations on the Sugar Colonies and Trade; addressed to two Committees nominated by the West-India Merchants, . . . With . . . 1. Four Letters concerning the Flourishing Condition . . . of the French Sugar Colonies . . . 2. Some Proposals . . . for the . . . Advancement of the British Sugar Colonies . . . 2nd edit. 8vo. London.

1739 The British Sailor's Discovery: or, the Spanish Pretensions confuted. Containing A Short History of the Discoveries and Conquests of Spain in America, with a particular account of the illegal and unchristian Means they made use of to establish their Settlement there; Proving that the sovereign sole Dominion claimed by the Crown of Spain to the West-Indies, is founded upon an unjustifiable Possession; . . . That America was discovered and planted by the Ancient Britons 300 years before Columbus conducted the Spaniards thither; . . . Also the Declaration of War against Spain by Oliver Cromwell, in 1655, translated from the Latin original; wherein the English Right to the West-Indies is plainly demonstrated. 8vo. London.

> Apparently written to excite the British Nation against the Spaniards. Relates to the dispute between Spain and England about the limits of Carolina and Georgia. Perhaps it is the same as the "Proposal for humbling Spain," published the same year.—Sabin.

A Description of the Windward Passage, and Gulf of Florida, with the Course of the British Trading-Ships to, and from the Island of Jamaica. Also an Account of the Trade Winds, and of the Variable

Winds and Currents on the Coasts thereabouts, at different Seasons of the Year. Illustrated with a Chart of the Coast of Florida, and the Islands of Bahama, Cuba, Hispaniola, Jamaica, and the adjacent smaller Islands, Shoals, Rocks, and other remarkable Things in the Course of the Navigation in the West-Indies. Whereby is demonstrated, The Precariousness of those Voyages to the West-India Merchants, and the Impossibility of their Homeward-Bound Ships keeping clear of the Spanish Garda Costa's: The Whole very necessary for the Information of such as never were in those Parts of the World. To which are added, Some Proposals for the better securing of the British Trade and Navigation to and from the West-Indies. Chart and plate. 4to. London.

LESLIE, CHARLES. A New and Exact Account of Jamaica, wherein The Ancient and Present State of that Colony, its Importance to Great Britain, Laws, Trade, Manners and Religion, together with the most remarkable and curious Animals, Plants, Trees, etc., are described: With a particular Account of the Sacrifices, Libations, etc., at this Day in use among the Negroes. 8vo. Edinburgh.

> 3rd edit., with the addition of An Account of Admiral Vernon's Success at Porto Bello and Chagre, Edinburgh, 1740.

1740 CARRANZA, DOMINGO GONZALES. A Geographical Description of the Coasts, Harbours and Sea Ports of the Spanish West Indies; particularly of Porto Bello, Cartagena and the Island of Cuba; with Observations of the Currents, and the Variations of the Compass in the Bay of Mexico, and the North Sea of America. Translated from a curious and authentic Manuscript, written in Spanish by Domingo Gonzales Carranza, his Catholick Majesty's principal Pilot of the Flota in New Spain, Anno 1718. To which is added, An Appendix, containing Capt. Parker's own Account of his taking the town of Porto Bello, in the Year 1601. With an Index, and a New and Correct Chart of the Whole; as also Plans of the Havannah, Porto Bello, Cartagena, and La Vera Cruz. 8vo. London.

The Present State of the Revenues and Forces, by Sea and Land, of France and Spain. Compar'd with those of Great Britain. Being an Essay to demonstrate the Disadvantages under which France must enter into the present War, if the natural Force of Britain is exerted. To which is added, An Appendix: Containing a View of those Countries of the Spanish West Indies that will probably be the seat of the present War. 8vo. London.

> Another edition, Dublin, 1740.
> This work relates entirely to America, Mexico, and Central America, the West Indies, Florida, the English Colonies in America, and a section of New Mexico.—Maggs, No. 502.

SLOANE, SIR HANS. A New History of Jamaica, from the Earliest Accounts, to the Taking of Porto Bello by Vice Admiral Vernon. In thirteen Letters from a Gentleman to his Friend . . . In which are briefly interspersed, The Characters of the Governors and Lieutenant-Governors: viz. Colonel D'Oyley (and twenty-four others). 2 maps. 8vo. London.

> 2nd edit., London, 1740; another edition, Dublin, 1741. Translated into French, London, 1751. See below.
> *Inter alia,* narratives are told of the buccaneers—Sir Henry Morgan, Bartholomew, Brasiliano, Lewis Scot, John Davis, and Edward Teach, and an account is given of the Scots settlement at Darien.—Quaritch. The work is seemingly anonymous, but it has been attributed to Sir Hans Sloane, the antiquarian.

> 1751    (In French.) Histoire de la Jamaïque, traduite de l'anglais (de Hans Sloane), par . . . (Raulin), ancien officier de dragons. 2 vols. 8vo. London.

ST. MICHEL, MAURICE DE. Voyage aux Isles Commercantes en Amérique. Paris, 1654.

> Pinkerton XVII cites this with the notation that it was translated into English by Stephens (Stevens?), London, 1740.

1741 CAMPBELL, JOHN. For that part of Spanish America lying within the West India Islands see his *A Concise History of the Spanish America,* under SOUTH AMERICA.

A Geographical and Historical Description of the Principal Objects of the Present War in the West Indies: viz. Cartagena, Puerto-Bello, La Vera Cruz, The Havana, and San Augustin. Shewing their Situation, Strength, Trade, etc. With An Account of the many Sieges they have undergone to the present Time. The whole Compiled from the most Authentic Memoirs, and Enlarged with many Curious Particulars not to be met with in former Authors. To which is prefix'd An Accurate Map of the West-Indies adapted to the work. 8vo. London.

> This contains much matter relating to Sir Henry Morgan and the Buccaneers.—Robinson, No. 20.

KEIMER, SAMUEL. Carribeana. Containing Letters and Dissertations, together with Poetical Essays, on various Subjects and Occasions: chiefly wrote by several Hands in the West-Indies, and some of them Gentlemen residing there. Now collected together in Two Volumes. Wherein are also comprised, divers Papers relating to Trade, Government, and Laws in General; but more especially, to those of the British Sugar Colonies, and of Barbados in Particular: As likewise the Characters of the most eminent Men that have died, of late years, in that Island. To which are added in an Appendix, Some Pieces never before Published. 2 vols. 4to. London.

> This was made up from the "Barbadoes Gazette," edited by Samuel Keimer, a printer, formerly of Philadelphia. It contains many curious epigrams, satirical poems, and love songs, and also historical notices relating to New England and other States. It is arranged in a stiff imitation of the "Tatler."—Sabin.

Some Memoirs of the First Settlement of the Island of Barbadoes, . . . Extracted from ancient Records, Papers, and Accounts, . . . Also the Laws and Constitution of Barbadoes. London.

1743  The American Traveller; being a new Historical Collection, carefully compiled from original Memoirs in several languages, and the most Authentic Voyages and Travels, containing a compleate account of that Part of the World, now called the West Indies, from its Discovery by Columbus to the Present Time. Portraits. 8vo. London.

> "This work was published in 18 numbers, and appears to be the commencement of an extensive work, but of which no more than this volume appeared. It commences with a long introduction on the rise, progress and improvement of navigation, which is followed by book 1, divided into two chapters: one on the peopling of America, and the other, which concludes the book, containing an account of the voyages of Columbus."—Rich, quoted by Sabin.

Memoirs of the First Settlement of the Island of Barbadoes, and other Carribbee Islands, from Ancient Records, Papers, and Accounts taken from Mr. Wm. Arnold, Mr. Samuel Bulkly, and Mr. John Summers, some of the First Settlers, the last of whom was alive in 1688, aged 82. 8vo. London.

1744-48  COLUMBUS, CHRISTOPHER. The Voyage of Don Christopher Columbus. In Harris II, 2-6.

COLUMBUS, CHRISTOPHER. The First Voyage of Christopher Columbus, in which he discovered the Lucayan Islands, and afterwards Cuba and Hispaniola, which opened a Passage from Europe to America, with his Return to Spain, and Reception by their Catholic Majesties. In Harris II, 3-16.

> Taken, the editor says, from one of the Spanish historians (probably Herrera).

The Second Voyage of the Admiral Don Christopher Columbus, to the West Indies, including an Account of all the Discoveries made by him in that Voyage. In Harris II, 16-27.

The Third Voyage of Admiral Don Christopher Columbus to the West-Indies, in which he first saw the Continent of America, including the Troubles to which he was exposed, and his being sent home in Irons. In Harris II, 27-39.

The Fourth Voyage of Admiral Don Christopher Columbus; and his Discoveries on the Continent, and the Islands in America; with an Account of his Return from that Voyage, and his Decease. In Harris II, 39-49.

The History of the several Discoveries and Settlements, and Conquests made by the Spaniards in the West-Indies, after the Death of the Admiral Don Christopher Columbus, to the Expedition of Ferdinand, or Hernan Cortes. In Harris II, 49-63.

1745 HARRIS, T.   Account of the Spanish Butcheries on the Native Indians. 8vo.   London.

> The title is from a bookseller's catalogue; probably "Old England Forever" with a new title-page.—Sabin.

Letter to a Member of Parliament concerning the Importance of our Sugar-Colonies to Great Britain. By a Gentleman who resided many years in the Island of Jamaica. 8vo.   London.

> Illustrating the ill effects of an additional tax on sugar, the author gives many interesting particulars of the cost of living during the N. American War, difficulties of marketing, slave labour, freight costs, production of rum, etc.—Bookseller's Note.

SMITH, WILLIAM (Rev.).   A Natural History of Nevis, and the rest of the English Leeward Charibee Islands in America. With many other Observations particularly, an introduction to the Art of Decyphering. In Eleven Letters from the Rev. Mr. Smith, sometime Rector of St. John's at Nevis, and now Rector of St. Mary's in Bedford; to the Revd. Mr. Mason, B.D. Woodwardian Professor, and Fellow of Trinity College in Cambridge. 8vo.   Cambridge.

1750 HUGHES, GRIFFITH (Rev.). The Natural History of Barbados. In Ten Books. Large folding map and numerous engraved plates. Fol. London.

> Book 1, General Account; 2, Of the Diseases peculiar to this and the neighbouring Islands; 3, Of Land Animals; 4, Of Vegetables; 5, Of Trees, Shrubs, and Plants of the Pomiferous kind; 6, Of the Bocciferous kind; 7, Of the Pruniferous kind; 8, Of the Siliquose kind; 9, Of the Shore and its Inhabitants; 10, Sea and its Inhabitants.—Bookseller's Note. There is a well-written article on this work in the *Monthly Review*, III, 197, which states that it is of no value to the naturalist. The book is handsomely printed, and the plates are finely executed from drawings by Ehret, and are colored only in large paper copies of the work. —Sabin.

Tobago, Or, a Geographical Description, Natural and Civil History, together with a full Representation of the Produce, and other Advantages arising from the Fertility, excellent Harbours, and happy Situation of that Island . . . Colored folding map. London.

> This work was written with the object of demonstrating the superior right of Great Britain to Tobago over that of France. It is an unusual work.—Maggs, No. 549.

1753 POOLE, ROBERT (M.D.). For an account of travels to the West Indies see his *The Beneficent Bee,* under WEST EUROPE.

1755 RAMBLE, JAMES. The Life and Adventures of James Ramble, interspersed with accounts of certain noble personages deeply concerned in the northern commotions in the years 1715. 2 vols. 12mo. London.

> This contains his adventures in the West Indies.—Sabin.

1756 BROWNE, PATRICK. Civil and Natural History of Jamaica: Foreign Trade, Revenue, Vegetable Productions (classified), Quadrupeds, Birds, Fishes, . . . 2 folding maps and 49 plates of birds, fishes, insects, animals. Fol. London.

> 2nd edit., (without the plates, which had been destroyed in a fire) with the addition of a Linnaean index and a map of Jamaica, London, 1789. Lowndes calls attention to a favorable review of this work by Samuel Johnson in the *Literary Magazine*. The author was a student of botany and a correspondent of Linnaeus.

A Letter from a Citizen of Port-Royal in Jamaica, to a Citizen of New York. Relating to some Extraordinary Measures lately set on Foot in that Island. 8vo. Dublin. (28 pp.)

1759 DILWORTH, H. W. The History of the Buccaniers of America: Being an Entertaining Narrative of the Exploits, Cruelties and Sufferings . . . of Noted Commanders. Copperplates. 24mo. London.

HILARY, WILLIAM.   Observations on the Changes of the Air and the Concomitant Epidemical Diseases, in the Island of Barbadoes, . . . 8vo. London.

1760   JEFFERYS, THOMAS.   For a description of the West Indies see his *The Natural and Civil History of the French Dominions in North and South America,* under NORTH AMERICA.

1762   For a description of the Spanish colonies in the West Indies see *An Account of the Spanish Settlements in America,* under SOUTH AMERICA.

ALLEN, ROBERT.   The Great Importance of the Havanna, set forth in an Essay on the Nature and Methods of carrying on a Trade to the South Sea and the Spanish West-Indies. By Robert Allen, Esq., who resided some years in the Kingdom of Peru.   8vo.   London.

> This probably relates more to South America than to the West Indies.

JEFFERYS, THOMAS.   Description of the Spanish Islands and Settlements on the Coast of the West Indies, compiled from Authentic Memoirs.   32 maps and plans.   4to.   London.

> This work was published when war had just broken out between England and Spain, and when England's attention was especially turned towards Spain's Colonies in America . . . Among the most interesting of the contents are the accounts of Florida, Pennsacola, and St. Augustine de la Florida.—Maggs, No. 465.

1763   CAMPBELL, JOHN.   Candid and Impartial Considerations on the Nature of the Sugar Trade; the comparative Importance of the British and French Islands in the West-Indies; with the Value and Consequence of St. Lucia and Granada, truly stated.   3 large folding maps. 8vo.   London.

> "Upon the whole, we think it a masterly performance."—*Monthly Review,* quoted by Sabin.

GRANT, JEREMIAH.   The Peregrinations of Jeremiah Grant, Esq., the West-Indian.   8vo.   London.

1766   The Privileges of the Island of Jamaica Vindicated; with an Impartial Narrative of the late dispute between the Governor and House of Representatives, upon the case of Mr. Olyphant, A member of that House. (With an Appendix, giving an Historical Account of the Establishment of the Colony, its Constitution and form of Government.) 8vo. London.

This work is noticed in the *Monthly Review*, XXXV, 473.

1768 FRERE, GEORGE. A Short History of Barbadoes, from its First Discovery and Settlement, to the End of the Year 1767. 8vo. London.

This work is attributed to Frere.

SANDBY, PAUL. Twenty-seven Views in North America and the West-Indies, with Descriptions in English and French. (See the same under NORTH AMERICA.)

1769 CHEVALIER DE * * * For an account of the West Indies see his *Voyages et Avantures,* under NORTH AMERICA.

1772 DELACROIX, JACQUES VINCENT. Memoirs of an American. 2 vols. 12mo. London.

French original, Lausanne and Paris, 1771. See below.
Cited by Monoghan. Delacroix was thought to have travelled in America.

1771 DELACROIX, JACQUES VINCENT. Mémoires d'un Américain avec une description de la Prusse et de l'Isle de Saint Dominique. Par l'Auteur des lettres d'Affi à Zurac et de celles d'un Philosophe sensible. 2 vols. 12mo. Lausanne & Paris.

1774. FOWLER, JOHN. A Summary Account of the Present Flourishing State of the respectable Colony of Tobago, in the British West Indies. Maps and plan. 8vo. London.

Reprinted, London, 1777.

The Importance of Jamaica to Great-Britain, consider'd. With some Account of that Island, from its Discovery in 1492 to this Time: and a List of the Governors and Presidents, with an Account of their Towns, Harbors, Bays, Buildings, Inhabitants, Whites and Negroes, etc. The Country and People cleared from Misrepresentation; the Misbehavior of Spanish Governors by entertaining Pirates, and plundering the Inhabitants and Merchants of Jamaica, and the Rise of the Pirates among them. An Account of their Fruits, Drugs, Timber and Dying Woods, and of the Uses they are apply'd to there: with a Description of Exotick Plants, preserved in the Gardens of the Curious in England; . . . Also of their Beasts, Birds, Fishes, and Insects; with their Eatables and Potables, Distempers, and Remedies. With an Account of their Trade and Produce; with the Advantages they are of to Great-Britain, Ireland, and the Colonies in North America, and the Commodities they take in Return from them, . . . In a Letter to a Gentleman. In which is added, A Postscript, of the Benefits which may arise by keeping of Carthagena, to Great-Britain and our American Colonies. 8vo. London.

> This was published while Admiral Vernon was making his unsuccessful attack upon Carthagena.

LONG, EDWARD.   The History of Jamaica: A General Survey of its Ancient and Modern State, with Reflections on its Settlements, Inhabitants, Climate, Products, Commerce, Laws, and Government, . . . 16 maps, plans, and views.   3 vols.   4to.   London.

> "The high station of the author at Jamaica, where he was Judge of the Admiralty Court, gave him every opportunity of procuring authentic materials, which have been digested with ingenuity and candour. The work has now become exceedingly rare".—Nichols, *Literary Anecdotes,* quoted by Sabin, who adds that the book is not so rare as this remark seems to indicate.

1775   JEFFERYS, THOMAS.   The West-India Atlas, or, A Compendious Description of the West-Indies, illustrated with 40 correct charts and maps, taken from actual surveys, together with an Historical Account of the Several Countries and Islands which compose that part of the World, their Discovery, Situation, Extent, Boundaries, Product, Trade, Inhabitants, Strength, Government, Religion, etc. By the late Thomas Jefferys, Geographer to The King.   Atlas fol.   London.

> This also includes, Florida, Louisiana, Venezuela, etc.—Maggs, No. 502.

1776   For a description of the West-Indies see *The North-American and West-Indian Gazetteer,* under NORTH AMERICA.

RAYNAL, GUILLAUME THOMAS (Abbé).   A Philosophical and Political History of the Settlements and Trade of the Europeans in the East and West Indies. Translated from the French by J. Justamond. Maps and portraits.   4 vols.   8vo.   London.

> This popular work was reprinted many times: 2nd edit., 5 vols., London, 1776; 4 vols., Dublin, 1776; 3rd edit., newly translated from the augmented French edition, 5 vols., London, 1777; with addition of his History of the Present War in America, Edinburgh, 1779; the same, 2 vols. in 1, Aberdeen; 6 vols., including his The Revolution in America, Edinburgh, 1782; "the best edition," 8 vols., London, 1783; again, 8 vols., London, 1788. French original, Amsterdam, 1770; augmented edition, Geneva, 1780. See below.
> This work is very comprehensive in its scope: it relates to trade in the Persian Gulf and with Arabia, the conquests of the Portuguese and Dutch in the East, Spanish conquests in South America, the Portuguese conquest of Brazil, the West Indies, the English colonies in North America, etc.—From Maggs, No. 502. The Abbé Raynal determined to increase the scope of the original work, published in

1770, and in 1780 he brought out the much enlarged Geneva edition, of which, according to Grimm, Diderot wrote more than one-third. A decree was issued by the parliament of Paris, May 21, 1781, against the author and his book, which obliged him to leave France.—Quaritch. The work was highly praised in Lord Gardenstone's *Travelling Memorandum*. He "may with reason be considered as one of the Authors of the French Revolution, from the republican, democratic, and licentious principles which are interspersed throughout that celebrated 'History'; and recommended by every grace and allurement of style. Shocked at the dreadful effects produced by his own writings, in the month of May, 1791, the Abbé appeared voluntarily at the bar of the National Assembly, and boldly expostulated with them on their rash and ruinous measures. The principal charge he brought against them was of a singular nature—that they had literally followed his principles, that they had reduced to practice the reveries and abstract ideas of a Philosopher, without having previously adapted and accommodated them to men, times, and circumstances." His address was received with evident displeasure, and he was prosecuted but allowed to retreat.—Nichols, *Literary Anecdotes*.

1770 RAYNAL, GUILLAUME THOMAS (Abbé). Histoire philosophique et politique des établissements et du commerce des Européens dans les deux Indes. 6 vols. 8vo. Amsterdam.

1780 RAYNAL, GUILLAUME THOMAS (Abbé). Histoire Philosophique et Politique des Etablissements et du Commerce des Européens dans les Deux Indes. 4 vols. with Atlas 1 vol. 5 vols. in all. Geneva.

RYMER, JAMES. Description of the Island of Nevis, with an Account of its Principal Diseases. London.

SINGLETON, JOHN. A Description of the West Indies, a Poem, in four Books: Containing References to Negro Trading, Nevis, St. Christopher, Vale of Sulphur, Deseada and Antigua, Wreckers and Pirates, Plantation Owners, Negro Burial, etc. By Mr. John Singleton, during his Excursions among those Islands. 4to. London.

Reprinted, with a slightly different title, Dublin, 1776; again, London, 1777. It was first printed at Bridge-Town, Barbadoes. See below.

The author was a member of the first regular theatrical company that came to America, arriving with Mr. Hallam and others on the *Charming Sally* at Yorktown, June 28, 1752; and opening a few months later at Williamsburg in the "Merchant of Venice." He also wrote the prologue for the company's first performance in Williamsburg, Sept. 5, 1752, and later for their opening in New York City.

1776 SINGLETON, JOHN. A General Description of the West-Indian Islands, as far as relates to the British, Dutch, and Danish Governments, from Barbadoes to Saint Croix. In Blank Verse. 8vo. Dublin.

1777 BYERS, JOHN (Surveyor). References to the Plan of the Island of Dominica. As surveyed from the Year 1765 to 1773. 8vo. London. (30 pp.)

COLUMBUS, CHRISTOPHER. The History of the Voyages of Christopher Columbus in order to discover America and the West Indies. 8vo. London.

1778   The Present State of the West Indies, containing an accurate Description
       of what parts are now possessed by the several Powers in Europe: to-
       gether with an authentick Account of the first Discoverers of these
       Islands and the Part adjacent, their Situation, Product, Trade . . . also
       their principal Bays and Harbours; with map of the West Indies.   4to.
       London.

1780   PATERSON, DANIEL (Lieut.-Col.).   A Topographical Description of
       Grenada; surveyed by Monsieur Pinel in 1763 . . . with the Addition of
       English Names, Alternations of Property, etc. . . . 4to.   London.   (13
       pp.)

       SUCKLING, GEORGE.   An Historical Account of the Virgin Islands in
       the West Indies, from their being settled by the English near a Century
       past, to their obtaining a Legislature of their own in the Year 1773;
       and the lawless State in which his Majesty's Subjects in those Islands
       have remained since that Time to the present.   8vo.   London.

1781   FOWLER, WILLIAM.   A General Account of the Calamities occasioned
       by the Late Tremendous Hurricanes and Earthquakes in the West-
       India Islands, Foreign as well as Domestic; with the Petitions to, and
       Resolutions of the House of Commons, in Behalf of the Sufferers at
       Jamaica and Barbados . . . Carefully Collated from Authentic Papers.
       8vo.   London.

           Allibone attributes this to William Fowler, M.D., and quotes "Fevers in the
       West Indies," 1860.—Sabin. See also the following item on the same subject.

       An History of Jamaica and Barbadoes, with an Authentic Account of the
       Lives Lost, and the Damage Sustained in each Island, by the late Hur-
       ricanes. To which is prefixed, A Sermon, preached on the Melancholy
       Occasion at St. Clements, Lombard Street.   4to.   London.

1782   BRUCE, PETER HENRY.   For his travels in the West Indies see his
       *Memoirs of Peter Henry Bruce,* under GENERAL TRAVELS AND
       DESCRIPTIONS (under date of 1772, which is given in error for
       1782).

           This also contains his adventures among the Creek and Cherokee Indians in
       Georgia, etc.

       For an account of the West Indies see *The Polite Traveller,* under NORTH
       AMERICA.

PULLEN, J. Memoirs of the Maritime Affairs of Great Britain, especially in relation to our concerns in the West-Indies. To which is prefix'd, the Original Letter of the Author to (and by the Command of) the Earl of Oxford, when High Treasurer of England, in relation to the South-Sea Company and the Trade they were assigned to carry on; in which the consequences of an ill Management in that respect are fully laid open, and the true nature of such a Commerce explained. . . . To which is added, Capt. Pain's Short View of Spanish America, containing a succinct deduction of Navigation, from the Original to the Discovery of the New World; and an account of the Extent, Quality, Riches, and Trade of his Catholic Majesty's Dominions there. 8vo. London.

STOKES, ANTHONY. For matter relating to the West Indies see his *View Of the Constitution of the British Colonies in North America,* under NORTH AMERICA.

1784 EDWARDS, BRYAN. Thoughts on the late Proceedings of Government, respecting the Trade of the West India Islands with the United States of North America . . . with postscript addressed to Lord Sheffield. 8vo. London.

> See also Edwards under 1797 below.

1785 TURNBULL, ——. Letters to a Young Planter; or Observations on the Management of a Sugar-Plantation. To which is added, the Planter's Kalendar. Written on the Island of Grenada, by an Old Planter . . . 8vo. London. (58 pp.)

> The author is probably Lieut. Gordon Turnbull. See Turnbull under 1795 below.

1787 MOSELY, BENJAMIN (M.D.) A Treatise on Tropical Diseases, and on the Climate of the West Indies. 8vo. London.

> 3rd edit., London, 1793.

> This was favorably reviewed in the *Gent. Mag.,* LX, 9-11. The author was appointed Surgeon-General of Jamaica. He was successful in treating dysentery, "which has been, and then was, the destruction of their armies, and the cause of the defeat of almost every enterprize in the war, by perspiration."—Quoted by Nichols, *Literary Anecdotes.*

1788 An Account of Jamaica. Newcastle-upon-Tyne.

HUNTER, JOHN (M.D.). Observations on the Diseases of the Army in Jamaica and on the best Means of preserving Health of Europeans in that Climate. 8vo. London.

>   The author was the most famous physician and surgeon in England in the 18th century.

WOODS, JOSEPH. Thoughts on Slavery of the Negroes, as it affects the British Colonies in the West Indies. 2nd edit. 8vo. London. (Printed for the author.)

>   The author's object seems to have been to prove "how well satisfied" the slaves were with their lot. . . . The author has confined his observations on the treatment and condition of slaves in the British colonies in the West Indies, to the island of Jamaica only.—From Sotheran.

1789   COKE, THOMAS. (Rev. Dr.). A Journal of his Visit to Jamaica, and of his Third Tour on the Continent of America. 12mo. London. (16 pp.)

>   See Coke under 1791-92 below and under 1793, NORTH AMERICA.

FRANCKLYN, G. Observations occasioned by the attempts made in England to effect the Abolition of the Slave Trade, shewing, the Manner in which Negroes are treated in the British Colonies in the West Indies. 8vo. London.

>   This was first printed at Kingston, Jamaica. It is an extraordinary production, suggesting that Jamaica was an earthly paradise for the Negro slave; ridiculing the efforts of Granville Sharp, whom the writer miscalls Glanville Sharpe.— Sotheran.

GRAVES, JOHN. A Short Account of the Bahama Islands, their Climate, Productions, etc. To which are added, some Strictures upon their relative and political Situation, the Defects of their present Government, etc., etc. By a Barrister at Law, late His Majesty's Solicitor-General of those Islands, and King's Counsel for the Provinces of Nova Scotia and New Brunswick. London.

>   1st edit., London, 1788. The pamphlet treats of certain grievances the inhabitants of those islands were suffering under and beseeches redress. See Sabin.

LUFFMAN, JOHN. A Brief Account of the Island of Antigua, together with the Customs and Manners of its Inhabitants as well White as Black; As also, an accurate Statement of the Food, Clothing, Labor, and Punishment of Slaves. In Letters to a Friend, written . . . in 1786, 1787, 1788. Map. 12mo. London.

>   2nd edit., revised, London. 1790.
>   "Contains nothing very interesting."—*Monthly Review*, Jan., 1790, quoted by Sabin.

1790 BECKFORD, WILLIAM. A Descriptive Account of the Island of Jamaica: with Remarks upon the Cultivation of the Sugar-Cane, throughout the different Seasons of the Year, and chiefly considered in a Picturesque Point of View; also, Observations and Reflections upon what would probably be the Consequences of an Abolition of the Slave Trade, and of the Emancipation of the Slaves. 2 vols. 8vo. London.

> "The author resided for several years in Jamaica and was largely concerned in its plantations and traffic; his work, in consequence, contains much valuable information."—Rich, quoted by Maggs, No. 502. The agitation of Wilberforce was beginning to alarm the planters.

SHEFFIELD, (JOHN BAKER HOLROYD, 1st Earl of). A Few Observations on the practicability of the present Project of Abolishing the Slave Trade. London.

> This edition was published anonymously; the 2nd edit., with author's name and many additions, London, 1791.

A Short Journey in the West-Indies, in which are interspersed curious anecdotes and characters ... 2 vols. 12mo. London.

> "A light composition, containing some very amusing sketches of West Indian manners, together with slight accounts of West Indian productions for the table. But the chief object of the work is to exaggerate the hardships of negro slavery."—*Monthly Review*, IV, 336, quoted by Sabin.

1791 ATWOOD, THOMAS. History of the Island of Dominica, containing a Description of its Situation, Climate, Extent, Mountains, Rivers, and natural Productions. 8vo. London.

> The author was chief judge of Dominica and later of the Bahamas.—D.N.B.

1791-92 COKE, THOMAS (Rev. Dr.). Journal of Dr. Coke's Third Tour through the West-Indies, and Fourth Tour of the Continent of North America. In Letters to John Wesley. 3 parts. London.

A Particular Account of the Insurrection of Negroes in St. Domingo, which began in August last, being a translation of the Speech made to the National Assembly the 3d of November, 1791, by the Deputies from the General Assembly of the French part of St. Domingo. 8vo. London. (Printed by order of the National Assembly, 1791.)

> 2nd edit., London, 1792.

RANDALL, MARIA.  Voyages to the Madeira, and Leeward Caribbean Isles, with sketches of the Natural History of these Islands.  12mo. Edinburgh.

Noticed in the *Monthly Review*, IX, 219.

1793  EDWARDS, BRYAN.  The History, Civil and Commercial, of the British Colonies in the West Indies.  9 maps, 8 plates and Tables of Exports.  2 vols.  4to.  London.

Reprinted, Dublin, 1793; 2nd edit., with numerous plates and large folding maps not issued with the 1st edit., 3 vols., London, 1794; an abridged edition, Dublin, 1798; again, abridged, but containing his Historical Survey of the French Colony in the Island of St. Domingo, London, 1798; enlarged edition, containing Historical Survey, 4 vols., London, 1801. With a Continuation to the "Present Time," 5 vols., London, 1819. Translated into French, Paris, 1801.

The additions have to do with the history of St. Domingo, Arthur Young's tour through the Barbadoes, St. Vincent, etc., in 1791-92, a relation of the Maroon Negroes, and the Maroon War, in Jamaica. With reference to this work, Dibdin remarks, "Obtain, by all the means, the History of those Islands, by Bryan Edwards, the 'facile princeps' of writers in his department."—Quoted by Maggs, No. 429. It was a deservedly popular work. See Edwards under 1796 and 1797 below.

MORETON, J. B.  Manners and Customs in the West India Islands. Containing various Particulars respecting the Soil, Cultivation, Produce, Trade, Officers, Inhabitants, etc. With the method of establishing and conducting a Sugar Plantation; . . . Also the Treatment of Slaves; and the Slave-Trade.  8vo.  London.

"The author was a negro driver. He has given a strange jumble of good advice, gross descriptions, licentious remarks, and bad poetry, mixed occasionally with texts of Scripture."—*Monthly Review*, IV, 337, quoted by Sabin.

1795  Memorial of the Agents in Behalf of the Principal Inhabitants and Proprietors of the Island of Martinique to the Duke of Portland.  Fol. London.

TURNBULL, GORDON (Lieut.)  A Narrative of the Revolt and Insurrection of the French Inhabitants in the Island of Granada.  By an Eye-Witness.  8vo.  Edinburgh.

WINTERBOTHAM, WILLIAM.  For matter relating to the West Indies see his *Historical, Commercial, Geographical and Philosophical View of the American United States,* under NORTH AMERICA.

1796  A Brief Enquiry into the Causes of, and Conduct pursued by, the Colonial Government for quelling the Insurrection in Grenada.  8vo.  London.

EDWARDS, BRYAN. Proceedings of the Governor and Assembly of Jamaica in regard to Maroon Negroes, with an Introductory Account containing Observations on the Disposition, Character, Manners and Habits of the Maroons, . . . 8vo. London.

1797 BULL, W. V. Narrative of the successful manner of cultivating the Clove Tree, in the Island of Dominica, one of the Windward Charibbee Islands. 8vo. London.

EDWARDS, BRYAN. An Historical Survey of the French Colony in the Island of St. Domingo, an account of its Ancient Government, Political State, Population, Productions and Exports: a narrative of the Calamities which have desolated the Country ever since the Year 1789, with some Reflections on their Causes and probable Consequences; and a Detail of the Military Transactions of the British Army in that Island to the End of 1794. Map. 4to. London.

This work was reprinted in the author's *History, Civil and Commercial, of the British Colonies in the West Indies*, from 1799 on. See Edwards under 1793 above. For a French reply to this Historical Survey see following item:

1797 CHARMILLY, M. LE COLONEL VENAULT DE, et WILLIAMSON, M. LE LIEUTENANT-GENERAL. Lettre à M. Bryan Edwards, Membre du Parlement d'Angleterre, et la Société Royale de Londres, Colon Propriétaire à la Jamaïque, en Refutation de son ouvrage, intitulé Vues Historiques sur la Colonie Française de Saint-Domingue, . . . 4to. London.

MUNOZ, DON JUAN BATISTA. The History of the New World, translated from the Spanish, with Notes by the Translator. Folding map of Hispaniola and engraved portrait of Columbus. Vol. I (all published). 8vo. London.

"This volume only reaches to the year 1500; the continuation never appeared in print as it was prohibited by the Spanish Government, being too enlightened and truthful; the work is preceded by a valuable critical review of the various writers on the subject."—Sabin.

WIMPFEN, BARON DE. A Voyage to St. Domingo, in the Years 1788, 1789, and 1790, translated from the original Manuscript by J. Wright. Maps. 8vo. London.

There is a citation saying that this work was translated into English in 1794. Lowndes states that the real name of the translator was William Gifford. French original, Paris, 1793. See below.

1793 WIMPFEN, BARON DE. Voyage à Saint-Domingue dans les années 1788, 1789, et 1790. 2 vols. Paris.

1798   LABORIE, P. J.   The Coffee Planter of Saint Domingo with an Appendix, containing a View of the Constitution, Government, Laws and State of that Colony, previous to the Year 1798. To which are added, some hints on the present state of the Island, under the British Government. 22 plates. 8vo. London.

> "A curious, and in some respects, a valuable performance. The author's knowledge of the French colonial system, under the ancient government, is accurate and profound. In no other book is so clear, exact, and perfect an account of the laws and constitution of St. Domingo, before the revolution, to be found."— *Monthly Review*, XXVIII, 355, quoted by Sabin.

MOORE, JAMES L.   The Columbiad: An Epic Poem on the Discovery of America and the West Indies by Columbus, in Twelve Books. 8vo. London.

1799   CAMPE, JOACHIM HEINRICH.   Columbus: or, the Discovery of America, as related by a Father to his Children, translated from the German, by Elizabeth Helme. Folding map of the West Indies. 2 vols. in 1. London.

LEMPRIERE, WILLIAM.   Practical Observations on the Diseases of the Army in Jamaica, as they occurred between the Years 1792 and 1797; on the Situation, Climate, and Diseases of that Island; and on the probable Means of lessening Mortality among the Troops, and among Europeans in Tropical Climates. Tables. 2 vols. 8vo. London.

> For Lempriere's African experiences see his *A Tour from Gibraltar to Tangier* under 1791, AFRICA.

1800   Antigua:   A Collection of Exotics from the Island of Antigua, by a Lady. 4 pp. of descriptive text, with 12 colored Plates. Fol. London.

> Deals with West Indian plants, and dedicated to the Countess of Galway.— Sotheran.

MACPHERSON, CHARLES.   Memoirs of the Life and Travels of the late Charles Macpherson, Esq., in Asia, Africa, and America . . . Investigation of the Nature, Treatment, and Improvement of the Negro, in the British and French West India Islands. Written by Himself. . . . 12mo. London.

> Noticed in the *Monthly Review*, XXXIV, 106.

ADDENDA

1847 COLUMBUS, CHRISTOPHER. Select Letters of Christopher Columbus, With Original Documents relating to the Discovery of the New World. Translated and edited by Richard Henry Major, F. S. A. Hak. Soc., ser. I, vol. 2. London.

> The 2nd edit. of this work appeared in 1870 as vol. 43. See under 1870 below.

1848 DRAKE, SIR FRANCIS. Sir Francis Drake his Voyage, 1595, by Thomas Maynarde, together with the Spanish Account of Drake's attack on Puerto Rico. Edited from the original MSS. by William Desborough Cooley. Hak. Soc., ser. I, vol. 4. London.

HELPS, ARTHUR. The Conquerors of the New World and Their Bondsmen, being a Narrative of the principal Events which led to Negro Slavery in the West Indies and America. 2 vols. 12mo. London.

> Includes Ca da Mosto's Voyage; Administration of Columbus in West Indies; Ovando's Government, etc.—Bookseller's Note.

1850 HAKLUYT, RICHARD. Divers Voyages touching the Discovery of America And the Islands adjacent, collected and published by Richard Hakluyt, Prebendary of Bristol, in the year 1582. Edited, with notes & an introduction by John Winter Jones, Principal Librarian of the British Museum. 2 maps. 1 illus. Hak. Soc., ser. I, vol. 7. London.

1858 CHAMPLAIN, SAMUEL. Narrative of a Voyage to the West Indies and Mexico, in the Years 1599-1602, Translated from the original and unpublished manuscript, with Biographical Notice and Notes by Alice Wilmere. Edited by Norton Shaw. 4 maps and 5 illus. Hak. Soc., ser. I, vol. 23. London.

1865 Certain Inducements To Well Minded People Who Are Here Straitned in their Estates or otherwise: or, Such as are willing, out of Noble and Publike Principles, to transport Themselves or some Servants, or Agents for them into the West Indies, for the Propagating of the Gospel and Increase of Trade. 4to. New York.

> The rare original was published in London about 1644.—Quaritch. One is tempted to remark on how trade follows the Bible.

1870 COLUMBUS, CHRISTOPHER. Select Letters of Christopher Columbus, with other Original Documents relating to his Four Voyages to the New World. Translated & edited by Richard Henry Major, F.S.A., Keeper of Maps, Brit. Mus., Sec. R.G.S. 2nd edit. 3 maps and 1 illus. Hak. Soc., ser. I, vol 43. London.

> 1st edit. appeared as vol. 2 in this series. See under 1847 above.

1881 BUTLER, NATHANIEL (Captain). The History of the Bermudas or Summer Islands. Attributed to Captain Nathaniel Butler. Edited from a MS. in the Sloane Collection, Brit. Mus., by General Sir John Henry Lefroy, R.A., K.C.M.G., C.B., F.R.S. Map and illus. Glossary. Hak. Soc., ser. I, vol. 65. London

1892 COLUMBUS, CHRISTOPHER. The Journal of Christopher Columbus during his First Voyage (1492-93), and Documents relating to the Voyages of John Cabot and Gaspar Corte Real. Translated, with Notes & an Introduction, by Clements R. Markham, C.B., F.R.S., ex-Pres. R.G.S. 3 maps and 1 illus. Hak. Soc., ser. I, vol. 86. London.

1893 COLUMBUS and VESPUCCI. The Spanish Letter of Columbus (printed at Barcelona in 1493). Reduced Facsimile, with Translation. The Latin Columbus Letter (printed at Rome in 1493). Reproduced in Facsimile, with a Preface.—Vespucci. First Four Voyages (printed under the title of "Lettera" at Florence in 1505). Reproduced in Facsimile, with a Translation. With 2 illus.—Hariot. Narrative of the First Plantation of Virginia (printed in 1588 and 1590). With Facsimiles of the engravings made by De Bry from John White's designs. 4 parts. 4to. London. Quaritch's Facsimiles.

1894-98 OLIVER, VERE LANGFORD. The History of the Island of Antigua, one of the Leeward Carribbees in the West Indies, from the First Settlement in 1635 to the Present Time. Maps, plans, portraits and other illus. 3 vols. Fol. London.

1899 DUDLEY, SIR ROBERT. The Voyage of Robert Dudley, afterwards styled Earl of Warwick and Leicester, and Duke of Northumberland, to the West Indies, 1594-95, narrated by Capt. Wyatt himself, and Abram Kendall, Master. Edited by (Sir) George F. Warner. Portrait, map, and facsimile. Hak. Soc., ser. II, vol. 3. London.

1902 TOSCANELLI, ——. Letter and Chart of Toscanelli on the Route to the Indies by way of the West, sent 1474 to Fernam Martins and later to Christopher Columbus. A critical study on the authenticity and value of these documents followed by various Texts and Translations, etc. Revised from the original French edition, with many additions and notes by H. Vignaud. 8vo. London.

1903 HAWKINS, SIR JOHN. First Voyage to the West Indies, October, 1562, to September, 1563. In Beazley I (from Hakluyt 1589). London.

> This and the two subsequent voyages of Hawkins' introduced the English nation to the African slave trade. On this first some 300 negroes were "got partly by the sword, and partly by other means."

HAWKINS, SIR JOHN. Second Voyage to the West Indies, October, 1564, to September, 1565. In Beazley I (from Hakluyt, 1589). London.

> On this voyage Hawkins touched at the shore of South America and Florida as well as at the West Indies.

HAWKINS, SIR JOHN. Third Voyage to Guinea and the West Indies, 1567-68. In Beazley I (from the State Papers, Domestic, etc.). London.

> This was the first venture that English ships made into the Gulf of Mexico. This account Hakluyt omitted from his 1598-1600 Voyages. See Hawkins under 1569 above.

INGRAM, DAVID. David Ingram's Relation of 1582. In Beazley I. London.

> Hakluyt thought Ingram was a liar and so omitted him from his 1598-1600 Voyages.

PHILLIPS, MILES. Miles Phillips' Discourse of 1583 (?). In Beazley I (from Hakluyt, 1589). London.

TONSON, ROBERT. His Voyage to the West Indies and Mexico, 1556-58. In Beazley I (from Hakluyt 1589). London.

> Tonson was a merchant of Andover. He states that he found a Scotchman in the city of Mexico who had been there since before 1536.

1907 DYOTT, WILLIAM (General). Dyott's Diary: 1781-1845: a Selection from the Journal of William Dyott, sometime General in the British Army and Aide-de-Camp to King George III. Edited by Reginald W. Jeffery, M.A. 9 Portraits. 2 vols. 8vo. London.

VESPUCCI, AMERIGO.   The Cosmographiae of Martin Waldsee-Mueller in Facsimile.  Followed by the Four Voyages of Amerigo Vespucci, with their translation into English, to which are added Waldsee-Mueller's Two World Maps of 1507.  With an Introduction by Prof. J. Fischer, S. J., and Prof. F. Von Wieser, edited by Prof. C. G. Herbermann.  4to.  Catholic Historical Society.  New York.

1916   VESPUCCI, AMERIGO.   Mundus Novus.  Letter to Lorenzo Pietro di Medici.  Translated by G. T. Northup.  Vespucci Reprints, Texts and Studies, V.  Princeton, N. J.

1922   SHAW, "JEN."   Journal of a Lady of Quality; being the Narrative of a Journey from Scotland to the West Indies, North Carolina, and Portugal in the years 1774-1776.  Edited by E. W. and C. M. Andrews.  8vo.  New Haven.

Other editions in 1927 and 1934.

1924   COLUMBUS, CHRISTOPHER.   Journal of the First Voyage to America by Christopher Columbus.  Introduction by Van Wyck Brooks.  American Explorers.  New York.

1924-29   English Conquest of Jamaica, 1655-56 (with other matter), edited by Bannister, Hall and others.  3 vols.  4to.  Camden Miscellany, vols. 13-15.  London.

1926   HARLOW, V. T.   A History of Barbados, 1625-1685.  2 maps.  8vo.  Oxford.

1928   English Voyages to the Carribean.  Spanish Documents concerning English Voyages to the Carribean, 1527-1568.  Selected from the Archives of the Indies at Seville.  By Miss Irene A. Wright.  Maps and plates.  Hak. Soc., ser. II, vol. 62.  London.

1929   COLUMBUS, CHRISTOPHER.   Select Documents illustrating the four Voyages of Columbus, including those contained in R. H. Major's Select Letters of Christopher Columbus.  Translated and edited with additional material, an introduction and notes, by Cecil Jane (vol. I, the first and second voyages).  Hak. Soc., ser. II, vol. 65.  London.

For the third and fourth voyages see under 1932 below.

1930 COLUMBUS, CHRISTOPHER. The Voyages of Christopher Columbus, Being the Journals of his First and Third, and the Letters Concerning his First and Last Voyages, to which is added the Account of his Second Voyage Written by Andrés Bernàldez. Now Newly Translated and Edited with Introduction and Notes by Cecil Jane. 5 maps. 4to. Argonaut Press. London.

1931 LABAT, JEAN BAPTISTE. Memoirs of Pere Labat, in the West Indies, 1693-1705, translated by J. Eaden. 8vo. London.

> There is a French edition of Labat's *Nouveau Voyage aux Isles de l'Amérique*, printed at The Hague, 1724.
> Labat went to the West Indies as a Dominican Missionary, and gives in this, his most famous work, details of all the Islands he visited, and notably of Martinique and Guadeloupe. He speaks also of many of the smaller islands; of some of them this is the only early information we possess. He gives accounts of the cultivation of tobacco, sugar, indigo, etc., and many anecdotes of the inhabitants.— Maggs, No. 432.

Narratives of the Discovery of America, edit. by A. W. Lawrence and J. Young. 8vo. London.

> See this item, under COLLECTIONS, ADD. I.

1932 COLUMBUS, CHRISTOPHER. Select Documents illustrating the four Voyages of Columbus. Translated and edited by Cecil Jane. Vol. 2. The Third and Fourth Voyages, with a supplementary Introduction by E. G. R. Taylor. 3 maps and 1 illus. Hak. Soc., ser. II, vol. 70. London.

English Voyages to the Spanish Main. Documents concerning English Voyages to the Spanish Main, 1569-1580. I. Spanish Documents. II. English Accounts, *Sir Francis Drake Revived* and others, reprinted. Translated and edited by Irene A. Wright. 2 maps and 1 illus. Hak. Soc., ser. II, vol. 71. London.

# VII

## Mexico

1569 HAWKINS, SIR JOHN. Hawkins made contact with Mexico at Vera Cruz. See this date, under WEST INDIES.

1578 GOMARA, FRANCISCO LOPEZ DE. The Pleasant Historie of the Conquest of the WEAST INDIA, now called New Spayne, Atchieued by the worthy Prince Hernando Cortes Marques of the valley of Huaxacac, most delectable to Reade: Translated out of the Spanishe tongue, by T(homas) N(icholas). 4to. London.

> Another edition, London, 1596. Earliest issue of the Spanish original, Saragossa, 1552. Other editions, Antwerp, 1554; and one dated 1551. See below.
> Gomara was one of the earliest and ablest of the Spanish historians of the New World. In 1540 he was Chaplain and Secretary to Cortes, and had access to many documents which have since disappeared. His purpose in the main work was to relate the whole range of the Spanish conquests in America down to the middle of the Sixteenth century.—Robinson, No. 23. It is curious to note that the translator makes no mention of the actual author's name, but gives his own name in full at the end of the Epistle Dedicatory. The preliminary leaves also contain a six-verse poem, in English, with six lines in each, and a twelve-line Latin poem, written by the Elizabethan poet Stephen Gosson, in praise of the Translator.—Maggs, No. 465. Gomara has generally been criticised for his partiality towards Cortes, but his attitude towards the Spanish in general was somewhat less favorable, and an edict of suppression against the book had nominal force for nearly two centuries.—Waldman.

> 1551 GOMARA, FRANCISCO LOPEZ DE. Historia de Mexico, con el descubrimiento de la Neuva España, conquistada por el muy illustre y valeroso Principe don Fernando Cortes. Antwerp.
>
> > It may be doubted whether this date has been accurately noted.

> 1552 GOMARA, FRANCISCO LOPEZ DE. La historia de Las Indias y conquista de Mexico. 2 parts in 1. Fol. Saragossa.
>
> > This is the earliest issue of the first edition, having the title-page dated 1552, instead of 1553, as do the usually recorded issues. The title also bears a slightly different and simpler wording, . . . The First Part relates to the subjugation of Peru. The Second Part gives an account of the Conquest of Mexico, and is that portion of the work by which its author is best known.—Maggs, No. 429.

> 1553 GOMARA, FRANCISCO LOPEZ DE. Hispania Victrix. Primera y Secunda parte de la historia general de las Indias, con todo el descubrimiento . . . Con la Conquista de Mexico, y de Nueva España. Woodcut of a bison. Fol. Saragossa.

> 1554-55 GOMARA, FRANCISCO LOPEZ DE. La Historia General de las Indias y Neuva Mundo, con mas la conquista del Peru y de Mexico. Cronica de la Neuve España con la conquista de Mexico, y otras cosas notables: hechas por el valeroso Hernando Cortes. 32 large engravings on wood. 2 vols. in 1. Fol. Saragossa.

According to Robinson, No. 23, the Antwerp edition of 1554 printed for Nucio was the authorised one. Robinson adds that Nucio printed the *Conquista de Mexico* the year previous with the intention of adding it to the *La Historia General* but never did.—The *Historia* begins, after the Spanish fashion, with the creation of the world and ends with the glories of Spain, though it is chiefly devoted to Columbus and the discovery and conquest of Peru; and the *Cronica* to the history and life of Cortes.—From Maggs, No. 612.

1604   ACOSTA, JOSEPH.   For matter relating to Mexico see his *Natural and Morall Historie of the East and West Indies,* under SOUTH AMERICA.

1648   GAGE, THOMAS.   The English-American his Travail by Sea and Land; or, A Nevv Svrvey of the VVest-Indias, containing a Journall of three thousand and three hundred miles within the main Land of America . . . with a New and Exact Discovery of the Spanish Navigation to those parts; And of their Dominions, Government, Religion, Forts, Castles, Ports, . . . with a Grammar of the Indian Tongue. By the true and painfull endeavors of Thomas Gage.   Fol.   London.

2nd edit., fol., London, 1655; 3rd edit., 8vo, London, 1677; 4th, 8vo, London, 1699; another, 8vo, London, 1702; 4th edit., enlarged by the author, London, 1711. Modern editions, Broadway Travellers, London, 1928; Argonaut Series, London (New York), 1929. Translated into French, Paris, 1676; also into Dutch, 1682, German, 1693, Spanish, and Portuguese (in manuscript). See below.

The book created a sensation when it appeared. In it the author describes Mexico and the wealth of South America, commenting upon the ease with which it could be conquered.—Maggs, No. 502. Gage originally belonged to the Dominican order, and served as a missionary priest in Mexico, going out in 1625. He afterwards joined the Church of England, and wrote this work, the first to give the World a description of the vast regions from which all foreigners had been jealously excluded by the Spanish authorities. It is supposed to have incited the attacks on the Spanish territories and colonies during Cromwell's time. Gage was appointed chaplain to the forces which captured Jamaica, where he died in 1656.—From Maggs, No. 549. The 22nd chapter, relating his journey to Rome, was left out in the 3rd edition, as is said, to its reflecting on the character of Archbishop Laud.—Lowndes. The author appears to have been a believer in witchcraft and sorcery, and admits many curious relations on these subjects.— Puttick and Simpson. Portions concerning Laud and rules for learning the Central American languages were issued separately.—D.N.B. Southey quoted this work in his notes on "Madoc," where he charged that Gage's account of Mexico was copied verbatim from Nicholas' *Conquest of Mexico* (see Gomara under 1578 above).

1655   GAGE, THOMAS.   A New Survey of the West-Indies: or, the English American his Travail by Sea and land: containing a Journall of Three thousand and Three hundred miles within the Main Land of America. Wherein is set forth his Voyage from Spain to St. John de Vlhua; and from thence to Xalappa, to Tlaxcalla, the City of Angels, and forward to Mexico; With the description of that great City, as it was in former times, as also at this present. Likewise, his Journey from Mexico . . . As also his strange and wonderfull Conversion and Calling from those remote Parts, to his Native Countrey. With his return through the Province of Nicaragua; and Costa Rica. . . . Also a New and Exact Discovery of the Spanish Navigations in those Parts . . . With a Grammar or some Rudiments of the Indian Tongue called Poconchi or Pocoman.   4 maps.   Fol.   London.

The work has been reset, and to the paragraph on page 202, a line for line reprint of the issue of 1648. It contains four maps, apparently none of them engraved for this work.—John Carter Brown.

1699   GAGE, THOMAS.  A New Survey of the West-Indies. Being a Journal of three thousand and three hundred Miles within the Main Land of America. By the only Protestant that ever was known to have travel'd these parts. Folding map of the West Indies, Gulf of Mexico, and adjacent coasts. 8vo. London.

1929   GAGE, THOMAS.  A New Survey of the West Indies, 1648. Edited with an Introduction by A. P. Newton. Illustrated. 8vo. Argonaut Series. London.

1676   (In French.)  Nouvelle Relation, contenant les voyages de Thomas Gage dans la Nouvelle Espagne, ses diverses avantures; & son retour par la Province de Nicaragua, jusques à la Havane. Avec la description de la Ville de Mexique. . . . 4 vols. 12mo. Paris.

This is the only French version to contain the Poconchi vocabulary. —From Quaritch. The translation was made at the command of Colbert.

The first French version with text abridged done at Paris, 1663, was collected by Thévenot for his *Relation des divers Voyages curieux* (1672, see under COLLECTIONS). With title changed to *Relation de Mexique et de la Nouvelle Espagne*, it appeared at Paris, 1676, with translation by M. de Carcavi for the Sieur de Beaulieu, in 2 vols. This contained practically the whole of the original except the early chapters and those parts most offensive to Roman Catholics.

1659   GORGES, FERDINANDO.  For a history of the Spanish proceedings in their conquests of the Indians see his *America Painted to the Life,* under NORTH AMERICA.

1675   LOZA, FRANCISCO.  The Holy Life of Gregory Lopez, a Spanish Hermite in the West Indies. Englished from the Spanish of Father Losa. 8vo. (Place?).

2nd edit., London, 1685.
For a Spanish account of Loza's life printed at Mexico City, 1613, see below. This contains curious particulars of New Spain, the author's solitary life among the Indian Chichinecos, several testimonials of divers bishops in Mexico, etc.— From Sabin.

1613   LOZA, FRANCISCO.  La Vida, que hizo el siervo de Dios Gregorio Lopez, en algunos lugares de esta Neuve España, y principalmente en el Pueblo de Sancta Fee, dos leguas de la Ciudad de Mexico, donde fue su dichoso transito. 12mo. Mexico City.

The famous Missionary, whose life is here described, was a man of mystery. He was supposed to be of noble lineage, but became a hermit. His whereabouts was traced and he was taken to Madrid and made a court page. Later he managed to go to Mexico, where he lived the life of a recluse, dying in 1596.—Maggs, No. 612.

1724 PHILIPS, MILES. Voyages and Adventures of Miles Philips, a West-Country Sailor. Containing a Relation of the inhuman Usage he met with from the Spaniards at Mexico, and the savage Indians of Canada, . . . 12mo. London.

> Philips was with Hawkins on one of his expeditions to the West Indies, and was taken prisoner in Mexico. He escaped and lived to tell his own story to Hakluyt.

SOLIS, ANTONIO DE. The History of the Conquest of Mexico by the Spaniards. Done into English from the Original Spanish by Thomas Townsend. Engraved portrait of Cortes by Vertue and 8 engraved plates and maps. Fol. London.

> Another edition, 12mo, Dublin, 1727; the whole translation revised and corrected by Nathaniel Hooke, 2 vols., 8vo, London, 1738; 3rd edit., 2 vols., 8vo, London, 1753. Spanish original, Madrid, 1684. See below.
> This was undoubtedly the most popular history of America that had then been written; and the number of editions published even up to the nineteenth century, in Spanish, French, Italian, English and German, testify to its popularity long after the initial interest of its historical information had passed. . . . His principal sources of inspiration for this history were the letters of Hernan Cortes, the works of Francisco Lopez de Gomara, Bernal Diaz del Castillo, and some miscellaneous documents. In addition to a full account of the relations between Cortes and Montezuma, there is an abundance of data concerning the intimate lives of the Indians . . . Solis became Secretary to the King of Spain (Charles II) and succeeded Antonio de Leon Pinelo as chief chronicler of the Indies.—From Maggs, No. 479.

> 1684 SOLIS Y RIBADENEYRA, ANTONIO DE. Historia de la Conquista de Mexico, Poblacion y Progressos de la America-Septentrional, conocida por el nombre de Nueva-España. Fol. Madrid.

1725-26 HERRERA, ANTONIO DE. For descriptions of the mainland under Spanish control see his *The General History of the Vast Continent and Islands of America,* under WEST INDIES.

1732 CARERI, JOHN FRANCESCO GEMELLI. For a description of Mexico see his *Voyage Round the World,* under CIRCUMNAVIGATIONS.

> "Humboldt and Clavigero have confirmed his local knowledge of Mexico, and found his book useful and veracious." He first published the famous Mexican map or picture of the Migration of the Aztecs.—Sabin.

NAVARETTE, DOMINGO FERNANDEZ. For an account of Mexico see his *An Account of the Empire of China,* under FAR EAST.

1740 CARRANZA, DOMINGO GONZALEZ. For an account of Mexico see his *A Geographical Description of the Coasts, Harbours, and Sea Ports of the Spanish West-Indies,* under WEST INDIES.

For matter relating to Mexico see *The Present State of the Revenues and Forces by Sea and Land*, under WEST INDIES.

1741   CAMPBELL, JOHN.   For a description of Mexico see his *Concise History of Spanish America*, under SOUTH AMERICA.

1744-48   The Expedition of Hernan Cortes for the Reduction of New Spain, from the Time of his being appointed to that Command, unto his being obliged to return to the Isle of Cozumel. In Harris II, 63-135.

> Revised, with large additions and brought down to 1748, by John Campbell. Fol.  London.

1759   DILWORTH, W. H.   The History of the Conquest of Mexico. By the celebrated Hernan Cortes. Containing a Faithful and Entertaining Detail of all his Amazing Victories, in that vast empire, its Laws, Customs, Religions, . . . A Work abounding with Strokes of Generalship, and the most refined Maxims of Civil Policy. To which is added, The Voyage of Vasco de Gama, extracted from Osorio, Bishop of Sylves. Published for the Improvement and Entertainment of the British Youth of both Sexes. 12mo.  London.

> Reprinted, Glasgow, 1785.

1774-78   CORTES, HERNAN.   The Conquest of Mexico. With an Introduction by Dr. Samuel Johnson. 10 engravings. In *The World Displayed* II.  4th edit.  London.

1777   ROBERTSON, WILLIAM.   For sections on Mexico see his *History of America*, under NORTH AMERICA.

1780   CHAPPE D'AUTEROCHE, JEAN.   For some descriptions of Mexico see his *A Voyage to California*, under NORTH AMERICA.

> This volume contains the best account of the City of Mexico previous to the work of Humboldt.—Pinkerton XVII.

1787   CLAVIGERO, FRANCESCO SAVERIO (Abbé).   The History of Mexico, Collected from Spanish and Mexican Historians, from Manuscripts and Ancient Paintings of the Indians. To which are added Critical Dissertations on the Land, the Animals, and Inhabitants of Mexico: translated from the original Italian by Charles Cullen. 2 maps and 25 full-page copperplate engravings. 2 vols.  4to.  London.

Italian original, Cesena, 1780-81. See below. The original text of this excellent history having been almost 'epuise,' there was brought out a Spanish translation under the title *Historia Antigua de Mexico,* 2 vols., 8vo, London, 1786.— Quoted.

A valuable work containing much learned research on the ancient history of Mexico.—Robinson, No. 23. "Clavigero was a native of Vera Cruz (born 1731, died at Bologna, 1787), a Jesuit and a thorough antiquarian, who spent thirty years of active research into the archaeology and antiquities of Mexico. His book, published originally in Italian, is a mine of precious historical documents, and contains valuable lists of others in the Mendoza, the Vatican, and the Boturini collections. All the other books that have been elaborated since on the same subject, instead of superseding Clavigero's, have tended rather to magnify its importance."—Stevens, quoted by Maggs, No. 479.

1780-81  CLAVIGERO, FRANCESCO SAVERIO (F.S.). Storia Antica del Messico cavata da' migliori storici spagnuoli, e da' manoscritti, e dalle pitture anticha degl' Indiani: divisa in dieci libri, e corredata di carte geografiche, e di varie figure: e dissertazioni sulla Terra, sugli Animali, e sugli abitatori del Messico. Numerous engraved plates of Mexican customs, views, portraits, etc. 4 vols. 4to. Cesena.

1799  CAMPE, JOACHIM HEINRICH. Cortez; or, the Conquest of Mexico: as related by, a Father to his Children, and designed for the Instruction of Youth, Translated from the German of J. H. Campe. By Elizabeth Helme. Folding map. 12mo. London.

Reprinted, Dublin, 1800.

1800  DIAZ DEL CASTILLO, BERNAL. The True History of the Conquest of Mexico, by one of the Conquerors. Written in the year 1568. Translated by Maurice Keatinge. Plan of Mexico City. London.

This is the first complete version in English, and was made from the Spanish version of Remon, Madrid, 1632. Keatinge's translation reissued in the Argonaut Series, New York, 1928, and Garcia's edition in the Broadway Travellers, London, 1928. An edition prepared from the sole existing copy of the original manuscript has been edited for the Hakluyt Society, London, 1908-1916. See below.

"It is noteworthy that some of the most striking accounts of exploration in Spanish America were written by common soldiers. . . . They interpreted the thoughts and sentiments of the subordinate class, and help one to see how the private soldier or common man viewed the enterprises in which he was engaged. The position of men of this class made a sharp contrast between their writings and the writings of leaders."—Dr. Moses, *Spanish Colonial Literature in South America,* quoted by Maggs, No. 442. This work was largely drawn on by Prescott for his *Conquest of Mexico.*

1908-1916  DIAZ DEL CASTILLO, BERNAL. The True History of the Conquest of New Spain. By Bernal Diaz del Xastillo, one of its Conquerors. From the only exact copy made of the Original Manuscript. Edited and published in Mexico, by Genaro Garcia, 1904. Translated into English, with Introduction and Notes, by Alfred Percival Maudslay, M.A., Hon. Professor of Archaeology, National Museum, Mexico. Maps. 5 vols. Hak. Soc., ser. II, vols. 23, 24, 25, 30, 40. London.

The original manuscript was always kept in Guatemala, first by the Author, and afterwards by his descendants, and still later by the Municipality of the Capitol. A copy of it was made in the 16th century and sent to Spain to King Philip II. It was published in Madrid by Friar Alonzo Remon, in 1632. Several editions followed. The English translation by Keatinge in 1800 was made from this edition.

But Remon extensively "corrupted" the text, as has been long known. . . . As all the later editions and translations were made from Remon's edition, the fact is that these are necessarily falsified editions also.— From the Introduction of Garcia in the Hakluyt Society edition.

1928 DIAZ DEL CASTILLO, BERNAL. The Discovery and Conquest of Mexico, 1517-1521. Edited by Sir E. Denison Ross and Eileen Power, from the only exact copy of the original MS. and published in Mexico by Genaro Garcia. Translated with Introduction and Notes by A. P. Maudslay. 8vo. Broadway Travellers. New York.

1928 DIAZ DEL CASTILLO, BERNAL. The True History of the Conquest of Mexico. Written in the year 1568 by Captain Bernal Diaz del Castillo, and translated by Maurice Keatinge. Introduction by Arthur D. Howden Smith. 2 vols. Argonaut Series. London.

1632 DIAZ DEL CASTILLO, BERNAL. Historia Verdadera de la Conquista de la Neuva-España. Escrita por el Capitan Bernal Diaz del Castillo, uno de sus Conquistadores. Sacada a luz por el P. M. Fr. Alonso Remon, Predicador y Coronista General del Orden de Nuestra Senora de la Merced Redempcion de Cautivos. Fol. Madrid.

## ADDENDA

1808-1814 MENONVILLE, NICOLAS JOSEPH THIERRY DE. Travels to Guaxoca Capitol of the Province of the same Name in the Kingdom of Mexico. In Pinkerton XIII, 753-876.

Menonville was botanist to the King Louis XVI. He planned to naturalize the nopal and cochineal insect in the French colonies. He set out for Mexico in 1776.

1858 CHAMPLAIN, SAMUEL. For a voyage to Mexico see his *Narrative of a Voyage to the West Indies and Mexico,* under WEST INDIES.

1860 PALACIO, DIEGO GARCIA DE Carta dirijida al Rey España. Published in the original, with translations, illustrative notes, map and biographical sketches, by E. G. Squier. 4to. New York.

This is a description of the ancient provinces of Guazacapan, Cuscatlan and Chiquimula, in the Audiencia of Guatamala; with an Account of the Languages, Customs and Religion of their Aboriginal Inhabitants, and a Description of the Ruins of Copan.—Bookseller's Note.

1868 CORTES, HERNAN. The Fifth Letter of Hernan Cortes To the Emperor Charles V, containing an Account of his Expedition to Honduras in 1525-26. Translated from the original Spanish by Don Pascual De Gayangos. Hak. Soc., ser. I, vol. 40. London.

1903 BODENHAM, ROGER (Master). His Trip to Mexico, 1564-65. In Beazley I (taken from Hakluyt, 1589). London.

CHILTON, JOHN. Travels in Mexico, 1568-1585. In Beazley I, taken from Hakluyt, 1589. London.

> These travels also refer to Hawkins's disaster at San Juan de Ulua. This is one of the most valuable Elizabethan accounts of these regions.—Beazley.

MACE, WILLIAM. The Voyage of the Dog to the Gulf of Mexico, 1589. In Beazley II (taken from Hakluyt, 1589). London.

> "A Brief Remembrance."

TONSON, ROBERT. For his voyage to Mexico see his *Voyage to the West Indies and Mexico,* under WEST INDIES.

1917 Narrative of Some Things of New Spain and of the Great City of Temestitan, Mexico. Written by the anonymous conqueror, a companion of Hernan Cortes. Translated into English and annotated by Marshall H. Saville. 8vo. The Cortes Society. New York.

1928 CORTES, HERNANDO. Five Letters, 1519-1526. The Conquest of Mexico seen through the eyes of its Conqueror, translated with Introduction, by J. Bayard Morris. 8 plates and maps. 8vo. Broadway Travellers. London.

1929 CORTES, HERNANDO. The Letters of Hernando Cortes, 1519-1526. Translated by J. Bayard Morris, with an Introduction. Edited by Sir E. Denison Ross and Eileen Power. With a Frontispiece Portrait. 8vo. Argonaut Series. New York.

> These Letters from Cortes to the Emperor represent the conquest of Mexico seen through the eyes of the Conqueror, the advance of the little Spanish force into a treacherous and hostile Kingdom; the seizure of Montezuma, finally the two years' journey overland to Honduras fraught with every imaginable hardship. Behind the letters rises a figure of truly Elizabethan proportions.—Bookseller's Note.

1932 DE SANAGUN, FRAY BERNARDINO. A History of Ancient Mexico, 1547-1577. Translated by Fanny R. Bandelier into English from the Spanish Version of Carlos Maris de Bustamente. 8vo. London.

> Charles L. Lummis, just before he died, in 1929 . . . described this book: "De Sanagun spent thirty years in preparation for writing his great book (which gives us more of the early history of Mexico from the inside than any other); but the General of the Franciscan Order seized his work, and it was many years before Fray Bernardino could get it back again, and renew his labors. He was already eighty when his remarkable book, which may be called by translation 'General History of the Things of New Spain,' was at last restored to him. He then began to rewrite it, the Aztec text in one column and the Spanish in another. For more than two centuries his book lay buried in the convent of San Francisco de Tolosa, in Navarre, Spain, and it was not until 1829 that it was printed, being then issued by the eminent Mexican scholar Bustamente. . . ."—Quoted.

# VIII

## Central America

1626 DRAKE, SIR FRANCIS. For an account of his third voyage "into the West Indies," 1572-73, see *Sir Francis Drake Revived,* under CIR-CUMNAVIGATIONS. See also Beazley II, London.

> This is the narrative of the expedition against Nombre de Dios, and besides is the source of most of our knowledge of Drake's exploits in Central America. It was on this excursion against the enemy that Drake gained his first view of the Pacific Ocean.

1648 GAGE, THOMAS. For his journey through Nicaragua see his *A New Survey of the West Indies,* under MEXICO.

1683 MORGAN, SIR HENRY. For an account of his capture of Panama see *The Present State of Jamaica,* under WEST INDIES.

1684 ESQUEMELING, JOHN. For relations of expeditions by the Bucca-neers on the Central American coast see his *The Bucaniers of America,* under WEST INDIES.

SHARP, BARTHOLOMEW. For an account of the taking of Panama by Sir Henry Morgan see his *The Voyages and Adventures of . . . in the South Sea,* under SOUTH AMERICA.

1697 DAMPIER, WILLIAM (Captain). For a description of the Isthmus of Darien see his *A New Voyage round the World,* under CIRCUM-NAVIGATIONS.

1699 DARIEN SCHEME.

> The ill-fated Scotch Darien Scheme was the project of Wm. Paterson (the founder of the Bank of England) for a Scotch Company with Headquarters on the Isthmus of Panama, as a counterpart to the British East India Company. (The expedition sailed in July, 1698.) William III opposed the idea, and the Spaniards and British Colonies in North America did all they could to ruin it; all this, combined with the unhealthy climate caused the colony to be an utter fail-ure. Scotland was an exceedingly poor country at this time, and the loss of some £100,000 invested in the scheme caused a great deal of suffering there and much bitterness against England for her refusal to support the colony. England, how-ever, was friendly to Spain at the time, and it was entirely against her policy to cause ill feeling by encouraging a colony established on what was generally considered as Spanish territory.—Maggs, No. 549. The affair produced innum-erable defenses and evoked as many replies. See Scott, *Bibliography of the Darien Company,* 1904, and Insh, *Papers relating to the Ships and Voyages of the Com-pany of Scotland trading to Africa and the Indies,* 1924. Some of these are cited below.

1699 BLACKWELL, ISAAC. A Description of the Province and Bay of
Darien: Giving a full Account of all its Situations, Inhabitants, Way
and Manner of Living and Religion, Solemnities, Ceremonies and Prod-
ucts; being vastly rich with Gold, Silver, and other Commodities. By
I. B. a well-wisher to the Company who lived there 17 years. 4to.
Edinburgh. (16 pp.)

> The one-page address to the reader is signed 'Isaac Blackwell,'
> whose initials appear on this title. "What I have written," says the
> author, "is both what I have seen and heard, and I have not perused
> one word of Mr. Dampier or Mr. Wafer's Books (who) were both
> my Shipmaits near six years in the South-Sea."—Quoted from Book-
> seller.

FERGUSON, ROBERT. A Just and Modest Vindication of the Scots
Design for the having established a Colony at Darien, with a brief
display, how much it is their Interest, to apply themselves to Trade,
and particularly to that which is Foreign. 8vo. London.

> By Robert Ferguson, the Plotter, wrongly ascribed to James
> Hodges. Ferguson was one of the chief contrivers of the Rye House
> plot, and chaplain in the rebel army. He gave information which led
> to the frustration of the machinations of Simon Fraser, twelfth Lord
> Lovat, against the Duke of Atholl. He was committed to Newgate
> for treason, 1704, admitted to bail and never tried.—Bookseller's Note.

FLETCHER, ANDREW. A Short and Impartial View of the Manner
and Occasion of the Scots Colony's coming away from Darien, in a Letter to a Person of Quality (by P. C.). London.

The History of Caledonia; or, the Scots Colony in Darien in the West
Indies. With an Account of the Manners of the Inhabitants, and
Riches of the Country. By a Gentleman lately Arriv'd. 8vo. London.

> Printed also at Dublin, 1699, in a volume containing seven other
> pieces.
> This interesting narrative contains an account of the "Erecting of
> the Company of Scotland trading to Africa and the Indies," of the
> opposition to it, its progress and arrival of the expedition at the Fort
> of New St. Andrew in Panama. A short description of Caledonia or
> Darien in Panama. Account of the Darien Indians, their manners and
> customs, their games and manner of hunting. Account of their settle-
> ment of Fort St. Andrew, etc.—Maggs, No. 442. The possibility of
> cutting a channel across the Isthmus is suggested but the idea is re-
> jected on account of the great obstacles of the mountains running
> across it.

A Letter giving a Description of the Isthmus of Darien: (where the Scots
Colonie is settled;) From a Gentleman who lives there at present.
With an Account of the Fertilness of the Soil, the Quality of the Air,
the Manners of the Inhabitants, And the Nature of the Plants, and
Animals, &c. And a particular Mapp of the Isthmus, and Entrance to
the River of Darien. 4to. Edinburgh. (12 leaves.)

A Short Account from, and Description of, the Isthmus of Darien, where
the Scots Collony are settled, with a particular map of the Isthmus
and entrance to the River of Darien. Folding map and cuts. 4to.
Edinburgh.

RIDPATH, GEORGE. A Defence of the Scots Settlement at Darien.
With an answer to the Spanish Memorial against it. And arguments
to prove that it is the interest of England to join with the Scots, and

prevent it. To which is added, A Description of the Country, and particular Account of the Scots Colony. 8vo. Edinburgh.

> The dedication is signed Philo-Caledon, who is said to be George Ridpath.—Maggs, No. 502.

The Defence of the Scots Settlement at Darien, Answer'd, Paragraph by Paragraph. By Philo-Britan. 8vo. London.

> This is an answer to Ridpath's "Defence," from an English point of view. The Scottish Parliament attributed it to Walter Herries or Harris, and ordered him to be prosecuted.—Quaritch.

1700 HODGES, JAMES (?). A Defence of the Scots Abdicating Darien: including an Answer to the Defence of the Scots Settlement there. Authore Britanno sed Dunensi. 8vo. Edinburgh.

> The introduction is an appeal to Scotchmen not to waste their money in the Scheme . . . The whole work is written in an extraordinary satirical manner, and raised tremendous indignation in Scotland, so much so that the Treasury was required to offer a reward of £6,000 scots for the arrest of the author, and the book was condemned to be burnt by the public hangman. At the time a certain Walter Herries was supposed to be the author, but Halkett and Laing attribute it to James Hodges.—Maggs, No. 549.

RIDPATH, GEORGE. An Enquiry into the Causes of the Miscarriage of the Scots Colony at Darien. Or, an Answer to a Libel entituled a Defence of the Scots abdicating Darien. Submitted to the Consideration of the Good People of England. 8vo. Glasgow.

> Generally ascribed to George Ridpath and written in defence of the colony.—Maggs, No. 549. The book was considered libellous by the English, and was burned by their hangman.—Scott, *Bibliography*.

A Short Vindication of Phil. Scot's Defence of the Scots abdicating Darien: being in Answer to the Challenge of the Author of the Defence of that Settlement, to prove the Spanish Title to Darien, by Inheritance, Donation, Purchase, Reversion, Surrender, or Conquest. 8vo. London.

> This volume includes many references to buccaneers who had visited Panama.—Maggs, No. 549.

A Full and Exact Collection of all the Considerable Addresses, Memorials, Petitions, Answers, Proclamations, Declarations, Letters, and other Publick Papers, Relating to the Company of Scotland Trading to Africa and the Indies, since the passing of the Act of Parliament, by which the said Company was established in June 1695, till November, 1700. 8vo. Edinburgh.

> This includes the Proclamations of the Governors of Jamaica, Barbadoes, New-York, and New England, against the Scotch colony. —Maggs, No. 549.

1702 BYRES, JAMES. A Letter to a Friend at Edinburgh From Rotterdam, Giving an account of the Scots affair in Darien. 8vo. (Place?).

1715 Memoirs of North Britain. 8vo. London.

> This contains an account of the Colony of Darien, with a Vindication of King William's Honor and Justice therein.—Sabin.

1726-27 Miscellanea Curiosa. In vol. 3 of this work is an account of the Scots colony at Darien. See under NORTH AMERICA.

1755 BORLAND, FRANCIS (Rev.). Memoirs of Darien Giving a short description of that Country. with an Account of the Attempts of the Company of Scotland, To Settle a Colonie in that Place. With a relation of some of the many Tragical Disasters which did attend that design. Written mostly in the Year 1700, while the Author was in the American Regions. Map. 8vo. Glasgow.

> Reprinted as the History of Darien, Glasgow, 1779.
> This is a very interesting narrative, with a coarse woodcut plan of Caledonia Harbor on page 9. The author says, "What passages he did not see himself, these he relates as he had them delivered by credible persons, who were eye-witnesses of them when they occurred; and the author being the only person of all the ministers who were sent abroad upon the service of Caledonia, that lived to return to his native country. Another surviving minister was the Rev. Archibald Stobo, who settled in Charleston in Carolina."—J. R. Smith, quoted by Sabin.

1774 CARSTARES, WILLIAM (Secretary of William III). State Papers and Letters chiefly concerning Scotland: Darien Expedition, Ferguson the Plotter, etc. 4to. London.

1849 The Darien Press. Being a Selection of Original Letters and Official Documents relating to the Establishment of a Colony at Darien by the Company of Scotland trading to Africa and the Indies, 1695-1700. Edited by J. Hill Burton. Plan and facsimiles. 4to. Bannatyne Club. Edinburgh.

1699 SHARP, BARTHOLOMEW (Captain). Journey over the Isthmus of Darien, and Expedition into the South Seas, written by himself in the year 1680. In Hacke's Collection. (See Hacke under 1699, COLLECTIONS.)

> Sharp was one of the semi-buccaneers that plundered the west coast of South America.

WAFER, LIONEL (Surgeon). A New Voyage and Description of the Isthmus of America, giving an Account of the Author's abode there, the form and make of the Country, the Coasts, Hills, Rivers, etc., Woods, Soil, Weather, etc., Trees, Fruit, Beasts, Birds, Fish, etc., the Indian Inhabitants, their Features, Complection, etc., their Manners, Customs, Employments, Marriages, Feasts, Hunting, Computation, Language, etc. With remarkable Occurrences in the South Sea, and elsewhere. Several copperplates. 8vo. London.

> 2nd edit., with additions, 8vo, London, 1704. Modern reprint, Cleveland, 1903; Hakluyt Society, London, 1933. Translated into French, Paris, 1706. See below.
> This work contains the best account that has yet been given, of the Isthmus of Panama, of the Indians there, and of the natural products, and contains many interesting items. It is in this edition that Wafer makes his strong appeal to the Government to make a settlement on the Isthmus, whereby—among other advantages—"a free passage by land, from the Atlantic to the South Sea, might easily be affected, which would be of the greatest consequence to the East India trade." . . . In 1681, whilst with the buccaneers (among them Dampier) marching across the Isthmus soon after the taking of Santa Maria, Wafer was injured by an explosion of gunpowder and was left behind among the Darien Indians, with whom he lived until he was eventually sent to the coast and taken on board Dampier's

sloop at Le Sound's Key (on the Atlantic side). Being a surgeon he was held in high esteem by the Indians and was able to gain all his information concerning them at first hand.—Maggs, No. 479. On account of his intimate knowledge of the Isthmus Wafer's name and experience were frequently invoked by the partisans of the Scots Settlement at Darien. Wafer took part in the privateering voyage of 1683 commanded by John Cook, in company with Dampier, Cowley, and Davis.

1704    WAFER, LIONEL. New Voyage and Description of the Isthmus of America, . . . with the Natural History of those parts by a Fellow of the Royal Society and Davis' Expedition to the Gold Mines, in 1702. Map and copperplates. 8vo. London.

1903    WAFER, LIONEL. A New Voyage to the Isthmus of America. Reprinted from the original edition of 1699. Edited by George P. Winship. 8vo. Cleveland.

1933    WAFER, LIONEL. A New Voyage and Description of the Isthmus of America. With Wafer's Secret Report (1688) and Nathaniel Davis's Expedition to the Gold Mines (1704). Edited by L. E. Elliot Joyce. 4 maps and 4 illus. Hak. Soc., ser. II, vol. 73. London.

1706    (In French.) Les Voyages de L. Waffer contenant une description très exacte de l'Isthme de l'Amérique et de toute la Nouvelle Espagne. Traduits de l'anglois par M. de Montirat. 2 maps. 12mo. Paris.

1704    DAVIS, NATHANIEL. Expedition to the Gold Mines in 1702. (In 2nd edit. of Wafer's *New Voyage*—see above.)

1708    WALLACE, —— (Dr.). Journal kept from Scotland to New Caledonia in Darien, with Account of that Country. In *Miscellanea Curiosa*. London. (See under COLLECTIONS.)

1732    W., M. The Mosqueto Indian and his Golden River. Being a familiar Description of the Mosqueto Kingdom in America, with a True Relation of the strange Customs, Ways of Living, Divinations, Religion, Drinking Bouts, Wars, Marriages, Buryings, etc., of those Heathenish People; together with an Account of the Product of their Country. Written (in or about the year 1699) by M. W. In Churchill VI, 283-298.

This tells of the coast of Honduras:

COCKBURN, JOHN. The Distresses and Adventures of John Cockburn, and five other Englishmen, at Porto Cavallo, and Journey from the Gulf of Honduras. 4to. London.

The date is questionable. This item is cited by Sabin as being taken from J. Bunstead's Catalogue. See following item.

1735    COCKBURN, JOHN (and Others). A Journey Overland, from the Gulf of Honduras to the Great South Sea. Performed by John Cockburn, and five other Englishmen, viz., Thomas Rounce, Richard Banister,

John Holland, Thomas Robinson, and John Ballman; who were taken by a Spanish Guarda-Costa, in the John and the Jane, Edward Burt Master, and set on Shoar at a Place called Porto-Cavalo, naked and wounded, as mentioned in several newspapers of October, 1731. Containing a variety of extraordinary Distresses and Adventures, and some New and Useful Discoveries of the Inland of those almost unknown Parts of America; As also, An exact Account of the Manners, Customs and Behavior of the several Indians inhabiting a Tract of Land of 2400 Miles; particularly of their Dispositions towards the Spaniards and English. To which is added, a curious Piece, written in the Reign of King James I. and never before printed, intiteled, A Brief Discovery of some Things best worth Noteinge in the Travels of Nicholas Withington, a Factor in the East-Indiase. Map. 8vo. London.

2nd edit., 8vo, London, 1740. Some copies of this date begin the title with: The Unfortunate Englishmen; or, . . . These also lack the account of Withington. Others begin: A Faithful Account, etc., and contain Withington's Discovery. 3rd edit., 12mo, London, 1773; 4th, 12mo, London, 1799. A French edition is mentioned by Rich, but no date is given.

"A curious and authentic narrative, and appeared so extraordinary as to be looked upon as little better than a romance."—Lowndes. "In the French title of this work, in the 'Bibliothèque des Voyages,' it is stated to be by Nicholas Withington; and Pinkerton's 'Collection of Voyages' XVII, 208, retranslates the title, and perpetuates the error. Similar instances are innumerable in the former work, and are all repeated, with additions, in the latter."—Rich.

1740 For matter relating to Central America see *The Present State of the Revenue and Forces, by Sea and Land,* under WEST INDIES.

1744 Original Papers relating to the Expedition to Panama. 8vo. London.

1744-48 The Discoveries made by the Spaniards in the Province called Golden Castile; their first Knowledge of the South Seas, and their Establishment of Panama, by which a Passage was opened up to the Discovery and Conquest of the great Empire of Peru. In Harris II, 136-142.

1753 HOUSTON, JAMES. For material on the Scots Darien Settlement see *The Works of James Houston,* under GENERAL TRAVELS AND DESCRIPTIONS.

1769 COOK, JAMES (Lieutenant). Remarks on a Passage from the River Balise, in the Bay of Honduras, to Merida; the Capital of the Province of Yucatan, In the Spanish West Indies. By Lieutenant Cook, Ordered by Sir William Burnaby, Rear Admiral of the Red, in Jamaica; With Despatches to the Governor of the Province; Relative to the Logwood

Cutters in the Bay of Honduras, In February and March 1765. 8vo. London. Map.

> At the same time of this reputed journey Cook was engaged in making a survey of Newfoundland.—Mrs. Cook said her husband never was in the Bay of Honduras.—*Edin. Cabinet* xxi, 287, note. But see the 1935 reissue of this item cited below.

> 1935 COOK, JAMES (Lieut.). Remarks on a Passage from the River Balie, in the Bay of Honduras, to Merida: The Capital of the Province of Jucatan in the Spanish West Indies. With Perspective by Muriel Haas. Reprinted from the 1769 edition. 12mo. New Orleans.

1789 The Case of his Majesty's Subjects having Property on the Mosquito Shore in America . . . Humbly submitted to the King's Most Excellent Majesty in Council, the Lords and Commons in Parliament, and the Nation of Great Britain at Large. 4to. London.

1799 BANNANTINE, J. Memoirs of Colonel Edward Marcus Despard. By James Bannantine, his Secretary when King's Superintendent of Honduras. 8vo. London.

# ADDENDA

1924 ALVAREDO, PEDRO DE. An Account of the Conquest of Guatemala in 1524. Edited by S. J. Mackie, with a facsimile of the Spanish Original, 1525. 8vo. Cortes Society. New York.

1937 LANDA, DIEGO DE (Friar). Yucatan Before and After the Conquest. With additional Documents, Maps and many illustrations. Translated by William Gates. The Maya Society. Baltimore.

> Fray Diego, an ardent Franciscan missionary of the middle decades of the 16th century, knew his Mayas intimately and at a time when they still held a knowledge of much of their culture, which they imparted to their inquisitor.— Quoted by Dauber and Pine. The original manuscript is lost, but a somewhat abbreviated later transcript was found in Spain and published with a French translation, by Brasseur de Bourbourg, in 1864. Brasseur, however, left unpublished nearly one-fourth of the manuscript, or all after sec. 42. Two Spanish editions followed, one also incomplete, and the other in a very rare folio, with many colored illustrations, as an Appendix to a translation of another equally rare French work by Leon de Rosny, on the decipherment of the Mayan hieroglyphics. No English edition at all has appeared until now.—From Dauber and Pine.

# IX

## South America

**1542 ASCHAM, ANTHONY.** A Lytle Treatise of Astronomy. London.

> This is the fifth book printed in English relating to America, or, if translations be excluded, the second; being preceded only by *A new interlude and a mery of the nature of the iiii elements* (see Rastell under 1510-1520, GENERAL TRAVELS AND DESCRIPTIONS) . . . The portion relating to America begins on the verso of C₂:—"Knowe that the people dwellynge in the countre of Brasili, beynge in that parte of the worlde called America, with all the portes and hauens called Canibales, where be founde many precious stones, and also the region of Giauntes, where Magellanus that passed the strayght and narowe see, beyonde America, dyd measure them to be ten fote longe, and also the yle Spagnolla, where groweth Lignum guaiacum, & also the yle Madagascar . . . hathe wynter when we haue sommer . . ."—Quoted by Quaritch.

**1568 THEVET, ANDRE.** The New found vvorlde, or Antarctike, wherin is contained wonderful and strange things, as well of humaine creatures, as Beastes, Fishes, Foules, and Serpents, Trees, Plants, Mines of Golde and Siluer: garnished with many learned aucthorities, trauailed and written in the French tong, by that excellent learned man, master Andrevve Thevet. And novv nevvly translated into Englishe, vvherein is reformed the errours of the auncient Cosmographers. 4to. London.

> Modern edition, Argonaut Press, London. French original, Paris, 1556. See below.
>
> This work, after that of Cartier's, is the oldest French book that speaks of New France, but its chief merit, though it is said to be full of errors and fables, lies in the fact that it forms the chief historical and official narrative of the expedition of Villegagnon in 1555 to Brazil, and the establishment formed there under the name of France Antarctique. This attempt to found a Protestant French colony in Brazil was a failure, and after several months' stay in that country Thevet returned to France. His book contains some material on French Canada. The translator was T. Hackit.

> **1556 THEVET, ANDRE.** Les Singvlaritez de la France antarctiqve nommée Amerique: & de plusieurs Terres & Islaes decouuertes de nostre temps. Par F. Andre Theuet, natif d'Angoulesme. Woodcut. 8vo. Paris.

**1578 GOMARA, FRANCISCO LOPEZ DE.** For an account of the conquest of Peru see the second part of *The Pleasant Historie of the Conquest of the Weast Indies*, under MEXICO.

**1581 ZARATE, AUGUSTIN DE.** The Strange and Delectable History of the Discoverie and Conquest of the Provinces of Peru, in the South Sea. And of the Notable things which there are found: and also of the bloudie civill warres which there happened for government. Written in foure bookes by Augustin Sarate, Auditor for the Emperor his Maiestie in the same provinces and firme land. And also of the ritche Mines of Potosi. Translated out of the Spanish tongue by T. Nicholas. Woodcut frontispiece and 6 woodcuts in the text. 4to. London.

> Modern edition, London, 1933. Spanish original, Antwerp, 1555. See below.
> Zarate was the Comptroller of Accounts for Castile, and was sent out as treasurer-general with the first viceroy, Blasco Nuñez de Vela, to examine into the financial affairs of Peru, where he remained many years. He carefully collected notes and material in his journal during his residence at Lima, and, on his return to Spain, began the compilation of a history from the discovery of Pizarro to the departure of Gasca. He had access to the best official sources of information, and his work is of great historical value.—Robinson, No. 41. "This work is, in fact, the foundation of all subsequent histories of the events to which it refers, and the narrative is given with force and simplicity. The characters of the different heroes are clearly and strongly drawn, and there is a long, distinct chapter on the appearance, conduct, and dispositions of Pizarro and Almagro. The accounts of the execution of Almagro, and of the assassination of Pizarro, are written with much spirit and picturesqueness; and the story of the misfortunes and final death of Atabaliba, the young Peruvian Inca, is very touching."—Quoted by Maggs, No. 502. Zarate was highly partial and his style, in addition, is tedious and difficult. —Waldman.

> 1933 ZARATE, AUGUSTIN DE. A History of the Discovery and Conquest of Peru, Books I-IV, translated from the Spanish by Thomas Nicholas, 1581. With an Introduction by D. B. Thomas. 8vo. Penguin Press. London.

> 1555 ZARATE, AUGUSTIN DE. Historia del Descubrimiento y Conquista del Peru, con cosas naturales que señaladamenta alli se hallan, y los successos que ha avido. La qual Escrivia Augustin de Carate, exerciendo el cargo de Contador general cuentas por su Magestad en aquella provincia, y en la de Tierra firme. 12mo. Antwerp.

1582 CASTANHEDA, FERNANDO LOPEZ DE. For Cabral's voyage to Brazil see The First Booke of *The Historie of the Discouerie and Conquest of the East Indies,* under EAST INDIES.

1589 DRAKE, SIR FRANCIS. For an account of Drake's attacks on Spanish American towns see his *A Summarie and True-Discourse of Sir Francis Drake's VVest Indian Voyage,* under WEST INDIES.

1594 ASHLEY, ROBERT. Of the Interchangeable Course or Variety of Things in the Whole World. London.

> This is a translation of a work by Louis Le Roy. Italian original, Venice, 1585. See below.

> 1585 LE ROY, LOUIS. La Vicissitvdine o Mvtabile Varieta delle Cose, nell' Vniverso di Lvigi Regio Francese: tradotta dal Signor Cavalier Hercole Cato. Venice.

> > In this work are several references to Peru, Brazil, and America, as "delle Terre Nouve."—Robinson, No. 20.

1596 CHAPMAN, GEORGE. De Guiana Carmen. London.

> The subject of this poem was Raleigh's discovery and proposed colonisation of Guiana.—*Cam. Hist. Eng. Lit.*, IV, v.

KEYMIS, LAWRENCE. A relation of the Second Voyage to Guiana. Performed and written in the yeare 1596. London.

> Keymis was sent out by Raleigh immediately after his return from the first voyage, to continue the exploration of the Orinoco. This voyage was Raleigh's last effort to found a colony. Keymis committed suicide after Raleigh's next and last futile voyage of 1616.—Waldman. This voyage, dedicated to Sir Walter Raleigh, is remitted into the third volume of Hakluyt's work. It was translated into Latin by Gotard Artus of Dantzig and printed at Frankfort, 1599.—Lowndes.

LODGE, THOMAS. A Margarite of America. 4to. London.

> This is a translation from the Spanish, made by Lodge 'being at sea four years before with M. Cavendish, in passing through the straits of Magellan.' Many sonnets, and metrical inscriptions are intermixed.—Lowndes.

RALEIGH, SIR WALTER. The Discoverie of the large, rich and bevvtiful Empyre of Gviana, with a relation of the great and Golden Citie of Manoa (which the Spaniards call El Dorado) And of the Prouinces of Emeria, Arromaniia, and other Countries, with their riuers, adioyning, Performed in the yeare 1595 by Sir W. Ralegh Knight, Captaine of her Maiesties Guard, Lo. Warden of the Stanneries, and her Highnesse Lieutenant generall of the Countre of Cornewall. 4to. London.

> Two more editions the same year. Reprinted in Hakluyt, 1598-1600; reprinted by the Hakluyt Society, London, 1848. A modern reprint, London, 1928. Translated into Latin, Nürnberg, 1598; into German, Nürnberg, 1599; into Dutch, together with Keymis' account, Amsterdam, 1617. See below and also under dates 1618, 1720, and 1751. See also Arber's *English Reprints*. A French account in Correal under 1722 below.
>
> Raleigh sent out a preliminary voyage to Guiana in 1594, he went himself in 1595, and sent Lawrence Keymis again in 1596.—Parks. This work was a justification of his expedition and a refutation of the charges that he had never been there himself. It won immediate popularity. Hume thought his narrative "full of the grossest and most palpable lies," but Schomburgh, editor of the Hakluyt Society reprint, has vindicated him.—*Cam. Hist. Eng. Lit.*, IV, iii. "In this work Raleigh gives an account of his second voyage (1595) and seems to confirm the marvellous tales concerning the Spanish city of El Doradó, which he calls by the Indian name of 'Manoa.' Camus says he described the country with the exactness of a person who had been born there, but that when he speaks of the richness of Guiana he seems to have been reduced by false appearances and the accounts of the natives and Spaniards, as he did when describing the Amazons and the people whose faces seemed placed on their breasts." Another writer, with perhaps greater justness, says: "Raleigh takes the utmost pains to state what he saw with his own eyes, what he was told by the Spaniards, or by the natives of the country, and what he inferred of the great riches of Guiana, from their accounts compared with his own observations."—Maggs, No. 590. This search for the El Dorado of the Spaniards had been going on since the expedition of Diego de Ordaz in 1511, who ascended the Orinoco as far as the Cataract of Allures. The Spanish attempts continued to the year of Raleigh's fruitless venture. The general results were of value geographically if not financially.

1848 RALEIGH, SIR WALTER. The Discovery of the Large, Rich, & Beautiful Empire of Guiana, With a Relation of the great and golden City of Manoa (which the Spaniards call El Dorado), etc., performed in the year 1595 by Sir Walter Raleigh. With some unpublished Documents relative to that country. Edited with copious explanatory Notes and a biographical Memoir by Sir Robert Hermann Schomburgh, Ph.D. Map. Hak. Soc., ser. I, vol. 3. London.

1928 RALEGH, SIR WALTER. The Discoverie of Guiana, edited from the original Text, with Introduction, Notes and Appendices of hitherto unpublished documents by V. T. Harlow. 2 maps and a portrait of Ralegh. 4to. Argonaut Press. London.

In the Introduction to the present work the romantic legend of Sir Walter as a "Deven Sea-Dog," which has persisted from the seventeenth century onwards, is examined in the light of the fresh documentary evidence; and the result is an important revelation of the great Elizabethan. The picture of Ralegh as the clever and sometimes rapacious business man is convincingly drawn. His privateering activities are shown to have been based on commercial considerations as strictly as those of any of his contemporaries. For him money-making was a life-long interest, because money spelt power. Furthermore, the reader is reminded that Ralegh has no claim to fame as a naval commander.— From Advertisement of volume.

1598 (In Latin.) Brevis et admiranda descriptio regni Guianae, auro abundantissimi, in America; seu Novus Orbis sub linea aequinoxiali situs, qui nuper admodum annis nimirum 1594-1595, et 1596, per Waltherum Raleigh equitum detectus est; paulo post jussu ejus duobus libellis comprehensus, ex quibus Iodocus Hondius tabla geographica adornavit, . . . Nürnberg.

1599 (In German.) Kurtze Wunderbare Beschreibung Dess Goldreichen Königreichs Guianae in America oder newen Welt unter der Linea Aequinoctiali gelegen. So newlich Anno 1594, 1595, unnd 1596, von den Wolgebornen Herrn Walthero Ralegh einem Englischen Ritter besucht worden. 6 engraved plates and a folding map. 4to. Nürnberg.

1617 (In Dutch.) Warachtighe ende grondige beschryvinghe van . . . Guiana . . . in America, by Noorden de rivier Orelliana. . . . Wat voor rijcke waren daer te lande . . . vallen, als . . . gout, . . . peerlen, balsem olie, langhe peper, . . . medicinale wortelen, droogheryen ende gommen. Item, zijde, catoen ende Brasilie-hout. Mitsgaders de beschrijvinge van . . . Emeria, Arromaia, Amapaia, ende Topago. Ontdeckt ende beschreven in 1595 en 1596. Waerachtighe ende grondighe beschryvinghe vande tweede zeevaert der Engelschen nae Guiana, ende de omliggende lantschappen. . . . Ontdeckt ende beschreven in 1596. 4to. Amsterdam.

1601 GALVANO, ANTONIO. For an account of the discovery of Brazil by Cabral see his *The Discoveries of the World*, under COLLECTIONS.

1604 ACOSTA, JOSEPH. The Naturall and Morall Historie of the East and West Indies: Intreating of the remarkable things of Heaven, of the Elements, Metalls, Plants and Beasts which are proper to that Country; Together with the Manners, Ceremonies, Lawes, Governments. and Warres of the Indians. Translated into English by E(dward) G(rimston). 4to. London.

Edited for the Hakluyt Society, London, 1879. Latin original (consisting of only two books), Salamanca, 1589; first edition in Spanish and first complete edition as well, Seville, 1590. See below.

Acosta is one of the earliest writers who has treated philosophically of America and its productions.—Rich. This is one of the most celebrated early works on America. It is especially important for its particulars concerning the state of South America at that time, and the early history of the Indians of Peru and Mexico. Acosta lived in America for seventeen years and was a missionary in Peru from 1571 to 1576, after which he stayed in Mexico for over two years. He was a careful and accurate observer of all that he saw . . . Part of the work was written during his stay in Peru, and was completed after his return to Spain. It became a standard authority and attained great popularity, being translated into nearly every European tongue.—Maggs, No. 465. Books V., VI., and VII. are entirely devoted to a relation of the history, customs, and wars of the Indians. This portion of the work is replete with the most curious details of the Aborigines before their peculiar customs had become modified by contact with the whites.—Robinson, No. 23.

1879 ACOSTA, JOSEPH DE. The Natural and Moral History of the Indies. By Father Joseph de Acosta. Reprinted from the English edition of Edward Grimston, 1604, and edited by Clements R. Markham, C.B., F.R.S. Vol. 1. The Natural History (Books I-IV.). Vol. 2. The Moral History (Books V-VII.). Hak. Soc., ser. I, vols. 60-61. London.

1589 ACOSTA, JOSEPH (Padre). De Natura Novi Orbis. Libri duo, et De Promulgatione Evangelii apud barbaros, sive de procuranda Indorum salute. Libri sex. 8vo. Salamanca.

1590 ACOSTA, JOSEPH. Historia Natural y Moral de las Indias, en que se tratan las cosas notables del cielo, y elementos, metals, plantas, y animales dellas: y los ritos, y ceremonias, leyes, y govierno, y guerras de los Indias. 4to. Seville.

1607 NICHOLL, JOHN. An Houre Glasse of Indian Newes. Or a true and tragicall discourse, shewing the most lamentable miseries, and distressed Calamities indured by 67 Englishmen, which were sent for a supply to the planting in Guiana in the yeare 1605. VVho not finding the saide place, were for want of victuall, left a shore in Saint Lucia, an Island of Caniballs or Men-eaters in the West-Indyes, vnder the Conduct of Captain Sen-Johns, of all which said number, onely a 11. are supposed to be still liuing, whereof 4. are lately returned into England. Written by John Nicholl, one of the aforesaid Company. 4to. London.

A Curious and very little-known book. The author was a member of the band of 67 Englishmen who attempted the establishment of another colony in Guiana; they were shipwrecked, rescued by the Spaniards, and Nicholl was imprisoned as a spy. He finally escaped to England and set himself to this doleful relation of his adventures and tribulations.—Waldman.

1611 LERIUS, JOHN. The History of America, Or Brasill, and the deploration of the people of Lappia. Written in Latin and now newly translated into English. By Ed. Aston. London.

See Boemus *The Manners, Lawes, and Cvstomes of all Nations,* 1611 edition, under 1555, GENERAL TRAVELS AND DESCRIPTIONS.

1613  HARCOURT, ROBERT.  A Relation of a Voyage to Guiana. Describing the Countrey, Climat, Scituation, Fertilitie, Provisions and Commodities of the Country. Together with the Manners, Customes, . . . of the People. Performed by Robert Harcourt, of Staunton on Harcourt Esquire. The Pattent for the Plantation of which Country his Maiestie hath granted to the said Robert Harcourt. 4to. London.

> 2nd edit., with some additions, 4to, London, 1626. Reprinted entire in the sixth edition of the *Harleian Miscellany.* Edited for the Hakluyt Society, London, 1926. See below.
>   The expedition set out on March 23, 1608/9 and the author returned to Bristol on February 2, 1609/10. The preface gives a sketch of the other settlements made or attempted in America by Spaniards and Englishmen. This account makes a valuable supplement to Raleigh's narrative of 1596.

1926  HARCOURT, ROBERT.  Harcourt's Voyage to Guiana. A Relation of a Voyage to Guiana, by Robert Harcourt, 1613. Edited by Sir Charles Alexander Harris, K.C.M.G., C.B., C.V.O. Hak. Soc., ser. II, vol. 60. London.

1618  RALEIGH, SIR WALTER.  A Declaration Of The Demeanour And Carriage Of Sir Walter Raleigh, Knight, as well in his Voyage, as in, and sithence his Returne; And of the true motiues and inducements which occasioned His Maiestie to Proceed in doing Iustice vpon him, as hath bene done. 4to. London.

> The first issue of this, the first edition, has incorrect pagination at the end. Raleigh's last trial and execution arose, as is well known, from his disobedience to King James's orders not to commit any hostilities against the Spaniards, on what was to become his final voyage—to Guiana in search of a fabulously rich mine, the position of which was known only to a Captain Kemys. His execution aroused considerable popular feeling and it was with the view of justifying their action this official account was issued by the Commissioners appointed to try him. Bacon has been regarded as the sole author of it, but (in the words of Spedding, Life, vol. VI, p. 383): "To call it Bacon's Declaration . . . is both inaccurate and misleading . . . its proper title is the official Declaration:—a declaration drawn up by the King's direction, penned by certain Councillors (Bacon being one), allowed by the Council and printed by authority. Bacon's rank in Council, together with his concern in the actual composition, entitle us to impute to him a large share of the responsibility, . . ."—From Quaritch.

RALEIGH, SIR WALTER.  Nevves of Sir Walter Rauleigh. With the True Description of Gviana: As also a Relation of the excellent Gouernment, and much hope of the prosperity of the voyage. Sent from a Gentleman of his Fleet, to a most especiall Friend of his in London. From the Riuer of Caliana, on the Coast of Guiana, Nouem. 17, 1617. Woodcut of Sir Walter Raleigh. 4to. London.

> Reprinted in Force's *Tracts,* vol. III, No. 4.—Sabin.
> The sender of the "Nevves" was "R. M."

1622  HAWKINS, SIR RICHARD.  The Observations Of Sir Richard Havvkins Knight, In His Voiage Into The South Sea. Anno Domini 1593. Fol. London.

Reprinted in Callander II, 3-142, 1766-68, taken from Purchas. Edited for the Hakluyt Society, London, 1847 and 1877. Modern edition, London, 1933. See below.

This is one of the best of all English narratives and adventurous seamanship. It is now rare.—Quaritch. "This work was in the press at the time of Hawkins' death, and was published shortly afterwards. It is a work of great interest, describing what he saw and the details of nautical life. . . . The account of the early part of the voyage is interesting from the intelligent description of sea life and of the places at which the ships touched. They lost many men by scurvy; the Dainty was nearly burnt by accident; and about the end of October, having a very large number of sick, they put into Santos in Brazil."—Sir J. K. Laughton. They afterwards passed the Strait of Magellan, plundered Valparaiso, and took prizes. In the Bay of St. Mateo, with the crew of the Dainty reduced to 75, they were attacked by two large Spanish ships, with a crew ten times as numerous, and after a stubborn fight lasting two days had to surrender. Hawkins was made a prisoner, and taken to Madrid, where he remained a prisoner for five years, until ransomed for £3000.—Sotheran. Sir Richard (who was the son of Sir John Hawkins) was one of those men who can write as well as fight. His Observations have become a classic, not only for the absorbing narrative which they embody, and for their descriptions of men and countries, but for another characteristic in which they are unique: they constitute the only detailed account, written by a contemporary, of life at sea in the Elizabethan age. They give us the work and the play, the food and drink, the sickness and the grumbling, and last of all the bulldog courage against odds, of the men who laid the foundations of England's greatness.—From the Advertisement to the Argonaut Press edition. Many illustrations might be given of Shakespeare's knowledge of sea affairs. Was it a mere coincidence that Ancient Pistol, hauled off to the Fleet with Falstaff in the last scene of Henry IV, part 2, uses a phrase which is employed in The Observations of Sir Richard Hawkins . . . existing in manuscript, we presume, when Shakespeare wrote the play? Or rather, were not Shakespeare and Hawkins quoting from a common original in the speech of the people? "Si fortuna me tormenta spero me contenta," says the Ancient. When Hawkins loses his pinnace at Plymouth, he also exclaims: "Si fortuna me tormenta, esperance me contenta."—Quoted by Robinson from *Cam. Hist. Eng. Lit.*, IV, p. 78.

1847 HAWKINS, SIR RICHARD. The Observations of Sir Richard Hawkins, Knt., In his Voyage into the South Sea in 1593. Reprinted from the edition of 1622, and edited by Capt. Charles R. Drinkwater Bethune, C.B. Hak. Soc., ser. I, vol. 1. London.

1877 The Hawkins' Voyages During the reigns of Henry VIII, Queen Elizabeth, and James I. Second edition. Edited by Clements R. Markham, C.B., F.R.S., ex-Pres. R.G.S. 1 illus. Hak. Soc., ser. I, vol. 57. London.

1933 HAWKINS, SIR RICHARD. Observations of Sir Richard Hawkins Knight in his Voyage into the South Sea, Anno Domini 1593. Edited from the Text of 1622. With Introductions, Notes, Appendices and Map, by James A. Williamson, D. Lit. Facsimile of title page. 4to. Argonaut Press. London.

1625 C(ROSS), W(ILLIAM). The Dutch Survey. Wherein are related and truly discoursed, the chiefest losses and acquirements, which have past betweene the Dutch and the Spaniards . . . with that which they have lost unto the Dutch and Persians, in Brasilia, Lima, and Ormus. 4to. London.

Pages 18 to 27 relate to America, and describe at length how the Dutch captured from the Portuguese the town and district of Todos los Sanctos (Bahia) in Brazil and also Callao, the port of Lima, with a long description of those parts of Brazil and Peru. This work is ascribed to William Crosse, the poet and translator, who flourished at that period. The Survey is probably a prose rendering based on a poem he wrote entitled "Belgiaes Troubles and Triumphs."—From Maggs, No. 479.

L'HERMITE, JACQUES. A True Relation of the Fleete which went vnder the Admirall Jaquis Le Hermite through the Straights of Magellans towards the Coasts of Peru, and the Towne of Lima in the West-Indies. With a Letter, Containing the present State of Castille in Peru. Herevnto is annexed an excellent Discourse which sheweth by cleare and strong Arguments how that it was both necessary and profitable for the Vnited Prouinces to erect a West-India Company, and euery true subject of the same ought to aduance it according to his power. Written by a Well-wisher of the Commonwealth. 4to. London. (36 pp.)

This is a translation of the Dutch original: Waerachtigh verhael, van het succes van de Vlote, of 1625. This appeared in Latin at Frankfort in 1628 and 1634. Thence it was translated into French and published in the Collection of Dutch East-India Voyages, Amsterdam, 1725. Then it was translated into English again and printed in Harris I, 66-77. Abstract in Callander II, 286-334. The Dutch edition of 1648 is given below.

According to Callander the author of this journal was Adolph Decker, a native of Strassburg, and Captain of Marines on board the Dutch fleet. Le Hermite was admiral of the Nassau fleet which was sent out to harass the Spaniards in the South Sea. It sailed April 29, 1623. It but moderately succeeded. Le Hermite died at Callao and the fleet finally proceeded to the East Indies. Le Hermite's name was given to the group of islands north of Cape Horn.

1648 L'HERMITE, JACQUES. Journal van de Nassausche vloot ofte beschrijvingh van de voyagie om den aertkloot onder J. l'Hermite en G. H. Schapenham, 1623-26. M. beschrijv. van de regeeringe van Peru door P. de Madriga . . . ockm. eenige discoursen de Oostind. vaert en de coopmanschap betreffende. 4to. Amsterdam.

This is a reprint of the edition of 1643, but with the addition of the account of an English voyage to Guiana in 1596 (Raleigh's), and some particulars relative to the navigation to the East Indies.—Hiersemann.

The Spanish Pilgrime; or, An Admirable Discovery of a Romish Catholicke. Showing how necessary and important it is, for the Protestant Kings, Princes, and Potentates of Europe, to make warre upon the King of Spaines owne Countrey; also where, and by what means, his Dominions may be invaded and easily ruinated; . . .   London.

Originally written in Castilian, this bitter attack on the ambitions of Philip II was translated into French in 1597 by J. D. Dralymont, and thence into English. The London publisher offered the pamphlet to his readers as an incomparable treasure, a rich storehouse and magazine full of precious speeches, true Histories, rare examples, etc. It relates, *inter alia,* to the exploits of the English under Norris and Drake in 1589, incidentally refers to the reasons that led Magellan with "great impatience and folly," to "discover the enterprise of Peru to the King of Castile" instead of to the King of Portugal.—Maggs, No. 442.

1626 BAERS, JAN ( ?). A plaine and trve Relation, of the going forth of a Holland Fleete the eleuenth of Nouember 1623, to the Coast of Brasile. With the Taking in of Saluedoe, and the chiefe occurrences falling out there, in the time of the Hollanders continuance therein. As also The coming of the Spanish Armado to Saluedoe, with the beleaguring of it, the accedints falling in the Towne the time of the beleaguring. And also, the great losse of Honour and Riches, and the hopefull Expectation of a Princely Land: the Excellencie thereof is truly (yet Briefly) discoueried, Lastly, The Reasons and Motiues mouing the Authour to the publishing thereof. All which are briefely, truly, and plainely set downe, without fraude or fauour. By I. B. that hath ben an eye and eare-witnesse of this subiect. Rotterdam.

> Sabin conjectures that "Johannes Baers" was the author who wrote the tract *Olinda* of 1630.—From John Carter Brown.

1627 A breefe Relation of the present state of the business of Guiana, Concerning the proceeding therein. . . . London.

> A broadside.—John Carter Brown.

1632 A Pvblication of Gviana's Plantation Newly undertaken by the Right Hon. the Earle of Barkshire (Knight of the most Noble Order of the Garter) and Company for that most famous River of the Amazons in America. Wherein is briefly shewed the Lawfulnesse of plantation in forraine Countries; hope of the natives conversion; nature of the River; qualitie of the Land, Climate, and people of Gviana; with the provisions for mans sustenance, and commodities therein growing for the trade of Merchandise: and manner of the Adventure. With an answer to some objections touching feare of Enemie . . . 4to. London. (24 pp.)

1640 News for this week from Noremberg . . . with something from Brazil. 4to. London.

1650 RALEIGH, SIR WALTER. Judicious and Select Essayes and Observations, By that Renowned and Learned Knight, Sir Walter Raleigh. Upon the first Invention of Shipping. The Misery of Invasive Warre, The Navy Royall and Sea-Service. With his Apologie for his voyage to Guiana. Portrait by Vaughan. 4 parts in 1 vol. 12mo. London.

> The Apologie was reprinted in Abridgement of his *History of the World,* London, 1698.

1655 PEAKE, THOMAS. For a description of parts of South America see his *America,* under WEST INDIES.

1656  FLECKNOE, RICHARD.  For an account of Brazil see his *A Relation of Ten Years Travells in Europe, Asia, Afrique, and America,* under GENERAL TRAVELS AND DESCRIPTIONS.

1660  CAMPANELLA, THOMAS.  His Advice to the King of Spain for attaining the universal Monarchy of the World, Particularly concerning England, Scotland and Ireland, how to raise Division between King and Parliament, to alter the Government from a Kingdome to a Commonwealth.  Thereby embroiling England in Civil War to divert the English from disturbing the Spaniard in bringing the Indian Treasure into Spain.  Also for reducing Holland . . . affirming . . . that if the King of Spain becomes Master of England and the Low Countries, he will quickly be Monarch of all Europe, and the greatest of the new World.  Translated into English by Ed. Chilmead. . . . With an admonitrie Preface by William Prynne.  4to.  London.

> A curious and interesting work.  Ch. 31 is entitled "Of the other Hemisphere and of the New World."  Ch. 32, "Of Navigation," also relates to America as well as other parts of the book.—Maggs, No. 479.

1661  PAGAN, —— (Count of).  An Historical and Geographical Description of the Great Country and River of the Amazones in America, Drawn out of divers Authors, and reduced into a better forme; with a Mapp of the River, and of its Provinces, being that place which Sir Walter Rawleigh intended to conquer and plant, when he made his Voyage to Guiana.  Translated into English by William Hamilton, and humbly offered to his Majesty, as worthy his Consideration.  Engraved folding map.  8vo.  London.

1667  WARREN, GEORGE.  An Impartiall Description of Surinam upon the Continent of Guiana, in America, with a History of several strange Beasts, Birds, Fishes, Serpents, Insects, and Customs, of that Colony, &c.  Worthy the Perusal of all, from the Experience of George Warren, Gent.  4to.  London.  (28 pp.)

> Reprinted in Osborne II, 919-937.
> An extremely interesting early account of Guiana.  Warren spent three years in one of the English settlements at that time in Surinam, which, however, were soon to be suppressed by the Dutch.—Maggs, No. 549.  He takes occasion to disprove that ancient opinion that "under the line or near it" was not habitable.  The English had a plantation there for trading for tobacco and sugar.

1671  MONTANUS, ARNOLDUS.  America: being the latest, and most Accurate Description of the New World; containing The Original of the Inhabitants, and the Remarkable Voyages thither.  The Conquest of the vast Empires of Mexico and Peru, and other large Provinces and

Territories, with the several European Plantations in those Parts. 65 engraved plates, 6 portraits, 30 folded views and 19 maps. Fol. London.

> This is a translation by John Ogilby from the *De Nieuwe en Onbekende Weereld* of Montanus. It sometimes bears Ogilby's name. It contains descriptions of various South American states and cities. See Montanus also under 1670 and 1671, FAR EAST.

1684 SHARP, BARTHOLOMEW (Captain). The Voyages and Adventures of Capt. Barth. Sharp and others, in the South Sea: being a Journal of the same. Also Capt. Van Horn with his Buccanieres surprizing of la Vera Cruz. To which is added the true Relation of Sir Henry Morgan his Expedition against the Spaniards in the West-Indies, and his taking Panama. Together with President of Panama's Account of the Same Expedition, translated out of Spanish. And Col. Beeston's Adjustment of Peace between the Spaniards and English in the West Indies. 8vo. London.

> This work was reprinted the next year as the 4th part of the 2nd edit., of Esquemeling's *History of the Buccaneers* (see under WEST INDIES). Reprinted in Hacke's Collection, London, 1699; a brief abstract in Callander II, 524-528. Translated into French, Rouen, 1712. See below.
>
> The account by the President of Panama was a letter he wrote concerning the actions of the Buccaneers. It was intercepted by them and sent to "Admiral" Morgan.—For two years and a half Sharp's party of buccaneers ranged up and down the western coast of South America, sacking and burning towns, capturing ships, ransoming sometimes, but killing often, quarreling among one another and gradually dwindling in number till it was no longer possible to carry on their plundering and rapine against the increasing forces of the Spanish authorities. At last in desperate state for stores, they sailed round the Horn for Barbadoes. There they met a King's vessel and, fearing capture, set sail for Antigua where the band was broken up, each man shifting for himself, and the ship handed over to seven unfortunates who had lost their all at play.—From Quaritch. Sharp was killed by the Spaniards at Cape Corrientes and his journals were published at London, 1699, two years after his death. For other expeditions to the Spanish American shores see Esquemeling under 1684-85, WEST INDIES.

> 1712 SHARP, ANDRE. Voyage aux Terres Magellaniques. Traduit de l'Anglais. Rouen.
>
>> So cited by Pinkerton XVII. Evidently it must be Bartholomew Sharp that is meant.

1688 GARCILASSO DE LA VEGA. The Royal Commentaries of Peru. In two Parts. The first Part treating of the Original of their Incas or Kings: of their Idolatry; of their Laws and Government both in Peace and War; of the Reigns and Conquests of the Incas: with many other Particulars relating to their Empire and Policies before such time as the Spaniards invaded their Colonies. The Second Part describing the manner by which that New World was conquered by the Spaniards. Also the Civil Wars between the Piçarrists and the Almagrians, occasioned by Quarrels arising about the Division of that Land. Of the

Rise and Fall of Rebels; and other particulars contained in that History. Illustrated with Sculptures. Written originally in Spanish, by the Inca Garcillasso de la Vega, and rendered into English, by Sir Paul Ricault. Portrait and numerous plates. Fol. London.

Edited for the Hakluyt Society, London, 1869 and 1871, and (in part) 1850. Spanish original, Lisbon, 1609. See below.

The author was a son of one of the conquerors of Peru, and by his mother a great grandson of the last of the Incas to rule Peru. He was proud of both paternal and maternal origin, and assumed the Spanish name of the first, while he was careful to assert his Incarial descent. He was a gentleman of refinement and possessed of much learning, speaking Spanish and Quichua from infancy. He was a most industrious and careful historian of the evil fortunes of his race, as well as a chronicler of the victories of its conquerors.—From Maggs, No. 502.

1850   Garcilasso's account of the journey of Gonzalo Pizarro is reprinted by the Hakluyt Society in *Expeditions into the Valley of the Amazons.* See under 1850 below.

1869-1871   GARCILASSO DE LA VEGA. The Royal Commentaries of the Yncas. . . . Translated and edited by Clements R. Markham. 2 vols. Hakluyt Society, ser. I, vols. 41 and 45. London.

1609   GARCILASSO DE LA VEGA. Primera Parte de los Commentarios Reales, que tratan del Origen de los Yncas, Reyes que fueron del Peru, de su Idolatria, Leyes, y govierno en paz y en guerra: de sus vidas y conquistas, y de todo lo que fue aquel Imperio y su Republica, antes que los Españoles passaran a el. Ecritos por el Ynca Garcilasso de la Vega, naturel del Cozco, y Capitan de su Magestad. 4to. Lisbon. Segunda Parte de los Commentarios Reales que tratan del Origen de los Yncas, Reyes que fueron del Peru, . . . de sus Vidas, y Conquistas, su Descubrimiento, y como lo ganaron los Españoles; las Guerras Civiles que huvo entre Pizarros, y Almagros, sobre la partiga de la Tierra; Castigo, y Levantamiento de Tyrannos, y de todo lo que fue aquel Imperio, y Republica, antes que los Españoles passaran a el. Escritos por el Inca Garcilasso de la Vega, Naturel del Cozco, y Capitan de su Magestad. 4to. Lisbon.

1692   BOYLE, R.   For advice how to observe the natural history of Guiana and Brazil see his *General Heads for the Natural History of a Country, Great or Small,* under NORTH AMERICA.

1694   NARBOROUGH, SIR JOHN.   For the account of his voyage in 1669 to the Straits of Magellan and up the west coast of South America see Robinson, under COLLECTIONS.

Narborough's journal as far as it goes and as it was completed for the voyage home by that of his lieutenant Nathaniel Peckett reprinted in Callander II, 422-519. Of this voyage there are two accounts—the one given in Callander, which was translated into French, Amsterdam, 1722; and the other by John Wood, an officer on board Narborough's ship, printed at London, 1699, in Hacke's Collection. This was also translated into French, Amsterdam, 1712. See below.

Narborough sailed in 1669 under commission from the British Admiralty to explore the west coast of North America from California north, and to investigate the possibility of a passage to the Atlantic in the North, and to open up trade with Chile as well. He failed to attain either object, for he got no further north than Valdivia, Chile. But he made good charts, especially of the Strait of Magellan, which were much superior to those previously in use.

1712 (In French.) Voyage aux Terres Magellaniques par Jean Wood; rédigé par le même. Traduit de l'anglais. Amsterdam.

1722 (In French.) Relations des voyages de Jean Narborough aux Terres Magellaniques. Rédigés et traduits de l'anglois. Paris and Amsterdam.

1697 DAMPIER, WILLIAM (Captain). For descriptions of the west coasts of South America see his *A New Voyage round the World,* under CIRCUMNAVIGATIONS.

> Similar references may be made to his voyage of 1703, to Cowley's, 1699, Funnell's, 1707, Cooke's, 1712, Rogers', 1712, Shelvocke's. 1726, Betagh's, 1728—all under CIRCUMNAVIGATIONS.

1698 ACUNHA, CHRISTOVAL DE (and Others). Voyages and Discoveries in South America, the First up the River of the Amazons to Quito in Peru, and back again to Brazil, by Christopher D'Acugna; the Second up the River of Plata and thence by Land to the Mines of Potosi, by M. Acarete (du Biscay); the Third from Cayenne into Guiana, in search of the Lake of Parima, reputed to be the richest Place in the World, by M. Grillet and Bechamel. 2 folding maps. 8vo. London.

> Acarete's voyage was issued separately, London, 1716. See below. Acunha's voyage was edited for the Hakluyt Society, London, 1859. See *Expeditions into the Valley of the Amazons* under 1859 below. Spanish original of Acunha, Madrid, 1641.
>
> The common explanation for the rarity of Acunha's work is its suppression by the Spanish government of Philip IV lest Portugal, which had been freed from Spain before the work came off the press, should profit by its information. It has been pointed out, however, by the editor of the Hakluyt Society edition that Portugal already knew as much. But according to Barcia (quoted by Sabin), its rarity is due to the small number of copies printed. Rich states that "it was probably not intended for sale, as it is not furnished with the licenses usually prefixed to books printed at that time. Acunha was accompanied by Artieda, a brother Jesuit, and the object of their voyage was to ascertain whether the treasures of Peru might not be brought to Europe by way of the River Amazon, without going through the South Sea (at that time much infested by pirates) and round Cape Horn."

> 1716 ACARETE DU BISCAY. A Relation of Mr. R. M.'s Voyage to Buenos-Ayres: and from thence by land to Potosi. Dedicated to the Honourable the Court of Directors of the South Sea Company. Small folding map. 12mo. London.
>
> > A scarce separately printed account. . . . It is an extremely interesting narrative of commercial ventures to the River Plate in the 1655-1660 period. R. M. was probably the gentleman who, as mentioned in the dedication, recommended the reprinting of the narrative.—Maggs, No. 612.

> 1641 ACUNA, CHRISTOVAL DE. Nvevo Descobrimiento del Gran Rio de las Amazonas. Por el Padre Christoval de Acuña, Religioso de la Suprema Generan Inquisicion, Al qval sue, y Seluzo por Orden de su Magestad, el año de 1639 Por la Provincia de Qvito en los Reynos del Peru. . . . 4to. Madrid.
>
> > This is the earliest published account of the River Amazon known to exist.

DELLON, CHARLES (M.D.). For an account of the coast of Brazil see his *Voyage to the East Indies,* under EAST INDIES.

FROGER, SIEUR FRANCOIS. A Relation of a Voyage made in the Years 1695, 1696, 1697, on the Coasts of Africa, Streights of Magellan, Brasil, Cayenna, and the Antilles, by a Squadron of French Men of War, under the Command of M. de Gennes. By the Sieur Froger, Voluntier-Engineer on board the English Falcon. Illustrated with divers strange Figures, drawn to the Life. 4 charts and 10 plates. 8vo. London.

> Extract in Callander III, 1-6. French original, Paris, 1698. See below.
> This book contains what is probably the first map of Rio de Janiero. . . . The expedition was undertaken for the purpose of founding a French settlement in the Straits of Magellan. Some French buccaneers who had preyed on the Spaniards round the coasts of South America, and in the South Seas, and who had settled for some time in the Straits of Magellan, proposed the project to De Gennes. A company was formed, but the project failed.—Robinson, No. 45. The account of the expedition is noteworthy for its details of natural history subject and for the accuracy of Froger's South American charts.—From Maggs, No. 534.

> 1698 FROGER, SIEUR FRANCOIS. Relation du'n Voyage fait en 1695, 1696, et 1697, aux côtes d'Afrique, détroit de Magellan, Brésil, Cayenne, et Isles Antilles, par une escadre de vaisseaux du Roi de France, commandée par M. de Gennes. 29 engraved plates and maps. 8vo. Paris.

A Relation of the great River of the Amazons in South America. London.

> So cited by Pinkerton XVII. It may be a garbled citation of Acunha's work above.

1699 LAS CASAS, BARTHOLOMEW DE. For an account of Spanish discoveries in South America see his *An Account of the First Voyages and Discoveries in America,* under WEST INDIES.

PONTIS, LOUIS DE. For a description of Carthagena and the country adjacent see his *A Genuine and Particular Account of the Taking of Carthagena,* under NAVAL EXPEDITIONS.

WOOD, JOHN (Captain). For his voyage to the Strait of Magellan see Hacke's Collection, under COLLECTIONS.

1700 RALEIGH, SIR WALTER. History of the World, to which is added his Premonition to Princes, his Apology for his Unlucky Voyage to Guiana, . . . 8vo. London.

Seventeen Years' Travels through the Kingdom of Peru. London.

> So cited by Pinkerton XVII. See Cieza de Leon under 1709 below.

1703  OVALLE, ALONSO DE.  An Historical Relation of the Kingdom of Chile, by Alonso de Ovalle of the Company of Jesus, a Native of St. Jago de Chile, and Procurator at Rome for that Place.  Translated out of Spanish into English.  By a Member of the Royal Society.  London.

> In Churchill III, 1-138 (first six books only); In Pinkerton XIV, 30-210 (first six books, with some omissions).  Spanish original, Rome, 1646; Italian version, Rome, 1646.  See below.
> The editions in Spanish and Italian were published simultaneously at Rome. The Spanish edition is, however, the more complete, and contains the series of interesting portraits not found in the Italian issue.—Maggs, No. 479.  (See Dr. Moses' *Spanish Colonial Literature in South America* for a description of this work.)  "Alonso de Ovalle became more widely known than most of the early Colonial historians, partly from the fact his 'history of Chile' was one of the first Chilean Books of which translations were published in Europe."—Dr. Moses. The work is divided into eight books in which the author treats of the natural state of the kingdom of Chile, the dispositions of its inhabitants, the coming of the Spaniards and their conquest of the country, the warfare with the Indians, etc.  The last two books deal with the work of conversion of the natives to Christianity.  The author says that he was impelled to write the book to dispel the general ignorance of his country and to publish the spiritual ministry of the Company of Jesus in the work of saving souls.

> 1646  OVALLE, ALONSO DE.  Historica Relacion del Reyno de Chile, y de las missiones, y ministerios que exercita en el la Compañia de Jesus. Fol.  Rome.
>
> > This edition contains maps and plans, numerous engraved plates, and woodcut views of Jesuit Colleges, plans of cities.

1708-1711  Voyage to the South-Seas, from 1708 to 1711; containing a journal of what happened most remarkable during this voyage, with the description of the Coasts of North America, from the Terre-del-Fuego to California.  From a Spanish Manuscript, entitled, The Pilot of the Coasts, etc.

> So cited by Pinkerton XVII, without place or date.

1709  CIEZA DE LEON, PETER DE.  The Seventeen Years Travels of Peter de Cieza through the Mighty Kingdom of Peru, and the large Provinces of Carthagena and Popayan in South America: from the City of Panama, on the Isthmus, to the Frontiers of Chile (translated by Captain John Stevens).  Maps and plates.  4to.  London.

> Included in Stevens' Collection, 1711.  Edited for the Hakluyt Society, London, 1864 and 1883.  Spanish original, Seville, 1553.  See below.
> "One of the most remarkable literary productions of the age of the Spanish conquest in America.  It is, in fact, the only book which exhibits the 'physical aspect of the country as it existed under the elaborate culture of the Incas.'" The author of this history was one of the greatest authorities on Peru, where he spent 16 years.  He started the work at Popayan in 1541 and finished it in Lima in 1550; the full chronicle consisted of four volumes, of which only the first was published, and deals with the geography, history and ethnology of Peru.  According to Leclerc, the three remaining books dealt respectively with: the history of the Incas; the Spanish conquest; and the history of the civil wars.—Maggs, No. 612.  See Cieza de Leon under 1913, 1917, and 1923, below.

1864  CIEZA DE LEON, PEDRO DE. The Travels of Pedro Cieza de Leon, A.D. 1532-50, From the Gulf of Darien to the City of La Plata, contained in the first part of His Chronicle of Peru (Antwerp, 1554). Translated & edited by Clements R. Markham. Hak. Soc., ser. I, vol. 33. London.

1883  CIEZA DE LEON, PEDRO DE. The Second Part of the Chronicles of Peru, 1532-1550. Translated and edited, with Notes and Introduction, by Clements R. Markham, C.B., F.R.S., ex-President R.G.S. Hak. Soc., ser. I, vol. 68. London.

1553  CIECA DE LEON, PEDRO DE. Parte Primera de la Chronica del Peru. Que Tracta la Demarcacion de sus Provincias: La Descripcion dellas. Las Fundaciones de las Nuevas Ciudades. Los Ritos y Costumbres de los Indios. Y otras Cosas Estrañas Dignas de ser Sabidas. Woodcuts depicting scenes from the life of the settlers in Peru. Fol. Seville.

1711  A View of the Coasts, Countries and Islands within the Limits of the South-Sea Company. Containing an Account of the Discoveries, Settlements, Progress and Present State; together with the Bays, Ports, Harbours, Rivers, Product, Trade, Manufactures, Riches, . . . of the several places: viz. From the River Aranoca to Terra del Fuego, and from thence through the South Sea to the farthest Bounds of the late Act of Parliament . . . establishing the New Company, . . . As also some useful Observations on the several Voyages that have been hitherto Published. Large folding map of South America by Moll. 8vo. London.

This work relates entirely to South America, and in it the whole of the coast is described, together with particulars regarding the Falkland Islands, Juan Fernandez, etc. A long description is given of the River Plate regions. The whole work is largely based on the voyages of the famous English buccaneers.— Maggs, No. 534.

1714  For an account of various Jesuit missions in South America see *The Travels of several Learned Missioners of the Society of Jesus,* under COLLECTIONS.

This contains an abridgement of a Spanish Relation, concerning the New Mission of the Moxos, in Peru, giving an account of the Life and Death of Father Baraza, the founder of these Missions, with an account of the life and customs of the Moxos Indians, the discovery of a new way over the Mountains of Peru, etc.—Maggs, No. 612.

SELKIRK, ALEXANDER. The Englishman: Being the Sequel of the Guardian. 8vo. London.

No. 26 of *The Englishman* is devoted to the Life and adventures of Alexander Selkirk, the prototype of Defoe's "Robinson Crusoe." Steele actually interviewed Selkirk on his return from his exile on the island of Juan Fernandez, rendering his account of added importance because of its authenticity.—Maggs, No. 580.

1715-18　Journal in which a cavalry soldier, nephew of Manuel Alves Barroza, briefly describes the voyages which he made from Lisbon to Rio de Janeiro, Pernambuco, Bahia, Cape Verde, Saint Vincent and Mazagan, etc., from September 1715 to October 1738. Fol. (No place given.)

　　　　So cited by Maggs, No. 585.

1717　FREZIER, AMEDEE FRANCOIS. A Voyage to the South-Seas, and along the Coast of Chili and Peru, in the Years 1712-14. Particularly describing the Genius and Constitution of the Inhabitants, as well Indians as Spaniards: Their Customs and Manners; their Natural History, Mines, Commodities, Traffick with Europe, . . . 37 engraved maps and plates, with plans of various cities. 4to. London.

　　　　Extract in Callander III, 386-439. French original, Paris, 1716. See below.
　　　　This work forms one of the most valuable of our early records of the Falkland Islands, and to Frézier we are indebted for the clearest contemporary account of the Navigation of the French seamen there. Most of these navigators, including Frézier himself, were from St. Malo, and thus the islands became known as the Malouines. To Frézier we are also indebted for the statement that "these Islands are certainly the same which Sir Richard Hawkins discover'd in 1593," a statement often quoted later at the time of the English, French, and Spanish claims to the Falkland Islands. This English edition is preferable to the original French edition of 1716, as it contains Dr. Edmund Halley's Postscript, correcting certain Geographical errors made by Frézier. Halley is of course most famous now as the discoverer of Halley's Comet. At the end is a 13 pp. account of the Joint Settlement in Paraguay. The work also contains an interesting account of guano at page 147.—Maggs, No. 612. This work was very useful in its day and in later times to navigators proposing to double Cape Horn. The author, who was "Engineer in Ordinary" to the French King, sailed from St. Malo Nov. 23, 1711.

　　　　1716　FREZIER, AMEDEE FRANCOIS. Relation du Voyage de la Mer du Sud aus Côtes du Chily et de Pérou, et du Brésil, fait pendant les années 1712-14. Maps and plates. 4to. Paris.

1720　RALEIGH, SIR WALTER. An Historical Account of the Voyages and Adventures of Sir Walter Raleigh . . . humbly proposed to the South Sea Company. London.

　　　　Published in 1720, but dated 1719. Defoe has been proposed as the author of this work.

1722　CORREAL, FRANCOIS. Voyages de Francois Corréal aux Indes Occidentales; contenant ce qu'il y a vue de plus remarquable pendant son séjour, depuis 1666 jusqu'en 1697; traduit de l'Espagnol: avec une relation de la Guiane de Walter Raleigh, et le Voyage de Narborough à la Mer du Sud par le Détroit de Magellan. Traduits de l'Anglois. 2 vols. Folding map. 8vo. Amsterdam.

　　　　This work is cited here for its versions of Raleigh and Narborough. The regions visited by Corréal include Mexico, the Terra Firma, Brazil, and Paraguay. Besides the narratives of Raleigh and Narborough, there are given the journal of the navigator Abel Jansen Tasman and an account of the Moxos mission in Peru.

1725 HERRERA, ANTONIO DE.   For a history of Spanish conquest and colonization in South America see his *The General History of the Vast Continent and Islands of America,* under WEST INDIES.

1726 BROCKWELL, C.   For a history of Brazil see his *Natural and Political History of Portugal,* under WEST EUROPE.

1732 BREWER, HENRY, and HERCKEMAN, ELIAS.   A Voyage to the Kingdom of Chili in America. Performed by Mr. Henry Brewer and Mr. Elias Herckeman, in the years 1642 and 1643. With a Description of the Isle of Formosa and Japan. Translated from the High Dutch Original, Printed at Frankford, upon the Maine, 1649. In Churchill I, 453-485.

> Reprinted in Callander II, 379-418.
> Brewer, one of the directors of the Dutch West India Company, commanded a ship which sailed with a fleet of five to set up trade with the natives, who were then in bad humor with the Spaniards. But the assistance of the latter was not well organized. Besides the Dutch showed themselves too eager for gold. Brewer died at Valdivia in August, 1643, and the command fell to Herckeman.

NIEUHOFF, JOHN.   For an account of travels in Brazil see his *The Voyages and Travels into Brazil and the East Indies,* under EAST INDIES.

> Nieuhoff's stay in Brazil extended from 1640 to 1649. He was a Dutch official there during the time the Dutch were making establishments in that country. His work was long considered a standard authority on Brazil.

SEPP, ANTHONY, and BEHME, ANTHONY.   An Account of a Voyage from Spain to Paraquaria: Performed by the Reverend Fathers Anthony Sepp and Anthony Behme both German Jesuits. Containing a description of all the remarkable things and the Inhabitants, as well as of the Missioners residing in that Country. Taken from the Letters of the said Anthony Sepp and published by his own Brother Gabriel Sepp. Translated from the High Dutch Original. In Churchill IV, 596-622.

> German original, Nürnberg, 1696. See below.
> The missioners, forty in number, arrived at Buenos Ayres about April 6, 1691. Buenos Ayres at that time was a collection of clay houses taking up two streets which crossed each other.

> 1696  SEPP, ANTHONY, and BOEHM, ANTHONY. Reisbeschreibung aus Hispaniam nach Paraquariam. Nürnberg.

TECHO, NICHOLAS DE (Father). The History of the Provinces of Paraguay, Tucuman, Rio de la Plata, Parana, Guaire and Uroasca, and something of the Kingdom of Chili in South America. In Churchill IV, 636-749.

> Techo was a priest of the Society of Jesus. His work was originally written in Latin. The editor of Churchill omits much matter dealing with the history of the Society, religious miracles, etc. The writer lived five years in the country. He celebrates, instead of conquest by soldiers and arms, the peaceable conquest of the Indians' souls. In 1645 there were 299 priests and 9 colleges among the Indians of that region.

1735 ATKINS, JOHN. For an account of Brazil see his *A Voyage to Guinea, Brazil, and the West Indies,* under GENERAL TRAVELS AND DESCRIPTIONS.

1740 CARRANZA, DOMINGO GONZALEZ. For a description of the ports of Porto Bello, and Carthagena see his *A Geographical Description of the Coasts, Harbours, and Sea Ports of the Spanish West-Indies,* under WEST INDIES.

1741 CAMPBELL, JOHN. A concise History of Spanish America; containing a succinct Relation of the Discovery and Settlement of its several Colonies: A circumstantial Detail of their respective Situation, Extent, Commodities, Trade, . . . And a full and clear Account of the Commerce with Old Spain by the Galleons, Flota, etc. As also of the Contraband Trade with the English, Dutch, French, Danes, and Portuguese. Together with an appendix, in which is comprehended an exact Description of Paraguay. Collected chiefly from Spanish Writers. 8vo. London.

> Republished, with new titles, London, 1742 and 1747. Translated into Dutch, Amsterdam, 1745-46. The 1747 version translated into Dutch, Amsterdam, 1750; into German, Soraw, 1763. See below.

> 1742 CAMPBELL, JOHN. A Compleat History of Spanish America, . . . 8vo. London.

> 1745-46 (In Dutch.) Historie van het Spansche Ryk in Amerika, . . . Maps and plates. Amsterdam.

> 1747 CAMPBELL, JOHN. The Spanish Empire in America, . . . By an English Merchant. 8vo. London.

> 1750 (In Dutch.) Beknopte Historie en tegenwoordigen staat van het Spaansche ryk in Amerika. Plates. 8vo. Amsterdam.

> 1763 (In German.) Das Spanische Reich in Amerika, oder kurze Beschreibung aller spanischen Pflanzstädte und Besitzungen. 4to. Soraw.

RAVENEAU DE LUSSAN. A Journal of a Voyage made into the South Sea, by the Bucaniers or Freebooters of America, from the year 1684-89. To which is added the Voyage of Montauban 1699. Translated from the French. London.

> See Esquemeling under 1684-85, WEST INDIES. French original, Paris, 1689. See below.
> A very famous and entertaining work. The author adopted the Buccaneering *profession* in order to obtain money to pay his creditors and to return to his fashionable life in Paris. According to his own account, he was a man of the highest principles and very devout, never allowing his crew to molest priests, nuns, or churches. After taking a Spanish town he would attend mass in the church or cathedral with his pirates before commencing to loot. He recounts a love affair with a wealthy Spanish widow in one of his captured towns and his adventures and ultimate safe arrival back in Paris.—Maggs, No. 612.

> 1689  RAVENEAU DE LUSSAN. Journal du Voyage fait à la Mer de Sud, avec les Filibustiers de l'Amérique en 1684 & années suivantes. 12mo. Paris.

1743  BULKELEY, JOHN (Gunner), and CUMMINS, JOHN (Carpenter). A Voyage to the South-Seas, in the year 1740-41, containing a faithful Narrative of the Loss of H. M. S. 'Wager,' on a desolate Island in Latitude 47 S., Longitude 81 : 40 W., with the Proceedings and Conduct of the Officers and Crew, . . . in Coasting the Southern Part of Patagonia, their Passage through the Streights of Magellan, Account of their Manner of living on Seals, Wild Horses, . . . their safe Arrival to the Brazil, interspersed with many entertaining and curious Observations not taken notice of by Sir John Narborough or any other Journalist. 8vo. London.

> 2nd edit., London, 1757. A modern reprint, London, 1928. See below and also Lieut. Byron's account of the same shipwreck under 1768 below, together with Campbell's, 1747, Morris', and Young's, 1751, below.
> The *Wager* was one of Commodore Anson's fleet (see Anson under 1748 below) which was proceeding up the west coast of South America to harass the Spanish possessions. The ship ran aground on a small island in the Northwest part of the Gulf de la Penas, and broke up. The distresses endured caused the crew to divide, some electing to stay with Captain Cheap, who by the way was about as amiable a character as Lieut. Bligh of the *Bounty* fame, and the others to take the long boats and make their way back to the east coast. Bulkeley and Cummins were of the latter group. The navigation of the perilous seas, amid vast swarms of unknown islands and channels along the west coast of Patagonia or Chile is as marvelous as the men's capacity to endure cold, wet, and hunger. The voyage was successfully accomplished with the help of Narborough's charts. If there is a more desolate and rain-ridden coast than that of southern Chile, it remains yet to be discovered. This expedition of Anson's has many chroniclers.

> 1928  BULKELEY, JOHN, and CUMMINS, JOHN. A Voyage to the South Seas in the Year 1740-41. Edited by Arthur D. Howden Smith. Contemporary illustrations reproduced. 8vo. Argonaut Series. London.

LOCKMAN, JOHN. For accounts of South America from Jesuit missionaries see his *Travels of the Jesuits into Various Parts of the World*, under COLLECTIONS.

1744 ANSON, GEORGE (Commodore). For an account of Commodore Anson's cruising expedition on the west coast of South America see this date, together with the dates 1745 and 1748, under CIRCUMNAVIGATIONS.

1744-48 BETAGH, WILLIAM (Captain). Capt. Betagh's Observations on the Country of Peru, and its Inhabitants during his Captivity. In Harris I, 240-256.

> Reprinted in Pinkerton XIV, 1-29.

A Concise History of the Discovery, Settlement, and Cultivation of Brazil by the Portugueze: the Conquest of the greatest Part of the Country by the Dutch, the Recovery thereof by the Portugueze, and the vast Advantages that have accrued to them of late Years from this noble Colony. In Harris II, 166-189.

The History of the Discovery and Conquest of the Empire of Peru by Francis Pizarro, together with the Discovery of Chili, and the Conquest of that Country, also. In Harris II, 143-166.

PYRARD, DE LAVAL, FRANCOIS. For his stay in Brazil see his *The Voyage of Pirard de Laval to the East Indies,* under EAST INDIES.

1747 CAMPBELL, ALEXANDER. The Sequel to Bulkeley and Cummins's Voyage to the South-Seas, or, the Adventures of Capt. Cheap, the Hon. Mr. Byron, Lieut. Hamilton, Alex. Campbell, and others, of H. M. S. the Wager, which was wreck'd on a desolate Island in the South-Seas, 1741, containing a faithful Narrative of the unparallel'd Sufferings of these Gentlemen, after being left on the said Island by the rest of the Officers and Crew, who went off in the Long-boat; . . . Their falling into the hands of the Indians, who carried them into New Spain, where they remained Prisoners of War, till sent back to Europe in 1746. 8vo. London.

> This was called in soon after it was published and suppressed, so that few copies are at present to be seen.—Sabin. The present work is a counterblast to the account published by Bulkeley and Cummins in 1743. See this date above.

LA CONDAMINE, CHARLES MARIE DE. A Succinct Abridgement of a Voyage made within the Inland Parts of South America; from the Coasts of the South-Sea, to the Coasts of Brazil and Guiana, down the River of the Amazons: As it was read in the Public Assembly of the Academy of Sciences at Paris, April 28, 1745. . . . To which is annexed,

A Map of the Maranon, or River of the Amazons, drawn by the same (*i.e.*, by La Condamine). 8vo. London.

> Reprinted in Pinkerton XIV, 211-269. French original, Paris, 1745-46. See below.
>
> The Paris Academy of Sciences conducted two researches in geodetic measurement to determine the configuration of the earth by measuring an arc of the meridian, one in Lapland, carried on by Maupertuis, Clairault, Camus, Abbé Outhier, and others, in 1736 (for an account of their voyage see Maupertuis and Outhier under 1808-1814, NORTH EUROPE); the other in 1735 executed by La Condamine at the equator on the high Andean plateau. They were assisted in the work by the Spanish Government, which appointed Ulloa as leader (see below under 1758). The job done, La Condamine returned to the east coast of the continent by descending the Amazon, the first time it was accomplished by a scientist.

1745-46   LA CONDAMINE, CHARLES MARIE DE. Relation abrégée d'un voyage fait dans l'intérieur de l'Amérique méridionale, depuis la côte de la mer du Sud jusqu'à celle du Brésil et de la Guyane, en descendant la rivière des Amazones; avec une lettre sur l'émeute populaire excitée à Cuenca au Pérou, contre le academiciens envoyés pour mesurer la figure de la terre. Avec une carte du Maranon, et une planche représentant l'émeute. 8vo. Paris.

1748   LOZANO, PEDRO. A True and Particular Relation of the Dreadful Earthquake which happen'd at Lima, the Capital of Peru, and the neighbouring Port of Callao, On the 28th of October, 1746. With an Account likewise of every Thing material that passed there afterwards to the end of November following. Published at Lima by Command of the Vice-Roy, And translated from the Original Spanish, By a Gentleman who resided many years in those Countries. To which is Added, A Description of Peru in General, with its Inhabitants; setting forth their Manners, Customs, Religion, Government, Commerce, etc. Interspersed with Passages of Natural History and Physiological Disquisitions; particularly an Enquiry into the Cause of Earthquakes. The whole illustrated with a Map of the Country about Lima; Plans of the Road and Town of Callao, another of Lima; and several Cuts of Natives drawn on the Spot by the Translator. 8vo. London.

> Sabin cites this as the second edition. He also lists another title of the same year, with some differences in wording, which may be the first. There is a translation into French of one of these or a similar work, The Hague, 1752. The Spanish original seems to have been printed at Lima. There is a Portuguese version, Lisbon, 1748. See below.
>
> The translator is said to be Henry Johnson, but Sabin quotes the *Gentleman's Magazine*, for 1784, for the statement: "It is a pretended translation from the Spanish." The French translation seems to have been done from a work by one named Hales. See the note to the same. Lima had suffered from two previous disastrous earthquakes—one in 1687 and another in 1586.

1748   LOZANO, PEDRO. A True and Particular History of Earthquakes. Containing a relation of that dreadful Earthquake which happened at Lima and Callao, in Peru, Oct. 28, 1746; published at Lima by Command of the Vice-Roy, and now Translated from the Original Spanish; also of that which happen'd in Jamaica in 1692, and of others in different parts of the world. Accurately describing the dreadful Devastations that have been made by these dreadful convulsions of the Earth's whereby Mountains have been thrown down, or removed to great distances; Cities, with all their Inhabitants swallow'd up in a moment; whole flocks and herds, with their keepers, ingilp'd in the tremendous chasms and openings of valleys; and large forests sunk, and forever buried in an instant. Extracted from Authors of unexceptionable Reputation, by Philolethus. 8vo. London.

1752 (In French.) HALES, ——. Histoire des tremblemens de terre arrivés à Lima, capitale du Pérou, et autres lieux; avec la description du Pérou, et des recherches sur les causes phisiques des tremblemens de terre. Traduite de l'anglois. 2 parts in 1 vol. 12mo. 4 maps and 3 plates. The Hague.

Le traducteur a ajouté à l'ouvrage de Hales, une relation du tremblement de terre de Lima et de Callao, précédé d'une description de ces deux villes; traduite de l'espagnol sur l'original imprimé à Lima. . . . A la fin de la 2 partie, il y a la traduction de deux lettres écrites à bord du vaisseau *La Grenade*, relatives au tremblement de terre arrivé au Port-Royal et à la Jamaïque, en 1692.—Leclerc, quoted by Bookseller.

This may be a translation of the second work cited above.

1748 LOZANO, PEDRO. Individual, e verdadeira Relaçao da extrema ruina, que padeceo a Cidade dos Reys Lima, Capital do Reyno do Peru, com o horrivel Terremoto, acontecido em a noite do dia 28 de Outubro de 1746; e da Total Assolaçao do Presidio, e Porto de Calho pela violente irrupçao do Mar, que a occasionou naquella Bahia. 4to. Lisboa.

1750 The African Company's Property to the Forts and Settlements in Guiana, in America, considered, and the Necessity of establishing a trade in a regulated Company. 8vo. London.

1751 MORRIS, ISAAC. A Narrative of the Dangers and Distresses which befel Isaac Morris, and Seven more of the Crew, belonging to the Wager Store-Ship, which attended Commodore Anson, in his Voyage to the South Sea; containing an Account of their Adventures, after they were left by Bulkeley and Cummins, on an uninhabited Part of Patagonia, on South America; where they remained about Fifteen Months 'till they were seized by a Party of Indians, and carried to Buenos-Ayres, and ransomed by the Governor, who sent them on board the Asia, a Spanish Man of War and confined them there above thirteen Months; when the Asia sailed for Europe. Interspersed with a Description of the Manners and Customs of the Indians in that Part of the World, . . . The Whole Serving as a Supplement to Mr. Bulkeley's Journal, Campbell's Narrative, and Ld. Anson's Voyage. By I. Morris, late Midshipman of the Voyage. 8vo. London.

"This narrative appears to be genuine, and is well and methodically written," etc.—*Monthly Review,* V, 156, quoted by Sabin.

RALEIGH, SIR WALTER. Works, Political, Commercial, and Philosophical; together with his Letters and Poems, with an Account of his Life, by Thomas Birch. Portrait. 2 vols. 8vo. London.

> Among other items this contains Orders to be observed by the Commanders of the Fleet and Land Companies under the Charge of Sir Walter Raleigh, bound for the South Parts of America; A Voyage for the Discovery of Guiana; An Apology for the Voyage to Guiana; and A Letter to Lord Carew touching Guiana.

YOUNG, JOHN (Cooper). An Affecting Narrative of the Unfortunate Voyage and Catastrophe of his Majesty's Ship Wager, one of Commodore Anson's Squadron in the South Sea Expedition. 8vo. London.

> Young was one of the crew that elected to go in the long boat with Bulkeley and Cummins after the wreck of the *Wager*, and was one of the thirty survivors out of a company of seventy that reached Brazil. This voyage of three thousand miles in an open boat with its constant exposure to shipwreck, and endurance of hunger quite matches that of Bligh's, recently made famous by the novel of Nordhoff and Hall.

1752 BLANCHARDIERE, COURTE DE LA (Abbé). A Voyage to Peru, performed by the (Ship) Conde of St. Malo, in the years 1745, 1746, 1747, 1748, and 1749. Written by the Chaplain. To which is added, An Appendix, containing the present State of the Spanish affairs in America in respect to mines, trade, and discoveries. 12mo. London.

> The author's "observations and descriptions are sensible, pertinent, and entertaining. He seems to have little of the priest, and nothing of the bigot about him; yet his sentiments are such as become the good Christian and the gentleman."— *Monthly Review*, IX, 294, quoted by Sabin. See Brignon under 1766-68 below.

OSORIUS, JEROME. For an account of the Portuguese discoveries in Brazil see his *The History of the Portuguese, during the Reign of Emmanuel,* under COLLECTIONS.

1756 ROLT, RICHARD. A New and Accurate History of South America: containing a particular Account of some Accidents leading to the Discovery of the New World; of the Discovery made by Columbus, and other Adventurers; of the several Attempts made to find out a North-East and North-West Passage. With a full Description of the Spanish Provinces of Chili, Paraguay, Peru, and Terra Firma. Of Guiana . . . of Cayenne . . . of Brazil . . . of that Part of Paraguay possessed by the Jesuits . . . and of the various Nations of Indians, . . . Large engraved map of South America. 8vo. London.

1758 BURKE, EDMUND. For an account of the Spanish and Portuguese settlements in the New World see his *An Account of the European Settlements in America,* under NORTH AMERICA.

JUAN, GEORGE, and ULLOA, ANTONIO DE. A Voyage to South-America: Describing at large the Spanish Cities, Towns, Provinces . . . on that extensive Continent . . . Together with the Natural History of the Country. And an Account of their Gold and Silver Mines . . . Translated from the original Spanish. (by John Adams). 7 maps and plates. 2 vols. London.

> Printed at Dublin, 2 vols., 1758; 2nd edit., revised and corrected, 2 vols., London, 1760; 3rd edit., with added matter, 2 vols., London, 1772. Extract in Callander III, 659-669; reprinted in Pinkerton XIV, 313-696, from the 5th edition of 1807. Spanish original, Madrid, 1748. See below.
>
> This voyage arose out of the desire of the French Government (through the Academy of Sciences at Paris) to send certain members of the Academy of Sciences to measure a degree of longitude in the equinoctial countries of Peru (see La Condamine under 1747 above). This request was not only accorded in the most courteous manner, but the King of Spain conceived the idea of sharing the honor of a scheme devoted to the advancement of knowledge, and sent two of the most scientific officers of the Spanish navy to accompany the expedition. This party carried on a series of operations of unexampled difficulty and encountered hardships and sufferings which demanded the strength of the strongest constitutions and the energy of minds stimulated by a love of science. Much information was collected and published, which has been reproduced in other works on South America.—Quoted by Maggs, No. 429. Antonio de Ulloa was a Spanish admiral and statistician. He was an able administrator and undertook the organization of the newly acquired dominion of Louisiana on behalf of the Spanish government, but was obliged to abandon the project owing to the opposition of the colonists. He was indefatigable in his scientific researches, and made a study of the properties of platinum and magnetism; introduced various improvements in the arts of engraving, and directed the execution of the geographical charts of Spain.—From Maggs, No. 546.

> 1772 JUAN, GEORGE, and ULLOA, ANTONIO DE. A Voyage to South America, describing the Spanish Cities, Towns, Provinces, . . . To which are added, by J. Adams, Occasional Notes and Observations, an Account of some parts of the Brazils hitherto unknown to the English Nation. Maps and plates. 2 vols. 8vo. London.
>
>> Adams, the translator, had lived for several years in those parts. This edition is said to be the best in English, and the French translation of 1752 next to the original in value on account of its plates, which number 55.

> 1748 JUAN, JORGE, and ULLOA, ANTONIO DE. Relacion Historica del viage a la America Meridional para medir algunos grados de meridiano terrestre, y venir por ellos en conocimiento de la verdadera figura y magnitud de la tierra, con otras varias observaciones astronomicas y phisicas. 43 maps, etc. 5 vols. 4to. Madrid.
>
>> For a work with a slightly different title but with reference to this expedition see below.

> 1748 JUAN, JORGE, and ULLOA, ANTONIO DE. Observaciones Astronomicas, y Phisicas, hechas de Orden de S. Magestad en los Reynos del Peru . . . de las quales se deduce la figura, y magnitud de la Tierra, y se aplica a la Navegacion. Frontispiece and diagrams. Fol. Madrid.

1759 DILWORTH, W. H. The Conquest of Peru, by Francis Pizarro. Containing an Authentic Detail of the Government, Religion, Laws, etc. Together with the Voyages of the First Adventures, particularly Ferdinand de Soto, for the Discovery of Florida. 12mo. London. (A chapbook.)

Muratori, L. A.   A Relation of the Missions of Paraguay wrote originally in Italian, and now done into English from the French Translation
(by F. E. de Lourmel, 1757).   Folding map.   8vo.   London.

> Another edition, with a different title, London, 1788. Italian original, Venice,
> 1743. See below.
> "The History of the Missions of the Jesuits in Paraguay, where they exerted
> an extraordinary influence and obtained almost supreme power, is full of interest.
> Most books on the subject are written by members of the order; but the fact that
> Muratori was not a Jesuit has given his history a character of impartiality not
> claimed for other authors. It was composed in great part from documents written
> by various Jesuit Missionaries and travellers, furnished to Muratori by Father
> Gaetan Cattanio, a missionary in Paraguay."—Maggs, No. 612. It is difficult to
> find a more fascinating story than this attempt of the Jesuits to establish a self-
> sustained community of natives, where foreigners were not admitted except under
> strictest regulations. See Graham, under GENERAL REFERENCE.

> 1788  MURATORI, L. A.   The Jesuits Travels in South America, Paraguay,
>       Chili, . . . With the Relation of Father Cagetan (Gaetan) Cattaneo.
>       Table and map. 16mo. London.

> 1743  MURATORI, A.   Il christianesimo felice nelle Missioni de Padri del la
>       compagnia di Gesu nel Paraguai. Folding map of South America. 4to.
>       Venice.

1760  JEFFERYS, THOMAS.   For an account of Spanish settlements in Spanish South America see his *The Natural and Civil History of the French
Dominions in North and South America,* under NORTH AMERICA.

1762  An Account of the Spanish Settlements in America. In Four Parts. I. An
account of the Discovery of America by the celebrated Christopher
Columbus, with a description of the Spanish insular Colonies in the
West Indies. II. Their settlements on the continent of North
America. III. Their settlements in Peru, Chili, Paraguay and Rio
de la Plata. IV. Their settlements in Terra Firma, Of the different
countries in South America still possessed by the Indians, . . . with a
description of the Canary Islands. Each part contains an accurate de-
scription of the settlements in it, their Situation, Extent, Climate, Soil,
Produce, former and present Condition, trading Commodities, Manufactures, the Genius, Disposition, and Number of their Inhabitants,
their Government both civil and ecclesiastic, together with a concise
Account of their chief Cities, Ports, Bays, Rivers, Lakes, Mountains,
Minerals, Fortifications, etc., with a very particular Account of the
Trade carried on between them and Old Spain, to which is annexed, A
Sufficient Account of the Climate, Produce, and Manufactures, Trade,
etc., of Old Spain. Map of America. 8vo. Edinburgh.

> At the end is "The accurate Accounts published by Authority, of the Siege
> and Surrender of the Havannah, the chief Town of the Island Cuba."—Sabin.

ALLEN, ROBERT. For an account of the trade to the South Sea, etc., see his *The Importance of the Havana,* under WEST INDIES.

1766 An Account of the Giants lately discovered, In a Letter to a Friend in the Country. 12mo. London. (31 pp.)

> Commodore Byron, on his return from his Voyage to the South Sea, reported that he had seen five hundred giants on horseback on the coast of Patagonia, an opinion that prevailed till quite recently. The object of the author of this tract was to ridicule and disprove the statement of Byron.—Sabin. In the *Philosophical Transactions* for 1764, there is an "Account of a very tall Man seen near the Straits of Magellan." See Coyer under 1767 below.

1766-68 BEAUCHESNE-GOUIN. Voyage to Magellanica. From the Journal of the Sieur de Villefort, ensign on Beauchesne's ship, and thence for the first time printed in English. Extract in Callander III, 56-66.

> This voyage ran from Dec. 17, 1690, to Aug. 6, 1701.

BRIGNON, HENRY. Voyage to Magellanica. In Callander III, 669-672.

> The history of this voyage was written by the Sieur de la Blanchardière, and printed at Paris in 1751. Though short it is of some importance as it gives a very different account of the passage round Cape Horn from that experienced by Anson, in that the passage was remarkably short and easy both coming and going. The departure from France was in November, 1745, and the return to St. Malo in March, 1749. This may be the same voyage as that listed under Blanchardière under 1751 above.

CAMARGO, ALPHONSO DE. Voyage to Magellanica. In Callander I, 201-203.

> This abstract is taken originally from Herrera, Decade 7, lib. i, cap. 8. It appears for the first time in English in Callander. Because of the difficulties attending the crossing the Isthmus of Panama, the Spaniards still persisted in the attempt to get into the South Seas by the Strait of Magellan. This expedition of three ships, which sailed from Seville in 1539, met with disaster in the Strait. Disgusted with their experiences in that region, they resolved to think no more of this passage and to fortify Nombre de Dios on the Isthmus.—From Callander.

CARJAVAL, JUTIERES DE, and LADRILLEROS, —— (Capt.). Voyage of . . . to Magellanica. Brief abstract in Callander I, 110-112.

> This account is taken from the Latin of Barlaeus, and Acosta's *Natural History of the Indies,* and the *Voyage aux Terres Australes* and appears for the first time in English. Carjaval, Bishop of Placentia, fitted out a fleet of four vessels to try the Strait of Magellan. Three were wrecked, but the fourth got to Lima. It was unable to proceed to the Moluccas, however. The ship was hauled up on dry land, and laid up as a monument to the enterprise. The date of the expedition is about 1523 or 1524.

FENTON, ——. Voyage to Magellanica, written by Vice-Admiral Ward. Given in original form in Callander I, 378-412.

> This voyage was made by a fleet of four ships in 1582. Its destination was China, but it was forced to return to England without even making the Strait of Magellan. Callander does not tell us his source.

FEUILLÉE, LOUIS. Voyage to Magellanica. Extract from the Journal of the physical, mathematical and botanical Observations made by Father Feuillée on the coasts of South America. In Callander III, 379-386.

> The author was correspondent of the Academy of Sciences and his observations were printed at Paris, 1714, 2 vols. He sailed from Marseilles, Dec. 14, 1707. The account appears for the first time in English.

FOUQUET, ——, and PEREE, ——. Voyage to Magellanica. Extract. in Callander III, 227-231.

> This account was written by a Jesuit aboard Peree's ship, and printed at Paris in 1707, with other letters of the Missionaries. The ships sailed from St. Malo Dec. 26, 1703. In a storm off Cape Horn Fouquet was lost.

GARCIA DE LOAISA. Voyage to Magellanica and Polynesia. Substance in Callander I, 112-118.

> This voyage, which is here given in English for the first time, is written up in Herrera, Decade III, lib. 7. et seq., Madrid, 1601. Some loose extracts of it are found in the Latin Collection of Barlaeus, and in the History of Argensola. See Gonzales de Oviedo, *Hist. Nat. de Ind.* I. ii. Oviedo was well acquainted with the adventures of Magellan and Garcia de Loaisa, having conversed with Sebastian Cano and Bastumante his companions. The former had brought home Magellan's flagship. The present expedition was destined for a voyage round the world, but on the voyage north on the west coast of South America, Garcia died and likewise successive commanders died or were poisoned.

LE BARBINAIS. Voyage to Magellanica. Extract in Callander III, 439-443.

> The history of this voyage was printed at Paris, 3 vols., 12mo, 1725 and 1728. It appears here for the first time in English. Nothing very material is related in it. Le Barbinais sailed from France in August, 1714, in a vessel freighted for Chile.

MURRAY, GEORGE (Hon.). Letter from the Hon. George Murray to Thomas Corbet, Esq., Secretary to the Right Honourable the Lords of Admiralty. Extract in Callander III, 654-659.

> This gives an account of the ships *Severn* and *Pearl,* after their separation from Anson's fleet at the passage of the Strait of Le Maire. They were forced to return to Rio de Janeiro. See Anson under 1748, CIRCUMNAVIGATIONS.

## SARMIENTO DE GAMBOA, PEDRO. Voyage to Magellanica. Abstract in Callander I, 363-378.

This extract is the first appearance in English of this voyage. Edited for the Hakluyt Society, London, 1894. First printed Spanish edition, Madrid, 1768. See below.

The history of this voyage is contained in Argensola's *History of the Conquest of the Moluccas* (see under 1708, EAST INDIES). It was afterwards translated into French, Amsterdam, 1706. In Acosta is another source for the voyage. Sarmiento appears to have been a vain empty man who paid little regard to the truth. Argensola follows him closely and even adds fables of his own. Acosta is more reliable. He says he got reliable information from Hernando Alonzo, the pilot of the ship.—From Callander. "In 1579, when Drake appeared in Peruvian waters, Sarmiento led an expedition in pursuit of him, but failed to overtake him. On his return, he received the Viceroy's orders to proceed to the Strait of Magellan, in order to intercept Drake there on his voyage back to England. At the same time he was under orders to fortify the Strait so as to prevent the passage of explorers or pirates who might undertake to follow Drake. . . . Sarmiento's account persuaded the King of Spain to fit out an extensive fleet for the purpose of transporting a considerable body of colonists, men with their families, to the inhospitable shores of the strait. Sarmiento was appointed to be the governor of the colony, but the command of the fleet was entrusted to the incompetent Diego Flores de Valdes, and his incompetence rather than the storms encountered caused the ruin of the enterprize."—From Dr. Moses' *Spanish Colonial Literature in South America,* quoted by Maggs, No. 612. Cavendish found the remnants of this ill-starred colony on his passage through the Strait.

1894 SARMIENTO DE GAMBOA, PEDRO. Narratives of the Voyage of Pedro Sarmiento de Gamboa to the Straits of Magellan, 1579-1580. Translated and Edited, with Illustrative Documents and Introduction, by Clements R. Markham, C.B., F.R.S., ex-Pres. R.G.S. Map. Hak. Soc., ser. I, vol. 91. London.

1768 SARMIENTO DE GAMBOA, PEDRO. Viage al Estrecho de Magellanes, 1579-1580, y Noticia de la Expedicion que despues hizo para poblare. 3 folding plates. 4to. Madrid.

> The Journal of Sarmiento was here printed from the original Manuscript in the Royal Library at Madrid, and edited by Don Bernardo Yriarte.—Maggs, No. 612.

## SIMON DE ALCAZOVA. Voyage to Magellanica. Brief abstract in Callander I, 124-127.

This account is taken from Herrera, Decade V, lib. vii, cap. 5. It has not been hitherto noticed by English compilers.—Callander. The voyage was an attempt made in 1534 to settle colonists in Peru. During a mutiny on board Alcazova was murdered, but the mutineers were punished. The expedition never reached Peru.

## ULLOA, FRANCISCO DE. Voyage to the North-West of California. In Callander I, 127-201.

The portion of his journal given here concerns the stretch from Acapulco north. It is taken from Hakluyt, who translated it from Ramusio.

## VESPUTIO, AMERIGO. Voyage to Magellanica, 1501. In substance and extract in Callander I, 53-63.

The First Four Voyages published in English, London, 1885; his Letters edited for the Hakluyt Society, London, 1894. See below, and also under 1907 and 1916, WEST INDIES.

The voyage of 1501 was Vespucci's third and was performed in the service of the king of Portugal. It explored the coast of South America from latitude 5° S. to latitude 50° S. Failure of proper recognition from the Spanish court led him to offer his talents to Emmanuel of Portugal. Of the four voyages credited to Vespucci modern scholars are inclined to accept as genuine only the second and third, though it may be added that there is some acceptance of the first. It was on the second voyage of 1499 that Brazil was discovered. How his name came to be attached to the New World is related in Waldseemüller's *Cosmographiae*, Saint Die, 1507. This *Cosmographiae Introductio* was a small text book which the geographer Waldseemüller composed to accompany a wall map delineating the latest additions to the known extent of the world. In it he inserted a sentence of extraordinary consequence: "But now that these parts have been more extensively examined, and another fourth part has been discovered by Americus Vespuccius, I do not see why we should rightly refuse to name it America, to wit the land of Amerigen or America, after its discoverer Americus, a man of sagacious mind, since both Europe and Asia took their names from women."—From Robinson, No. 20.

1885 VESPUCCI, AMERIGO. The First Four Voyages of Amerigo Vespucci. Translated from the rare original edition (Florence, 1505-06); with some preliminary notices by M(ichael) K(erney). 4to. London.

> The first translation in any modern language of the extraordinarily and highly important work of Vespucci, in which he described his first four voyages (1497-98, 1499-1500, 1501-02, 1503-04).—Quaritch.

1894 VESPUCCI, AMERIGO. The Letters of Amerigo Vespucci And other Documents illustrative of his career. Translated, with Notes & an Introduction, by Clements R. Markham, C.B., F.R.S., ex-Pres. R.G.S. Map. Hak. Soc., ser. I, vol. 90. London.

VILLEGAGNON, ——. Voyage to South America. Account of voyage taken from Purchas. In Callander I, 212-277.

> After reaching Rio de Janeiro, Villegagnon sent two ships on to the South. They sailed as far as latitude 55° S., where violent storms stopped them and made them return. The account contains interesting descriptions of the life of the savages they encountered. This voyage belongs to 1555. See Thevet under 1568 above.

WAFER, LIONEL (Surgeon). Voyage to Magellanica. Portion of his voyage with Capt. Davis, one of the buccaneers with whom he returned from the South Sea around Cape Horn. In Callendar II, 673-692.

> Wafer was surgeon on several of the vessels of the buccaneers, and made a number of voyages with Capts. Sharp, Swan, Cooke, Dampier, and others from 1677 to 1683. For his enforced sojourn in the Isthmus of Panama see under 1699, CENTRAL AMERICA.

1767 COYER, GABRIEL FRANCOIS (Abbé). A Letter to Doctor Matay, Secretary to the Royal Society; containing an Abstract of the relations of travellers of different nations, concerning the Patagonians; with a more particular account of the several Discoveries of the latest French and English Navigators, relative to this gigantic race of men, including a full reply to the objections made to their existence. 16mo. London.

French original, Bruxelles, 1767. See below. See also *An Account of the Giants lately discovered* under 1756 above.

1767 COYER, GABRIEL FRANCOIS (Abbé). Lettre au Docteur Maty, sur les géans Patagones. 12mo. Bruxelles (*i.e.,* Paris).

1768 BYRON, JOHN (Lieut.). The Narrative of the Honourable John Byron (Commodore in a Late Voyage round the World) containing an Account of the Great Distresses suffered by Himself and his Companions on the Coast of Patagonia, from the Year 1740, till their Arrival in England, 1746. With a Description of St. Jago de Chili, and the Manners and Customs of the Inhabitants. Also a Relation of the Loss of the Wager Man of War, one of Admiral Anson's Squadron. Written by Himself, and now First Published. Frontispiece. 8vo. London.

2nd edit., London, 1768; Dublin, 1768; London, 1769; 1778 (a chap-book edition) ; 1780; 1782; 1785 in 12mo. Translated into French, Paris, 1799 (doubtless there were earlier French versions.) See below and also Bulkeley and Cummins under 1743 above.

As is well known, this narrative supplied the poet Lord Byron with materials for the shipwreck of his hero in Canto II of "Don Juan," whose distresses are compared with "those related in my grand-dad's 'Narrative'." Byron, then a lieutenant on board the *Wager,* prefered to remain with the captain to joining the group seeking to escape from their predicament in the long boat. Had he done otherwise he would have reached England much sooner.—The Fate of the *Wager* led to an alteration in the laws of naval service. The rule was that the pay of a ship's company ceased immediately upon her wreck. The new rule was that "in the future, every person entering the service of His Majesty's navy should be held attached to that service, and be entitled to pay, maintenance, or emoluments belonging to his station until such time as he should be regularly discharged by an order of the Admiralty or of his superior officer."—From *Edin. Cabinet,* XXIX, 193-4.

1799 (In French.) Voyage à la mer du Sud, complétant la Relation du voyage d'Anson, avec un Extraict du second voyage du Byron autour du monde. Traduit de l'anglais par A. de Cantwell. Paris.

1769 BANCROFT, EDWARD. An Essay on the Natural History of Guiana, In South America. Containing a Description of many curious Productions in the Animal and Vegetable Systems of that Country. Together with an Account of the Religion, Manners, and Customs of several Tribes of its Indians. Interspersed with a Variety of Literary and Medical Observations. In several Letters from a Gentleman of the Medical Faculty, During his Residence in that Country. 8vo. London.

The author was a naturalist and a chemist. He made several visits to America.

CHARLEVOIX, FRANÇOIS XAVIER DE (Father).   The History of Paraguay, containing amongst many other New, Curious, and Interesting Particulars of that Country, a Full and Authentic Account of the Establishments formed there by the Jesuits from among the Savage Natives in the very Centre of Barbarism, Establishments allowed to have realised the sublime Ideas of Fénelon, Sir T. More and Plato. 2 vols.   8vo.   London.

> Printed also at Dublin, 1769. French original, Paris, 1756. See below.
> "The most complete and satisfactory work on Paraguay, and the only one in which the vast system of the Jesuits is fully developed, the position of the author affording him peculiar opportunities for its examination."—Quoted by Maggs, No. 612. For a discussion of the Utopia formed there by the Jesuits see Graham, *Vanished Arcadia,* 1901, under GENERAL REFERENCE.

> 1756  CHARLEVOIX, F. X. (Pere).   Histoire du Paraguay. 7 engraved maps and plans.   3 vols.   4to.   Paris.

1771  BOUGAINVILLE, LOUIS DE.   The History of a Voyage to the Malouine (*i.e.,* Falkland) Islands, made in 1763 and 1764, under the command of M. de Bougainville, in order to form a Settlement there, and of Two Voyages to the Streights of Magellan, with an Account of the Patagonians.   Translated from Dom Pernety's Historical Journal.   16 maps and plates.   4to.   London.

> An edition, 8vo, Dublin, 1772; 2nd edit., 4to, London, 1773. French original, Paris, 1770. See below.
> This expedition is often listed under the name of Pernetty, who wrote up the journal.—This voyage to the Falkland Islands and Patagonia was undertaken by Bougainville, at his own expense, for the purpose of colonising them for France. The settlement excited the jealousy of the Spaniards, and the French Government gave it up to them, on condition of their indemnifying Bougainville.—Maggs, No. 491. The conflicting claims of England, France, and Spain to possession of the Islands created a constant series of imbroglios for three centuries. At the present time the group is under the dominion of Great Britain, but Argentina is asserting her right to their ownership. For an interesting description of them in 1838, see Darwin's *Voyage of the Beagle,* ch. IX.

> 1770  PERNETTY, ANTOINE JOSEPH (Dom).   Histoire d'un voyage aux isles Malouines, fait en 1763 et 1764, avec des observations sur le Détroit de Magellan et sur les Patagons. Nouvelle édition refondue et augmentée d'un discours préliminaire, de remarques sur l'histoire naturelle, etc.   Plates.   2 vols.   8vo.   Paris.

> This edition contains the additions of Delisle de Sales.

JOHNSON, SAMUEL.   Thoughts on the late Transactions respecting Falkland's Islands.   8vo.   London.

> 2nd edit., London, 1771; printed at Dublin, 1771.
> "In 1771 he published 'Thoughts . . .' in which, upon materials furnished him by ministry, and upon general topicks expanded in his richest style, he successfully endeavoured to persuade the nation that it was wise and laudable to suffer the questions of right to remain undecided, rather than involve our country in another war. . . . His descriptions of its (war's) miseries in this pamphlet, is one of the finest pieces of eloquence in the English language."—Boswell. See also Penrose under 1775 below.

LOEFLING, PEDER. For an abstract of part of his travels in South
America see Bossu under this date, NORTH AMERICA.

> Swedish original, Stockholm, 1758. See below.
> The author was one of Linnaeus' travelling students. He died while in South
> America from a fever.

> 1758 LOEFLING, PETER. Iter hispanicum, eller Resa til Spanska Länderna
> uti Europa och Amerika, forrätad ifrån Ar 1751 til Ar 1756, med
> Beskrifningar och Ron öfver de Märkvärdigaste Växter, utgifven Efter
> Dess Frånfålls af Carl Linnaeus. Stockholm.

1772 ADAMS, JOHN. A Voyage to South America, describing at large,
The Spanish Cities, Towns, Provinces, etc., on that extensive Continent. Maps and plates. 2 vols. 8vo. London.

1774 FALKNER, THOMAS (Father). A Description of Patagonia, and the
Adjoining Parts of South America: containing an Account of the Soil,
Produce, Animals, Vales, Mountains, Rivers, Lakes, . . . of those
Countries; the Religion, Government, Policy, Customs, Dress, Arms,
and Language of the Indian Inhabitants; and some Particulars relating
to Falkland's Islands. By Thomas Falkner, who resided near Forty
Years in those Parts. 2 maps. 4to. Hereford.

> Another edition, London, 1777. Modern Facsimile edition, Lakeside Press,
> Chicago, 1937. Noticed in the *Journal des Scavans*, 1775, II, 509.
> Father Falkner lived in the regions south and west of the La Plata nearly
> forty years and often made the journey from Buenos Aires up the Parana to Cor-
> dova and Santa Fé, and to the Southern Interior and the Lakes. The greatest
> commerce of the country was cattle and horses. The publication of his book led
> the Spanish Government to survey the coast of Patagonia and to form settlements
> upon it. The maps are by Kitchen.—Quaritch. The work also contains an ac-
> count of the language of the Moluches with a grammar and a short vocabulary.

1775 (?) FALKNER, THOMAS (Father). Of the Patagonians. Formed from
the relation of Father Falkner, a Jesuit, who had resided among them
thirty eight years; and from the different Voyagers who had met with
this tall race. 4to. Darlington.

> The date 1788 has also been given to this item. This was printed at the private
> press of George Allen, Esq., for his friend Thomas Pennant. Falkner assisted ma-
> terially in perpetuating the tradition of the tall stature of the Patagonians. He
> asserts that such was their height, that, when in a sitting posture, they were almost
> as tall as the commodore of the ship. Navigators who preceded Falkner had made
> similar statements; but recent visitors, who have seen many of the natives, state
> that they are no taller than Europeans.—From Sabin.

PENROSE, BERNARD (Surgeon's Mate). An Account of the last Expedition to Port Egmont, in Falkland's Islands, in the year 1772. Together with the Transactions of the Company, of the Penguin Shallop
during their stay there. 12mo. London.

1776    The History of North and South America, containing an Account of the first Discoveries of the New World, the Customs, Genius, and Persons of the original Inhabitants, . . . 2 vols.  12mo.  London.

1777    KINDERSLEY, —— (Mrs.).  For an account of Brazil see her *Letters from the Island of Teneriffe, Brazil and the Cape of Good Hope,* under AFRICA.

MARMONTEL, ——.  The Incas; or, the Destruction of the Empire of Peru.  2 vols.  12mo.  London.

> Reprinted twice in Dublin, 1771; London, 1787; Dublin, 1792.

Papers relative to the late Negotiations with Spain; and the taking of Falkland's Island from the English.  4to.  London.

> This was published partly at the instigation of Samuel Johnson (see Johnson under 1771 above). The material is taken from a "Manuscript Letter-Book, containing the official Admiralty Correspondence relating to the Disputes between England, France and Spain over the Falkland Islands, or Islas Malvinas, from 1765 to 1770, apparently written by the Secretary to the Admiralty, Philip Stevens."—From Maggs, No. 532.

ROBERTSON, WILLIAM.  For accounts of South America see his *History of America,* under NORTH AMERICA.

1780    COOPER, —— (Rev.).  The History of South America.  Containing the Discoveries of Columbus, the Conquest of Mexico and Peru, and the Other Transactions of the Spaniards in the New World.  Copperplate cuts.  London.

> Reprinted, 18mo, London, 1789; 12mo, Albany, 1793.
> The plates are by A. Reid, and are early specimens of American art.—Sabin.

1781    FERMIN, PHILIPPE.  An Historical and Political View of the Present and Ancient State of the Colony of Surinam, in South America; with the settlements of Demerary and Issequibo; Together with an account of its Produce for twenty-five Years past.  By a Person who lived there for ten years.  8vo.  London.

> French original, Maestricht, 1778.  See below.
>
> 1778  FERMIN, PHILIPPE.  Tableau historique et politique de l'Etat ancien et actuel de la Colonie de Surinam.  Maestricht.

1785    ROCH, JOHN.  The Surprizing Adventures of John Roch, Mariner, of Whitehaven; Containing A genuine Account of his cruel Treatment during a long Captivity amongst the Indians, and Imprisonment by the Spaniards, in South America. With his Miraculous Preservation and Deliverance by Divine Providence, And Happy Return to the Place of his Nativity, After being Thirteen Years amongst his inhuman Enemies. 12mo. Liverpool.

Reprinted, 8vo, Dumfries, 1788.

1786 The History of the Conquest of Peru. Plates. 18mo. London.

1788 DALRYMPLE, SIR JOHN. Memoirs of Great Britain and Ireland, with Appendix Account of an intended Expedition into the South Sea by Private Persons in the late War. 4to. Edinburgh.

Other parts of the Appendix relate to Jucutan and Honduras, and the Rio de la Plata. The proposed Expedition was intended against Spanish Commerce, via Australia, New Zealand, and Juan Fernandez, to the Coast of South America. Frequent mention is made of Capt. Cook.—Maggs. No. 562.

1791-94 A General Idea of the Monuments of Peru. London.

"An extract from the following works: 'Mercurio Peruano de historia Literatura, y noticias publicas,' 12 vols., Lima, 1791-94."
So cited by Pinkerton XVII.

1793 PENNANT, THOMAS. The Literary Life of Thomas Pennant. By Himself. Portrait and Plates. 4to. London.

This contains an appendix on the Patagonians, and includes notices of Falkner, a Jesuit (see Falkner under 1775 above), with an account of travels in Bolivia, La Plata, and the Strait of Magellan. Pennant travelled extensively in England and Scotland, but abroad was a mind-traveller.

1796 STEDMAN, JOHN GABRIEL (Captain). Narrative of a Five Years' Expedition against the Revolted Negroes of Surinam in Guiana on the Wild Coast of South America, from 1772-77, elucidating the History of the Country, and describing its Productions—*viz.*, Quadrupeds, Birds, Reptiles, Trees, Shrubs, Fruits, and Roots, with an Account of the Indians of Guiana and Negroes of Guiana. 81 plates by Blake, Bartolozzi, Holloway, etc. 2 vols. 4to. London.

Translated into French, Paris, 1799. See below.
In 1772, Stedman, who was in the Scots Brigade in Holland, volunteered to accompany an expedition sent out by the States-General to subdue the revolted negroes in Dutch Guiana. His narrative of this service is a model of what such a book should be. Its rules for marching and fighting amid tropical swamps anticipate those laid down for the Ashanti expedition. The field of his curiosity embraced not only all branches of natural history, but also economical and social conditions. His descriptions of the cruelties practiced upon the negroes, and of the moral deterioration resulting to their masters, forms one of the most vivid indictments of slavery that have ever been penned. . . . Quoted by Maggs, No. 442.

1799 (In French.) Voyage à Surinam et dans l'intérieur de la Guiane. Avec des détails sur les Indiens de la Guiane et les Négres. Traduit de l'anglais par P. F. Henry. 44 plates. 4 vols. 8vo. Paris.

1797  MUNOZ, DON JUAN BAPTISTA. The History of the New World
      . . . Translated from the Spanish, with Notes by the Translator. Por-
      trait of Columbus and map of Espanola. Vol. I (all printed). 8vo.
      London.

> See Munoz this date, under WEST INDIES.

1798  BLACK, JOHN. An Authentic Narrative of the Mutiny on Board the
      Ship Lady Shore; with Particulars of a Journey through Part of
      Brazil: in a Letter, dated "Rio Janeiro, Jan. 18, 1708," to the Rev. John
      Black, Woodbridge, Suffolk, from Mr. John Black, one of the sur-
      viving Officers of the Ship. 8vo. Ipswich.

> The "Lady Shore" sailed from Portsmouth during the Mutiny in the Fleet,
> for the convict settlement at Port Jackson in Australia. The soldiers on board
> were mutinous before they sailed and actual mutiny broke out off the Brazilian
> coast. The Captain and first mate were murdered and the remaining officers, pas-
> sengers and some convicts set adrift in the long boat. These managed to reach
> the coast of Brazil and after various adventures reached Rio Janeiro. The ship
> was taken by the mutineers into Monte Video.—From Maggs, No. 638.

      COLNETT, JAMES. A Voyage to the South Atlantic and round Cape
      Horn into the Pacific Ocean for the purpose of extending the sper-
      maceti whale fisheries and other objects of commerce by ascertaining
      the Ports, etc., in certain Islands and Coasts in those Seas. 6 charts
      and 9 tables, with portrait of P. Stephens. 4to. London.

> Colnett had sailed with Capt. Cook on his last voyage and also with Capt.
> Meares in his voyage to Vancouver Island. After calling at Rio de Janeiro the
> *Rattler* sailed round Cape Horn, and up the American coast to the Gulf of Cal-
> ifornia.—From Maggs, No. 549.

1799  BRITTON, JOHN. The Enterprising Adventures of Pizarro, preceded
      by a brief sketch of the Voyages and Discoveries of Columbus and
      Cortez: to which are subjoined the Histories of Alonzo and Cora, on
      which Kotzebue founded his two celebrated Plays of the Virgin of the
      Sun and the Death of Rolla. Also varieties and oppositions of criti-
      cisms on the Play of Pizarro: with biographical sketches of Sheridan
      and Kotzebue. Frontispiece of Mr. Kemble as Rolla, rescuing Alonzo's
      child from Pizarro. 8vo. London.

      CAMPE, JOACHIM HEINRICH. Pizarro, or the Conquest of Peru:
      being a continuation of the Discovery of America, for the use of Chil-
      dren and Young Persons. 12mo. London.

> Reprinted, Birmingham, 1800.
> The translator was doubtless Elizabeth Helme. See Campe under this date,
> WEST INDIES and MEXICO.

RAMEL, —— (General). Narrative of the Deportation to Cayenne, of Barthélemy, Pichegru, Willot, Marbois, La Rue, Ramel, etc., in consequence of the Revolution of the 18th Fructidor (September 4, 1797). Containing a variety of important facts relative to that Revolution, and to the Voyage, Residence and Escape of Barthélemy, Pichegru, etc. 8vo. London.

> See below for the Sequel.

RAMEL, —— (General). Secret Anecdotes of the Revolution of the 18th Fructidor; and New Memoirs of the persons deported to Guiana, written by themselves: containing . . . A Narrative of Events that took place at Guiana subsequent to the escape of Pichegru, Ramel, etc. . . . Forming a Sequel to the "Narrative of General Ramel." Translated from the French. 8vo. London.

> Reprinted, London, 1800.

1800 AIME, J. J. JOB. Narrative of the Deportation to Cayenne and Shipwreck on the Coast of Scotland, of J. J. Job Aimé, written by himself. With Observations on the Present State of that Colony, and of the Negroes; and an Account of the Situation of the deported Person at the time of his Escape. 8vo. London.

> This relates to the deportation to French Guiana of nearly 600 Royalists. No food or shelter was provided and two-thirds of them perished miserably within a few months. Various incidents of naval interest are described.—Maggs, No. 534.

Letters from Paraguay, 1796-98, Comprising 33 letters. 8vo. London.

SEMPLE, J. G. (Lisle). The Life of Major J. G. Semple Lisle: containing a Faithful Narrative of his alternate vicissitudes of Splendour and Misfortune. Portrait. 8vo. London.

> This includes his adventures in South America, description of the Province of Rio Grande, etc.—Sabin.

## ADDENDA

1806  BARROW, JOHN.  For views and plans of the city and harbor of Rio de Janeiro see his *Voyage to Cochinchina,* under FAR EAST.

1808-1814  BOUQUER, ——.  An Abridged Relation of a Voyage to Peru undertaken by Gentlemen of the Royal Academy of Sciences to measure the Degrees of the Meridian near the Equator, whereby to infer the Figure of the Earth.  Translated from the French.  In Pinkerton XIV, 270-312.

> See La Condamine under 1747 and Ulloa under 1758 above.  One part of this account was read in public in the Assembly of the Royal Academy of Sciences, Nov. 14, 1744.  Bouquer was one of the company of geodocists accompanying La Condamine.  The expedition left France in May, 1735.

1818-1829  HUMBOLDT, ALEXANDER VON, and BONPLAND, AIME.  Personal Narrative of Travels to the Equinoctial Regions of the New Continent during the years 1799-1804, translated by Helen Maria Williams.  8 maps.  7 vols. in 6.  8vo.  London.

> Reissued in Bohn's Library, 3 vols., 12mo, London, 1852.  There is a supplementary vol. VII which contains further information relating to Cuba.
> On June 5, 1799, Humboldt and Bonpland, armed with powerful recommendations, sailed . . . to the Canary Islands . . . Thence they proceeded to Caracas in Venezuela, and in Feb., 1800, left the coast for the purpose of exploring the course of the Orinoco.  "This trip, which lasted four months, covered seventeen hundred and twenty-five miles of wild and uninhabited country, had the important result of establishing the existence of a communication between the water-systems of the Orinoco and the Amazon and of determining the exact position of the bifurcation. . . ." After a stay of two months in Cuba they crossed over to Cartagena, ascended the Magdalena, and finally reached Quito, Jan. 6, 1802.  Enroute to Lima they made an expedition to the sources of the Amazon.  "At Callao Humboldt observed the transit of Mercury, and studied the fertilising properties of Guano, the introduction of which into Europe was mainly due to his writings.  After a year's stay in Mexico and a short visit to the United States, they returned to Europe." In this famous expedition Humboldt may justly be regarded as having laid the foundation of the science of physical geography and meteorology in their larger bearings.  His services to geology were mainly based on his attentive study of the volcanoes of the New World.—From Maggs, No. 612.

1857  BENZONI, GIROLAMO.  History of the New World.  By Girolamo Benzoni, of Milan.  Showing his Travels in America, from A.D. 1541 to 1556, with some particulars of the Island of Canary.  Now first Translated and Edited by Admiral William Henry Smyth, K.S.F., F.R.S., D.C.L.  19 illus.  Hak. Soc., ser. I, vol 21.  London.

> Italian original, Venice, 1565.

1859 Expeditions into the Valley of the Amazons, 1539, 1540, 1639. Containing the Journey of Gonzalo Pizarro, from the Royal Commentaries of Garcilasso Inca de la Vega; the Voyage of Francisco de Orellano, from the General History of Herrera; and the Voyage of Cristoval de Acuña. Translated and Edited by Clements R. Markham, C.B., F.R.S., ex-Pres. R.G.S. Map and List of Tribes in the Valley of the Amazon. Hak. Soc., ser. I, vol. 24. London.

1861 URSUA, PEDRO DE, and AGUIRRE, LOPE DE. The Expedition of Pedro de Ursua and Lope de Aguirre, in Search of El Dorado and Omagua, in 1560-61. Translated from Fray Pedro Simon's "Sixth Historical Notice of the Conquest of Tierra Firma, 1627," by William Bollaert, F.R.G.S. With an Introduction by Clements R. Markham, C.B., F.R.S., ex-Pres. R.G.S. Map. Hak. Soc., ser. I, vol. 28. London.

1862 GUZMAN, DON ALONZO ENRIQUEZ DE. The Life and Acts of Don Alonzo Enriquez de Guzman, a Knight of Seville, of the Order of Santiago, A. D. 1518 to 1543. Translated from an original & inedited MS. in the National Library at Madrid. With Notes and an Introduction by Clements R. Markham, C.B., F.R.S., ex-Pres. R.G.S. Illus. Hak. Soc., ser. I, vol. 29. London.

1865 ANDAGOYA, PASCUAL DE. Narrative of the Proceedings of Pedrarias Davila in the Provinces of Tierra Firma or Castilla del Oro, and of the discovery of the South Sea and the Coasts of Peru and Nicaragua. Written by the Adelantado Pascual de Andagoya. Translated and Edited, with Notes and an Introduction, by Clements R. Markham, C.B., F.R.S., ex-Pres. R.G.S. Map. Hak. Soc., ser. I, vol. 34. London.

1870 COLUMBUS, CHRISTOPHER. For an account of his fourth voyage, which took Columbus to the coasts of South America, see *Select Letters of Christopher Columbus*, under WEST INDIES. See also *The Voyages of Christopher Columbus*, under 1929, WEST INDIES.

1871 CABECA DE VACA, ALVAR NUNEZ. For an account of his discoveries in the La Plata regions see this date, under NORTH AMERICA.

1872 Discovery of Peru. I. Report of Francisco de Xeres, Secretary to Francisco Pizarro. II. Report of Miguel de Astete on the Expedition to Pachamac. III. Letter of Hernando Pizarro to the Royal Audience of

Santo Domingo. IV. Report of Pedro Sancho on the Partition of the Ransom of Atahuallpa. Translated and Edited, with Notes and an Introduction, by Clements Markham, C.B., F.R.S., ex-Pres. R.G.S. Map. Hak. Soc., ser. I, vol. 47. London.

Narratives of the Rites and Laws of the Yncas. Translated from the original Spanish MSS., and Edited, with Notes and an Introduction, by Clements R. Markham, C.B., F.R.S., ex-Pres. R.G.S. Hak. Soc., ser. I, vol. 48. London.

1874  STADE, HANS. The Captivity of Hans Stade of Hesse in 1547-1555, among the Wild Tribes of Eastern Brazil. Translated by Albert Tootal of Rio de Janeiro, and annotated by Sir Richard Francis Burton, K.C. M.G. Bibliography. Hak. Soc., ser. I, vol. 51. London.

> Another translation from the original German edition, Marburg, 1557, by Malcolm Letts, Broadway Travellers, London, 1928; Argonaut Series, New York, 1929.
> Southey used Stade's account in his *History of Brazil.*—Sabin. This is the true history of the romantic adventures of Hans Stade, the Hession adventurer, who set sail for Brazil, in 1547 to seek his fortune, and was taken captive two years later, by the Tupinamba Indians, whilst assisting the Portuguese in one of their earliest Brazilian settlements at Santo Amaro. He remained nine months, in their hands, escaped on board a French ship for Dieppe, then went to London and Antwerp in 1566.—Maggs, No. 546.

1889  The Conquest of La Plata, 1535-1555. I. Voyage of Ulrich Schmidt to the Rivers La Plata and Paraguai, from the original German edition, 1567. II. The Commentaries of Alvar Nuñez Cabeza de Vaca. From the original Spanish Edition, 1555. Translated, with Notes and an Introduction, by H. E. Don Luis L. Dominguez, Minister Plenipotentiary of the Argentine Republic. Map. Bibliography. Hak. Soc., ser. I, vol. 81. London.

1907  History of the Incas By Pedro Sarmiento de Gamboa, 1572. From the MS. sent to King Philip II. of Spain. And the Execution of the Inca Tupac Amaru, 1571, by Captain Baltasar de Ocampo, 1610. (Brit. Mus. Add. MSS. 17, 585.) Translated and edited by Sir Clements R. Markham, K.C.B. 2 maps and 10 illus. Supplement. A Narrative of the Vice-Regal Embassy to Vilcamambal 1571, and of the Execution of the Inca Tupac Amaru, Dec. 1571. By Friar Gabriel de Oviedo, of Cuzco, 1573. Translated by Sir Clements R. Markham, K.C.B. Hak. Soc., ser. II, vol. 22. London.

1911 STORM VAN'S GRAVESANDE. The Rise of British Guiana, compiled from his despatches, by C. A. Harris, C.B., C.M.G., Chief Clerk, Colonial Office, and J. A. J. de Villiers, of the Brit. Mus. Maps. and illus. 2 vols. Hak. Soc., ser. II, vols. 26-27. London.

Early Spanish Voyages, edited, with Notes and an Introduction, by Sir Clements R. Markham, K.C.B. 3 maps and 9 illus. Hak. Soc., ser. II, vol. 28. London.

1913 CIEZA DE LEON. The War of Quito. Translated and Edited by Sir Clements R. Markham, K.C.B. Hak. Soc., ser. II, vol. 31. London.

See Cieza under 1709 above.

1917 CIEZA DE LEON. The War of Chupas. Translated and edited by Sir Clements R. Markham, K.C.B. Hak. Soc., ser. II, vol. 42. London.

SANCHO, PEDRO. An Account of the Conquest of Peru. Translated into English and annotated by Philip Ainsworth Means. 8vo. The Cortes Society. New York.

1920 MONTESINOS, FERNANDO. Memorias Antiguas Historiales del Peru by Lic. Fernando Montesinos. Translated and edited by Philip Ainsworth Means, M.A. 10 plates. Hak. Soc., ser. II, vol. 48. London.

1921 PIZARRO, PEDRO. Relation of the Discovery and Conquest of the Kingdoms of Peru. Translated into English and annotated by Philip Ainsworth Means. 2 vols. 8vo. The Cortes Society. New York.

1922 FRITZ, SAMUEL. Journal of the Travels and Labours of Father Samuel Fritz in the River of the Amazons between 1686 and 1723. Translated from the Evora MS., and edited, with Introduction and Notes, by the Rev. Dr. George Edmundson. 2 maps. Hak. Soc., ser. II, vol. 51. London.

MAGALHAES, PEDRO DE. The Histories of Brazil. Translated into English for the first time and annotated by J. B. Stetson. With a facsimile of the Portuguese original, 1576. Frontispiece and plates. 2 vols. 8vo. The Cortes Society. New York.

1923   CIEZA DE LEON.   The War of Las Salinas.   One of the civil wars of
       Peru in the sixteenth century.   Translated and edited by Sir Clements
       R. Markham, K.C.B.   Hak. Soc., ser. II, vol. 54.   London.

1924   Colonising Expeditions to the West Indies and Guiana, 1625-1667.   Edited
       by Vincent T. Harlow, B.A., B.Litt., F.R.Hist.S.   6 maps and 2
       plates.   Hak. Soc., ser. II, vol. 56.   London.

         These narratives, hitherto unpublished, record the early efforts of English ad-
       venturers to explore and occupy regions in the New World, made famous by the
       buccaneers of the sixteenth century. They thus form a vital link between the
       voyages of Hawkins and Raleigh and subsequent colonial history—From notice of
       the book.

1934   CARVAJAL, GASPAR DE.   The Discovery of the Amazon, According
       to the Account of Friar Gaspar de Carvajal and other Documents.   Ed-
       ited, with translations from the sixteenth century MSS. with annota-
       tions, by H. C. Heaton.   8vo.   American Geographical Society.   New
       York.

# X

## South Seas

(The items listed under this section and those under AUSTRALIA are so closely related that each of the latter could as well be cited here as under its own caption. Likewise a goodly portion of the discoveries in the South Seas are incidents, sometimes of the nature of accidents, in the larger enterprise of circumnavigating the globe. Hence to avoid a constant succession of cross references it is recommended here that the sections AUSTRALIA and CIRCUMNAVIGATIONS be generously consulted.)

1595    Transitus expeditus in mare Australe Sinam, Cataiam, etc.   London.

So entered in *Stationers' Register*, Jan. 19, 1595.

1617    QUIROS, PEDRO FERNANDES DE.   Terra Australis Incognita, or a a new Southerne Discoverie, containing a fifth part of the World. Lately found out by Ferdinand de Quir, a Spanish Captaine. Never before published. Translated by W. B.  4to.  London.  (27 pp.)

Another edition, London, 1723; an account in Harris I, 63-65; a reprint of one of the Memorials taken from Purchas, in Callander II, 142-191; another one in Dalrymple. An abridged account of the voyage taken from Torquemado (Seville, 1615) is included in Callander. A reprint of the Memorial printed in 1610, Sydney, 1874. Accounts of the voyage edited for the Hakluyt Society, 2 vols., London, 1904. See also Hakluyt Society edition of Prado's journal, London, 1929, under this date below. Which one of the fifty Memorials presented by Quiros to the King and Council is the original of the item listed above is not known to the editor. For the Spanish edition of 1610, see below.

After his return to Spain from this voyage of 1606, Quiros spent seven long poverty-stricken years memorializing the authorities for funds and ships to prosecute further discoveries for the vast Antarctic Continent, which he believed he had sighted and had named Australia del Espiritu Santo, which, however, turned out to be part of the group now known as the New Hebrides, some 1400 miles from Australia. Of the fifty Memorials which he wrote only eight are extant. The high cost of printing led to their circulation in manuscript. This fact, together with the order of Philip III to call them in, lest their contents reveal geographical secrets to foreigners, accounts for their scarcity. To get rid of this importunate navigator the king finally sent him out to Peru with pretended orders to assist him but in reality with instructions to do nothing. Luckily Quiros died at Panama before he discovered the deception. Quiros had already made the voyage to the South Seas as pilot to Mendana in 1595. With two ships and a launch he sailed from Callao in Peru in 1606 on the voyage listed above. As he sighted island group after island group he grew more confident and when he saw continuous coast lines (in the New Hebrides group) he believed that his dream had come true, and that his eyes rested on a mass of land that stretched from Terra Australis to and even beyond Tierra del Fuego. He took ceremonious possession of this continent in the name of the Church, the Pope, and the King, and held to his death the notion that he had added these dominions to the crown of Spain and had opened the way to the conversion of millions of souls. In the storms that struck them while about to continue the exploration, Quiros unaccountably turned back and made for Acapulco, Mexico, and in 1607 arrived at Madrid, where he vainly endeavored to persuade the court to send him out again.

The question to what nation belongs the honor of first sighting the shores of Australia, whether French, Portuguese, Dutch, or Spanish, has been variously answered; but the latest pronouncement by Henry N. Stevens, in his Introduction to the volume *New Light on the Discovery of Australia* (Hakluyt Society, 1929), is that the Dutch may rightfully claim, on the basis of unquestionable documents, to be the first, when William Janszoon, in the *Duifken,* sailing through the Torres Straits from the west sighted the coast line of Australia in the Gulf of Carpentaria. A few months later, however, in the same year of 1605-06, the Spanish under Don Diego de Prado, who succeeded Quiros in command, approaching from the east discovered the Straits themselves as well as the lands adjacent. Something of ironic humor lies in the fact that neither was aware that his eyes had actually beheld the elusive Terra Australis. For the part that Tasman played in the discovery of Australia see Tasman under 1694 and 1744-48, AUSTRALIA. For discoveries by Dampier and Cook see the former under 1703, and the latter under Hawkesworth, 1773, CIRCUMNAVIGATIONS.

1874    QUIROS, PEDRO FERNANDES DE. Account of a Memorial presented to (Philip III of Spain) concerning the Population and Discovery of . . . Australia the Unknown, its Riches and Fertility. Reprint of the 1610 Spanish edition, with translation and introduction by W. A. Duncan. 4to. Sydney.

1904    QUIROS, PEDRO FERNANDES DE. The Voyages of Pedro Fernandez de Quiros, 1595-1606. Translated and Edited by Sir Clements Markham, K.C.B., Pres. R.G.S., Pres. Hakluyt Society. With a Note on the Cartography of the Southern Continent, and a Bibliography, by Basil H. Soulsby, F.S.A., Superintendent of the Map Department, British Museum. 3 maps. 2 vols. Hak. Soc., ser. II, vols. 14-15. London.

1610    QUIROS, PEDRO FERNANDES DE. Memorial dio a S. M. sobre el descubrimiento que hizo en 1606 de las tierras australes, y Submario breve y derrotero del viaje que hizo el capitan P. F. Quiros, de nacion portugues, en el descubrimiento de las tierras incognitas de la parte austral del mar del Sur, que salio del Peru por fin del año 1605. (Place?).

    This is hazarded as being the original memorial of the translation given above.

1876-1882    QUIROS, PEDRO FERNANDES DE. Historia del descubrimiento de las regiones Australes hecho por el General Pedro Fernandez de Quiros. 3 vols. Biblioteca Hispana-Ultramarina. 8vo. Madrid.

1621    HEYLYN, PETER. For a disourse on the endeavour to disover the Terra Australis Incognita, or the Southern Continent, see his *Microcosmvs,* 1652 edition, under GEOGRAPHY.

1652    HEYLYN, PETER. For details of the voyages to the South Seas by Magellan, Hawkins, Quiros, Sibald de Veert, Le Maire, Saavedra, etc., see his *Cosmographia,* under GEOGRAPHY.

1662    MANDELSLO, JOHANN ALBRECHT VON. For descriptions of the Philippines see his *Voyages and Travels,* under EAST INDIES.

1692    HYDE, T. An Account of the Famous Prince Giolo, Son of the King of GILOLO, now in England . . . with a Description of the Island of Gilolo, and the adjacent Isle of Celebes, their Religion and Manners, written from his own mouth. Portrait. 4to. London.

This title is already cited under EAST INDIES. It is repeated here for the additional information reported.

This is a very picturesque and probably somewhat untrue account of the Malasian Prince brought to England by Captain Dampier in 1691. The Prince was a native of Meangis in the island of Gilolo and was chiefly famous for the intricate tattooings with which his body was covered. He was sold by Dampier and exhibited as a curiosity; he died at Oxford not many months after landing. This pamphlet was doubtless issued as an advertisement by the showmen who had purchased him. A long account of him is given in Dampier's Voyages.— Quaritch. It may be that the account was written by Thomas Hyde the orientalist.

1707 DAMPIER, WILLIAM (Captain).  Capt. Dampier's Vindication of his Voyage to the South-Seas in the Ship St. George. . . . With some small Observations for the Present on Mr. Funnell's Chimerical Relation of the Voyage round the World.  4to.  London.  (8 pp.)

For Funnell's Voyage see this date, under CIRCUMNAVIGATIONS. Dampier had been charged with cruelty to his crew by J. Welbe.

1732 Discovery of the Islands of Salomon. A Fragment Relation.  In Churchill IV, 622-635.

This is probably taken from Quiros, who is brought into the narrative and made to give reasons for going again upon the same voyage of discovery. The date of this voyage seems to be about 1595.

1740 A Voyage into the South Sea; translated from the English (into Dutch). Amsterdam.

So cited by Pinkerton XVII.

1757 HOLMESBY, JOHN.  Voyage and Adventures to the Southern Ocean, 1737.  London.

So cited by Chavanne.

1766 SCHOOTEN, HENRY.  The Hairy Giants, or a Description of Two Islands in the South Sea called by the Names Benganga and Coma, translated by P.M. Gent.  Maps.  8vo.  London.

This title looks suspiciously like a fictitious account.

1766-68 BOUVET DE LOZIERS, J. B. C.  Voyage to Magellanica.  Extract in Callander III, 641-644.

The journal of this voyage was printed at Paris and thence inserted in the Memoirs of Trevoux, February, 1740. The above extract is the first appearance of any portion of it in English. The object of the expedition was the search for the more or less mythical "Gonneville's" Island, supposedly discovered in the early sixteenth century. The maps had placed it south or southwest of Africa, but it failed to turn up where sought for. However, a small, snow-covered island was sighted to which was given the name Cape Circumcision. This island was rediscovered in fairly recent times and has been called Bouvet's Island. Bouvet's experiences with the ice proved of service to Cook in his second voyage of circumnavigation. (See Cook under 1777, CIRCUMNAVIGATIONS, and also De Gonneville this current date below.) The expedition set out in 1738 and returned to France in 1739.

CANTOVA, ANTONY.   Voyage to the Caroline Islands.   Extract from the Lettres Edifiantes et Curieuses.   In Callander III, 23-40.

This account, which appears here for the first time in English, was taken from De Brosses. These islands are said to have been discovered by the Spaniards in 1686, but like many another discovery, they had to be sought for again. As they gradually reappeared to man's knowledge, the Jesuits in the Philippines felt impelled to establish a mission there, which was at last accomplished by Father Juan Antonio Cantova in 1722. He was murdered in 1733 by the natives of Mogmog, near Falalep. (See Heawood, *Geographical Discoveries*, 412.)

CLAIN, —— (Father), and GOBIEN, LE (Father).   Account of the New Philippines.   Extracts from the Lettres Edifiantes et Curieuses. In Callander III, 9-23.

These letters are to be found in tome I and tome IV of the *Lettres Edifiantes et Curieuses*, written by the Jesuit missionaries in the East Indies and the Far East, edited by Du Halde and Le Gobien. They are supplemented here by an account of a later date (1710), written apparently by the captain of the vessel touching there. The New Philippines was the name given to the Carolines by the Jesuits of the Philippines.

DAMPIER, WILLIAM (Captain).   Voyages to Magellanica and Polynesia.   In a revised form in Callander II, 556-673.

The editor has "digested" the several relations of Dampier in their "proper order of time," and has done some pruning. For the most part he lets Dampier speak in his own language. (See Dampier under dates 1697-1703, under CIRCUMNAVIGATIONS.)

GAETAN, JUAN, and TORRE, BERTRAND DELLE.   Voyage to Polynesia.   An Extract from a Journal kept by the Spanish Pilot.   In Callander I, 203-212.

The journal was printed at Venice in folio, 1550, and was included in Ramusio's Collection. According to Callander, it had never before appeared in English. These voyagers sailed from some port on the west coast of Mexico and continued around the world to Europe. It has to do with the famous line of demarcation and the alleged efforts of the Portuguese to get the Spice Islands by making false charts.

GOBIEN, LE (Father).   History of the Ladrone or Marian Islands.   Extract in Callander III, 40-56.

The original was printed at Paris in 12mo, 1700. It consists, for the most part, of interesting accounts of the attempts of the Jesuits to plant the Catholic faith in these islands. This is the first appearance in English of any part of it.

GONNEVILLE, BINOT PAULMIER DE.  Voyage to Australia.  Short extract in Callander I, 63-73.

This was extracted from a judicial declaration made by the above before the Admiralty in France, July 19, 1505, and inserted in the *Mémoires touchant l'Etablissement d'une Mission Chrétienne dans la Terre Australe*, printed at Paris by Cramoisy, 1663.  The author of this account was a great grandson of a native of Australia or of the southern world, whom Gonneville had brought into France on his return from those parts, and whom he married to one of his relatives on his having embraced Christianity.  Gonneville's journals were lost when he was captured by the English as he was returning home.  The author above mentioned collected his materials from the traditions and the judicial declaration named above.  The claim is made that this voyage discovered Terra Australis sixteen years before Magellan made his circumnavigation.—From Callander's Introduction.  Gonneville's name is attached to the mythical land sought for by Bouvet.

GUALLE, FRANCISCO DE.  Voyage to Polynesia.  An account in Callander I, 412-423.

This voyage started from Acapulco, Mexico, in March, 1582.  It took in the Philippines, Macao, China, and seems to have run near Japan.  The return was by way of the coast of California, and ended in 1584.  The author says that his account was written in Spanish and translated verbatim into Low Dutch by Linschoten.

KEYTS, —— (Captain).  Voyage to Australia.  Abstract in Callander II, 519-523.

Keyts sailed from Banda July 19, 1678, for the coast of New Guinea, taking the same course as Vink had done in 1663.

MENDOZA, ALVAR DE.  Voyage to Polynesia.  Abstract taken from Herrera's General History and the Portuguese History of Lopez Vaez.  Never before translated into English except the small Extracts from Vaez in Hakluyt.  In Callander I, 277-283.

This expedition started from Peru in 1567 to make discoveries in the South Seas.  Among the groups it sighted were the Solomon Islands.  As a result of the voyage plans were made to colonize these islands, but having learned that Drake had found his way into the South Seas, the authorities abandoned the project.

SAAVEDRA, ALVAR DE.  Voyage to Polynesia and Australasia.  Given in substance in Callander I, 119-122.

An account of this voyage is given in Herrera, Decades IV.  This expedition was fitted out by Cortes for the discovery of the Spice Islands.  It sailed from Mexico Oct. 31, 1526.  In the Moluccas they found some of Magellan's men and some of Garcia de Loaisa's.

VINK, —— (Captain).  Voyage from Banda to New Guinea.  Short abstract in Callander II, 420-422.

Two small frigates were sent out by the Dutch at Batavia to examine the coasts of New Guinea.  They met with some opposition from the natives.  The journal offers little information.

WINTER, JOHN.  Voyage to Magellanica.  In Callander I, 337-355.

> Winter was associated with Drake on his voyage round the world. He turned back from the Strait of Magellan and made for home.

1767  BYRON, JOHN (Commodore).  For an account of his discoveries in the South Seas see his *Voyage round the World,* under CIRCUMNAVI-GATIONS, and the item following here.

1773  BYRON, JOHN (Commodore).  This voyage of 1764-66, together with Carteret's and Wallis's of 1766 and Cook's of 1768, all circumnavigations, were done officially for the Admiralty by Hawkesworth. See under both COLLECTIONS and CIRCUMNAVIGATIONS this date.

> Beginning with Byron's the voyages to the South Seas for the next thirty years are remarkable, not for conquest and plunder, but for the steady progress in correcting errors of former navigators and in filling up blank spaces on the map with new discoveries. In this work the French assisted very materially. Byron's instructions were to locate the elusive Davis Island and the lost Pepys Island, as well as to make new finds. His discoveries in the Pacific were not as rich as were those of Carteret and Wallis and fall immeasurably below those of Cook. He failed to fix the islands wanted though he thought he had found in the Falklands Pepys Island. These he claimed in the name of King George, notwithstanding that Bougainville had planted a French colony there but a short time before. For Byron's adventures and misfortunes occasioned by the wreck of the Storeship *Wager,* during Commodore Anson's voyage of 1740 see *The Narrative of the Honourable John Byron* under 1768, SOUTH AMERICA.

CARTERET, PHILIP (Captain).  For his discoveries in the South Seas see his *Voyage round the World,* under CIRCUMNAVIGATIONS.

> Carteret and Wallis started out together in the ships *Swallow* and *Dolphin* three months after Byron's return home. They separated at the Strait of Magellan and prosecuted their discoveries independently of each other. Carteret failed to find Davis Island at the spot marked on the chart, but he sighted Pitcairn Island,which was to become the last refuge of the mutineers of the *Bounty.* His discoveries further on in the region of New Britain and New Ireland were of fundamental importance. He reached home in March, 1769.

WALLIS, SAMUEL (Captain).  For his discoveries in the South Seas see his *Voyage round the World,* under CIRCUMNAVIGATIONS.

> Well might the natives of Tahiti exclaim "Woe the day!" when Wallis dropped anchor off their doorstep, for they were destined to exchange their primal innocency, liberty, and unblemished health for white man's vices, domination, and diseases. While the fatal beauty of this Island of the Ever Young proved to be its own undoing, it has brightened the life of man by serving as a release for the imagination, a port of call for every wandering "White Wings in the South Seas," a refuge for jaded Gauguins, and a final resting-place for the homeless beachcomber. Had Wallis made no further contributions to geography, he has won honor enough by being the first white discoverer of Tahiti. By establishing friendly relations with the inhabitants and by suggesting this spot as the proper place for making observations of the transit of Venus he prepared the way for Cook's famous voyage of 1768.

COOK, JAMES (Captain). For his discoveries in the South Seas see Hawkesworth's *An Account of the Voyages undertaken . . . for Making Discoveries in the Southern Hemisphere,* under COLLECTIONS and CIRCUMNAVIGATIONS.

> Hawkesworth relates only Cook's first voyage. For his second and third of 1772-75 and 1776-1780, see Cook under dates 1777 and 1785, CIRCUMNAVIGA-TIONS, as well as the intervening titles. The field of discovery is already described under the items cited.

(Banks, Queen Oberea, Omai, and Cook called forth the efforts of poets and poetesses, satirists and elegists. A few samples of these literary productions are listed below, not as belonging to the bibliography of travel, but merely as curiosa.)

1773   Epistle from Mr. Banks, voyager, monster-hunter and amoroso to Oberea, Queen of Otaheite. 4to. London.

1774   Epistle, moral and philosophical, from an Officer at Otaheite to Lady Gr-v-n-r. 4to. London.

> Genuine Account of Omiah, a Native of Otaheite . . . lately brought over to England by Capt. Furneaux, 1774. London Magazine, Aug., 1774.
>
> > Omai became the sensation of London and was referred to in any number of diaries, letters, and memoirs of the period. Dr. Johnson refused to be impressed with Boswell's account of his elegant table manners. Reynolds painted his portrait arrayed in a long robe worn by no Tahitian either before or since. The flattering attention paid him in England threw him off his balance and on his return to his native islands on Cook's third voyage he cut no great figure with his countrymen. A more promising specimen of the "noble savage" was Prince Lee Boo, a native of the Pelew Islands (see under 1789 below).
>
> SCOTT-WARING, J. Epistle from Oberea, Queen of Otaheite, to Joseph Banks. 4to. 2nd edit. London.
>
> > There were at least five editions of this piece published the same year.
>
> > Second Letter from Oberea, Queen of Otaheite, to Joseph Banks. 4to. London (no date).

1775   An Historic Epistle from Omiah to the Queen of Otaheite, being his Remarks on the English Nation. Fol. London.

1780   FITZGERALD, W. Ode to the Memory of the late Captain Cook. 4to. London.

> Letter from Omai to the . . . Earl of ****** (Sandwich), translated from the Ulaietean tongue. 8vo. London.
>
> SEWARD, ANNA. Elegy on Captain Cook, to which is added An Ode to the Sun. 4to. 2nd edit. London.

1786   At the Theatre Royal in Covent Garden, this present Monday, May 8, 1786, The Duenna . . . to which will be added for the 4th time, a new pantomime called Omai; or, A Trip round the World . . . with a procession exactly representing the dresses, weapons and manners of the inhabitants of Otaheite, New Zealand, etc., . . . and the other countries visited by . . . Cook. (A poster.)

1788  WOLCOT, JOHN ("Peter Pindar"). Sir Joseph Banks and the Emperor of Morocco: a tale (in verse). Fol. 4th edit. London.

1789  Death of Captain Cook: a grand serious-pantomimic ballet . . . as performed at the Theatre Royal, Covent Garden. 8vo. London.

1790  Narrations d'Omai, insulaire de la Mer du Sud, ami et compagnon de voyage du Capitaine Cook. Ouvrage traduit de l'O-taitien par M. K. . . . Publié par le Capitaine L. A. E. (Abbé G. A. R. Baston). Portrait. 4 vols. 8vo. Rouen.

1794  WOLCOT, JOHN ("Peter Pindar"). Sir Joseph Banks and the thief-takers (in verse) ; Sir Joseph Banks and the boiled fleas (in verse). In his *Works,* vol. II, 187-206 ; 283-7 ; 393-7. London.

PARKINSON, SYDNEY. Fifteen Plates from Voyage to the South Seas, mostly relating to Otaheite. 4to. London.

Parkinson was the draughtsman to Joseph Banks. For his account of Cook's first voyage to the South Seas see his *A Journey of a Voyage to the South Sea in His Majesty's Ship the Endeavour,* under CIRCUMNAVIGATIONS.

1774  FREVILLE, A. F. J. DE. Voyages dans la Mer du Sud, par les Espagnoles et les Hollandois. Traduit de l'anglois. Paris.

This was translated from the English of Alexander Dalrymple.—Chavanne. "Il faut joindre à ce volume: Hydrographie, ou Histoire des nouvelles découvertes faites dans la Mer du Sud, en 1767-1770. Rédigé par Fréville. 2 vols. Paris.—From Chavanne.

1775  ELLIS, JOHN. A Description of the Mangostan and the Bread-Fruit; the first, esteemed one of the most delicious; the other, the most useful of all the Fruits in the East-Indies. To which are added, Directions to Voyagers, for bringing over these and other Vegetable Productions, which would be extremely beneficial to the Inhabitants of our West India Islands. 4 engraved plates illustrative of the Mango and the Bread-Fruit, and methods for transporting them. 4to. London.

The reports of the excellence of the Bread-fruit tree in Tahiti led to several expeditions whose purpose in part was the introduction of this tree into the West Indies. Among them was Bligh's fateful voyage in the *Bounty.* Ellis was described by Linnaeus as a "bright star of natural history," and as the "main support of natural history in England." . . . He imported various American plants and seed, and also sent out others to America.—Maggs, No. 491.

1776  FORSTER, JOHN REINHOLD. Characteres Generum plantarum quas in itinere ad insulas maris Australis collegrunt, descripterunt, delinearunt, 1772-75. 75 plates. 4to. London.

The first specimens of the natural productions of those remote countries in the South Seas which Dr. Forster and his Son were sent out with Capt. Cook, at the national expence, to collect and describe. It contains 75 new genera of plants.—Nichols, *Literary Anecdotes.*

1778 FORSTER, JOHN REINHOLD. For observations on natural history of the islands of the South Seas see his *Observations made during a Voyage round the World,* under CIRCUMNAVIGATIONS.

PINGRE, ALEXANDRE-GUY. A Memoir relating to the Discoveries made in the South Sea during the Voyages of the English and French round the World. London (?).

> This item is cited by Chavanne under the date of 1758, but inasmuch as it was read before the Academy of Sciences at Paris, Dec. 23, 1766, and Jan., 1767, and was printed at Paris in 1778, it seems probable that the date 1778 is more nearly correct. Moreover Pingré made voyages to the South Seas in 1767, 1768-69, and 1771, which were published in 1768, 1773, and 1778.
> Pingré was a French astronomer, who is credited with publication of the first nautical almanack.

TRUSLER, JOHN (Rev. Dr.). A Descriptive Account of the Islands lately discovered in the South-Seas, giving a full detail of the present state of the Inhabitants, their Government, Religion, Language, Manners, Customs, etc., from the first Discovery to the present time, carefully collected, digested and systematically arranged from Mendana, De Quiros, Schouten, Tasmen, Dalrymple, Bougainville, Byron, Carteret, Wallis, Hawkesworth, Parkinson, Fourneaux, Forster, Cook, and others; with some Account of the country of Kamtschatka, a late Discovery of the Russians. 8vo. London. Folding map.

> Trusler is known for his *Hogarth Moralized.*

1779 FORREST, THOMAS (Captain). Voyage to New-Guinea, and the Moluccas, from Balambangan, including an Account of Magindano, Sooloo, and other Islands, performed in the Tartar Galley belonging to the Honourable East India Company, 1774-76: to which is added, a Vocabulary of the Magindano Tongue. Portrait, numerous plates, map and plans. 4to. London.

> 2nd edit., with an Index, London, 1780; an edition, Dublin, 1779. Translated into French, Paris, 1780; into German (without the vocabularies), Hamburg, 1782. It also appeared in the *Göttinger Magazin.* See below.
> A very interesting work, as far as it relates to the manners and customs of the people.—Pinkerton XVII. This work supplies what is wanting in Sonnerat, as it is full on the physical and moral character of the inhabitants, and on their language, mode of life, and trade.—Lowndes. This voyage was one of examination and enquiry rather than discovery, and the additions made to geographical knowledge were corrections of detail rather than startling novelties.—Maggs, No. 491.

1780 (In French.) Voyage aux Moluques et à la Nouvelle Guinée, fait sur la galère la Tartare, 1774-76, par Ordre de la Compagnie Angloise, avec Vocabulaire de la Langue Magindano. Folding map and 28 plates. 4to. Paris.

1781 (In German.) Des Schiffhauptmanns Forrest Nachrichten von der Insel Magindano. In Georg Forster's Sämmtliche Schriften, vol. IV, (Leipzig, 1843). From *Göttinger Magazin* (1781).

WALLIS, SAMUEL (Commander R.N.). The Injured Islanders; or, The Influence of Art upon the Happiness of Nature. 4to. London.

This poem concerns Oberea, Queen of Tahiti, after her fall from power. —Maggs, No. 562. Wallis, it will be remembered, commanded the South Sea expedition related in Hawkesworth.

1786 SAMWELL, DAVID. For his account of venereal diseases introduced into the Sandwich Islands see his *A Narrative of the Death of Captain Cook,* under Cook, 1784, CIRCUMNAVIGATIONS.

TURNBULL, WILLIAM. Inquiry into the Origin and Antiquity of the Lues Venerea; with Observations on its Introduction and Progress in the Islands of the South Seas. 8vo. London.

1787 ANDERSON and FORSTER, R. A Catalogue of the different Specimens of Cloth, collected in the three Voyages of Captain Cook, with a particular Account of the Manner of Manufacturing the same in the various Islands of the South Seas; extracted from the Observations of Mr. Anderson and R. Forster. 4to. London.

Anderson had served as surgeon on board the *Resolution* during Cook's second voyage, and on the third voyage as naturalist.

1788 KEATE, GEORGE (F.R.S.). An Account of the Pelew Islands situated in the Western Part of the Pacific Ocean, composed from the Journals of Captain Henry Wilson and some of his Officers who, in August 1783, were there shipwrecked in the "Antelope." Portraits of Capt. Wilson and Prince Lee Boo, maps, and plates of views, antiquities, etc. 4to. London.

2nd edit., London 1788; an edition, Dublin, 1788; a chapbook edition, Perth, 1788; 3rd edit., London, 1789; another edition, Dublin, 1793. A Supplement from the journals of the *Panther* and *Endeavour,* Hon. East India Co., etc., by Rev. John Pearce Hockin, was added to the London edition of 1803. Translated into French, Paris, 1788; into Dutch, Rotterdam, 1789. See below.

In August, 1783, the *Antelope,* commanded by Henry Wilson, of the East India Company's Marines, ran on a rock near one of the Pelew Islands, and became a wreck. This group of islands had been sighted by the Spaniards and others, but had never been explored. Captain Wilson and his crew escaped safely to shore. He and his men were well treated by the natives, and in time

they managed to build a small vessel from the wreck, in which they were able
to reach Macao, taking with them Prince Lee Boo, or Liby, one of the king's
sons. Wilson brought him to England where he was lionized and created a
very good impression; he, however, unfortunately died of small-pox.—From
Maggs, No. 491. On the death of the Prince the East India Company sent out
two vessels, the *Panther* and the *Endeavour,* under Captain McCluer to convey
the sad news to Abba Thulle, King of the Pelew Islands, together with some
presents of seeds, plants, etc. McCluer finally married one of the native women
and lived there fifteen months, when, growing tired of solitude, he managed to
reach China in a native boat without compass or other instruments. He returned
to the islands for his family and sailed for Calcutta. Meeting the Bombay
frigate he sent some of his party on board her. After leaving Calcutta he was
never heard of again.—From Maggs, No. 491. Fanny Burney records meeting
Keate, but she gives no flattering description of him. He seems to have been
enormously conceited over his poems, with which, in the words of the *Biographia Dramatica,* he "obliged the world." He dressed up the style of the sea-
men's journals much as did Hawkesworth those of Cook and Banks.

1788 WILSON, HENRY. The Shipwreck of the Antelope East-India Packet,
H. Wilson, Esq. Commander, on the Pelew Islands, situated in the
West Part of the Pacific Ocean, in August, 1783, containing the subsequent Adventures of the Crew with a singular Race of People
hitherto unknown to Europeans. Plate. 8vo. London.

It is difficult to judge from the title whether this is a reprint
of Keate or another work covering the same ground.

1788 (In French.) Relation des îles Pelew situées dans la partie occidentale
de l'Océan Pacifique, composée sur les journaux et les communications
du capitaine Henri Wilson et de quelques-uns de ses officiers, qui en
août mil sept cent quatre vingt trois, y ont fait naufrage sur l'Antelope,
paquebot de la compagnie des Indes orientales, traduit de l'anglais de
George Keate. Portrait, map, and plates. 2 vols. 8vo. Paris.

1789 (In Dutch.) Beschryving van de Pelew Eilanden, gelegen in het westlyh
gedeelte van den Stillen Oceaan, welke in Augustus 1783 aan dezel-
ven schipbreuk geleden hebben met de Antelope een paketboot in
dienst van de Engelsche Oostindische Maatschappy door G. Keate.
Portrait, map and plates. 4to. Rotterdam.

1789 LEE BOO, PRINCE. The Interesting and Affecting History of a Na-
tive brought to England by Capt. Wilson, to which is prefixed a Short
Account of those Islands, with Sketch of the Manners and Customs.
Frontispiece. 18mo. London.

The pathetic fate of Prince Lee Boo in dying of small pox while in England aroused much interest. He seems to have been a very lovable, docile native with far more natural endowment than the more fortunate Omai, the native
of Tahiti, who was safely returned to his islands. The Prince's father had let
him go in the expectation that the son would on his return bring with him some
of the blessings of civilization which would improve the conditions of life in
Pelew.

1790 BLIGH, WILLIAM (Lieutenant). A Narrative of the Mutiny on board
His Majesty's Ship Bounty; and the subsequent Voyage of Part of
the Crew, in the Ship's Boat, from Tofoa, one of the Friendly Islands,
to Timor, a Dutch Settlement in the Dutch East Indies. Plate and
charts. 4to. London.

Another edition, Dublin, 8vo, 1790. Translated into French, Paris, 1790; into Dutch, Rotterdam, 1790. See below. The official account of Bligh's voyage and the mutiny was published at London, 1792. See latter date below.

1790 (In French.)  Relation de l'enlèvement du Navire "Le Bounty," apparte-nant du Roi d'Angleterre, & commandé par le Lieutenant Guillaume Bligh; avec le voyage subséquent de cet Officier & d'une partie de son équipage dans la mer du Sud, jusqu' à Timor, établissement Hollan-dais aux îles Moluques. Traduit par Daniel Lescallier. 3 maps and 14 page introduction by the translator, concerning Tahiti, etc. Paris.

1790 (In Dutch.)  Verhaal van de Mutiny, aan boord van het Engelsch Kon-ingsschip de Bounty. 4to. Rotterdam.

1791 FLEURIEU, C. P. C., COMTE DE.  Discoveries of the French in 1768 and 1769, to the South-East of New Guinea, with the subsequent Visits to the same Lands by English Navigators, who gave them new Names. To which is prefixed, an Historical Abridgement of the Voyages and Discoveries of the Spaniards in the same Seas. By M.*****, formerly a Captain in the French Navy. Translated from the French.  12 fold-ing plates and charts of the Solomon Islands and New Guinea.  4to. London.

French original, Paris, 1790. See below.
This volume is distinguished by the most laborious research, singular acute-ness, and critical discrimination.—*Edin. Cab.* XXI, 237, note.  Count Fleurieu, famous French statesman and scientist, was the leading light in the early his-tory of French South Sea exploration. . . . The maps in the volume are very curious and interesting. They were based on actual discoveries and on Fleurieu's theories. When D'Entrecasteaux returned from his fruitless search for La Pérouse, it was found that these theories were in the main details correct.— Maggs, No. 491. In the narrative of the English expeditions to these regions there is a relation of Captain Cook's recognition of the Tierra Austral del Es-piritu Santo of Quiros as the New Hebrides, as well as of Cook's discovery of New Caledonia in 1774.

1790 FLEURIEU, C. P. C., COMTE DE.  Découvertes des Francois en 1768 & 1769, dans le Sud-Est de la Nouvelle Guinée. Et Reconnaissances postérieures des même Terres par des Navigateurs Anglois qui leur ont imposé de nouveaux noms; précédés de l'Abrégé historique des Naviga-tions & des Découvertes des Espagnols dans les mêmes Passages. 12 folding plates and charts. Paris.

MORTIMER, GEORGE (Lieutenant).  Observations and Remarks made during a Voyage to the Islands of Teneriffe, Amsterdam, Maria's Islands near Van Diemen's Land; Otaheite, Sandwich Islands; Owhy-hee, the Fox Islands on the North West Coast of America, Tinian, and from thence to Canton, in the Brig Mercury, commanded by John Henry Cox, Esq.  4to.  London.

Another edition, Dublin, 1791. Translated into Dutch, Leyden, 1793. See be-low.
A hasty voyage of ten months and one day, containing but little informa-tion.—Lowndes. It contains some curious details concerning the Mutiny of the *Bounty* and Captain Cook.—Maggs, No. 549.

1793 (In Dutch.) Waarnemimgen en aanmerkungen geduur eene reize naar
Teneriffe, van Diemansland, Sandwich-Eiland, de Noord-West-Kust
van Amerika enz onder bevel van J. H. Cox. Uit het Engelsch vertaald d. J. D. Pasteur. Leyden.

1792 BLIGH, WILLIAM (Lieutenant). A Voyage to the South Sea, Undertaken by Command of His Majesty, for the purpose of conveying the
Bread-Fruit Tree to the West Indies, in his Majesty's Ship the Bounty,
commanded by Lieutenant Wm. Bligh, including an account of the
Mutiny on Board the Said Ship, and the Subsequent Voyage of part
of the Crew, in the Ship's Boat, from Tofoa, one of the Friendly
Islands, to Timor, a Dutch Settlement in the East Indies. Portrait,
folding maps and plans. 4to. London.

Another edition, Dublin, 1792; again, London, 1794; Translated into French,
Paris, 1792; into German, Berlin, 1793. In 1831 Sir John Barrow published an
account of the mutiny and the later fortunes of the mutineers, which was reprinted in the Oxford Classics, with an Introduction by Admiral Sir Cyprian
Bridge, Oxford, 1914. The story is retold along with Bligh's second voyage on
the same errand by Ida Lee, London, 1920. See below. The expedition has gained
wide recognition in recent years by the three novels of Charles Nordhoff and
James N. Hall, and the moving picture reproduction. See also Christian under
1798, Smith under 1815, Morrison under 1935, and Irving under 1936 below. For
a purported narrative by Fletcher Christian in the form of letters see Christian
under date of 1796, FICTITIOUS VOYAGES AND TRAVELS.
For some time the project of transplanting the bread fruit tree from the
South Sea Islands to the West Indies had engaged the attention of various merchants and naturalists, and in 1787 the ship *Bounty* under command of Lieutenant
Bligh was dispatched to Tahiti for the purpose of collecting the young plants
and conveying them to the West Indies. This work of collecting was successfully carried out. But while at the Island of Aitutaki, of the Cook or Hervey
group, the crew, under the leadership of Fletcher Christian, master mate,
mutinied. Bligh with eighteen others was put into the ship's launch along with
a few provisions and some instruments and set adrift. After a voyage of 3600
miles and forty-one days the launch succeeded in reaching Timor and Java in
the Dutch East Indies, where the emaciated unfortunates were taken in by the
Dutch and hospitably treated. Bligh bought a small schooner and continued on
to England. Meanwhile the mutineers divided into two parties. Sixteen landed
at Tahiti and were for the most part eventually captured by the *Pandora,* sent
out to apprehend them, and carried to England where they were tried and, with
the exception of some three, were executed. The other nine remained with the
*Bounty,* and, after taking on six native men and twelve women, cruised around
until they sighted Pitcairn Island, where they landed, destroyed the ship, and
formed a settlement. Dissensions arose between the natives and the whites with
the consequent mortality of all but one white man, Alexander Smith, who assumed the name of John Adams. The story of peace and idyllic tranquility that
followed belongs to the accidental contacts with the island made by Captain Folger of the American ship *Topaz* (October, 1808), who sent in a report of his
discovery. The next visit to the island was made by two English frigates in
1814, which forwarded the official account to England. This was followed by the
visit of Capt. Beeching in the *Blossom* in 1825, who reported the population to
number sixty-six. In 1830 Captain Woldegrave found the population had grown
to seventy-nine. Later on the population had increased so much that the British
government moved a portion of them to another island, some of whom, however,
becoming homesick returned to Pitcairn. It is generally agreed that the main
cause of the mutiny was the intolerable harshness of Bligh's temper. For an
account of the capture of some of the mutineers see Edwards under 1915 below.
Byron's poem, "The Island," was based on the story of the relations that existed
between the sailors and the native women.

1794  BLIGH, WILLIAM (Lieutenant).  An Account of the Mutinous Seizure of the Bounty; with the succeeding Hardships of the Crew. To which are added, Secret Anecdotes of the Otaheitean Females. Frontispiece of the "Pirates seizing Captain Bligh." London.

> The date is approximate. The anecdotes told of the "Otaheitean Females" in this scarce account were doubtless such as readers desired to believe.

1920  BLIGH, WILLIAM (Captain).  Captain Bligh's Second Voyage to the South Sea. Edited by Ida Lee. Maps and illustrations. 8vo. London.

> This is partly retold from the logs of Bligh and others. Bligh's log books were written in 1791-93, the years of the expeditions. This time the bread fruit shoots were safely conveyed to the West Indies, but the labor was largely in vain, for the inhabitants of those islands never took to the new food.

1936  IRVING, LAURENCE. William Bligh. His Narrative of his Voyage to Otaheite: with an Account of the Mutiny and of his Boat Journey to Timor.  New York.

1792  (In French.)  Voyage à la Mer du Sud, entrepris par ordre de S. M. britannique, pour introduire aux Indes la jaquier. Avec une relation de la révolte à borde de son vaisseau. Traduit de l'anglois par F. Soulès. Avec carte. 8vo. Paris.

1793  (In German.)  Reise in das Südmeer. Translated from the English by Georg Forster. 8vo. Berlin.


1792-93  PAGES, PIERRE MARIE FRANCOIS.  For an account of a voyage towards the South Pole see his *Travels round the World in 1767-1771,* under CIRCUMNAVIGATIONS.


1793  HAMILTON, GEORGE.  For an account of the expedition sent in search of the mutineers of the *Bounty* see his *A Voyage round the World,* CIRCUMNAVIGATIONS. For a modern edition of this voyage see Edwards under 1915 below.


1798  CHRISTIAN, FLETCHER.  Voyages and Travels of Fletcher Christian, and a Narrative of the Mutiny on board H.M. Ship Bounty at Otaheite. From the French. London.


1799  An Account of Discoveries in the Southern Pacific-Ocean. London.

> So cited by Pinkerton XVII.


POPHAM, SIR HOME.  Description of Prince of Wales Island in the Streights of Malacca, with its Advantages and Resources. 2 folding charts. 4to. London.

WILSON, JAMES (Captain). A Missionary Voyage to the Southern Pacific Ocean performed in the years 1796, 1797, 1798, in the ship Duff, commanded by Captain James Wilson. Compiled from Journals of the Officers and the Missionaries, and illustrated with Maps, Charts, and Views, Drawn by Mrs. William Wilson, and engraved by the most eminent Artists. With Discourse on the Geography and History of the South Sea Islands, and Appendix. 4to. London.

> Translated into German, Weimar, 1800. See below.
> This voyage was undertaken by the London Missionary Society for the purpose of establishing a mission in Tahiti. A settlement of twenty-five persons was formed. The king of the Islands, Pomare I, befriended them, but they met with continual difficulties from the civil wars, and finally had to flee to Australia, returning, however, in 1815 to Tahiti. . . . Many valuable details regarding Tahiti, the Fiji Islands, the Marquesas, etc. A new group of islands was found among the Santa Cruslands and named the Duff Group. . . . Maggs, No. 491. Not only the missionaries but the crew as well were selected with the utmost care for this undertaking. Consequently the natives were much non-plussed, being unaccustomed to such virtuous conduct on the part of sailors. Some of the missionaries established themselves at other island groups, but success did not immediately attend any of their efforts at Christianizing the Polynesians. The account is of extraordinary interest for its fresh and sometimes naive viewpoint, and for its descriptions of customs passed over by the nautical and geographical explorer.

> 1800 (In German.) Beschreibung einer englischen Missionsreise nach dem südlichen stillen Ocean 1796-98. Übersetzt von Sprengel. Maps. Weimar.

1800 History of the Otaheitean Islands, from their first Discovery to the present Time, including an Account of the Institutions, Manners, Customs, Religion, Ceremonies, etc., of the People Inhabiting the Friendly, Sandwich Society Islands, and the Marquesas. With an historical sketch of the Sandwich Islands. To which is added, An Account of a Mission to the Pacific Ocean, 1796-98. 12mo. Edinburgh.

> The mission referred to is that set forth in the preceding item of the Voyage of the Duff.

LABILLARDIERE, JACQUES JULIEN HOUTON DE. For an account of explorations among the New Zealand, New Guinea, and Solomon Island groups see his Voyage in Search of La Pérouse, under CIRCUMNAVIGATIONS, and La Pérouse's Voyage round the World, under 1798 of the same section.

PENNANT, THOMAS. The view of the Malayan Islands, New Holland, and Spicy Islands. . . . Folded maps. 4to. London.

> This forms vol. IV of Pennant's Outlines of the Globe.

## ADDENDA

1808   WEBBER, J.   Views in the South Seas, from Drawings by the late James (John) Webber, Draughtsman on board the *Resolution,* 1776-1780, with a Descriptive Letterpress of the various Scenery. 16 colored plates from the original drawings in the possession of the Admiralty Board. Fol. London.

> John Webber was the son of a Swiss sculptor who had settled in England. His portrait of his brother exhibited at the Royal Academy in 1776 seen by Dr. Solander led to his appointment as draughtsman to Cook's last voyage.—From Maggs, No. 491. The original drawings illustrated scenes and incidents observed on Cook's third voyage. They included views of the Hawaiian Islands, Vancouver Island, New Zealand, etc.

1808-1814   DAMPIER, WILLIAM (Captain).   Account of the Philippines. From his Voyages, vol. I, 7th edit., 1729. In Pinkerton XI, 1-67.

DE GUIGNES, ——.   For an account of the Philippines see his *Observations on the Philippine Islands and the Isle of France,* under FAR EAST.

1810   An Authentic Narrative of Four Years Residence at Tongataboo, One of the Friendly Islands, by ——, who went thither in the Duff, under Captain Wilson, in 1796; with an Appendix by an eminent writer. 8vo. London.

> Another edition, London, 1815. This one is a little fuller in title; it gives the name as George V.—, which is identified by Halkett and Laing as George Veeson.
>
> An interesting and scarce narrative. The author went out to Tonga nominally as a Missionary, but left them and intermarried with the natives, with whom he lived for two years. When the missionaries were murdered, he escaped the massacre. The narrative is very well written, and describes the author's voyage to Rio de Janeiro, Australia, and so to Tahiti. A long account is given of Tahiti and Eimeo and events there. Voyage from Tahiti to Tonga and events there. The author's declension from the Missionaries and marriage with a Tongan girl, and life among the natives. His prosperity, and customs of the natives. War at Tonga, and murder of the Missionaries. The author's escape from the South Sea Islands, and return to America and England.—Maggs, No. 491.

1815   SMITH, ALEXANDER.   The Life of Alexander Smith, Captain of the Island of Pitcairn, one of the Mutineers on board His Majesty's Ship Bounty; commanded by Lieut. Wm. Bligh. Written by Smith himself on the above island, and bringing the accounts from Pitcairn, down to the year 1815. 8vo. Boston.

> As noted under Bligh, 1792, above, Smith assumed the name of John Adams, after the death of all the other men on the island.

1868 MORGA, ANTONIO DE. The Philippine Islands, Moluccas, Siam, Japan, and China, at the close of the 16th Century. By Antonio de Morga, 1609. Translated from the Spanish, with Notes & a Preface, and Letter from Luis Vaez de Torres, describing his Voyage through the Torres Straits, by Lord Stanley of Alderley. 2 illus. Hak. Soc., ser. I, vol. 39. London.

> Spanish original, Mexico, 1609. See below.
> This work is extremely rare. . . . De Morga is less remarkable for his literary merits than for his qualities as a jurist and administrator and a commander. His book is rather an historical than a geographical work, but the account of Alvaro de Mendana's second voyage by his pilot Fernandez de Quiros, given by De Morga, is of great importance.—From Maggs, No. 491.

> 1609 MORGA, ANTONIO DE. Sucesos de las Islas Philipinas. 4to. Mexico.

1891 CROZET, ——. Crozet's Voyage to Tasmania, New Zealand, the Ladrone Islands, and the Philippines in 1771-72, translated by H. Ling Roth, with preface and brief reference to the Literature of New Zealand, by Jas. R. Boosé Map, plates and illus. 8vo. London.

> French original, Paris, 1783. See below.
> In this voyage the Crozet or the Marion Islands were discovered. It is usually known as Crozet's Voyage, and was drawn up by the Abbé Rochon, who proposed accompanying the ill-fated expedition. The vessels left Mauritius in Oct., 1771, and sailed via the Cape, Crozet Islands, Tasmania, New Zealand, Guam, Manilla, and home. A month was spent at the Bay of Islands where Marion and 26 of his crew were massacred by the New Zealanders, June, 1772, and the command was transferred to Crozet. An excellent description of New Zealand, productions, natives and their habits, is given. . . . From Maggs, No. 491.

> 1783 CROZET, ——. Nouveau Voyage à la mer du Sud, commencé sous les ordres de M. Marion. Cette Relation a été rédigée d'après les Plans & Journaux de M. de Crozet. On a joint à ce Voyage un Extrait de celui M. de Surville dans les mêmes Passages. 7 engraved plates. 8vo. Paris.

1896 BANKS, SIR JOSEPH. For his account of Otaheite, New Zealand, Australia, etc., printed from his own journal written during Cook's first voyage see his *Journal during Capt. Cook's First Voyage . . ., 1768-1771,* under Hawkesworth, CIRCUMNAVIGATIONS.

1901 MENDANA, ALVARO DE. The Voyage of Mendana to the Solomon Islands in 1568. Edited by the Lord Amherst of Hackney and Basil Thomson. Maps and illus. 2 vols. Hak. Soc., ser. II, vols. 7-8. London.

1903 GONZALEZ, DON FELIPE (Captain). The Voyage of Captain Don Felipe Gonzalez in the Ship of the Line San Lorenzo, with the Frigate Santa Rosalia in company, to Easter Island, in 1770-1771. Preceded by an Extract from Mynheer Jacob Roggeveen's Official Log of his Discovery of and Visit to Easter Island in 1722. Translated, Annotated, and Edited by Bolton Glanvill Corney, Companion of the Imperial Service Order. With a Preface by Admiral Sir Cyprian Bridge, G.C.B.   3 maps and 4 illus.   Bibliography.   Hak. Soc., ser. II, vol. 13. London.

> For Roggewein's circumnavigation see *Commodore Roggewein's Expedition . . . for the Discovery of Southern Lands* under 1744-48, CIRCUMNAVIGATIONS.

1912   HAYES, SIR JOHN.   His Voyage and Life, 1767-1831, with an Account of Admiral D'Entrecasteaux's voyage of 1792-93, by Ida Lee.  Portrait and illus.   8vo.   London.

> Hayes' voyage produced much useful information. He circumnavigated Australia, surveyed and mapped Tasmania, and besides he was the first European to penetrate the Great Barrier Reef. He also established a settlement on New Guinea, and endeavored to secure it for the British crown. Some interesting details concerning the disappearance of La Pérouse and the search for him are included in the work.

1913-18   The Quest and Occupation of Tahiti, by Emissaries of Spain during 1772-76, told in Despatches and other contemporary Documents, translated into English and compiled, with Notes and Introduction, by B. Glanvill Corney, I.S.O.   Charts, plans, and illus.   3 vols.   Hak. Soc., ser. II, vols. 32 (1913), 36 (1915), 43 (1918).

1915   EDWARDS, EDWARD (Captain), and HAMILTON, GEORGE (Surgeon.)   Voyage of the *Pandora* despatched to Arrest the Mutineers of the *Bounty* in the South Seas, 1790-91, with Introduction by Sir Basil Thomson.   Folding map.   8vo.   London.

> Capt. Edwards was as rigid and inflexible a disciplinarian as was Bligh but without the great qualities of mind that must be allowed the latter. The mutineers on board were all but suffered to drown when the *Pandora* was wrecked on the Barrier Reef had not final permission been obtained to knock off their irons. As it was, four of them perished in the wreck.   See Hamilton under 1793, CIRCUMNAVIGATIONS.

1924   FANNING, E. (Captain).   Voyages and Discoveries in the South Seas, 1792-1832.   Illus.   8vo.   Salem.

> This is Publication No. 6 of the Marine Research Society. It is an interesting account of one of the early American voyagers. The original was published in 1833.

1935   MORRISON, JAMES.   The Journal of James Morrison, Boatswain's Mate of the *Bounty*, describing the Mutiny and subsequent Misfortunes of the Mutineers, together with an account of the Island of Tahiti, with an Introduction by Owen Rutter.   4 engravings.   8vo.   London.

> This journal has heretofore appeared only in extracts. See Bligh under 1792 above.

# XI

## Australia

1617 QUIROS, PEDRO FERNANDES DE. For his connection with the discovery of Australia see under 1617, SOUTH SEAS.

1694 TASMAN, ABEL JANSEN (Captain). For an account of his voyage to Tasmania and New Zealand see Robinson's Collection, under COLLECTIONS.

> An abstract of his journal in Harris I, 325-336; reprinted in Callander II, 355-379; a new translation by Rev. C. G. Woide, printed in Burney's *Chronological History of Discoveries in the South Sea,* vol. III, London, 1803. A modern edition by J. E. Heeres, Amsterdam, 1898. See below.
>
> The above account is probably the earliest in English of Tasman's famous voyage of 1642, in which he discovered Tasmania, called by him Van Diemen's Land, and New Zealand. This short account is based upon that by Dirk Rembrantse, published in Holland about 1678. In his long introduction the author speaks of explorations toward the South Terra Incognita, and suggests that the Dutch had made great discoveries there which they had never divulged, . . . and writes "Tis probable by Abel Jansen Tasman's Navigation, that New Zealand, New Carpentaria, and New Holland, are a vast prodigious Island, which he seems to have encompassed in his voyage, setting out from Batavia to Maurice Isle . . . he fell upon those new Tracts of Land called Van Diemen's, and afterwards upon New Zealand, to the South-East of New Holland; returning to Batavia through part of the South Sea (wherein he discovered new Islands) and so Northwards to New Guinea to the Molucco's, and Java."—From Maggs, No. 491. For many years the only account of Tasman's voyage was to be found in a curtailed version of his journal, published at Amsterdam, 1674, and in a more copious relation inserted in Valentyn's *East India Descriptions.* About 1711 a MS. journal, supposed to be the original, fell into the hands of Sir Joseph Banks, and was found to be much more complete than any previous narrative. This was translated into English by Rev. C. G. Woide, and published by James Burney as stated above. It commences: "Journal or Description by me, Abel Jansz Tasman, of a Voyage from Batavia for making discoveries of the unknown South Land, in the year 1642. May God Almighty be pleased to give His Blessing to this Voyage! Amen."—From *Edinburgh Cabinet,* XXI, 143, note. The Dutch original was never published entire; perhaps it was never intended to be, for the Dutch East India Company, like the Spaniards and the Portuguese, kept many discoveries secret to prevent results being utilized by other nations. The first complete and exact version is that edited by Heeres.
>
> For the answer to the question who and what nation first sighted Australia see under Quiros, 1617, SOUTH SEAS, and Prado y Tovar under 1929 below. Preceding Tasman a number of Dutch voyagers had been sent out from Batavia to the western shores of this new-old continent, but the results had been isolated contacts which were to remain separate pieces for some time to come. The Dutch East India Company were not so much interested in pure geographical discovery as in new regions to exploit and new usable trade routes to South America, although their instructions to Tasman included settling the question whether Australia and New Guinea were one continuous land mass and had any connection with the Antarctic continent. However much Tasman's voyage disproved the common assumptions, he was unaware of the fact. His second voyage of 1644 confirmed him in the same error, but it did prove that land discovered by early explorers in the Gulf of Carpentaria was a part of that found on the western and northwestern coasts.

1898 TASMAN, ABEL JANSZOON. Journal of his Discovery of Van Diemen's Land and New Zealand in 1642, with Documents relating to his

Exploration of Australia in 1644, facsimile reproduction of the Original Manuscript, with English translation and Life of Tasman, by J. E. Heeres. 5 facs. maps. Fol. Amsterdam.

1697  DAMPIER, WILLIAM (Captain).   For his two voyages to Australia in 1688 and 1699, which record the earliest English contacts with that continent, see under 1697-1709, CIRCUMNAVIGATIONS.

A reprint of the account of New Holland, taken from vol. III, 1729 edition, in Pinkerton XI, 464-497.

Dampier's approach to Australia was made from the Indian Ocean, and consequently his experiences with that barren, desolate coast were bound to react unfavorably with regard to either land or inhabitants. In the 1709 volume, which is part II of vol. III, it is stated that he was commissioned to survey "all islands, shores, capes, bays, creeks, and harbours, fit for shelter as well as defence, to take careful soundings as he went, to note tides, currents, winds, and the character of the weather, with a special view to the settling of the best districts. To observe the disposition and commodities of the natives," etc., of what is now Australia. Dampier's recommendations were not of a character to encourage further immediate voyages to this continent. With Cook's discoveries on the east coast a new era opened up for English interest in Australia.

1744-48  PELSAERT, FRANCOIS (Captain).   The Voyage and Shipwreck of Capt. Francis Pelsart, in the Batavia, on the Coast of New Holland and his succeeding Adventures. In Harris I, 320-325.

An abstract published in Callander II, 335-354; and abstract taken from De Brosses in Pinkerton XI, 428-438. It was translated into French by Thévenot from the original Dutch and included in vol. I of his Collection. Dutch original, Amsterdam, 1648. See below.

Pelsaert sailed from the Texel, October, 1628. His object was to continue the exploration of the western coast of Australia. The voyage ended in mutinies, murder, and shipwreck, but Pelsaert managed to reach Batavia alive.—His account of Australia was sufficiently dismal to deter the Dutch from trying to settle on that "barren" continent. Through him Europe got its first description of the kangaroo.—From Maggs, No. 491.

1648  PELSAERT, FRANCOIS. Ongeluckige Voyagie van het Schip Batavia nae Oost-Indian . . . van Persien, . . . en gebleven is op de Abrollos van Fredrick Houtman . . . in de Jaren 1628 en 1629. 4to. Amsterdam.

1764  SERIMAN, ZACARIA.   Viaggi di Enrico Wanton alle Terre Incognite Australi, ed ai Regni delle Scimie e de' Cinocefali.   Portrait, folding map, and 32 engraved plates. 4 vols.   8vo.   Berne.

This work purporting to be the account of the voyage of a certain Englishman to the unknown land of Australia and two other unknown countries named Scimie and Cinocefali, was the composition of a Venetian named Zaccaria Seriman. Italian editions were also published at Venice and London.—Maggs, No. 491. There is a Spanish edition in 3 vols., Madrid, 1778, which states that this work was translated from "Idioma Ingles al Italiano," and from the latter into Spanish by Joaquin de y Guzman. The names of the unknown regions of Scimie and Cinocefali make the piece suspect as a fictional effort.

1766-68 VLAMINGH, WILLEM DE (Captain). Voyage to Australasia. Extract from the Journal of Vlamingh printed at Amsterdam, 1701. In Callander III, 6-9.

> This voyage, which began at the Texel in 1696, had for one of its objects the search of a Dutch East Indiaman supposed to have been lost somewhere on the coasts of New Holland, in the route from the Cape of Good Hope to Batavia. It surveyed the whole western shore of Australia more completely than had been done before. The charting and surveys of the coast and islands and bays was of considerable value. Vlamingh came across the plate set up by Dirck Hartog in his voyage of 1616 to this coast. This he carried off but left one with the same inscription in its stead. This in turn was found, half buried in the sand, by Captain Hamelin of the French expedition of 1801, and was fastened to a new post. In 1818 it was brought away by Louis de Freycinct to France. See Heawood, *Geographical Discovery.*

1767 ROBERTSON, ——. Voyage de Robertson aux terres australes, traduit sur le MSS. Anglois. 12mo. Amsterdam.

> In German, Amsterdam, 1768. See below. Apparently this has not appeared in English.

> 1768 ROBERSTON, ——. Reise in die mittaglichen Länder, oder nach Australien. Plates. 8vo. Amsterdam.

1773 COOK, JAMES (Captain). For accounts of Cook's visit to Australia in 1770 see Hawkesworth under COLLECTIONS and CIRCUM-NAVIGATIONS, and following items.

> After observing the transit of Venus at Tahiti, Cook in compliance with his instructions took up the work of further discovery. The most momentous result of this voyage was the survey of the eastern coast of Australia, the navigation of the Great Barrier Reef, and the finding of a passage through Endeavour Strait into Torres Strait, and so on to Timor. In his preface to his second voyage Cook gives Torres credit for the discovery of the Strait bearing his name. Formal possession in the name of King George was taken of the entire east coast.

1787 EDEN, WILLIAM. The History of New Holland, from its first Discovery to the present Time, with a particular Account of its Produce and Inhabitants, and a Description of Botany Bay, also a List of the Naval, Marine, Military and Civil Establishments, to which is prefixed An Introductory Discourse on Banishment by the Rt. Hon. W. Eden. Folding map of New Zealand and chart of passage from England to Botany Bay. 8vo. London.

> 2nd edit., with 5 additional leaves to the preface, London, 1787.
> The author of this curious and interesting book was afterwards first Lord Auckland. He confines himself to authentic accounts, and gives relations of the wreck of Pelsart off the west Coast of Australia; the two visits of Dampier to Australia, . . . Captain Furneaux' Account, and a long account of Capt. Cook's Australian exploration and discoveries.—Maggs. No. 491.

1789  KING, ——. Account of the Settlement of Port Jackson.  London.

> So cited by Pinkerton XVII.
>
> This is probably Lieut. Philip Gidley King, who was commissioned by Governor Phillip to superintend the transportation of convicts to Norfolk Island for settlement, of which he became first governor. See King under 1791-92 below.


PHILLIP, ARTHUR (Governor).  The voyages of Governor Phillip to Botany Bay, with an Account of the Establishment of the Colonies of Port Jackson and Norfolk Island, compiled from authentic papers, to which are added the Journals of Lieuts. Shortland, Watts, Ball, and Capt. Marshall, with their Discoveries. Portraits, folding maps and charts, and 55 engravings of views and natural history. 4to. London.

> 2nd and 3rd edits., London, 1790; abridged, Dublin, 1790. Maggs, No. 491, cites a Dublin edition of 1790 as an Irish Chapbook version with the full text, in which is described the foundation of Sydney. Translated into German, Stuttgart, 1789, and Berlin, 1794; into French, Paris, 1791. See below.
>
> Arthur Phillip was the first governor of New South Wales. In 1786 he was assigned the duty of forming a convict settlement in Australia, and on May 13, 1787, he sailed with the "first Australian fleet" for Botany Bay. He landed Jan. 18, 1788, but not being satisfied with Botany Bay, he founded his new settlement in Port Jackson on Jan. 26, 1788, naming it Sydney, after Thomas Townshend Viscount Sydney, then Secretary of State. This is an exceedingly important and valuable work.—Maggs, No. 491. The history of the establishment of New South Wales as a colony is one of vicissitudes, among which may be mentioned near starvation of the whole colony and near mutinies of the troops and the convicts.

> 1789  (In German.)  Reise nach der Botany Bai auf Neu Holland. Small folding map. Stuttgart.

> 1794  (In German.)  Reise nach Neu-Südwallis, . . . Phillip, Arthur, Tagebuch . . . in der neu Kolonie in Port Jackson, June 1790-Jan. 1792; Hamilton, G., Reise um die Welt in der Fregatte Pandora, Capitaine Edwards, 1790-1792. In 1 vol. 8vo. Berlin.

> 1791  (In French.)  Voyage du Gouverneur Phillip à Botany-Bay, avec une description de l'établissement des Colonies du Port Jackson et de l'ile Norfolk. Faites sur des papiers authentiques, obtenus des divers départments, auxquels on a ajouté les journeux des lieutenants Shortland, Watts, Ball, et du capitaine Marshall, avec un récit de leurs nouvelles découvertes. Traduit de l'anglois (par A.-L. Millin). 8vo. Paris.


SHORTLAND, JOHN (Lieutenant, later Captain).  The Voyage of Governor Phillip to Botany Bay.  London.

> This is a narrative of the expedition made during a voyage of Lieutenant Shortland while guarding a fleet of transports from New South Wales to England.—*Edinburgh Cabinet* XX1, 276. Shortland, who had sailed with Governor Phillip on the outbound voyage to Botany Bay, was sent back home in command of a fleet of four transports. He took a new route north of New Guinea and thus extended the range of geographical knowledge of the South Sea archipelagos. He reached England but not without experiencing terrible suffering from disease among his crew. He later died of a gunshot wound received in a fight with a French frigate in the West Indies.

TENCH, WATKIN (Captain). Narrative of the Expedition to Botany Bay; with an Account of New South Wales . . . To which is subjoined a List of the Civil and Military Establishments at Port Jackson. 8vo. London.

> 3rd edit., "to which is now added, A Postscript, dated Sydney Cove, Oct. 1, 1788," London, 1789; another edition, Dublin, 1789. Translated into French, Paris, 1789, of which there are two titles. See below and also Tench under 1793 below.
> The Postscript referred to above relates to Norfolk Island, and to the sending a party of convicts to the head of Port Jackson to build a new settlement. Tench kept a daily journal, and his narratives, "written in an admirable literary style, are regarded by the best authorities as the most accurate, most orderly, vivacious, and valuable descriptions of life in the colony in its first days."— Quoted by Maggs, No. 491. Tench was a captain of marines and sailed with the first convict fleet to Australia, where he resided four years.

> 1789 (In French.) Voyage à la Baie Botanique, avec une description du nouveau pays de Galles méridionales, de ses habitans, de ses productions, . . . et quelques détails relatifs à M. de la Peyrouse, pendant son séjour à la Baie Botanique. A laquelle on a ajouté le récit historique, de la découverte de las Nouvelle Hollande, et des différens voyages qui ont été faites par les Européens. 8vo. Paris.

> 1789 (In French.) Relation d'une expédition à la Baye Botanique, située dans la Nouvelle Hollande, sur la côte nommée par le Capitaine Cook, Nouvelles Galles méridionales, avec des observations sur les habitans de cette contrée, et la liste de l'Etats civil au Port Jackson, traduit de l'anglais par C**** P**** (Charles Pougens). 8vo. Paris.

1790 COOK, JAMES (Captain). A Description of Botany Bay on the East Side of New Holland, in the Indian Seas, where Government means to form a Settlement for the reception of Male and Female Convicts, sentenced by the Laws of this Country to Transportation, from Captain Cook's Voyage. 8vo. Lancaster. (8 pp.)

> This description was probably drawn from the account of Cook's first voyage.

History of Botany Bay in New Holland. London.

WHITE, JOHN (Surgeon). Journal of a Voyage to New South Wales, to Botany Bay, Port Jackson, in 1787-1789 . . . With 65 colored plates of nondescript animals, birds, lizards, serpents, trees, and other natural products. 4to. London.

> Translated into German, Berlin, 1791; into Swedish, Upsala, 1793; into French, Paris, 1795. See below.
> The Dedication of this narrative is dated from Sydney Cove, Port Jackson, 1788. The illustrations were considered at the time to represent nondescripts, but the editor obtained the assistance of John Hunter, Dr. Smith, and Dr. Shaw for the scientific descriptions given in the book.—Quaritch. White was Surgeon-General to the Settlement, and went out to Australia in 1787 with the convict transports in charge of H.M.S. *Sirius*. He gives an extremely interesting account of the voyage and early life in New South Wales. The long appendix, occupying the second half of the volume, is very important. It describes the natural history of the new Colony.—Maggs, No. 491. White's account gives many circumstances omitted by Governor Phillip and other writers.—Lowndes.

1791    (In German.)  Tagebuch einer Reise nach Neu-Süd-Wallis.  Map und 4
taf.  (Together with)  Bligh, Wm. Bericht von dem Aufruhr an Bord
des Schiffs Bounty.  Unternehmungen der Gesellschaft zur Beförderung
der Entdeckungen in Innern von Afrika.  R. Norris: Reise nach dem
Hoflager des Königs von Dahomey Bossa Ahadi, 1772.  Berlin.

1793    (In Swedish.)  Resa till Nya Holland åren 1787-88, i sammandrag af S.
Odmann.  4 Tabler.  Upsala.

> This has an appendix entitled, Utdrag af Capt. J. Cook's dag-bok
> hallen under dess Segling vid Nya Hollands Kust, år 1770.—Hierse-
> mann.

1795    (In French.)  Voyage à la Nouvelle-Galles du Sud, à Botany Bay, au
port Jackson, en 1787-1789.  Traduit de l'anglois avec des notes critiques
et philosophiques sur l'histoire naturelle et les moeurs par Ch. Pougens.
2 parts in 1 vol.  2 plates.  8vo.  Paris.

**1791-92  KING, PHILIP GIDLEY (Lieutenant).  For his account of Norfolk
Island see under Phillip this date below.**

> King, whose sea experience began at the age of twelve, was sent in 1788 to
> Norfolk Island, a barren scrub-covered place, with a petty officer, a surgeon's
> mate, two marines, two men supposed to be skilled in the cultivation of flax,
> nine male and six female convicts, for the purpose of forming a branch colony.
> King turned out to be a very able administrator and was rewarded with the
> office of governor of the island. Later he became governor of New South Wales.

**PHILLIP, ARTHUR (Governor).  Extracts of Letters from Arthur
Phillip, Esq., Governor of New South Wales, to Lord Sydney; to
which is annexed a Description of Norfolk Island, by Philip Gidley
King, Esq., and an Account of Expenses incurred in transporting Convicts to New South Wales, . . . In 2 parts.  4to.  London.**

**1792  PHILLIP, ARTHUR (Governor).  Copies and Extracts of Letters from
Governor Phillip giving an Account of the Nature and Fertility of the
Land in and adjoining to any Settlement in New South Wales.  4to.
London.**

**1793  HUNTER, JOHN.  An Historical Journal of the Transactions at Port
Jackson and Norfolk Island, with the Discoveries which have been
made in New South Wales and in the Southern Ocean since the Publication of Governor Phillip's Voyages, . . . including the Journal of
Governor Phillip and King, and of Lt. Ball, and Voyages from the
first Sailing of the Sirius in 1787 to the Return of that Ship's Company to England in 1792.  Portrait, maps, and plates.  4to.  London.**

> An edition in 8vo abridged from the 4to edition, London, 1793.  Translated
> into German, Nürnberg, 1793-94.  See below.
> This is an extremely valuable work for the early history of the English
> settlement of Australia.  Hunter went out to New South Wales as second in com-
> mand of H.M.S. *Sirius*, conveying the first batch of convicts to Botany Bay.  The

*Sirius* returned to the Cape of Good Hope for stores, thus circumnavigating the globe, but was wrecked on Norfolk Island on her trip back to Australia. When Phillip resigned the governorship of New South Wales, Hunter was appointed in his stead. As governor he was not exactly a success, but as sailor he was much esteemed.—Maggs, No. 491. Under the administration of Hunter the exploration of the coast line of Australia made rapid progress.

> 1793-94 (In German.) Historische Nachrichtung von den merkwürdigsten Ereignissen auf Port Jackson und der Norfolk's Insel seit Errichtung der Englischen Niederlassung bis 1792. 2 bde. Portrait, 3 Karten und 6 Tafeln. Nürnberg.

TENCH, WATKIN (Captain). A Complete Account of the Settlement at Port Jackson, in New South Wales, including an accurate Description of the Situation of the Colony; of the Natives; and of its Natural Productions. With a map of the hitherto unexplored country. 4to. London.

> Translated into German, Hamburg, 1794. See below.

> 1794 (In German.) Geschichte von Port Jackson in Neu-Holland von 1788 bis 1792, nebst einer Beschreibung der Insel von Norfolk. Hamburg.

1794 BARRINGTON, GEORGE. A Voyage to Botany Bay, with a Description of the Country, Manners, Customs, Religion, . . . of the Natives. To which is added, his Life and Trial. 8vo. London.

> 4th edit., London, 1796. For the sequel to this voyage see Barrington under 1801 below. In 1810 appeared a collected account. Translated into French, Paris, 1797. See below.
> The author, whose real name was Waldron, was a pickpocket, who running away from home had joined a band of strolling players. He was twice sentenced to hard labor, and finally to transportation to Botany Bay.—D.N.B. On the voyage he prevented the vessel's being seized by the convicts, was recommended to the favorable consideration of the Governor, and in 1792 obtained the first warrant of emancipation ever issued. Later he rose to be high constable of Paramatta, and wrote several works, including the famous line, "We left our country for our country's good."—Maggs, No. 491.

> > 1797 (In French.) Voyage à Botany Bay, avec une description du pays, des moeurs, des coûtumes et de la religion des natifs, traduit de l'anglais sur la troisième édition. 8vo. Paris.

1795 PARKER, JOHN. For some account of a voyage which touched at Botany Bay see his *A Voyage round the World,* under CIRCUMNAVIGATIONS.

1796 A New and Correct History of New Holland, with Description of Botany Bay and particularly Port Jackson, together with an Account of the Manners and Customs of the Inhabitants, . . . By a Society of Gentlemen. 12mo. Glasgow.

1798  LA PEROUSE, JEAN FRANCOIS DE GALOUP, COMTE DE. For his contacts with Australia see *A Voyage round the World in 1785-88*, under CIRCUMNAVIGATIONS.

1798-1802  COLLINS, DAVID. An Account of the English Colony in New South Wales: with Remarks on the Dispositions, Customs, Manners, . . . of the native Inhabitants of that Country. To which are added some particulars of New Zealand, compiled from the MSS. of Lieut. Governor King (and an account of a voyage performed by Capt. Flinders and Mr. Bass.) 3 charts, 23 plates (those of natural history colored), and 11 text illus. 2 vols. 4to. London.

> Vol. I appeared in 1798. A 2nd edit. of the whole, London, 1804.
> This work, apart from its singular, almost painful, interest as a narrative, is of special value as the first official account of the infant colony. It includes an account of the discovery of Bass's Strait from Bass's Journal. After the publication of the second volume Collins was offered and accepted the governorship of another projected settlement in Australia. An attempt to found one on the southeastern coast of Port Phillip proving a failure, he crossed to Van Diemen's Land (now Tasmania), and there, on the 19th Feb., 1804, he laid the first stone of the present city of Hobart Town.—Quaritch.

## ADDENDA

1801  BARRINGTON, GEORGE. Sequel to Barrington's Voyage to New South Wales: comprising a Narrative of the Behaviour of the Convicts, Progress of the Colony, . . . with Official Register of Crimes, Trials and Executions of the Convicts. 2 vols. in 1. 8vo. London.

> See Barrington under 1794 above.

1859  Early Voyages to Terra Australis, now called Australia. A Collection of Documents, and Extracts from early MS. Maps, illustrative of the History of Discovery on the Coasts of that vast Island, from the Beginning of the Sixteenth Century to the Time of Captain Cook. Edited with an Introduction by Richard Henry Major, F.S.A., Keeper of Maps, Brit. Mus., Sec. R.G.S. 5 maps. Hak. Soc., ser. I, vol. 25. London.

1868  TORRES, LUIS VAEZ DE. For the Letter describing his voyage through the Torres Strait see Morga: *The Philippine Islands*, under SOUTH SEAS; also Prado y Tovar under 1929 below.

1900-05  COOK, JAMES (Captain).  Illustrations of Australian Plants, collected in 1770 during Captain Cook's Voyage round the World in H.M.S. "Endeavour." Fol. London.

> Part I. 100 plates, with 31 pages of descriptive text, 1900. Part II. 143 plates, with 41 pages of descriptive text, 1901. Part III. 77 plates, with 26 pages of descriptive text, including Index to whole work, and 3 maps, 1905. These plates had to wait until our day before they were put on the printing press.

1929  PRADO Y TOVAR, DON DIEGO DE (Captain).  New Light on the discovery of Australia as revealed by the Journal of Capt. Don Diego de Prado y Tovar. Edited by Henry N. Stevens, M.A., with annotated translations from the Spanish by George F. Barwick, B.A.  Maps and plates.  Hak. Soc., ser. II, vol. 64.  London.

> Included with Prado's Journal is Torres' Letter of July 12, 1607, the Report of the Council of State with Letter of Luis Vaez de Torres, and other documents. The editor in his Introduction gives a resumé of the conflicting claims of the Dutch, French, Portuguese, and Spanish to priority of discovery of Australia (see Quiros under 1617, SOUTH SEAS), and points out the confusion resulting from the error made by early map makers in identifying Terra Australis Incognita with Australia. He makes much of Prado's *Relacion*, which had dropped out of sight until modern times, in clearing up the mystery surrounding Quiros' return to Mexico after he had got separated from his sister ship in a gale off the Island of Espiritu Santo. Prado, being unable to agree with Quiros, his senior officer, had himself transferred to the ship commanded by Torres and with him continued the voyage of exploration. It is made evident that the popular notion which attributed the discovery of Australia to Quiros must be once for all abandoned, as the latter's nearest approach to that continent was the Island of Espiritu Santo, which is fourteen hundred miles away. Instead the honor of first sighting land belonging to Australia on this voyage must be shifted to Prado, who, however, must remain in ignorance of the fact, unless his spirit is still permitted to hold converse with Mother Earth. See Tasman under 1694 above.

# XII

## Directions For Travelers

1498 Informacon for pylgrymes unto the holy londe. London (?).

> So cited by Parks, who gives dates of reprints as 1515, 1524. Modern reprint, London, 1893. See below.

> 1893 Information for Pilgrims into the Holy Land, edited by E. Gordon Duff. 4to. London.
>
> > As was stated in the note to this edition under NEAR EAST, this book was intended to help travellers in their pilgrimages to Jerusalem. It contains useful directions for travel in the East and a set of phrases required by travellers.

A Book for Travellers. Printed at Westmestre by William Caxton. Fol. London.

> 35 leaves printed in double columns, without numerals, signatures or catchwords. This work, from Caxton's press, may be considered a compendium of almost every known topic: theology, household matters, birds, beasts, fishes, fruits, viands, drinks, merchandise, arts, etc., etc. It also embraces the several orders of society. See Ames' *Typographical Antiquities* by Dr. Dibdin, i, 315-317, and *Bibliotheca Spenceriana*, iv, 319-324.—Lowndes.

1575 TURLER, JEROME. The Traveiler of Jerome Turler, divided into two bookes, the first conteining a notable Discourse of the Maner and Order of traveiling oversea, or into strange and foreign Countries, the second comprehending an excellent Description of the most delicious Realme of Naples in Italy; a work very pleasant for all persons to reade, and right profitable and necessarie unto all such as are minded to traveyll. 16mo. London.

> Latin original, Argentorati, 1574. See below.

> 1574 TURLER, JEROME. De Perigrinatione et agro neapolitano, libri II. Scripti ab Hieronymo Turlero. Omnibus perigrinantibus utiles ac necessarii; ac in eorum gratiam nunc primum editi. Argentorati.

1589 MEIER, ALBERT. Certaine briefe and speciall instructions for Gentlemen, merchants, students, Souldiers, marriners . . . employed in service abrode or anie way occasioned to serve the kingdomes and governements of forren Princes (translated by Philip Jones). 12mo. London.

> Latin original, Helmstadt, 1587. See below.

> 1587 MEIERUS, ALBERTUS. Methodus describendi regiones, urbes et arces, et quid singulis locis praecipue in perigrinationibus homines nobiles ac docti animadvertere, observare et annotare debeant. Helmstadt.
>
> > This was a traveller's handbook to neighboring countries and remains an interesting comment on land travel in the sixteenth century. Meier was a Dane who Latinized his name to Meierus.—From Parks.

1592 LIPSIUS, JUSTUS. A Direction for Trauailers taken (by Sir John Stradling) out of J. Lipsius (his Epistola de peregrinatione italica), and enlarged for the behoofe of the right honorable Lord, the young Earle of Bedford, being now ready to Travell. 4to. London.

> Sir John Stradling enjoyed a great reputation for learning in his day.—D.N.B.

1593 ELIOT, JOHN. The Parlement of Pratlers. London.

> Modern reprint, London, 1928. See below.
> This gives us a fairly complete picture of the normal out of pocket gallant. For it is to this audience that Eliot directs his book; not to school children but to men likely to make the grand tour. . . . He gives us the best portrait of that section of daily life which we are most apt to conjure up by the adjective "Elizabethan."—From the Introduction to the modern edition. There is a French translation on the opposite pages.

> 1928 ELIOT, JOHN. The Parlement of Pratlers, a Series of Elizabethan Dialogues and Monologues illustrating Daily Life and the Conduct of a Gentleman on the Grand Tour, extracted from Ortho-Epia Gallica, a book on the correct Pronunciation of the French Language written by John Eliot, and published in 1593. Edited by Jack Lindsay, and illustrated by Hal Collins. 8vo. Fanfrolico Press. London.

1597 BACON, FRANCIS. Of Travel. (In his *Essays*.) London.

> Reprinted in the 1612 and 1625 editions, London.
> "Travel in the younger sort, is a part of education, in the elder, a part of experience."

1599 A Discourse to knowe the scituation and custommes of forayne cities without travailinge to see them. London.

> So entered in the *Stationers' Register*. See Lewkenor following.

1600 LEWKENOR, SAMUEL. A Discourse Not Altogether Vnprofitable Nor Vnpleasant for such as are desirous to know the situation and customes of forraine Citties without trauelling to see them. Containing A Discourse of all those Citties wherein doe flourish at this day priueleged Vniuersities. . . . 4to. London.

> An interesting work by the nephew of Sir Richard Lewkenor. Although mentioning certain of the other attractions of the cities dealt with, the author was chiefly concerned with the Universities and it is to this fact that the work owes its importance.—Quaritch.

1602 BRITTON, NICHOLAS. A merry Dialogue betwixt Twoo Trauellers Lorenzo and Dorindo. London.

> So entered in the *Stationers' Register*.

1604 BRETON, NICHOLAS. Grimello's Fortune, with his Entertainment in his Travaile. London.

1605 DALLINGTON, SIR ROBERT. For his *Method for Trauell* see his *The View of Fraunce* under 1604, WEST EUROPE.

1606 PALMER, SIR THOMAS. An Essay of the Meanes hovv to make our Trauailes, into forraine Countries, the more profitable and honourable. Folding tables. 4to. London.

> Here Palmer discussed the advantages of foreign travel, and some of the political and commercial principles which the traveller should understand. The book is dated from Wingham, where the author is said to have kept, with great hospitality, sixty Christmases without intermission.—Quoted from D.N.B. The work contains several references to America, the manners and customs of the Indians, etc.—Robinson, No. 41.

1611 The Italian Traveller of Benvenuto Italian professor these 9 years past of his owne native tongue, in London. The first and second parte which doth contayne dialogues. London.

> So entered in the *Stationers' Register*.

1613 SIDNEY, SIR PHILIP (and Others). Profitable Instructions: describing what speciall Observations are to be taken by Travellers in all Nations, States, and Countries; pleasant and profitable. By the three much admired, Robert late Earle of Essex, Sir Philip Sidney, and Secretary Davison. 12mo. London.

> 2nd edit., London, 1633; Osborne I, liv-lvii, for the letter of the Earl of Essex.
> The first piece in this little work consists of 'Instructions for Travellers,' presumed to be by Secretary Davison, comprising useful hints for inquiry. After these a new title appears: 'Two excellent Letters concerning Travell. One written by the late Earle of Essex, the other by Sir Phillip Sydney.'—Lowndes. See also Sidney under 1746 below.

1616 B., J. The Merchants Avizo. Very necessary for their Sonnes and Servants, when they first send them beyond the Sea, as to Spaine and Portingale, or other Countries. Made by their hearty welwiller in Christ, I. B. Merchant. 4to. London.

> Another edit., London, 1640.
> The first stanza of the Address to the Reader runs as follows:

> > "When Merchants trade proceeds in peace,
> > And labours prosper well:
> > Then Common-weales in wealth increase,
> > As now good proofs can tell."

> From Maggs, No. 594. In the dedication the author states that he has been careful to so order the work that it "shall be lawfully permitted to be seene and read in any parts beyond the sea." The extraordinary rarity of the work is probably accounted for by its having been taken abroad by merchants and apprentices as was the author's intention, and having been lost or fingered to pieces in the course of commerce.—Robinson, No. 19.

1617 HALL, JOSEPH (Bishop). Quo Vadis? A Just Censure of Travell as it is undertaken by the Gentlemen of our Nation. London.

> Bishop Hall was a voluminous author, a supporter of episcopacy under the approval of Laud, was impeached and imprisoned in 1642 and his cathedral desecrated. He published controversial works against the Brownists and Presbyterians, besides poems, meditations, and devotional tracts. His best known work was *Mundus Alter et Idem* (see under 1609, FICTITIOUS VOYAGES AND TRAVELS).

1622 CAPEL, SIR ARTHUR. Reasons against the travelling of my grandchild Arthur into parts beyond the sea. (Place?)

> Cited by Ascoli, *Angleterre devant l'Opinion Française*, I, 474, footnote, Paris, 1930.

PEACHAM, HENRY. The Compleat Gentleman, fashioning him absolute in the most necessary and commendable Qualities concerning Minde or Bodie that may be required in a noble Gentleman. London.

> 2nd edit., London, 1634; 3rd edit., London, 1661. Reprinted in Tudor and Stuart Library, with introduction by G. S. Gordon, Clarendon Press, Oxford, 1906.
> This was written for William Howard, Lord Arundel's youngest son, eight years old, to whom he was tutor. It was intended to supply a want in the equipment necessary to perfect English youth. It is a record of the manners and education and way of thinking characterizing the better sort of Cavalier gentry before the Civil War. It belongs to the great literature of Courtesy and was a protest against slovenliness in the education of his time, aiming by precept and example to remedy the condition. Peacham believed that Englishmen should know their own country first, quoting Lord Treasurer Burleigh, who said, "If anyone came to the Lords of the Counsell for a License to travaile, hee would first examine him of England: if he found him ignorant, would bid him stay at home and know his owne countrey firste." See the chapter "Of Travaile."

1630 GOODALL, BAPTIST. The Tryall of Trauell, or 1. The Wonders in Trauell. 2. The Worthes of Trauell. 3. The Way of Trauell. In three bookes Epitomized, By Baptist Goodall, Merchant. 4to. London.

> "An excessive rare volume of poems. . . . Among the Worthes of Trauell the author records:
>
> > 'Collumbus and Magellian prowdly ventur'd,
> > Then Drake, Vesputius, and our Forbish enter'd:
> > But the South regiones what they are unheard,
> > The words of wealth thence to our hands accrue
> > And the many fertile Colonies insue.'
>
> It is dedicated to Elizabeth, Queen of Bohemia."—Sabin.

1633 GREVILLE, FULKE, LORD BROOKE. A Letter of Travell, to his Cousin Grevil le Varney. (In Certaine Learned and Elegant Works of the Right Honorable Fulke, Lord Brooke.) London.

HEYWOOD, THOMAS.   The English Traveller.   London.

1637   WOTTON, SIR HENRY.   Letter of Instruction to John Milton, about to travel. (In *Life and Letters,* edited by Pearsall Smith, Oxford, 1907.)

1641   WADSWORTH, JAMES.   The European Mercury: Describing the Highways and Stages from place to place, through the most remarkable parts of Christendome. With a Catalogue of the principall Fairs, Marts, etc. throughout the same. Useful for all Gentlemen who delight in seeing foraign Countries; and instructing Merchants where to meet their convenience for Trade.   London.

   Described in *Gentleman's Magazine,* 1811, Part I, 446-447, which suggests that the date of printing must have been 1639, "for at the end of the book it says: Imprimatur Tho. Wykes, March (?) 23, 1639." For the career of this informer and spy see under 1629, WEST EUROPE.

1642   HOWELL, JAMES.   Instructions for Forriene Travell; shewing by what Cours, and in what Compasse of time, one may take an exact Survey of the Kingdomes and States of Christendome and arrive to the Practical Knowledge of Languages to good purpose. Portrait of Prince Charles. 12mo.   London.

   Another edition, London, 1650. A modern reprint, edited by Edward Arber, London, 1868.

1643   A Direction for the English Traveller, by which he shall be inabled to coast about all England and Wales. 4to.   London.

1652   EVELYN, JOHN.   For a discussion of travel see the preface to his *The State of France,* under WEST EUROPE.

1656   OSBORNE, FRANCIS.   Advice to a Son. Or Directions for your better Conduct, through the various and most important Encounters of this Life. I. Studies, &c. II. Love and Marriage. III. Travell. IV. Government. V. Religion. 12mo.   London.

   Five editions were published in this same year. 6th edit., Oxford, 1658; another, London (?), 1673.
   Included in this volume, making two volumes in one, is additional matter: I. Politicall Reflections upon the Government of the Turks. Nicholas Machiavel. The King of Sweden's Descent into Germany, etc. The Advice was his chief publication. The warnings against women with which he plied his son form the most interesting passages. . . . On 27th July, 1658, the vice-chancellor, Dr. John Conant, summoned the Oxford booksellers before him and bade them sell no more copies of Osborne's book; but this direction caused the "Advice," according to Wood, to "sell better."—D.N.B., quoted by Sotheran.

1662  HOWELL, JAMES.  A New English Grammar, whereunto is annexed
      A Discours or Dialog containing a Perambulation of Spain and Portu-
      gall which may serve for a direction how to travell through both Coun-
      tryes.  London.

      See Howell's *La Perambulacion de España,* under WEST EUROPE.

1664  NEALE, SIR THOMAS.  Treatise of Direction how to travell safely
      and profitably into forraign Countries.  8vo.  London.

      D.N.B. cites this publication under date of 1643.

1665  GERBIER, BALTHAZAR (Knight).  Subsidium Peregrinatibus, or an
      Assistance to a Traveller in his convers with: 1, Hollanders; 2, Ger-
      mans; 3, Venetians; 4, Italians; 5, Spaniards; 6, French; written to a
      Princely Traveller for a Vade Mecum.  12mo.  Oxford.

      This curious little work is not a guide to the different foreign languages,
      but to the manners and customs of different countries, and the kind of conversation
      most likely to appeal to their inhabitants.  For instance, "The French are accus-
      tomed to ask at the very first sight of a stranger whether he be Homme d'esprit;
      the Germans, if he be a Gentleman; the Spaniards, if he be a Cavallero; the
      Venetians and Genovesi, if he be Rich; the Italians, if he be Ingenious; the Low-
      Dutch, if he be an Honest Man."—Quoted.  Gerbier was master of the ceremonies
      to King Charles I.

1668  GAILHARD, J.  For directions to travellers in Italy see his *The Present
      State of the Princes and Republicks of Italy,* under WEST EUROPE.

      See Gailhard under 1678 below.

1670  BLOME, RICHARD.  For a "Treatise of Travel" see his *A Geographical
      Description of the Four Parts of the World,* under GEOGRAPHY.

      LASSELS, RICHARD.  For his instructions concerning travel see his
      *The Voyage of Italy,* under WEST EUROPE.

      LASSELS, RICHARD.  A Letter of Advice to a young Gentleman Leav-
      ing the University, concerning his Behavior and Conversation in the
      World.  Dublin.

1671  LEIGH, EDWARD.  Three Diatribes or Discourses: First of Travel, or
      a Guide for Travellers into Foreign Parts; Secondly, of Money and
      Coyns; Thirdly, of Measuring of the Distance betwixt Place and Place.
      12mo.  London.

      Another edition, with the title, The Gentleman's Guide, etc., 8vo, London,
      1780.

1673 MERITON, GEORGE.   For directions to travellers see his *A Geograph-ical Description of the World*, under GENERAL TRAVELS AND DESCRIPTIONS.

1678 GAILHARD, J.   The Compleat Gentleman, or Directions for the Educa-tion of Youth, as to their breeding at home, and Travelling abroad. In Two Treatises. 8vo. London.

> The title states that Gailhard "hath been Tutor abroad to several of the No-bility and Gentry."

1683 M., J.   The Traveller's Guide, and the Countries Safety. Being a Declar-ation of the Laws of England against Highwaymen; what is requisite and necessary to be done by such Persons as are robbed, in order to re-cover their Damages; against whom they are to bring their Action, and the manner how it ought to be brought. Illustrated with variety of Law Cases, Historical Remarks, Customs, Usages, Antiquities, and Authen-tick Authority. 12mo. London.

> Reprinted, London, 1692.

1688 CARR, WILLIAM.   For directions how to travel in the Low Countries see his *Remarks of the Government of several Parts of Germany*, etc., under WEST EUROPE.

A Letter of Advice to a Young Gentleman of an Honorable Family, now in his Travels beyond the Seas; for his more safe and profitable conduct in the three great Instances, of Study, Moral Deportment and Religion. In three Parts. By a True Son of the Church of England.   London.

1691 For instructions to travellers see *An Accurate Description of the United Netherlands*, under WEST EUROPE.

1692 BOYLE, ROBERT.   General Heads for the natural History of a Coun-try, great or small, drawn out for the use of Travellers and Navigators. Imparted by the late Honourable Robert Boyle Esq. F.R.S.; ordered to be published in his Life time at the request of some curious persons: to which is added, Other directions for Navigators, etc., with particular Observations of the most noted Countries of the World, by another hand. 12mo. London.

> A scarce little work of considerable American interest, containing many amusing tales which Boyle and his editor (possibly Denis Papin) had apparently received from navigators. Pp. 102-6, for example, are headed, "Enquiries for Virginia and Bermudas," in which he asks for a "particular Account of the

(well known) Spider in the Bermudas, said to be Large and Beautiful for its Colours," etc. He also desires further information concerning the "Gigantic Natives of Cheasapeak" and the particulars of that sea water "where ships do soonest rot as in the Streights of California the Sea looks red, with innumerable Worms that are in it." It contains also "Enquiries for Guiana and Brasil," etc. —From Maggs. No. 580.

1693 For necessary instructions to travellers see *Travels through Flanders, Holland, Germany, Sweden, Denmark,* under CONTINENTAL EUROPE.

1695 CARR, WILLIAM. For instructions to travellers see *The Travellour's Guide, and Historian's faithful Companion,* under GENERAL TRAVELS AND DESCRIPTIONS.

MISSON, MAXIMILIAN. For instructions to travellers in France and Italy see his *A New Voyage to Italy,* under WEST EUROPE.

1699 LAS CASAS, BARTHOLOMEW DE. For the Art of Travelling see his *An Account of the First Voyages and Discoveries made by the Spaniards in America,* under WEST INDIES.

This is added by the translator.

LOCKE, JOHN. Some Thoughts concerning Education. 4th edit. London.

1700 BALFOUR, SIR ANDREW (M.D.). Letters containing Directions and Advices for Travelling through France and Italy. 12mo. Edinburgh.

1705 TOLAND, JOHN. For instructions to travellers see his *The Agreement of the Customs of the East Indies,* under EAST INDIES.

1718 Laws concerning Travelling, etc.: Robbery, Accidents, bad Ways, Extortions of Innkeepers, Regulation of Coaches, Chairs, etc., in London, etc. 8vo. London.

1722 The Gentleman's Pocket Companion for Travelling into Foreign Parts. Illustrated with maps. With three dialogues in six European Languages, etc. London.

1725 For instructions to travellers see *Travels through Flanders, Holland, Germany, Sweden, and Denmark,* under WEST EUROPE.

1726  For an essay on travelling see *Letters describing the Character and Customs of the English and French Nations,* under WEST EUROPE.

1727  HYDE, EDWARD, EARL OF CLARENDON.   A Dialogue concerning Education in *A Collection of Several Tracts.*  London.

1729  The Practical Physician for Travellers, whether by Sea or Land.  Giving Directions how Persons on Voyages and Journies may remedy the Diseases incident to them, without the sorry Assistances they often meet with on the Seas or Roads. . . . By a Member of the College of Physicians.  8vo.  London.

1739  WEST, GILBERT.   On the Abuse of Travelling: A Canto in Imitation of Spenser.  London.

> Printed in Dodsley's *Collection of Poems by Several Hands,* vol. II, London, 1766 edition.
> In this satirical and moral poem West decries the evils likely to attend foreign travel.  See letter from Gray to Richard West, Florence, July 16, 1740. Gray's letter goes on to say:  "Mr. Walpole and I have frequently wondered you should never mention a certain imitation of Spenser, published last year by a namesake of yours, with which we are all enraptured and enmarvailed."  The argument of the poem seems to be that Englishmen should not be lured into internationalism and away from love of their own country by travel. The "argument" stanza preceding it reads:
>
> > "Archimage tempts the Red-Cross Knight
> > From love of Fairy land,
> > With shew of foreign pleasures all,
> > The which he doth withstand."

1742  POOLE, ROBERT.   For the Traveller's Useful Vade Mecum see his *A Journey from London to France and Holland,* under WEST EUROPE.

1746  SIDNEY, SIR PHILIP.   Sir Philip Sidney to his Brother Robert Sidney when he was on his Travels; advising him what circuit to take; how to behave, what Authors to read, etc.  In *Letters and Memorials of State,* collected by Arthur Collins.  London.

1753  JEFFRIES, DAVID.   Traité des Diamans et des Perles . . . Par David Jeffries.  Ouvrage traduite de l'Anglois.  8vo.  Paris .

> The English original has not come to the notice of the editor.  The work contains some advice to travellers.

1757 TUCKER, JOSIAH (Rev. Dr.). Instructions for Travellers. London.

> This is a dialogue on conditions in England to show the kind of information which travellers should always try to obtain. The design was carried out to absurd extremes by Count Leo Berchtold, who highly commended the work (see Berchtold under 1789 below). The author became Dean of Gloucester in 1758. He wrote numerous articles on economic, political, and religious subjects.

1758 The Bear-Leaders: or Modern Travelling stated in a proper Light, in a Letter to the Rt. Hon. the Earl of *****. London.

1763 HURD, RICHARD (Bishop). Dialogues on the Uses of Foreign Travel, considered as a Part of an English Gentleman's Education between Lord Shaftesbury and Mr. Locke. (Addressed to Robert Molesworth, Esq.) 8vo. London.

> 2nd edit., London, 1764; reprinted, London, 1765, with the Author's name, under the title Dialogues Moral and Political, with Letters on Chivalry. This edition contains a preface, then first published, on the manner of writing Dialogues. Noticed in the *Journal des Scavans,* 1764, VII, 248.

1764 ROCQUE, JOHN. The Traveller's Assistant, being a General List of the Post Roads, etc., from Cornhill, London, to the Capitals of each Empire, Kingdom, Province in Europe, likewise from each Capital to their Respective Post Towns. 8vo. London.

1766 SHARP, SAMUEL. For advice to travellers intending to cross the Alps see his *Letters from Italy,* under WEST EUROPE.

1768 THICKNESSE, PHILIP. Useful Hints to those who make the Tour of France, in a series of Letters written from that Kingdom. London.

> 2nd edit., London, 1770.
> Advice from this much travelled man ought to be of value. See Thicknesse under 1766, WEST EUROPE.

1770 MILLARD, JOHN. For his *Gentleman's Guide in his Tour through France* see under WEST EUROPE.

1774 D'AULNOY, MARIE-CATHERINE (Countess of). For instructions how to travel in Spain see her *The Lady's Travels into Spain* under 1691, WEST EUROPE (the 1774 edition).

1782 See *The Traveller's Vade Mecum through the Netherlands, and Parts of France and Germany,* under WEST EUROPE.

1784    ANDREWS, JOHN (Dr.).    Letters to a Young Gentleman in setting out
        for France.    London.

1787    BERCHTOLD, COUNT LEOPOLD.    An Essay to Direct and Extend
        the Inquiries of Patriotic Travellers; with further Observations on the
        Means of preserving the Life, Health, and Property of the inexpe-
        rienced in their Journies by Land and Sea.    Also a Series of Questions,
        interesting to Society and Humanity, necessary to be proposed for So-
        lution to Men of all Ranks and Employments and of all Nations and
        Governments, comprising the most serious Points relative to the Ob-
        jects of all Travels.    To which is Annexed a List of English and for-
        eign Works intended for the Instruction and Benefit of Travellers, a
        Catalogue of the most interesting European Travels which have been
        published in different Languages from the earliest Times down to Sep-
        tember 8th, 1787.    8vo.    London.

    Apparently a second volume was projected but unfortunately seems not to
    have been published.  Presumably it would have contained the List of Travels
    and Travellers promised in the title.  If the traveller found the answers to all the
    questions proposed for each place in this thick first volume, he would need sev-
    eral lifetimes to complete the tour of a single kingdom.  This work is an expan-
    sion of the *Instructions for Travellers* by Josiah Tucker (see Tucker under 1757
    above).

        KNOX, VICESIMUS.    On the Manner of Writing Voyages and Travels.
        In *Essays Moral and Literary* (9th edit., London, 1787), I, 221-231.

    This essay really belongs to a section of Directions for Writers, but in the
    want of such it is placed in this section as being nearest of kin.

        MARTYN, THOMAS.    For directions how to tour Italy see his *The
        Gentleman's Guide in his Tour through Italy,* under WEST EUROPE.

1793    For directions for travelling in Germany see *A Tour through Germany,* un-
        der WEST EUROPE.

1799    TAYLOR, JOHN (Major).    For directions to travellers see his *Travels
        to India 1789,* under EAST INDIES.

1800    STARKE, MARIANA.    For information for travellers see her *Travels
        on the Continent for the Use and Particular Information of Travellers,*
        under WEST EUROPE.

## ADDENDA

1857 WEY, WILLIAM.   For advice to travellers in the Near East see his *The Itineraries of William Wey,* under NEAR EAST.

1870 BORDE, ANDREW.   For aids to travellers see his *Fyrst Boke of the Introduction of Knowledge,* under NEAR EAST.

# XIII

## Geography

(It has been pointed out by E. G. R. Taylor, *Tudor Geography,* that geography owes a great debt to astronomy and hence to astrology, that the cosmographer was in the first instance an astronomer and mathematician, so that many geographical works are to be found embedded in numerous astronomical and mathematical works.)

1480  HIGDEN, RANULF. Polychronicon.

>Written in Latin and translated into English by John of Trevisa in 1387. It was published by Caxton in 1480 (according to Taylor; in 1482 according to D.N.B.). It contains "The descrypcion of . . . Britayne and Ireland," and a Mappa Mundi, i.e., a verbal description of the known world compiled from many sources, from Pliny, Isidore, and Macrobius down to Giraldus Cambrensis. It is thoroughly typical of its day.—From Taylor.

1503  ARNOLD, RICHARD. The Copy of the Carete Cumposynge the Cyrcuet of the Worlde and the Cumpace of every Yland. Antwerp ( ? ).

>Reprinted, London, 1521. Modern edition, London, 1811.—Parks. Reprinted by R. Wyer, 1535, under the title of Mappa Mundi, and by the same publisher at about the same time under the title of Rutter of the Distances from one Porte to another, as an addendum to the Compost of Phtolomaeus.—From Taylor. For the Compost see the following item.
>
>This is a section from Arnold's *Chronicle* and a verbal Mappa Mundi of the crudest character, really compiled at second-hand from Aristotle, Isidore, and Ptolemy.—From Taylor.

1532 (?)  Here begynneth the Compost of Phtolomeus. Translated from the French. 8vo. London.

>Later editions: London, 1535 (?), 1540, 1545 (?); corrected, 1551-62; 1635. See *Short Title Catalogue.* For an undated version of a work by Ptolemy and a modern reprint of his Geography see below. The 3rd edition, undated, adds "The Rutter of the Distances from one Porte or Countree to another," noted under Arnold above. The work deals mainly with the Mediterranean regions. It can be described as scraps from Ptolemy, mainly astrology, with a very little geography. —From Parks.
>
>The numerous versions of Ptolemy printed in the sixteenth century on the continent and their relative scarcity with English imprints reflect on the slowness with which the study of geography was taken up by the English. The *Geographike Syntaxis* of this famous mathematician, astronomer, and geographer of Egypt was far in advance of its day in its scientific attitude towards the subject of geography and in its projections of maps, and exerted for nearly thirteen centuries an influence that almost amounted to a tyranny in the field of mapping. The first edition of Donis's Latin translation appeared in 1482 and the first printing of the Greek text was that edited by Erasmus and published at Basel in 1533. For the advance made by Mercator over Ptolemy see Mercator under 1635 below.

>1561-62  PTOLEMY, CLAUDIUS. The Compost of Phtolemeus Prince of Astronomye: Very necessarye, and profytable, for all suche as desyre the knowledge of the Science of Astronomye. London.
>
>>Quoted for sale by Robinson, No. 59, who calls it an unknown edition of the "Quadripartium" in English, and regards it as the edition entered in the *Stationers' Register* for this date. It was issued by

Thomas Colwell, and bears a remarkable resemblance to the undated edition issued by Colwell's predecessor Robert Wyer about 1540.—Robinson, No. 59.

? PTOLOMAEUS, CLAUDIUS. Universalis Tabula; in quatres continentis partes, Europa, Africa & Asia, quatenus ipsus tempore innotuerant, delineatae sunt. 30 double-page maps (including the Sphere showing America and marking Maryland, Virginia, New Jersey, Charles Town, etc.). Corrected by Philip Lea. Fol. London.

It is a question whether this work gets anything from Ptolemy besides his name.

1932 PTOLEMY, CLAUDIUS. Geography of, translated into English and edited by Edward Luther Stevenson, based upon Greek and Latin MSS., and Important Late Fifteenth and Early Sixteenth Century Editions, including Reproductions of the Maps from the Erner MS. ca. 1560, with Introduction by Joseph Fischer, S. J. 29 double-page collotype plates and numerous illus. Fol. New York Public Library.

1550 PROCLUS. The Description of the Sphere or Frame of the Worlde . . . Englyshed by Wyllyam Salysburye. London.

Translated for Salisbury's "cosen John Edwards of Chyrcke Esquyer," after "I had walked myself round about all Paules Churchyard from shop to shop" and found no English book on the subject. Proclus was an Athenian scientist of the fifth century A.D., and his book was a standard medieval text. Salisbury himself was a Welsh philologist.—Parks.

1551 RECORDE, ROBERT. The Castle of Knowledge, containing the explication of the Sphere. London.

This is rather a book on astronomy than on geography. Recorde was the first writer in English on arithmetic, geometry, astronomy, and the first to introduce algebra in English. He taught mathematics and other subjects at Oxford and Cambridge. He died in prison, probably for debt.—D.N.B. This work is an instance of the new interest in mathematical geography. It was dedicated to Queen Mary, with a letter to Cardinal Pole. It is probably the Introductio in Geometriam atque Cosmographiam listed by Bale. It formed part of Frobisher's ship library. It was written directly to further the search for a route to Cathay.—From Taylor.

1553 MUNSTER, SEBASTIAN. For an English version of his Cosmographia, see Eden, under COLLECTIONS.

1559 CUNNINGHAM, WILLIAM. The cosmographical Glasse, conteining the pleasant Principles of Cosmographie, Geographie, Hydrographie, or Nauigation. Compiled by VVilliam Cuningham Doctor in Physicke . . . In this Glasse you will beholde the Sterry Skie, and Yearth so wide, the Seas also, with windes so colde, Yea and thy selfe all these to guide: What this Type meane first learne a right, So shall the gayne thy trauail quight. London.

This interesting book, which is very rarely found complete, is one of the most artistic productions of Day's press—both in typography and illustrations:

indeed, it is superior to any book which had appeared in English up to this time. It is dedicated to Robert Dudley, Queen Elizabeth's favorite, afterwards Earl of Leicester . . . The portrait of Cunningham, at the age of 28, is the best to be found in any English book of the sixteenth century . . . The last three pages of the text are devoted to "A Perticular Description of suche partes of America, as are by trauaile founde out," in which Columbus is not mentioned, the discovery being attributed to Vespucci.—Quaritch. This is an elementary treatise, mainly on mathematical geography; not up to date, but the first substantial English work on geography.—Parks. It follows closely continental models provided by the cosmographies of Apian and Orontius Finaeus . . . It shows the difficulty of matching theoretical knowledge with the practical instruments then in use.—From Taylor.

1566  PLINY.  A Summarie of the Antiquities, and wonders of the Worlde, out of the sixteene first bookes. Translated out of the French of P. de Changy by I. A.  London (?).

> Reprinted 1585 and 1587 as The Secrets and wonders of the worlde. The complete Pliny was translated by Philemon Holland in 1601.—Parks.

1567  MIZALDUS, A.  Cosmographie, seu Mundi Sphaerae . . . Ejusdem Geographica Quaedam.  12mo.  London(?).

1572  DIONYSUS PERIEGETES.  The Surueye of the Worlde, or Situation of the Earth, as much as is inhabited. Englished by Thomas Twine. 8vo.  London.

> The original of this work, known as Periegesis, was a description of the habitable world written in Greek hexameters by Dionysius Periegetes, also known as Lybicus or Africanus. Nothing certain is known of the date of writing or of the nationality of the author, but he is supposed to have been an Alexandrian of the time of Hadrian. The work was popular in ancient times as a school book. It was translated into blank verse in 1789 by J. Free.—From *Encycl. Brit.*, 13th edit. A Latin version done by Antonius Becharius was printed at Venice in 1478.

MUNSTER, SEBASTIAN.  A Brief Collection and Compendious Extract of Straunge and Memorable Thinges, gathered oute of the Cosmographye of S. Munster . . . 8vo.  London.

> Reprinted, London, 1574.
> The *Cosmographia Universalis* of Sebastian Munster was printed at Basel, 1544. See also Eden under 1553, COLLECTIONS. "Munster occupies a peculiar position as a cartographer; he far surpasses most of the map-drawers of his time in his exertions to get access to the latest information regarding the history, ethnology, and geography of the countries he describes. His bulky cosmography will therefore always remain an important source for the history of civilisation of the period in which he lived."—Nordenskiöld, *Facsimile Atlas,* quoted by Maggs, No. 491. Among his maps are those of the whole world and of America, neither of which shews any representation of a "Terra Australis." Munster, the most famous German geographer of his age, was a frank disbeliever in the existence of a great Southern Continent.—From Maggs, No. 491.

1573  BOURNE, WILLIAM.  For a Hydrographical Discourse of the five ways to Cathay see his *Regiment of the Sea* under the 1580 edition of this work, NAVIGATION I. This discourse was inspired by the Frobisher voyages.

P(OWELL), D(AVID). Certaine brief and necessarie Rules of Geographie, serving for the understanding of Chartes and Mappes. London.

> This is an elementary treatment of circles, parallels, and meridians and other conventions of the map. It indicates the rising interest among Englishmen in cosmography.—Taylor.

1578 BOURNE, WILLIAM. For cosmography see his *A Booke called the Treasure for traueillers,* under NAVIGATION I.

1585 MELA, POMPONIUS. The rare and singular Worke of Pomponius Mela, the Cosmographer, concerning the Situation of the World, . . . A Booke right pleasant and profitable for all sortes of Men: but speciallie for Gentlemen, Merchants, Mariners, and Travellers translated out of Latine by Arthur Golding, Gentleman. 4to. London.

> Another edition, with the addition of Polyhistor, London, 1590; the Latin text (three books) after the recension of Gronovius, Glasgow, 1725; the Latin text, Eton, 1761. There is a Latin edition, Salamanca, 1482, which may be the original of the above translation. See below.
> Of Pomponius Mela nothing is known, but he is believed to have lived in the time of the Emperor Claudius . . . It is written in a clear and simple style, and notwithstanding its conciseness is enlivened with interesting descriptions of manners and customs.—From Maggs, No. 429. With the exception of Pliny's *Natural History,* this is the only formal treatise on geography in classical Latin. It agrees in general with Greek writers from Eratosthenes to Strabo. It divided the earth into five zones, of which two only were inhabitable. It also, unlike the Greek writers, asserted the existence of a southern temperate region, which was inaccessible because it was cut off from the northern region by a terrifically hot zone intervening. It followed closely the Greek geographical accounts in its descriptions of the eastern part of the earth, but went beyond them in its account of the western part of Europe, as would be expected of a Spanish subject of imperial Rome. It was the first to name the Orcades or Orkneys, which it locates pretty accurately. —From *Encycl. Brit.,* 13th edit.

> 1590 MELA, POMPONIUS. The rare and singular Worke of Pomponius Mela, of the Situation of the World, . . . Whereunto is added, that learned work of Iulius Solinus Polyhistor, with a necessary Table for thys Booke. Translated into Englyshe by Arthur Golding, Gentleman. 4to. London.

> For Golding's translation of Solinus see under 1586 below.

> 1761 MELA, POMPONIUS. De Situ Orbis. 27 engraved maps. 4to. Eton.

> > This text was edited by John Reynolds, an Eton Master, who prepared it from the most reliable manuscripts in England and Ireland.— Maggs, No. 580.

> 1482 MELA, POMPONIUS. Cosmographia sive de situ orbis. Salamanca.

1586 SOLINUS, CAIUS JULIUS (Polyhistor). The excellent and pleasant Worke of Iulius Solinus Polyhistor, translated out of Latin into English, by Arthur Golding, Gent. 4to. London.

A Latin version (the original?), Venice, 1498. See below.

Solinus, whose curious woodcut map of the world describes America as *Terra Incognita*, was a Roman geographer, probably of the third century. His book was originally called "Collecteanea Rerum Memorabilium," to which he afterwards gave the title "Polyhistor"—a name which has since been transferred to the author.—Maggs, No. 465. The greater part of this work is taken from Pliny's *Natural History* and Mela's *Cosmographia*. It was revised in the sixth century under the title of Polyhistor. It was a popular work in the Middle Ages. Golding was a friend of Sir Philip Sidney whom he assisted in translating De Mornay's *Truth of Christianity*. Other translations by him are Ovid's *Metamorphoses*, and Caesar's *Commentaries*.

1498 SOLINUS, CAIUS JULIUS. De memorabilibus Mundi. 4to. Venice.

1591 COOKE, FRANCIS. The Principles of Geometrie, Astronomie, and Geographie. London.

1592 TANNER, ROBERT. A Briefe Treatise for the Vse of the Sphere. 8vo. London.

> Later editions: London, 1616 and 1620.

1593 HUES, ROBERT Tractatus de Globis et eorum vsu, accomodatus iis qui Londini editi sunt anno 1593. 8vo. London.

> The Hakluyt Society edition (1888) gives date of 1592 and D.N.B. of 1594. This latter date may be that of another edition, as is stated by the editor of the 1888 edition. Reprinted, London, 1611; done into English, London, 1639; 12th Latin edition, and 2nd in English, London, 1659; last Latin edition, Oxford, 1668. Edited for the Hakluyt Society, London, 1888. Translated into Dutch by Isaac Pontanus, whose notes accompanied the English edition of 1659. See below.
>
> The globes mentioned were those constructed by Emery Molyneux. They were two feet and two inches in diameter and represented both the celestial and terrestrial spheres. In 1603 they received additions from the discoveries of Barents in Nova Zembla, and of English and Dutch explorers in the North Polar regions, and indicated the tracks of Drake and Cavendish around the world. Almost as soon as the globes were made, a manual for their use was published by Dr. Hood (see Hood under 1592, NAVIGATION I), as well as by Robert Hues. The latter went on several voyages, one of them being with Cavendish on his circumnavigation of 1586-88. He had considerable knowledge of the requirements of navigation, and he issued this tract to supply the needs of mariners.

> 1611 HUES, ROBERT. Tractatus de Globis, Caelesti et Terrestri, ac eorum vsu: Conscriptus; a Roberto Hves, Anglo. London.

> 1639 HUES, ROBERT. A Learned Treatise of the Globes, both Coelestiall and Terrestriall: with their several uses. Written first in Latine, by Mr. Robert Hues: and by him so published. Afterwards illustrated with Notes, By Io. Isa. Pontanus. And now lately made English, for the benefit of the vnlearned. By John Chilmead, M.A., Christ-Church in Oxon. 8vo. London.

> > The *Stationers' Register* names Edmond Chilmead as the translator.

1888 HUES, ROBERT. Tractatus de Globis et eorum usu. A Treatise descriptive of the Globes constructed by Emery Molyneux, and Published in 1592. Edited, with annotated Indices and an Introduction by Clements R. Markham, C.B., F.R.S., ex-Pres. R.G.S. To which is appended, Sailing Directions for the Circumnavigation of England, and for a voyage to Gibraltar, from a XVth Century MS., edited by James Gairdner, with Glossary by E. Delmar Morgan. Frontispiece and map. Hak. Soc., ser. I, vol. 79. London.

1595 DAVIS, JOHN. The Worldes Hydrographical Discription. Wherein is proued not onely by aucthorite of writers, but also by late experience of trauellers and reasons of substantiall probabilitie that the worlde in all his Zones, Clymats and places, is habitable and inhabited, and the Seas likewise vniuersally Nauigable without any naturall anoyance to hinder the same whereby appeares that from England there is a short and speedie passage into the South Seas, to China, Molucca, Phillipina, and India, by Northerly Nauigation, to the renowne, honour and benifit of her Maiesties state and Communalty. 8vo. London.

The author here gives an account of his search for the Northwest Passage and the discovery of the Strait bearing his name. He uses the arguments of Sir Humphrey Gilbert in support of the theory of a way to China north of America. —Quaritch. See Gilbert under 1576, NORTHWEST PASSAGE.

1596 BLAGRAVE, JOHN. Nova orbis terrarum descriptio. London.

For other works by Blagrave see under 1585 and 1590, NAVIGATION I.

1599 ABBOT, GEORGE. For "Abbot's Geography" see his *Briefe Description of the Whole Worlde,* under GENERAL TRAVELS AND DESCRIPTIONS.

1602 A Geographical Dictionary: In which are described the most eminent Countreys, Towns, Ports, Seas, Streights, and Rivers of the whole World: very useful for the understanding of all Modern Histories. London.

5th edit., 12mo, London, 1687.

ORTELIUS, ABRAHAM. Abraham Ortelius his Epitome of the Theatre of the Worlde Nowe latlye, since the Latine, Italian, Spanishe, and Frenche editions, Renewed and Augmented, the Mappes all newe grauen according to Geographicall measure. By Michael Coignet, Mathematitian of Antwerp. Beeing more Exactlye set forth, And amplefyed with larger descriptions, then any done heere to fore. (This is followed by) An Addition to the Epitomies of Abraham Ortelivs his littel Theatre, Nevvly corrected, augmented, and adorned vvith Geo-

graphical measures, By Michael Coignet, Professour of the Mathemat-
ick Arte in Antwarpe.  8vo.  London.

> Another edition, London, 1606. Latin original, Antwerp, 1570. See below.
> An interesting and curious Elizabethan Geography, by one of the most famous
> geographers of the 16th century. Scarce with the English text.—Maggs, No. 442.
> This is really an atlas the original issue of which contained 53 finely colored en-
> graved and decorative maps. How it came to be compiled is related in a letter of
> Radermacher, the friend of Ortelius, to the latter's nephew, Jacob Cools. It ap-
> pears that his master, Aeidius Hooftman, a celebrated Antwerp merchant, had
> a passion for buying geographical maps, . . . "but as the unrolling of the large
> maps of that time proved to be very inconvenient, I suggested . . . binding as
> many small maps as could be had into a book which might be easily handled:
> Hence the task was entrusted to me, and through me to Ortelius, of obtaining
> from Italy and France as many maps as could be found printed on one sheet of
> paper. In this way originated a volume of about thirty maps . . . and its use
> proved to be so convenient that it induced our friend Abraham (Ortelius) to ex-
> tend its benefit to scholars in general, and to collect the maps of the best authors
> in a volume of uniform size."—From Maggs, No. 491.

1606 ORTELIUS, ABRAHAM. Theatrvm Orbis Terrarvm Abrahami Orteli
      Antwerp. Geographii Regii: The Theatre of the whole world: set
      forth by that Excellent Geographer Abraham Ortelius, . . . in Hebrew,
      Greeke, and Latine. London.

> This edition contains the "Life of Abraham Ortell," written first
> in Latin by Francis Sweert of Antwerp, and translated into English
> by W. B. The maps were printed in Antwerp.—John Carter Brown.
> The translator and printer was John Norton.

1570 ORTELIUS, ABRAHAM. Theatrum orbis terrarum. Fol. Antwerp.


1607 STAFFORDE, ROBERT. Speculum topographicum; or the topograph-
      icall glasse. 4to. London.


STAFFORDE, ROBERT. A Geographicall and Anthologicall Description of all the Empires and Kingdomes, both of Continent and Islands
in the terrestrial Globe. Relating their Scituations, Manners, Customes, Prouinces, and Gouernments. 4to. London.

> Later editions: 4to, London, 1618 and 1634.


1611 HOPTON, ARTHUR. Speculum topographicum; or, the topographicall
      glasse. 4to. London.

> See Stafforde under 1607 above.


1615 GRIMSTON, EDWARD. The Estates, Empires, and Principalities of
      the World represented by ye description of Countries, Maners of In-
      habitants, Riches of Provinces, Forces, Gouernment, Religion, and the
      Princes that have gouerned in every Estate, translated out of French.
      Fol. London.

1621 HEYLYN, PETER. Microcosmvs, or a Little Description of the Great World. A Treatise Historicall, Geographicall, Politicall, Theologicall. 4to. Oxford.

> A popular work frequently reissued. 2nd edit., augmented and revised by the author, Oxford, 1625; 3rd edit., revised, Oxford, 1627; other editions: 1629, 1632, 1633, 1636, 1637, 1639. A new and much enlarged edition, under the title of Cosmography, London, 1652; reprinted, London, 1657, 1666, 1670, 1673, and 1703, with various corrections. For some of these see below.
> Heylyn presented a copy of his work to the Prince of Wales; the book fell into the hands of James I, who took offense at a passage which said that "France is a greater and more famous kingdom" than England. Heylyn explained that "is" was a mistake for "was," and that the passage referred to the time of Edward III. The clause was omitted, however, in subsequent editions.—D.N.B., quoted by Sotheran. Concerning America, Heylyn remarks that "this great tract of Land ought, and that most aptly, to bee called the New World: New, for the late discovery; and World, for the vast spaciousness of it. The most vsuall; and yet somewhat improper name, is America because Americus Vespucius discovered it: but sithence Columbus gave us the first light to discerne these countries, and Sebastianus Cabot touched at many parts of the continent; . . . why is it not as well called Columbana, Sebastiana, or Cabotia"?—From Maggs, No. 465. Heylyn would have found the answer to his question in Waldseemüller's *Cosmographiae Introductio*, of 1507.

1652 HEYLYN, PETER. Cosmographie, in Four Books, contayning the Chorographie and Historie of the Whole World, and all the principall Kingdomes, Provinces, Seas, and Isles, Thereof. Fol. London.

> Book IV contains the Chorography and History of America; the other books cover Europe, Asia, and Africa, including Scotland and England at the same period with Appendix on the endeavor to discover Terra Australis Incognita, or the Southern Continent. This curious discourse on Terra Australis describes its supposed immense size to be as large as Europe, Asia, and Africa! There are special sections devoted to Terra del Fuego, Solomon Islands, New Guinea, Mundus Alter et Idem ("a witty and ingenious invention of a learned Prelate," i.e., Bishop Hall—see under 1609, FICTITIOUS VOYAGES AND TRAVELS), Utopia. (a country first discovered by Sir Thomas More), New Atlantis (discovered by Sir Francis Bacon), Faerie Land, The Painters Wives Island, Lands of Chivalrie, and the New World in the Moon. There are details of the voyages of Quiros, Magellan, Hawkins, Sibald de Weert, Le Maire, Saavedra, etc.—From Maggs, No. 491. Robert Vaughan engraved the maps of Europe, Africa, and America, and John Goddard that of Asia.—John Carter Brown.

1703 HEYLYN, PETER. Cosmography: the Chorography and History of the Whole World improved with an historical Continuation to the present times. By Edmund Bohun. 5 maps. Fol. London.

1625 CARPENTER, NATHANIEL. Geography Delineated . . . in Two Books, containing the Sphaericall and Topicall Parts thereof. Numerous geographical diagrams. 2 vols. 4to. Oxford.

> 2nd edit., corrected, 4to, Oxford, 1635.
> California is mentioned as the fifth continent. The author remarks that, by a Spanish chart taken by the Hollanders, it has been discovered to be an island, and not part of the Continent as supposed.—Sabin.

1627  SPEED, JOHN.  The Theatre of the Empire of Great Britaine; Presenting an Exact Geography of the Kingdomes of England, Scotland, Ireland, and the Iles adioyning . . . 67 double-page maps.  Fol.  London.

> A new edition, with added matter, London, 1676. See Speed under 1631 below.
> This well-known antiquarian and map-maker is equally famous for his *History of Great Britain,* 1611. He was a member of the Society of Antiquarians.

1631  SPEED, JOHN.  A Prospect of the Most Famous Parts of the VVorld. Viz., Asia, Affrica, Evrope, America. VVith the Kingdomes therein contained . . . Performed by Iohn Speed . . . Together with all the Prouinces, Countries, and Shires, contained in large Theator (*sic*) of Great Brittaines Empire. Portrait and maps. 2 vols. in 1.  Fol.  London.

> The first part consists of 22 maps, each surrounded by views of towns and figures in a typical costume. Of especial interest is one of America, which gives the western coast of North America very defectively, showing California as an island, but is full of detail elsewhere; . . . and a map of the "Invasions of England." The second part incorporates the "Theatre of Great Britaine" (see preceding item), . . . It contains a map of Great Britain, a map of Great Britain and Ireland, with views of London and Edinburgh, one of the Anglo-Saxon Heptarchy, with figures of ancient warriors and historical events, . . . 58 maps of the counties of England and Wales, . . . The engravers were R. Elstracke, Abr. Goos, D. Grijp, Jac. Hondius, J. Norden, C. Saxton, and Ev. Sijmons.—From Sotheran. For the edition of 1676 see below.

> 1676  SPEED, JOHN.  The Theatre of the Empire of Great Britain, presenting an exact Geography of the Kingdom of England, Scotland, Ireland, and the Isles adjoyning; together with a Prospect of the most Famous Parts of the World, viz., Asia, Africa, Europe, America. (To this new edition are added) The Description of his Majesty's Dominions abroad; with a map engraven to each description, viz., New England, New York, Carolina, Florida, Virginia, Maryland, Jamaica, Barbadoes, . . . Complete series of 96 engraved maps. London.

> There is another title of this date which runs:

> An Epitome of Mr. John Speed's Theatre of the Empire of Great Britain, and of his Prospect, etc. (Along with the other additions there follows) The Empire of the Great Mogul with rest of the East-Indies, The Empire of Russia. Engraved frontispiece and 90 engraved maps. London.

1635  MERCATOR, GERARDUS, and HONDIUS, JODOCUS.  Historia Mundi: or Mercator's Atlas, Containing his Cosmographicall Description of the Fabricke and Figure of the World. Lately rectified in divers places, as also beautified and enlarged with new Mappes and Tables; by the studious industry of Iudocus Hondy. Englished by W(ye) S(altonstall) Generosus, and Coll. Regin. Oxoniae. Nearly 200 engraved maps.  Fol.  London.

> An edition, translated by Henry Hexham, Amsterdam, 1636; Saltonstall's (with 56 pp. of introduction not in the first edition), London, 1637; Hexham's again, Amsterdam, 1641. Latin original, Duisberg, 1585. See below.
> Mercator's descriptive texts to these maps were rather unorthodox to theologians, and he faced the danger of being charged with heresy. The first part of

his Atlas appeared in 1585; it was completed with the addition of other maps by Rumold, after the death of Mercator in 1592. Mercator, together with Ortelius, freed geography from the domination of Ptolemy. Hondius was a Dutch engraver, who came to England from Ghent. He is known for the large globes he made for his illustrations to the voyages of Drake and Cavendish.

1636 MERCATOR, GERARDUS, and HONDIUS, JODOCUS. Gerardi Mercatoris et I. Hondii, Atlas, or a Geographicke description of the Regions, Countries and Kingdomes of the world, through Europe, Asia, Africa and America, represented by new, exact Maps. Translated by Henry Hexham, Quarter-Master to the Regiment of Colonel Goring. 2 vols. Fol. Amsterdam.

1585 MERCATOR, GERARDUS, and HONDIUS, JODOCUS. Atlas, sive Cosmographicae Meditationes de Fabrica Mundi. Duisberg.

SWAN, JOHN. Speculum Mundi, or a Glasse representing the Face of the World. 4to. Cambridge.

2nd edit., enlarged, Cambridge, 1645.

1646 A Prospect of the most Famovs Parts of the World; viz., Asia, Africa, Evrope, America . . . England, Wales, Scotland, and Ireland described . . . Numerous little copperplate maps. London.

This is cited by Robinson, No. 20, without author's name. But evidently it is an edition of Speed's work (see under 1631 above).

1649 GERBIER, BALTHAZAR. The first Lecture of an Introduction to Cosmographie: being a Description of all the World. Read publiquely at Sir Balthazar Gerbier's Academy. London.

Gerbier was a painter, architect, and courtier, a native of Germany, who came to England, and after being taken up by the Duke of Buckingham, entered into various diplomatic undertakings for the English court. He shifted his residence from England to France and back again to England. He finally turned his attention to architecture.—D.N.B.

1657 CLARKE, SAMUEL (Rev.) A Geographicall Description of all the Countries in the Knowne World as also of the Chiefest Cityes, Famousest Structures, Greatest Rivers, Strangest Fountaines, &c. Together with rarest Beasts, Birds, Fishes, &c. which are the Least knowne amongst vs. 2 parts. Portrait. Fol. London.

4th edit., fol., London, 1670-71, with additions; with another title, London, 1708 and 1712. See below and also under Clarke, 1671.

1670-71 CLARKE, SAMUEL (Rev.). A Geographical Description of all the Countries in the Knowne Worlde; . . . To which is added, a True and Faithful Account of the Four Chiefest Plantations of the English in America, to wit: Virginia, New England, Bermudas, Barbadoes; as also of the Natives of Virginia and New England—their Religion, Customs, Fishing, Hunting, . . . Collected by Samuel Clarke. Fol. London.

1708  CLARKE, SAMUEL (Rev.). A New Description of the World. Or, a Compendious Treatise of the Empires, Kingdoms, States, Provinces, Countries, Islands, Cities and Towns of Europe, Asia, Africa, and America: . . . An Account of Natures of the People . . . With several remarkable Revolutions, and delightful Histories. 12mo. London.

1658  FAGE, ROBERT. Cosmography, or A Description of the Whole World, with Some General Rules touching the use of the Globe . . . London.

> Later editions: 8vo, London, 1663, 1667, and 1671, with additions. See below.

1667  FAGE, ROBERT. Cosmography Or, A Description of the Whole World, Represented (by a more exact and certain Discovery) in its Situation, Commodities, Inhabitants, and History: Of Their Particular and Distinct Governments, Religions, Arms, and Degrees of Honour used amongst them. Enlarged with very many and rare Additions. Very delightful to read in so small a volume. 8vo. London.

> Mostly relates to America.—Sabin.

1659  MOXON, JOSEPH. A Tutor to Astronomie and Geographie, or an Easie and speedy way to know the use of both the Globes, Coelestial and Terrestrial, in six books. Diagrams. 4to. London.

> Reprinted, London, 1674; 4th edition, London, 1686; 5th, London, 1699. See below.
> Moxon was hydrographer to Charles II in 1660.

1674  MOXON, JOSEPH. A Tutor to Astronomy and Geography, or an Easie and Speedy Way to know the Use of both the Globes, Coelestial and Terrestrial. Teaching the Rudiments of Astronomy and Geography. Problems in the Art of Navigation, . . . more fully set forth than either Gemma Frisius, Metius, Hues, Wright, Blaew, or any others. Numerous copperplates and woodcuts. 4to. London.

> Dedicated to Samuels Pepys, Esq., Principal Officer of Navy, this very scarce Tutor includes the following Problems in the Art of Navigation: To keep a Journal by the Globe, Steer in the Night by the Stars, How to platt on the Globe New Land never before discovered, How to know the distance of your ship from two known points or Capes of Land, Of Tides, Variations of the Compass, To find a Course, etc.—Bookseller's Note.

1686  MOXON, JOSEPH. A Tutor to Astronomy and Geography, . . . with the Ancient Poetical Stories of the Stars, collected from Dr. Hood, and a Discourse of the Antiquity, Progress, and Augmentation of Astronomie, Fourth Edition, Corrected and Enlarged, with Appendix shewing the Use of the Ptolemaick Sphere. Portrait, engravings on copper and wood-cuts. 4to. London.

PETAVIUS, DIONYSIUS. The History of the World; or, An Account of Time. Compiled by the learned Dionisius Petavius and Continued by others to the Year of our Lord, 1659. Together with a Geographicall Description of Europe, Asia, Africa and America. Portrait and folding map. Fol. London.

> Another edition the same year.
> The map is a fine and most interesting example . . . North and South America are most fully delineated, with many curious little "observations," . . . California is shown as an island.—Robinson, No. 19. The author, Denys Petau, **was** a brilliant French Jesuit scholar, who died in 1652.

1670 BLOME, RICHARD. A Geographical Description of the Four Parts of the World taken from the Notes and Workes of the famous Monsieur Sanson, Geographer to the French King, and other eminent Travellers and Authors. To which are added, the Commodities, Coyns, Weights, and Measures of the Chief Places of Traffick in the World; compared with those of England (or London), as to the Trade thereof. Also, a treatise of travel, and another Traffick, wherein the matter of Trade is briefly handled. Illustrated with a variety of useful and delightful maps (some folding), and figures. Fol. London.

> See Blome under 1673 and 1683 below for other geographical works. Blome was a voluminous publisher and compiler who was distinguished by the magnificence of his output. Nicolas Sanson was a famous map maker of France in the seventeenth century whose work was distinguished by great delicacy of drawing.

1671 CLARKE, SAMUEL (Rev.). A Mirror, or Looking-Glass both for Saints and Sinners, wherein is Recorded as Gods Great Goodness to the one so his Seveare Judgment against the other, whereunto is added, A Geographical Description of all the knowne World; as allso of the Chiefest Citys both Ancient and Modern, . . . 2 vols. 8vo. London.

> See Clarke under 1657 above.

1672 VARENIUS, BERNHARD. Geographia generalis, in qua affectiones generales tellures explicantur, ab Isaaco Newton. 8vo. Cambridge.

> 2nd edit., 1681; made English by William Dugdale, 2 vols., London, 1734, 1736. A Latin version, Amsterdam, 1664. See below and also Blome under 1683 below.
>
> A work formerly held in considerable estimation.—Quoted.

> 1734 VARENIUS, BERNHARD. A Compleat System of General Geography, improved by Sir Isaac Newton and Dr. Jurin, and translated into English by Mr. Dugdale, revised by P. Shaw. 2 vols. 8vo. London.
>
> > Dugdale was a well known antiquarian remembered for his *Monasticon Anglicanum* (1655-1673).

> 1664 VARENIUS, BERNHARD. Geographia generalis, in qua affectiones generales tellures explicantur. Frontispiece and maps. 8vo. Amsterdam.

1673 BLOME, RICHARD. Britannia; or, a Geographical Description of the Kingdoms of England, Scotland, and Ireland (and Wales; also the Isles and Territories belonging to His Majesty in America). 50 maps. Fol. London.

1675 LEYBOURN, WILLIAM. An Introduction to Astronomy and Geography, being a plain and easie Treatise of the Globes. Diagrams. 8vo. London.

> The author was a teacher of mathematics and professional land surveyor in London. He is said to have begun life as a printer, but as early as 1648 he appears as joint author with Vincent Wing of the first book on astronomy in English. Its title was "Urania Practica," and it was adapted to the comprehension of beginners. Leybourn's works all grew out of his teaching and were deservedly popular.—D.N.B.

1676 Geographical Cards, printed from Copper Plates, designed and fitted to all our known English Games at Cards; faithfully representing the several Kingdoms, Countreys, and parts of the whole World, with the Latitude and Longitude of all Places: whereby Geography may familiarly and easily be learned by all sorts of People. London.

L., D. For a geography "fitted to all Capacities" see his *A most exact and accurate Map of the Whole World,* under MAPS AND ATLASES.

A Perspective Glass, by which you may see the situation of all the Countreys and Islands in the World. Together with a Description of each part distinct; as likewise all the Kingdoms and Islands. London.

1680 The English Atlas, Volume First; containing a Description of the Places next the North Pole, as also of Muscovy, Poland, Sweden, Denmark, and their several dependencies. With a general Introduction to Geography, and a large Index containing the Longitudes and Latitudes of all the particular Places; thereby directing the Reader to find them readily in the Maps. Published according to the directions of William Lord Bishop of St. Asaph, Sir Christopher Wren, Dr. Isaac Vossius, Dr. Po. Pell, Dr. Tho. Gale, and Mr. Robert Hooke. Fol. London.

> Concerning this work Arber, *Term Catalogues,* states that this "English Atlas, produced at the Sheldonian Theatre, Oxford, in Eleven volumes, and sold by Moses Pitt in London, for two pounds a volume and twenty-two pounds a set, was probably the most costly work produced in England at that time." Of the eleven volumes projected only those noted here seem to have been published. See below.

> 1681 The English Atlas, Volume Two, containing the Description of the Northern Parts of the Empire of Germany; (i. e.,) both the Saxonies, Brandenburgh, Masnia, Mechlenburgh, Bremen, with the Territories adjoyning the Palatinate of the Rhine and the Kingdom of Bohemia.
>
> The announcement of this volume contains the news that the third and fourth volumes are in preparation.

> 1682 The English Atlas, the Fourth Volume (but third published), containing a Description of . . . the Netherlands.
>
> Announcement that all the remaining volumes are in press.

1683   The English Atlas, Volume Three (the fourth published), containing the
Description of the remaining part of the Empire of Germany, viz.,
Schwaben, The Palatinate of Bavaria, Arch-Dukedome of Austria,
Kingdom of Hungary, Principality of Transylvania, the Circle of
Westphalia; with the neighboring Provinces.

MORDEN, ROBERT.   Geography Rectified: or, A Description of the
World, in all its Kingdoms, Provinces, Countries, Islands, Cities,
Towns, Seas, Rivers, Bayes, Capes, Ports, . . . 63 maps.   4to.   Lon-
don.

> 2nd edit., London, 1688; 3rd edit., enlarged, London, 1693; 4th, enlarged,
> London, 1700.
> In the first edition about sixty pages are given up to America.—Sabin. In
> the third edition the town of New York is described as containing five hun-
> dred well-built houses.—Robinson, No. 20. Morden was in the business of mak-
> ing maps and globes.

1682   CLIFFORD, PEREGRINE.   Compendium Geographicum: or, A more
Exact, Plain, and Easie Introduction into all Geography than yet extant, after the latest Discoveries or Alterations. Very Useful, especially for Young Noblemen and Gentlemen, the like not Printed in England. By Peregrine Clifford, Chamberlayne of the Inner Temple, Gent.
8vo.   London.

> 2nd edit., with additions, London, 1684.

1683   BLOME, RICHARD.   Cosmography and Geography. In Two Parts. The
First containing the general and absolute part of Cosmography and
Geography; being a Translation from that eminent and much esteemed
Geographer, Varenius, wherein are at large handled all such Arts as
are necessary for the true knowledge thereof. To which is added, The
much wanted Schemes, omitted by the Author. The Second Part, being a Geographical Description of all the World, taken from the Notes
and Works of the famous Monsieur Sanson, late Geographer to the
French King. To which are added, About an Hundred Cosmographical, Geographical, and Hydrographical, Tables of several Kingdoms
and Isles of the World; With their chief Cities, Des-Ports, Bays, etc.
Maps.   Fol.   London.

> Another edition, fol., London, 1693. This has in addition the County Maps of
> England drawn from Speed. It contains 61 maps outlined in colors, comprising
> one of the hemispheres, 10 European, 38 English, and 12 other foreign ones,
> and 3 astronomical plates. All the plates, with the exception of those of the
> English colonies, are large size and folded, and pp. 423-493 with 2 large maps
> are devoted to North and South America.—Maggs, No. 502.

MIEGE, GUY.   A New Cosmography, or Survey of the whole world, in
six ingenious and comprehensive Discourses; with a previous Discourse, being a new Project for bringing up Young Men to Learning.
8vo.   London.

> The author came to England from Lausanne in 1661, and was made ambas-
> sador extraordinary to Russia, Sweden, and Denmark in 1663. See also Miège
> under 1683, NORTH EUROPE.

1685 DUVAL, PIERRE (Sieur). Geographia Universalis. The Present State of the World, giving an Account of the several Religions, Customs, and Riches, of each People, the Strength and Government of each Polity and State, the curious and most remarkable Things in every Religion; with other particulars necessary to the Understanding of History, and the Interests of Princes. Written originally, at the Command of the French King, for the Use of the Dauphin, by the Sieur Duval, Geographer in Ordinary to his Majesty; made English by Farrand Spence. 8vo. London.

> 2nd edit., corrected and enlarged, London, 1691. Translated by the Earl of Dartmouth.—Bookseller's Note.

PEMBLE, WILLIAM. A Briefe Introduction to Geography, containing a Description of the Grounds and general part thereof. Very necessary for young students in that Science. 4to. Oxford.

> Another notice of this item under this date states that it is the 6th edition.

SELLER, JOHN. Atlas Minimus: or, A Book of Geography, shewing all the Empires, Monarchies, Dominions, Principalities, and Countries, in the whole World. 51 maps, including 12 of America. London.

> Seller, who was hydrographer to Charles II, published many volumes of maps of different parts of the world toward the close of the seventeenth century.

SELLER, JOHN. A New Systeme of Geography Accomodated with New Mapps of all the Countries of the whole World. With Geographical Tables. 25 double paged maps, all in colors, an hour dial with revolving disc, not colored, etc. In all 29 illus. London.

1688 BOHUN, EDMUND. A Geographical Dictionary . . . of all the Countries, Provinces, Remarkable Cities, Universities, Ports, Towns, . . . of the Whole World . . . with a short Historical Account of the same and their present State. Maps. 8vo. London.

> 2nd edit., London, 1691; 3rd edit., enlarged, fol., London, 1693; 4th, begun by Bohun and continued by John A. Bernard, London, 1695; again London, 1702; this last reprinted London, 1710. See below.

>> 1693 BOHUN, EDMUND. A Geographical Dictionary . . . continued, corrected, and enlarged with great additions throughout, and particularly with what ever in the Geographical part of the voluminous Moreri and Le Clerc, occurs observable, by Mr. Bernard. Together with all the Market Towns, Corporations, and Rivers in England; wanting in both the former Editions. Fol. London.

>> 1710 BOHUN, EDMUND, and BERNARD, JOHN A. A Geographical Dictionary representing the present and Antient Names and States of all the Countries, Kingdoms, Provinces, Remarkable Cities, Univer-

sities, Ports, Mountains, . . . begun by Edmund Bohun, since corrected, and enlarged with Great Additions, to which are added, the General Praecognita of Geography, and the Doctrine of the Sphere, . . . Fol. London.

1691 ECHARD, LAURENCE. A most Compleat Compendium of Geography, General and Special; Describing all the Empires, Kingdoms, and Dominions, in the whole World: Shewing their Bounds, Situations, Dimensions, Ancient and Modern Names, History, Government, Religions, Languages, Commodities, Divisions, Subdivisions, Cities, Rivers, Mountains, Lakes, with their Archbishopricks and Universities. In a more plain and easie Method, more Compendious, and (perhaps) more Useful than any of this bigness. To which are added, General Rules for making a large Geography; very necessary for the right Understanding of the Transactions of these Times. Collected according to the most late Discoveries and agreeing with the choicest and newest Maps. 2 maps. 12mo. London.

> 2nd edit., London, 1691; 3rd edit., improved, 16mo, London, 1693. See also Echard under 1792 below.

WYCHE, SIR PETER. The World Geographically describ'd in fifty-two Copper Plates. (Made up in cards and sheets.) London.

1692 ECHARD, LAURENCE. The Gazetteer's, or Newsman's, Interpreter; being a Geographical Index of all the considerable Cities, Patriarchships, Bishopricks, Universities, Dukedoms, . . . ; Imperial and Hans Towns, Ports, Forts, Castles, . . .; in Europe: shewing in what Kingdoms, Provinces, and Countries, they are in; nigh what River or Seas, . . . they stand; their distances from other places, with their Longitude and Latitude, etc. London.

> 2nd edit., corrected and much enlarged, London, 1693; later editions: London, 12mo, 1707; 8vo, London, 1716-18; London, 1724; 12mo, London, 1732; 8vo, London, 1744;—all of these enlarged to include Asia, Africa, and America. That of 1732 is said to be the thirteenth edition.

1693 GORDON, PATRICK. Geography Anatomiz'd; or, the Geographical Grammar. Being a Short and Exact Analysis of the whole Body of Modern Geography after a new and curious Method. To which is subjoyned, The Present State of the European Plantations in the East and West Indies. 16 maps. 8vo. London.

> 2nd edit., London, 1699; 3rd edit., corrected, 8vo, London, 1702; and so on to the 19th edit., London, 1749.

The Great Historical, Geographical, and Poetical Dictionary; . . . London.

> This is a general compendium taken from all sorts of historical, chronological, lexicographical, and geographical works.

1695 Thesaurus Geographicus. A New Body of Geography: or, a Compleat Description of the Earth: containing: I., By way of Introduction, the General Doctrine of Geography . . .; II., A Description of the known Countries of the Earth . . .; III., The Principal Cities and most considerable Towns in the World...; IV., Maps of every Country of Europe, and general ones of Asia, Africa, and America, fairly engraved on Copper . . . And also particular Draughts of the chief fortified towns of Europe. Collected with great care . . . by several hands. With an Alphabetical Table of all the Towns Names. Fol. London.

1698-1712 HUDSON, JOHN, DODWELL, H., and WELLS, E. Geographiae Veteris Scriptores Graeci Minores, cum Interpretatione Latina, Dissertationibus, ac Annotationibus. 4 frontispieces and 4 maps. 4 vols. (in Greek and Latin). 8vo. Oxford.

> The third volume contains the Supplement from Arabic writers. See Hudson under 1698, NEAR EAST.

1700 FER, A. D. A Short and Easy Method to Understand Geography. Wherein are Describ'd the form of Government of each Country. . . . With an Abridgement of the Sphere, and the use of Geographical Maps. Made English by a Gentleman of Cambridge. London.

> The date is approximate.

TEMPLEMAN, THOMAS. A New Survey of the Globe, or an Accurate Mensuration of all the Empires, Kingdoms, Countries, States, and Islands in the World. A collection of all the Noted Sea Ports in the World. The whole engraved on 35 copperplates. Obl. fol. London.

> The date is approximate. In Puttick and Simpson is cited an edition under 1776. See below.

> > 1776 TEMPLEMAN, THOMAS. A New Survey of the Globe; . . . Also the Settlements and Factories belonging to the English, Dutch, French, Portuguese, Spaniards, etc., in the East and West Indies, Africa, and other Parts. 35 plates. Obl. fol. London.

WELLS, EDWARD. For a Geographical Treatise adapted to the Use and Design of the maps referred to see his *A New Sett of Maps,* under MAPS AND ATLASES.

> To spare disappointment it may be stated that there is no such "Geographical Treatise," at least in the 1700 edition.

1701 MOLL, HERMAN. Moll's System of Geography, a New and Accurate Description of the Earth in all its Empires, Kingdoms, and States, illustrated with History and Topography, with Index to all the places mentioned, and a General Index of Remarkable Things; the Second

Part, containing the Description of Asia, Africa, and America, written in Latin by Joan Luyts, and English'd with large additional accounts of the East Indies and the English Plantations in America. Numerous maps. Fol. London.

> See Moll under 1711-1717 and 1739 below, and also under 1709, 1719, and 1732, MAPS AND ATLASES. Moll was an indefatigable maker of maps and geographies who came to England from Holland.

1703  CELLARIUS, CHRISTOPHORUS.  Notitia Orbis Antiquiae, sive Geographia Plenior, Ab ortu Rerum-publicarum ad Constantinorum tempora Orbis terrarum faciem declarans. Ex vetustis probatisque monumentis collegit, et Novis Tabulis Geographicis, . . . Adjectus est Index copiosissimus locorum & aliarum rerum Geographicarum. Numerous double page maps. 4to. Cambridge.

1704  S., M. Enchiridion Geographicum. Or, A Manual of Geography. Being a Description of all the Empires, Kingdoms, and Dominions of the Earth. 8vo. Edinburgh.

1708-1725  SENEX, JOHN.  Modern Geography . . . to which is added, the Geography of the Ancient World . . . 34 maps. Fol. London.

> Senex was one of the best known engravers of the eighteenth century.

1709  CHURCHILL, A., and J.  The Compleat Geographer, or the Chorography and Topography of all the known Parts of the Earth. To which is premised, An Introduction to Geography, and a Natural History of the Earth and Elements. Containing a true and perfect Account of 1st. The Situation, Bounds and Extent, Climate, Soil, Production, History, Trade, Manufactures; The Religion, Manners and Customs of People; with the Revolutions, Conquests, and other Changes, of all the Countries of the Earth. 2dly. The several Provinces that every Kingdom or State is divided into. 3dly. The Principal Cities, and most considerable Towns in the World. The Magnitude, principal Buildings, Antiquity, present State, Trade, History, etc. As also the Situation, with the Distances and Bearings from other Towns: Together with all the necessary Pieces of Natural History. The whole containing the Substances of at least 150 Books of Modern Travels, faithfully abstracted and digested into Logical Order; . . . To which is added, Maps of every Country, fairly Engrav'd in Copper, according to the latest Surveys and newest Discoveries; mostly engraved by H. Moll. Fol. London.

> 3rd edit., London, 1719; 4th edit., London, 1723.
> This work was printed for A. and J. Churchill, the compilers of a Collection of Voyages (see under 1704, COLLECTIONS), who very likely had a large hand in its editing. Some copies have a map of North America showing California as an Island in the "Pacifick."

A Geographical Description of the whole World; in a Pack of Cards: useful for all, especially Young Gentlemen. London.

1711-17    MOLL, HERMAN. Atlas Geographicus: or, a Compleat System of Geography, Ancient and Modern . . . with Discoveries and Improvements to this time, . . . Maps by Moll and Tables by Sanson. 5 vols. 4to. London.

>   Vol. III appeared in 1712; vol. V in 1717. There were at least five editions. See the one listed under 1747 below. See also under 1711, SOUTH AMERICA.

>   1717    MOLL, HERMAN. Atlas Geographicus: or, A Compleat System of Geography—Vol. V., America, containing what is of most Use in Blaeu, Varenius, Cellarius, Cluverius, Luyts, Baudrand, Sanson and the Royal Commentaries of Peru, with numerous Maps of North and South America, and the West Indies. 4to. London.

>   1747    MOLL, HERMAN. A Complete System of Geography, being a Description of all the Countries, Islands, Cities, Chief Towns, Harbours, Lakes, Rivers, etc., of the Known World, Situation, Extent, and Boundaries of the Empires, Kingdoms, Republics, their Climate, Soil, and Produce, principal Buildings, Manufactures, Religion, Government, Manners, Customs, and whatever is curious and remarkable in the works of Art, and Nature, extracted from several hundred Books of Travel and History. 70 maps engraved by E. Bowen (full page). 2 vols. Fol. London.

>   >   "This work extracted from several hundred books of Travels and History, is brought down to the present Time (1747). Preserving all that is useful in the fourth and last edition of the Complete Geographer."

1712    H., T. A Short Way to Know the World, or the Rudiments of Geography by T. H. 8vo. London.

>   This is written in the form of Questions and Answers. Part V deals with America and includes some curious statements.—Bookseller's Note.

1721    For the geography of the ancients see *Geographica Classica,* under MAPS AND ATLASES.

SENEX, JOHN. A New General Atlas, containing a Geographical and Historical Account of all the Empires, Kingdoms, and other Dominions of the World: with the Natural History and Trade of each Country. 34 engraved folding maps, each 23x20, including 8 relating to America, and 14 engraved plates containing 784 Coats of Arms of the Subscribers to the work. Fol. London.

1726    PASCHOUD, ——. Historical-Political Geography . . . of the several Countries of the World. 2nd edit., with additions. 2 vols. 8vo. London.

WATTS, I. The First Principles of Astronomy and Geography. Folding plates. 8vo. London.

1727 SALMON, THOMAS. For a general description of the world see his *The Modern History,* under GENERAL TRAVELS AND DE-SCRIPTIONS.

1730 FRESNOY, LANGUET DU (Abbé). A New Method of Studying History, Geography, and Chronology, with Bibliography (forming vol. II). 2 vols. 8vo. London.

> See also Fresnoy under 1747 below.

1738 MAUPERTUIS, PIERRE-LOUIS MOREAU DE. For his geographical measurement of a degree of the meridian at the Polar Circle see under 1808-1814, NORTH EUROPE.

> (The date—1738—of the first translation of this memoir came to the notice of the editor after vol. I had gone to press.)

1739 MOLL, HERMAN. The Present State of All Nations: their Persons, Habits, Arts, Sciences, Trades, Plants, Animals, and Minerals. 5 (?) vols. Engraved maps and plates on copper. 4to. Dublin.

> As Dublin seldom got the first printing of such works, this is probably not the first issue but Moll's *Atlas Geographicus* with wording of title changed. See Moll under 1711-1717 above.

1740 MARTIN, BENJAMIN. The Description and Use of both the Globes, the Armillary Sphere, and Orrery, exemplified in a large and select Variety of Problems in Astronomy, Geography, Dialling, Navigation, Sphereical Trigonometry, Chronology, etc. Also a New Construction of each Globe, by an Apparatus exhibiting the Phoenomena of the Earth and Heavens exactly as they are, and adapting the same to every Age of the World. 2nd edition, corrected and enlarged with the Addition of many useful Subjects; and an Appendix of Chronology, or the Doctrine of Time. Copperplates. 8vo. London.

> The date is approximate.

1743-47 BICKHAM, GEORGE. The British Monarchy; or, a New Chorographical Description of all the Dominions subject to the King of Great Britain . . . Folding map showing all the British possessions in America. Fol. London.

> A beautiful work published over a number of years. Practically every page contains one or more beautiful vignettes of scenery, famous houses, etc.—From Bookseller's Note.

1744  PURRY, JOHN PETER. A Method for Determining the best Climate of the Earth, On a Principle, to which all Geographers and Historians have been hitherto Strangers. In a Memorial presented to the Governors of the East India Company in Holland, for which the Author was obliged to leave that Country. Translated from the French. London.

1745  A Geographical Dictionary, containing a brief Description of all the Countries, Empires, Cities, Towns, Mountains, Rivers, Capes, . . . of the World, with their Situations. Translated from the French. 8vo. London.

> This title reads like that of Bohun's under 1688 above.

1746  HUBNER, ——. Introduction to the Study of Geography, in Two Parts, translated from the High Dutch, by J. Cowley. Folding maps. 12mo. London.

1747  FRESNOY, LANGUET DU (Abbé). Geographia Antiqua et Nova, or a System of Antient and Modern Geography, translated from the French with great additions and improvements, from Ptolemy, Strabo, Cellarius, etc. 33 maps engraved on copper. 4to. London.

1748  NEWBERY, JOHN. Geography made Familiar and Easy to Young Gentlemen and Ladies; being the Sixth Vol. of the Circle of the Sciences. 32mo. London.

1751  HARRIS, JOSEPH. Description and Use of the Globes. Folding plates. 8vo. London.

1754  SALMON, THOMAS. Salmon's New Geographical and Historical Grammar, wherein the Geographical Part is truly modern and the Present State of the Kingdoms of the World is rendered entertaining and instructive. Engraving and 23 maps by Jefferys. 8vo. London.

> Another edition, London, 1757, and again, London, 1772; Edinboro, 1782, and 13th edition, London, 1785. See also Salmon under 1756 below.
> Salmon was a traveller as well as a geographer; he made the voyage around the world with Commodore Anson in 1740-44.

1756  BLAIR, JOHN. Chronology and History of the World, illustrated in LVI Tabels, with 14 Maps, and a Dissertation of the Rise and Progress of Geography. Fol. London.

> Other editions: London, 1768 and 1779; with continuations, London, 1790, 1803, etc.
> Lowndes speaks of this work as highly valuable and highly useful.

A New Guide to Geography; . . . 2nd edit., improved and corrected. Map. 12mo. London.

SALMON, THOMAS. The Modern Gazetteer; or, a Short View of the Several Nations of the World. Absolutely necessary for rendering the Public New, and other Historical Occurrences intelligible and entertaining . . . the Situation and Extent of all the Empires, Kingdoms, States, Provinces, and Chief Towns in Europe, Asia, Africa, and America, . . . 8vo. London.

1757  DEMARVILLE, ——. The Young Ladies Geography, or Compendium of Modern Geography. Numerous colored maps. 2 vols. 8vo. London.

1759  A New Geographical Dictionary. 2 vols. Fol. London.

> See Barrow under 1763 below for the same title.

Universal Gazetteer. Description of the Empires, Kingdoms, Cities, Towns, Lakes, Mountains, . . . in the known World, with an Account of Produce, Revenue, Battles, and other Transactions which have rendered them remarkable. 4 maps. 8vo. London.

> 2nd edit., London, 1760.

1760  MARTIN, BENJAMIN (?). Gazetteer of the Known World. London.

1762  For the *American Gazetteer* see this date, under NORTH AMERICA.

BÜSCHING, ANTHONY FREDERICK. System of Geography, translated from the German. 36 maps. 6 vols. 4to. London.

> Of this work it has been said, though the minuteness of Büsching is generally tiresome and superfluous, yet we can pardon it for the accuracy of its details. —Lowndes.

1763  BARROW, JOHN. A New Geographical Dictionary, containing a Full and Accurate Account of the several Parts of the Known World, Europe, Asia, Africa, and America, their Revenues, Produce, Trade, Commerce, . . . Numerous copperplate engravings of costume, views, maps. 2 vols. Fol. London.

1764-65  FENNING, D., COLLIER, J., and Others. A New System of Geography, or, a General Description of the World, Containing a Particular and Circumstantial Account of all the Countries, Kingdoms, and States of Europe, Asia, and America. Numerous engraved maps, many folding, as well as views of the principal cities, etc. 2 vols. Fol. London.

1770  Description of the Four Parts of the World, viz., Europe, Africa, Asia, America. 12mo. London (?).

> A scarce chap-book.—Sabin.

GUTHRIE, WILLIAM. A New System of Modern Geography, . . . 4to. London.

> Frequently reprinted. It was also reproduced as: A Geographical, Historical and Commercial Grammar, etc. Sometimes the two titles were combined. Sabin cites a sixth edition under the first title as of 1795; a sixteenth edition under the second title as of 1796. See below for the full title of the 1795 edition.

> 1795 GUTHRIE, WILLIAM. A New System of Modern Geography, a Geographical, Historical and Commercial Grammar and Present State of the Several Kingdoms of the World, the Astronomical Part by J. Ferguson, containing the Planets, Situation and Extent of Empires, their Climates, Productions, Natural Curiosities, Natural History, Manners, Customs and Habits of the People, Science, Manufactures, etc., Table of Coins of all Nations, and a Chronological Table of Remarkable Events. 2 vols. 4to. London.

1773  WATSON, F. New and Complete Geographical Dictionary, containing Full and Accurate Description of the several Parts of the Known World, as divided into Continents, Islands, Oceans, . . . to which is prefixed Introductory Dissertation, with engraved maps and plates. London.

1775  PAVOLERI, J. New Geographical Tables, exhibiting at one view all Empires, Kingdoms, Climates, Cities, Religions, Languages, Curiosities, . . . (With movable honary circle.) 8vo. London.

1776  JEFFERYS, THOMAS. For a geographical description of America see his *The American Atlas,* under MAPS AND ATLASES.

For a gazetteer of North American and West Indian colonies see *The North-American and the West-Indian Gazetteer,* under NORTH AMERICA.

1778 MIDDLETON, CHARLES THEODORE. A New and Complete System of Geography, containing a full Description of Europe, Asia, Africa, and America; . . . Customs, Names, Genius, Tempers, Habits, . . . 120 engravings, maps, etc. 2 vols. Fol. London.

1782 MARTIN, WILLIAM FREDERICK. The Geographical Magazine; . . . of Asia, Africa, Europe, and America. 2 vols. 4to. London.

MILLAR, G. H. The New and Universal System of Geography: being a complete History and Description of the whole World, including all the valuable Discoveries in Voyages and Travels. Maps and 120 copperplates. 4 vols. Fol. London.

789 BANKES, T. (Rev.). A Modern, Authentic and Complete System of Universal Geography, containing a Genuine History and Description of the Whole World . . . Whole Sheet Maps forming a Complete Atlas. . . . Cook's Voyages and other Discoveries; The whole forming a Complete Collection of Voyages and Travels. Numerous engraved maps and plates. 2 vols. Fol. London.

> The date is approximate. An edition, London, dated 1790 and one dated 1791. See below. The maps were done by Thomas Bowen, the well known cartographer who died 1790.

> 1791 BANKES, T. (Rev.). Geography, Antient and Modern, including all the latest Discoveries from Columbus to the death of Captain Cook, a Genuine Guide to Geography, Astronomy, Navigation, the discoveries of Captain Cook, Byron, Carteret, Wallis, Forrest, . . . and an account of the Pewlew Islands and Botany Bay. Maps by Bowen and nearly 200 engravings by Grignion. 2 vols. Fol. London.

> > Date is approximate.

1791 A Short Compendium of Ancient and Modern Geography translated from the French by Mr. de Lanségüe. 8vo. London.

1792 MORSE, JEDIDIAH. For a geographical view of the American Continent see his *The American Geography,* under NORTH AMERICA.

1793 RENNELL, JAMES (Major). Elucidations of the African Geography. 4to. London.

> 2nd, 3rd, 4th Memoirs on the same, London, 1798.

1794 BALDWYN, G. A. A New Royal, Authentic, Complete and Universal System of Geography; or, a modern History and Description of the Whole World, containing new, full, and accurate descriptions of Europe, Asia, Africa, and America, including Voyages and Travels, . . . Numerous full page maps and over 100 copperplates depicting the various dresses of the inhabitants of different countries, etc. Fol.   London.

1795   D'ANVILLE, J. B. B.   A Complete Body of Ancient Geography.   13 large maps of Ancient Rome, Greece, etc.  Fol.   London.

1798-1800   PENNANT, THOMAS.   Outlines of the Globe.   Vols. I and II, The View of Hindostan; vols. III and IV, The View of India, extra Gangem, China, Japan, Malaya Islands, New Hollands, and the Spicy Islands, 3 folding maps and 23 engravings.   4 vols. in 2.   4to. London.

   This is sometimes found in four separate volumes.

1800   COOKE, G. A.   System of Universal Geography, containing an Accurate Description of Europe, Asia, Africa, and America, Description of the Inhabitants, Trade, Commerce, Customs, Ceremonies, Amusements, New Discoveries, Accounts of Early Travellers, Voyages and Travels, . . . Numerous copperplates and maps of America, Australia, New Zealand, South Seas, Africa, etc.  2 vols.   4to.   London.

   IBN HAUKAL.   The Oriental Geography of Ibn Haukal, an Arabian Traveller of the Tenth Century.   Translated from a manuscript in his own possession, collated with one preserved in the Library of Eton College by W. Ouseley.   4to.   London.

   RENNELL, JAMES (Major).   For the circumnavigations of Africa and other geographical matters see his *The Geographical System of Herodotus,* under AFRICA.   See also Rennell under 1788, EAST INDIES.

## ADDENDA

1858   HERODOTUS.   The History of Herodotus, a new English Version, edited with copious Notes and Appendices illustrative of the History and Geography of Herodotus, from the most recent sources of information, by G. Rawlinson, assisted by E. Rawlinson and J. G. Wilinson.   Maps and illus.   4 vols.   8vo.   London.

1873 BEVAN, W. L., and PHILLOTT, H. W. Medieval Geography, an Essay in illustration of the Hereford Mappa Mundi, 2 photographic reproductions. 8vo. London.

1887 SCHONER, JOHANN (Professor). A Reproduction of his Globe of 1523 long lost. With New Translations and Notes on the Globe by Henry Stevens of Vermont. Edited with an Introduction and Bibliography by C. H. Coote. Cuts and Facsimiles, and 3 folding Maps in Facsimile. 12mo. London.

1897 INDICOPLEUSTES, COSMAS. See his *Topographia Christiana,* under NEAR EAST.

1912 Book of the Knowledge of all the Kingdoms, Lands and Lordships that are in the World . . . Written by a Spanish Franciscan Friar in the Middle of the XIV Century; published for the first time, with Notes, by Marcos Jimenez de la Espada. Translated and Edited by Sir Clements R. Markham, K.C.B. 20 colored plates. Hak. Soc., ser. II, vol. 29. London.

1912-16 STRABO. The Geography of Strabo, literally translated, with Notes, by H. C. Hamilton and W. Falconer. 3 vols. 8vo. Bohn's Library. London.

1919 BADDELEY, JOHN F. For discussion of the progress of geographical knowledge of northern Asia see his *Russia, Mongolia, China,* under FAR EAST.

1931 BARLOW, ROGER. A briefe Summe of Geographie, 1540-41. Edited by Prof. E. G. R. Taylor, D.S.C. Hak. Soc., ser. II, vol. 69. London.

See Encisco under 1578, WEST INDIES.

# XIV

## Navigation

### I. The Art

(For a list of Treatises on the subject of navigation from before the time of Columbus to the reign of James I see Appendix A of the Hakluyt Society volume for 1926.)

1561 CORTES, MARTIN. The Arte of Nauigation, Conteining a compendious description of the Sphere, with the making of certayne Instruments and Rules for Nauigation, and exemplified by many Demonstrations. Written by Martin Cortes, Spaniarde, Englyshed out of Spanishe by by Richarde Eden. 4to. London.

> Frequently reprinted, with additions and corrections: London, 1572, 1579, 1584, 1589, 1596, 1609, corrected and augmented by J. Tapp, 1609, and 1615. Spanish original, Seville, 1551. See below.
>
> This work revolutionized the science of navigation and was the first to point out the deflection of the needle. Though in great demand in England after Eden's translation, all editions are very rare, and hardly any copies with both the folding map and the complete set of volvelles have survived.—Quaritch. It was translated at the suggestion of Stephen Borough, chief pilot of the Russian trade for the Muscovy Company, who made the masters of trade realize that the more universal experience of the Spaniards in navigation, their skillful use of the stars, their greater knowledge of making one's way over the sea must be utilized if English navigators were to compete successfully with Spain and Portugal. Early English expeditions had to depend very much on pilots from the Mediterranean lands. Eden wanted Englishmen to learn these secrets of land, sea, and stars so that they could pilot their own ships.

> 1551 CORTES, MARTIN. Breve Compendio de la Sphera y de la arte de navegar, con nuevos instrumentos y reglas, exemplificado con muy subtiles demonstraciones. With various revolving and other geographical and astronomical diagrams, including a full page map of America. Fol. Seville.
>
> > The work also contains notice of the discovery of Peru, the Strait of Magellan, Brazil, Rio de la Plata, Canary Islands, the Indies, etc.— From Maggs, No. 479.

1567 BOURNE, WILLIAM. An Almanacke and prognostication for iii yeres with serten Rules of navigation. London.

> New edition, 1571.
>
> The Rules were the prelude to a series of works popularizing scientific methods of Navigation and Survey. They were also the germ of his *Regiment for the Sea*. See below under 1574.

1574 BOURNE, WILLIAM. A Regiment for the Sea; Conteyning most profitable Rules, Mathematical experiences, and perfect knowledge of Navigation, for all Coastes and Countreys; most needful and necessary to all seafarying Men and Travellers, as Pilots, Mariners, Merchants, etc., exactly derived and made by William Bourne. 4to. London.

> Taylor states that this work was published in 1573; elsewhere it is generally listed under 1574. Reprinted, London, 1576(?), 1577, 1580, 1587, 1592 corrected by Thomas Hood, 1596 enlarged by Hood, 1611, 1620, 1631 (list cited by Parks); other dates met with are 1583 and 1628. See below.
> This is the best work of the day on the subject of navigation of the sea.— *Cam. Hist. Eng. Lit.*, IV, v. This work embodies the results of both reading and experience. It has to do with, among other things, a table of the Declination of the Sun, taking of position in the southern hemisphere, and especially with the variation of the compass. The success of the work probably encouraged Bourne to further books on navigation.—From Taylor. See Bourne under 1578 below.

1583 BOURNE, WILLIAM. A Regiment for the Sea; containing Necessarie matters for all sorts of Travailers; whereunto is added an hydrographical Discourse touching the five several passages into Cathay; corrected, and amended, by Thomas Hood, M.D., who hath added a new Regiment and table of declination with the mariner's guide, and a perfect sea card thereunto belonging; with figure. London.

1577 DEE, JOHN. General and Rare Memorials pertayning to the perfect Arte of Navigation. Annexed to the Paradoxal Cumpas, in Playne: now first published: 24 years, after the first Invention thereof. London.

> This is the general title of the whole work; the title of the first volume (all that got published) was the *Pety Navy Royall.* Vol. II, finished in 1576 and lost, was called Queen Elizabeth her Arithmetical Tables Gubernatick: for Navigation by the Paradoxall Cumpass and Navigation in Great Circles. Vol. III was finished and burnt (probably because politically dangerous). Vol. IV, called the Great Volume of Famous and Rich Discoveries, written in 1577. The great part— from chapter 7 on—is preserved in the British Museum, though badly damaged by fire.—Taylor. Dee played an important part in the general work of exploration of the day, and was adviser to a number of adventures overseas. He was a close friend of the great cartographers of Europe, and an advanced mathematician, who helped to make the country conscious of the close connection between mathematics, navigation, and cartography. For detailed accounts of his work and influence see Parks, 49-50, and Taylor, chapters V-VII. See also Dee under 1577, COLLECTIONS.

1578 BOURNE, WILLIAM. Inuentions or Deuices very necessary for all Generales and Captaines, or Leaders of Men as well by Sea and by Land. 4to. London.

BOURNE, WILLIAM. A booke called the Treasure for traueilers, deuided into fiue Bookes or partes, contayning very necessary matters, for all sortes of Trauailers, eyther by Sea or by Lande. . . . Numerous woodcut diagrams. 4to. London.

> The book is dedicated to Sir William Winter under whom Bourne served, most probably as a gunner on the Gravesend bulwark. The contents of the five books is explained in the dedication as follows: ". . . the fyrst is Geometrie perspectiue, the second Booke is appertainying unto Cosmographie, the thirde Booke is Geometrie general, the fourth Booke is Statick, and the fyfth and last Booke is appertayning vnto natural Philosophie . . ." In the second book chapters eight

and nine give the latitude and longitude and the length of the longest summer day of numerous places in America and the West Indies, . . . the concluding chapter of the fifth book contains the author's opinion as to how America and all the then newly discovered lands became peopled. He believed that America was part of the mythical island of Atlantis, and that the Atlantic Ocean was full of mud. . . . —Quaritch.

GUEVARA, ANTONIO DE. A Booke of the Invention of the arte of Navigation, and of the great travelles which they do passe which sail in gallies . . . Translated by Edward Hellowes. 8vo. London.

> Spanish original (place ?), 1539. Another Spanish edition, Antwerp, c. 1545. See below. The English version seems to have been translated from the latter.
> A very scarce and curious little work on navigation. The author, Antonio de Guevara, was the Bishop of Mondonedo and accompanied the Emperor Charles V on many of his voyages as Chaplain and Chronicler. . . . The ten chapters into which this . . . book is divided deal with the earliest legends regarding navigation, the first inventors of galleys and how they began their work; the dangers of navigation, and of the many philosophers who never ventured in the sea; . . . of the difficulties and risks run by passengers on galleys; . . . of the articles with which a navigator must be supplied on embarking in a galley.—From Maggs, No. 508.

> 1539 GUEVARA, ANTONIO DE. Aguja de marear y de sus inventores. (Place ?.)

> 1545 GUEVARA, ANTONIO DE. Libro de los inventores del Arte de Marear y de muchos trabajos que se passan en las Galeras. (Together with) Libro llamado Menosprecio de corte y Alabaça de Aldea. 2 works in 1 vol. 12mo. Antwerp.

>> The date is approximate.

1579 TAISNIER, JOANNES. A very necessarie and profitable Booke concerning Nauigation, compiled in Latin by Ionnes Taisnierus, a publike professor in Rome, Ferraria, & other Uniuersities in Italie of the Mathematicalles, named a treatise of continuall Motions. Translated into Englishe, by Richard Eden. 4to. London.

> On 3a Eden states: "By whiche description, some doo vnderstand that the knowledge of the longitude myght be so founde, a thyng doubtlesse greatly to be desyred, and hytherto not certaynely knowen, although Sebastian Cabot on his death bed tolde me that he myght not teache any man. But I thinke that the good olde man, in that extreme age, somewhat doted, and had not yet euen in the article of death, vtterly shaken of all worldlye vayne glorie." . . . The date has been conjectured to be 1577, but the British Museum Catalogue gives 1579.—From John Carter Brown. The "greatlye to be desyred" knowledge of the longitude was still being sought for throughout the eighteenth century. See Williams under 1755 below.—The Frenchman Taisnier was tutor to the pages of Charles V, and went with the Emperor to Tunis in 1535, later settling in Cologne. His work De Natura magnetis Eden brought home with him for translation.—Taylor.

1581 BOROUGH, WILLIAM. Discovrs of the Variation of the Compas, or magneticall Needle. 4to. London.

> The author was a navigator who sailed with his brother Stephen as a common seaman in 1553, 1556, and 1557, and made other voyages, one of which was an attempt to discover a passage to Cathay in 1568. He was vice-admiral to

Drake on the expedition to Cadiz in 1587, when he was put under arrest for questioning the latter on the wisdom of attacking Lagos. He commanded a vessel against the Armada. Accounts of his voyages are given in Hakluyt.—D.N.B.

MEDINA, PEDRO DE.  The Arte of Navigation, wherein is contained all the rules, declarations, secrets, and advises, which for good Navigation are necessarie and ought to be known and practised, made by master Pedro de Medina, directed to the right excellent and renowned Lord Don Philippo, prince of Spain and of both Sicilies.  London.

> Reprinted, London, 1595. Spanish original, Valladolid, 1545. See below. The Antwerp edition of 1580 was the copy which was found at Ice Haven, Nova Zembla, in 1871, left there by Barents in 1596.
> Medina, with Cortes, may be said to have been the founder of the literature of seamanship. He was entrusted by King Philip II with the examination of pilots and sailing-masters for the West Indies, taught navigation, and was held in high esteem as a cosmographer. This book was popular with the successors of Columbus, and was translated into several languages.—From Maggs, No. 508.

1545  MEDINA, PEDRO DE.  Arte de Navegar, en que se contenen todas las reglas, Declaraciones, Secretos, y Avisos, que a la buena navegacion son necessarios, y se deven sabar, Dirigida al serenissimo y muy esclarescido señor, Don Phelipe principe de España, y de las dos Sicilias. Fol.  Valladolid.

NORMAN, ROBERT.  The newe attractive, containyng a short Discourse of the Magnet or Lodestone.  Also certaine necessarie rules for the Art of Navigation.  Also a Discourse of the Variation of the Compas, by William Borough.  London.

> Reprinted, London, 1585, 1592, 1596, 1609, 1614.—Parks; also London, 1720.

1585  BLAGRAVE, JOHN.  The Mathematical Jewel, shewing the making, and most excellent Use of a singular Instrument so called: in that it performeth with wonderfull dexteritie, whatsoever is to be done, either by Quadrant, Ship, Circle, Cylinder, Ring, Dyall, Horoscope, Astrolabe, Sphere, Globe, or any such like heretofore divised: yea or by most tables commonly extant: and that generally to all places from Pole to Pole, . . . by John Blagrave of Reading Gentleman, and well willer to Mathematicks, who hath cut all the prints or pictures of the whole worke with his own hands.  London.

> An early book on mathematics. See Blagrave under 1590 and 1596 below.

TURNBULL, CHARLES.  A perfect and easie Treatise of the Use of the Celestiall Globe.  London.

> Reprinted, London, 1597.

1587 TANNER, ROBERT. A Mirror for Mathematiques . . . Contayning also an order howe to make an . . . Astrolabe. London.

> See Tanner also under 1592 below.

1589 BLUNDEVILLE, THOMAS. A Briefe Description of universal Mappes and Cardes . . . and also the Uses of Phtolomey his Tables. 4to. London.

1590 BLAGRAVE, JOHN. Baculum Familliare, a book of the making and use of a Staffe. London.

HOOD, THOMAS. The Use of the Celestial Globe in Plano. London.

HOOD, THOMAS. The Use of . . . the Crosse Staffe and the Jacobs Staffe. London.

> Reprinted, London, 1595 and 1596.

1592 DIGGES, LEONARD. Prognostication everlasting . . . where-unto is added by T. Diggs his sonne, A perfect Description of the Celestiall Orbes . . . also certaine Errors by him noted, usually practised in Navigation. London.

> Digges the son was a friend of Dee and a knowing man in mathematics and practical instruments.

HOOD, THOMAS. The Use of both the Globes. London.

TANNER, ROBERT. A Briefe Treatise for the Use of the Sphere. London.

1594 BLUNDEVILLE, THOMAS. Mr. Blundeuile His Exercises, containing sixe Treatises . . . 4to. London.

> 2nd edit., enlarged to eight treatises, London, 1597; 3rd edit., London, 1606; succeeding editions: 1613, 16—(?), 1622, 1636, 1637. See below.
> This was a very popular work. It was made up of several parts consecutively folioed, with separate titles to each part. This Elizabethan Norfolk squire is oftener mentioned for his books on horsemanship; his writings on which, his translations from the Italian, and his books on science show him to have been one of the numerous men of varied interests whom that wonderful age produced.—From Robinson, No. 19.

>> 1597 BLUNDEUILE, THOMAS. M. Blundeuile His Exercises, containing eight Treatises . . . verie necessarie to be read and learned of all yoong Gentlemen that haue not bene exercised in such disciplines, and yet are

desirous to haue knowledge as well in Cosmographie, Astronomie, and Geographie as also in the Arte of Nauigation, in which Arte it is impossible to profite without the helpe of these, or such like instructions

. . . The second edition, Corrected and augmented by the Author. 6 folding woodcuts and numerous diagrams throughout the text. 4to. London.

Of the seven or eight editions the sixth of 1622 is said to be the rarest extant, and the fifth is said to have disappeared entirely. The separate titles to the eight treatises are as follows:

A briefe Description of the tables of the three speciall right lines belonging to a Circle, called Signes, lines Tangent, and lines Secant . . . written by Maister Blundeuile, 1593. London.

A plaine Treatise of the first principles of Cosmographie, and specially of the Spheare, representing the shape of the whole world: . . . Written by M. Blundevill of Newton Flotman, Anno Dom. 1594.

A Plain description of Mercator his two Globes, that is to say, of the Terrestriall Globe and of the Celestiall Globe, and of eyther of them . . . Whereunto is added a briefe description of the two great Globes lately set foorth by M. Molinaxe: and of Sir Francis Drake his first voyage into the Indies (also Cavendish's circumnavigation) . . .

A plaine and full description of Petrus Plancius his vniuersall Mapp, seruing both for sea and land, and by him lately put foorth in the yeare of our Lord, 1592. In which Mappe are set downe many more places, as well of both the Indies as of Afrique, together with their true Longitudes and Latitudes than are to be found either in Mercator his Mappe, or in any other moderne Map whatsoeuer . . . A Mappe meete to adorne the house of any Gentleman or Marchant that delighteth in Geographie, and therewith this Booke is also meete to be bought, for that it plainly expoundeth euerything contained in the said Mappe. Written in our mother tongue by M. Blundeuill . . . 1594.

A very brief and most plain description of Master Blagraue his Astrolabe, which he calleth the Mathematicall Iewell. Together with the diuerse vses thereof, and most necessarie for seamen. . . .

A Nevv and necessarie Treatise of Nauigation containing all the chiefest principles of that Arte. Lately collected out of the best Moderne writers by M. Blundeuile, and by him reduced into such a plaine and orderly forme of teaching as euery man of a meane capacitie may easily vnderstand the same. . . .

A breife Description of vniuersall Maps and Cards, and of their vse, and also the vse of Ptolomy his Tables together with their true order of making the saide Tables, and of all other Mappes and Cardes as well vniuersall as particular, and that according to the doctrine of the best Geographers that be or haue beene in these latter daies. . . .

The trve Order of Making of Ptolomie his Tables, and also the making of all other tables Maps or Cardes, as well vniuersall as particular, and that according to the doctrine of best Geographers, . . . Plainely set forth in ovr natiue speech by Master Blundeuile . . . 1597.

DAVIS, JOHN.   The Seamans Secrets.   London.

> Reprinted, London, 1607, 16—(?). 1626, 1633; 8th edit., London, 1657. For fuller title see 1633 edition below.
> This work was very popular and managed to supplant Cortes' work (see under 1561 above) in favor.

> 1633   DAVIS, JOHN.   The Seamans Secrets. Divided into two parts, wherein is taught the three kindes of sayling, Horizontall, Paradoxall, and Sayling vpon a great Circle. Also an Horizontall Tyde-Table for the easie finding of the ebbing and flowing of the Tydes, with a Regiment newly calculated for the finding of the Declination of the Sunne, and many other most necessary Rules and Instruments, not heeretofore set forth by any. Newly corrected and amended, and the fifth time Imprinted.
> The Second Part of this Treatise of Navigation. Wherein is Tavght the nature and most necessary vse of the Globe, with the Circles, Zones, Climates, and other distinctions, to the perfect vse of Sayling. By which most excellent Instrument is performed all that is needfully required to the full perfection of all the three kindes of Navigation. London.

> The "Paradoxall Sayling" was doubtless based on the use of Dee's Paradoxall Compass, by which the master was enabled "to lay a course along a succession of rhumbs which would make an approximation to great circle sailing."—Quoted from Taylor. Davis had made three voyages in search of the Northwest Passage in 1585, 1586, and 1587. See under 1595, NORTHWEST PASSAGE.

1596   BLAGRAVE, JOHN.   Astrolabium vranicum general beinge a necessarye and pleasant solace and recreation for Navigatours in their longe Journeys contayning the vse (of) an Instrument or generall Astrolabe newly devised for them to bringe them skillfullye acquaynted with the Planettes and constellacions and their courses movinges and apparances called 'the Vranicall Astrolabe.'

> So entered in the *Stationers' Register.*

HOOD, THOMAS.   The Marriner's Guide set forth in the forme of a dialogue, wherein the use of the plaine sea carde is brieflie and plainlie delivered to the commoditie of all sorts as have delight in navigation. 4to.   London.

> This is usually bound up with Bourne's *Regiment of the Sea.* Hood edited later editions of Bourne. See Bourne under 1574 above.

1597   BARLOW, WILLIAM.   The Navigators Supply.   London.

> This Barlow was bishop of St. David's and brother to Roger Barlow (see under 1931, GEOGRAPHY).

1598   HOOD, THOMAS.   The Making and Use of a Sector.   London.

LAKEMAN, MATHIAS SIJVERTS.  A Treatyse very necessarye for all sea-faringe men, in the which by way of Conference between two Pilotes are many necessarye thinges disclosed; besides the most desired arte of shooting East and Weste, and the observacions of the sune, by Mathias Sijverts Lakeman alias Sofridus.  Translated from the Dutch by John Wolfe.  London.

1599  STEVIN, SIMON.  The Haven finding Art.  Translated from the Dutch by Edward Wright.  London.

> 2nd edit., London, 1610.  Dutch original, Leyden, 1599.  See below.

> 1599  STEVIN, SIMON.  De Haven vinding.  Leyden.

WRIGHT, EDWARD.  Certaine Errors in Navigation Detected and Corrected By Edward Wright.  London.

> 2nd edit., London, 1610; 3rd edit., with added material, 4to, London, 1657.
> Added to the third edition is the Haven finding Art of Stevin above.—Wright an eminent mathematician discovered the true method of projecting charts by increasing the distance between meridians, which is erroneously attributed to Mercartor.—Introduction to the Hakluyt Society volume 59 for 1878. In the Dedication the author complains that part of his works has been unjustly forestalled, another part stolen, and a third lately published by another in his own name. The preface is, in fact, a treatise on the art and progress of navigation.—Lowndes.

1602  BLUNDEVILLE, THOMAS, and GILBERT, WILLIAM.  The Theoriques of the Seven Planets, shewing all their diverse motions, and all other Accidents, called Passions, thereunto belonging . . . A Booke most necessarie . . . for all Pilots and Sea-men, or any others that love to serve the Prince on the Sea, or by the Sea to travell into Forraine Countries, . . . There is also hereto added, the making, description, and use, of two most ingenious and necessarie Instruments for Sea-men, to find out thereby the latitude of any place upon the Sea or Land . . . first invented by M. Doctor Gilbert, a most excellent Philosopher, . . . 58 engravings of instruments, diagrams, etc., and tables.  4to.  London.

> Gilbert published an excellent work on the magnet and its properties in 1600, which led Dryden to predict, in his epistle to Dr. Charlton, "Gilbert shall live till loadstones cease to draw."—Maggs, No. 585.

LINTON, ANTHONY.  Newes of the Complement of the Art of Navigation. And of the mightie Empire of Cataia. Together with the Straits of Anian.  4to.  London.

1605  POLTER, R.  The Pathway to Perfect Sayling.  London.

> This was written in 1586 but not published till 1605. The date is given as 1644 in the Hakluyt Society volume, No. 59, 1878, App. A. It has been called "an absurd little book."

1615 TAPP, JOHN. The Seaman's Kalendar, or an Ephemerides of the Sun, Moon, and most notable Fixed Stars; also rules for finding the Prime, Epact, Moon's Age, time of high water, and the Courses, distances, and soundings, of the Coasts of England, Scotland, Ireland, and France. And a Table of Latitude and Longitude of the principal ports, etc. Now enlarged with a new exact Table of the North Star, and of sixty-five of the principal Fixed Stars; their coming upon the Meridian, with their right ascension and declination; and a discovery of the long hidden secrets of Longitude. By H. Bond. And many other Rules and Tables very useful in Navigation. By H. Phillippes. 4to. London.

> This is the 5th edition. The book seems to have been a standard work. Tapp was a bookseller and a friend of Capt. Luke Fox, the explorer of Hudson's Bay (see under 1635, NORTHWEST PASSAGE). According to the D.N.B. he was the author of the Arte of Navigation, translated from the Spanish by Richard Eden and now "corrected" . . . by J.T., 1596. This refers to the work of Cortes (see under 1561 above). Another edition, 4to, London, 1679; again, London, 1696.

1616 BARLOW, WILLIAM. Magneticall Aduertisements: or Divers Pertinent observations, and approued experiments concerning the nature and properties of the Load-stone: Very pleasant for knowledge, and most needfull for practise of trauelling, or framing of Instruments for Trauellers both by Sea and Land. 4to. London.

> "Science is indebted to Barlow for some marked improvements in the hanging of compasses at sea, for the discovery of the difference between iron and steel for magnetic purposes, and for the proper way of touching magnetic needles, and of piercing and cementing load stones. Anthony à Wood endorses Barlow's statement that 'he had knowledge in the magnet twenty years before Dr. William Gilbert published his book on that subject' and adds that he was 'accounted superior, or at least equal to that doctor for a happy finder out of many rare and magnetical secrets.' "—D.N.B., quoted by Robinson, No. 19. See Blundeville and Gilbert under 1602 above.

1624 ASHLEY, JOHN. Speculum nauticum; a looking glasse for sea-men. 4to. London.

> Another edition, 1673. See below.

> 1673 ASHLEY, JOHN. Speculum Nauticum. A Looking-glass for Seamen; wherein they may behold how, by a small Instrument, called the Plain Scale, all nautical questions are very easily and demonstratively performed. Whereunto are added many new propositions in Navigation and Astronomy, and also a new way of Dialling; with an appendix containing the use of all Sea Instruments. 9th edit. 4to. London.
>
> > Apparently the labors of H. Phillippes and Wm. Leybourn were drawn on in this volume.

1625 HAGTHORPE, JOHN. Englands-Exchequer. Or, a Discourse of the Sea and Navigation, with some things thereto coincident concerning Plantations. Likewise Some particular Remonstrances, how a Seaforce might be profitably imployed. Wherein by the way, is likewise set downe the great commodities and Victories the Portingalls, Spaniards, Dutch, and others, haue gotten by Nauigation and Plantations, in the West-Indies and elsewhere. Written as an incouragement to our English Nation to affect the like, who are better prouided then any of those. London.

1626 SMITH, JOHN (Captain). An Accidence or the Pathway to Experience. Necessary for all Young Sea-men or those that are desirous to goe to Sea, briefly shewing the Phrases, Offices, and Words of Command, Belonging to the Building, Ridging, and Sayling, A Man of Warre; And how to manage a Fight at Sea. Together with the Charge and Duty of every Officer, and their Shares: Also the Names, VVeight, Charge, Shot, and Powder, of all sorts of great Ordnance. With the vse of the Petty Tally. 4to. London.

> An enlarged and rearranged edition under the title of A Sea-Mans Grammar, London, 1627; 2nd edit. of this new title, London, 1653; again, London, 1691. See below.
> The author describes the duties of all the officers of the ship as well as her timbers and sails, and adds many quaint illustrations of the use of sea terms, and the manner of working the ship and giving battle. The excellence of his maxims caused a great demand for the book.—Waldman. This is the Captain John Smith of Virginia fame. See under 1624, NORTH AMERICA.

> 1627 SMITH, JOHN (Captain). A Sea-Mans Grammar, With the Plaine Exposition of Smiths Accidence for young Sea-men, enlarged. Diuided into fifteene Chapters: what they are you may partly conceiue by the Contents. London.

> 1653 SMITH, JOHN (Captain). A Sea-Mans Grammar: Containing Most plain and easie directions, how to Build, Rigge, Yard, and Mast any Ship whatsoever. With the plain exposition of all such terms as are used in a Navie and Fight at Sea. Whereunto is added, a Table of the Weight, Charge, Shot, Powder, and the dimensions of all other appurtenances belonging to all sorts of great Ordnance. With divers practical Experiments in the Art of Gunnery. Also the Charge and Duty of every Officer in a Ship and their Shares: With the use of the Petty Tally . . . 4to. London.

1632 DELAMAIN, RICHARD. The Making, description and vse of a small Instrument called a Horizontal Quadrant. 8vo. London.

> Another edition, 1639(?).

1633 GELLIBRAND, HENRY. An Appendix concerning Longitude. London.

> This was subjoined to *The Voyage of Captain Thomas James, in the South Sea.* See James under 1633, NORTHWEST PASSAGE, and also Gellibrand under 1674 below.

1636   BEDWELL, WILLIAM.   The Way to Geometry, being necessary and usefull for Astronomers, Geographers, Land-Meters, Sea-Men, Engineers, Architecks, Carpenters, Paynters, Carvers, etc.   Translated from the Latin of Peter Ramus.   London ( ? ).

1642   SALTONSTALL, CHARLES (Captain).   The Navigator, or the theorie and practic Principles of the Art of Navigation.   Portrait of author by W. Marchall.   4to.   London.

1643   BLAEU, WILLIAM JOHNSON.   The Sea-Beacon, containing a Briefe Instruction in the Art of Navigation; and the Description of the Seas and Coasts of the Easterne, Northerne, and Westerne Navigation; Collected and Compiled together, out of the Discoveries of many Skilfull and expert Sea-men, by William Johnson Blaev, and Translated out of Dutch into English by Richard Hynmers.   Newly avgmented and corrected of many faults . . . Woodcuts, numerous copperplate sea-charts, and landscape woodcuts depicting "How these lands doe shew themselves at sea."   Fol.   Amsterdam.

1644   MANWAYRING, SIR HENRY.   The Sea-mans Dictionary: or, An Exposition and Demonstration of all the Parts and Things belonging to a Shippe: Together with an Explanation of all the Termes and Phrases used in the Practique of Navigation.   4to.   London.

> 2nd edit., London, 1670.
> Sir Henry Manwayring commanded the *Unicorn* in the Ship Money Fleet of 1636. He presented this work to the Duke of Buckingham when the latter held the position of Admiral.—Maggs, No. 508. The work belongs to the literature recording the advances made in scientific knowledge of navigation. The author helped to spread a knowledge of the practical things that concerned the sea profession, and he did so for the assistance of the gentlemen captains of the time, which was one of naval decay—the fleet of Charles I being greatly demoralized and mutinous. The book throws a side-light upon some of the short-comings of some of the cavalier officers.—*Cam. Hist. Eng. Lit.*, IV, v. The matter of the book is arranged alphabetically, in the manner of a glossary or dictionary.

NORWOOD, RICHARD.   The Sea-Man's Practice: containing a Fundamentall Probleme in Navigation, experimentally verified, . . . London.

> Another edition, London, 1712. See below.
> Various editions of this work were issued over a period of about a hundred years. As a young man Norwood was sent out to make a survey of the Island of Bermuda. He also measured, in 1633-35, the distance between London and York, "partly by chain and partly by pacing." From observations of the sun's altitude, he determined the difference in latitude of the two cities, and thus calculated the length of a degree of the meridian. His results were an excess of only about 600 yards. His chief additions to the art of navigation were his endeavors, as related in the above book, to remove one of the greatest obstacles, that of not knowing the true length of a nautical mile. His measurements gave 2,040 yards,

about 12 yards too much. He is also credited with the discovery of the "dip" of the magnetic needle.—Maggs, No. 585. In 1651 Norwood issued a work on trigonometry with reference to its use in the "three principal kindes of sayling."

1712 NORWOOD, RICHARD. The Seaman's Practice: containing a fundamental Problem in Navigation, experimentally verified: namely, touching the Compass of the Earth and Sea, and the Quantity of a Degree in our English Measures. With certain Tables and other Rules used in Navigation: The Latitude of the principal Places in England: the Variation of the Compass: The finding of the Currents at Sea. 4to. London.

1653 GUNTER, EDMUND. Workes, containing the Description of the Sector, Cross-staff, and other instruments: with a cannon of Artificial Sines and Tangents. Together with a new Treatise on Fortification. London.

Another edition, London, 1673. See below.

1673 GUNTER, EDMUND. Works. Containing the Description and Use of the Sector, Cross-staff, Bow, Quadrant, and other Instruments. With a Canon of Artificial Sines and Tangents to a Radius of 10.00000 parts, and the Logarithms from an Unite to 10000. The Uses whereof are illustrated in the Practice of Arithmetick, Geometry, Astronomy, Navigation, Dialling and Fortification. And some questions in Navigation added by Mr. Henry Bond. To which is added the Description and Use of another Sector and Quadrant, both of them invented by Mr. Sam. Foster, furnished with more Lines and differing from those of Mr. Gunter's, both in form and manner of Working. By William Leybourn. Numerous plates and diagrams. 4to. London.

Best edition of this eminent mathematician's works.—Lowndes.

1659 COLLINS, JOHN. The Mariners Plain Scale New Plain'd: Or, a Treatise shewing the ample Uses of a Circle equally divided, or of a Line of Chords and equal Parts, Divided into Three Books or Parts. . . . I. The first containing Geometrical Rudiments, and shewing the Uses of a Line of Chords, in resolving of all Proportions relating to Plain or Spherical Triangles, with Schemes suited to all the Cases derived from Proportions, and the full Use of the Scale in Navigation . . . II. The second shewing the Uses of a line of Chords, in resolving all the Cases of Spherical Triangles . . . III. The third Part shewing the Uses of a Line of Chords in resolving all the Cases of Spherical Triangles Stereographically that is on the Circular Projection with Dyalling . . . Of great Use to Sea-men. Folding engraved plate and numerous diagrams in the text. 4to. London.

Collins was the great authority of his period in the study of Mathematical Science.—Maggs, No. 585.

MOXON, JOSEPH. For works on astonomy and navigation see under GEOGRAPHY, especially the 1674 edition.

1660  NEWTON, JOHN.   Mathematical Elements, in III Parts.  The first, being a Discourse of Practical Geometry, the three Parts of continued Quantity, Lines, Planes, and Solids.  The Second, a Description and Use of the Coelestial and Terrestrial Globes.  The Third, the Delineation of the Globe upon the Plain of any Great Circle, according to the Stereographick or Circular Projection.  Engraved portrait and 14 engraved plates of Globes on stands, scales, diagrams, etc.   4to.   London.

> This relates partly to the science of navigation, with chapters on the Art of Navigation in General, Variation of the Compasse, Dividing the Log-line. Sailing by the plain Chart, Sayling by Mercator's Chart, etc.—Maggs, No. 508.

1661  PHILIPOT, THOMAS.   An Historical Discourse of the first Invention of Navigation, with probable Causes of the Variation of the Compasse; likewise some Reflections upon the Name and Office of Admirall.   4to. London.

1664  SERLE, GEORGE.   Dialling Universal.  Shewing by an easie and speedy Way, how to describe the Houre-lines upon all sorts of Plains in any Latitude whatsoever: Performed by certain Scales set upon a small portable Rvler.  The Second Edition furnished with these varieties. . . . with an Appendix: Shewing the Use of the Scales in resolving of the most useful Questions appertaining to Astronomie, Navigation and Geography.  Folding copperplates of scales, woodcuts and numerous diagrams.   4to.   London.

> This work supplies rules for finding the sun's azimuth, which had been wanting heretofore.

1669  LEYBOURN, WILLIAM.   Nine Geometrical Exercises for Young Seamen and others that are studious in mathematical practices.   London.

PHILLIPPES, H.   The Geometrical Seaman, or the Art of Navigation performed by Geometry; shewing how the Three Kinds of sailing, viz., by Plain Chart, Mercator's Chart, or a Great Circle, may be performed by a plain Rule and a pair of Compasses.   3rd edit.   4to.   London.

SELLER, JOHN.   Practical Navigation, or an Introduction to that whole Art; containing several Geometrical, Astronomical, Geographical, and Nautical, Definitions, etc.; Tables of the Sun's declination and true place; an Almanack of the Moon for eight years; the calculation of plain and spherical Triangles; the description and use of most Instruments in Navigation: with an Appendix of the Virtues of the Loadstone.   4to.   London.

> Later editions: London, 1679 and 1739.
> Seller was a compass maker.

STURMY, SAMUEL (Captain). The Mariners Magazine, or Sturmy's Mathematical and Practical Arts, containing the description, makeing, and use of the most usefull instruments for all artists and navigators. The Arts of Navigation at large, a new Way of surveying of Land, gaging, gunnery, astronomy, and dyalling, performed geometrically, instrumentally, and by calculable volvelles. Numerous engravings and diagrams, including the movable volvelles. Fol. London.

2nd edit., revised and corrected by John Colson, fol., London, 1679; 3rd edit., London, 1694. Swift is known to have used this work in Gulliver's second voyage.

WAKELEY, ANDREW. The Mariner's Compass Rectified: with an Appendix containing the Description of and use of all those instruments used in the Art of Navigation; with a Table of the Longitude and Latitude of Places. 8vo. London.

3rd edit., corrected, London, 1684; another, London, 1753 and 1789.

1670 NORRIS, RICHARD. Observation of the Tide, and how to turn a Ship out of the Straights Mouth, the Wind being Westerly. See Roberts, A., *Adventures of Mr. T. S., an English Merchant,* under AFRICA.

1671 BOHUN, R. A Discourse Concerning the Origine and Properties of VVind. With an Historical Account of Hurricanes, and other Tempestuous Winds . . . 4 copperplates. 8vo. Oxford.

This important book is one of the first in which the Aristotelian theories of the wind are compared with the monsoons, typhoons, trade and other winds of the world, of which the ancients knew nothing. The references to America are both numerous and interesting.—Quaritch.

1672 LEYBOURN, WILLIAM. Pan Organon, or an Universal Instrument performing all such conclusions Geometrical and Astronomical as are usually wrought by the Globes, Spheres, Sectors, Quadrants, Planispheres, or other the like instruments, yet in being, with ease and exactness in the practice of Geometry, Astronomy, Dialling, Geography, Trigonometry, Projection, . . . London.

1674 GELLIBRAND, HENRY. The Epitome of Navigation; Containing the doctrine of plain and Spherical Triangles, and their use and application in plain sailing, Mercator's sailing, and great Circle sailing; as also in Astronomy and Geography; and Rules for finding the variation of the Compass, and correcting the Course; together with the tables of the Sun's and Stars' right Ascension and Declination, of the Latitude and Longitude of places. Likewise a Traverse Table, a perpetual Almanack, and other things very useful in Navigation, as Logarithms, Sines and Tangents, and Canons.  London.

> Another edition, London, 1680.
> Gellibrand was a mathematician, and Gresham professor of astronomy, 1677; he was prosecuted by Laud for bringing out an almanack in which he substituted protestant martyrs for Romish saints, but was acquitted.—D.N.B.

OUGHTRED, WILLIAM.  Mathematical Recreations: or, a Collection of many Problems extracted out of the Ancient and Modern Philosophers: as, Secrets and Experiments in Arithematick, Geometrie, Horolography, Navigation, Chymistry, Water-Works, Fire-Works, . . . London.

1675 COLSON, NATHANIEL.  The Marriner's New Calendar; Containing the principles of Arithematick and Geometry, with the extraction of the Square and Cube root; also rules for finding the Prime, Epact, Moon's Age, times of High Water, with Tables for the same; also the Sun's place, etc., the Latitude and Longitude; description and use of the Quadrant, Forestaff, and Nocturnal; the Problems of plain sailing and Astronomy, wrought by Logarithms, and plain, and Gunter's Line with a Rutter for the Coasts of England, Scotland, Ireland, France, etc. with variety of other things for the benefit of the Sailors, and other ingenious persons.  4to.  London.

> Frequently reprinted: London, 1697; 4to, London, 1713 and 1716; 12mo, London, 1749; 4to, London, 1751; revised edition, Dublin, 1754. Included in the last edition cited is The Compleat Irish Coaster. See also Tapp under 1615 above.

1678 BOND, HENRY.  The Longitude Found, or, a Treatise shewing an easie and speedy way, as well by night as by day, to find the Longitude; having but the Latitude of the place, and the Inclination of the Magnetical Inclinatory Needle.  Since the first publication of it, some Needles were made so ill as not to answer expectations; but now such experiments have been made, before the Royal Society and many others, as have been to their great satisfaction; not only that the needles were well made, but that the Inclination agrees with that assigned in the Treatise. . . . London.

NORWOOD, MATTHEW.  The Seaman's Companion; being a plain Guide to the Understanding of Arithmetick, Geometry, Trigonometry, Navigation, and Astronomy.  Applyed chiefly to Navigation; and furnished with a Table of Meridional parts to every third Minute.  With excellent ways of keeping a Reckoning at Sea; also a Catalogue of the Longitude and Latitude of the Principal places in the World: with other useful things.  3rd edit., corrected and amended.  4to.  London.

NORWOOD, RICHARD. Norwood's Epitome. An Application of the Doctrine of Triangles in the use of the plain Sea-Chart, and Mercator's Chart: with Tables and Artificial Sines and Tangents, . . . Also Logarithms for one to a thousand, with the Tables of the Sun's right Ascension and Declination; and of the principal Fixed Stars; also an universal Almanack. Newly revised and corrected by R. Norwood. 8vo. London.

1680 Practical Navigation; being an Introduction to the whole Art. Containing Geometrical definitions and Problems; the doctrine of plain and Spherical Triangles; plain, Mercator, and great Circle sailing, etc.; the use of Instruments, Azimuth, Ringdialling Variation Compass, Forestaff, Quadrant, Plow, and Nocturnal, Plain Scale, Gunter's Scale, Civial Quadrant; the use of the Globes, Inclinatory Needle; the motion of the Sun and Stars; . . . With great variety of other matters, fitted for the capacity of all Saylors and others. London.

1682 PERKINS, P. The Seaman's Tutor, explaining Geometry, Cosmography, and Trigonometry; with requisite Tables of Longitude and Latitude of Sea-Ports, Traverse Tables, Tables of Easting and Westing, Meridian miles, Declinations, Amplitudes, Refractions, use of the Compass, Calendar, Measure of the Earth's Globe, use of Instruments and Charts, Difference of sayling, estimation of a Ship's way by Log and Log Line, Currents, etc. Compiled for the use of the Mathematical School in Christ's Hospital in London. 12mo. London.

> This is the first navigation class book used in the Bluecoat School, and has for a frontispiece a plate of "One of the Children Educated in Christ's Hospital." —*Cam. Hist. Eng. Lit.*, IV, v.

1684 RATCLIFF, THOMAS. A Pocket Companion for Sea-men: wherein is contained Plain, and Mercator's Sailing, by Vulgar Arithemetic and Tables ready calculated, fitted to the meanest Capacity. To which is added, The Whole Art of Gunnery, and Guaging of Vessels, measuring of Board and Timber, according to the best method. 8vo. London.

> Author was a "Mariner and Practitioner of these Arts above forty Years."

1685 BOTELER, NATHANIEL. Six Dialogues about Sea-services, between an High Admiral and a Captain at Sea, concerning, 1. The Commanders in Chief. 2. The Common Mariner. 3. The Victualling out of Ships. 4. The Names of all parts of a ship. 5. The choice of the best Ships of War. 6. The Sailings, Signals, Chases, and Fights. 8vo. London.

> Author was "lately Commander and Captain in one of his Majesties Royal Ships of War" (in title). The book had evidently been written some years before.

He was an experienced student of his profession, and had considerable knowledge of the internal economy of ships of war. It is one of the most interesting volumes dealing with the sea service that appeared within the century.—*Cam. Hist. Eng. Lit.*, IV, v.

NEWHOUSE, CAPTAIN DANIEL. The whole Art of Navigation; in Five Books, containing 1. The Principles of Navigation and Geometry. 2. The Principles of Astronomy. 3. The practical part of Navigation. 4. The Description and Use of such Instruments as are useful in taking Observations at Sea; and therein the use of a large new Sinical Quadrant, performing with more exactness than any yet extant, all Questions relating to Navigation, rendered as easie as to be understood by the meanest Capacity. 5. Useful Tables in Navigation: wherein those of the Sun's and Stars' Declination and right Ascension, etc., are newly calculated. The whole delivered in very easie and familiar Stile, by way of a Dialogue between a Tutor and a Scholar: approved by the ablest Mathematicians, and by his Majesties Command. 4to. London.

NORWOOD, MATTHEW. Norwood's System of Navigation; teaching the whole Art in a way familiar, easie, and practical, than hath been hitherto done: shewing the Projection of the plain Scale, the Sphere in plano, Astronomical Problems, Traverse Tables, right lin'd Triangles; geometrically by Tables of Sines, Tangents, Logarithms, and by Gunter's Rule, applied to plain, and Mercator, Sayling, etc., etc. 4to. London.

1686  ATKINSON, JAMES. The Seaman's new Epitome: containing the Doctrine of Triangles, both plain and special; with the use and application thereof in Navigation, viz., in Plain, Mercator's and Great-Circle Sailing; likewise in Astronomy and Geography and Rules for finding the variation of the Compass, and correcting the course; also to work an observation of the Sun, or Star to find the latitude thereby. Also a new Method to keep an exact Journal at Sea, more compleat than hitherto, a Table of Meridional parts, with their explanation and use; . . . Carefully corrected by James Atkinson, Teacher of the Mathematicks. 8vo. London.

> Later editions, 2 vols. in 1, with 6 engraved plates, Dublin, 1715, and 1725; Dublin, 1735; and 1739. A Supplement to make the Epitome a complete system of navigation, with folding plates, London, 1736; in 8vo, 1747. Revised and corrected by W. Mountaine, 8vo, London, 1765.

1688  SINCLAIR, GEORGE. The Principles of Astronomy and Navigation; or, A Clear, Short, yet Full Explanation, of all Circles of the Celestial and Terrestrial Globes, and of their Uses, being the whole Doctrine of the Sphere, and Hypotheses to the Phenomena of the Primum Mobile. To which is added A Discovery of the Secrets of Nature, which are found in the Mercurial-Weather-Glass, etc. As also a New Proposal for Buoying up a Ship of any Burden from the Bottom of the Sea. Edinburgh.

> Sinclair, a professor of Philosophy and Mathematics at Glasgow, was one of the first in Scotland who devoted attention to the study of physics, then held, as he laments, of little account. In 1655 he was associated with an unnamed experimenter, probably Maule of Belgium, the inventor of the diving bell, using the new invention in exploring the contents of the ship Florida, a relic of the Armada, wrecked on the Isle of Mull. He was also one of the first in Scotland to utilise the barometer, which he styled the baroscope, as a means of measuring altitudes and also the depth of mines, although he based his calculations on erroneous principles.—Maggs, No. 505.

1691 HALE, THOMAS. An Account of New Inventions and Improvements made necessary for England, relating to English Shipping, Naval Philosophy, etc. London.

1692 PARTRIDGE, SETH. The Description and Use of an Instrument called the Double Scale of Proportion, by which instrument all questions in arithmetic, geometry, astronomy, navigation, gunnery, etc., may be most accurately and speedily performed without the assistance of either pen or compasses. Folding diagrams. 8vo. London.

1695 BREWSTER, SIR FRANCIS. Essays on Trade and Navigation, in Five Parts. The first part. 8vo. London.

NARBOROUGH, SIR JOHN. The Mariner's Jewel, a dictionary of naval terms. London.

1698 SAVERY, THOMAS. Navigation Improved, or the Art of Rowing Ships of all Rates in Calms, with a more easy, swift, and steady motion than Oars can. Also a Description of the Engine that performs it. London.

1699 MOYLE, JOHN. Chirurgus Marinus, or, the Sea Chirurgion, being instructions to junior Chirurgie Practitioners who design to serve at sea in this imploy. London.

LOVE, JAMES. The Mariner's Jewell: or, a Pocket Companion for the Ingenious. Containing Decimal Arithmetick; Extraction of the Square Root; to know the Burthen, and how to rig a Ship, . . . proper direc-

tions for making of Masts . . . new list of the Royal Navy . . . Guide
for Pursers and Stewards . . . the most usual Terms at Sea explain'd,
etc. London.

> 2nd edit., 1700; another, 1724. See also C., J. under 1703 below, and Love
> under 1707 below.

1700  SENEX, JOHN.  A Pocket Book.  Containing several Choice Collections
in Arithmetic, Astronomy, Geometry, Surveying, Dialling, Navigation,
Astrology, Geography, Measuring, Guageing.  Illustrated with a Per-
petual Almanack, the Signs of the Zodiac, Fortification, four Maps of
Europe, Asia, Africa, and America, and a considerable number of
Tables, all engraved. 8vo. London.

> The date is approximate.

1702  JONES, WILLIAM.  A New Compendium of the Whole Art of Navigation; containing the elements of Plain Trigonometry, and its Application to Plain, Mercator's and Middle-Latitude Sailing.  Together with
the most Useful and Necessary Problems in Astronomy.  Also the
Method of finding the Variation of the Compass, working on Observation, the Reason and Use of the Log-Line, Allowances for Lee-way;
with new Tables of the Sun's Declination. Various diagrams. 12mo.
London.

> The author was the father of the celebrated orientalist, Sir William Jones.

MORDEN, R.  An Introduction to Astronomy, Geography, Navigation,
And other Mathematical Sciences Made easy by the Description and
Uses of the Coelestial and Terrestrial Globes.  In Seven Parts.  8 en-
graved plates. 8vo. London.

RENAU, D'ELISAGARAY BERNARD.  The Theory of Working
Ships at Sea. Translated by S. J. from the Original of D'Elisagaray
Bernard Renau. Folding plates shewing the manoeuvering of vessels.
8vo. London.

> The date is approximate.

1703  C., J.  The Mariner's Jewell, Or a Pocket Companion for the Ingenious.
Containing Decimal Arithmetick, Extraction of the Square Root, to
know the Burthen, and how to Rig a Ship.  With an Exact Method for
Gunners, Carpenters, Boatswains; whereby to know the Expence of
their Stores Monthly.  Likewise the Compleat Shipwright; with Directions for making Masts and Yards. Sea Terms explained; with Di-

rections how to work a Ship at Sea, With other things needful for Sea-
faring Men. London.

> See under Love, James, above 1700. This reads like an identical piece of
> work.

1703-05 DAMPIER, CAPTAIN WILLIAM. A Discourse of Winds, Breezes,
Storms, Tides, and Currents. In Vol. II. of his Voyages. See same
under CIRCUMNAVIGATIONS.

1705 JUSTICE, ALEXANDER. A General Treatise of the Dominion of the
Sea; and a Compleat Body of the Sea Laws: Containing what is most
Valuable on that Subject in antient and Modern Authors; . . . and Ad-
judg'd Cases in several Courts concerning Trade and Navigation. By
A. J. 2nd edit. 4to. London.

> 3rd edit., with large Additions, and Improvements. And a New Appendix. . . .
> 2 plates, 4to, London, 1707.

1706 BULL, DIGBY. A Letter of Advice to all Worthy and Ingenuous Merchants . . . and to all Ingenuous and Ingenious Artists in Astronomy,
Geography, and Navigation, shewing an exact, easie, and speedy way to
know the longitude of all places in the world where the European Merchants have their Agents to make observations. 4to. London.

1707 L(OVE), J(AMES). The Sea-Man's Vade Mecum: Containing The
most Necessary Things for qualifying Seamen of all Ranks, viz. I.
Vulgar and Decimal Arithmetick. . . . II. An exact Sea Dictionary.
III. What Winds will carry a Ship from one Port to another. . . . IV.
The Theory and Practice of Gunnery. . . . V. His Royal Highness
Prince George's Regulations of Officers. VI. A compleat List of the
Royal Navy. VII. Trigonometry, apply'd to Plain, Oblique and Mer-
cator Sailing. VIII. An Abstract of all the Acts of Parliament relating
to Seamen. . . . Figures in the text; portrait of Cloudesley Shovel.
12mo. London.

> See Love under 1700 above, and Mountaine under 1747 below.

1713 HARRIS, JOHN. The Description and Uses of the Celestial and Terrestrial Globes; and of Collins' Pocket Quadrant. 4th edit. 1 plate.
8vo. London.

1714 WARD, J. A Practical Method to discover the Longitude at Sea by a
new contrived Automaton, With an Account of the Author's new Instrument for taking the Latitude, etc. 12mo. London.

1718 STEELE, SIR RICHARD, and GILLMORE, JOSEPH. An Account of the Fish-Pool, consisting of a Description of the Vessel so call'd, lately invented and built for the Importation of Fish alive, and in good health, from parts however distant. A Proof of the Imperfection of the Well-Boat hitherto used in the Fishing Trade. The True Reasons why ships become stiff or crank in sailing, with other improvements, very useful to all persons concern'd in Trade and Navigation. Likewise a Description of the Carriage intended for the Conveyance of Fish by Land, in the same good condition as in the Fish-Pool at Sea. Woodcuts. 8vo. London.

1720 CORNWALL, HENRY (Captain). Observations upon several Voyages to India out and home; as also Remarks on the Ports and Places touched at in that Voyage; with some account of the Genius of the Natives and Inhabitants, their Customs, Laws and the Trade of the Several Countries. Illustrated with 61 curious copper plates, representing the several Harbours, Headlands, Rocks, Shoals, and Sands in the Places herein mentioned. Fol. London.

> A very scarce and curious work on Navigation. The author writes in his Preface, "Having sail'd many Years to East-India by the Help of Draughts and Books, which Experience shew'd me to be erroneous, I resolv'd to note those Errors, and publish this Book for a general Good." . . . Quoted by Maggs, No. 508.

1723 Navigation New Modelled, or a treatise of Geometrical, Arithmetical, Instrumental and Practical, teaching how to keep a reckoning in Latitude and Longitude without tables or instruments, together with all necessay tables, and the projection of the Sphere Orthographick and Stereographick. 2nd edit., with the addition of Spherical Trigonometry and Astronomy, by Henry Wilson. Many folding diagrams. 8vo. London.

1739 COMINE, WILLIAM. Improvements in Navigation and Philosophy, which contains: 1, Easy Method of finding the Longitude at Sea, also of finding the Latitude, etc. 8vo. London.

1743 SQUIRE, JANE. A Proposal to Determine our Longitude. Folding Plate. 8vo. London.

1744-48 HARRIS. For an account of Navigation see Introductions to his Collection of Voyages, the 1744-48 edition, under 1705, COLLECTIONS.

1747 MOUNTAINE, WILLIAM. The Seaman's Vade-Mecum, and Defensive War by Sea: containing the Proportion of Rigging, Masts, and Yards, weight of Anchors, sizes and weights of Cables and Cordage, List of the Navy. The exercise of the Small Arms, Bayonet, Granadoes and Great Guns, Duty of Officers, etc. Also shewing how to prepare a Merchant-Ship for a close Fight . . . Chasing . . . Defensive-fighting . . . Naval Fortification . . . Essay on Naval Book-keeping, etc. 2 engraved views of a ship and its rigging and 2 other plates. 8vo. London.

> Reprinted, 12mo, London, 1767 and 1783.

1750 BARROW, J. Navigatio Britannica: Or a Complete System of Navigation in all its Branches, both with regard to theory and practice. Containing Geometry, plane and spherical trigonometry, and the doctrine of the sphere; Sailing by the plane chart, etc.; the Nature of Currents, lee-way, variation, etc.; the Method of keeping a journal at Sea; etc. Folding plates. 8vo. London.

COLLING, JOHN. The Description and Use of Four several Quadrants, two great ones, and two small ones. With the Use of a Diagonal-Scale and Semicircle. Each of them accommodated with Lines and Circles, for the resolving of proportions instrumentally, in Chronology, Astronomy, Altimetria, Longimetria, Navigation, Dialling. 6 woodcut diagrams of sundials, etc. 4to. London.

1752 LOCKE, RICHARD (and Revised by an ingenius Mathematician). The New and Universal Problem to Discover the Longitude at Sea. Further explained and illustrated, in which is geometrically demonstrated, that not only the Longitude and course, but also the Distance run, is corrected by the same observation of Latitude and Distance run. . . . 8vo. London. (40 pp.)

1754 MURRAY, MUNGO. A Treatise on Ship-Building and Navigation; to which is added an English Abridgment of another Treatise on Naval Architecture, by M. Duhamel. Plates. 4to. London.

> A Plain, ingenious, and perspicuous treatise.—Lowndes.

ROBERTSON, J. The Elements of Navigation. Plates, maps, and various diagrams. 2 vols. 8vo. London.

> Another edition, 8vo, 2 vols. in 1, London, 1780.

1755  EMERSON, WILLIAM.  Navigation; or the Art of Sailing upon the Sea.  7 engraved plates of diagrams.  8vo.  London.

> 2nd edition, corrected and enlarged, 8vo, 1764.
> The work includes a table of sea terms and a table of latitude and longitude. —Maggs, No. 534.

WILLIAMS, ZACHARIAH.  An Account of an Attempt to ascertain the Longitude at Sea by an exact Theory of the Variation of the Magnetic Needle; with a Table of the Variations at Sea at the most remarkable Cities in Europe, from the year 1660 to 1680.  4to.  London.

> Williams "had long been known to philosophers and seamen for his skill in magnetism and his proposal to ascertain the longitude by a peculiar system of the variation of the compass."—Boswell.  He hoped to win the great parliamentary grant or reward offered for the successful solution of this long puzzling problem. Dr. Johnson, who had mastered his principles and experiments, wrote this pamphlet for him.  Williams was the father of the blind lady who lived under Johnson's roof.  The work was translated into Italian by Signor Baretti, according to Lowndes.

1757  HASELDEN, THOMAS.  The Seaman's Daily Assistant, being a Short, Easy, and Plain Method of Keeping a Journal at Sea, etc.  4to.  London.

> Other editions in 1769 and 1777.  For latter see below.
> The author was teacher of mathematics in the Royal Navy.

> 1777  HASELDEN, THOMAS.  The Seaman's Daily Assistant, Being A Short, Easy, and Plain Method of Keeping a Journal at Sea; In which are contained Rules Shewing How the Allowances for Leeway, Variation, Heave of the Sea, Set of Currents, etc., are to be made, and to correct the Dead-Reckoning by an Observation, in all Cases. . . . Diagrams. 4to.  London.

1759  News-Reader's Pocket-Book (The) or a Military and Naval Dictionary explaining the most difficult Terms made use of in Fortification . . . Navigation, Ship-Building, etc.  12mo.  London.

WILKINSON, J.  The Seaman's Preservative: or, Safety in Shipwreck. To which are added Admonitions and Precepts, to prevent, by various and easy methods, the diseases incident to Seafaring People.  8vo. London.

> Until Captain Cook's Second Voyage, scurvy was the disease most to be dreaded.

1769  FALCONER, WILLIAM.  An Universal Dictionary of the Marine: or a Copious Explanation of the Technical Terms and Phrases employed in the Construction, Equipment, Furniture, Machinery, Movements and

Military Operations of a Ship. Illustrated with original designs of Shipping with separate views of masts, sails, yards, and rigging. 4to. London.

> Later editions, 4to, 1771, with "To which is annexed, a Translation of the French Sea-Terms and Phrases." A new edition corrected, 4to, 1776. Again in 4to, 1784.
>
> An important, old naval work. This author is better known now for his celebrated poem The Shipwreck. He was purser to H.M.S. *Swiftsure* when he published this work.—Maggs, No. 508. He was lost at sea on the *Aurora*.

1772 MOORE, JOHN HAMILTON. The Practical Navigator, and Seaman's New Daily Asistant. . . . Exemplified in a Journal kept from London to the Island of St. Maries, and back again to Falmouth. 8vo. London.

> According to Lowndes, by 1814 nineteen editions had appeared.

1773 ADAMS, JOHN. The Young Sea-Officer's Assistant, both in his Examination and Voyage. In 4 parts. 4to. London.

> The same author also wrote a Treatise on the Globe, to which Dr. Johnson provided a Dedication to the King.

1774 CHAMBERS, W. The Universal Navigator, or a Comprehensive Treatise on Navigation. Charts. 8vo. London.

1777 HUTCHINSON, WILLIAM. Treatise on Practical Seamanship, with Hints and Rewards Relating thereto: Designed to Contribute something towards fixing Rules upon Philosophical and Rational Principles; to make Ships and the Management of Them; and also Navigation, in General more Perfect and Consequently less Dangerous and Destructive to Health, Lives and Property. 4to. London.

> 2nd edit., considerably enlarged, with 12 engraved plates of sailing vessels, etc., 4to, 1787.
>
> The author was a mariner and dock master at Liverpool.

WADDINGTON, ROBERT. An Epitome of Theoretical and Practical Navigation, containing a complete system of that art, greatly improved, etc. Folding chart and 4 folding plates of diagrams. 4to. London.

1780 For "many things useful in the Art of Navigation" see *The English Pilot* (*for Africa*) under NAVIGATION II.

1782 COOK, CAPTAIN, LIEUT. KING, and BAYLY, WILLIAM. The original Astronomical Observations made in the Course of a Voyage to the Northern Pacific Ocean, for the Discovery of a North-East, or North-West Passage. Plate. Published by Order of the Commissioners. London.

1783 HARRIS, JOSEPH. The Description and Use of the Globes, and the Orrery. To which is prefix'd, by way of Introduction, a brief Account of the Solar System. Folding plates. 8vo. London.

1792 MUDGE, THOMAS, JR. Narrative of Facts Relating to Time-keepers, for Discovery of Longitude at Sea. With astronomical Observations. London.

NICHELSON, WILLIAM. A Treatise on Practical Navigation and Seamanship, with Remarks, Observations, and Directions for Managing and Conducting a Ship . . . to make Ships, and the Management of them, and also Navigation in General more Perfect. Engraved frontispiece and 4 full-page engraved plates of ships. 4to. London.

Another edition, 1796. See Hutchinson under 1777 above.

1793 GOWER, R. H. Treatise on the Theory and Practice of Seamanship: Containing the general Rules for manoeuvering Vessels. By an Officer in the Service of the East India Company. Folding plate. 8vo. London.

1794 The Ship-Master's Assistant and Owners Manual, concerning Privateers, Ballast, Pilots, Slave Trade, and much other Practical Matter. 8vo. London.

1795 STEELE, DAVID. Seamanship, both in Theory and Practice. Engraved frontispiece and folding plates. 8vo. London.

1796 KELLY, P. Practical Introduction to Spherics and Nautical Astronomy, among other matter, the Discovery of a Projection for Clearing the Lunar Distances in order to find the Longitude at Sea. Folding plates. 8vo. London.

1800 The Ship Owner's Manual, or Sea-Faring Man's Assistant; Containing a General System of Maritime Laws. 8vo. London.

## II. Charts and Sailing Directions

1528  GARCIE, PIERRE.  The Rutter of the Sea, with the Laws of the Isle of
Auleron.  Translated from the French and printed by R. Copland.
London.

> Reissued 1536 (?), 1541 (?), and with the addition of a Rutter of the North,
> 1560 (?), 1565 (?) (said to be the earliest routier known: see Markham, Hak-
> luyt Society volume 1880).  Pollard gives the dates as 1555 (?), 1555 (?), 1555,
> 1560 (?).—Cited by Parks. French original, Rouen, n.d. See below.
> It is said that all succeeding rutters had their origin in this one. It is a book
> for pilots, showing the channels, soundings, shoals, routes and ports for ships ply-
> ing between England and France in the wine trade. Apparently it was a popular
> work. See also Taylor, p. 63, who explains that the "Laws of the Isle of Auleron"
> was a code of laws dealing with the sea dating from 1266.

> 1536  GARCIE, PIERRE.  The Rutter of the Sea, with the Havens, Rodes,
> Soundynges, Kennynges (an English measurement of 20 miles),
> Wyndes, Floodes, and Ebbes, Daungers and Costes of dyvers Regions,
> with the Laws of the Yle of Auleron and the Judgmentes of the See.
> 16mo. London.

>> Apparently this was the first book printed by Thomas Petyt. Cop-
>> land, the original printer, was a pupil of Wynkyn de Worde, and a
>> poet and translator.

> (?)  GARCIE, PIERRE.  Le Routier de la Mer iusques un fleuve de jourdain
> nouvellement imprimé a Rouen. Rouen.

>> Pierre Garcie was a shipmaster of St. Giles sur Vie (Vendée).
>> The earliest version extant in French is that dated 1542, but the work
>> must have been printed early in the century.—From Taylor.

1581  The Carde or Rutter of the Sea lyenge between Holland and Ffryselande.

> So entered in the *Stationers' Register.*

1584  NORMAN, ROBERT.  The Safegard of Sailers, or great Rutter (for
Northern Europe).  Translated from the Dutch.  London.

> Reprinted 1587, 1590, 1600, 1605 augmented by Edward Wright, 1612, 1640.—
> Listed by Parks. See below for title of 1587 edition.
> Norman, the translator, was a mathematical instrument maker and a writer
> on the compass.—D.N.B.

> 1587  NORMAN, ROBERT.  The Safeguard of Sailors: or Great Rutter. Con-
> taining the Courses, Distances, Depthes, Soundings, Floudes and Ebbes,
> with the markes for the entringes of sundry Harboroughs bothe of Eng-
> land, France, Spaine, Ireland, Flaunders, and the Sounds of Denmark,
> with other necessarye Rules of common Navigation. Translated by
> Robert Norman, Hydrographer. London.

1588  WAGENAER, LUCAS JANSZ.  The Mariner's Mirrour, together with
the Rules and Instruments of Navigation, first made by Luke Wagenaer of Enchuisen, and now fitted with necessarie additions for the

use of Englishmen by Anthony Ashley. . . . Heerin also may be understood the Exploits late atchieued by the Lord Admiral of England (referring to the pursuit of the Armada up the English Channel), and some former Seruices don by Sir. Fra. Drake.   Fol.   London.

> In two parts, with charts by Theodore de Bry, A. Ryther, Jodocus Hondius, and Joan. Rutlinger.—Lowndes. This was a popular work and was many times reprinted. A Dutch version, Leyden, 1584; first Latin edition, Leyden, 1586. See below.
>
> Luke Jansen Wagenaer was one of the most distinguished cartographers of the 16th century, and one of the first Dutch men to write on the subject of navigation. He was born at Enckuisen about 1550 and was brought up in the Merchant service. He published in 1584 an Atlas containing charts—the first proper Marine Atlas. The following year a second part was ready and the work republished with 44 charts. In 1586 several extra maps were added and a Latin edition, translated by Martin Everaerts of Bruges, was issued, probably for foreign circulation. The maps were accompanied with brief sailing directions, . . . According to Nordenskiöld, this work opened up a new period in the history of Marine literature. Owing to the great popularity and importance of the work subsequent Portulan Atlases were called Wagoners after the author's name. The charts comprise those for Holland, Southern and Eastern England, Eastern Scotland, Norway and the Baltic, Northern and Western France and Spain and Portugal.—From Maggs, No. 534. Sir Thomas Browne, writing to his son Thomas, a naval officer, says "Waggoner you will not be without, which will teach the particular coasts, depths of roades, and how the land riseth upon the several points of the compass."—Sir Anthony Ashley, the translator, had made the voyage with Drake and Norris to Spain in 1599. He was Secretary of War in the "honorable voyage unto Cadiz," and was knighted in 1596. He became Clerk of the Privy Council.—D.N.B.

1584 WAGENAER, LUCAS JANSZ. Spieghel der Zeevaardt van de Navigatie der Westersche Zee.   Fol.   Leyden.

1586 WAGENAER, LUCAS JANSZ. Speculum nauticum super navigatione maris Occidentalis confectum, continens omnes oras Maritimas Galliae, Hispaniae et praecipuarum partium Angliae, in diversis mappis maritimis comprehensum, una cum usu et interpretatione earundem, . . . 45 portulan charts and 1 revolving and 2 other diagrams. 2 parts in 1. Fol.   Leyden.

1589 BLUNDEVILLE, THOMAS. See his *Briefe Description of universal Mappes,* under NAVIGATION I.

1615 TAPP, JOHN. For material on courses, soundings, distances, etc., see his *The Seaman's Kalendar,* under NAVIGATION I.

1618 DAVIS, JOHN. A Ruter . . . for Readie Sailings into the East Indies. London.

> Davis made a voyage to the East Indies as pilot and captain.

1639 COLOM, JACOB. The first Part The first Book of the fierie Sea-Colvmne, wherein The Description of the Whole North Sea. With

Previlege of the High and Mighty Lords the States General, for twelve yeares. Amsterdam.

> The maps are not paged or numbered and legends are in Dutch only.—John Carter Brown. Another edition, with different title, London, 1640. See below. See also Doncker under 1699 below.

> 1640 COLUMNE, JACOB. The Fierie Sea-Columne, wherein are shewed the Seas, and Sea-Coasts, of the Northern, Eastern, and Western Navigation, manifestly inlightened, and the failings and mistakes of the former Light or Sea-Mirrours amended. London.

1643 BLAEU, WILLIAM JOHNSON. For a description of seas and coasts see his *The Sea-Beacon,* under NAVIGATION I.

1668 GOOS, PETER. The Sea-Atlas or the Watter-World, wherein are described all the Sea-Coasts of the Knowne World. Very Usefull and necessary for all Shipmasters, Pilots and Seamen, as allso for Marchants and Others. 40 portulan maps in contemporary coloring. Fol. Amsterdam.

> The exceedingly rare English issue of Peter Goos' famous portulan atlas.— Maggs, No. 549. Dutch original, Amsterdam, 1666. See below.

> 1666 GOOS, PETER. De zee-atlas, ofte water-weereld. Waer in vertoont werden all de zee-kusten van het bekende des aerdbodems. 40 charts. Fol. Amsterdam.

> > For a Dutch title very similar and of the same date see Doncker under 1699 below.

1669 CHILDE, L. A Short Compendium of the New and much Enlarged Sea-Book, or Pilots Sea-Mirror, containing the Distances and Thwart Courses of the Eastern, Northern, and Western Navigation, newly enlarged and amended, by several Experienced Navigators, and now for the Benefit and Encouragement of our Sea-men, translated into English, and calculated accordingly to 20 Leagues for a Degree. 4to. London.

> This may be an enlarged edition of the *Fierie Sea-Columne.* See Colom under 1639 above, 1640 edition.

1671 The English Pilot, with surveys by Jonas Moor and descriptions of Sands, Shoals and Buoys by Captain Gilbert Crane and Captain Thomas Brown, Leder Brethren of the Trinity House. London.

SELLER, JOHN. A Description of the Sands, Shoals Buoyes, Beacons, Roads, Channels, Sea-Marks, on the Coasts of England, from the South Forland to Orfordness; shewing their bearings and distances from the most eminent place on the Land, with the depth of Water on them as well as in the Channels between them. Being accomodated with a new and exact draught of the Sands, according to the said Description. Fol. London.

1671-72.  SELLER, JOHN.  The English Pilot. Book I.—Describing the Sea-Coasts, Capes, Head-Lands, Soundings, Sands, Shoals, Rocks and Dangers. The Bayes, Roads, Harbors, Rivers and Ports in the whole Northern Navigation. Book II.—Describing the Sea-Coasts, Capes, Head-Lands, Soundings, . . . in the Southern Navigation; shewing the Courses and Distances from one place to another; Ebbing and Flowing of the Tides and Currents; the Ebbing and Flowing of the Sea. Being also accomodated for the necessary use of Seamen, with Tables of the Sun's Declination, and an Ephemeris of the Moon, and a large Table of the Tides. Being furnished with new and exact Draughts, Charts, and Descriptions, gathered from the latest and best discoveries that have been made by divers able and experienced Navigators of the English Nation. 50 colored charts, and numerous woodcuts. Fol.  London.

> This work seemingly appeared under differing titles but with much the same stuff. See Seller under 1672 and 1675; Thornton under 1703; and *The English Pilot* under 1689 below. The latter is headed *The Fourth Part of the General English Pilot* and the former the *Third Part*. Seller was a general publisher of maps and hydrographer to the King.

1672  SELLER, JOHN.  The Coasting Pilot: containing a Description of the Sands, Shoals, Rocks and Dangers; the Bayes, Beacons, Roads, Channels and Sea Marks, upon the Coasts of England, Holland, and Flanders. With Directions for bringing a Ship to an Anchor in any Road; or to carry them into any Harbour on the said Coasts. Published for the better security of his Majesties Royal Navy in this present Expedition; and is very useful for any Masters and Pilots employed in his Majesties Service. Gathered from the practice and experience of divers able and experienced Navigators of our English Nation.  London.

1675  SELLER, JOHN.  Atlas Maritimus, or the Sea Atlas; being a Book of Maritime Charts describing the Sea-Coasts, Headlands, Sands, Shoals, Rocks and Dangers. The Bays, Roads, Harbors, Rivers and Ports, in most of the known parts of the world. Views, portraits of Drake, Rawleigh and other early navigators, and 20 two-fold maps including those of North and South America, the West Indies, etc. Fol.  London.

1677 BOURNE, WILLIAM. The Safeguard of Sailors; or, A Sure Guide for Coasters, describing the Courses, Distances, Soundings, Sands, Rocks, and Dangers: the Bayes, Rivers, Ports, Buoys, Beacons, and Seamarks, . . . upon the Sea-Coasts of England, Scotland, Ireland, France, Flanders, Holland, Jutland and Norway; also the Flouds and Ebbs, and setting of the Currents, with Directions for bringing a Ship into the Principal Harbours on the said Coasts. 3 folding charts, woodcuts in text. 4to. London.

> It has been conjectured that the author was a son of the elder William Bourne (see under 1574, NAVIGATION I). Even the casual reader of these titles cannot miss being struck with the generous way in which authors helped themselves to each other's phraseology.

1689 The English Pilot. The Fourth Book; containing Charts of the North Part of America, or Hudson's Bay, . . . Newfoundland, the Islands of Jamaica, Barbadoes, Bermuda, Hispaniola, . . . a General Chart of the West Indies, a new Map of Carolina, and Maps of Virginia, Maryland, Pennsylvania, New Jersey, New York, with Parts of New England. London.

> Among the later editions, all of which were much amplified by new surveys and discoveries, may be cited those of 1707, 1728, 1742, 1767. Naturally the later charts were much superior to the one cited above. Their range extends from Hudson's Bay to the "River Amazones." The 1767 edition, Dublin, which had its maps engraved expressly for it, differs materially from the London editions of the work, as it contains generally more minute particulars.

1682 RINGROSE, BASIL. The South Sea Waggoner. London.

> The date is approximate. Ringrose was one of the buccaneers that ravaged the Darien coast and shipping. He returned to England in 1682, but went back to his old profession and was killed in Mexico in 1686. His journal was published with Esquemeling's *Bucaniers of America* as the second volume. See Esquemeling under 1684-85, WEST INDIES.

1685 HACKE, WILLIAM (Captain). A Wagoner of the South Sea, describing the Sea Coast from Acapulco to Albemarle Isle. 148 colored portulan charts, illuminated and decorated, and descriptive sailing instructions written on them. Fol. Wapping.

> Gosse cites an edition of 1690. This one states the range to be from Acapulco to the Strait of Lemaire.
> For Hacke's compilation of voyages see under 1699, COLLECTIONS.—The author of this remarkable volume was one of the famous group of English buccaneers of the 1690-1710 period. . . . It was on the knowledge of South American harbors and ports gained by these men that Hacke bases his charts.—From Maggs, No. 549.

1699 DONCKER, H. The lightningh columne, or sea-mirrour, contaighningh the sea-coasts of the Northern and Eastern (and) Western Navigation. . . . As alsoo the situation of the Northernly countries, as Islands, . . .

Old Greenland, Spitsbergen and Nova Zembla, . . . With a brief instruction of the art of navigation. . . . 2 parts in 1 vol. 67 charts and numerous maps and figures in the text. Fol. Amsterdam.

Dutch original, Amsterdam, 1666. See below.

1666 DONCKER, H. De zee-atlas ofte water-waerelt, vertoonende alle de zeekusten van het bekende des aerd-bodems, met een generale beschrijvinge der selve. 32 charts in color. Fol. Amsterdam.

See Colom, 1640 edition, under 1639, and Goos under 1668 above.

1700 RALEIGH, SIR WALTER. A Discourse on Sea Ports, Principally of the Port and Haven of Dover, written by Sir Walter Raleigh, with useful Remarks, etc., by Sir Henry Sheere. 4to. London.

Reprinted in *Harl. Misc.,* IV, 1744.

1701 MOUNT, RICHARD. The Sea Coasts from Calais to Bayone, describ'd in 15 large charts, surveyed and printed by Order of the French King, copy'd from the original at Paris. 15 double-page engraved charts. Fol. London.

Another edition, London, c. 1715: again, London, 1730. See below.

1715 MOUNT, RICHARD. The Sea-Coasts of France from Calais to Bayone. Described in Fifteen Large Charts, Surveyed and Printed by order of the French King. From the Original, done at Paris, and the Remarks explained in English, and Published for the use of His Majesty's Royal Navy. 15 engraved double-page charts. Fol. London.

1703 THORNTON, JOHN. The English Pilot. Third Book, describing the Sea Coasts, Capes, Headlands, Straits, Ports, etc., in the Oriental Navigation. London.

Whether this forms part of the *English Pilot* begun by Seller is unknown to the editor of this bibliography. See Seller under 1670-71 above.

1704 SELLER, JEREMIAH, and PRICE, CHARLES. The English Neptune: or, a new Sea Atlas. Describing the Sea-Coasts, Capes, Head-Lands, Straits, Soundings, Sands, Shoals, Rocks and Dangers . . . 29 maps colored. Fol. London.

This seems to be another rewording of the *English Pilot* cited under 1671-72 above.

1722 BARLOW, E. An Exact Survey of the Tide, Explicating its Production and Propagation, Variety and Anomaly, in all Parts of the world; especially near the coasts of Great Britain and Ireland. With a Preliminary Treatise concerning the Origin of Springs, Generation of Rain and Production of Wind. 2nd edit., with curious Maps. 12 maps. 8vo London.

1728  Atlas Maritimus & Commercialia; or, A General View of the World so far
as relates to Trade and Navigation, describing all the Coasts, Ports,
Harbours, and noted Rivers, . . . together with a Large Account of the
Commerce carried on by Sea between the several Countries of the
World, as likewise Inland Trade by means of Navigable Rivers . . . to
which are added Sailing Directions for all the known Coasts and
Islands on the Globe, with a Sett of Sea-Charts . . . 54 folding maps
and sea-charts and 5 smaller diagrams. Fol. London.

> This atlas consists of two parts, with separate title pages. That of the Sec-
> ond Part reads: A General Coasting Pilot, containing directions for sailing into
> and out of the Principal Ports and Harbours thr'out the known World . . . by
> Nathaniel Cutler. The work was published anonymously, but it was probably the
> work of John Harris, John Senex, and Henry Wilson. It contains a full-page
> comment by Dr. Edmund Halley on the new globular projection, in which he says
> that in this Atlas the Projection is different from anything that has yet appeared,
> and gives it his approval.—Robinson, No. 32. This is said to be the first atlas
> on Mercator's projection.

1730  THORNTON, ——. A New and Correct Chart of the North Part of
America from New Found Land to Hudson's Bay. Engraved map,
17¼ by 22 in. London.

> The date is approximate. See under 1758 below.

1732  BOLLAND, RICHARD (Captain). A Draught of the Streights of Gibraltar, with some Observations upon the Currents thereunto belonging. In Churchill IV, 782-784.

> The date of these Observations is 1675.

1739  For directions to navigators in the West Indies see *A Description of the
Windward Passage, and Gulf of Florida,* under WEST INDIES.

1744  COLLINS, GREENVILE (Captain). Great Britain's Coasting Pilot, being a New and Exact Survey of the Sea Coast of England and Scotland, with the Setting and Flowing of Tides, Directions for the knowing of any Place, and How to harbour a Ship in the same with safety.
Numerous large charts, several of which have interesting views of
towns and places mentioned. Fol. London.

> Another edition, London, 1749.

1745  A Description of the Coast, Tides, and Currents, in Button's Bay, And in
the Welcome: Being The Northwest Coast of Hudson's Bay, from
Churchill River, in 58° 56′ North Latitude, to Wager River or Strait
in 65° 25′ taken from Sergt's, Crow's, Napier's and Smith's Journals,

made in the Years 1722, 1737, 1740, 1742, 1743, and 1744. Also, From
the Discoveries made in 1742, in the Voyage in the Furnace Bomb, and
Discovery, Pink, commanded by Captain Middleton and Captain
Moor; Shewing from these Journals, a Probability, that there is a
Passage from thence to the Western Ocean of America. 8vo. Dub-
lin. (27 pp.)

> This is doubtless a repercussion of the Middleton-Dobbs controversy. See
> Middleton under 1743, NORTHWEST PASSAGE.

1753  GREEN, J.  Remarks in Support of the New Chart of North and South
      America; in Six Sheets. 4to. London. (48 pp.)

      JEFFERYS, THOMAS.  Chart, comprising Greenland, with the Coun-
      tries and Islands about Baffin's and Hudson's Bays, New Britain,
      Prince William's Land, Straits of Dowis, etc. London.

1757  MEAD, JOSEPH.  An Essay on Currents at Sea; by which it appears
      that the Sea is not a Fluid in a State of Rest . . . but that the Currents
      of the Guiph of Florida, also on the Coast of Brasil, and the Northern
      In-draught on this Western Coast, are Currents in Circulation, kept up
      by different Densities in this Earth and its Motion round its Axis. 8vo.
      London.

1758  A New and Correct Chart of the North Part of America from New Found
      Land to Hudson's Bay. An engraved map 21¾ by 17 inches. London.

1759 (?)  Directions for Navigating the Gulf and River of St. Laurence, with a
      particular account of the Bays, Rocks, Shoals, etc. Founded on ac-
      curate observations and experiments made by the officers of H.M.'s
      Fleet. By order of Charles Saunders, Esq., Vice Admiral of the Blue,
      and Commander in Chief of the British Naval Forces in the Expedi-
      tion against Quebec in 1759. 4to. London.

1769  COOK, JAMES, LANE, M., GILBERT, J., GAUDY, J.  The New-
      foundland Pilot, containing a collection of Directions for sailing round
      the whole Island, . . . and part of the coast of Labrador. London.

      > Later editions, London, 1775 and 1784.

1772  BRAHM, WILLIAM GERARD DE.  The Atlantic Pilot. Calculated for
      the safe conduct of Ships in their Navigation from the Gulph of Mex-
      ico along Cuba and the Martieres, through the New Bahama Chan-

nel, to the Northern parts of his Majesty's Dominions on the Continent of America, and from thence to Europe. By William Gerard de Brahm, His Majesty's Surveyor General of the District of North America. 3 charts. 8vo. London.

1775 CALLENDAR, G. Nautical Remarks and Observations for the Chart of the Harbor of Boston. Composed from different Surveys, but principally from that taken in 1769, by G. Callendar. 4to. London. (11 pp.)

A Chart of the Gulf of St. Lawrence. Composed from a great number of actual surveys and other material regulated and connected by Astronomical Observations. 25 by 20 in. London.

Chart of North and South America, including the Atlantic and Pacific Oceans, with the nearest Coast of Europe, Africa and Asia. Arctic Regions. Fol. London.

DUNN, SAMUEL. The Navigator's Guide to the Oriental or Indian Seas. London.

> Dunn was an astronomer and mathematician and mathematical examiner to the East India Company.

JEFFERYS, THOMAS. An Exact Chart of the River St. Lawrence, from Fort Frontenac to the Island of Anticosti shewing the Soundings, Rocks, Shoals, etc., with Views of the Lands and all necessary instructions for navigating that river to Quebec. With inset maps of the Seven Islands, Passage from Cape Torment into the South Channel of Orleans Island, Road of Tadousac, and printed instructions for sailing up the river. 3x2 feet. London.

•JEFFERYS, THOMAS. The North-American Pilot for Newfoundland, Labrador, the Gulf and River of St. Lawrence: being a Collection of Sixty Accurate Charts and Plans, drawn from Original Surveys: taken by Captain James Cook and Michael Lane, Surveyors, and Joseph Gilbert, and other Officers in the King's Service. . . . Chiefly engraved by the late Thomas Jefferys, . . . on Thirty-six large Copper Plates. (Part II) The North American Pilot for New England, New York, Pennsylvania, Maryland, and Virginia; Also the two Carolinas, and Florida. Drawn from the Original Surveys, taken by Captain John Gascoigne, Joshua Fisher, Jacob Blamey, and other Officers. Fol. London.

> Reprinted several times before the close of the century, sometimes in 2 vols.

It was Cook's successful and accurate surveys of the St. Lawrence and off Newfoundland that led to his being put in charge of the expedition sent to the South Seas, which resulted in the British annexation of Australia.—Maggs, No. 491.

Sailing Directions for the North American Pilot: Containing the Gulf and River St. Lawrence, the whole Island of Newfoundland, including the Straits of Bell-Isle, and the Coast of Labrador. . . . 9 parts. 4to. London.

1776  HOLLAND, SAMUEL.  Charts of the Coasts and Harbors of New England.  Surveyed under the Direction of the Lords of Trade, by Samuel Holland. Fol. London.

1777-79  The Atlantic Neptune, published for the use of the Royal Navy of Great Britain by J. F. W. Des Barres Esq. under the directions of the Right Hon. the Lords Commissioners of the Admiralty. Maps, charts and colored views. 2 vols.  Fol.  London.

> Three more volumes complete this series of four sets of charts. These follow here:

> 1778  Charts of the Coast and Harbours in the Gulf and River of St. Lawrence, from surveys taken by Major Holland, surveyor-general of northern North America and his assistants, by order of the lords commissioners for trade and plantations in the years 1765-68. Composed and published by command of Government for use in the Royal Navy.

> 1778  Charts of the Coast and Harbours of New England, from Surveys taken by Samuel Holland . . . Together with several useful additional surveys, soundings, views, etc., taken by various officers on the spot.

> 1778  Charts of the several Harbours and Parts of the Coast of North America, from New York to the Gulf of Mexico.

>> The four series bound in 5 vols. imperial folio, 148 charts and colored views, of which a large proportion are in two states. The dates given for the complete collection are 1774-1781.
>> The most splendid collection of Charts, Plans, and Views ever published. The English Government spared no expense in order to make it a monument worthy of the nation. The book is extraordinarily difficult to collate, as there was no regular sequence, and no copies exactly agree.—Robinson, No. 41. For a detailed list of 136 items, see Quaritch Cat. No. 539.

1778  CHANDLER, J.  Coasting Directions for the North and South Channels of the River Thames: also Directions from Lowestoff-Roads to the Downs, and up the King's and Queen's Channels to London. To which are added, Directions for the British Channels from Scilly to the Downs: with a corresponding Tide-table. 4to. London.

1779 ROMANS, BERNARD, (and Others). The Compleat Pilot for the Gulf Passage; or Directions for sailing through the Gulf of Florida, or New Bahama channel, and the neighbouring parts. By Capt. Bernard Romans, Capt. W. Gerrard de Brahm (and others). 8vo. London.

> Another edition, 8vo, London, 1789; the Sailing Directions reprinted, London, 1794 and 1799.

1780 The English Pilot (for Africa), describing the Sea-Coasts, Capes, Headlands, Bays, Roads, Harbours, Rivers, and Ports: with the exact Appearances and Representations of the most Principal Marks, Lands, . . . on the West-Coast of Africa; from the Straits of Gibraltar to the Cape of Good Hope . . . shewing many things useful in the Art of Navigation. 19 large double-page maps (one of which includes North and South America), and numerous woodcuts in the text "shewing how the lands appear from the sea." Fol. London.

> See Seller under 1671-72 above.

HERBERT, WILLIAM, NICHELSON, WILLIAM (and Others). The New Directory of the East Indies. Containing I. The first Discoveries made in the East-Indies by European Voyagers and Travellers. II. The Origin, Construction, and Application of the Nautical and Hydrographical Charts. III. The Natural Causes . . . of the Trade-Winds, Monsoons, and Currents throughout the Indian Oceans and Seas, etc. IV. A Description of the Sea-Coasts, etc. V. Directions for Navigating, etc. The whole being a work originally begun upon the plan of the Oriental Neptune, augmented and improved by William Herbert, Mr. William Nichelson, and Others; and now methodised, corrected, and further enlarged by Samuel Dunn, Teacher of the Mathematical Sciences, London. 5th edit. 4to. London.

1782 JEFFERYS, THOMAS. Neptune Occidental (from the West India Pilot). A Compleat Pilot for the West-Indies . . . with their Bays, Harbours, Keys, Rocks, Land-Marks, Depths of Water, . . . Done from Actual Surveys . . . 25 engraved charts on 28 plates. Fol. London.

1784 The Atlas of Plates to Cook's Voyages, containing a large Folding Map, a Chart of the American Coast, and 59 Plates. Atlas Fol. London.

> The date is approximate.

ROBERTS, HENRY. General Chart exhibiting the discoveries made by Captn. James Cook in this and his two preceding Voyages, with the tracks of the ships under his command. 1 sheet. London.

> There were several editions of this map.

1785  RITCHIE, JOHN (Captain).  Directions for Sailing in the Northern Part of the Bay of Bengal.  London.

> Sailing Directions for the Coast of Chittagong, 1761, were published as an Appendix to Ritchie.

1786  STEPHENSON, JOHN, and BURN, GEORGE.  The Channel Pilot, comprehending the English and French Coasts from the Thames Mouth to the Bay of Biscay, with Sailing Directions from Observations and Actual Surveys.  25 folding maps engraved on copper, including the Tide Table, with movable Index of Tides.  Fol.  London.

1787  POWNALL, THOMAS (Governor).  Hydraulic and Nautical Observations on the Currents in the Atlantic Ocean, Forming an Hypothetical Theorem for Investigation.  Addressed to Navigators By Governor Pownall, F.R.S. & F.S.A.  To which are annexed some notes By Dr. Franklin.  Map.  4to.  London.  (17 pp.)

SAYER, ROBERT.  Catalogue of Pilots, Neptunes, and Charts, both general and particular for the navigation of all the seas and coasts of the universe.  8vo.  London.

1793  MOORE, JOHN HAMILTON.  Sailing Directions for the West Indies and Coasts of America . . . 8vo.  London.

Le Petit Neptune Français, or, French Coast of Flanders, Channel, Bay of Biscay, and Mediterranean.  To which is added, the Coast of Italy from the River Var to Orbitello; with the Gulf of Naples, and the Island of Corsica.  42 charts.  4to.  London.

RENNELL, JAMES (Major).  Observations of a Current that often prevails to the Westward of Scilly; endangering the Safety of Ships that approach the British Channel.  Chart.  4to.  London.

1794  CHURCHMAN, JOHN.  Magnetic Atlas, or Variation Charts of the whole terraqueous Globe.  4to.  London.

JEFFERYS, THOMAS.  Complete Pilot for the West Indies, including the British Channel, Bay of Biscay, and all the Atlantic Islands, done from actual surveys of the observations of the most experienced navigators.  29 engraved copperplates, with ships at sea, historical observations and profiles of the coast.  Fol.  London.

The Oriental Navigator; or, New Directions for Sailing to and from the East Indies. Also for the use of the country ships, trading in the Indian and China Seas; to New Holland, etc., collected from Manuscripts, Journals, Memoirs and Observations of the most experienced Officers in the Hon. East India Company's service. 4to. London.

1795 MALHAM, J. The Naval Gazetteer, or Seaman's complete Guide, containing full and accurate Account, alphabetically arranged, of the several Coasts of all Countries and Islands in the known World, with description of Bays, Capes, Channels, Currents, Harbours, Tides, etc. Set of folding charts. 2 vols. 8vo. London.

1798 ARROWSMITH, AARON. Charts of the Pacific Ocean (in 9 sheets) drawn from a great number of printed and MS. Journals; (with) Reduced Chart of the Pacific Ocean from the one published in 9 sheets. 10 sheets. Fol. London.

> This shows the navigators' routes, including those of Cook's three voyages. —*Cook Bibliog.*

1799 DALZEL, ARCHIBALD. New Sailing Directions for the Coast of Africa. London.

1800 CHANDLER, J., DISTON, J., EUNSON, G., and ADAMS, J. The New Seaman's Guide and Coaster's Companion, containing Sailing Directions, Magnetic Courses, Tables of Latitude and Longitude, etc. 8vo. London.

The Oriental Navigator, being a necessary Companion to the complete East India Pilot, in two large volumes of Charts and Plates. 4to. London.

## ADDENDA

1897 For a history of charts and early sailing directions see Nordenskiöld, *Periplus,* under GENERAL REFERENCE.

# XV

## Maps And Atlases

### A Selected Cartography

(The history of cartography as illustrating the progress of geographical knowledge is a forbidden field to any but the inner circle of specialists. Therefore the selected cartography listed in this section maintains a respectful silence on the famous maps of the fifteenth and sixteenth centuries and contents itself with referring the curious to A. E. Nordenskiöld's *Facsimile Atlas to the Early History of Cartography* (Stockholm, 1889), which is regarded as being well-nigh exhaustive in its treatment. What the reader will find below is a random selection from the common run of publications, sufficient, however, it is believed, to evidence the intensely active desire of English cosmographers to keep pace with the discoveries of English navigators. As nearly all the works cited in these two volumes contain maps, it was thought futile to load these pages with repeated cross references.)

1572 MUNSTER, SEBASTIAN. For comment on Munster as a cosmographer see *Cosmographia Universalis,* under GEOGRAPHY.

1602 ORTELIUS, ABRAHAM. For his famous work dealing with maps see his *Epitome of the Theatre of the Worlde,* under GEOGRAPHY.

1589 BLUNDEVILLE, THOMAS. See his *A Briefe Description of universal Mappes and Cardes,* under NAVIGATION I.

1627 SPEED, JOHN. For a large collection of maps see his *The Theatre of the Empire of Great Britaine* and his *A Prospect of the Most Famous Parts of the VVorld* under this date and that of 1631, GEOGRAPHY.

1635 MERCATOR, GERARDUS. For his pioneer work in modern mapping see his *Historia Mundi,* under GEOGRAPHY.

1640-1679 SANSON, NICOLAS, (and others). A Unique Collection of 312 large double-page Maps of the World. The Heavens, the Continents, Countries, Empires, Monarchies, Republics, etc., also Maps illustrating St. Paul's Journeys, The Voyage of Aeneas, The Expeditions of Alexander the Great, and a series of Maps of the Dioceses of France, engraved on copper, with the coasts and boundaries outlined in various colors by hand, many maps having their titles in fine decorative and emblematic borders, with coats-of-arms, crests, etc., the majority engraved by Nicholas Sanson, and the remainder by his son, G. Sanson, Tavernier, De La Rue, and others. 2 vols. Fol. Paris (n.d. and 1640-1679).

Not being an English work this item does not properly fall within the limits of this bibliography. It is cited here, however, to bring to notice the workmanship of one of the most famous map-engravers of France, N. Sanson. Besides, the title illustrates the happy custom of the times to collect in one volume scattered single maps, whose existence otherwise would have been rather ephemeral.

1668  A Map of the Whole World; or the Orb Terrestrial, in Four Parts, Asia, Europe, Affrica, America. 4to. London.

The descriptive text to this map runs to 193 pp., and makes the work a geography. See L., D. under 1676 below.

1672  MORDEN, ROBERT.  A Map of the Seventeen Provinces, in which the situation and distance of the principal Cities, Towns, Rivers, Castles, and other remarkable places are exactly described. All which, with much care and diligence, was Collected from the large Provincial Maps by Rob. Morden at the Atlas in Cornhill; and by William Berry, . . . London.

Morden was one of those publisher cosmographers, who, along with Senex, Blome, Moxon, Seller, Bohun, Moll, etc., kept the seventeenth century presses busy with issues and reissues of maps and geographies.

A New Map of all the World, drawn according to the best descriptions and latest discoveries that have been made by Englishmen or Strangers. Together with apt descriptions down the sides, teaching the use of it and other Maps. 4 feet in length and above 3 feet in depth. London.

1673  MOXON, JOSEPH.  The English Empire in America described in a Map, containing six foot in length and four foot and a half in depth, beginning Eastward at Newfoundland, and proceeding Westwards to New Scotland, New England, New York, New Jersey, Maryland, Virginia, Carolina; all contiguous to each other on the Continent: together with the Islands of New Providence, Jamaica, . . . Tobago, etc. With pertinent Descriptions, down the sides and under the Map, declaring the Nature of the Soil in each Country, the Product, Commodities, and Strength, of each place; the Policies, Laws, Customs, and Manner of living, etc. London.

A New Map of the Trading Part of America, both Continent and Islands; shewing also the excellent situation of Isthmus and Panama, and the Island of Jamaica for trade, or design, beyond all other parts of India. London.

1676  GARRETT, JOHN.  A Book of Maps exactly describing Europe, both the present as now it standeth, and the antient State thereof, with the

Distribution of Places, and original names of Kingdoms, Provences, Islands, Rivers, Cities, etc. Being very necessary to the furtherance, help, and light, of the pleasant and profitable study of Histories, Ecclesiastical, Poetical, or Chronological. General map and 11 others. London.

L., D.   A Most Exact and Accurate Map of the whole world, or the Orb Terrestrial described in four plain Maps, viz. Asia, Europe, Africa, America; containing all the known and most remarkable Capes, Ports, Bays, Isles, etc. Together with their Situation, Commodities, . . . : and a new and exact Geography, especially their Longitudes and Latitudes in Alphabetical order, and fitted to all Capacities. 4to. London.

1680  BERRY, WILLIAM.   A Collection of Twenty Maps by William Berry, including Three of America. All colored. Fol. London.

> The date is approximate.

A Map of North America divided into its Principal Parts, where are distinguished the Severall States which belong to the English, Spanish and French. Boundaries in color. London.

> The date is approximate.

MORDEN, ROBERT.   Atlas Terrestris, containing 78 double-page maps, engraved on copper, rivers and outlines colored. 6 by 6¼ in. 8vo. London.

> In this California is shown as an island.

1685  SELLER, JOHN.   Atlas Terrestris: or a Book of Mapps, of all the Empires, Monarchies, Kingdoms, Regions, Dominions, Principalities, and Countreys in the Whole World accomodated with a Brief Description of each particular Country. With engraved border to title bearing portraits of Davies, Raleigh, Willoughby, Smith, Drake, and Cavendish and at foot a view of old London, etc., and 24 double-page maps, mostly colored, including several American maps. Fol. London.

> The date is approximate.

1696-1733  POPPLE, HENRY.   A Map (colored) of the British Empire in America, with the French and Spanish Settlements Adjacent, and Four Small Inset Views of New York, Quebec, etc. 20 by 20½ in. Included in an Atlas of Sixty-Seven Maps of Europe and Asia, by Vischer, Allard, Wilson, Silva, De Wit, and others. Fol. London (?).

This is another collection of heterogenous maps published over a run of years. Most of the engravers are from the continent of Europe.

1699 A New Atlas; or Travels and Voyages in Europe, Asia, and America, through the most renowned parts of the World, performed by an English Gentleman in nine years. 8vo. London.

This title shows a curious misuse of the term Atlas, which since Mercator introduced it, has been restricted to a collection of maps in book form and has stood its ground against the attempts to employ Theatre, Speculum or Mirror, Geographia, Cosmographia, and Chorographia in its place. The work listed above is printed in fuller title under GENERAL TRAVELS AND DESCRIPTIONS this date.

1700 A New Map of North America shewing its Principal Divisions, Chief Cities, Townes, Rivers, Mountains, etc. 19¾ by 14¾ in. Oxford.

This was probably issued by Edward Wells.

A New Map of South America Shewing its General Divisions, Chief Cities & Townes; Rivers, Mountains, etc. 19¾ by 15 in. Oxford.

A New Map of the terraqueous globe according to the latest discoveries and the most General Divisions of it, into Continents and Oceans. 20¼ by 14¾ in. Oxford.

SELLER, JOHN. America. 28 copperplate maps. London.

The date is approximate. This item is cited by Sabin who refers the reader to Stevens' "Nuggets," No. 2447.

WELLS, EDWARD. A New Map of the most Considerable Plantations Of the English in America Dedicated to his Highness William Duke of Gloucester. 19¼ by 14½ in. Oxford.

The main engraving depicts New England, New York, New Jersey, Pennsylvania, Maryland, and Virginia. There are inset maps of Carolina, Nova Scotia, Jamaica, the Bermudas and Barbadoes.—Quaritch.

WELLS, EDWARD. A New Map of the East Indies, Taken from Mr. de Fer's Map of Asia, shewing their chief Divisions, Cities, Towns, Ports, Rivers, Mountains, etc. 19½ by 14½ in. Oxford.

To the East are depicted the Philippines and the Molucca Islands.—Quaritch.

WELLS, EDWARD.  A New Sett of Maps, both of antient and present geography: together with a Geographical Treatise particularly adapted to the Use and Design of these Maps.  47 large maps, including three of America.  Fol.  Oxford.

> As stated in a note to this item under GEOGRAPHY, there is no "Geographical Treatise." Another edition, with 41 maps, London (?) 1722; again, London, 1730.

WELLS, EDWARD.  Present Asia Distinguisht into its general Divisions or Countries together with their Capital Cities, chief Rivers, Mountains, &c.  20¼ by 14¾ in.  Oxford.

> Showing to the East the Pacific, "Companies Land," the Philippines and the Moluccas.—Quaritch. These maps published by Wells are all dedicated to the Duke of Gloucester and are engraved by different artists.

1702  BOYER, ——.  The Draughts of the most remarkable fortified Towns of Europe, in 44 Copper-plates; with a Geographical Description of them, and the History of the Sieges they have sustained, and the Revolutions they have undergone, for above the 100 Years past.  To which is prefixed, An Introduction to Military Architecture, or Fortification; . . . A Book very useful to all Gentlemen and Officers in the Army.  London.

1703  ALLINGHAM, WILLIAM.  A Short Account of the Nature and Use of Maps; as also some Short Discourses of the Division of the Earth into Zones, Climates, and Parallels, with the properties of the several inhabitants thereof.  To which is subjoined, A Catalogue of the Factories and Places now in possession of the English, French, Dutch, Spanish, Portuguese, and Danes, both in the East and West Indies; with Seven Tables very useful in Geography and Navigation.  8vo.  London.

1708  SENEX, JOHN.  Map of South America.  Corrected from the Observations communicated to the Royal Societies of London and Paris.  38 by 27 in.  Colored.  London.

> The date is in doubt. An interesting map in which the Southern Atlantic is denominated the "Ethiopic Ocean." Shewing the various sea routes of early navigators. With numerous curious notes round the coast line and the interior on Indian tribes, mines, explorations, etc.—Robinson, No. 41.

1708-1725  SENEX, JOHN.  Atlas, containing 34 large folding coloured Maps, including 2 of America.  Atlas Fol.  London.

> The maps comprise the Solar System, the World, Europe, Asia, Africa, North America, South America, Gt. Britain, Ireland, Seven United Provinces, Ten Spanish Provinces, etc., etc.

1709   MOLL, HENRY.   Atlas Manuale; or, a New Sett of Maps of all the
         Parts of the Earth, as well Asia, Africa and America as Europe,
         wherein Geography is Rectify'd by Reforming the old maps according
         to the modern Observation, and the Coasts of all Countries are laid
         down, agreeable to Mr. E. Halley's own map, . . . mostly perform'd by
         Herman Moll.   43 double-page maps, including 9 of America.   8vo.
         London.

> The advertisement states that these maps have been corrected on the new
> system of obtaining longitude by observation of the eclipses of Jupiter's satellites.
> —Quoted.

1710   A New Map of North America, shewing its principal Divisions, Chief
         Cities, Townes, Rivers, Mountains, etc.   Folding sheet, 17 by 21 in.,
         engraved by M. Burghers.   London.

> This map may be a reissue of one of Wells' noted under 1700 above.—It
> shews California as an island lettered "New Albion discovered by Sir Francis
> Drake in 1577."—Quoted.

         SENEX, JOHN.   A General Atlas of the World.   34 folding maps, in
         contemporary coloring, engraven and revised by Senex.   38 by 27 in.
         Fol.   London.

1710-1720   MOLL, HERMAN.   The World Described, or a New and Correct
         Sett of Maps.   Consisting of 30 large folding maps colored in outline.
         Fol.   London.

> The date is approximate.

1713   MOLL, HERMAN.   Map of Africa.   Engraved and outlined in colors,
         3 ft. 2 in. by 1 ft. 11 in.   Small inset view of the Cape and Plans of the
         Fort of Good Hope, James Fort, St. Helena, Cape Coast Castle.   Lon-
         don.

         MOLL, HERMAN.   Engraved Map of Asia, the East Indian Archipela-
         go, New Guinea and New Britain, outlined in color.   Small insets, in-
         cluding plan of Bombay and Sallset Island.   3 by 2 ft.   London.

         MOLL, HERMAN.   A Map of the East-Indies and the adjacent Coun-
         tries: with the Settlements, Factories and Territories, explaining what
         belongs to England, Spain, France, Holland, Denmark, Portugal, etc.,
         with many remarks not extant in any other map.   Inset plans of Ban-
         tam and Madras, views of Goa and Surat.   3 by 2 ft.   London.

1714  PRICE, C.   Map of the World in Two Hemispheres, laid down from the newest discoveries and most exact observations by C. Price. Colored. 3 ft. 5½ in. by 2 ft. 2 in.   London.

1715  MOLL, HERMAN.   Map of North America "according to ye newest and most exact observations." 24 by 38 in., outlines colored.   London.

> The left portion of the map is occupied by a large ornamental dedication to Lord John Somers, an engraved view of a Newfoundland curing station, and insets of Boston Harbor, Ashley and Cooper Rivers, Havana, etc.—Bookseller's Note.

1717 MEAD, ——.   The Construction of Maps and Globes. In Two Parts. 18 engraved plates of map projection. 8vo.   London.

1719  MOLL, HERMAN.   Atlas of the World, Europe, Asia, East Indies, Africa, North America, Dominions of the King of Great Britain on ye continent of North America, new map of the North parts of America claimed by France under ye names of Louisiana, Mississippi, Canada and New France, West Indies, South America, Limits of ye South Sea Company, Denmark and Sweden, Great Britain, England and Wales, Scotland, Ireland, Germany, Hungary, Transylvania, and The Suisse, Netherlands, France, Spain and Portugal, Italy, Turkish Empire, Roman Empire, etc. Atlas Fol.   London.

MOLL, HERMAN.   A New and Correct Map of the Whole World, shewing ye Situation of its Principal Parts, . . . Outlined in colors, 40 by 25 in.   London.

> This shows most of Australia and parts of Tasmania and New Zealand.— Maggs, No. 491.

MOLL, HERMAN.   A New and Correct Map of the World, Showing Kingdoms, Ports, Trade Winds, etc., with most remarkable tracks of bold attempts to find North East and North West Passages. With 30 early maps of Asia, Africa, with view of Cape Coast Castle and Fort, 2 maps of America, New Scotland, New York, Virginia, Canada, West Indies, Limits of the South Sea Company, views of Towns and other maps. Fol.   London.

MOLL, HERMAN.   A Catalogue of a New and Compleat Atlas, or a Set of 27 Two-Sheet (colored) Maps. Included are 3 maps of North and South America, and nearly all bear views of towns, forts, etc., all on guards and folded three times. Fol.   London.

1720 PRICE, C. South America, corrected from observations by C. Price, coasts and outlines in color (with ornamental title of natives, curious swans which swim with their whole bodyes always under water), shewing the journies of Magellan, La Roche, Sharp, etc.

> The date is approximate.

1720-1775 A Contemporary Collection of 22 important Maps by various cartographers made up about the year 1775 and bound as a North American Atlas, including Montresor's famous plan of New York City, plans of the operations before Quebec in 1759, plan of New Orleans, etc. Atlas Fol. London.

1721 Geographia Classica: The Geography of the Ancients. A Collection long wanted, and Publish'd for the Use of Schools. A series of 29 double-page maps engraved on copper of the Old World and its several kingdoms and provinces. 4to. London.

> These maps are intended to illustrate the classics. See also Moll under 1732 below.

SENEX, JOHN. For a set of 34 general maps see his *A New General Atlas,* under GEOGRAPHY. (In these California is still shown as an island.)

1729 MOLL, HERMAN. Atlas Minor: or, a New and Curious Set of Sixty-two Maps, in which are shewn all the Empires, Kingdoms, Countries, States, in all the known Parts of the Earth; . . . Composed and laid down by Herman Moll Geographer. Double-page engraved. 4to. London.

> Another edition, 4to, London, 1732.

1732 MOLL, HERMAN. Thirty-two New and Accurate Maps of the Geography of the Ancients, as contained in the Greek and Latin Classicks, wherein the several Empires, Kingdoms, and Provinces, the chief Cities, Towns, etc., mentioned in Herodotus, Homer, Vergil, Ovid, Caesar, Livy, etc., are represented. 4to. London.

POPPLE, HENRY. A Map of the British Empire in America, with the French and Spanish Settlements adjacent thereto; engraved on twenty sheets. By Henry Popple. Fol. London.

> Reissued in 1733 and 1740. See also Popple under 1735 below.
> Engraved by Wm. Henry Toms, and up to its date the largest and best map of America. The Index map forms the 21st sheet. Colored copies are to be preferred. The maps also contain views of Niagara Falls, New York, Quebec, etc.— Sabin.

1735   POPPLE, HENRY.  The British Empire in America, with the French, Spanish, and Hollandish Settlements adjacent thereto.  Series of 6 colored engraved maps, each 24 by 20 in.  Amsterdam.

> This famous series of maps was first published at London in 1732, in a still larger scale. . . . These six maps have descriptions at the top in French and elsewhere in English.—Maggs, No. 532.

1739   The Seat of War in the West Indies, containing new and accurate plans of the Havana, La Vera Cruz, Cartagena and Puerto Bello (taken from the Spanish draughts) also of San Augustin and the Bay of Honda in Cuba . . . likewise a chart or map of the West Indies . . . in order to demonstrate that the Havana is the only place the possession of which can possibly secure our trade to the West Indies, and prevent Spanish depredations.  5 plans on 1 sheet (22 by 19 in.).  London.

1744   A Map of North America With the European Settlements & whatever else is remarkable in ye West Indies from the latest and best Observations.  R. W. delin. 18¾ by 14¾ in.  London.

1746-1757   In the *London Magazine or Gentleman's Monthly Intelligencer* for the years 1747 to 1757 appear numerous maps, plans, plates and portraits relating mostly to North America.

1747   BOWEN, EMANUEL.  Collection of 75 Maps engraved on copper. 16 by 10½ in.  Fol.  London.

> Lists the usual American regions, North and South. Another collection by Bowen, dated 1770, contains maps of Negro-land, East Indies, Africa, a general map of America, and at the end a New and Accurate Map of the British Dominions in America by Kitchin, 1763, size 28 by 22½ in. This collection contains only 36 maps, 15 by 9½ in., fol.

1750   HOMAN, ——.  Atlas of the World.  34 double-page maps, engraved on copper, colored, and decorated with coats-of-arms, cherubs, nature scenes, plans of cities.  24½ by 21½ in.  Fol.  London.

> The date is approximate.

1750-1790   A Collection of Thirty-Seven Folding Maps, all colored in Outline, some fully colored, by Thos. Jefferys, J. Bayly, De l'Isle, Robert de Vaugondy, J. Pallairet.  Average size 20½ by 26½ in., with elaborately engraved cartouches.  Fol.  London.

> The maps include "Mappemonde," Northwest Coast of America, the whole Continent of America, North America (engraved by R. W. Scale, 1768), map of the Roman Empire, etc., all of which exhibits an eclectic temper on the part of the collector.

1752 BOWEN, EMANUEL. Complete Atlas . . . of the known World. 68 engraved maps (some with outlines colored), with vignette inscriptions, including 20 early maps of Virginia and Maryland, New Jersey, Pensilvania, New York, etc.; Newfoundland, Cape Breton, etc.; Harbor Plans of Boston, Providence, etc. Obl. fol. London.

> This work lays down the latitudes and longitudes of the principal places in the world.

1753 GREEN, J. Remarks in support of the new chart of North and South America; in six sheets . . . 4to. London.

1755 EVANS, LEWIS. A General Map of the Middle British Colonies, in America; Viz. Virginia, Mariland, Delaware, Pensilvania, New-Jersey, New-York, Connecticut, and Rhode Island: Of . . . the Country of the Confederate Indians . . . Of the Lakes Erie, Ontario and Champlain, And of Part of New-France: Wherein is also shewn the antient and present Seats of the Indian Nations. . . . A map 26⅛ by 19¾ printed on silk, lightly colored. Philadelphia.

> This map is quoted here for the following information: A rare and important map . . . of which no copy printed on silk is recorded by Henry Stevens in his monograph of Lewis Evans and his map. In that work he wrote: "The Map of 1755 for a long period was the principal prototype for the cartography of British North America . . . its indirect influence can be traced in almost every other map of North America made down to the end of the century." The map displays a wonderfully high standard of accuracy, especially when the vast extent of the country covered and its unsettled and even partially unexplored state is taken into account . . ." "Of additional interest is the fact that the printer was Benjamin Franklin."—From Quaritch.

FRY, JOSHUA, and JEFFERSON, PETER. A Map of the most Inhabited part of Virginia, containing the whole Province of Maryland with part of Pensilvania, New Jersey, and North Carolina. Drawn in 1751. Colored engraved map, on two large sheets each 48 by 16 in. London.

> An important map marking the latest explorations, and engagements with the French up to 1754.—Maggs, No. 442.

MITCHELL, J. A Map of the British and French Dominions in North America. With the Roads, Distances, Limits and Extent of the Settlements, Humbly Inscribed to the Earl of Halifax, and the other Right Honourable the Lords Commissioners for Trade & Plantations . . . Thos. Kitchin sculp. Published for the Author Feb. 13th, 1755, according to Act of Parliament. Large map, 53½ by 76½ in., lightly colored; divided into 32 pieces and mounted on linen. London.

> Another issue, fol., London, 1775.
> This is an official map prepared under the instructions of the Lords of Trade and Plantations from surveys in 1750.—Quaritch.

1758  BOWEN, EMANUEL.   Atlas Minimus, a new set of Pocket Maps of the several Empires, Kingdoms and States of the known World, with Historical Extracts relating to each drawn and engraved by J. Gibson. 52 maps in contemporary color, size 4½ by 3 in.   18mo.   London.

1760  BOWEN, EMANUEL.   Map (in two parts) of the British and French Settlements in North America, exhibiting their just Boundaries, French Encroachments, etc. 10 by 21 in.   London.

> The date is approximate.

JEFFERYS, THOMAS.   For maps of the French Colonies in North and South America see his *The Natural and Civil History of the French Dominions in North and South America,* under NORTH AMERICA.

1760-1775  Collection of seven engraved Maps from the *London Magazine* comprising the St. Lawrence and Siege of Quebec; Town and Fortifications of Montreal; Map of the Cherokee Nation; Philippine Islands; Quebec; Louisbourg; and Halifax, Nova Scotia. Also portrait of Wolfe.   4to and 8vo.   London.

1761  DURY, A.   A New General and Universal Atlas. Engraved 45 maps on 39 Plates (outlines colored) by Kitchin and others. Includes Canada, North and South America, West Indies, etc.   4to.   London.

1763  ANDREWS, P. and J.   A Set of Plans and Forts in America. Reduced from actual Surveys. Index and 30 plans engraved by P. and J. Andrews.   4to.   London.

> An extremely rare little Atlas illustrating the campaign against Canada and Nova Scotia. Reprinted in 1765.—From Maggs, No. 549.

1765  DURY, A.   A Chorographical Map of the King of Sardinia's Dominions on Twelve Sheets taken from the famous map of Borgonia and a Chorographical Map of the Republic of Genoa on Eight Sheets, taken from the map by Chalfrion. With Index maps comprising 18 double-page colored maps.   Fol.   London.

1768-1771  KITCHIN, THOMAS.   A General Atlas: or, Description at Large of the Whole Universe. Complete collection of title and 11 large colored maps on 22 sheets and engraved on 44 large copper-plates.   London.

This was reissued in 1773, 1780, 1782, and 1786-87, being brought down to date with the succeeding years. See below.

The Map of North America describes the Passage by land to California discovered by Father Kino.—From Maggs, No. 442.

1773 KITCHIN, THOMAS. A General Atlas, describing the whole Universe: being a compleat and new Collection of the most approved Maps extant, corrected . . . and augmented from the latest Discoveries, the whole being an Improvement of the Maps of D'Anville and Robert. 35 large folding colored maps engraved on 62 copperplates by Thomas Kitchin and others, after those of the above mentioned, John Rocque, Thos. Jefferys, and others. Imp. fol. London.

Many of the maps have historical designs.

1782 KITCHIN, THOMAS. A General Atlas, Describing the Whole Universe. Being a Complete and New Collection of the most Approved Maps extant . . . augmented from the latest discoveries, down to 1782. Series of 23 engraved maps, outlined in color, on 62 copperplates. Fol. London.

This map includes: Map of the World, in two sections; America, in two sections; North America and the West Indies with insert of California, in two sections; Chart of the St. Lawrence; Course of the Mississippi by Lieut. Ross; South America and the Falkland Islands, in two sections.—Maggs, No. 580.

1770 COLLET, —— (Captain). A Compleat Map of North Carolina from an actual Survey. By Captn. Collet, Governor of Fort Johnson. Engraved by I. Bayly. 43¾ by 28⅞ in. London.

A New Map of the most Considerable Plantations of the English in America. Engraved by Sutton Nichols. 14 by 18 in. London.

The date is approximate.

A New Map, wherein the British Empire and its Limits, according to the Definitive Treaty of Peace in 1763, are accurately described, and the Dominions possessed by the Spaniards, the French, and other European States. With insets of "A particular Map of Baffin and Hudson's Bay," and a "Map of the country between Montreal, Albany and Oswego." Large colored folding map. London.

The date is approximate. There is another map, made of two sheets stuck together, 46½ by 41 in., with much the same wording, dated 1777.

774 DUNN, SAMUEL. West Indies, containing the Coasts of Florida, Louisiana, New Spain and Terra Firma, with all the Islands. Single sheet 22 by 16 in., engraved surface 18 by 11. in. Colored in outline. London.

A Map of the most Inhabited part of New England, containing the Provinces of Massachusets Bay and New Hampshire, with the Colonies of Conecticut and Rhode Island; Divided into Counties and Townships; the whole composed from actual Surveys and its Situation adjusted by Astronomical Observations. Engraved, outlined in colors, 42 by 39 in., with inset "Plan of Boston Harbour from an Accurate Survey," and inset "Plan of the Town of Boston," also decorative title-piece representing the landing of the Pilgrim Fathers at Plymouth Rock in 1620. Wm. Faden. London.

A New Introduction to the Knowledge and Use of Maps; to which is added, an Appendix, containing Remarks on Dr. Solander and Mr. Bank's Voyage to the Southern Hemisphere, and also some late Discoveries near the North Pole. Map. 12mo. London.

> Solander and Banks accompanied Capt. Cook on his first voyage to the South Seas. See Hawkesworth under 1773, CIRCUMNAVIGATIONS.

SENEX, JOHN, and MAXWELL, ——. The English Atlas. 31 maps, the majority being double-page, 27 by 38 in., engraved and colored. Fol. London.

> This comprises maps chiefly of the Old World.

1774-1785  A Collection of eleven Maps. Fol. London.

> These portray various portions of the United States, Canada, the sea-board colonies, Florida, Louisiana, etc., mostly published by Faden.

1775  JEFFERYS, THOMAS. For a set of 40 charts and maps accompanying an historical and descriptive account of the West Indies see his *The West India Atlas*, under WEST INDIES.

A Map of Pennsylvania Exhibiting not only the Improved Parts of that Province, but also its extensive Frontiers: laid down from Actual Surveys and chiefly from the late map of W. Scull Published in 1770 . . . 53⅜ by 27⅛ in. London (?)

1776  The American Military Pocket Atlas: Being an approved Collection of Correct Maps, both General and Particular, of the British Colonies, especially those which are now, or probably may be, the Theatre of War. Taken principally from the Actual Surveys and judicious Observations of Engineers De Brahm and Romans, Employed in his

Majesty's Fleets and Armies. Maps varying in size from 27 by 21 in. to 18 by 13½ in., six in number, colored in outline. 8vo. London.

An important collection of contemporary Revolutionary maps. They were compiled for the use of British mounted officers, and so the volume was called a "Holster Atlas." The work was dedicated to Governor Pownall, who was instrumental in having it prepared.

DUNN, SAMUEL. The British Empire in Northern America, improved from the Surveys of Capt. Carver. Folded single sheet, 22 by 18½ in. London.

JEFFERYS, THOMAS. The American Atlas, or a Geographical Description of the whole Continent of America; wherein are delineated at large its several Regions, Countries, States, and Islands, and chiefly the British Colonies, composed from Numerous Surveys, several of which were made by order of Government by Major Holland, Lewis Evans, William Scull, and others. . . . Engraved on 48 copperplates, colored in outline. Fol. London.

Another edition, 49 copperplates, London, 1778.
A very useful and valuable collection; the maps, which are on a large scale, were mostly executed by the surveyors of the various colonies between the years 1762-1766.—Quaritch.

SAYER, R., and BENNETT, J. A Map of the Theatre of War in North America with the Roads and a Table of the Distances. Engraved colored map, with description under "Compendious Account of the British Colonies in North America," in three columns. 21½ by 30 in. Folded to 4to size. London.

The map contains an inset "Evans' Polymetric Table of America showing the Distances between the Principal Towns, Forts, and other Places in the British Colonies." The lower portion of the sheet contains the "Compendious Account of the Colonies."—Maggs, No. 429.

1776-77 A Collection of American Maps, mostly concerning the War of Independence. 8 maps in 1 vol. Fol. London.

A brief outline of their range is given below.

1. A map of the inhabited part of Canada, from the French Surveys, . . . by Claude Joseph Sauthier, engraved by Wm. Faden. 1777.

2. A Map, drawn and tinted by hand, of the different lines of communication from Canada to New England, . . . n.d.

3. A Topographical Map of the North Part of New York Island, exhibiting the plan of Fort Washington, now Fort Kynphausen, . . . 1777.

4. Bowles' Map of the Seat of War in New England, . . . 1776.

5. A Topographical Map of Hudson's River, with the Channels, depth of water, rocks, shoals, &c., and the country adjacent . . . 1776.

6. A Map of the Province of New York, reduc'd from the large drawing of that province compiled from actual surveys by order of His Excellency William Tryon, Esq., Captain General and Governor of the same . . . 1776.

7. A Plan of the Operations of the King's Army under the command of General Sir William Howe, K.B., in New York and East New Jersey, against the American forces commanded by General Washington, from the 12th of October to the 28th of November 1776 . . . 1777.

8. A Plan of the City and Environs of Philadelphia. Surveyed by N. Scull and G. Heap. . . . 1777.

1777   The North American Atlas, selected From the most Authentic Maps, Charts, Plans, etc., Hitherto Published. Fol. London.

    This consists of 26 folio maps, etc., of the British colonies in North America and Florida, etc. Faden also published a series of plans of the battles of the Revolutionary War, which are sometimes bound up with this atlas.—Sabin.

1779   Map of South America, containing Tierra Firma, Guayana, New Granada, Amazonia, Brasil, Pieru, etc., from M. D'Anville. Colored. Folded to large 8vo. case. London.

    RENNELL, JAMES (Major). Bengal Atlas, containing maps of the seat of War. London.

    Another edition, London, 1791.

1780   BOWLES, ——. Universal Atlas, a Collection of the most Accurate Maps of all the known Countries of the World, displaying the whole surface, whether habitable or uninhabitable, of the terraqueous Globe, by John Palairet, revised and improved by other eminent geographers. 38 colored maps, engraved on copper, with engravings of natives, scenes, historical quotations, etc. 21½ by 15 in. London.

    The maps of the world show the tracks of Anson, Cook, Bougainville, and other discoverers. There are among the usual American maps, those of the Independent States, showing Indian towns, also the Ouasioto Mountains, "through which there is not yet any occupied path," etc.—Bookseller's Note.

1781   BERRY, WILLIAM. Map of the World: Europe; Asia; Africa; North America; South America; Ireland; France; Spain; Rhine and the Rhone; . . . Germany; United Provinces of the Netherlands; Denmark; Catholick Provinces of the Low Countries; Italy; The Alps; Poland; Hungary; Turkey; etc. Colored maps in fol. London.

    Map of the Dutch Settlements of Surinam, Demerary, Issequibo and Berbeices and the Islands of Curassoa, etc. 10 by 14 3/6 in. London.

1781-1815  FADEN, WILLIAM.  Atlas of 59 engraved Maps, outlined in color, and many folding; together with printed leaf of contents. Large fol. London.

1783-1800  RUSSELL, J.  A Collection of Nine Folding Maps of the various parts of North and South America and West Indies.  London.

1785  POCOCK, EBE.  Map of the World, in colors, printed on the outside of a fire-balloon, about 5 ft. in height and 3 ft. 6 in. in width when inflated. London.

> The date is given by Maggs, No. 429, as about 1785, but it would appear to be considerably later, for this authority states that shown on the map are the tracks of famous discoverers, such as Cook, Vancouver, La Pérouse, of whom the last two made their voyages in the 1790's.

1786  A New Map of the Whole Continent of America, divided into North and South and West Indies. Wherein are exactly described the United States of North America, as well as the Several European Possessions according to the Preliminaries of Peace signed at Versailles January 20th, 1783. Compiled from Mr. D'Anville's Map of that Continent, with the addition of the Spanish Discoveries in 1775 to the North of California, and corrected in the several parts belonging to Great Britain, from the original Materials of Governor Powell (Pownall?). With insert map of the Countries adjoining to Baffin's and Hudson's Bays, and lists of all the possessions in America belonging to the various countries. 2 large sheets (each 4 ft. by 21 in.).  London.

> Reissued, London, 1794.

RENNELL, JAMES (Major).  Map of Bengal, Bahar, Oude and Allahabad, with part of Agra and Delhi, exhibiting the Course of the Ganges, from Hurdwar to the Sea. Dissected on canvas, 3 ft. 6 in. by 2 ft. 5 in.  London.

1787  BOULTON, S.  Africa with all its States, Kingdoms, Republics, . . . by S. Boulton; with inset of the Gold Coast, engraved descriptive text on the Cape Government, . . . 2 parts. 40 by 48 in.  London.

> See Boulton under 1794 below.

1787  Map of Asia and its Islands, according to D'Anville, divided into Empires, Kingdoms, States, Regions, etc., With the European Possessions and Settlements in the East Indies and an exact delineation of all the Discoveries made in the Eastern Parts by the English under Captain Cook. 2 sheets, each 20 by 46 in.  London.

PLAYFAIR, WILLIAM.  The Commercial and Political Atlas, which represents at a single view, by means of Copper Plate Charts, the most important public Accounts of Revenues, Expenditures, Debts, and Commerce of England.  40 copperplates.  4to.  London.

> This includes charts and descriptions for: Exports and Imports to and from the West Indies; to and from all North America, 1770-1782; to and from the U.S.A., Spanish West Indies, Greenland, Bermuda, etc.—Maggs, No. 502.

1787  SAYER, R.  Kingdom of Poland with its dismembered Provinces.  19 by 26 in.  Outlines colored.  London.

1789  BANKES, T. (Rev.).  For an atlas of the whole world see his *A Modern Authentic and Complete System of Universal Geography,* under GEOGRAPHY.

1790  SAYER, R.  European and Asiatic Russian Empire from Maps of the Academy of St. Petersburg.  18¾ by 50½ in.  Outlines colored.  London.

SAYER, R.  New Map of Spain and Portugal.  18¾ by 25½ in.  Outlines colored.  London.

1790-1794  Old Maps of Denmark, Scandinavia, and Germany, outlined in colors, dissected and mounted on linen, the three folding into 8vo case.  London.

> Comprises: Faden's Denmark, 28¾ by 21 in., 1790; Delarochette's Scandinavia and the Danish Islands, 29 by 20½ in., 1794; Laurie and Whittle's Germany, 26¾ by 19 in., 1794.—Bookseller's Note.

1794  ARROWSMITH, A.  Map of the World on a Globular Projection, exhibiting the nautical researches of Capt. J. Cook, with all the recent discoveries to the present time.  London.

BOULTON, S.  Africa, with all its States, Kingdoms, Republics, Islands, etc., enlarged from D'Anville's Map, with a chart of the Gold Coast, by S. Boulton, with a description of Trade, Produce, Customs, etc., boundaries colored.  2 sections each 46 by 20 in.  London.

FADEN, WILLIAM. Chart of the North West Coast of America and North East Coast of Asia explored in the Years 1778 and 1779. Prepared by Lieut. Henry Roberts under the immediate inspection of Capt. Cook. 24 by 31 in. in colors. 2nd edit. London.

KITCHIN, THOMAS. South America with its several Divisions, according to the Possessions of the European Powers. Engraved colored map. 21 by 17 in. London.

1796 Fifty Old Engraved Maps and Views of the Chinese Empire. Copperplates and engravings. 22 by 15 in. London.

> This contains full page engravings of curious views, natural history and ceremonies, etc.—Bookseller's Note.

1797 FADEN, WILLIAM. Map of America or the New World wherein are introduced all the known parts of the Western Hemisphere from the Map of D'Anville with the necessary alterations and the additional discoveries made since the year 1761. 24 by 31 in. in colors. London.

1798 Atlas Minimus Universalis, or a Geographical Abridgement. 55 maps engraved. 8vo. London.

KITCHIN, THOMAS. A New Universal Atlas augmented from D'Anville and Robert, with improvements by Rennell, and others. 104 folding colored maps, with engraved vignettes. Fol. London.

RENNELL, JAMES (Major). A Map shewing the progress of discovery & improvement in the Geography of North Africa. London.

See *The African Association* under 1790, AFRICA.

1800 CHAUCHARD, —— (Captain). A General Map of Germany, Holland, Netherlands, Switzerland, The Grisons, Italy, Sicily, Corsica, and Sardinia. 25 large folding maps. Fol. London.

Map of North and South America, showing the newest Discoveries, States, etc. 19 by 21 in. London.

## ADDENDA

1874 BREVOORT, J. C. Verrazano the Navigator. Notes on Giovanni Da Verrazano and on a Planisphere of 1520 Illustrating his American Voyage of 1524. With a Reduced Copy of the Map. 8vo. New York.

1889 NORDENSKIÖLD, A. E. Facsimile Atlas to the Early History of Cartography, with Reproductions of the most important Maps printed in the fifteenth and sixteenth Centuries; translated from the Swedish original by Ekelöf and Clements R. Markham. 51 large maps printed as plates and 84 of somewhat smaller size printed in the letterpress, reproducing the rarest and most important maps which were printed in the fifteenth and sixteenth centuries. Fol. Stockholm.

> An admirably scientific work, which may be regarded as almost exhaustive of the subject. Jomard and Santarem might be said to have produced an imperfect first volume of an Illustrated History of Cartography treating irregularly upon the manuscript sources; Nordenskiöld's atlas might be called the complete second volume dealing with the entire printed or engraved material. It is indispensable as furnishing by far the best apparatus for studying the growth of geographical science, and the gradual enlargement of knowledge with regard to the surface of the globe.—Quaritch.

1892 HARRISSE, HENRY. For an essay on cartography and description of 240 maps and 40 maps of globes, etc., see his *Discovery of North America,* under GENERAL REFERENCE.

1894-99 Remarkable Maps of the XVth, XVIth & XVIIth Centuries reproduced in their original size. 6 parts in four port-folios, with supplement to part II and part III. Fol. Amsterdam. (Frederik Muller & Co.)

> A most important collection of reproductions of early maps. All but two in the first part and many in the other parts depict America. Only 100 sets printed. The contents are listed below:
>
> I. The Bodel-Nyenhuis Collection at Leyden. 9 maps on 14 sheets.
>
> II-III. The Geography of Australia as delineated by the Dutch cartographers of the 16th century. Edited by Mr. C. H. Coote. 14 and 7 maps, with a Supplement issued four years later containing a reproduction of part of Huych Allardt's map of India.
>
> IV. Nicolaes Witsen's map of Northern Asia, on 6 sheets. Also 3 maps of the world.
>
> V-VI. Maps of various parts of Europe, delineated in the 15th & 16th centuries, chiefly from the Isaac Vossius Collection in the Library of Leyden University. 26 maps on 30 sheets.—From Quaritch.

1895 WINSOR, JUSTIN. For reproductions of maps contemporaneous with the period discussed see his *The Mississippi Basin,* which treats of the Struggle in America between the English and French, 1697-1763. 8vo. Boston.

1908  BJORNBO, AXEL ANTHON, and PETERSEN, CARL S.    Anecdota
      Cartographica Septentrionalia. Printed at the expense of the Royal
      Danish Society of Sciences. The English Translation by Sophia Bertel-
      sen. 11 plates, 3 colored. Fol.  Copenhagen.

> Besides first and foremost contributing to the elucidation of the cartography
> of Schleswig-Holstein, Denmark, Norway, Sweden and Finland; the work also
> gives new contributions to the geographical history of the surrounding countries,
> Germany, Holland, Russia; it contains printed uniques from Hamburg and Ant-
> werp, and presents original maps or copies of maps by the Dutchmen Cornelis
> Anthoniszoon, Simon van Salinghen, and Joris Carolus, by the Germans Nicolaus
> Cusanus and Henricus Martellus, by Marcus Jordan from Holstein and by Tycho
> Brahe's Scandinavian pupils. But above all it presents a new and not unimportant
> source for the history of the exploration of North America and Polar lands.—
> Quaritch.

1912  LOWERY, W.  For a list of maps of the Spanish possessions within the
      present limits of the United States, 1502-1820 see under BIBLIOG-
      RAPHIES.

1916  STEVENSON, E. L.  Genoese World Map, 1457. Facsimile with Criti-
      cal Text. Plates. 8vo.  New York.

1924  A Map of the World Designed by Gio. Matteo Contarini, engraved by
      Fran. Roselli, 1506. Map 24½ by 16 in. Fol. British Museum, Lon-
      don.

> "The map reproduced here was purchased by the British Museum in 1922.
> The introduction to the facsimile was written by Mr. J. A. J. de Villiers, Deputy
> Keeper of Printed Books, . . . The lists of names, with reference to the latitude
> as given in the map, has been compiled by Mr. F. P. Sprent, Assistant Keeper,
> to whom is also due the transliteration of the inscriptions in the cartouches. . . ."
> —A. W. Pollard, quoted by Quaritch. Quaritch also adds that this is the first
> printed map known in which the discoveries made in the New World by Colum-
> bus and his contemporaries are represented. No other copy is known.

⋅1926  FITE, E. D., and FREEMAN, A.  A Book of Old Maps delineating
       American History from the Earliest Days down to the Close of the
       Revolutionary War. 74 facsimiles of maps. Fol.  London (?).

      HUMPHREYS, ARTHUR L.  Old Decorative Maps and Charts. With
      illustrations from Engravings in the MacPherson Collection, and a
      Catalogue of the Atlases, etc., in the Collection of Henry Stevens. 79
      full page plates, 19 of which in color. 4to.  London.

1927   CHUBB, THOMAS.   The printed Maps in the Atlases of Great Britain and Ireland, 1579-1870, with Introduction by F. P. Sprent, with biographical notes of the map makers, engravers and publishers. Numerous facsimiles. 4to. London.


SPRENT, F. R.   Francis Drake's Voyage Round the World, 1577-1580. Two Contemporary Maps. Reproduced in Facsimile. With an Introduction and Description by Mr. F. R. Sprent. 2 maps. Fol. London.


1928   STEVENS, HENRY N.   The First Delineation of the New World and the First Use of the Name America on a Printed Map. An Analytical Comparison of Three Maps—with an argument—that the earliest is the one discovered in 1893 and now in the John Carter Brown Library. Large folding maps in pocket. 4to. London.


1932   BROWN, BASIL.   For a general guide to Atlases, Maps and Charts see his *Astronomical Atlases, Maps and Charts* under GENERAL REFERENCE.


1935   CORTESAO, ARNANDO (Dr.).   Cartografos portugueses dos seculos XV e XVI. 2 vols. 4to. Lisbon.

> Two thick volumes of more than 400 pages each and 56 plates reproducing contemporary Portuguese maps and charts, the majority of which are hitherto unpublished, besides other illustrations in the text, and numerous documents.—From the Announcement of the work by Quaritch.

# XVI

## Military Expeditions

1637 VINCENT, PHILIP. For an account of the war against the Pequot Indians see his *A True Relation of the Late Battell fought in New England*, under NORTH AMERICA.

1639 ZARAIN AGA. A Relacion of the Late Siedge and taking of the City of Babylon by the Turke. As it was written from thence by Zarain Aga, one of his Captaines, to Caymaran, his Brother, Vice-Roy in Constantinople . . . Translated out of the Turkish, into the Italian Language, by the Drugerman to the State of Ragouza. And Englished by W. H. London.

> A letter on p. 22 transmitting the Relacion is signed by William Holloway (of Ragusa). Woodcut representing the siege.—From John Carter Brown.

1655 S., I. A Brief and Perfect Journal of the late Proceeding and Success of the English Army in the West-Indies, continued until June the 24th, 1655; together with some Quaeres inserted and Answered, published for the Satisfaction of all who desired truely to be informed in these Particulars, by I. S., an Eye-Witnesse. 4to. London.

> "This tract fills an important gap in the History of the English Possessions in the West Indies. The Expedition was fitted out by Cromwell, and the fleet commanded by Admiral Penn, father of William Penn."—Stevens. This Cromwellian expedition, commanded by Robert Venables (the author of the "Experienced Angler") and William Penn (the founder of Pennsylvania) was almost a failure. It aimed at the capture of Hispaniola, but after a disgraceful defeat at the hands of the Spaniards, the force was withdrawn to Jamaica. Here they were more fortunate; the Spaniards were so few in number that they evacuated the town and permitted the landing of the expedition.—Robinson, No. 20.

1670 A Relation of the Siege of Candia. From the first Expeditions of the French Forces under the Command of M. de la Fueillade, Duke of Roannez, to its Surrender, the 27th of September, 1669. Written in French by a Gentleman who was a Voluntier in that Service, and faithfully Englished. 8vo. London.

1673 A Narrative of the Siege and Surrender of Maestricht, to the most Christian King. On the 30th of June. Fol. London.

1675-77 For King Philip's War Tracts see this date under NORTH AMERICA.

1683　DE QUESNE, ——. An Account of Monsieur De Quesne's late Expedition at Chio: together with the Negotiation of Monsieur Guilleragues, the French Ambassador at the Port, in a letter written by an Officer of the Grand Vizir's to a Pacha, Translated into English. 4to. London.

1684　A Journal, or, a Most Particular Account of all that Passed in the late Siege of Vienna, written by a principal Officer, who was in town during the Siege. Translated out of High Dutch. 12mo. London.

　　PETER A VALCARAN (JOHN). A Relation or Diary of the Siege of Vienna. Folding plan. 4to. London.

　　TAAFE, FRANCIS, COUNT. Count Taafe's Letters, from the Imperial Camp to his Brother, the Earl of Carlingford, here in London, giving an Account of the most considerable Actions, both before and at the raising the Siege of Vienna; together with several Remarkable Passages afterward in the Campagne against the Turks in Hungary, . . . 4to. London.

1685-87　A True and Exact Relation of the Imperial Expedition in Hungaria, with a Journal of the Siege and Taking of Buda. Folding plate. 4to. London.

　　　　The journal was written by a Mr. Trevelyan.

1686　An Historical Description of the Glorious Conquest of the City of Buda, the Capital of Hungary, by the Victorious Arms of the Thrice Illustrious and Invincible Emperor Leopold I, under the Conduct of his most serene Highness, the Duke of Lorraine, and the Elector of Bavaria. 4to. London.

1687　A Most Exact Description of the Taking that important Fortress of Buda; Shewing the whole Action of storming it, Sept. 2, 1686. By the Imperial, Bavarian, and Brandenburgh Forces: and other remarkable Actions during the Siege, with the Names of all Places in the City. 4to. London.

1688　A Journal of the Venetian Campaigne, 1687. 4to. London.

1689   BYFIELD, NATHANIEL.   For an account of the revolt in New England see his *An Account of the late Revolution in New England,* under NORTH AMERICA.

A Journal of the Siege of Mentz, under the Command of His Serene Highness, the Duke of Lorrain, and the Confederate Princes.   4to.   London.

1690   A Journal of the late Motions and Actions of the confederate Forces against the French in the United Provinces and Spanish Netherlands: with Remarks on the most considerable Cities, Towns, and Fortifications, in those Countryes: with an exact list of the Army. Written by an English Officer who was there during the last Campagne.   London.

1693   REYARD, NICHOLAS (Colonel), and LODOWICK, CHARLES (Colonel). A Journal of the late Transactions of the French at Canada, with the Manner of their being repulsed by His Excellency Benjamin Fletcher.   4to.   London.   (11 leaves.)

1694   D'AUVERGNE, EDWARD.   The History of the Campagne in the Spanish Netherlands, Anno Dom. 1694. With the Journal of the Siege of Huy.   London.

The Gentlemen's Journal for the War; being an Historical Account and Geographical Description of several strong Cities, Towns, and Ports of Europe. With authentick Draughts of the Fortifications of every Place, made by order of the French King, for the use of the Duke of Burgundy. Engraven on copperplates . . . Part III. Containing a Description and Draughts of the ensuing Cities and Towns, Viz. Liege, Coni, Oudenard(e), Phillipsburg.   London.

1695   An Exact Account of the Siege of Namur: with a Perfect Diary of the Campagne in Flanders.   4to.   London.

An Exact Journal of the Siege of Namur: Giving a Particular Account of the severall Sallies and Attacks, and other most remarkable Passages from the first Investing of the Place.   4to.   London.

1698   An Exact and Faithful Journal of the Famous Siege of Barcelona.   4to.   London.

1702 Campagna Miravigliosa, or, an Exact Journal of the Imperial Army's Advance into, and Incampments in Italy, under the Command of Prince Eugene of Savoy, by an Officer of the German Army, made English by William Barton. 4to. London.

1708 FRIEND, JOHN. An Account of the Earl of Peterborough's Conduct in Spain, chiefly since the raising the Siege of Barcelona, 1706, to which is added the Campagne of Valencia. 2nd edit. London.

1712 DUMMER, JEREMIAH. A Letter to a Friend in the Country, on the Late Expedition to Canada: With an Account of the former Enterprizes, a Defence of that Design, and the Share the Late M . . . rs had in it. 8vo. London.

A Letter to a Noble Lord concerning the Late Expedition to Canada, (offering Satisfaction in Three Points. I. Of what Importance the Conquest of the Country would have been to the Crown, and whether it would have answered the Expense of the Great Armament that was made against it. II. Whether the Expedition was well concerted? And, lastly, if the Ill Success of it ought wholly to be charged on New England, as People here are made to Believe). 8vo. London.

1720 WALKER, SIR HOVENDEN. A Journal: or Full Account of the late Expedition to Canada. With an Appendix, containing Commissions, Orders, Instructions, Letters, Memorials, Courts-Martial, Councils-of-War, etc. relating thereunto. 8vo. London.

> This item is described under NAVAL EXPEDITIONS.

1742 OGLETHORPE, JAMES. An Impartial Account of the late Expedition against St. Augustine. With an Exact Plan of the Town, Castle and Harbour of St. Augustine, and the adjacent Coast of Florida. 8vo. London.

1744 KIMBER, EDWARD. A Relation or Journal of a Late Expedition to the Gates of St. Augustine on Florida, Conducted by Gen. Oglethorpe. London.

> Modern reprint, Boston, 1935. See below and also Mackay and Oglethorpe under 1742, NORTH AMERICA.

> 1935 KIMBER, EDWARD. A Relation or Journal of a Late Expedition to the Gates of St. Augustine on Florida, Conducted by Gen. James Oglethorpe, etc. Reprinted from the London, 1744 edition, with bibliographical notes by Sidney A. Kimber. Portrait and facsimile. 8vo. Boston.

1745 BRINDLEY, J.   The Theatre of the Present War in the Netherlands and upon the Rhine, etc.   Maps and plans.   London.

GIBSON, JAMES.   A Journal of the Late Siege by the Troops from North America, against the French at Cape Breton, the City of Louisbourg, and the Territories thereunto belonging.   Surrendered to the English, on the 17th of June, 1745, after a Siege of Forty-eight Days. By James Gibson, Gentleman Voluntier at the above Siege.   Large engraved folding plate, "A Prospect of the City of Lewisbourg.   Also the Harbours and Garrisons on the Island of Gaspey or Cape Breton in North America," etc.   8vo.   London.

> This work is dedicated to the Commissioned Officers who took part in the siege of Louisbourg, and in the 8-page Introductory Preface the author gives an account of the City, and of certain dangerous exploits in which he had taken a part.  Then follows a valuable record of the siege itself, in the form of a daily journal . . .—From Maggs, No. 465.  This event and its subsequent issues called forth a great many pamphlets.  See items from this date on, under NORTH AMERICA.

1746 The French and Indian War.   The Beginning, Progress and Conclusion of the Late War; with other Interesting Matters considered.   And a Map of the Lands, Islands, Gulphs, Seas, and Fishing-Banks, comprising the Cod Fishing in America annexed, . . . Folding map.   London.

> A rare book on the French and Indian War.  It relates largely to fishing rights and interests in Nova Scotia and Newfoundland.—Robinson, No. 61.

1747 PEPPERELL, SIR WILLIAM.   An Accurate Journal and Account of the Proceedings of the New-England Land Forces during the late Expedition against the French Settlements on Cape Breton, to the time of the Surrender of Louisberg.   Containing a just Representation of the Transactions and Occurrences, and of the Behaviour of the said Forces . . . All sent over, by General Pepperell himself, to his friend Capt. Henry Stafford at Exmouth, Devon.   Exeter.

> Reprinted, London, 1758.  See below and also Durell under 1745, NORTH AMERICA.
> The author fitted out this expedition against Louisbourg at his own expense and at a great personal loss.  This letter is to bring these facts to the attention of the public and the Government.  At the Treaty of Aix-la-Chappelle, 1748, Cape Breton was restored to France, but in 1758, having been recaptured by the British, the above Journal was reprinted at London to enlighten the public on the importance of the place and of Cape Breton and the necessity of keeping them. Louisbourg was the strongest fortress on the eastern coast of America, and its reduction by a colonial force evoked the greatest admiration both in England and America.  This author was born in New England and distinguished himself as Commander of the Colonial forces that captured the fortress.—From Robinson, No. 20.

1758  PEPPERELL, SIR WILLIAM. An Accurate and Authentic Journal of the Taking of Cape Breton, in the year 1745. Together with a Computation of the French Fishery in that part of the World: both sent over by Gen. Pepperell, who commanded in that Expedition, in a letter to his friend Captain Henry Stafford, . . . From which will appear the Importance of that Island, and the danger we shall be in of losing our superiority at sea, should it now be restored to France. 8vo. London.

SHIRLEY, WILLIAM. A Letter from William Shirley, Esq. Governor of Massachusett's Bay, to the Duke of Newcastle, with a Journal of the Siege of Louisbourg, and other Operations of the Forces in North America, during the Expedition against the French Settlements on Cape Breton, published by authority. 8vo. London. (32 pp.)

1754  WASHINGTON, GEORGE. The Journal of Major George Washington. With an additional Map. London.

> The most esteemed memento of the French and Indian War, which was issued before the war commenced, however. Washington was sent out in 1754 to reconnoiter the territory west of the Alleghenies, to treat with the French and demand the withdrawal of the Indians. The Journal contains a very full account of his actions, and was so urgently required by Governor Dinwiddie that, as the youthful officer says, it was reprinted almost before the last page had time to dry. It is Washington's earliest publication, and extremely rare. The original edition bears the imprint of William Hunter of Williamsburg; another edition appeared in London during the same year. The latter edition was very likely printed from the manuscript, which is now preserved in the Public Record Office in London.—Waldman.

1755  BRADDOCK, EDWARD (General). For an account of the expedition to Virginia see under NORTH AMERICA.

1757  A Review of the military Operations in North America, from the Commencement of the French Hostilities on the Frontiers of Virginia, 1753, to the Surrender of Oswego, Aug. XIV, 1756. 3 vols. 4to. London.

1758  An Authentic Account of the Reduction of Louisbourg, in June and July, 1758. 4to. London.

> This refers to the second capture of the fortress by the British and Colonial troops.

Six Plans of the Different Dispositions of the English Army, Under the Command of the Late General Braddock, in North America. I. Line of March with the whole Baggage. II. Plan of the Disposition of the advanced Party of four hundred Men to protect the Workers while clearing the Road. III. Encampment of the Detachment sent from the little Meadows. IV. Line of March of the Detachment sent from the little Meadows. V. Plan of the Field of Battle on the 9th of July 1755. VI. A Map shewing the Rout and Encampment of the Army. By an Officer. Fol. London.

1759 An Accurate and Authentic Journal of the Siege of Quebec, 1759. By a Gentleman in an eminent Station on the Spot. 8vo. London.

> Another edition, 12mo, Dublin, 1759.

BRADSTREET, JOHN. An Impartial Account of Lieut. Col. Brad- street's Expedition to Fort Frontenac. To which are added, A few Re- flections on the Conduct of that Enterprise, and the Advantages result- ing from its Success. By a Volunteer on the Expedition. 8vo. Lon- don.

MONCRIEF, —— (Major). A Short Account of the Expedition Against Quebec, commanded by Major-General Wolfe in the year 1759. By an Engineer upon that Expedition. With a Plan of the Town and Basin of Quebec, and part of the adjacent Country, showing the principal En- campments and Works of the British Army, and those of the French Army during the Attack in 1759. 8vo. London.

> The date is approximate.

1760 A Journal of the Siege of Quebec. To which is annexed, a correct Plan of the Environs of Quebec, and of the Battle fought on the 13th of Sep- tember 1759; Together with a particular Detail of the French Lines and Batteries, and also of the Encampments, Batteries and Attacks of the British Army, and the Investiture of that City under the Command of Vice Admiral Saunders, Major General Wolfe, Brigadier-General Monckton, and Brigadier-General Townshend. Drawn from the Or- iginal Surveys, taken by the Engineers of the Army. Engraved by Thomas Jefferys, Geographer to his Majesty. 4to. London.

A New Military Dictionary: or the Field of War. Containing a Particular and Circumstantial Account of the most Remarkable Battles, Sieges, Bombardments, and Expeditions, Whether by Sea, or Land, Such as relate to Great Britain and her Dependencies . . . By a Military Gentle- man. . . . Fol. London.

> This contains plates, portraits, maps, and plans of Ontario, Crown Point, etc.

PATRICK, J. Quebec; A Poetical Essay, In Imitation of the Miltonic style; being a regular Narrative of the Proceedings and Capital Transactions performed by the British Forces under the Command of Vice-Admiral Saunders and Major-General Wolfe, in the glorious Expedition against Canada, in the Year 1759. The Performance of a Volunteer on board His Majesty's Ship Somerset, during the Passage Home from Quebec. The whole embellished with entertaining and explanatory notes. 4to. London. (30 pp.)

1761 CAMBRIDGE, RICHARD OWEN. An Account of the War in India, between the English and French, on the Coast of Coromandel, from 1750 to 1760, with a Relation of the late Remarkable Events on the Malabar Coast, and the Expeditions to Golconda and Surat, and the Operations of the Fleet, compiled from original Papers. Folding maps and plans by T. Jefferys, also views of forts, etc. 4to. London.

> 2nd edit., London, 1762.
> This contains Col. Lawrence's Narrative of the War on the Coasts of Coromandel, from the beginning of the Troubles to 1754; the Expedition against Angria, 1755; Journal of the Siege of Fort St. George, 1758-59, by J. Call, Chief Engineer; Col. Forde's Expedition to Golconda, and Proceedings of the Commissaries at Madrass, etc.—Bookseller's Note.

1762 GARDINER, RICHARD. Memoirs of the Siege of Quebec, etc. 4to. London.

1763 Complete History of the Origin and Progress of the late War to 1763; Naval and Land Campaigns of the French and British in America; etc. 2 vols. 8vo. London.

ORME, ROBERT. History of the Military Transactions of the British Nation in Indostan, from 1745; with a dissertation on the Establishments made by Mahomedan Conquerors in Indostan. Folding map. 4to. London.

See Orme under 1763-1778, EAST INDIES.

ROCQUE, M. A. America. A Set of Plans and Forts in America. Reduced from Actual Surveyes. 30 maps and plans (one folding) and the earliest printed map of Albany. 12mo. London.

> An extremely rare and important little book. It is valuable for the history of the Canadian War, being almost the sole source of information on the frontier forts. This work contains the Duyckinck Map of New York City, and the earliest printed map of Albany. There are also maps of Quebec, Montreal, Halifax, Fort Ontario, etc.—From Robinson, No. 45.

1765  ROGERS, ROBERT (Major).  Journals of Major Robert Rogers: Containing An Account of the Several Excursions he made under the Generals who commanded upon the Continent of North America during the late War. From which may by (*sic*) collected the most Material Circumstances of every Campaign upon that Continent, from the Commencement to the Conclusion of the War.  8vo.  London.

> Another edition, 16mo, Dublin, 1769. See below.
> "Rogers, a native of New Hampshire, commanded a body of Provincial Rangers, and stood in high repute as a partisan officer . . . I have no hesitation in following his account of the expedition up the Lakes."—Parkman, *Conspiracy of Pontiac,* quoted by Robinson, No. 20. See Rogers under 1765, NORTH AMERICA.

> 1769. ROGERS, ROBERT (Major).  Journals . . . containing the most Material Circumstances of every Campaign (during the French and Indian War) to which is added, An Historical Account of the Expedition against the Ohio Indians in the year 1764, under Henry Bouquet. 16mo.  Dublin.
>
> > For this last expedition see William Smith under 1766, NORTH AMERICA. See also Rogers under 1765, NORTH AMERICA.

1766  LALLY, —— COUNT.  Memoirs of Count Lally, from his embarking for the East Indies, as Commander in Chief of the French Forces in that Country to his being sent Prisoner of War to England, after the Surrender of Pondicherry.  Map.  8vo.  London.

SMITH, WILLIAM.  For an account of the expedition against the Indians of the Ohio in 1764 see this date under NORTH AMERICA.

1769  HAZARD, JOSEPH.  The Conquest of Quebec. A Poem. Plan of Quebec.  4to.  Oxford.  (20 pp.)

1772  MANTE, THOMAS.  The History of the Late War in North America. London.

> This is generally accepted as the best of the general histories that began to come out after the Treaty of Paris in 1763. The author was an engineer officer. His History gives a careful, fair and accurate account of the causes of the war, describes in detail and with understanding the course and effect of the military operations, and best of all, contains 18 superb maps and plans. . . . His account of Washington's narrow escape from assassination in 1753 at the hands of a treacherous Indian guide is capital reading.—Waldman.

1775  A Journal of the March of a Party of Provincials from Carlisle to Boston and from thence to Quebec; begun the 13th of June, and ended the 31st of December, 1775. To which is added, an Account of the Attack and Engagement at Quebec the 31st of December, 1775. 12mo. Glasgow.

A very rare piece. It is the journal of a company of riflemen under Captain William Hendricks and John Chambers, sent from a Gentleman in Quebec to his friend in Glasgow. The Americans under General Montgomery were defeated and made prisoners. The account of the engagement at Quebec is not by the American Officer who wrote the journal, but by the gentleman who sent it to Glasgow.—Sabin.

1776   Relation du bombardment et siège de Quebec, par un Jésuite du Canada; With an English Translation by Rev. Thomas Alcock. 12mo. London.

1779   A Brief Examination of the Plan and Conduct of the Northern Expedition in America, in 1777. And of the Surrender of the Army under the Command of Lieutenant General Burgoyne. 8vo. London.

1780   BURGOYNE, JOHN (Lieut.-Gen.). A State of the Expedition from Canada, as laid down before the House of Commons, and verified by Evidence, with an Appendix of Authentic Documents, and an Addition of many Circumstances which were prevented from appearing before the House by the Prorogation of Parliament. Written and Collected by himself, and dedicated to the Officers of the Army he commanded. 6 maps and plans. 4to. London.

> 2nd edit., 8vo, London, 1780; 3rd edit., 1780-81. A Supplement appeared in 1780. See below.
> "The materials of his interesting story will be held in high estimation by the historians who shall record the events of the unhappy war, to which they owe their birth."—*North American Review,* quoted by Puttick and Simpson. In his *State of the Expedition from Canada* he proved that his army was one-half the size he had demanded, and in every way was badly provided.—D.N.B. General Burgoyne will always interest Americans, but his career was remarkable enough otherwise. He attacked Lord Clive, surrendered at Saratoga, directed the impeachment of Warren Hastings, wrote lively plays, and was buried in Westminster Abbey.—Sotheran.

> 1780   BURGOYNE, JOHN (Lieut.-Gen.). A Supplement to the State of the Expedition from Canada, containing General Burgoyne's Orders, respecting the Principal Movements, and Operations of the Army to the Raising of the Siege of Ticonderoga. 4to. London.

>> This work was originally published without Burgoyne's authority. See *Monthly Review* XLII, 492.—Sabin.

An Enquiry into, and Remarks upon the Conduct of Lieut. Gen. Burgoyne. The Plan of operation for the Campaign of 1777, the instructions from the Secretary of State, and the Circumstances that led to the Loss of the Northern Army. 8vo. London.

> See *Monthly Review* LXV, 174. A poetical piece, called the *Blockade of Boston,* has been attributed to General Burgoyne . . . For Burgoyne's original Letters see *Mass. Hist. Soc. Coll.,* vol. 2; for a Proclamation dated July 10, 1777, see *New Hamp. Hist. Soc. Coll.,* vol. 2.—Sabin.

HALL, WILLIAM CORNWALLIS (Captain). The History of the Civil War in America. Vol. 1. Comprehending the Campaigns of 1775, 1776, and 1777. By an Officer of the Army. Folding map. 8vo. London.

> Only one volume appeared.

HOWE, WILLIAM (Lieut.-Gen., Lord). Narrative of . . . , in a Committee of the House of Commons, of the 29th of April, 1779, relative to his Conduct during his late Command of the King's Troops in North-America; to which are added, some Observations on a pamphlet, entitled, "Letters to a Nobleman." London.

> 3rd edit., London, 1781.
> Lord Howe "solemnly declared that, although preferring conciliation, his brother and himself stretched their powers to the utmost verge of their instructions, and never suffered their efforts in the direction of conciliation to interfere with the military operations."—D.N.B., quoted by Sotheran.

MURRAY, JAMES (Rev.). An Impartial History of the Present War in America; containing an Account of its Rise and Progress, the Political Springs thereof, with its Various Successes and Disappointments, on both sides. 23 portraits and folding plan of Boston and the Battle of Bunker Hill. 2 vols. 8vo. Newcastle upon Tyne.

> This work is mainly sought for on account of the portraits, which include:— Washington, Franklin, John Hancock, Putnam, Gates, Arnold, Gage, Sullivan, Howe, Burgoyne, Grey, Lee, Clinton, Tarleton, Lord Howe, etc.—Maggs, No. 549.

1786 DRINKWATER, JOHN (Captain). The History of the Siege of Gibraltar (1779-1783), with a Description and Account of that Garrison. 2 folding panoramic views and 4 folding plans. 2nd edit., corrected. London.

> 3rd edit., 4to, London, 1786; an edition, 8vo, London, 1844. A modern edition, London, 1905.

1787 FULLARTON, WILLIAM. A View of the English Interests in India and an Account of the Military Operations in the Southern Parts of the Peninsula during 1782, 1783 and 1784. In two Letters. 8vo. London.

SIMCOE, JOHN GRAVES (Lieut.-Col.). A Journal of the Operations of the Queen's Rangers, from the end of the Year 1777, to the Conclusion of the Late American War. 10 colored engraved folding plans of various affairs. Exeter.

One of the most important and valuable works on the American War. The book was printed for private circulation only, and not for sale. According to Mr. Rich, its existence was almost unknown until a copy turned up in the Chalmers Sale in 1841.—Maggs, No. 465.

TARLETON, SIR BANASTRE. A History of the Campaigns of 1780 and 1781 in the Southern Provinces of North America. 4to. London.

> Another edition, Dublin, 1787.
> "Valuable as containing documents otherwise difficult of access."—D.N.B., quoted by Sotheran. Tarleton was a distinguished soldier on the British side during the Revolutionary War and is remembered for his brilliant campaign in the southern states. He also assisted Clinton earlier in the capture of New York. After the surrender of Yorktown he returned to England, where he received further military honors.

1788 MACLEAN, NEIL (Captain). The Complaint of Mr. Neil Maclean, to the Honourable the Commons of Great Britain, in Parliament Assembled. 8vo. (No place, printer, or date, is given. Privately printed, c. 1788.)

> Extremely rare. The author served under General Wolfe during the French and Indian War, and a letter is printed in the appendix certifying that he was held in high esteem by that general. The succeeding years he lived in the colonies, and at the outbreak of the Revolutionary War he was offered the command of a regiment in Connecticut. On refusing he had to flee the district and took service again in the British forces. The remainder of the narrative, over 100 pages, is a graphic account of his experiences and adventures throughout the whole period of the war. He seems to have had a high opinion of himself. The purpose of the pamphlet was first to secure money owing him by Government, and second, to claim formal and solemn thanks for having saved Quebec by his intimidations of General Montgomery and so having scared the forces away from that city.—From Robinson.

1793 DIROM, —— (Major). The Campaign in India, ending in the war with Tippoo Sultan, 1792; the siege of Seringapatam, etc. 9 illus., maps, etc. 4to. London.

1794 MOOR, EDWARD. Narrative of the Operations of Captain Little's Detachment and the Maharatta Army against Tippoo Sultan; siege of Darwar, Seringapatam, etc. 8 illus., maps, etc. 4to. London.

STEDMAN, C. The History of the Origin, Progress and Termination of the American War, by C. Stedman, who served under Sir. W. Howe, Sir H. Clinton, and the Marques Cornwallis. 2 vols. 15 maps. 4to. London.

1798 WILLYAMS, COOPER (Rev.). An Account of the Campaign in the West Indies in the year 1794 under the Command of Lieut-Gen. Sir Charles Grey and Vice-Admiral Sir John Jervis, with the Reduction of the Islands of Martinique, St. Lucia, Guadalupe, Marigalante, etc. Maps and plans. 4to. London.

## ADDENDA

1846  SENTER, ISAAC.  The Journal of Isaac Senter, Physician and Surgeon to the Troops Detached from the American Army Encamped at Cambridge, on a Secret Expedition Against Quebec Under the Command of Col. Benedict Arnold.  8vo.  Philadelphia.

1857  MELVIN, JAMES.  A Journal of the Expedition to Quebec 1775 Under Command of Col. Benedict Arnold.  21 portraits and views including 2 rare early copperplate views of Quebec and Montreal and rare portraits of George III and Gen. Carleton.  8vo.  New York.

1867  The Invasion of Canada in 1775, Including the Journal of Captain Thayer, with Notes and Appendix by Edwin M. Stone.  4to.  New York.

1880  Journal of the Siege of York in Virginia (By a French Engineer) September-October, 1781.  In *Magazine of American History*, IV, 449-452.  New York.

> See the following item.

> 1931  Journal of the Siege of York-town.  Unpublished journal of the Siege of York-town in 1781 operated by the General Staff of the French Army, as recorded in the hand of Gaspard de Gallatin and translated by the French Department of the College of William and Mary.  8vo.  Government Printing Office, Washington.

> Cited by Monoghan.

1887  SULLIVAN, JOHN (Major-Gen.).  Journals of the Military Expedition of Major-General Sullivan against the Six Nations of Indians in 1779.  With Records of the Centennial Celebrations.  Prepared by Frederick Cook.  Portraits and maps.  8vo.  Auburn, N. Y.

1903  ANDRE, JOHN (Major).  André's Journal: An Authentic Record of the Movements and Engagements of the British Army in America from June 1777 to November 1778, as recorded from Day to Day by Major. John André.  Edited by Henry Cabot Lodge.  2 vols.  4to.  Bibliophile Society.  Boston.

1908  SPILSBURY, —— (Captain).  A Journal of the Siege of Gibraltar, 1779-1783.  Illus.  8vo.  London.

# XVII

## Naval Expeditions

1578  GREEPE, THOMAS.  The true and perfect Newes of the woorthy and valiaunt exploytes, performed and doone by that valiant Knight Syr Frauncis Drake: Not onely at Sancto Domingo, and Carthagena, but also nowe at Cales, and uppon the Coast of Spayne.  4to.  London.

> Excessively rare. Apparently only two or three other copies are known. The American voyage is described in verse by Greepe, who, in his dedication to George Clifford, Earl of Cumberland, explains that he has written it for "the vulgar sorte of people in the Realme." At the end is printed a letter from Sir Francis Drake written from aboard her Majesties good Ship the Elizabeth Bonaventure, in which he describes the fight at Cadiz.—Quaritch.

1589  DRAKE, SIR FRANCIS, and NORRIS, SIR JOHN.  Ephemeris expeditionis Norreysii & Draki in Lusitaniam.  4to.  London.

> English version, 4to, London, 1589. See below.
> Whether the Latin or the English version was the earlier printed it is difficult to determine. Probably both appeared at the same time. The English account has been reprinted entire by Collier, and is reviewed at length in his Bibliographical Catalogue, Vol. I.—Robinson, No. 26. This important little publication refers to the expedition which Elizabeth sent to Portugal in 1589 under the joint command of Sir John Norris and Sir Francis Drake, to the assistance of Dom Antonio, pretender to the Portuguese throne. Reprisals were also due for the Spanish Armada. The expedition returned in July . . . without having achieved any decisive results. The Latin publication gives an account of the expedition in diary form, when preparations were being made at Plymouth to the 3rd of July.—From Maggs, No. 528. The expedition played great havoc with the Spanish ships and harbors, but on land was tragically unsuccessful. Enormous numbers were lost out of sickness.—From Quaritch.

> 1589  DRAKE, SIR FRANCIS.  A True Coppie of a Discourse written by a Gentleman, employed in the late Voyage of Spaine and Portingale; Sent to his particular friend, and by him published, for the better Satisfaction of all such, as hauing been seduced by particular Report, haue entred into Conceipts tending to the Discredit of the Enterprise, and Actors of the same.  4to.  London.

1591  HAWES, JOHN.  The valiant and most laudable fight by the Centurion of London against fiue Spanish Gallies . . . 4to.  London.

> So cited in the *Short Title Catalogue.*

RALEIGH, SIR WALTER.  A Report of the truth of the fight about the Isles of Acores, this last Sommer, Betwixt the Revenge, one of her Majesties Shippes, and an Armada of the King of Spaine.  4to.  London.

> This is said to be Raleigh's first published quarto tract. It was put out anonymously. Edward Arber edited in 1871 (12mo) "The Last Fight of the

Revenge at Sea," a copy of which was in Tennyson's library with passages marked. In his Manuscript Notes he remarks: "The story of the Revenge is finely told by Sir Walter Raleigh."—From Robinson, No. 61.

1595 ROBERTS, HENRY. Lancaster his Allarums, honorable Assaultes, and surprising of the Block-houses and Store-houses belonging to Fernand Bucke in Brasill. With his braue attempt in Landing in the mouth of the Ordinaunce there, which were Cannons Culuering, Cannon periall and Savres of brasse, with other sundry his most resolute and braue attempts in that Covntry. From whence he laded of their spoyles and rich commodities he there found fifteene good Ships, which was Sinemon, Sugar, Pepper, Cloues, Mace, Callow-cloth and Brassel-wood with other commodities. With the names of such men of worth hauing charge within this most honorable attempt lost their liues. Published for their eternall Honor by a VVelvviller. Woodcut. London.

> Lancaster had returned to England in 1594 with rich booty from the East Indies, and sailed in November on the expedition described in this volume . . . A fuller account is to be found in Hakluyt's *Voyages* (1600), III, 708.—From John Carter Brown.

1596 SAVILLE, HENRY (Captain). A Libell of Spanish Lies: found at the Sacke of Cales, discoursing the fight in the West Indies twixt the English Navie, being fourteene Ships and Pinasses and a Fleete of twentie saile of the King of Spaine, and of the death of Sir Francis Drake. With an answer briefly confuting the Spanish lies, and a short Relation of the fight according to Truth. London.

> It will be remembered that Drake died during an unsuccessful expedition in the West Indies while conducting attacks on the Spaniards in that quarter in company with Sir John Hawkins.

1599 A True Report of a voyage made this last Summer by a fleete of 73. shippes, sent forth at the command and direction of the states generall of the vnited prouinces, to the coast of Spaine and the Canary-Isles: And in what sort the said fleet tooke the principall town, and two Castles of the Grand Canaria . . . with the successe of part of the saide fleete in their returne homeward. Which set saile for Spaine the 25. of May, and returned home the 10. of Septemb. 1599. 4to. London.

> Apparently unique. This is really the first issue of "The Conquest of the Grand Canaries, made this last summer." of the *Short Title Catalogue*.—From Quaritch. The fleet was commanded by Jacob Cornelicz Van Neck.

The Voyage of the right Ho. George Earle of Cvmberland to the Azores. . . . 1589. London.

> This account is to be found in some copies of Edward Wright's *Certaine Errors in Navigation* (see under NAVIGATION I). Found in Hakluyt II, 155, 2nd part; reprinted in Pinkerton I, 804-809; in Beazley II. Translated into Dutch,

Pieter Van der AA (see under COLLECTIONS II). For life and voyages of Cumberland see below.
This privateering adventure sailed in June, 1589.

> 1920 CUMBERLAND, GEORGE (Third Earl of). His Life and his Voyages: a Study from Original Documents, by G. C. Williamson. 21 portraits, plates, facsimiles, etc. 8vo. Cambridge.

1601  The Algiers Voyage against the Pirates, under the Command of Sir Mansell, Vice-Admiral of England. 4to. London.

1614  SQUIRE, WILLIAM. News from Marmora; or a Relation sent to the King of Spain of the good successe of a Voyage which it hath pleased God to give in taking and supressing of Marmora a port in Barbary, by the Armado and Hoast Royall. Translated from the Spanish. 4to. London.

1617  A Fight at Sea by the Dolphin of London, against Five of the Turks' Men-of-War, Jan. 12, 1616 (-17). 4to. London.

> See Beazley, *Voyages and Travels,* II.

1621  Algiers Voyage, in a Journall, or briefe Reportary of all Occurrents hapning in the Fleet of Ships sent out by the Kinge his most excellent Majestie, as well against the Pirates of Algiers, as others. 4to. London.

A True Relation of a wonderfull Sea Fight betweene two great and well appointed Spanish Ships, and a small English Ship. 4to. London.

> An abridgement of the above, Amsterdam, 1621.

1622  The True Relation of that vvorthy Sea Fight which two of the East India Shipps had with 4 Portingals of great force and burthen, in the Persian Gulph, with the Lamentable Death of Captaine Andrewe Chilling, with other Memorable Accidents in that Voiage. Printed this 2. of July. 4to. London. (22 pp.)

1625  The Dvtch Svrvey; wherein are related and truly discoursed the chiefest Losses and Acquirements which have past betweene the Dutch and Spaniards in these last four yeares Warres of the Netherlands, with a comparative ballancing and estimation of that which the Spaniards haue got in the Dutchies of Cleeve and Iuliers. with that which they haue lost vnto the Dutch and Persians in Brasilia, Lima, and Ormus. 4to. London. (3 pp.)

Dedicated to Cromwell, signed W. C.—Puttick and Simpson.

1626 CEBES, EDWARD, LORD. A Jovrnall and Relation of the action which by his Majesties Commandement Edward, Lord Cecyl, Baron of Putney, and Viscount of Wimbledon, Admirall, and Lieutenat Generalall of his Majestyes Forces, did vndertake vpon the Coast of Spaine, 1625. 4to. London.

This tract was probably privately printed.—Lowndes.

SMITH, JOHN (Captain). A trve Relation of a brave English Stratagem, practised lately vpon a Sea-Towne in Galizia (one of the Kingdomes in Spaine), and most valiantly and successfully performed by one English Ship alone of 30 Tonne, with no more than 35 Men in her. As also, With two other remarkeable Accidents betweene the English and Spaniards, to the glory of our Nation. London.

1637 DUNTON, JOHN (Mariner). A True Journall of the Sally Fleet, with the Proceedings of the Voyage . . . Published by John Dunton, Master of the Admirall call'd the Leopard. Whereunto is annexed, a List of Sally Captives names, and the places where they dwell, and a Description of the three Townes in a Card. Folding map. 4to. London.

Reprinted in Osborne II, 491-98.
The author had at one time been a prisoner of the pirates, but had redeemed himself from Sallee. He was then sent out as master and pilot on a Sallee man-of-war, with 21 Moors and some Flemish renegadoes, to the coast of England to take prisoners. He brought the boat to the Isle of Wight where he was captured and detained as a pirate. Upon trial he was released, and then was put in command of an expedition to effect the release of Christian captives. Some 399 prisoners were thus rescued. Dunton states that his only son of ten years of age was a slave in Algiers and like to be lost to him forever. The year of the expedition was 1636.

1639 Tvvo famovs Sea-Fights Lately made, Betwixt the Fleets of the King of Spaine, and the Fleets of the Hollanders. The one, in the West-Indyes: The other, The Eight of this present Moneth of February, betweixt Callis and Gravelin. In the former, the Hollanders suffered. In the latter, the Spaniard lost. Two Relations not vnfit for these Times to animate Noble Spirits to attempt and accomplish brave Actions. London.

The first part is translated from a Spanish account printed in Seville, 1638. A number of ballads on these sea fights were entered at Stationers' Hall in September and October, 1639.

1648  RICH, ROBERT (Earl of Warwick). The Navall Expedition of the Right Honourable, Robert, Earle of Warwick, (Lord High Admiral of England) against the Revolted Ships: Being a true and perfect Relation of the whole Expedition, from their first setting out from Chatham, to their returne againe into the Downes. . . . London.

1650  CARTER, MATTHEW. Relation of that as honourable as unfortunate Expedition of Kent, Essex, and Colchester; by M. C. a Loyall Actor in that Engagement, Anno Dom. 1648. London.

> This tract records several particulars not noticed by Lord Clarendon, and our general historians.—Lowndes.

1653  BLAKE, ROBERT (Admiral). A True Relation of the late Great Seafight as it was sent in a Letter to his Excellency the Lord General Cromwell. From Gen. Blake and Gen. Monck. Wherein is a List of what Dutch Ships were taken and sunk, with the number of the Prisoners, . . . 4to. London.

> This fight took place on Feb. 18, 1653, and is known as the Battle off Portland. The English lost the "Sampson" which foundered after the fight, captured the "Struisvogel" and destroyed various Dutch vessels.—Maggs, No. 508.

BLAKE, ROBERT, and MONCK, GEORGE. A Relation of the Engagement of the Fleet of the Commonwealth of England, under the Command of Gen. Blake, Gen. Deane, and Gen. Munke, with the Dutch Fleet, under the Command of Van Tromp. 4to. London.

> The English naval Victory of the "First Battle of the North Foreland," June 2-3, 1653. Eleven Dutch vessels were captured and 1350 prisoners taken. No English vessels were lost.—Maggs, No. 508.

The Common-wealths great Ship Commonly called the Soveraigne of the Seas, built in the yeare 1637. . . . With all the Fights wee have had with the Hollander . . . Plates in the text; woodcut of a ship under full sail, with inscription at the top: The Soveraigne of the Seas, . . . London.

> On pp. 24-25: A true Relation of a most bloody, treacherous, cruell Designe of the Dutch in the New Netherlands in America in supplying the Indians with Arms and Ammunition, to burn and slay the English on a Sabbath day when they were at meeting. This is a reprint of the Second Part of the Tragedy of Amboyna.—Lowndes.

VIOLET, THOMAS. A true Narrative of some remarkable Proceedings concerning the Ships Samson, Salvador and George, their Silver and Lading, and several Prize-Ships depending in the High Court of Admiraltie. Fol. London.

1656 STAYNER, SIR RICHARD. A True Narrative of the late Success which it hath pleased God to give to some part of the Fleet of this Commonwealth upon the Spanish Coast, against the King of Spains West-India Fleet in its Return to Cadiz: being the substance of several letters writ and sent by the Generals of the Fleet upon this occasion. London.

> Stayner, with three powerful ships, attacked the Spanish treasure Fleet Sept. 9th, 1656, near Cadiz. The one that remained in their possession was a prize of £600,000; but it was stated that their loss was not less than nine million dollars or nearly two million pounds sterling.—From Maggs, No. 442.

1659 A Book of the Continuation of Forreign Passages, that is, of the Peace made between this Commonwealth and that of the United Provinces of the Netherlands, with all the Articles of that Peace, Apr. 5, 1654; and the Articles of Peace, Friendshipp and Entercourse agreed between England and Sweden in a Treaty of Upsall, May 9, 1654; as also the substance of the Articles if the Treaty of Peace betwixt England and France, . . . ; From General Blake's Fleet, the Turks in Argier do consent to deliver up all the English slaves, and desire a firme Peace forever, and in Tunnis Road we battered the Castle of Portoferina and set on fire their fleet in the Harbour, Apr. 9, 1655; moreover an attempt on the Island of Jamaica and taking the Towne of St. Iago de la viga, beating the enemy from their Forts and Ordnance, being a body of 3,000 men, and so took possession of the Island, May 10, 1655. With a full Description thereof. With a true Narrative of the late Successe, which it hath pleased God to give to some part of the Fleet of this Commonwealth, the Speaker, the Bridgewater, the Plimouth Frigots, against the King of Spains West India Fleet: the value of what is taken and possessed by the calculation of the Spaniards about nine millions of pieces of eight, and 350 prisoners, and all this without the losse of one vessel of the English, 1656. 8 engraved plates in the text, portraits of Pope Alexander VII, Ludwig XIV, Christine of Sweden, Naval actions, etc. 4to. London.

> The Spanish fleet on its way home from the West Indies was waylaid by the English, and the majority of the ships captured or sunk. Many important Spanish gentlemen and merchants, including the Governor of Havana, were made prisoners.

1658 DOYLEY, EDWARD. A Narrative of the Great Success God hath been pleased to give His Highness Forces in Jamaica, against the King of Spains Forces; Together with a true Relation of the Spaniards losing their Plate-Fleet, As it was Communicated in a Letter from the Governour of Jamaica. London. (6 pp.)

> This affair is described in the item just preceding.

1659   The Faithfull Scout impartially communicating the most remarkable In-
telligence, and Chief Occurrences, from all Christian Kings, Princes,
States, and Common-Wealths; with the proceedings of the English,
Swedish, Dutch, and Danish Fleets, throughout the Sound and Baltic
Seas. 4to. London. (8 pp.)

1671   BALTHORPE, JOHN.   The Streights Voyage, or St. David's Penman;
being a description of the most remarkable passages that happened in
the first Expedition against the Turks of Argier, Sir John Harmon,
Commander, Rere Admiral of His Majesties' Fleet; beginning May
1669, ending April 1671. 12mo. London.

PALMER, ROGER, EARL OF CASTLEMAINE.   A Short and True
Account of the material Passages in the war between the English and
the Dutch. London.

SPRAGGE, SIR EDWARD (Admiral).   A True and Perfect Relation
of the Happy Successe and Victory obtained against the Turks of Ar-
giers at Bugia, by his Majesties Fleet in the Mediterranean . . . together with an Exact List of the Turks Ships, Burnt and Destroyed,
with the Names of their Commanders, . . . Fol. London. (8 pp.)

1673   Relation of the Re-Taking of the Island of St. Helena, and Three Dutch
East-India Ships. 4to.   Edinburgh. (4 pp.)

> See Beazley, *Voyages and Travels,* II.
>
> The East India Company had settled St. Helena in 1660, but soon after the
> outbreak of war with Holland in 1672 the Island was captured by the Dutch only
> to be retaken by Capt. Richard Munde in the *Assistance,* with three other vessels.
> . . .—Maggs, No. 508.

1679   TOSIER, JOHN (Captain).   A Narrative of his Embassye and Command to the Captain General and Governor of Havannah to demand
His Majesty of Great Britain's subjects kept prisoners there.   London.

1680   A True Relation of a Great and Bloody Fight between the English and the
Moors before Tangiere, and of the Bravery and Heroick Exploits by
the English. Fol. London. (4 pp.)

> The date is approximate.
> The attempt of the English to get settled in Tangier was finally abandoned
> in 1684, but not until they had learned that the way to defeat the Moors was to go
> out after them.

1681   An Exact and Faithful Account of the Late Bloody Engagement between Captain Booth, Commander of the Adventure, and Hodge Allii, Captain of the Two Lions and Crown of Algier, otherwise called the Great Genoese, a Ship of 40 Guns, 327 Turks and Moors, and 88 Christian Slaves on Board. On the 16th and 17th of September, 1681, as it was communicated from the said Captain to his Friend at Cadiz: And thence by Letter, of the 18th of October, New-Stile, communicated to his Friend, in London. 4to. London. (1 sheet.)

    This concerns the taking of two Algerian Pirates and the rescuing of 88 Christian slaves.—Maggs, No. 630.

1691   A True and Faithful Relation of the Proceedings of the Forces of their Majesties K. William and Q. Mary, in their Expedition against the French, in their Caribby Islands in the West Indies, under the Conduct of his Excellency Christopher Codrington. 4to. London.

1698   PONTIS, LOUIS DE (Mons.). An Account of the Taking of Carthagena by the French in the Year 1697, containing all the Particulars of that Expedition. Large engraved map in two folding sheets. 8vo. London.

    Another account issued, London, 1699. See below.
    An interesting and accurate account of the expedition to the West Indies and attack on Carthagena, in which the city was plundered by the French to the value of more than one million pounds. The fleet returning by way of Newfoundland fell in with the English fleet, under Admiral Nevil, but escaped after a short engagement.—Bookseller's Note. The attacking force consisted of French men-of-war and a large contingent of buccaneers. The French admiral has nothing too bad to say of his allies, calling them cowards, pirates, mutineers, rabble, and other opprobrious names.—Gosse.

    1699   PONTIS, LOUIS DE (Mons.). A Genuine and Particular Account of the Taking of Carthagena by the French and Buccaniers, in the Year 1697. 8vo. London.

    1699   PONTIS, LOUIS DE (Mons.). Monsieur de Pontis' Expedition to Carthagena: being a Particular Relation, I, Of the Taking and Plundering of that City by the French in the Year 1697 . . . III. Of their Passing by Commodore Norris at Newfoundland . . . Illus. with a Large Draught of the City of Carthagena, its Harbours and Forts. 8vo. London.

    There was another edition, 8vo, London, 1740.

1699   Die Lunca, 17 April, 1699: a Petition of the Houses of Parliament to His Majesty in Regard to Capt. Charles Desborow, employed in the Expedition to Newfoundland. 4to. London. (8 pp.)

    An account of several incidents which took place off Newfoundland and at St. John's, Newfoundland, resulting in a court-martial and suspension of Capt. Norris.—Bookseller's Note.

1703   BURCHETT, JOSIAH.   Memoirs of Transactions at Sea during the War with France, 1688-1697.   8vo.   London.

> Several expeditions of American interest are described, including Voyages to Newfoundland and the West Indies.—Thorp. Burchett, of humble origin, was at the age of 14 taken by Samuel Pepys, the then Secretary of the Admiralty, about 1680, into his service as body servant and clerk. After remaining with Pepys for more than seven years he incurred his master's displeasure and was discharged.—Sotheran. See Burchett under 1704 and Lillingston 1704 below; also Burchett under 1720 below.

An Impartial Account of all the Material Transactions of the Grand Fleet and Land Forces from their first setting out from Spithead, June 29, till his Grace the Duke of Ormond's Arrival at Deal, November 7, 1702. In which is included a particular Relation of the Expedition at Cadiz, and the Glorious Victory at Vigo. By an Officer that was present.   4to.   London.

1704   B., C. M.   A Journal of the Expedition of Her Majesty's Fleet, under the Command of Sir George Rooke, from the time of their leaving Lisbon in Portugal, till their Arrival in the Bay of Altea, being June the 7th, 1704.   Folding map of Portugal.   Fol.   London.

> This relates to the movements of the Anglo-Dutch fleet prior to the battle of Velez Malaga, of the fleet's appearance off Barcelona and of the escape of the French fleet into Toulon.—Maggs, No. 534.

BURCHETT, JOSIAH.   Mr. Burchett's Justification of his Naval-Memoirs, in answer to Reflections made by Coll. Lillingston, on that part which relates to Cape Francois and Port de Paix. With some short Observations on our West-India Expeditions.   8vo.   London.

> See Burchett under 1703 above and the item of Lillingston following below.

LILLINGSTON, LUKE (Colonel).   Reflections on Mr. Burchett's Memoirs, or, Remarks on his Account of Captain Wilmot's Expedition to the West Indies.   8vo.   London.

> Burchett evidently made some unfavorable remarks concerning Col. Lillingston's conduct in the West Indian Naval operations during 1694-97, and in this work the Colonel gives further particulars concerning the expeditions against Martinique and St. Domingo in which he was in command of the landing parties. —Maggs, No. 534.

MONSON, SIR WILLIAM.   Naval Tracts.   In Six Books.
   1.   A Yearly Account of the English and Spanish Fleets during the War in Queen Elizabeth's Time; with Remarks on Actions on both Sides.

2. Actions of the English under James I and Discourses upon that Subject.

3. The Office of the Lord High Admiral of England and of all the Members and Officers under him; with other Particulars to that Purpose.

4. Discoveries and Enterprises of the Spaniard and Portuguese; and several other Remarkable Passages and Observations.

5. Divers Projects and Stratagems tender'd for the Good of the Kingdom.

6. Treats of Fishing to be set up on the Coasts of England, Scotland, and Ireland, with the Benefit that will accrue by it to all his Majesty's Kingdoms; with many other things concerning Fish, Fishery, etc.

These memorials and tracts were originally brought to notice in Churchill's Collection, 1704 edition, and were reprinted in the 1732 edition. They have since been reprinted in the *Navy Society Records.*—They contain details of the greatest importance concerning early English naval history, and now are first printed from the original MS., written in the days of Queen Elizabeth and James I.— From Maggs, No. 546. His purpose was to describe the acts and enterprises of Englishmen at sea, to deal with the duties of seamen, to touch upon the voyages and conquests of the Spaniards and Portuguese, to discover the benefits of fishing upon the coast, etc. He was apparently the first Englishman to make a critical examination of the work of seamen afloat in his own time as well as of some of his predecessors and successors at sea. His views are those of a vigilant, sagacious, and thinking officer.—*Cam. Hist. Eng. Lit.* IV, v.

ROOKE, SIR GEORGE. A Narrative of Sir George Rooke's late voyage to the Mediterranean, where he Commanded as Admiral of the Confederate Fleet. With a Description of Gibraltar; . . . An Account also of the Naval Battel fought betwixt the Confederates and French King's Fleets: with a Judgment of the Event. 4to. London.

The Journal of Sir George Rooke published by the Navy Records Society, London, 1897. See below.
This relates to the capture of Gibraltar by the British and the battle of Velez Malaga. The author closes with advice concerning the better arrangement of ship's guns.—Maggs, No. 534.

1897 ROOKE, SIR GEORGE. Journal of Sir George Rooke, Admiral of the Fleet, 1700-02. Introduction and Notes by Oscar Browning. Maps. 8vo. Navy Records Society. London.

1708 SHOVELL, SIR CLOUDSLEY. Secret Memoirs of the Life of Sir Cloudsley Shovell, Kt. Admiral of Great Britain, containing his Birth, Education and Rise, with a full Account of all the Naval Battels since the Revolution . . . and a more exact Relation of the Enterprise upon Toulon than any yet extant. Portrait by Van der Gucht. 8vo. London.

1711  Journal of an Expedition Performed by the Forces of our Soveraign Lady
Anne. . . Queen, . . . Under the Command of the Honourable Francis
Nicholson, General and Commander in chief, in the Year 1710 for the
Reduction of Port Royal in Nova Scotia, or any other Place in those
Parts in America, then in Possession of the French. 4to. London.
(24 pp.)

1716  GRANTHAM, SIR THOMAS.  An Historical Account of some Memorable Actions, Particularly in Virginia; Also Against the Admiral of Algier, and in the East Indies: Performed for the Service of his King
and Country. 8vo. London.

1720  BURCHETT, JOSIAH.  A Complete History of the most Remarkable
Transactions at Sea, from the Earliest Accounts of Time to the Conclusion of the last War with France, wherein is given an Account of
the most considerable Naval Expeditions, Sea Fights, Strategems, Discoveries, and other Maritime Occurrences that have happen'd among
all Nations which have flourished at Sea. Portrait engraved by Vertue
and 9 folding charts. Fol. London.

>   Among the expeditions related are Leake's proceedings with a Squadron to
> Newfoundland; Captain Stafford Fairborn's to Newfoundland; Mons. Pontey's
> coming to Newfoundland; Admiral Aylmer's expedition to Port Royal in Nova
> Scotia; and the unsuccessful expedition against Quebec under Sir Hovenden
> Walker; and a number of expeditions to the West Indies.

WALKER, SIR HOVENDEN.  A Journal: or Full Account of the late
Expedition to Canada. With an Appendix containing Commissions,
Orders, Instructions, Letters, Memorials, Courts-Martial, Councils-of-
War, etc. relating thereunto. 8vo. London.

>   The author, after distinguishing himself in the West Indies, was placed in
> command of the Naval Forces in the Expedition to Canada in 1711. Ill luck at-
> tended that enterprise, eight transports being cast away, and nearly 900 soldiers
> drowned . . . Sir Hovenden was arraigned for his conduct. He underwent great
> persecution, his name being struck from the list of Admirals, as well as from
> half-pay lists.—Robinson, No. 20. See Nichols, *Literary Anecdotes* I, 178-180,
> for an account of its leader.

1724  GRANVILLE, SIR RICHARD.  Original Journals of Sir Richard Granville, viz. I. Of the Expedition to Cadiz in Spain, Anno 1625, with the
Charge delivered by the Earl of Essex and Nine other Colonels, against
the Viscount Wimbledon, General of that Voyage, with his Answer,
containing a Full Relation of the Defeat thereof; II. Of the Expedition
to the Isle of Rhee in France, Anno 1627, containing an Account of
the most Material Passages happening at and after our landing there,
now first published from their respective Manuscripts. 8vo. London.

1727 COLLIBER, SAMUEL. Columna Rostrata: or, a Critical History of the English Sea Affairs; wherein all the Remarkable Actions of the English Nation at Sea are described. 8vo. London.

> A large part of this volume relates to affairs in America.—Puttick and Simpson.

1729 CORBETT, T. An Account of the Expedition of the British Fleet to Sicily, in the years 1718, 1719, 1720. . . . Collected from the Admiral's MSS. and other original papers. 8vo. London.

1732 DU GUAY-TROUIN, RENE. The Memoirs of M. du Gué-Trouin, Chief of a Squadron in the Royal Navy of France, and Great Cross of the Military Order of St. Lewis. Containing all his Sea-Actions with the English, Dutch, and Portugueze, in the late Wars of King William and Queen Mary. Translated from the French by a Sea-Officer. 12mo. London.

> This was translated from the surreptitious Dutch edition of 1730. These are the Memoirs of one of the most illustrious French seamen and corsairs. He inflicted many defeats on English and Dutch warships and in 1711 captured Rio de Janeiro from the Portuguese.—Maggs, No. 508. The first official French edition was published in 1740 at Paris. See below.

> 1740 DU GUAY-TROUIN, RENE. Mémoires de Monsieur Du Guay-Trouin, Lieutenant Général des Armées Navales de France. Portrait plan and plates. 4to. Paris.

1737 DOWNING, CLEMENT. A Compendious History of the Indian Wars; with an Account of the Rise, Progress, Strength, and Forces of Angria the Pyrate. Also the Transactions of a Squadron of Men of War under the Commodore Matthews, sent to the East Indies to suppress the Pyrates. To which is annex'd . . . an Account of the Life and Actions of John Plantain, a notorious Pyrate at Madagascar; . . . 12mo. London.

1738 A Faithful Narrative of the Capture of the Ship Derby (belonging to the Honourable East India Company, Abraham Anselm Commander) by Angria the Pirate, on the Coast of Mallabar, December 26, 1735, . . . 8vo. London.

SANDWICH, JOHN MONTAGU, EARL OF. A Voyage Round the Mediterranean, 1738-39; with Memoirs of the Author's Life by John Cooke, Portrait of the Author, chart of his course, and plates. 2nd edit. London.

> Another edition, with Life, London, 1799. See below.

1799 SANDWICH, JOHN MONTAGU, EARL OF. A Voyage Round the Mediterranean performed by the late Earl of Sandwich in the years 1738 and 1739. Written by himself. Embellished with a portrait of his lordship and illustrated with several engravings, antient buildings and inscriptions with a chart of his course. To which are prefixed— Memoirs of the noble author's life by John Cooke, M.A. Chaplain to his lordship and one of the chaplains of Greenwich Hospital. Portrait, map, 23 plates. 4to. London.

1739 BYNG, SIR GEORGE. An Account of the Expedition of the British Fleet to Sicily, in 1718, 1719, and 1720, under the command of Sir George Byng (afterwards Viscount Torrington), Admiral and Commander in Chief of His Majesty's Fleet, and H. M. Commissary and Plenipotentiary to the several Princes and States of Italy, from the Admiral's manuscripts. 8vo. London.

> Viscount Torrington was the father of the unfortunate John Byng whose unskilful handling of the ships under his command at Minorca caused his court martial and execution in 1757.

JENKINS, CHARLES (Captain). Spanish Insolence, corrected by English Bravery, being an Historical Account of the many signal Naval Atchievements obtained by the English over the Spaniards, from 1350 to the present time. 8vo. London.

> Largely concerning the Anglo-Spanish rivalry in America and the West Indies.—Bookseller's Note. A similar though fuller title of the same date is recorded below.

> 1739 JENKINS, CHARLES. England's Triumph: or, Spanish Cowardice expos'd. Being a Compleat History of the many Signal Victories gain'd by the Royal Navy and Merchant Ships of Great Britain, for the term of Four Hundred Years past, over the insulting and haughty Spaniards. Wherein is particularly related A True and genuine Account of all the Expeditions, Voyages, Adventures, etc., of all the British Admirals from the Time above-mentioned whose Successes have already filled all Europe with Amazement. By Captain Charles Jenkins, who has too sensibly felt the effects of Spanish Tyranny. 2 plates and 1 table. 12mo. London.
>
> > Originally issued in 24 numbers. A large part of this scarce volume pertains directly or indirectly to America, containing accounts of various expeditions of Hawkins, Drake, Raleigh, and many others, from 1567 to 1730.—Sabin.

LESLIE, CHARLES. For an account of the Victory of Admiral Vernon at Porto Bello and Chagre see his *A New and Exact Account of Jamaica,* under WEST INDIES.

1740 CARRANZA, DOMINGO GONZALES. For an account of Capt. Parker's taking the town of Porto Bello in 1601 see his *A Geographical Description of the Coasts, Harbours, and Sea Ports of the Spanish West Indies,* under WEST INDIES.

1743 An Account of the Expedition to Carthagena, with explanatory Notes and Observations. 8vo. London.

> At least three editions, London, 1743; Edinburgh, 1743.
> Admiral Vernon had blown up the defences of Porto Bello and so became the hero of the hour. Confident of further success he made an attack three months later on Carthagena; but here he found defences of the port too strong to be captured without the aid of some seven or eight thousand troops. The events of the siege are related by Smollett in *Roderick Random,* where the incompetence in handling the sick, the brutal treatment of the ordinary seaman in the Royal Navy, and the wretched accommodations on board such ships are detailed with the passion of one who had experienced such a way of life. The disaster called forth many charges and replies. Some of these listed in the following items. The above Account is ascribed to Admiral Sir C. Knowles.

1744 A Journal of the Expedition to Carthagena, with Notes. In Answer to a late Pamphlet entitled, An Account of the Expedition to Carthagena. 8vo. London.

> 2nd edit., 8vo, London, 1744.
> This is ascribed to General Wentworth.

Authentic Papers relating to the Expedition against Carthagena. Containing Original Letters between the Admiral (Vernon) and the General (Wentworth), their Councils of War, etc. Also Letters between the Vice-King of Santa Fe, Governor of Carthagena, and the Admiral. 8vo. London.

Journal of the Expedition to La Guira and Porto Cavallos in the West Indies, under the Command of Commodore Knowles. In a Letter from an Officer on board the Burford to his Friend in London. 8vo. London.

MATTHEWS, THOMAS (Admiral). Authentic Letters from Admiral Matthews to the Secretary of State on his Expedition to the Mediterranean. London.

> Through his failure to maintain the blockade at Toulon the Admiral was charged with having neglected to give the necessary orders, and with having fled from the enemy and given up the chace, though there was every chance of success. The trial dragged on for years, and he was dismissed in 1747.—D.N.B. This was the occasion of numerous pamphlets as usual.

A Narrative of the proceedings of His Majesty's Fleet in the Mediterranean, and the combined Fleets of France and Spain, from 1741 to March, 1744, . . . Folding maps and plans. 8vo. London.

1746   Original Letters to an Honest Sailor. 8vo. London.

> These interesting letters were addressed to Admiral Vernon by Admiral Sir Charles Wager, W. Pulteney, Lord Cathcart, Speaker Onslow, Holles Duke of Newcastle, Lord Chancellor Hardwicke, Lord Vere, Beauclerk, and Admiral Byng, and contain some interesting particulars relative to the expeditions to the West Indies, Peru, Mexico, etc., from 1730 to 1745.—Sabin.

Some Seasonable Advice from an Honest Sailor, to whom it might have Concerned, for the Service of the C——n and C——y. 8vo. London.

> An interesting naval pamphlet, dealing entirely with naval matters, operations of the Privateers, manoeuvers in the West Indies, reference to the Louisbourg expedition.—Maggs, No. 502.

A Specimen of Naked Truth, from a British Sailor. 8vo. London. (30 pp.)

> It was for publishing this pamphlet, relating to the expeditions against the Spanish possessions in America, that Admiral Vernon was struck off the list of flag officers.—Puttick and Simpson.

A Letter to a certain Eminent British Sailor. Occasion'd by his Specimen of Naked Truth. From a zealous Asserter of his Merit, and sincere Well-wisher to his Person. 8vo. London.

> This relates to Admiral Vernon's exploits in the West Indies at Portobello and Carthagena, and includes his letter to the Governor of Jamaica with the answer, etc.—Maggs, No. 502.

1747   An Authentic Account of the late Expedition to Bretagne, conducted by Richard Lestock, Admiral of the Blue, and Lieut.-Gen. St. Clair, Commander-in-Chief of the Land Forces. 8vo. London.

1750   A Journal or Narrative of the Admiral Boscawen's Voyage to Bombay in the East-Indies, Benjamin Braund Commander, with Remarks on her Remarkable Quick Passage thither, and some Surprising Events that occurr'd during the same anno 1749, by a Young Gentleman; . . . also Thoughts on Trade, Duties, Smuggling, Shipwrecks, etc. 8vo. London.

> See A *Journal of a Voyage to the East Indies* under 1756 below.

1753-56   HOWARD, LEONARD (M.D.). A Collection of Letters and State Papers, from the Original Manuscripts of many Princes, Great Personages, and Statesmen, together with some curious and scarce Tracts, and Pieces of Antiquity, Religion, Political, and Moral. 2 parts in 1 vol. 4to. London.

This commences with a long letter concerning the Expedition of Admiral Penn and Venables against the Island of Hispaniola, during the Protectorship of Oliver Cromwell; also some interesting Letters of Sir George Calvert and others.—Sabin.

1756 A Journal of a Voyage to the East Indies, and back to England under the Command of Admiral Edward Boscawen and Major John Mompesson, 1747-1750. 4to. Edinburgh.

> The naval expedition was sent against the French at Pondicherry. It was unsuccessful owing to bad weather and the incapacity of the engineers, and cost the lives of 1,065 British and of about 200 French. In the operations Ensign Clive, afterwards Lord Clive, gained his first military distinction.—Maggs, No. 534.

Seamen's Letters. London.

> These are referred to and quoted in Maud Wyndham's *Chronicles of the Eighteenth Century* I, 146 ff. See Wyndham under GENERAL REFERENCE.

The State of Minorca, and its lost Condition, when A-1 B-g appeared off that Island. 8vo. London.

> For the Byng affair see Byng under 1739 above.

1757 A Genuine Account of the late Grand Expedition to the Coast of France, under the Conduct of Admirals Hawke, Knowles, and Broderick, General Mordaunt, . . . By a Volunteer in the said Expedition. 8vo. London.

> An account of the unsuccessful expedition against Rochefort, condemning the conduct of the sailors and marines after the capture of the Island of Aix.—Maggs, No. 534.

The Secret Expedition impartially disclos'd: or, an Authentick, faithful Narrative of all Occurrences that happened to the Fleet and Army commanded by Sir E—— H—— and Sir J—— M——, from its first sailing to its return to England. With apparent Reasons for not landing the Infantry, and many other interesting particulars, not yet made Publick. By a Commissioned Officer on board the Fleet, and Graduate of the University, . . . 8vo. London.

> Another account, with the names of the chief performers spelled out, is given below.

1759 A Genuine Account of the late Secret Expedition to Martinico and Guadeloupe, under Commodore Moore and General Hopson. Written at Guadeloupe, By a Sea-Officer who went out with Commodore Hughes. 8vo. London. (23 pp.)

> A Reprint of newspaper articles.—Sabin.

GARDINER, RICHARD. An Account of the Expedition to the West-Indies, against Martinico, Guadeloupe, and other Leeward Islands; subject to the French King. By Richard Gardiner, Esq., Captain of the Marines on board His Majesty's Ship Rippon, on the Expedition. Maps and plans. 4to. London.

> 2nd edit., London, 1760; 3rd edit., Birmingham, 1762; in French, Birmingham, 1762.
> These last three items seemingly refer to the same event.

MOLYNEUX, THOMAS MORE. Conjunct Expeditions: or Expeditions that have been carried on jointly by the Fleet and Army, with a Commentary on a Litoral War. 2 parts. Maps. 8vo. London.

> The various expeditions to Canada and the West Indies are mentioned and commented upon.—Sabin.

1760 For accounts of naval expeditions see *The Naval Chronicle,* under GENERAL REFERENCE.

WALKER, GEORGE (Commodore). Voyages and Cruises of Commodore Walker. 2 vols. London.

> Reprinted, London, Dublin, 1762. A modern reprint in the Sea Farers' Library, London, 1928. See below.
> The story of Commodore Walker's voyages makes delightful reading. Especially memorable is the Commodore's journey to London with his lady prisoner, a French woman, accompanied by his sailors variously mounted and accoutred, who thus sought to do him honor. The difference between a sailor's life in the merchant marine and the Royal Navy is vividly brought home.

> 1928 WALKER, GEORGE (Commodore). Voyages and Cruises of Commodore Walker. With Introduction and Notes by H. S. Vaughan. 8 plates and 2 maps. Seafarers' Library. London.
>
> It is stated that this is the first reprint since 1762.

1762 An Authentic Journal of the Siege of the Havana. By an Officer. To which is prefixed, A Plan of the Siege of the Havana, shewing the Landing, Encampments, Approaches, and Batteries of the English Army. With the Attacks and Stations of the Fleet. Plan. 8vo. London.

> This has to do with the operations of the fleet and army under Admiral Pocock and the Earl of Albemarle in the siege and capture of Havana. The following item deals with the same expedition.

MACKELLAR, PATRICK. A Correct Journal of the Landing of His Majesty's Forces on the Island of Cuba, and of the Siege and Surrender of the Havannah, Aug. 13, 1762. Together with a List of the Men of War taken and surrendered with the City, and the Return of Guns, Mortars, and Principal Stores. 8vo. London.

1765 CORNISH, SIR SAMUEL, and DRAPER, SIR WILLIAM. A plain Narrative of the Reduction of Manilla and the Philippine Islands. 8vo. London.

> Reprinted in *The Field of Mars,* vol. 2, London, 1781.
> This book is described in an article on The Philippine Islands, by Lucy M. J. Garnett, *Fortn. Rev.,* No. 379, N.S., vol. 70., July 1st, 1898. The Narrative was published by Rear-Admiral Cornish and Brig.-Gen. Draper, in reply to accusations of infringement of the capitulations made against these officers by the Spaniards.—Library of Congress. Manila was captured by the English in 1762.

1779 A Candid and Impartial Narrative of the Transactions of the Fleet, under the Command of Lord Howe, from the Arrival of the Toulon Squadron, on the Coast of America, to the time of his Lordship's Departure for England, with Observations. By an Officer then serving in the fleet. 8vo. London.

> 2nd edit., revised and corrected, with a Plan of the Situation of the Fleet, within Sandy-Hook, London, 1779.
> This work gives praise to Lord Howe and abuse of the Ministry, particularly Lord Sandwich.—Sabin.

1779-1780 HERVEY, FREDERICK. For accounts of naval expeditions see his *Naval History of Great Britain,* under GENERAL REFERENCE.

1788 DALRYMPLE, SIR JOHN. Memoirs of Great Britain and Ireland, from the Battle of La Hogue till the Capture of the French and Spanish Fleets at Vigo. 2 vols. in 1. 4to. Edinburgh.

> This is a collection of his papers and essays first published 1771, and reissued in 1788 with a continuation to the capture of the enemy's fleets at Vigo. This continuation contains an important Appendix, comprising, firstly, "Account of an intended Expedition into the South Seas by Private Persons in the Late War." Secondly, "Letter to Captain Roberts . . . on the subject of an Expedition into the South Seas." Thirdly, "Project of an Expedition to the Coast of Jucatan and of Honduras." Fourthly, "Weakness of the River La Plata."—From Maggs, No. 502.

1790 SUTHERLAND, DAVID (Captain). A Tour up the Straits from Gibraltar to Constantinople, with the leading Events in the present War between the Austrians, Russians, and Turks. 8vo. London.

1795 CROOKSHANKS, JOHN. The Conduct of John Crookshanks, Esq. late Commander of His Majesty's Ship the Lark, relating to his Attempt to take the Glorioso, a Spanish Ship of War, in July 1747: containing the Original Orders, Letters, Papers, that passed in consequence of that affair, between Captain Crookshanks, Admiral Knowles, the Secretaries of the Admiralty, and others. With a Plan, shewing the Positions of the Ships. 8vo. London.

An interesting narrative, relating to various parts of North America, containing letters and papers of Admiral Knowles, commander at Cape Breton, Robert Kirke, and others. For an answer see Erskine (R.), Knowles (Admiral), also . . . "Letter from a Gentleman in the Country to a Member of Parliament in Town; containing Remarks upon a Book lately published, entitled 'The Conduct and Treatment of John Crookshanks, Esq., late Commander of His Majesty's Ship the Lark.' "—Sabin.

1796    Narrative of the Proceedings of His Majesty's Fleet under the Command of Earl Howe from the second of May to the second of June, M.DCC.XCIV. 4to. London.

1798    NELSON, HORATIO (Admiral).    An Authentic Narrative of the Proceedings of His Majesty's Squadron, under Command of Rear-Admiral Sir Horatio Nelson, from its sailing from Gibraltar to the Conclusion of the Glorious Battle of the Nile; drawn up from the Minutes of an Officer of Rank in the Squadron. 8vo. London.

1800    SMITH, SYDNEY.    The English Expedition to Egypt. In *Edinb. Rev.,* vol. 2, p. 53.

## ADDENDA

1802    WILLYAMS, COOPER.    A Voyage up the Mediterranean in His Majesty's Ship the Swiftsure, one of the Squadron under the Command of Rear-Admiral Sir Horatio Nelson, K.B., Now Viscount and Baron Nelson of the Nile and Duke of Bronte in Italy. With a Description of the Battle of the Nile on the First of August, 1798, and a detail of Events that occurred subsequent to the Battle in various parts of the Mediterranean. 43 plates in colored aquatint. Fol. London.

1864    The Operations of the French Fleet under the Count de Grasse in 1781-82, as described in two contemporaneous journals. Illus. 8vo.   Bradford Club Series, no. 3.   New York.

Edited by John D. G. Shea. The Chevalier de Goussencourt was apparently a pseudonym; the second was written by a person friendly to de Grasse, if not by de Grasse himself. A journal of the cruise of His Most Christian Majesty, under the command of the Count de Grasse-Tilly, in 1781 and 1782. By the Chevalier de Goussencourt (translated from the MS.), pp. 25-133. Journal of an officer in the naval army in America, in 1781 and 1782. Amsterdam, 1783, pp. 136-185.—Monoghan.

1894-1932    For journals, letters, naval tracts, papers relating to expeditions, etc., see *Navy Society's Publications,* under GENERAL REFERENCE.

1903  The Destruction of the Portuguese Carracks by English Seamen, 1592-94. In Beazley II (from the Hakluyt of 1598-1600).  London.

The Unfortunate Voyage of the *Jesus* to Tripoli, in 1584.  In Beazley I (from the Hakluyt of 1589, and original publication of 1587).  London.

1927  NARBOROUGH, SIR JOHN.  Expedition to Tripoli.  Reprinted in full in Teonge from Charnock's *Biographia Navalis* I, 247-250.  See Teonge below.

TEONGE, HENRY (Chaplain).  The Diary of Henry Teonge, Chaplain on board H.M.'s Ships *Assistance, Bristol* and *Royal Oak*, 1675-1679.  Transcribed from the original Manuscript and edited with an Introduction and Notes by G. E. Manwaring.  8 illus.  Broadway Travellers' Series.  London.

> Teonge is often forced to relate how his sermons on board ship were interrupted by commands to change sail or prepare for battle.

1931  PASLEY, SIR THOMAS.  Private Sea Journals, 1778-1782, when in charge of the *Glasgow, Sybil,* and *Jupiter*.  Edited by R. M. S. Pasley.  Illus. and maps.  8vo.  London.

1934  BARLOW, EDWARD.  Journal of his Life at Sea in King's Ships, East and West India-Men, and other Merchantmen, from 1659 to 1703, transcribed by Basil Lubbock.  16 colored plates and 64 reproductions from Barlow's drawings.  2 vols.  8vo.  London.

> One of the charms of this journal is its variety.  Edward Barlow voyages everywhere, he suffers shipwreck, stranding, imprisonments, etc.  There is hardly an aspect of sea life which Barlow does not experience or touch upon.  He fought against the Barbary Pirates; at the battle of Lowestoft, 1665; captured by the Dutch in the Straits of Banca, 1672; two Voyages to the West Indies, 1678-1681; Various Voyages to India, China, &c.  Barlow was not only a superb sea-man, but an artist, and his drawings are of considerable ability.—Bookseller's Note.

1936  INGRAM, BRUCE S.  (Editor).  Three Sea Journals of Stuart Times.  Being, first, The Diary of Dawtrey Cooper, Captain of the *Pelican* of the Navy of his Majesty King Charles I.  Kept during the Expedition under the Earl of Lindsey to relieve La Rochelle in the Year of our Lord 1628.  Secondly, The Journals of Jeremy Roch, Captain of the King's Navy, describing some remarkable voyages and adventures at sea during the reigns of their Majesties Charles II, James II, and William III, together with a description of the Grand Engagements between the English and Hollander in the year 1666, in which he took an active part. Thirdly, The Diary of Francis Rogers, London Merchant. Kept on his voyages to the East Indies, the West Indies and elsewhere in the years 1703 and 1704, describing many strange sights and adventures in different parts of the Globe. Edited and Transcribed from the original Manuscripts by Bruce S. Ingram. 16 illus. 8vo. London.

# XVIII

## Adventures, Disasters, Shipwrecks

1595 HASLETON, RICHARD. Strange and wonderful Things happened to Rd. Hasleton, borne at Braintree in Essex, in his ten yeares Trauailes in many Forraine Countries. Penned as he delivered it from his own Mouth. Woodcuts. 4to. London.

> Reprinted in Beazley II, London, 1903.
> This is a brief account of capture by Algerine pirates, servitude in the galleys, escapes, imprisonment by the Inquisition, and final return home.

1612 Relation of an Englishman shipwrecked on the Coast of Camboya. London.

> So cited by Pinkerton XVII.

1614 DAVIES, WILLIAM. A True Relation of the Travailes and most miserable Captivitie of William Davies, Barber-Surgeon of London, under the Duke of Florence. Wherein is truly set downe the manner of his taking, the long time of his Slaverie, and meanes of his Deliverie, after eight yeeres and ten Moneths Captivitie in the Gallies. 4to. London.

> Chapter V is entitled "The Description and discovery of the River of the Amazons." The author states that he was a gentleman by birth and served in many naval and military operations. On Jan. 28, 1597-98 he sailed in a trading-ship to the Mediterranean; his ship was attacked by six galleys of the Duke of Florence; he was taken to Leghorn, where he worked as a slave for eight years and ten months. He was ransomed by a captain of a Florentine ship who desired to take him as a doctor on an expedition to the River Amazon. On returning to Italy he was again attacked, this time by an English pirate, but escaped to shore. He was arrested by the Inquisition, lived on bread and water in an underground unlighted dungeon for sixteen days, and then removed to another prison. An English shipowner helped him to escape, and after sailing about the Mediterranean, he reached London in 1614 and wrote a full and interesting account of his travels.—Maggs, No. 508.

1641 Sad Nevvs from the Seas. Being a true Relation of the Losse of that good Ship called the Merchant Royall, which was cast away ten leagues from the Lands end, on Thursday night, being the 23 of Septem. last, 1641, having in her a world of treasure, as this story following doth truly relate. Woodcut. London.

1650 FOSTER, NICHOLAS. A Briefe Relation of the late Horrid Rebellion acted in the Island Barbadoes, in the West Indies. Wherein is contained their Inhumane Acts and Actions, in Fining and Banishing the well

affected to the Parliament of England (both men and women) without the least cause given them so to doe, etc. Acted by the Waldronds
and their Abettors, Anno, 1650. Written at Sea by Nicholas Foster.
16mo. London.

1664　JOHNSON, WILLIAM.　Sermon and Narrative of the Dangers and Deliverances at Sea, with the Name of the Master and those that suffered,
also the Owners of the Ship. 8vo. London.

> Reprinted, 3rd edit., 12mo, London, 1672, under different title; 6th edit., Lon-
> don, 1769. See below.
> A very interesting and well written account of the shipwreck of the *William
> and John* of Ipswich, in 1648, on the coast of Norway near Fredrikstad, and of
> other escapes of the author from a watery grave.—From Maggs, No. 508.

> 1672　JOHNSON, WILLIAM.　Deus Nobiscum. A Narrative of a Great De-
> liverance at Sea, with the Name of the Master, Ship, and those that
> Suffered. Also a Sermon preached on their Return. 12mo. London.

1671　A Description of a Great Sea Storm, that Happened to some Ships in the
Gulph of Florida, in September last; Drawn up by one of the Company, and sent to his Friend at London. Fol. London.

> A broad sheet in verse.—Puttick and Simpson.

1675　JANEWAY, JAMES.　Mr. James Janeway's Legacy to his Friends: containing twenty-seven famous instances of God's Providence in and
about Sea-Dangers and Deliverances; with the Names of Several that
were Eye-witnesses to many of them. Engraved portrait. 12mo. London.

> Most of these shipwrecks, etc., took place off the coast of New England or
> in North American waters. The author was a native of Salem, Mass.—Maggs,
> No. 508. The "Epistle to the Reader" is signed John Ryther. He gives accounts
> of 29 (the number in the later editions) wrecks, etc., . . . and also gives his au-
> thorities, usually some person concerned in the disaster.—Maggs, No. 549.

1676　CUSACK, G.　The Grand Pyrate: Or, the Life and Death of Capt. George
Cusack The Great Sea Robber, with an Accompt of all notorious Robberies both at Sea and Land. Together with his Tryal, Condemnation,
and Execution. Taken by an Impartial Hand. 4to. London.

> Cusack travelled in New England and Virginia.

1682　ROWLANDSON, MARY.　For an account of captivity among the Indians of New England see under NORTH AMERICA.

1682 SMITH, WILLIAM, and HARSHFIELD, JOHN. A Full Account of the late Shipwreck of the Ship called The President, which was cast away in Montz-Bay in Cornwall on the 4th of February last, as it was deliver'd to His Majesty (both in writing and Discourse), by William Smith and John Harshfield, the only Persons that Escaped in the said Wreck. Together with all the remarkable Adventures in the said Voyage from their Sailing out of the Sound of Plimouth, on May-Day, 1682. Particularly their Engagement with Six Pirate-Ships at once on the Coast of Malabar. The whole Relation being taken in private Conference with the said William Smith. Fol. London. (8 pp.)

1685 PHELPS, THOMAS. A True Account of the Captivity of Thomas Phelps, at Machaness in Barbary, and of his strange escape in Company of Edmund Baxter and others, as also of the Burning of two of the greatest Pirat-Ships belonging to that Kingdom, in the River of Mamaora: upon the Thirteenth day of June, 1685. 4to. London.

> Reprinted in Osborne II, 498-510.
> Phelps' vessel the *Success,* of London, was captured by Algerine pirates Oct. 5, 1684, and he was carried as prisoner to Sallee and marched inland to Mekinez. On May 29, 1685, he and three others made their escape, reached the sea shore and put out to sea in a row boat, and were picked up by the Lark-Frigate, Captain Leighton. Upon Phelps' proposal an expedition was sent in to the harbor against two pirate boats at anchor, which were burnt with the loss of only one man to the English.—From Maggs, No. 534.

1689 PITMAN, HENRY. A Relation of the Great Sufferings and Strange Adventures of Henry Pitman, Chyrurgeon to the late Duke of Monmouth. 4to. London.

> Pitman was transported to the Barbadoes, and subsequently escaped and fled to Central America.—Puttick and Simpson.

1696 The Tryals of Joseph Dawson, Edward Forseith . . . for several Piracies and Robberies by them committed, in the Company of Every (Avery) the Grand Pirate, near the Coasts of the East-Indies; and several other Places on the Seas. Giving an Account of their villainous Robberies and Barbarities at the Admiralty Sessions, begun at the Old-Baily on the 29th of October, 1696, and ended on the 6th of November. London.

1700 DICKINSON, JONATHAN. For an account of the shipwreck of Robert Barrow see this date, under NORTH AMERICA .

1708  GEARE, ALLEN.  Eben-Ezer: or a Monument of Thankfulnesse: Being a true Account of a late miraculous Preservation of 9 Men in a small Boat, which was inclosed within Islands of Ice about 70 Leagues from Land, and continuing in Distress 20 Days; with the most remarkable Passages which happened in their Voyage from Plymouth to the New-foundland, in the Ship called the Langdon Frigate, Capt. Arthur Holdsworth Commander; with a List of the Names of those that sur-vived, and can witness to the Truth of this Relation. Written by Allèn Geare, Chief Mate of the Ship, who was a Principal Sherer both in the Misery and the Mercy. 8vo.  London.  (8 pp.)

> Reprinted in Osborne II, 787-792.
> The boat was bound for Newfoundland on a fishing trip and got stuck in the ice. A few saved themselves, among them the mate, by taking to the small boat and, with the assistance of fishermen, finally landed at St. Johns.

1711  DEAN, JOHN.  A True Account of the Voyage of the Nottingham Gal-ley of London, John Deane Commander, from the River Thames to New-England, Near which place she was cast away on Boon-Island, Dec. 11, 1710, by the Captain's Obstinacy, who endeavour'd to betray her to the French, or run her ashore; with an account of the False-hoods in the Captain's Narrative. And a faithful Relation of the Ex-tremities the Company were reduc'd to for Twenty-four Days on that Desolate Rock, where they were forc'd to eat one of their Companions who died, but were at last wonderfully deliver'd. The whole attested upon Oath, by Christopher Langman, Mate, Nicholas Miller, Boat-swain and George White, Sailor in said Ship. 8vo.  London.  (36 pp.)

> Revised and reprinted, with additions, 8vo, London, 1726; London, 1727; London, 1730; "now proposed for the last edition during the Author's Lifetime," London, 1738; 5th edit., London, 1762.

1712  SELKIRK, ALEXANDER.  Providence displayed: or, a very Surprising Account of one Mr. Alexander Selkirk, written by his own Hand.  4to.  London.

> An account, with slight change in title, London, 1800. See below.
> This tract is printed nearly verbatim from the narrative given by Capt. Woodes Rogers in his *Cruising Voyage round the World* (see this under this date as well as Capt. Cooke's *A Voyage to the South Sea*, CIRCUMNAVIGA-TIONS, and Steel's *The Englishman*). Reprinted in *Harl. Misc.* V.

>> 1800  SELKIRK, ALEXANDER.  Providence displayed; or, the remarkable Adventures of Alexander Selkirk, of Largo, Scotland, . . . By Isaac James. Map of the Island and 24 cuts. 12mo. London.

1715  EVANS, KATHERINE, and CHEEVERS, SARAH.  A Brief History of the Voyage of Katherine Evans and Sarah Cheevers to the Island of Malta, where the Apostle Paul suffer'd shipwreck, and their cruel sufferings in the Inquisition there, for near four years; occasion'd by the Malice of the Monks and Friers against them, and their several Conferences with them, and how they came to be delivered from thence, and their safe return home to England, with a short relation from George Robinson, of the sufferings which befel him in His Journey to Jerusalem and how he was preserved from the Hands of Cruelty, when the Sentence of Death was passed 'against him, 1715, *also* A Brief Discovery of God's Eternal Truth, written in the *Inquisition of Malta,* by Katherine Evans. First printed in the year 1663, in one volume. 12mo. London.

> Another issue, with a slight change of title, London, 1715. See below.

1715 EVANS, KATHERINE, and CHEVERS, SARAH. This is a short Relation of some of the Cruel Sufferings (for the Truth's Sake) of Katherine Evans and Sarah Chevers in the Inquisition in the Isle of Malta, who have suffered there above three years, by the Pope's Authority, there to be deteined till they dye. Which Relation of their sufferings is come from their own hands and mouths, as doth appear by the following Treatise. These two Daughters of Abraham were passing to Alexandria, and to Colicia . . . but the provision which the Inhabitants and Knights of Malta, (called Christians) provided for them, is the Inquisition. 12mo. London.

1720 AVERY, JOHN. The King of the Pirates; being an Account of the famous Enterprises of Captain Avery, the mock King of Madagascar, with his Rambles and Piracies, in two Letters from Himself during his stay at Madagascar, and once since his escape from thence. 8vo. London.

> This contains an interesting account of his proceedings, with Capt. Sharp, Capt. Gawkins, Goiguet, and other pirates, in nearly every part of America. See also Johnson, *A General History of the Pyrates* under 1724, GENERAL REFERENCE.

FALCONER, RICHARD (Captain). Voyages, Dangerous Adventures and Imminent Escapes of Captain Richard Falconer, containing the Laws, Customs, and Manners of the Indians in America, his Shipwreck, his Marrying an Indian Wife, his Narrow Escape from the Island of Dominico, . . . intermixed with the Voyages and Adventures of Thomas Randal, his Shipwreck in the Baltic, his being taken by the Indians of Virginia, . . . 8vo. London.

> Later editions: 8vo, London, 1724; London, 1734; 12mo, London, 1764, with the addition of A Great Deliverance at Sea, by W. Johnson, D.D.; 6th edit., corrected, London, 1769.
> According to Halkett and Laing the author of this work was W. R. Chetwood.

1723 AUBIN, —— (Mrs.). The Life of Charlotta Du Pont, an English Lady, taken from her own Memoirs; giving an Account how she was trepan'd by her Stepmother to Virginia, how the Ship was taken by some Madagascar Pirates, of her Marriage in the Spanish West Indies, . . . 8vo. London.

1724 PHILIPS, MILES. The Voyages and Adventures of Miles Philips, A West-Country Sailor. Containing A Relation of his various Fortune both by Sea and Land; the inhuman Usage he met with from the Spaniards at Mexico; and the Sufferings he and his Companions underwent by their Confinement and Sentence in the Spanish Inquisition. Together with A Natural Description of the Countries he visited, and particular Observations on the Religion, Customs and Manners of their respective Inhabitants. Written by Himself in the plain Style of an English Sailor. 12mo. London.

1725 LURTING, THOMAS. The Fighting Sailor Turned Peaceable Christian, Manifested in the Convincement and Conversion of Thomas Lurting, With a Short Relation of Many Great Dangers and Wonderful Deliverances he met withal. First written for private satisfaction, and now Published for General Service. 12mo. London. (47 pp.)

> A curious narrative. The author gives a lengthy account of Admiral Blake's attack on Santa Cruz in the Canaries in 1657. About this time Lurting became a Quaker and describes his hardships on declining to fight. The second half of the volume describes how in 1663 Lurting was mate to one George Pattison when their vessel was taken by an Algerine pirate off Majorca. Without any bloodshed Lurting was able to regain control of the vessel and landed the Moors on the coast of Barbary rather than sell them into slavery. On returning to the Thames King Charles II heard of the boat's arrival and paid it a visit, and on hearing the story said that the Turkish prisoners should have been brought to him. To which Lurting replied that he thought it better for them to be in their own country, at which the King smiled!—Maggs, No. 534.

1726 ASHTON, PHILIP. Memorial; or, an Authentick Account of the Strange Adventures and Signal Deliverances of Mr. Philip Ashton, who, after he had made his escape from the Pirates, liv'd on a desolate Island for about 16 months, . . . with a short Account of Mr. Nicholas Merritt, who was taken at the same time; to which is added, a Sermon on Dan. iii, 17, by John Barnard, V.D.M. 12mo. London.

> Philip Ashton was a native of Marble Head in Massachusetts, and on the 15th of June, 1722, with Nicholas Merritt, his kinsman, was taken prisoner by the Pirate Low, at Port Rossaway, Cape Sable, and carried into the West Indies, Central America, etc. He returned after long wanderings and many hardships to New England, and landed at Salem, May 1st, 1726. Mr. Barnard, the minister of Marble Head, preached a sermon upon the joyful occasion of his return to his native town. The book is full of incident, and little known to the book collectors of New England.—Puttick and Simpson.

1727 (?) FOX, JAMES (Captain). Seizure of the Ship Industry, And the Consequent Sufferings of Capt. James Fox and his Companions; Their Captivity Among the Esquimaux Indians in North America; and the Miraculous Escape of the Captain; The Disasters which attended the Mutineers, Interspersed with Anecdotes, Descriptions, etc. Also, the Providential Escape and Suffering of Captain Boyce In the year 1727. Folded plate. 12mo. London. (28 pp.)

1728 An Authentic Relation of the many Hardships and Sufferings of a Dutch Sailor, who was put on shore on the Uninhabited Isle of Ascension, by Order of the Commander of a Squadron of Dutch Ships. 8vo. London. (28 pp.)

> A very rare account of the marooning of a Dutch sailor who died after five and a half months, but left behind him a journal of his sufferings, which was found in his tent by some English sailors in Jan. 1726.—Maggs, No. 508.

1730 DALTON, JAMES. The Life and Actions of James Dalton, a noted Street Robber, . . . With accounts of his running away with the Ship when he was first transported, and likeways the Tricks he played in New York, the Bermudas, Virginia, Carolina, and other parts of America, taken from his own mouth while in Newgate. 12mo. London.

1732 MAY, CHARLES. An Account of the Wonderful Preservation of the Ship Terra Nova of London, Peter Daniel Commander, Homeward-bound from Virginia. Written by Charles May, Mate in the said Ship. In Churchill VI, 343-354.

> After sailing from Port Royal, Jamaica, Dec. 24, 1688, the crew encountered storms that broke all over the ship and flooded the interiors, drowning all the live stock carried for provisions. The account is full of good detail, described in the nautical terms of the day. It was written Feb. 2, 1698/9.

1740 ،DEAN, JOHN. A True and Genuine Narrative of the whole Affair relating to the Ship Sussex, as sent to the Directors of the Honourable East India Company; from the time she was deserted by the Officers and greatest part of the Crew, till she was unfortunately wreck'd on the Bassas de India. Also a particular Account of the many Hardships and Distresses of Sixteen Brave Sailors who staid on Board. By John Dean, the only surviving Person of them all. 8vo. London.

> The author was a sailor on board the Sussex, which sprung a leak during a storm to the east of the Cape of Good Hope. The officers and a majority of the crew, believing that the vessel would sink, transferred to the Winchester East Indiaman, which was close by; sixteen sailors, however, chose to stand by the vessel. They reached St. Augustin's Bay, Madagascar, in safety, whence they intended to sail for Mozambique, but the vessel ran on the Bassas de India rocks . . . and became a wreck. Nine of the crew set off for the shore in the pinnace,

three of whom were drowned by the boat capsizing. After various distresses Dean managed to get rescued by an English vessel and reached Bombay.— Maggs, No. 508.

1741   CARTWRIGHT, CHARLES.   A Faithful Narrative of the unfortunate Charles Cartwright, who, in his voyage to Jamaica, was Taken by a Spanish Privateer, and carried into St. Sebastian, his Hard Usage there, and wonderful Escape from thence.   8vo.   London.

1743   ANNESLEY, JAMES.   Memoirs of an Unfortunate Young Nobleman (James Annesley, Earl of Annesley) return'd from a Thirteen Years Slavery in America, where he had been sent by the Wicked Contrivances of his Cruel Uncle.   By Himself.   12mo.   London.

> Seemingly reprinted the same year with a Part the Second, 8vo, London; other publications on the same case: 8vo, London, 1744; London, 1745; London, 1769. See below.
> James Annesley (1715-1760) was the son of Lord Altham, a dissolute spendthrift. In 1716 Lord and Lady Annesley separated, and the child, after living with his father as a legitimate son for some years, was left to shift for himself. On the death of Lord Altham (1727) his brother, afterwards Earl of Anglesey, succeeded to the title and contrived to get his nephew sent to America, and there sold as a slave for a period of seven years. During this period he managed to escape and endeavouring to return and prove his identity, was retaken and according to the colonial laws was sentenced to a further term of servitude for breaking his bond. At the end of his slavery, in 1740, he managed to enter one of the ships of Admiral Vernon's fleet as a sailor, and telling his story to the officers was brought back to England by Vernon, and an action for ejectment was brought against Lord Anglesey, his uncle. He was declared legitimate, but being without funds, died before the case could be prosecuted further.—Robinson. The incident was used by various novelists, such as Smollett in *Peregrine Pickle,* Scott in *Guy Mannering,* Charles Reade in *The Wandering Heir,* and perhaps Stevenson in *Kidnapped.*

> 1743   ANNESLEY, JAMES.   Memoirs of an Unfortunate Young Nobleman. . . . Part II., by the author of the First, in which is continued the History of Count Richard, concluding with a Summary View of the Tryal. 2 vols. 8vo.   London.

> 1744   Fortune's Favourite, containing Memoirs of the Many Hardships and Sufferings . . . of Jacobo Anglicano, a Young Nobleman . . . trepanned into Slavery which he suffer'd for Thirteen Years, with the Manner of his Escape from it. 8vo.   London.

> 1745   The Case of the Hon. James Annesley, being a Sequel to the Memoirs of an Unfortunate Young Nobleman. 8vo.   London.

> 1769   The History of an Unfortunate Young Nobleman returned from a Thirteen Years' Slavery in America. 2nd edit., revised. 8vo.   London.

1745   CAREW, BAMPFYLDE-MOORE.   The Life and Adventures of Bampfylde-Moore Carew, the noted Devonshire Stroller and Dog-Stealer; as related by Himself, during his Passage to the Plantations in America.   Exeter.

There are a number of accounts of this vagabond's life: Goadby's Apology, London, 1749; 6th edition of this, with additions, 12mo, London, 1756; 8th edit., London, 1768; 9th edit., 12mo, London, 1775; again, London, 1788; etc. One which purports to be collected and amended from his own writings, by Thomas Price, London, n.d. Modern edition, London, 1931. See below. The work listed above relates his life and adventures no further than the time of his deportation to America. The others carry them on.

"Carew was born in Devonshire, was tried at Exeter about 1739 or 1740, and banished to Maryland, where he went at the cost of the public. He gives an amusing account of the country and his adventures in Maryland, Virginia, New Jersey, New York, and Connecticut, till he embarked for England. His accounts of how he bamboozled and bled Whitefield, Thos. Penn, Gov. Thomas, and others of good repute, are amusing, true or not."—Stevens.

1768 GOADBY, ROBERT. An Apology for the Life of Mr. Bampfylde-Moore Carew, commonly called the King of the Beggars: being an Impartial Account of his Life, from his leaving Tiverton School, at the age of Fifteen, and entering into a Society of Gypsies, to the present Time; wherein the Motives of his Conduct will be explain'd and the great Number of Characters and Shapes he has appear'd in through Great Britain, Ireland, and several other Places of Europe, be related; with his Travels twice through great Part of America. Large engraved folding portrait. 12mo. London.

Carew is said to have dictated this life himself.—Maggs, No. 465.

1788 GOADBY, ROBERT. The Life and Adventures of . . . And a Dictionary of the Cant Language, used by the Mendicants. Engraved portrait. London.

n.d. PRICE, THOMAS. The Compleat Mendicant, or Unhappy Beggar; being the Life of Bampfylde Moore Carew, an Unfortunate Gentleman, the Remarkable Adventures that befel him in 23 years Pilgrimage; . . . 8vo. London.

One suspects that the author of this account was also among the bamboozled.

1931 CAREW, BAMPFYLDE-MOORE. The King of the Beggars, edited by C. H. Wilkinson. Frontispiece and map. 8vo. Oxford.

LE SAGE, ——. The Adventures of Robert Chevalier, call'd De Beauchêne, Captain of a Privateer in New France. By Monsieur Le Sage . . . 2 vols. 12mo. London.

This contains an account of his residence among the Indians of North America, and his being sold as a slave in New England, and is said by the author to be a veritable narrative.—Sabin.

1747 HOUSTOWN, JAMES (M.D.). Memoirs of the Life and Travels of James Houstown, M.D. (Formerly Physician and Surgeon-General to the Royal African Company's Settlements in Africa, and late Surgeon to the Royal Assiento Company's factories in America), From the Year 1690 to this Present Year 1747. Containing a great Variety of curious Observations that occurred during the Course of above Thirty Years Travels in divers Foreign Parts. Collected and Written by his own Hand. 8vo. London.

Reprinted, with additional introductory matter, 8vo, London, 1753.

This was originally published under the name of Jacob Bickerstaff. It was also put forth with a different title the same year. It is a very curious book, by a Scotch Adventurer, who was concerned in the Darien settlement. He was surgeon to the Assiento Company's factories in America, and passed most of his life trading and negotiating in Central America and the Spanish Main. The author gives much information on Colonial affairs, civil, military, and naval.—Sabin.

1750-51  WILLS, WILLIAM.  A Narrative of the very Extraordinary Adventures and Sufferings of Mr. William Wills, late Surgeon on Board the Durrington Indiaman, Captain Richard Crabb, in her late voyage to the East-Indies, under the Convoy of Admiral Boscawen. Being a continued Series of Cruelty and Oppresion . . . Together with an Account of his banishment to Goa, and his Voyage to Brazil, under Captain Kinsey, Commodore of a Portuguese Squadron. 2 parts in 1.  8vo. London.

A very curious narrative. The early pages give some account of practical joking on board. The Surgeon and Captain of the "Durrington" quarrelled over a lady passenger, the former being put under guard with a very scanty food allowance. . . . He was illegally tried at Bombay, disgraced and banished to Goa On his return to England, via Brazil, another trial was held, an account of which was published later.—Maggs, No. 521.

1755  BARKER, ROBERT.  Narrative of the Sufferings of Robert Barker, Carpenter on board the Thetis Snow, of Bristol, in her Voyage to the Coast of Guinea and Antigua.  8vo.  London.

Another edition, London, 1762.

The *Thetis* was a small slaver plying between the Guinea Coast and the West Indies.

RAMBLE, JAMES.  For an account of his adventures in the West Indies see his *The Life and Adventures of James Ramble,* under WEST INDIES.

1758  Memoirs of a Protestant, condemned to the Galleys of France for his Religion. Written by Himself, comprehending an Account of the various Distresses he suffered in Slavery; and his Constancy in supporting almost every Cruelty that bigotted Zeal could inflict or Human Nature sustain; also a Description of the Galleys, and the Service in which they are employed. The Whole interspersed with Anecdotes relative to the General History of the Times, for a Period of Thirteen Years; during which the Author continued in Slavery, 'till he was at last set free at the Intercession of the Court of Great Britain. Translated from the Original, just published at the Hague, by James Willington.  2 vols.  12mo.  London.

This is included in a bibliography of Goldsmith's works by Iolo Williams, *Seven Eighteenth Century Bibliographies,* London, 1924.

WILLIAMSON, PETER. For an account of his captivity among the Indians of North America see his *French and Indian Cruelty Exemplified in the Life of Peter Williamson,* under NORTH AMERICA.

1761 SUTHERLAND, JAMES (Lieut.). A Narrative of the Loss of His Majesty's Ship, the Litchfield, Captain Barton, on the Coast of Africa. With an account of the Sufferings of the Captain and the surviving part of the Crew, in their Slavery under the Emperor of Morocco. 8vo. London.

> Later edition, London, 1768.
> The ship ran aground on the west coast of Morocco during a storm and became a total wreck. The survivors of her crew were taken captives by the Moors and were ultimately ransomed, with other British subjects, for 170,000 dollars. Capt. Barton was tried for loss of his vessel and was honorably acquitted.— Maggs, No. 508.

1762 FALCONER, WILLIAM. The Shipwreck. A Poem in Three Cantos. By a Sailor. Folding map and folding plate. 4to. London.

> This poem was highly praised in its day for its "terrific sublimity and wild beauty," as it is today for its technical accuracy. The author was thought to have rivalled Virgil in his description of storms and wind tossed ships. Falconer was a common sailor when he wrote the piece, but as a reward and an encouragement to others he was made purser on board a royal frigate. He enjoyed this honor but a short time, for his ship, the *Aurora,* on which he sailed, disappeared from man's ken and likewise the purser.

1764 NEWTON, JOHN (Rev.). An authentic Narrative of some Remarkable and Interesting Particulars in the Life of . . . (Rev. John Newton) communicated in a Series of Letters of the Rev. Mr. Haweis. Small folding map of the Guinea Coast. 12mo. London.

> The record of John Newton's twenty years of wandering life at sea. He later obtained the curacy of Olney, became the close friend of Cowper, and with Cowper published "Olney Hymns."—Bookseller's Note. Some portions of his wanderings Newton communicated in letters to his wife. See below.

> 1793 NEWTON, JOHN. Letters to a Wife, written during Three Voyages to Africa from 1750-54, by the Author of Cardiphonia. 2 vols. 12mo. London.
>
> > *Cardiphonia,* or the *Utterance of the Heart,* was published in 2 vols., London, 1780-81.

1766 HARRISON, DAVID (Captain). The Melancholy Narrative of the Distressful Voyage and Miraculous Deliverance of Captain David Harrison of the Sloop Peggy, of New York, on his Voyage from Fayal . . . to New York, until relieved by Capt. Evers of the Virginia Trade. Written by Himself. 8vo. London.

1771  DUBOIS-FONTANELLE, J. G.  The Shipwreck and Adventures of Monsieur Pierre Viaud, a Native of Bordeaux, and Captain of a Ship. Translated from the French by Mrs. Griffith.  8vo.  London.

> An interesting account of the shipwreck of the French Brigantine *Tigre,* Capt. Lacouture, on God Island, near Apalachicola on the coast of Florida in 1766, and of the Author's Travels along the coast and final rescue by a British detachment from Saint-Marc des Apalaches, to which fort he was taken; and of his final twenty-four days' voyage round to St. Augustine, and so to New York. —Maggs, No. 625.

1774  GREEN, WILLIAM.  The Sufferings of William Green; being a Sorrowful Account of his Seven Years Transportation to Marblehead, Massachusetts.  12mo.  London.

SMETHURST, GAMALIEL.  For a narrative of adventure among the Indians see his *Narrative of an Extraordinary Escape,* under NORTH AMERICA.

1776  PURNELL, THOMAS.  The following is a true and faithful Account of the Loss of the Brigantine Tyrrell, Arthur Coghlan, Commander; with the Misfortunes attending the said Vessel's Crew.  By Thomas Purnell, Chief Mate thereof.  4to.  London.  (8 pp.)

> This is dated "Hoxton, Sept. 1766," and signed "Thomas Purnell." After the author's shipwreck he landed at Marble Head near Boston, and thence proceeded homewards by way of North Carolina.—Sabin.

1779  PHILLIPS, —— (Captain).  Reciprocal Love, or the Adventures of Captain Phillips contained in Letters to an Officer stationed at an Interior Post in North America, including many interesting Events.  8vo.  London.

1782  ANDERSON, ——.  History of the Life and Adventures of Mr. Anderson, containing his strange Varieties of Fortune in Europe and America.  8vo.  Berwick.

PRENTICE, S. W.  Narrative of a Shipwreck on the Island of Cape Breton, in a Voyage from Quebec, 1780.  By S. W. Prentice, Ensign of the 84th Regiment of Foot.  12mo.  London.

> 2nd edit., 12mo, London, 1783; 3rd edit., London, 1783.
> An interesting narrative related with moderation and good sense.—Sabin.

1783  DALRYMPLE, ALEXANDER.  An Account of the Loss of the Grosvenor Indiaman, commanded by Captain John Coxon, on the 4th of August, 1782 (inferred from the Portuguese Description of the Coast of Africa to have happened between 28° and 29° S.), with a Relation of Events which befel those Survivors who have reached England, viz., Robert Price, Thomas Lewis, John Warmington, and Barney Larez, being the Report given in to the East-India Company by Alexander Dalrymple. 8vo. London.

See Carter under 1791 below for another account.

INGLEFIELD, —— (Captain). Narrative concerning the Loss of his Majesty's Ship the Centaur, of 74 Guns; and the miraculous Preservation of the Pinnace, with the Captain, Master and the Crew, in a Traverse of near 390 Leagues on the great Western Ocean. 8vo. London.

1783-1796 An Account of the Loss of H.M.S. *Deal Castle* off the Island of Porto Rico, 1787.—Captain Inglefield's Narrative concerning the loss of H.M.S. *The Centaur*, 1783.—Smith, C. A Narrative of the Loss of the *Catherine, Venus* and *Piedmont* (Transports), and the *Thomas, Golden Grove*, and *Aeolus* (Merchant Ships), near Weymouth, 1796.— The Habitable World Described, maps, 1788.—In 1 vol. 8vo. London.

1784 KEATING, MAURICE (Major). The Genuine Narrative of the Life and Transactions of Major Maurice Keating, The noted Pirate and Murderer, who was executed on Monday the 27th of December, 1784, at Cuckold's-Point, near Port Royal, in the Island of Jamaica . . . To which is added, A True and Faithful Account of the Loss of the Brigantine Tyrrill, And the uncommon Hardships suffered by the Crew. 8vo. London. (16 pp.)

1785 ROCH, JOHN. For an account of his captivity among the Indians of South America see his *The Surprizing Adventures of John Roch,* under SOUTH AMERICA.

Sabin spells the name Roach and puts the date as 1784 and states that the cover title reads The Second Edition.

1786 MERITON, HENRY, and ROGER, JOHN. A Circumstantial Narrative of the Loss of the Halsewell, East-Indiaman, Capt. Richard Pierce, which was unfortunately wrecked at Seacombe in the Isle of Purbeck. Compiled by the two chief Officers, who happily escaped the dreadful Catastrophe. 12mo. London.

SEMPLE, JAMES GEORGE ("Major"). Memoirs of the Northern Impostor, or Prince of Swindlers. Being faithful Narrative of the Adventures and Deceptions of James George Semple, commonly called Major Semple . . . with an Account of his devices . . . and his Trial and Sentences . . . 8vo. London.

> This adventurer, who was transported from England for fraud, served in the British forces and was captured and held prisoner 1776-77. See Semple under 1800 below.

1787  BOYS, WILLIAM. An Account of the Loss of the Luxborough Galley, by Fire, on her Voyage from Jamaica to London; with the Sufferings of the Crew, in the year 1727. 4to. London.

> A summary of this story is given in Nichols, *Literary Anecdotes* IX, 24-25. This narrative is a story of almost unparalleled horror in its relation of acts of cannibalism. Boys was second mate of the ship.

HAWKINS, JAMES (Captain). An Account of the Loss of his Majesty's Ship Deal Castle, commanded by Captain James Hawkins, off the Island of Porto Rico, during the Hurricane in the West-Indies, in 1780. 8vo. London. (48 pp.)

> See *Monthly Review,* LXXVI, 267.—Sabin.

LE BEAU, TIMOTHY. Barbarian Cruelty: or, an Accurate and Impartial Narrative of the Unparallelled Sufferings & almost incredible Hardships of the British Captives belonging to the Inspector Privateer, Capt. Rd. Veale . . . Originally published by T. Troughton, of London; now republished by Timothy Le Beau, of Exeter, his Fellow-Sufferer, in that dreadful Captivity. Exeter.

1788  For an account of the shipwreck of the Antelope, in 1783, see Keate, *An Account of the Pelew Islands* under 1788, SOUTH SEAS.

1789  VASSA, GUSTAVUS. Interesting Narrative of the Life of Olaudah Equiano or Gustavus Vassa, the African. Written by Himself. Portrait and plates. 12mo. London.

> 3rd edit., enlarged, London, 1790; another edition, 8vo, Dublin, 1791; London, 1794.
> The author tells of his life in Africa, his being kidnapped and sent to Virginia as a slave, his adventures in the West Indies, shipwreck on the Bahama Banks, etc.—Maggs, No. 502.

WALTON, WILLIAM. For an account of captivity among the Indians of Pennsylvania see his *A Narrative of the Captivity and Sufferings of Benjamin Gilbert and his Family,* under NORTH AMERICA.

1791 CARTER, G.  A Narrative of the Loss of the Grosvenor East Indiaman, which was unfortunately wrecked upon the coast of Caffraria . . . On the 4th of August, 1782, compiled from the examination of John Hynes, one of the Unfortunate Survivors. Frontispiece and 3 plates. 8vo. London.

> See Dalrymple under 1783 above and Reenen under 1792 below.

1792 REENEN, JACOB VAN.  Journal of a Journey from the Cape of Good Hope, undertaken in 1790 and 1791 by Jacob van Reenen and others of his Countrymen in search of the Wreck of . . . the Grosvenor. With additional Notes by E. Riou. 4to. London.

VERNON, FRANCIS V.  Voyages and Travels of a Sea Officer. 4to. Dublin.

> This presents the Revolution from the angle of a junior naval officer.— Bookseller's Note.

1793 BRISTOW, JAMES. A Narrative of the Sufferings of James Bristow, belonging to the Bengal Artillery, during Ten Years' Captivity with Hyder Ally and Tippoo Saheb. 8vo. London.

1795 MOORE, MARK.  The Memoirs and Adventures of Mark Moore, late an Officer in the British Navy. Interspersed with a Variety of original Anecdotes, selected from his Journals, when in the Tuscan, Portuguese, Swedish, Imperial, American, and British Service, in each of which he bore a Commission. Written by Himself. 8vo. London.

> Moore was by birth an American, and an officer in the British navy, afterwards an "itinerant play-house adventurer," etc.—Sabin.

PALMER, T. F.  A Narrative of the Sufferings of T. F. Palmer, and W. Skirving, during a Voyage to Botany Bay, 1794, being by the High Court of Justiciary in Scotland, found guilty of sedition, and sentenced to be there transported, the one for seven, the other for fourteen years. Interspersed with remarks, on the Cruelties inflicted on the other Passengers and Convicts, by the Captain of the Surprise Transport in which they sailed. Portrait. 8vo. London.

> Palmer was a Unitarian Minister who joined a Society at Dundee, known as the "Friends of Liberty," who demanded Universal Suffrage and Short Parliaments. He was convicted of sedition and transported for seven years. On the conclusion of his sentence he set off on a trading expedition to the South Seas. He was unsuccessful at New Zealand and Tonga and was wrecked at the Fijis and taken prisoner by the Spaniards at the Mariana Islands, where he died from dysentery.—Maggs, No. 644.

1796   SMITH, C.   A Narrative of the Loss of the Catherine, Venus, and Pied-
       mont Transports, and the Thomas, Golden Grove, and Aeolus Mer-
       chant Ships, near Weymouth, on Wed. 18th Nov. last. Published for
       the Benefit of the Unfortunate survivor from one of the Wrecks and
       her Infant Child. 8vo.   London.

       The fleet was bound for the West Indies.—Maggs, No. 508.

1797   CRESPEL, EMANUEL.   For his shipwreck and hardships ensuing see
       his *Travels in North America,* under NORTH AMERICA.

       MORRIS, P.   An Interesting Narrative of the Voyage, Shipwreck, and
       . . . Adventures of one Drake Morris. 12mo.   London.

       There is an item entitled *The Travels of Mr. Drake Morris* under 1755,
       FICTITIOUS VOYAGES AND TRAVELS.

1798   MACKAY, WILLIAM.   A Narrative of the Shipwreck of the Juno, on
       the Coast of Aracan, and of the singular Preservation of 14 of her
       Company on the Wreck, without food, during a period of 23 days. 8vo.
       London.

       Translated into German, Hamburg, 1800. See below.

       1800   (In German.)   Geschichte des Schiffbruchs der Juno an der Küste von
              Arracan in Ostindien. 12mo.   Hamburg.

1799   RAMEL, —— (General).   A Narrative of the Deportation to Cayenne,
       of Barthélmy, Pichegru, Willot, La Rue, Ramel, etc. In consequence
       of the Revolution of the 18th Fructidor (September 4, 1797). Contain-
       ing a Variety of important facts relative to that revolution, and to the
       voyage, residence and escape of Barthélmy, Pichegru, etc. From the
       French of General Ramel . . . 8vo.   London.

1800   BARRY, THOMAS.   For a narrative of adventures and captivity among
       the Indians see his *Narrative of the Singular Adventures and Captivity
       of Mr. Thomas Barry,* under NORTH AMERICA.

       GREGORY, WILLIAM.   A Visible Display of Divine Providence; or,
       the Journal of a Captured Missionary, designated to the Southern Pa-
       cific Ocean, in the Second Voyage of the Duff, commanded by Captain
       Thomas Robson captured by Le Grand Buonaparte off Cape Frio: in-
       cluding every remarkable Occurrence which took place on board the
       . . . Duff, Le Grande Buonaparte, etc., in the Province of Paraguay,
       Spanish South America, and in Portugal, on the return home, in 1798

and 1799. By William Gregory, one of the Missionaries. 8vo. London.

> For the first voyage of the *Duff* on her missionary expedition to the South Seas see James Wilson, *A Missionary Voyage to the Southern Pacific Ocean under 1799*, SOUTH SEAS.

A Narrative of the Loss of the Ship Hercules, commanded by Captain Benjamin Stout on the Coast of Caffraria, the 16th of June, 1796, also circumstantial details of his Travels through the Southern Deserts of Africa. 12mo. Hudson, N.Y.

SEMPLE, J. G. (Major). The Life of Major J. G. Semple Lisle; containing a Faithful Narrative of his Alternate Vicissitudes of Splendor and Misfortune. Portrait. 8vo. London.

> Autobiography of this celebrated adventurer, including a full account of the mutiny of the "Lady Shore," in which he was being carried as a convict to Australia, and of the adventures of the landing party in their journey to Rio Janeiro. —Maggs, No. 644. For this mutiny see John Black under 1798, SOUTH AMERICA.

## ADDENDA

1805 SAUNDERS, DANIEL (Jr.). A Journal of the Travels and Sufferings of Daniel Saunders, Jr. A Mariner on board the Ship Commerce, of Boston, Samuel Johnson Commander, which was cast away near Cape Morchet, on the coast of Arabia, July 10, 1792. 16mo. Hudson, N.Y.

1809 Authentic Narrative of the Wreck of His Majesty's Ship Sceptre of 64 Guns, Capt. Valentine Edwards, in Table Bay, Cape of Good Hope, November 6, 1799, including the Melancholy loss of upwards of Three Hundred and Fifty of the Crew, Captain, Officers, &c., and the Miraculous Preservation of the Rest, interspersed with Interesting Particulars and Cursory Observations. Also the sufferings of Don Joseph Pizarro, &c. . . . Folding plate of the wreck. 12mo. London.

> The book also contains two other accounts; firstly, of the fate of the various vessels comprising the Spanish expedition sent out to prevent Anson sailing into the South Seas, relating to Buenos Aires, Rio de Janeiro, Valdivia, etc.; secondly, the "Dreadful Sufferings of M. de St. Germain, M. de Chilly, &c." whose caravan was attacked by 1,200 Arabs between Suez and the Mediterranean Sea.—Maggs, No. 546.

1812  DALYELL, SIR J. G.  Shipwrecks and Disasters at Sea, or Narratives of Noted Calamities and Deliverances resulting from Maritime Enterprise, with Expedients for Preserving Life. 2 maps. 3 vols. 8vo. Edinburgh.

> New edition, unabridged, 12mo, London, 1846-1854.
> Many of the wrecks listed above are included in these doleful volumes of human suffering. As is well known, Byron utilized this work in composing the second canto of his *Don Juan.*

1820  A Narrative of the Loss of the Winterton East Indiaman, wrecked on the Coast of Madagascar in 1792; and of the Sufferings connected with that Event, etc. Map and 2 engraved views of the wreck. 8vo. Edinburgh.

> The survivors of this wreck, after living for some time in Madagascar, were able to proceed to Mozambique, whence they sailed for Bombay, being, however, captured by a French privateer and taken to Mauritius.—Maggs, No. 521.

1827  JOHNSTON, CHARLES.  For a narrative of capture by the Indians see under NORTH AMERICA.

1831  SEAWARD, SIR EDWARD.  Narrative of his Shipwreck and consequent Discovery of certain Islands in the Caribbean Sea, 1733-1749, edited by Miss J. Porter. 2 vols. 8vo. London.

1836  ELLMS, CHARLES.  Shipwrecks and Disasters at Sea, or Historical Narratives of the most noted calamities, and providential deliverances from fire and famine, on the ocean. Compiled by Charles Ellms. Illus. 12mo. Boston.

1840  A Narrative of the Loss of H.M.S. Royal George, of 108 Guns, sunk at Spithead, August 29th, 1782; with a concise Account of Colonel Pasley's Operations on the wreck in 1839 and 1840. 4 plates. 16mo. Portsmouth.

1841  DRAKE, SAMUEL G.  Tragedies of the Wilderness: or, True, and Authentic Narratives of Captives who have been carried away by the Indians, from the various Frontier Settlements. Illus. 12mo. Boston.

> Thirty-one Indian captivities, unabridged.—Dauber & Pine.

1896  POTE, WILLIAM (Jr.).  For a narrative of his captivity among the Indians in the French and Indian War see his *Journal during his Captivity in the French and Indian War,* under NORTH AMERICA.

1897 MILET, PIERRE (Father). For a relation of captivity among the Oneida Indians see under NORTH AMERICA this date.

1900 BATTELL, ANDREW. The Strange Adventures of Andrew Battell of Leigh in Essex. Edited by Ernest George Ravenstone, F.R.G.S. Maps. Bibliography. Hak. Soc., ser. II, vol. 6. London.

1903 MUNDAY, ANTHONY The Captivity of John Fox. From Hakluyt, 1589. In Beazley I. London.

1924 JACKSON, WILLIAM (Captain). The Voyage of Captain William Jackson (1642-45). Edited by V. T. Harlow. Camd. Misc. XIII. London.

> This recounts some raiding expeditions in the West Indies.

1925 KELLY, SAMUEL. An Eighteenth Century Seaman, whose days have been few and evil, to which is added Remarks, etc., on places he visited during his Pilgrimage in this Wilderness. Now edited, with Introduction, by Crosbie Garstin. London.

1929 SEAVER, J. E. For a relation of captivity among the Indians see his *A Narrative of the Life of Mrs. Mary Jemison,* under NORTH AMERICA.

1934 BARLOW, EDWARD. See his *Journal of his Life at Sea, in King's Ships, East and West Indiamen,* under NAVAL EXPEDITIONS.

# XIX

## Fictitious Voyages and Travels

1581 CARTHENIE, JOHN. The Voyage of the Wandering Knight. Deuised by John Carthenie, a Frenchman. London.

> Reprinted, London, 1607; 1609 (?); 1626 (?).
> This was translated by William Goodyear from the French of Jean de Cartigny. It is an allegorical voyage, dedicated to Sir Francis Drake, who is commended for his modesty as compared with the boastful claims of other voyagers. It describes the travels of the Wandering Knight in the World of Folly, his final redemption from Sin by Faith, and his safe arrival in the City of Heaven. The work is briefly analysed by Louis B. Wright in his *Middle Class Culture in Elizabethan England*.

1609 HALL, JOSEPH (Bishop). The Discovery of a New World; or, A Description of the South Indies, hetherto unknowne. By an English Mercury. 8vo. London.

> The title was entered at Stationers' Hall, January 18, 1608-09, by Thomas Thorpe. The British Museum assigns 1620 as the year of issue, but doubtfully. —John Carter Brown. This translation of Hall's *Mundus Alter et Idem* was done by John Healey. The 2nd edit., with some differences in title, London, 1684. The first six chapters of the Latin original were translated into English by Dr. Wm. King before 1711 (see Morley's *Ideal Commonwealths*, 1896). Latin original, Frankfort, 1605. See below.
> The author gives an account of the manners of the inhabitants of an imaginary country in the southern hemisphere; this is really a satire on the London of his day. According to the *Encycl. Brit.*, it "is said to have furnished Swift with hints for Gulliver's Travels."—Robinson, No. 56.

> 1684 HALL, JOSEPH. The Travels of Don Francisco de Quevedo, through Terra Australis Incognita, discovering the Laws, Customs, Manners and Fashions, of the South Indians. A Novel. Originally in Spanish. 16mo. London.
>
> > See A. Esdaile, *A List of English Tales*.

> 1605 HALL, JOSEPH (Bishop) Mundus Alter et Idem, sive Terra Australis ante hac semper incognita longis itineribus peregrini Academici nuperrime lustrata. Auth: Mercurio Britannico. 5 curious engraved folding maps of fanciful representations of the Terra Australis. 12mo. Frankfort.
>
> > "This strange composition, sometimes erroneously described as a political romance, to which it bears no resemblance whatever, is a moral satire in prose, with a strong undercurrent of bitter gibes at the Romish Church and its eccentricities, which sufficiently betrays the author's main purpose in writing it. It shews considerable imagination, wit, and skill in latinity, but it has not enough of verisimilitude to make it an effective satire, and does not always avoid scurrility. The manuscript had been entrusted some years before to a friend named Knight, who was responsible for its publication." "Whalley, in his Inquiry into the learning of Shakespeare, states: 'I cannot forbear mentioning a Latin book of Bishop Hall's, equally valuable and forgotten, called 'Mundus Alter et Idem,' where under a pretended description of the Terra Australis, he gives us a very ingenious satire on the vices and follies of mankind.' "—Quoted by Maggs, No. 580.

1619 CERVANTES SAAVEDRA, MIGUEL DE. The Trauels of Persiles and Sigismunda. A Northern History . . . The first Copie, beeing written in Spanish; translated afterward into French; and now, last, into English. 4to. London.

1636 LLOYD, DAVID. The Legend of Captain Jones, relating his Adventures to Sea, his first Landing and Strange Combat, Furious Battles, his relieving of Kamper Castle, Admirable Sea Fight with the Gallies of Spain, his being taken Prisoner, and Hard Usage, Liberation and Return to England. 4to. London.

> Reprinted, London, 1648; in 2 parts, 12mo, London, 1656; 8vo. London, 1671. See below .
>
> Lloyd is exclusively remembered by this jeu d'esprit, produced soon after he left Oxford. It is a genial if somewhat coarse burlesque upon the extravagant adventures of a sea-rover called Jones, who, says Wood, "lived in the reign of Queen Elizabeth, and was in great renown for his exploits . . ." Elsewhere Wood says that the "legend" was a burlesque upon a Welsh poem entitled "Awdl Richard John Greulon"; but the view that Jones was not an altogether mythical person seems to derive support from the fact that, in his "Rehearsal Transposed" Andrew Marvell says, apropos of the "Legend," "I have heard that there was indeed such a captain, an honest brave fellow; but a wag that had a mind to be merry with him hath quite spoiled his history."—From Maggs, No. 574.

> 1671 LLOYD, DAVID. The Legende of Captaine Jones; relating his Adventure at Sea; his first landing, and strange Combat with a mighty Bear, . . . 8vo. London.

1638 GODWIN, FRANCIS (Bishop). The Voyage of Domingo Gonzales to the Moon. London.

> Reprinted in *Harl. Misc.* XI, 1808-1811; in *Anglia* X, 428-450.—Eddy, *Gulliver's Travels*.

HERBERT, THOMAS. Some Yeares Travels into Africa and Asia. London.

> Cited by Eddy, *Gulliver's Travels*.

WILKINS, JOHN (Bishop). The Discovery of a World in the Moone; or, a Discourse tending to prove 'tis probable there may be another habitable World in that Planet. 12mo. London.

> 2nd edit., London, 1638; 3rd, revised and enlarged, London, 1640.

1641 A Description of the famous Kingdom of Macaria. 4to. London.

> This little treatise, composed in the form of a novel, was designed to intimate a new model of government as the proper means to reconcile the breach which was then beginning between King Charles and his Parliament. It is reprinted in the first volume of the *Harleian Miscellany*.—Lowndes.

1668    A Relation of the Countrey of Jansenia: wherein is treated of the Singularities founde therein: the Customs, Manners, and Religion, of its Inhabitants. Written in French; and Englished by P. B. 8vo. London.

NEVILLE, HENRY. The Isle of Pines; or, A Late Discovery of a fourth Island in Terra Australis Incognita. Being a True Relation of certain English Persons, who in the days of Queen Elizabeth, making a Voyage to the East India, were cast away, and wrecked upon the Island near to the Coast of Terra Australis Incognita, and all drowned, except one Man and four women, whereof one was a Negro. And now lately Anno Dom. 1667, a Dutch ship driven by foul weather there by chance have found their Posterity (speaking good English) to amount to ten or twelve thousand persons, as they suppose. The whole Relation follows, written, and left by the Man Himself a little before his death, and declared to the Dutch by his Grandchild. 4to. London. (9 pp.)

> Reprinted, 12mo (19 pp.), London, 1768. Dutch version (perhaps the original?), Rotterdam, 1668. See below.
> This rare piece has been ascribed respectively to H. Neville, George Pine, and Cornelius van Sloetten. The last named person is certainly the author of another piece on the same subject.—Sabin. The details of the narrative are necessarily of a somewhat coarse and indecent character.—Robinson, No. 20.

1668    (In Dutch.)   Sprecht Verhaal van't Eiland van Pines, en des zelfs Bevolking: Of laatste Ontdekking van een vierde Eiland in Terra Australis Incognita . . . Rotterdam.

1671    SCHOOTEN, HENRY. The Hairy Giants: Or, A Description of Two Islands in the South Sea, called by the name of Benganga and Coma: Discovered by Henry Schooten of Harlem; In a Voyage begun January 1669, and finished October 1671. Also a perfect Account of the Religion, Government, and Commodities of those Islands; with the Customs and Manners of the Inhabitants, which are of an extraordinary stature, namely, Twelve Feet high, or thereabouts. Written in Dutch by Henry Schooten; and now Englished by P. M. Gent. Map 4to. London.

See *Monthly Review,* XXXV, 471.—Sabin.

1673    HEAD, RICHARD. The Floating Island; or, a New Discovery, relating the strange Adventure on a late Voyage, from Lambethana to Villa Franca, alias Ramallia, to the Eastward of Terra del Templo: By three Ships, viz., The *Pay-naught, Excuse, Least-in-Sight,* under the Conduct of Captain *Robert Owe-much:* Describing the Nature of the Inhabitants, their Religion, Laws and Customs. Published by Frank Careless, one of the Discoverers. 4to. London.

Richard Head (1637-1686) was born at Carrickfergus, son of a nobleman's chaplain who was murdered by the Irish rebels in 1641. His writings were amusing but of a very indelicate nature and appealed to the Restoration public. He lost his life at sea, whilst on a voyage to Plymouth. The present work is a sort of scurrilous account of life in London.—Maggs, No. 644. See Head under 1674 below.

1674 HEAD, RICHARD. The Western Wonder: Or, O Brazeel, an Inchanted Island (discovered); with a Relation of Two Ship-wracks in a dreadful Sea-storm in that discovery. To which is added, a Description of a Place, called Montecapernia, relating the Nature of the People, their Qualities, Humours, Fashions, Religion, . . . 4to. London.

A purely imagined narrative, after the style of the "Isle of Pines" (which the author cites as a "monstrous Fiction"), Swift's Gulliver's Travels, etc. Containing a three-page poem on "A great Sea-storm described, which hapned in the discovery of O Brazeel."—Maggs, No. 572. The name O Brazeel suggests the Irish Hy Brasil, the land of the ever-young, located far out in the Western Sea.

1675 BARNES, JOSHUA. Gerania: A New Discovery of a Little Sort of People, antiently discoursed of, called Pygmies, with a lively Description of their Stature, Habit, Manners, Buildings, Knowledge and Government, being very delightful and profitable. 12mo. London.

Reprinted, 8vo, London, 1750.
This work may have furnished Swift some hints for his *Voyage to Lilliput.* Barnes was a precocious poet, who published *Sacred Poems* at the age of 15. He also published an edition of Homer.

1679 VAIRASSE, DENIS (d'Alais). The History of the Sevarites or Sevarambi: a Nation inhabiting part of the third Continent, commonly called Terrae Australes Incognitae. With an Account of their admirable Government, Religion, Customs, and Language. Written by one Captain Siden, a worthy person, who, together with many others, was cast away upon those Coasts, and lived many years in that Country. Together with "the Second Part more wonderful and delightful than the First." 2 vols. in 1. 12mo. London.

The Part II of this work does not correspond with the French and probably was not written by Vairasse. A translation was published in 1727 as Part III of *Gulliver's Travels.*—From Eddy. Another edition, with preface by Thomas Skinner, London, 1738. French original, Paris, 1677-79. See below.
This Extraordinary Voyage is described at length by Atkinson, *The Extraordinary Voyage in French Literature from 1700 to 1720.* It belongs to that group of fictitious narratives purporting to be truthful accounts of voyages made by Europeans to then little known lands. Based upon realistic detail they are in the main satires or criticisms of the existing state of society.

1677 VAIRASSE, DENIS (d'Alais). Histoire des Sévarambes, peuples qui habitent une partie du troisième continent ordinairement appelé Terre Australe . . . 5 vols. 12mo. Paris.

The good Southey felt that there was a want of moral and religious feeling in the book, but he admitted that it was no ordinary work.

1682   A Discovery of Fonseca In a Voyage to Surranam, The Island so long
sought for in the Western Ocean. Inhabited by Women with the Account of their Habits, Customs and Religion. And the Exact Longitude
and Latitude of the Place, taken from the Mouth of a Person cast
away on the Place in a Hurricane, with the Account of their being cast
away. 4to. London. (8 pp.)

> This is signed I. S. Reprinted, Dublin, 1682. There is another work dated
> London, 1708, with much the same title. It may be the same piece or the story
> reworked. See under 1708 below.

1687   BERGERAC, CYRANO DE. The Comical History of the States and
Empires of the Worlds of the Moon and Sun. Written in French by
Cyrano Bergerac. And newly Englished by A. Lovell. 2 vols. in 1.
8vo. London.

> Another English version by Derrick was published, London, 1754. A mod-
> ern edition, translated with Introduction and Notes, by Richard Aldington,
> Broadway Translations, London, c. 1925. French original, Paris, 1657-1662.
> This is the best known of the philosophic voyages of which the French geni-
> us was so prolific in the seventeenth century. For the indebtedness of Swift
> to this work see Eddy. The original voyage to the moon was supposed to have
> been written as early as 1648; that to the sun was begun about 1650 and left un-
> finished. The early French editions, and consequently the English translations
> after them, were cruelly expurgated, for the Church kept a watchful eye open
> for heresies and sceptical views. These voyages, like others of the age, were not
> Utopias, but satires upon existing institutions, upon humbugs, prejudices, literal
> belief in the Old Testament, and the fundamental evil nature of man.

> 1754   BERGERAC, CYRANO DE. A Voyage to the Moon . . . A Comical
> Romance. Done from the French of Monsieur Cyrano de Bergerac,
> by Mr. Derrick. London.

> 1657   BERGERAC, CYRANO DE. Histoire Comique, par Monsieur de Cy-
> rano Bergerac. Contenant les Estats et Empires de la Lune. 12mo.
> Paris.

> > The edition of 1662 must be the one that contains the first print-
> > ing of the *Voyage to the Sun.*

1687-1694   MARANA, GIOVANNI PAOLO. Letters writ by a Turkish Spy,
who lived five and forty Years undiscover'd at Paris, giving an impartial Account to the Divan at Constantinople, of the most remarkable
Transactions of Europe, and discovering several Intrigues and Secrets
of the Christian Courts (especially that of France), from the Year
1637 to the Year 1682. 8 vols. 12mo. London.

> 2nd vol. appeared under pseudonym, Muhammad, London, 1690; 7th vol.,
> London, 1693; and 8th and last, London, 1694. An edition, 8 vols., 8vo, London,
> 1702; London, 1718; 8 vols., 12mo, London, 1741; again, 8 vols., 12mo, London,
> 1770. Translated into French, Cologne, 1717. See below.
> This is usually ascribed to Giovanni Paola Marana. But in Boswell it is re-
> corded that Johnson reported that Mrs. Manley affirmed her father, Roger Man-
> ley, to have written the first two volumes. Dunton stated, however, that most
> of the letters were composed by a hack writer named South under the direction

of Dr. Robert Midgley. Some of the editions pretend that the work was originally written in Arabic and translated into Italian, thence into English. It is probable that Italian was the original language of the work. With it and Montesquieu's *Lettres Persannes* begins that succession of Letters from a Chinese Spy, Letters from an Armenian, etc., that ran such a marked vogue in the eighteenth century as a method of social criticism.

> 1717 (In French.) L'Espion dans les cours des princes chrétiens, ou lettres et mémoires d'un Envoyé secret de la Porte dans les cours de l'Europe, où l'on voit les découvertes qu'il a faites dans toutes les Cours où il s'est trouvé, avec une dissertation curieuse de leurs forces, politique et religion; traduit de l'anglois par * * *. Nouvelle édition augmentée dans le corp de l'ouvrage. 6 vols. 12mo. Cologne.

1688 BEHN, MRS. APHRA. A Discovery of New Worlds, from the French; to which is prefixed a Preface, by way of essay on translated prose; wherein the Arguments of Father Tacquet, and others, against the System of Copernicus are likewise considered and answered. 8vo. London.

> Another edition, London, 1790.
> The original is said to be from Fontenelle.

1692 A Voyage to the World of Cartesius, written originally in French and now translated into English (by T. Taylor). Astronomical diagrams. 8vo. London.

> 2nd edit., London, 1694.
> Gabriel Daniel is stated by Halkett and Laing to be the original author. It has been ascribed to Defoe, but not very successfully.

1693 FOIGNY, GABRIEL. A New Discovery of Terra Incognita Australis, or the Southern World. By James Sadeur a French-man. Who being Cast there by a Shipwrack, lived 35 years in that Country and gives a particular Description of the Manners, Customs, Religion, Laws, Studies, and Wars, of those Southern People; and of some Animals peculiar to the Place; with several other Rarities. These Memoirs were thought so curious, that they were kept Secret in the Closet of a late Great Minister of State, and never published till now since his Death. Translated from the French Copy printed at Paris. 12mo. London.

> French original, Geneva, 1676. See below.
> It is of interest to note that, in the English edition, John Dunton, its translator and publisher, anglicises the name "Terra Australis" into Australia, and the inhabitants into Australians. Purchas has also used the name earlier, when his publisher misprinted the word Australia. Later writers, including Hawkesworth, adopted and repeated the wrong spelling, which is now, of course, in general use.—From Maggs, No. 491. This is probably the most famous of all the accounts of Terra Australis, which in this case is about 3,000 leagues in length and 400 or 500 leagues in breadth, and contains about "fourscore and 16 millions" of inhabitants. It is a fantastic mixture of the marvellous and the realistic, and is intended to be a conscious, logically argued attack on the Christian tradition. For analysis of its material and purpose see Atkinson, *The Extraordinary Voyage in French Literature 1700 to 1720.*

1676 FOIGNY, GABRIEL. La Terre Australe connue: c'est-à-dire la description de ce pays inconnu jusqu'ici, de ses moeurs et de ses coûtumes. Par Mr. Sadeur, avec les avantures qui le conduisirent en ce continent . . . 12mo. Geneva.

1703 Iter Lunare, Or a Voyage to the Moon. Containing some Considerations of the Nature of that Planet. The Possibility of getting thither. With other pleasant Conceits about the Inhabitants, their Manners and Customs. 8vo. London.

> An edition of 1704 names the author as David Russen of Hythe in Kent.— *Term Catalogues.* For more voyages to the moon see Defoe under 1705; *Miscellanea Aurea* under 1720; *Pythagorolunister,* n.d.; Daniel, 1751 below.

1704 PSALMANAAZAAR, GEORGE. An Historical and Geographical Description of Formosa, an Island subject to the Emperor of Japan: the Religion, Customs, Manners of the Inhabitants: the Author's Travels, Conferences with the Jesuits in Europe, and Conversion to Christianity, by George Psalmanaazaar, Native of the said Island, now in London. Map and copperplates. 8vo. London.

> 2nd edit., London, 1705. Modern reprint, Library of Impostors, London, 1926. Translated into French, Amsterdam, 1705. See below.
> The author, whose real name has never been found out, was one of the most celebrated impostors of all times. Born supposedly in the south of France, he got a good education, but being poor he took to the road and led the life of an adventurer. He suffered himself to be converted to the Anglican Church by the chaplain of a regiment in Holland and was passed on to the Bishop of London, who with full faith in his claims, sent him to Oxford to make a translation of the Catechism into Formosan. Doubt at once arose over the authenticity of his narrative. The author finally repented of his life of imposture and gave himself up to hackwork and naturally to a life of poverty. He won the deep respect of Dr. Johnson, who said he would as soon think of contradicting a bishop as Psalmanaazaar. His Memoirs published in 1764 is a remarkable document. For a pleasant essay on the man and his work see Bracey, *Eighteenth Century Studies,* 1925.

> 1926 PSALMANAAZAAR, GEORGE. Historical and Geographical Description of Formosa. Edited by N. M. Penzer. 16 illus. reproduced from the original edition. 8vo. Library of Impostors. London.

> 1705 (In French.) Description de l'Ile Formosa en Asie. 8vo. Amsterdam.

An Enquiry into the Objections against George Psalmanazaar of Formosa. In which the Accounts of the People, and Language by Candidius, and other European Authors, and the Letters from Geneva, and from Suffolk about Psalmanazaar, are proved not to contradict his Accounts. To which is added, George Psalmanazaar's Answer to Mons. D'Almavy of Sluice (Sluys). Folding plate. London. n.d.

1705 DEFOE, DANIEL. A Journey to the World in the Moon, . . . London.

DEFOE, DANIEL. A Second and more strange Journey to the World in the Moon. London.

DEFOE, DANIEL. The Consolidator, or, Memoirs of Sundry Transactions from the World in the Moon, translated from the Lunar Language, by the Author of the True-born English Man. 8vo. London.

> This prose satire contains the first hints of many of the ideas which Swift afterwards embodied in Gulliver, and also a great many sly hits at all the authors of the times from Dryden to Tom D'Urfey.—Bookseller's Note.

1706 D'URFEY, TOM. Wonders in the Sun or the Kingdoms of the Birds. London.

> This is obviously based on Cyrano de Bergerac's works.

1708 EBN-TOPHAIL. Hai Ebn Yokdhan. Translated from the Arabic by Simon Ockley. London.

> This is an imaginary philosophical voyage. The author was an Arabian who lived towards the close of the 12th century in Spain. This work was translated by Moses Narboniensis into Hebrew and into Latin by Pococke, 1671. Several English versions were made from the Latin. Its fundamental principles are that without the aid of instruction we can learn how to meet our physical wants and by contemplation we can learn of the existence of the Deity.—Dunlop, *History of Prose Fiction.* Ockley was an orientalist, whose *History of the Saracens,* 1708-1718, was the main source of Mohammedan history for generations. He also translated other works from the Arabic.—D.N.B.

1708 MISSON, FRANCOIS MAXIMILIEN. A New Voyage to the East-Indies by Francois Leguat and his Companions. Containing their Adventures in Two Desert Islands, Accounts of remarkable things at the Cape of Good Hope, the Island of Mauritius, at Batavia, the Island of St. Helena and other places on their Route . . . Numerous plates and maps. 8vo. London.

> Reprinted by the Hakluyt Society, London, 1890. It appeared in French, London and Amsterdam, 1708; also in Dutch, Utrecht, 1708.
> For an account of this extraordinary mixture of fact and fiction, which has long fooled learned editors, see Leguat under 1708, EAST INDIES. A lengthy analysis of the work has been made by Atkinson, *The Extraordinary Voyage in French Literature 1700 to 1720.*

Pasquinia, or an Account of Pasquin's Travels. 4to. London.

A Voyage to the New Island Fonseca, near Barbadoes. With some Observations made in a Cruize among the Leward Islands. In Letters from Two Captains of Turkish Men of War, driven thither in the Year 1707. Translated out of Turkish & French. London. (44 pp.)

> To be driven from the shores of Europe to the West Indies by a storm ought to be the occasion for observation. The only approach to this feat of long

distance endurance is the drifting from the Gulf of Lyons to the Cyclades related in Canto II of Byron's *Don Juan.*

1719   DEFOE, DANIEL.   The Life and strange surprizing Adventures of Robinson Crusoe of York, Mariner.   London.

> Of this popular work there were many editions both old and modern, together with numerous continuations. Concerning Alexander Selkirk, the original of the hero, see Woodes Rogers under 1712 and Cooke under 1712, CIRCUMNAVIGATIONS.

1720   Miscellanea Aurea: or the Golden Medley. Consisting of I. A Voyage to the Mountains of the Moon, . . . II. The Fortunate Shipwreck, or a Description of New Athens. . . . III. Alberoni, or a Vindication of the Cardinal. IV. The Secret History of the Amours of Don Alonso. . . . 8vo.   London.

> This was written chiefly, if not wholly, by Thomas Killigrew Jr.—Bookseller's Note.

1724   DEFOE, DANIEL.   A Continuation of the Life and Adventures of Signor Rozelli, Late of the Hague, Giving an Account of all that befell him . . . in a Series of the most diverting History and Surprizing Events ever yet made Publick. 11 full-page engraved plates. 8vo. London.

1725   DEFOE, DANIEL.   A New Voyage round the World, by a Course never sailed before, being a Voyage undertaken by some Merchants, who afterwards proposed the Setting up of an East-India Company in Flanders. Copperplates. 8vo.   London.

> Of this work there were many later editions. It is regarded as the last of Defoe's generally accepted works of fiction. Its descriptions of the lower parts of South America, doubtless based on actual accounts, are notable for their veracity.

1726   BOYLE, ROBERT (Captain).   The Voyages and Adventures of Captain Robert Boyle, in several parts of the World. Intermixed with the Story of Mrs. Villars an English Lady, with whom he made his surprising Escape from Barbary, to which is added, The Voyage, Shipwreck and Miraculous Preservation of Richard Castleman, Gent., with a Description of the City of Philadelphia, and the Country of Pennsylvania. 8vo.   London.

> Frequently reprinted. There is an edition of 1726 with a slightly different title; 2nd edit., 8vo, London, 1728; London, 1735; London, 1787; 12mo, London, 1794. Translated into French, Amsterdam, 1730. See below.
> This interesting adventure novel is ascribed to various authors, *e.g.,* Defoe, William Rufus Chetwood, and Benjamin Victor. Castleman's visit to Philadelphia is believed to be authentic; it contains an account of the Indians with a specimen of their language.

1787 BOYLE, ROBERT (Captain). The Voyages and Adventures of . . . Likewise including the History of an Italian Captive and the Life of Don Pedro Aquilio, . . . Full of various and amazing turns of Fortune. Engraved plate of the Indians attacking Boyle's ship. 12mo. London.

1730 (In French.) Les voyages et avantures du Capitaine Robert Boyle . . . avec la Relation du voyage, du Naufrage & de la conservation miraculeuse du Sr. Castleman, où l'on voit une description de la Pennsylvanie & de Philadelphie sa capitale. 7 engraved plates. 2 vols. in 1. 12mo. Amsterdam.

DEFOE, DANIEL. The Four Voyages of Capt. George Roberts; being a Series of Uncommon Events, which befell him in a Voyage to the Islands of the Canaries, Cape de Verde, and Barbadoes, from whence he was bound to the Coast of Guiney. The manner of his being taken by three Pyrate Ships . . . Folding map and four plates. 8vo. London.

This work is usually attributed to Defoe. See same under AFRICA.

SWIFT, JONATHAN. Travels into several remote Regions of the World. In Four Parts. By Lemuel Gulliver, first a Surgeon, and then a Captain of several Ships. Portrait and 6 plates. 2 vols. London.

Of this famous work there were many subsequent editions, imitations, and continuations. See under 1731 and Munchausen, 1785, below. For a study of its sources see Eddy, *Gulliver's Travels.*

1727 BRUNT, SAMUEL (Captain). A Voyage to Cucklo-Gallinia, with a Description of the Religion, Policy, Customs and Manners of that Country. 8vo. London.

DORRINGTON, E. The Hermit, or the Unparalleled Sufferings and Surprising Adventures of Mr. Philip Quarll, with his discovery upon an Uninhabited Island in the South Seas. Map. 8vo. London.

Frequently reprinted; some editions list the author's name as Peter Longueville. See below.

1750 QUARLL, PHILIP. The Hermit: or the Unparalleled Sufferings and Surprising Adventures of Mr. Philip Quarll, an Englishman, lately discovered by Mr. (Edward) Dorrington, a Bristol Merchant, upon an uninhabited Island in the South Sea, where he has lived about fifty Years . . . and will not come away; with the most material Circumstances of his Life . . . how he went to Sea a Cabin-boy . . . turned singing Master . . . married three Wives . . . was pardoned by King Charles II., turned Merchant, and was shipwrecked on this desolate Island on the Coast of Mexico. Plan. 12mo. London.

This is the 7th edition. The preface states that "every Incident herein selected is real Matter of Fact."

1728 HATCHETT, WILLIAM. The Adventures of Abdalla son of Hanif, sent by the Sultan of the Indies to make a Discovery of the Island of Borico, where the Fountain, which restores the Past Youth, is supposed to be found. Also an Account of the Travels of Rouschen a Persian Lady to the Topsy-Turvy Island, undiscovered to this day. The whole intermixed with several curious and instructive Histories. Translated into French from an Arabian MS. found at Batavia by Mr. de Sandison, and now done into English by William Hatchett, Gent.; and adorned with eight curious Cuts, etc. 8vo. London.

PYTHAGOROLUNISTER. A Journey to the World in the Moon. A Dream. Containing an Historical Relation, (as received from a Lunar Philosopher) from above an Hundred Years last past to the present Time, of the Most Material Occurrences, as to the Religion, Politics, &c. of the Inhabitants of that Globe. And particularly their Manner of Elections. 8vo. London. (n.d.)

1730 MONTESQUIEU, CHARLES DE SECONDAT (Baron de). Persian Letters. Translated from the French by John Ozell. London.

> Modern edition, Broadway Translations, London, 1923. French original, Amsterdam, 1721. See below.
> These are charming, witty letters alleged to have been exchanged between a wealthy Persian in Paris with his household in Persia, containing the usual social criticisms. They were published anonymously and are said to have "sold like loaves." The work is much indebted for its knowledge of Persia to the travels of Chardin and Tavernier (see under 1678 and 1686, CENTRAL ASIA).

> 1923 MONTESQUIEU, CHARLES DE SECONDAT (Baron de). Persian Letters. Translated by John Davidson, with Introduction. 8vo. Broadway Translations. London.

> 1721 MONTESQUIEU, CHARLES DE SECONDAT (Baron de). Lettres Persanes. Amsterdam.

1731 The Travels of Mr. John Gulliver, Son to Capt. Lemuel Gulliver, translated from the French, by J. Lockman. 2 vols. 12mo. London.

> The French original may be the continuation of *Gulliver's Travels* by the Abbé Desfontaines, known as *Le Nouveau Gulliver*, Paris, 1730.

1733 TYSSOT, SIMON (de Patot). The Travels and Adventures of James Massey, translated from the French by Stephen Whatley. 8vo. London.

> Another edition, London, 1743. French original, Bordeaux, 1710. See below.
> This story is full of the usual matter of voyages to designated ports, shipwrecks on strange lands, manner of life of Austral peoples, etc., but it differs from most of such stories by being extremely well written. For a detailed analysis of

its contents see Atkinson, *The Extraordinary Voyage in French Literature 1700 to 1720.*

1710 TYSSOT, SIMON (de Patot). Voyages et avantures de Jacques Masse. 12mo. Bordeaux.

1735 LYTTLETON, GEORGE (later Baron). Letters from a Persian in England to his Friend at Ispahan; the Persian Letters continued: or, The Second Volume of Letters from Selim at London to Merza at Ispahan. 2 vols. 8vo. London.

> These are much inferior to Montesquieu's Letters, by which they were obviously inspired. They testify, however, to the strong hold that oriental stuff had upon eighteenth century England. Lyttleton, an elegant dilettante and a liberal patron of literature, is better known for his *Dialogues of the Dead.*

1736 VAUGHAN, WILLIAM OWEN GWIN. Voyages, Trials, and Adventures, with the History of his Brother Jonathan, Six Years a Slave in Tunis. 2 vols. 12mo. London.

1738 LUCCA, GAUDENTIO DI (Signor). Memoir of: Discovery of an Unknown Country in the Desert of Africa, as Ancient, populous, and Civilized, as the Chinese, with an Account of their Antiquity, Origins, Religion, Customs, Polity, . . . 8vo. Dublin.

> Later editions, with slightly different title, 8vo, London, 1748; 12mo, London, 1763; 8vo, London, 1776. See below.
> This is often, but erroneously, attributed to Bishop Berkeley.—Halkett and Laing.

>> 1776 LUCCA, GAUDENTIO DI. The Adventures of Sign. Gaudentio di Lucca. Being the Substance of his Examination before the Fathers of the Inquisition at Bologna in Italy: Giving an Account of an Unknown Country in the Deserts of Africa, . . . Copied from the original MSS. in St. Mark's Library at Venice; with critical Notes of the learned Sign. Rhedi. Translated from the Italian. 8vo. London.

>> This admirable work is partly a romance and partly a scheme of patriarchal government.—Bookseller's Note.

1739 HOLMESBY, JOHN (Captain). The Voyages, Travels, and Wonderful Discoveries of Capt. John Holmesby. Containing a series of the most Surprising and Uncommon Events, which befel the Author in his Voyage to the Southern Ocean, in the Year 1739. 12mo. London.

> The phrasing of this title makes this volume suspect as a work of fiction.

1741 COCK, SAMUEL (Captain). Voyage to Lethe by Capt. Samuel Cock, sometime commander of the good ship the *Charming Sally.* 8vo. London.

> This is a reissue; apparently there is an earlier edition.

D'ARGENS, MARQUIS (John Baptist de Boyer).  Chinese Letters, being a philosophical, historical and critical Correspondence between a Chinese Traveller at Paris, and his Countrymen in China, Muscovy, Persia and Japan. 12mo. London.

> Other editions, with slightly different title, London, 1765; Dublin, 1766. See below.

> 1765  D'ARGENS, MARQUIS.  The Chinese Spy, or Emissary from the Court of Pekin, commissioned to examine into the Present State of Europe, translated from the Chinese. 6 vols. 8vo. London.

STRETZER, THOMAS.  A New Description of Merryland, containing a Topographical, Geographical, and Natural History of that Country. 3rd edition. 8vo. Bath.

1742  HOLBERG, LEWIS (Baron).  The Journey of Nicholas Klimius to the World Underground. Translated from the original Latin. London.

> According to Eddy this was written originally in Danish, and translated into German, French, Latin, and English. Its date of composition is in doubt, but it may have been composed between 1720 and 1732. The only date of English versions cited by Eddy is that of 1828. Editions of 1742 and 1746 in English cited by Maggs.
> For the relation of this voyage to *Gulliver's Travels* see Eddy, *Gulliver's Travels*. The author was the celebrated Norwegian dramatist. The work was a satire directed against the abuses in government.

1745  The Secret History of Persia. London.

1750  COYER, GABRIEL FRANCOIS.  A Discovery of the Island Frivola, or, the Frivolous Island. Translated from the French. Now privately handed about in Paris, and said to be agreeable to the English Manuscripts concerning that Island and its Inhabitants. 2nd edition. 8vo. London. (40 pp.)

> A burlesque publication, having reference to Lord Anson's voyage round the world. A Dutch translation also appeared. "It is happily conceived, very ingeniously executed, and has met with universal applause, not only in France, but in almost every country upon the continent where it has followed the book upon which it is founded and has very justly merited that title which it now bears."— Translator's Preface. Lowndes characterized it as "A satirical romance on the French nation."—From Sabin. See Anson under 1748, CIRCUMNAVIGATIONS.

GWENETT, AMBROSE.  The Life, Strange Voyages, and Uncommon Adventures of Ambrose Gwenett, Formerly known to the Public as, The Lame Beggar . . . Containing an Account of . . . His Voyage to the West-Indies. London.

> The date is approximate. Defoe has been suggested as the author.

1751 DANIEL, JOHN. The Life and Astonishing Adventures of John Daniel, Containing the Melancholy Occasion of his Travels, his Shipwreck with one Companion on a Desolate Island. . . . His Accidental Discovery of a Woman for his Companion. Also a description of a most surprising Engine, invented by his son Jacob, on which he flew to the Moon, with some Account of its Inhabitants. His return and accidental fall into the Habitation of a Sea-monster, with whom he lived two years. . . . His Residence in Lapland and Travels to Norway, from whence he arrived at Aldborough, and further transactions till his death in 1711, aged 97. London.

> Reprinted in the Library of Impostors, London, 1926.

PALTOCK, ROBERT. The Life and Adventures of Peter Wilkins, a Cornish Man; relating particularly his Shipwreck near the South Pole, his wonderful Passage thro' a subterraneous Cavern into a kind of New World . . . his extraordinary conveyance to the Country of Glums and Gawrys, or Men and Women that Fly. Likewise a Description of this strange Country, with the Laws, Customs, and Manners of its Inhabitants and the Author's remarkable Transactions among them. Taken from his own Mouth . . . by R. S., a passenger in the Hector. . . . 6 plates, one folding. 2 vols. 8vo. London.

> Reprinted, 2 vols., 12mo, Dublin, 1751; 2nd edit., Berwick, 1784. Reprinted in Weber's *Collection of Popular Romances*, 1812, Edinburgh. Modern reprint, London, 1925.
> "There are few romances which exhibit so many proofs of poetical imagination, yet there are few which have met with so much neglect."—Weber. "Paltock's fame rests enduringly on his original and fascinating romance," 'Peter Wilkins.' Coleridge is reported to have spoken of it in terms of enthusiastic admiration. Southey in a note on a passage of the 'Curse of Kehama' says that Paltock's winged people 'are the most beautiful creatures of imagination that ever were devised,' and adds that Sir Walter Scott was a warm admirer of the book. With Charles Lamb at Christ's Hospital the story was a favorite, while Leigh Hunt never wearied of it."—D.N.B. It has been suggested that Paltock named his hero after John Wilkins, Bishop of Chester, who had definitely foreseen the possibility of flying.—Bookseller's Note.

1753 BINGFIELD, WILLIAM. The Travels and Adventures of William Bingfield, Esq.; containing as surprizing a Fluctuation of Circumstances, both by Sea and Land, as ever befel one Man. With an accurate Account of the Shape, Nature, and Properties of that most furious Animal, the Dog-Bird. Printed from his Own Manuscript. Folding frontispiece of the author attended by a "Dog-Bird." 2 vols. 8vo. London.

> A very rare romance in the style of Robinson Crusoe.—Bookseller's Note.

1755 MORRIS, DRAKE. The Travels of Mr. Drake Morris, Merchant in London. Containing his Sufferings and Distresses in Several Voyages at Sea. Written by Himself. 8vo. London.

> A scarce and curious account of the buccaneers by a captive who was forced to join them in the Island of Tortuga. The work also contains an account of the author's adventures at Fernando Po, in Abyssinia, and other parts of Africa. —Maggs, No. 534. This account is stated by Maggs, No. 580, to be a fiction.

A Voyage to the World in the Centre of the Earth . . . their persons and Habits described, with several other Particulars, in which is introduced the History of an Inhabitant of the Air, written by himself, with some Account of the Planetary Worlds. 12mo. London.

> Contains an account of the vehicle in which the author flew in the air.— Bookseller's Note.

1756-1766 AMORY, THOMAS. The Life of John Buncle, Esq. containing various Observations and Reflections, made in several Parts of the World, and many extraordinary Relations. 2 vols. 8vo. London.

1757 HELLEN, ROBERT. Letters from an Armenian in Ireland to his Friends in Trebisond, . . . translated in the year 1756. 8vo. London.

> These letters contain the usual social and political criticisms. The century was to put up with still more letters of this type.

1760 JOHNSTONE, CHARLES. Chrysal: or, the Adventures of a Guinea. Wherein are exhibited Views of several striking Scenes in America, England, Holland, Germany, and Portugal. By an Adept. 2 vols. 12mo. London.

> Frequently reprinted. London, 1762, 1763, 1768, 1771, 1775, 1783, 1794. This was a masterly and caustic satire. A key to the characters is to be found in Davis' "Ohio," pp. 13-21.—Sabin. See *Monthly Review,* XXIII, 137.

SHEBBEARE, JOHN. The History of the Excellence and Decline of the Constitution, Religion, Laws, Manners and Genius of the Sumatrans, and of the Restoration thereof in the Reign of Amurath the Third. 2 vols. 8vo. London.

> Later editions: London, 1787; London, 1800.
> This is a satire on Whig policy and a panegyric on George III. For his *Letters to the People of England,* in which he attacks the Government's policies see under 1756-57, NORTH AMERICA.

1762 GOLDSMITH, OLIVER. Chinese Letters. London.

> This series of entertaining observations on English life appeared first in Newbery's *Public Ledger.* They are better known by the title of the *Citizen of the World,* under which they were published in the collected edition, 2 vols., 12mo, London, 1762.

1764 BURGH, JAMES. An account of the First Settlement, Laws, Form of Government, & Policie of the Cessares, a People of South America. In 9 Letters, from Mr. Vander Neck, one of the Senators of that Nation to his Friend in Holland. With Notes by the Editor. London.

> "The Cessares are a race of white Indians in Chili, about whom, however, very little is known. The present work adds nothing to our information respecting them, being merely a new version of Sir Thomas More's 'Utopia.' It was written, according to Nicholas, by the celebrated author of 'Dignity of Human Nature,' Mr. Burgh."—Rich. The book is not worth the space it occupies here; it is as veracious as "Peter Wilkins," but not so imaginative.—Sabin.

1767 ROBERTSON, ——. Voyage aux Terres Australes, traduit sur le Manuscrit Anglois. 8vo. Amsterdam.

> A curious fictitious work. The author states that, as a young man, he sailed with Sir Francis Drake, as lieutenant of the "Elizabeth." When far to the west of Chile the expedition approached land, which Drake took for a new continent. The author was given command of a small vessel with a crew of ten and sent to examine the coast. Unluckily he had not been provided with an anchor, and during the night was blown out to sea. The next day he discovered a rich and fertile land, in fact, Australia, and goes on to describe his adventures. The work was really written as an attack on the French Government and various French public men of the time.—Maggs, No. 574.

1771 WILLIAMSON, DAVID. A True Narrative of the Sufferings of David Williamson, Mariner, left by his ship on Fernandopoo, an island on the Guinea Coast, and delivered thence by a Portuguese Ship, 1771, written by Himself; wherein is given an Account of the Island; its extent, soil, and produce; also a Description of the Persons and Manners of the Natives. London.

> The date is only a guess, as none is given. This may be a "True Narrative."

1775 JOHNSTONE, CHARLES. The Pilgrim: or, a Picture of Life. In a Series of Letters, written mostly from London by a Chinese Philosopher to his Friend at Quang-Tong. Containing Remarks upon the Laws, Customs, and Manners of the English and other Nations. Illustrated by a Variety of curious and interesting Anecdotes, and Characters drawn from real life. 2 vols. in 1. 8vo. Dublin.

1776 KING, WILLIAM (Judge of the High Court of Admiralty). A Voyage to Cajamai (i.e., Jamaica). London.

> This is probably based not on a factual voyage to the Island, but on accounts read. It ridicules the matter-of-fact details customary with writers on travels.

1778  BOWMAN, H.  Travels into Carnovirria, Taupciniera, Olfactaria and Auditante; (a satire addressed to Sir J. Banks and Dr. Solander). 8vo. London.

> For other skits of like nature see Cook under 1773, SOUTH SEAS.

1785  RASPE, RUDOLPH ERICH.  Baron Munchausen's Narrative of his Marvelous Travels and Campaigns in Russia. 8vo. Oxford.

> 2nd edit., considerably enlarged, Oxford, 1786; 3rd edit., enlarged, London, 1786; 5th, London, 1787; 7th, with a *Sequel,* London, 1792. Modern reprint of the 7th, Broadway Translations, London, 1930. Translated into German (from the 2nd edit.) by Gottfried August Bürger, London (but printed in Göttingen), 1786. For German originals see following paragraph.
>
> For a discussion of the authorship of these tales, their sources, etc., see the Introduction to the Broadway Translations volume. Strange to say, there actually existed a flesh and blood Baron von Münchhausen, who was given to relating tall tales of his war and hunting days. These lived a verbal life until 1781, when they appeared in vols. VIII and IX of *Vade Mecum für lustige Leute,* a Berlin periodical. They were then taken over by Raspe, who was then living in England, and with some manipulation published anonymously at Oxford. For other reference to Raspe see the same under 1776, WEST EUROPE.

> 1787  RASPE, RUDOLPH ERICH.  Gulliver Revived; containing singular Travels, Campaigns, Voyages, and Adventures in Russia, The Caspian Sea, Iceland, Turkey, Egypt, Gibraltar, up the Mediterranean, on the Atlantic Ocean, and through the centre of Mount Etna into the South Sea; also An Account of a Voyage into the Moon and Dog-star, with many extraordinary Particulars relative to the Cooking Animal in those Planets, which we here call the Human Species, by Baron Munchausen. The fifth edition, Considerably enlarged, and ornamented with a variety of explanatory Views, engraved from Original Designs. London.

> 1930  RASPE, RUDOLPH ERICH.  The Travels of Baron Münchausen. Gulliver Revived or The Vice of Lying Properly Exposed. . . . Together with the Sequel containing The Adventures of Baron Münchausen in Russia. Edited by William Rose. With an Introduction. Illus. by Alfred Crowquill. 8vo. Broadway Translations. London.

1789  HURD, RICHARD.  An Account of the Shipwreck and Captivity of Mr. D. Bression, with a Description of the Deserts of Africa. 2 vols. London.

> This work a fiction?

1796  CHRISTIAN, FLETCHER.  Letters from Mr. Fletcher Christian, containing a Narrative of the Transactions on board His Majesty's Ship Bounty, before and after the Mutiny, with his subsequent Voyages and Travels in South America. 8vo. London.

> A scarce work, which is, of course, entirely fictitious, although many of the early details were based on correct information.—From Maggs, No. 644. See Bligh under 1792, SOUTH SEAS.

HAMILTON, ELIZA. Translation of the Letters of a Hindoo Rajah, with a preliminary Dissertation on the History, Religion and Manners of the Hindoos. 2 vols. 8vo. London.

> A work of fiction, describing the prevalent customs and manners of England. Dedicated to Warren Hastings.—Bookseller's Note.

1797 Travels before the Flood. Translated from the Arabic. 2 vols. in 1. London.

> "Oriental record of Men and Manners in the Antediluvian World, as told in conversations between the Caliph of Bagdad and his Court."

1798 Human Vicissitudes; or Travels into Unexplored Regions. 2 vols. 8vo. London.

> A fictitious account of Travels in South Africa, etc.—Maggs, No. 580.

MONTGOMERY, WILLIAM. The Extraordinary Adventures of William Montgomery in the Unexplored Regions of Amazonia; An account of his Captivity among the Oromara Indians, a Description of their Manners, Customs, and Wars; and the Escape of the Captive with the daughter of their Chief. 16mo. London. (30 pp.)

> This is not dated but is undoubtedly earlier than 1800. It may be a true narrative, but it reads a bit awry. Sabin directs the reader to Field's *Essay toward an Indian Bibliography.*

# XX

## General Reference

ADLER, ELKAN. Jewish Travellers. The Writings of Jewish Travellers from the Ninth to the Eighteenth Centuries. Edited and translated, with an Introduction, by Elkan Adler. 8 plates and a map. Broadway Travellers. London, 1930.

ALEXANDRE, —— (Capitaine). La Situation économique et sociale des Etats Unis à la fin du XVIIIth siècle d'après les voyageurs français. Paris, 1926.

ALLIBONE, SAMUEL AUSTIN. A Critical Dictionary of English Literature and British and American Authors living and deceased, from the earliest Accounts to the latter half of the Nineteenth Century. Supplement by John F. Kirk. 5 vols. Philadelphia, 1891-96.

AMERICAN EXPLORERS SERIES. Edited by Professor John Bach McMasters, 12mo. New York. (Many of these appeared previously in the Trailmakers Series.)

> Butler, Sir Wm. Francis (General). The Wild Northland, 1872-1873. 1904 (Trailmakers Series).
>
> Cabeza de Vaca, Alvar Nunez. The Journey of, from Florida to the Pacific, 1528-1536. 1905 (Trailmakers Series).
>
> Champlain, Samuel de. The Voyages and Explorations of, 1604-1616. 2 vols. 1912.
>
> Colden, Cadwallader. A History of the Five Indian Nations of Canada. 2 vols. 1904 (Trailmakers Series).
>
> Columbus, Christopher. Journal of the First Voyage to America by Christopher Columbus. 1924.
>
> Coronado, Francisco Vasquez de. The Journey of, from the City of Mexico to the Buffalo Plains of Texas, Kansas and Nebraska, 1540-1542. 1922.
>
> De Soto, Hernando. Narrative of the Career of, in the Conquest of Florida, 1539-1542. 2 vols. 1922.
>
> Harmon, Daniel William. A Journal of Voyages and Travels in the Interior of North America, 1800-1819. 1922.

La Salle, Réné Robert Cavalier, Sieur de. The Journeys of, as related by his Followers. 2 vols. 1922.

Lewis and Clark. History of the Expedition under the Command of, 1804-1806. 3 vols. 1904 (Trailmakers Series).

AMERICAN ORIENTAL SOCIETY. Journal. Complete set from the commencement to 1932, being vols. 1-50, bound in 61 vols. 8vo. London, 1849-1932.

The Journal contains texts, translations, and many important articles by some of the foremost orientalists.

ANDERSON, J. English Intercourse with Siam in the Seventeenth Century. London, 1890.

ARBER, EDWARD (Editor). An English Garner. Ingatherings from our History and Literature. 8 vols. London, 1895-97.

This reprints a number of rare voyages and adventures.

—— (Editor). The Story of the Pilgrim Fathers, 1606-1623, As told by themselves, their Friends, and their Enemies. 8vo. London, 1897.

ARCHER, A. B. Stories of Explorations and Discovery. Cambridge, 1915.

ARGONAUT PRESS. Travel Series edited by N. M. Penzer, M.A., F.R.G.S. London, 1925—. (In progress.)

Cabots, The Voyages of the. Edited by James A. Williamson, 13 maps. 1929.

Chardin, Sir John. Travels of, in Persia. Introduction by Brig.-Gen. Sir Percy Sykes. 1925.

Columbus, Christopher. The Voyages of. Translated and edited by Cecil Jane. 5 maps. 1930.

Cook, James. The Three Voyages of. Edited by Lieut-Commander R. T. Gould. 8 vols. 1931.

Dampier, William. A New Voyage Round the World. Introduction by Sir Albert Gray. 1927.

Dampier, William. Dampier's Voyages and Discoveries. With an Introduction by Clennell Wilkinson and a Note on the Discourse of Winds by A. C. Bell. 1927.

Drake, Sir Francis. The World Encompassed by. Edited by Sir Richard Carnac Temple. 1926.

East Indies. A New Account of. Edited by Sir William Foster. Maps and illus. 1931.

Frobisher, Martin. The Three Voyages of. Edited by Vilhjalmur Stefansson. Maps, bibliography, etc. 1936.

Hawkins, Sir Richard. The Observations of, in His Voyage into the South Sea. Edited by James A. Williamson. 4 maps. 1933.

Polo, Marco. The Most Noble & Famous Travels of. By John Frampton. 1929.

Ralegh. Last Voyage of. Edited by V. T. Harlow. Portrait and maps. 1932.

Ralegh, Sir Walter. The Discoverie of the Large and Bewtiful Empire of Guiana by. Edited by V. T. Harlow. Frontispiece and 2 folding maps. 1928.

Schouten, Francois and Joost. A True Description of the Mighty Kingdoms of Japan and Siam. Edited by C. R. Boxer. 11 plates and 7 maps. 1935.

A Spanish Voyage to Vancouver and the North-West Coast of America. Translated from the Spanish by Cecil Jane. 1930.

Varthema, Ludovico Di. The Itinerary of. Translated by John Winter Jones. Illus. and maps. 1928.

ASHER, G. M. A Bibliographical and Historical Essay on the Dutch Books and Pamphlets relating to New Netherland and to the Dutch West-India Company and to its possessions in Brazil, Angola, etc., as also on the Maps, Charts, etc., of New Netherland, with Facsimiles of the Map of New Amsterdam. Compiled from the Dutch Public and Private Libraries and from the Collection of Mr. Frederick Muller in Amsterdam. Facsimile reproduction of Visscher's Map. 4to. Amsterdam, 1854-1867.

ASIATIC SOCIETY OF BENGAL, 1796-1836. Asiatick Researches, or, Transactions of the Society instituted in Bengal, for inquiring into the History and Antiquities, the Arts, Sciences, and Literature, of Asia. Complete set, being Vols. 1-20, with General Index, 21 vols. Facsimiles, maps, etc. Calcutta, 1796-1836.

The best edition of the Transactions.—Bookseller's Note.

——— Journal of the Asiatic Society of Bengal. A set of all three parts from the commencement in 1832 to the conclusion in 1904, with the New Combined Series thereafter to 1932, about 150 vols. Calcutta, 1832-1932.

> This set is being completed. The parts of the original series will be bound separately as follows:—Part I. History, Literature and Antiquities. Part II. Natural History. Part III. Anthropology. After 1904 all three parts are combined in the New Series.—Bookseller's Note.

ATKINSON, GEOFFREY. The Extraordinary Voyage in French Literature before 1700. 8vo. Paris, 1920.

——— The Extraordinary Voyage in French Literature, from 1700 to 1720. 8vo. Paris, 1922.

> Frequently cited in this bibliography.

——— La Littérature géographique française de la Renaissance. Repertoire bibliographique. 300 reproductions. 4to. Paris, 1927.

——— Les Relations de Voyages du XVII siècle et l'évolution des idées. Contribution à l'étude de la formation de l'esprit du XVIII siècle. 8vo. Paris, n.d. (after 1922).

AYDER ALI KHAN. The History of Ayder Ali Khan, Nabob-Bahader; or, New Memoirs concerning the East Indies, with Historical Notes, by M. M. D. L. T. Map. 2 vols. 8vo. London, 1784.

BABEAU, A. Les voyageurs en France depuis la Renaissance jusqu'à la Revolution. Paris, 1885.

> Among the voyagers discussed are Le Tasse, de Thou, Montaigne, M. Lister, duchesse de Longueville, Mme. de Sévigné La Fontaine, Ch. de Brosses, Franklin, A. Young, Goethe, etc.

BAKER, J. N. L. A History of Geographical Discovery and Exploration. 50 maps. 8vo. London, 1931.

> This book is an attempt to give a connected account of the history of geographical discovery and exploration from classical times to the present day. It is divided into two parts, the first of which covers the period up to the end of the eighteenth century, while the second continues the story to recent times The whole work is illustrated by fifty maps, most of which show the routes of the more important explorers, but a few are outline sketches of important maps at certain periods. Thus the progress of exploration can be compared with the contemporary ideas of theoretical geographers.—Heffer and Sons. Frequently cited in this bibliography.

BARBOUR, JAMES S. History of William Paterson and the Darien Company, with illustrations and appendices by James S. Barbour. 8vo. Edinburgh, 1907.

> Owing to the stock having been destroyed by fire, the above is now a scarce book.—Bookseller's Note.

BARRINGTON, GEORGE. The Memoirs of George Barrington, containing every remarkable circumstance, from his Birth to the Present Time. 8vo. London, 1800 (?).

> See Barrington under 1794 and 1801, AUSTRALIA.

BARRINGTON, G. W. Remarkable Voyages and Shipwrecks. Collection of 38 authentic and extraordinary sea narratives. Illus. 8vo. London, 1890 (?).

BARROW, SIR JOHN. A Chronological History of Voyages into the Arctic Regions; undertaken chiefly for the purpose of Discovering a North-East, Northwest, or Polar Passage between the Atlantic and Pacific: from the earliest periods of Scandinavian Navigation to the Departure of the Recent Expeditions, under the orders of Captains Ross and Buchan. Folding map and 3 woodcuts. 8vo. London, 1818.

> More than any other man not actually employed in its operations, he had contributed to the splendid results obtained in the XIXth century. Point Barrow, Cape Barrow, and Barrow Straits in the polar seas, attest to the estimation in which his friendship was held by the explorers of his time.—D.N.B.

—— The Naval History of Great Britain, with the Lives of the most Illustrious Admirals and Commanders, &c. Maps (including America), portraits, engravings. 4 vols. 12mo. London, 1770.

BATES, E. S. Touring in 1600. 8vo. Boston, 1911.

> A very entertaining and useful account of methods of travelling at the beginning of the 17th century.

BEAGLEHOLE, J. C. The Exploration of the Pacific. Maps. 8vo. London, 1934.

> All European investigators and adventurers have their place in the story, from Magellan, Mendana and Quiros, Schouten, Tasman to the three brilliant and consummating voyages of James Cook.—Heffer and Sons.

BEAZLEY, C. R. The Dawn of Modern Geography. A History of Exploration and Geographical Science from the Conversion of the Roman

Empire to the Early Years of the Fifteenth Century, with an Account of the Achievements and Writings of the Early Christian, Arab and Chinese Travellers and Students. With reproductions of the principal maps of the times. 3 vols. 8vo. London, 1897-1906.

> Vol. III covers the "History of Exploration and Geographical Science, from the middle of the Thirteenth to the Early Years of Fifteenth Century" (c. A. D. 1260-1420).

—— The Discovery of North America (The Cabots). Maps. London, 1898.

—— Prince Henry The Navigator, Hero of Portugal and Modern Discovery, 1394-1460, with Geographical Progress in the Middle Ages. Illus. London, 1896.

> Reprinted, London, 1903.

BEER, G. R. DE. Early Travellers in the Alps, with many reproductions of contemporary woodcuts and engravings, also a Bibliography. 8vo. London, 1930.

> This book is based on a number of accounts of wanderings in the Central Alps, from the sixteenth to the end of the eighteenth centuries, and attempts to show what touring in those parts was like in those early days. Cited in this bibliography.

BESSON, MAURICE. The Scourge of the Indies: Buccaneers, Corsairs, and Filibusters, from original texts and contemporary engravings, translated by Everard Thornton. Colored plates and many text illustrations. 4to. London, 1929.

BIGGAR, H. P. The Precursors of Jacques Cartier, 1497-1534. A Collection of documents relating to the early history of the Dominion of Canada, edited by H. P. Biggar. Ottawa, 1911.

—— The Voyages of the Cabots and of the Corte-Reals to North America and Greenland, 1497-1503. 8vo. Paris, 1903.

BINGLEY, W. Biographical Conversations on the Most Eminent Voyageurs from Columbus to Cook, designed for the use of Young Persons. 8vo. London, 1818.

BLAIR, EMMA HELEN, and ROBERTSON, J. A. The Philippine Islands, 1493-1803. Explorations of early navigators, descriptions of the Islands and their People, their History and Records of the Catholic Missions, as related in contemporaneous Books and Manuscripts, shewing the Political, Economic, Commercial and Religious Conditions of those Islands from their earliest relations with European Nations to the Beginning of the Nineteenth Century. Maps, portraits, and other illus. 55 vols. 8vo. Cleveland, 1903-09.

BÖHME, M. Die grossen Reisesammlungen des 16. Jahrhunderts und ihre Bedeutung. Strassburg, 1904.

> This is concerned with early collections of travels.

BOLTON, HERBERT EUGENE. Rim of Christendom. The Life Story of Eusebio Francisco Kino, Pacific Coast Pioneer. New York, 1936.

> Father Kino was a member of the first expedition that reached the shores of the Pacific Ocean by traversing California (1684). He left in his trail many pueblo missions that have since become towns. This work is based on an exhaustive research for diaries, letters, and documents in the archives of Mexico and Europe.

BONAFFI, E. Voyages et Voyageurs de la Renaissance. Paris, 1895.

> This contains La Cour en voyage; Kozmital, Récit de son voyage (1465) en Allemagne, Flandre, Angleterre, Espagne et Italie. Voyage de Charles-Quint en Espagne par mer (1517), etc.—Bookseller's Note.

BOURNE, H. R. F. English Seamen under the Tudors. 2 vols. London, 1868.

> Vol. I deals with voyages of explorations and with trade.

BOWEN, C. M. Elizabethan Travel Literature. *Blackwood's Magazine,* October, 1916, 489-498.

BRACEY, ROBERT. Eighteenth Century Studies. 8vo. Oxford, 1925.

> Chapters on Boswell's Corsica; Johnson's Lobo's Abyssinia; Labat's Voyage aux Isles de l'Amérique; Butler's Travels in France; and Psalmanazaar.

BREBNER, JOHN BARTLETT. Forerunners of the North American Migrations. A Study in the Motives of the Early Explorers, 1492-1806. Pioneer Historical Series. London, 1933.

BRENDON, J. A. Great Navigators and Discoverers. Illus. and maps. 8vo. London, 1929.


THE BROADWAY TRAVELLERS. Edited by Sir E. Denison Ross and Eileen Power. All illustrated. Translations and reprints from the best travel-books drawn from all countries and ages. 8vo. London, 1926—. (In progress.)

> Andrade, Ruy Freyre de. Commentaries. 1930.
>
> Battuta, Ibn. Travels in Asia and Africa, 1325-1354. 1929.
>
> Bontekoe, W. Y. Memorable Description of the East Indian Voyage, 1618-1625. 1929.
>
> Bruce, G. W. Brazil and the Brazilians. n.d.
>
> Bruce, James. Journey to the Source of the Nile, 1768-1773. n.d.
>
> Carletti, Francesco. Voyages of, 1594-1602.
>
> Chang-Chun. Travels of an Alchemist to the Court of Ghingiz Khan, 1221-1224. 1931.
>
> Clavijo. Embassy to Tamerlane, 1403-1406. 1928.
>
> Cortes, Hernando. Five Letters, 1519-1526. 1928.
>
> D'Aulnoy, Madame. Travels in Spain, 1691. 1930.
>
> Desideri, Ippolito. An Account of Tibet, 1712-1727. 1932.
>
> Diaz, Bernal. Discovery and Conquest of Mexico, 1517-1521. 1928.
>
> Don Juan of Persia. A Shi'ah Catholic, 1560-1604. 1926.
>
> Eden, Hon. Emily. Up the Country—Letters from India, 1837 on. 1930.
>
> Gage, Thomas. A New Survey of the West Indies, 1648. 1928.
>
> Guerreiro, Father. Jahangir and the Jesuits. 1930.
>
> Hall, Capt. Basil. Travels in India, Ceylon and Borneo. 1931.
>
> Herbert, Thomas. Travels in Persia, 1627-1629. 1928.
>
> Huc and Gabet. Travels in Tartary, Thibet and China, 1844-1846. 2 vols. 1928.
>
> Jarric, Father Pierre du. Akbar and the Jesuits: an account of Jesuit Missions to the Court of Akbar. 1926.
>
> Jewish Travellers: a Selection. 1930.
>
> Lescarbot, Marc. Nova Francia: a Description of Acadia, 1606. 1928.
>
> Lewis, Monk. Journal of a West Indian Proprietor. 1929.
>
> Locke, J. C. (Editor). The First Englishmen in India. 1930.
>
> Macdonald, John. Memoirs of an Eighteenth Century Footman; the Life and Travels of, 1745-1779. 1931.

Mandelslo, Johann Albrecht von. Voyages and Travels of, 1638-1640. n.d.

Marco Polo. Travels. 1931.

Sherley, Thomas and Anthony. Literary Remains of. (Persia and Turkey.) n.d.

Staden, Hans. The True History of his Captivity, 1557. 1928.

Tafur, Pero. Travels and Adventures, 1435-1439. 1926.

Tenreszo and Rotta. Travels of. n.d.

Teonge, Henry. Diary, 1675-1679. 1927.

Thevet, André. The New-Founde World of Antarticke, 1568. n.d.

BROWN, BASIL. Astronomical Atlases, Maps and Charts: An Historical and General Guide, illustrated throughout with many full-page reproductions from contemporary charts and prints. 4to. London, 1932.

    The various works and authors have been written up more or less in review form so as to make the subject interesting to a variety of astronomers, collectors and others: this volume is therefore not intended, or put forward,. as a complete classified catalogue, although the author has endeavoured to include a greater proportion of early works than has previously been done by other writers who have attempted lists of titles on astronomical history. The illustrations will be found of great value and interest—they are reproduced with remarkable clarity—to all astronomical students. The volume is concluded with a short bibliography and an index.—Bookseller's Note.

BROWN, WILLIAM (M.D.). The History of the Christian Missions of the XVI-XIXth Centuries in all parts of the Globe, with Appendix, including List of Translations of the Holy Scriptures into Languages of the Heathen and Muhammedan Nations. 3 vols. 8vo. 3rd edit., enlarged. London, 1864.

BRUCE, J. Annals of the Honourable East India Company, from 1660-1707-8. 3 vols. 4to. London, 1810.

    Bruce was historiographer to the East India Company and had charge of their official records.—Davies, *Bibliography of British History.*

BUNBURY, E. H. A History of Ancient Geography among the Greeks and Romans from the earliest Ages till the Fall of the Roman Empire. Maps. 2 vols. 8vo. 2nd edit. London, 1883.

BUREAU OF AMERICAN ETHNOLOGY. Reports. Various years. 4to. Washington, D.C., 1880-1927.

    A number of translations of early Spanish voyages and travels in North America are to be found here.

BURNEY, JAMES (Captain, F.R.S.). A Chronological History of North-Eastern Voyages of Discovery and of the early Eastern Navigations of the Russians. London, 1819.

A Chronological History of the South Sea or Pacific Ocean. 45 maps and plates. 5 vols. London, 1803-1817.

> The most important general history of early South Sea discoveries, containing practically everything early on the subject, collected from all sources, with most important remarks concerning them by Capt. Burney, who was a great authority on the subject.—Hocken, *Bibliography of New Zealand.* "This important and comprehensive work brings the history of Pacific discovery down to 1764, when Hawkesworth continues it."—Maggs No. 491.. Burney was a brother of the delightful chronicler of domestic affairs, Fanny Burney, later Madame D'Arblay. He served as lieutenant on Cook's last two voyages.

—— History of the Buccaneers of America. 2 folding and 1 full-page maps. London, 1816.

> Reprinted, London, 1912.

BURPEE, L. J. The Search for the Western Sea. The Story of the Exploration of Northwestern America. Plates, portraits, and maps. London, 1908.

> A work of great value.—Baker, *Geographical Discovery.* Included is a useful bibliography.

CAMBRIDGE HISTORY OF AMERICAN LITERATURE. Edited by W. P. Trent (and others). 4 vols. New York, 1917-1921.

> For travel material see the following chapters of vol. I:
>
> Bk. I, ch. i. Travellers and Explorers, 1583-1763, by George P. Winship.
>
> Bk. II, ch. i. Travellers and Observers, 1763-1846, by Professor Lane Cooper.
>
> Bibliographies at end of volume.

CAMBRIDGE HISTORY OF ENGLISH LITERATURE. Edited by A. W. Ward and A. R. Waller. 14 vols. New York, 1907-1917.

> For travel material see the following chapters of vol. IV:
>
> Chap. III. Sir Walter Raleigh, by Louise Creighton.
>
> Chap. IV. The Literature of the Sea from the Origins to Hakluyt, by Commander Charles N. Robinson, R.N., and John Leyland.
>
> Chap. V. Seafaring and Travel: The Growth of professional Textbooks and Geographical Literature, by Commander Charles N. Robinson, R.N., and John Leyland.
>
> Bibliographies at end of volume.

CAMBRIDGE MODERN HISTORY.   Edited by Sir A. W. Ward and others.   13 vols.   London, 1907-1925.

> Vol. VII, The United States, has good lists of authorities.

CAMDEN SOCIETY'S PUBLICATIONS.   4to.   London, 1838-1934.

> This set runs to over 210 volumes. From 1898 on it has been·edited for the Royal Historical Society. The Camden Society was founded to perpetuate and make accessible the little known materials for the civil, ecclesiastical, and literary history of Great Britain. It reprints some voyages and expeditions.

CAMPBELL, GORDON (Vice-Admiral).   Captain Cook, R.N., F.R.S. Circumnavigator of the Globe.   Maps and illus.   London, 1936.

CAMPBELL, JOHN (Dr.).   Lives of the Admirals and other Eminent British Seamen . . . our discoveries, plantations, and commerce.   4 vols. 8vo.   London, 1748.

> Reprinted, 4 vols., Dublin, 1748; enlarged, London, 1750; London, 1779. This last edition has considerable American interest as it includes Naval transportations of the late and present war (i.e., the American Revolution), and an account of the recent discoveries in the Southern Hemisphere.—Bookseller's Note.

CARY, M., and WARMINGTON, E. H.   The Ancient Explorers.   15 maps.   8vo.   London, 1929.

> This volume discusses the aims and methods of ancient pioneers of travel, Egyptian, Mesopotamian, Greek and Roman, and sets forth their actual discoveries. It narrates in detail, with maps, the opening up of the Mediterranean, of the Atlantic and Indian Oceans, and of the three continents of the Old World.—Heffer and Sons.

CHARNOCK, JOHN.   Biographia Navalis, or Impartial Memoirs of the Lives and Characters of Officers of the Navy.   4 vols.   8vo.   London, 1794-98.

—— An History of Marine Architecture, including an enlarged view of the nautical regulation and naval history, both civil and military, of all Nations, especially of Great Britain, etc.   3 vols.   London, 1800.

CHATTERTON, E. KEBLE.   English Seamen and the Colonization of America.   26 illus.   London, 1930.

> The story of the early voyages of discovery and settlement in the new World leading up to colonization and finally independence.—Bookseller's Note.

CLARKE, JAMES STANIER. The Progress of Maritime Discovery, from the earliest period to the Close of the Eighteenth Century, forming an extensive system of Hydrography. 3 engraved plates, 5 charts and 10 vignettes. 4to. London, 1803.

CLAUVEL, CHARLES. In the Wake of "The Bounty" To Tahiti and Pitcairn Islands. Illus. Sydney, 1933.

COBHAM, C. D. Excerpta Cypria, Material for a History of Cyprus, translated and transcribed by C. D. Cobham, with an appendix on the bibliography of Cyprus. 4to. Cambridge, 1908.

> Comprises:—Extracts from over eighty writers, from the first to the nineteenth century, relating to Cyprus. "Mr. Cobham is known to students of Cypriote History and Antiquities by his valuable 'Bibliography of Cyprus,' of which four editions have appeared, and a fifth, considerably increased, is appended to the present volume, and many of the extracts are from works which are very rare and difficult of access."—*Athenaeum*, quoted by Bookseller.

COLLINGRIDGE, GEORGE. The Discovery of Australia. A Critical, Documentary and Historic Investigation concerning the Priority of Discovery in Australasia by Europeans before the Arrival of Lieut. James Cook, in the "Endeavour" in the year 1770. 8 illus. and maps. 4to. Sydney, 1895.

CORBETT, J. S. Drake and the Tudor Navy. With the History of the Rise of England as a maritime Power. 2 vols. 8vo. London, 1895-99.

> Excellent bibliographical notes are to be found in this work.

CORTES, HERNANDO. The Despatches of, now first translated into English from the original Spanish, with an Introduction and Notes, by George Folsom, one of the Secretaries of the New York Historical Society, etc. 8vo. New York, 1843.

CROUSE, NELLIS M. In Quest of the Western Ocean. Illus. and maps. 8vo. New York, 1928.

> This book traces in good detail the efforts of explorers to discover the route to the "Western Sea."

CULLEN, —— (Dr.). Isthmus of Darien Ship Canal; with a Full History of the Scotch Colony of Darien. Maps, views of the country and original documents. 8vo. London, 1853.

CUST, LIONEL. History of the Society of Dilettanti. Compiled by Lionel Cust and edited by Sir Sydney Colvin. Reissued with Supplementary Chapter. 4to. London, 1914.

> This contains detailed information on the archaeological discoveries of the eighteenth century in the Near East in which the Society was interested. It throws good light on the work of Wood at Palmyra, Stuart and Revett at Athens, and Chandler in Ionia.

DANVERS, F. C. The Portuguese in India; being a History of the Rise and Decline of their Eastern Empire. Plates. 2 vols. 8vo. London, 1894.

DARK, R. The Quest of the Indies. Portraits of Marco Polo, Prince Henry, Albuquerque, Cortes, Pizarro, etc. 8vo. Oxford, 1920.

DAVIS, JOHN. Davis, the Navigator. A Life of: 1550-1605. By Clements R. Markham. Illus. and maps. London, 1889.

DAWSON, S. E. The Saint Lawrence Basin and its Border-Lands; being the Story of their Discovery, Exploration and Occupation. Maps and illus. 8vo. London, 1905.

DECOSTA, B. F.. The Pre-Columbian Discovery of America by the Northmen. Maps. 8vo. 2nd edit. London, 1890.

DRAKE, SAMUEL G. Old Indian Chronicle. 4to. Boston, 1836.

—— The Book of the Indians; or Biography and History of the Indians of North America, from its First Discovery to the year 1841. Folding map, 12 portraits of Indian Chiefs and others, besides 6 other engravings. 8vo. 8th edit., with large additions and corrections. Boston, 1841.

> A very excellent and carefully compiled collection of the materials of Indian history. It is the result of a life-time of labor, by one who has spared no pains to be at the same time faithful to the completeness and truthfulness of history.— Bookseller's Note.

DULLES, F. R. Eastward Ho. The first English Adventurers to the Orient—Richard Chancellor, Anthony Jenkinson, James Lancaster, William Adams, Sir Thomas Roe. 20 illus. 8vo. London, 1931.

DUNBAR, SEYMOUR. A History of Travel in America. Maps, colored plates, and other illustrations reproduced from early engravings, etc. 4 vols. Indianapolis, 1915.

DUNCAN, ——. Duncan's Modern Traveller. Popular Description, historical and topographical, of the various Countries of the Globe, Europe, Asia, Africa, and America. Profusely illus. with maps and engraved views. 25 vols. 8vo. London, 1929.

DUNLOP, JOHN. The History of Fiction: Being a Critical Account of the most celebrated Prose Works of Fiction, from the earliest Greek Romances to the Novels of the Present Day. 3 vols. 8vo. London, 1814.

> This work of reference still maintains its position as an authority to be consulted.

EAMES, WILBERFORCE. Bibliographical Essays, A Tribute to Wilberforce Eames. 8vo. Cambridge, Mass., 1924.

> Among the Essays is one entitled Elizabethan Americana, by G. Watson Cole.

EDDY, WILLIAM A. Gulliver's Travels. A Critical Study. Princeton Univ. Press, 1923.

> Discusses Philosophic, Fantastic, and Realistic voyages of fictitious types in relation to *Gulliver's Travels*. With bibliographies. Cited in this bibliography.

EDINBURGH CABINET LIBRARY: including Voyages Round the World; Discoveries in Polar Regions; Lives and Voyages of Drake, Dampier, and Cavendish; Northern Coasts of America, Persia, Mesopotamia, Marco Polo, etc. By Murray Fraser, and others. Illus. 14 vols. Edinburgh, 1833.

> 3rd edit., 38 vols., 12mo, Edinburgh, 1835-37.
> References in this bibliography are to the 3rd edition. An historical account of travels, explorations, expeditions, biographies, etc., compiled from originals and other accounts. With plates and notes. Bibliographical reference sources at bottom of pages. Quotes freely from originals.

EDINBURGH MAGAZINE, 1757-66, vols. 1-6; and The Newcastle Magazine 1759. Containing articles and references to Wolf's Campaign in Canada, American Indians, West Indies, etc. 5 maps of Louisberg, St. Lawrence from Anticosti to Quebec, Martinico, Guadaloupe, Quebec. 7 vols. 8vo. Edinburgh, 1757-62.

EDINBURGH REVIEW.   Iceland and its Explorers.  *Edinb. Rev.,* 1876, vol. 291, pp. 222-250.


EINSTEIN, LEWIS.  Italian Renaissance in England: the Scholar, Courtier, Traveller, etc. Bibliography. 10 illus.  New York, 1902.


ELIAS, EDITH L.  The Book of Polar Exploration.  Color plates and numerous full page half tone illus.  Romance of Knowledge Series. 8vo.  London, 1936.

> This fascinating volume gives an account of expeditions to the North and South Polar regions from the early days of Arctic exploration to the recent adventures of Shackleton.—Bookseller's Note.


ELLIOT, SIR H. M.  The History of India as told by its own Historians: the Muhammedan Period.  The posthumous Papers of the late Sir H. M. Elliot, edited and continued by Professor John Dowson. 8 vols. 8vo.  London, 1867-77.

> A work so comprehensive and laborious that it can never be superseded. All future writers on Indian history must inevitably come to this treasury of recondite information, in which 154 distinct works in Arabic and Persian, by authors belonging to many centuries, are described, criticised, calendared and extracted. There are, besides, references to a great many other books. The divisions are general works on India, general and particular works on the Muhammedan history and the Mughal Empire, special national historians, and early geographers, and the time-limits of the subject may be roughly described as A.D. 1000-1750, although the general and the local books frequently overstep the earlier boundary.—Bookseller's Note.


ELLIS, WILLIAM (L.M.S.).  Narrative of a Tour through Hawaii, or Owhyhee, with the History, Traditions, Manners, Customs, and Manners of the Inhabitants of the Sandwich Islands.  7 plates. Folding map. 8vo.  London, 1826.


——  Polynesian Researches during a residence of nearly 6 years in the South Sea Islands, descriptions of the Natural History and Scenery, remarks on the History, Mythology, Traditions, Arts, Government and Customs of the inhabitants  Folding maps, plates of idols, tombs, etc., and wood engravings. 2 vols. 8vo.  London, 1830.

> One of the earliest instances of ethnological research by a missionary, and valuable for its information on the mythology, traditions, customs, etc., of the South Sea Islanders while still little sophisticated by Europeans.—Bookseller's Note. "The publication of this work went far to redeem the character of missionaries in the eyes of some who had thought of them all as ignorant and narrow-minded men."—D.N.B.

EVELYN, JOHN. Navigation and Commerce, Their Original and Progress. Containing A succinct Account of Traffick in General; its Benefits and Improvements: Of Discoveries, Wars and Conflicts at Sea, from the Original of Navigation to this Day; with Special Regard to the English Nation; Their several Voyages and Expeditions, to the Beginning of our late Differences with Holland; In which His Majesties Title to the Dominion of the Sea is asserted, against the Novel and later Pretenders. 8vo. London, 1674.

> For reference to this work see under COLLECTIONS.

EVERETT, W. Arctic Expeditions and their Results. London, 1863.

FAGIN, N. BRYLLION. William Bartram: Interpreter of the American Landscape. 8vo. John Hopkins Monographs in Literary History. Baltimore, 1933.

> This work puts Bartram into some interesting relations with the esthetic and intellectual trends of the times, and presents with considerable detail his influence on the romantic poets of the early nineteenth century. It also includes a good bibliography of travel literature and criticism.

FAVENC, ERNEST. History of Australian Exploration, 1788-1888. Maps and facsimile. 8vo. Sydney, 1888.

FISCHER, JOSEPH. The Discoveries of the Norsemen in America, with special relation to their early cartographical representation, translated by B. H. Soulsby. Bibliography, facsimiles of early maps and manuscripts, and cuts. 8vo. London, 1903.

FISKE, JOHN. The Discovery of America (see especially vol. I). Boston, 1898.

FORBES, HARRIETTE M. New England Diaries, 1602-1800. A Descriptive Catalogue of Diaries, Orderly Books and Sea Journals. Compiled by Harriette M. Forbes. 8vo. Topsfield, Mass., 1925.

FORCE, PETER. Tracts and other Papers relating principally to the Origin, Settlement, and Progress of the Colonies in North America, from the Discovery of the Country to the year 1776. 4 vols. 8vo. Washington, 1836-1846.

—— American Archives: Consisting of a collection of authentic Records, State Papers, . . . etc., the whole forming a documentary History of the Origin and progress of the North American Colonies; of the Causes and Accomplishment of the American Revolution . . . in six series. (The second title is) "American Archives" fourth series, to the Declaration of Independence. 6 vols. Fol. Plus fifth series, 3 vols. folio. Washington, 1848-1853.

> The above 9 volumes of this great storehouse of British Colonial and American history are all that have appeared.—Dauber & Pine.

FORDHAM, SIR HERBERT GEORGE. Maps: History, Characteristics, and their Uses. 6 plates. Cambridge, 1925.

—— Some Notable Surveyors and Map-Makers of the 16th, 17th and 18th centuries and their Work. A Study in the History of Cartography. 9 illus. 8vo. Cambridge, 1929.

—— Studies in Carto-Bibliography, British and French, and in the Bibliography of Itineraries and Road-Books. Frontispiece. 8vo. Oxford, 1914.

FORSTER, JOHANN REINHOLD. Magazin von merkwürdigen neuen Reisebeschreibungen aus fremden Sprachen übersetzt und mit Anmerckungen begleitet. Bd. 1-15. Numerous plates and maps. Berlin, 1790-98.

—— Magazin von merkwürdigen neuen Reisebeschreibungen aus fremden Sprachen übersetzt und mit Anmerckungen begleitet. Bd. 1-30. 57 plates and 13 maps. Vienna, 1792-1804.

> This is apparently an enlarged edition of the preceding item.

FOSTER, SIR WILLIAM. England's Quest of Eastern Trade. Maps. 8vo. Pioneer History Series. London, 1933.

> This is the story of the men who tried to reach Cathay by one way or another. It contains many names not mentioned in the D.N.B. The author was formerly historiographer to the India Office. In the compilation of the present work he has covered a very extensive field of research and closes his narrative with the East India Company fully launched and regular trade opened with China and the Far East at the end of the eighteenth century.—Bookseller's Note.

—— The English Factories in India, 1634-36, a Calendar of Documents in the India Office, British Museum, and Public Record Office. With frontispiece and index. 8vo. Oxford, 1911.

—— Letters received by the East India Company from its Servants in the East. Transcribed from the 'Original Correspondence' series of India Office Records, 1602-1617. Edited by W. Foster, with Introduction by F. C. Danvers. 6 vols. 8vo. London, 1896-1902.

FROUDE, J. A. English Seamen in the Sixteenth Century, Lectures delivered at Oxford. Easter Terms, 1893-94. 8vo. London, 1895.

> Reprinted, London, 1922.

FÜLÖP-MILLER, RENE. The Power and Secret of the Jesuits. Translated by F. S. Flint and D. F. Tait. Garden City, 1930.

> See Chapter V on the Far East, North America, and South America. A full bibliography is appended to the volume.

GERINI, G. E. Researches on Ptolemy's Geography of Eastern Asia (Further India and Indo-Malay Peninsula). 2 maps. 8vo. London, 1909.

GIBLIN, R. W. The Early History of Tasmania. (The Geographical Era, 1642-1804.) 3 plates and 12 charts. 8vo. London, 1928.

> "Here the author, a Tasmanian, has traced the development of European knowledge concerning the island from the time of its discovery by Tasman to 1803 and 1804, when the first settlements were made."

GOLDEN HIND SERIES. Biographies of the great explorers edited by Milton Waldman. Illus. and maps. 8vo. New York, 1927—.

> Dampier. By Clennell Wilkinson. 1929.
>
> Drake. By E. F. Benson. 1927.
>
> Frobisher. By William McFee. 1928.
>
> Grenville. By J. C. Squire. n.d.
>
> Hawkins. By Philip Gosse. 1930.
>
> Hudson. By Llewelyn Powys. 1927.
>
> Magellan. By E. F. Benson. 1930.
>
> Raleigh. By Milton Waldman. 1928.
>
> Scott. By Stephen Gwynn. 1930.
>
> Smith. By E. Keble Chatterton. 1927.

GOSLING, W. G. Labrador: Its discovery, exploration and development. Plates. 8vo. London, 1910.

GOSSE, PHILIP. The Pirates' Whos's Who. Giving particulars of the Lives and Deaths of the Pirates and Buccaneers. Illus. London, 1924.

    Cited in this bibliography.

GRAHAM, R. B. CUNNINGHAME. Vanished Arcadia, being some Account of the Jesuits in Paraguay, 1607-1767. Map. 8vo. Revised edition, London, 1924.

    See Muratori under 1759, SOUTH AMERICA.

GRANT, W. L. (Editor). The Makers of Canada. Biographies of the Leading Explorers, Statesmen, Soldiers, Churchmen, Patriots. Written by well-known Scholars and Covering the History of Canada from Champlain to Laurier and from the Atlantic to the Pacific. With the Oxford Encyclopedia of Canadian History. By L. J. Burpee. Illus. with portraits and full-page plates. Complete in 12 vols. 8vo. London, 1926.

GRAY, EDWARD. Leif Eriksson, Discoverer of America. A.D. 1003. Maps. 8vo. Oxford, 1930.

GREELY, A. W. (Major-General). Handbook of Polar Discoveries. Maps. London, 1897.

    Fourth edit., 1910.
    Bibliographies are to be found at the ends of chapters. The work is planned topically, each part of which is done chronologically. There is detailed information on various polar regions and interests.

GREENLAND, Vol. I. The Discovery of Greenland, Exploration and Nature of the Country. Published by the Commission for the Direction of the Geological and Geographical Investigations in Greenland. London, 1928.

GREY, C. European Adventurers of Northern India, 1785 to 1849. Edited by H. L. O. Garrett. Illus. 8vo. Lahore, 1929.

    The present work represents some six years of labour in the archives of the Punjab Government, as well as the consultation of a very large number of contemporary memoirs and other works, a full bibliography of which will be found in the appendix.—Preface, cited by Bookseller.

GUILFORD, E. L. Travellers and Travelling in the Middle Ages. 8vo. London, 1924.

GUILLEMARD, F. H. H.  The Life of Ferdinand Magellan.  8vo. London, 1890.

> This is still the best life of Magellan.—Baker, *Geographical Discovery.*

HAKLUYT, RICHARD (The two).  The Original Writings and Correspondence of the Two Richard Hakluýts.  Introduction and Notes by E. G. R. Taylor, D.Sc. 2 vols. Hak. Soc., ser. II, vols. 76-77.  London, 1935.

> These volumes are a boon to the student of the early efforts made by these two Englishmen to stimulate an interest in geographical discovery and overseas colonization.

HAKLUYT SOCIETY PUBLICATIONS.  Series I, vols. 1-100, London, 1848-1898; Series II, vols. 1-77, London, 1899-1936.  Extra Series, vols. 1-33, London, 1903-07.

> "Established in 1848, the Hakluyt Society has for its object the printing of rare and valuable Voyages, Travels, Naval Expeditions, and other geographical records. Books of this class are of the highest interest to students of history, geography, navigation, and ethnology; and many of them, especially the original narratives and translations of the Elizabeth and Stuart periods, are admirable examples of English prose at the stage of its most robust development. . . . The Society has not confined its selection to the books of English travellers, to a particular age, or to particular regions. Where the original is foreign, the work is given in English, fresh translations being made, except where it is possible to utilise the spirited renderings of the sixteenth or seventeenth centuries."—From the Prospectus. See also under BIBLIOGRAPHIES.

HALKETT, SAMUEL, and LAING, JOHN.  Dictionary of Anonymous and Pseudonymous English Literature.  4 vols.  4to.  London, 1882-1888.

> A new and enlarged edition by James Kennedy, W. A. Smith and A. F. Johnson.  6 vols.  8vo.  London, 1926.
> This work was begun by Halkett and completed by Laing .

HALL, D. G.  Early English Intercourse with India, 1587-1743.  London, 1928.

HARING, C. H.  The Buccaneers in the West Indies in the XVIIIth Century.  10 maps and illus.  London, 1910.

> Philip Gosse refers to this as a "most scholarly and interesting work."

HARLEIAN MISCELLANY.  A Collection of scarce, curious, and entertaining Pamphlets and Tracts, as well in Manuscript as in Print, selected from the Library of Edward Harley, second Earl of Oxford. Interspersed with historical, political, and critical Annotations, by the late William Oldys, Esq., and some additional Notes by Thomas Park, F.S.A. 12 vols. 4to. London, 1808-1813.

> 1st edit., with preface by Dr. Samuel Johnson, 10 vols., 4to, London, 1744-46. For a selection see Savage below.
> The famous library of Robert Harley, Earl of Oxford, was sold by his widow in 1742 to Thomas Osborne, bookseller, for £13,000, which was less than the cost of the bindings. The MSS. remained in her possession until 1753, when they were bought by Parliament for £10,000. At the same time was acquired by the trustees appointed by Parliament the library of Sir Hans Sloane. These two libraries, together with the Cottonian MSS., secured in 1700, were turned over to the trustees in 1753, and so was formed the nucleus of the great library of Great Britain in the British Museum.

HARRISSE, HENRY. The Discovery of North America. Numerous reproductions of maps. 4to. London, 1892.

> A critical, documentary, and historic Investigation, with an Essay on the Early Cartography of the New World, including Descriptions of Two Hundred and Forty Maps or Globes existing or lost, constructed before the year 1536; to which are added a Chronology of One Hundred Voyages westward, Projected, Attempted, or Accomplished between 1431 and 1504; Biographical Accounts of the 300 Pilots who first crossed the Atlantic; and a Copious List of the Original Names of American Regions, Caciqueships, Mountains, Islands, Capes, Gulfs, Rivers, Towns, and Harbours.—Maggs, No. 479.

HART, F. R. Admiral of the Caribbean. London, 1923.

> This contains an interesting chapter on Sir Henry Morgan.—Gosse.

HEARNE, THOMAS. Reliquiae Hearnianae: The Remains of Thomas Hearne, M.A., of Edmund Hall (Oxford University). Being Extracts from his MS. Diaries, Collected, with a Few Notes, by Philip Bliss. 3 vols. 8vo. London, 1869.

> App. XVII of vol. III consists of "Excerpts from a Catalogue of the Library of Thomas Hearne." Qt ite a number of travel books are listed here. The comments of this unyielding non-juror on his colleagues and on public events, on books and their authors, are pithy and pungent. Some of these have been cited in this bibliography.

HEAWOOD, EDWARD. A History of Geographical Discovery in the Seventeenth and Eighteenth Centuries. Numerous illus. and maps. 8vo. Cambridge, 1912.

> Frequently cited in this bibliography.

HEERES, J. E. The Part Borne by the Dutch in the Discovery of Australia, 1606-1765. Folding maps and illus. 4to. London, 1899.

HERVEY, FREDERICK, and Others. Naval History of Great Britain, from the earliest Times to the Rising of Parliament in 1779, including the Naval Expeditions and Sea Fights, and particularly recording the Glorious Achievements in the last War, etc. 5 vols. 8vo. London, 1779-80.

> Containing the attractive series of folding maps, portraits and plates. There are five maps of North America, South America, etc. Portraits of General Wolfe, Admirals Hawke, Anson, Keppel, Boscawen, etc.—Bookseller's Note.

An Historical Account of the Circumnavigation of the Globe and of the Progress of Discovery in the Pacific, from the Voyage of Magellan to the Death of Cook. Illus. 8vo. Edinburgh, 1836.

HOVGAARD, WILLIAM. The Voyages of the Norsemen to America. Plates and maps. 8vo. New York, 1914.

HOWARD, CLARE. English Travellers of the Renaissance. Illus. 8vo. London, 1914.

> This utilizes largely directions, advices, etc., on travel and to travellers. A selected bibliography is appended.

HOWLEY, J. P. The Beothucks, or Red Indians, the Aboriginal Inhabitants of Newfoundland, profusely illustrated with drawings and plates depicting implements and ornaments, etc. 4to. London, 1915.

> Contents:—Fifteenth, Sixteenth, Seventeenth Century Narratives of Voyages. Eighteenth Century Notes from Journals, Parliamentary Papers, Letters, etc. Nineteenth Century Reports of Expeditions, Correspondence, Narratives of Travel, etc. Also Narrative of a Journey Across the Island of Newfoundland in 1822.— Bookseller's Note.

HUDSON, G. F. Europe and China. A Survey of their Relations in History. 3 maps. 8vo. London, 1931.

> The author, one of the foremost of the rising historians of Oxford, has made a special study of the history of the far east of Asia, and this book includes the results of research on the spot. Starting with the earliest written references to the impact of East upon West, which go back as far as Herodotus, he traces the course of relations through the ancient world and the middle ages up to the end of the eighteenth century.—Bookseller's Note.

HUET, ——. Memoirs of the Dutch Trade in all the States, Empires and Kingdoms in the World, showing its Rise and Amazing Progress; After what manner the Dutch Manage and Carry on their Commerce, etc., translated from the French by Mr. Samber. 8vo. 2nd edit. London, 1719.

HUISH, R.  The North-West Passage, a History of the most remarkable voyages made in search of, from the earliest periods.  Illus.  8vo.  London, 1851.

IL MERCURIO ITALICO. . . . The Italian Mercury: or, A General Account concerning the Literature, Fine Arts, Useful Discoveries, etc., of all Italy.  Plates.  2 vols.  8vo.  London, 1789.

> In English and Italian.  It contains a history of discovery in America, with a facsimile of the map of Andrea Bianco, a Venetian, of 1436, in which the Antilles are delineated, before the discovery of Columbus.—Sabin.

INSH, G. P. (Editor).  Darien Shipping Papers, Papers relating to the Ships and Voyages of the Company of Scotland Trading to Africa and the Indies 1697-1707, edited by G. P. Insh.  Chart and plates of the Arms of the Company.  8vo.  Scottish Historical Society.  Edinburgh, 1924.

IORGA, N.  Les Voyageurs Français dans l'Orient Européen.  Poitiers, 1928.

> The author is a professor at the University of Bucharest.  The period covered ranges from XVth to the XIXth centuries.  The account is both descriptive and analytical.  Frequently cited in this bibliography.

——  Une Vingtaine de Voyageurs dans l'Orient Européen (pour faire suite aux Voyageurs Français dans l'Orient Européen).  Paris, 1928.

> The travellers are drawn from several nationalities; the voyages are given in summaries.  Frequently cited in this bibliography.

IRVING, WASHINGTON.  Life and Voyages of Columbus.  3 vols.  Revised edition.  New York, 1868.

> The first edition of this appeared in four volumes in 1824.

JACK, ROBERT LOGAN.  Northmost Australia: Three Centuries of Exploration, Discovery, and Adventures in and around Cape York.  16 maps and 39 illus.  2 vols.  8vo.  London, 1921.

> This is an investigation of the narratives of explorers in this region both by land and sea, many of which are from unpublished documents.

JAYNE, K. G.  Vasco da Gama and his Successors.  London, 1910.

JOHNSON, CHARLES (Captain).  A General History of the Pyrates, from their first Rise and Settlement in the Island of Providence, to the present time. With the remarkable Actions and Adventures of the two Female Pyrates Mary Read and Anne Bonny; contain'd in the following Chapters, I. Of Capt. Avery; II. Of Capt. Martel; III. Of Capt. Teach; IV. Of Capt. Bonnet; V. Of Capt. England; VI. Of Capt. Vane; VII. Of Capt. Rackam; VIII. Of Capt. Davis; IX. Of Capt. Roberts; X. Of Capt. Anatis; XI. Of Capt. Worley; XII. Of Capt. Lowther; XIII. Of Capt. Low; XIV. Of Capt. Evans; XV. Of Capt. Phillips; XVI. Of Capt. Spriggs. And of their several Crews. To which is added, a Short Abstract of the Statute and Civil Law, in relation to Piracy. 2nd edit., with considerable Additions. 3 plates. London, 1724.

> 3rd edit., London, 1725; Dublin, 1725; 4th, London, 1726; again (said to be the best), London, 1734. Modern edition, London, 1926. Translated into French, Paris, 1726. See below.
> This popular work appeared originally in 73 weekly numbers.—Philip Gosse. Gosse considers this the greatest work on pirates ever written. This edition is an enlargement of the extremely rare first edition, with different engraved plates. Sabin says of it that it embodies many items relating to the colonial history of British America nowhere else extant.—Robinson.

—— A General Historie of the Pyrates. 4th edit. 2 vols. London, 1726.

> At the end of Vol. I. an account is given of the notorious Shetland Pirate Captain Smith, alias Gow. Vol. II is largely devoted to the amazing career of the French Pirate Misson, who combined practical social reform with his regular profession. Also more brief biographies of other distinguished members of what may be named the Madagascar "group."—Gosse.

—— A General History of the Lives and Adventures of the most Famous Highwaymen, Murderers, Street-robbers, &c.; to which is added, a Genuine Account of the Voyages and Plunders of the most Notorious Pyrates, interspersed with several Diverting Tales and Pleasant Songs, and adorned with the Heads of the most remarkable Villains, curiously engraven on copper, including Sawney Beane, Tho. Savage, Whitney robbing a Usurer, Capt. Edward England, Captain Bartholomew Roberts, Capt. Lowther, Capt. Low, Capt. Morgan, John Cottington, Tom Waters, Jack Sheppard, Jonathan Wild, Burnworth, Blewitt, Sarah Malcolm, &c. 23 plates. Fol. London, 1734.

> To all intents a reissue of "Lives of Noted Highwaymen, Robbers, Thieves, and Pickpockets," 1711, by Captain Alexander Smith. Johnson added a number of his pirates to it.—Gosse. Many of these pirates were famous for their exploits on the American coast.

—— The History and Lives of the most Notorious Pirates, and their Crews; from Captain Avery, who first settled at Madagascar, to Captain John Gow, and James Williams, his lieutenant, etc., who were hanged at Execution Dock June 11, 1725, for Piracy and Murder; and afterwards hanged in Chains between Blackwall and Debtford. 16 quaint woodcuts of various pirates, including Capt. John Evans, the noted Welch Pirate, Capt. Martel, Capt. Teach, Capt. Vane, Mary Read, etc. London, 1780.

> The date is approximate. Most of these piracies were committed in American waters.—Maggs, No. 442. This work is probably based on Johnson.

—— A Complete Newgate Calendar, being Captain Charles Johnson's General History of the Lives and Adventures of the Most Famous Highwaymen, Murderers, Street-Robbers and Account of the Voyages and Plunders of the Most Notorious Pyrates, 1734; Captain Alexander Smith's Compleat History of the most Notorious Highwaymen, etc., 1719; The Tyburn Chronicle, 1768; The Malefactor's Register, 1796; George Borrow's Celebrated Trials, 1825, etc., etc. Collated and Edited with some Appendices by J. L. Raynor and G: T, Crook. 28 plates. 5 vols. 8vo. Navarre Society. London, 1926.

—— (In French.) Histoire des Pirates anglois depuis leur établissement dans l'sle de la Providence jusqu'à présent. Traduit de l'anglois. 12mo. Paris, 1726.

JOHNSTONE, SIR HARRY. History and Description of the British Empire in Africa: Early Discoveries, Native Movements, Development, etc. 6 maps and 250 illus. 8vo. London, 1910.

—— The Opening Up of Africa. 12mo. Home University Library. London, 1911.

JUSSERAND, J. J. English Wayfaring Life in the Middle Ages (XIVth Century). Translated from the French by Lucy Toulmin Smith. Illus. 8vo. London, 1909.

KELLY, J. A. England and Englishmen in German Literature of the 18th Century. Columbia Univ. Press. New York, 1921.

This contains some references to travels.

KENT, ——. Biographia Nautica. 3 vols. London, 1777.

KER, W. P. The Elizabethan Voyagers, in his *Collected Essays.* Vol. 1. London, 1925.

KITSON, A. The Life of Captain James Cook. New York, 1907.

This is considered to be the best life of Cook.—Quoted.

KOHL, J. G. A History of the Discovery of the East Coast of North America . . . from 990 to . . . 1578. 8 vols. *Documentary History of the State of Maine.* Portland, Me., 1869-1909.

This gives a full account of voyages to the northeast coast of America by all nations, with many documents and maps. Especially valuable for the Cabot voyages and for maps.—Read, *Bibliography of British History.*

LAFITAU, JOSEPH FRANCIS. Histoire des découvertes et conquestes des Portugais dans le Nouveau Monde. 4 vols. 12mo. Paris, 1734.

> L'auteur donne des détails très etendus et très exacts sur les coûtumes, les moeurs, la religion des sauvages de l'Amérique, et notamment de ceux du Canada. Il avait été à même de bien connaitre ces peuples ayant vécu longtemps chez les Iroquois (*Biog. Univ.*).—On y trouve un grand détail de moeurs . . . Aussi n'avions-nous rien de si exact sur ce sujet. Le paralléle des anciens peuples avec les Américains a paru fort ingénieux, et suppose une grande connäissance de l'antiquité.—Charlevoix. This work is cited here because of its value as a work of reference.

LATOURETTE, K. S. Voyages of American Ships to China, 1784-1844. 8vo. New Haven, 1927.

LEDIARD, T. Naval History of England . . . from the Norman Conquest . . . to the Conclusion of 1734. Fol. London, 1735.

LEE, IDA. Early Explorers in Australia, from the log-books and journals, including the Diary of Allan Cunningham, Botanist, from March 1st, 1817, to November 9th, 1818. Portraits, illus., and maps. London, 1925.

LEYDEN, JOHN (M.D.). Historical Account of Discoveries and Travels in Africa, enlarged and completed by Hugh Murray. 2 vols. 8vo. Edinburgh, 1817.

> A very valuable and highly instructive work.—Lowndes.

LOCKE, JOHN. The Whole History of Navigation from its Original to this time (1704). London, 1704.

> See the Preface to Churchill's *Collection of Voyages,* 1704 edition. Reprinted in Locke's Works, vol. X, London, 1801.

LOCKE, J. C. The First Englishmen in India. Letters and Narratives of sundry Elizabethans written by themselves, edited with Introduction and Notes, by J. C. Locke. 8vo. Broadway Travellers. London, 1930.

LONG, W. H. (Editor). Naval Yarns, Letters and Anecdotes; comprising Accounts of sea fights and wrecks, actions with pirates and privateers, etc., from 1616 to 1831. London, 1899.

LOW, C. B. Maritime Discovery, A History of Nautical Exploration from the Earliest Times. 2 vols. 8vo. London, 1881.

LOWERY, WOODURY. The Spanish Settlements within the present limits of the United States, 1513-1561. Maps. 8vo. New York, 1901.

—— The Spanish Settlements within the present limits of the United States. Florida, 1562-1574. Maps. 8vo. New York, 1911.

MAJOR, R. H. The Discoveries of Prince Henry the Navigator, and their results; being the Narrative of the Discovery by Sea, within one Century, of more than Half the World. Portraits, maps, etc. 2nd edit. London, 1877.

MANHART, GEORGE B. Studies in English Commerce and Exploration in the Reign of Elizabeth; England and Turkey; the Rise of Diplomatic and Commercial Relations, by Albert L. Rowland; English Search for a North-West Passage, in the time of Queen Elizabeth, by George B. Manhart. 8vo. Philadelphia, 1924.

MALAKES, ERNEST. French Travellers in Greece (1771-1820)—an early phase of French Phil-Hellenism. Philadelphia, 1925.

MARCIAN OF HERACLEA. Periplus of the Outer Sea, East and West, and of the Great Islands therein. A Translation from the Greek text, with commentary. 8vo. London, 1927.

MARINE RESEARCH SOCIETY. Publications of. Illus., plates, portraits, maps, plans, 25 vols. Salem, Mass., 1923-1934.

MARKHAM, SIR CLEMENTS R. Lands of Silence: History of Arctic and Antarctic Exploration. 50 maps and illus. 8vo. Cambridge, 1921.

MASON, JAMES. Ice-World Adventures; or Voyages and Travels in the Arctic Regions, from the Discovery of Iceland to the English expedition of 1875. London, 1876.

MASON, OTIS TUFTON. Primitive travel and transportation. Government Printing Office, Washington, D.C., 1896. "From the Report of the Department of the U.S. National Museum" for 1894, pp. 237-593.

MAUGHAM, H. NEVILLE. The Book of Italian Travel, 1580-1900. New York and London, 1903.

MAXWELL, CONSTANTIA. The English Traveller in France 1698-1815. London, 1932.

> Descriptive account of what the travellers saw. Selected bibliography.

MAYNARD, THEODORE. De Soto and the Conquistadores. Illus. 8vo. New York, 1930.

McCLYMONT, JAMES. The Discoveries made by Pedraluarez Cabral and his Captains. 8vo. London, 1909. (16 pp.)

—— Essays in Historical Geography and on Kindred Subjects. London, 1921.

> This is concerned with early Spanish explorers, the Wreck of the *Tryall* near Java, etc.

MEAD, WILLIAM E. The Grand Tour in the 18th Century. 8vo. Boston, 1914.

> A work to be consulted for the interchange of culture, directions for travellers, and objectives for the Grand Tour. A bibliography is appended.

MEIGS, J. F. The Story of the Seaman: being An Account of the Ways and Appliances of Seafarers and of Ships from the Earliest Times until now. Maps and plates. 2 vols. 8vo. Philadelphia, 1924.

MERENESS, NEWTON D. Travels in the American Colonies, 1690-1783. New York, 1916.

> Gives texts of Diaries and Journals.

MESICK, J. L. English Travellers in America. Columbia Univ. Studies in English and Comparative Literature. New York, 1922.

MORSE, WILLIAM INGLIS. The Land of the New Adventure (the Georgian Era in Nova Scotia). 97 plates. Folding map. 8vo. London, 1932.

> This book deals with the life of Nova Scotia during the early days of the eighteenth century, and it collects together the evidence of social intercourse between England and Nova Scotia during these formative years. The book is divided

into three main sections or chapters, No. I being a Survey of Nova Scotia: geography, drift of population, transportation and purveying of news, exportations and importations of goods between England and Nova Scotia, the social scene, and the art of the period. Chapters II and III deal with Early Churches and Monumental Art of Nova Scotia.—Bookseller's Note.

MOSES, BERNARD (Dr.). Spanish Colonial Literature in South America. 32 illus. and a map. 8vo. London, 1922.

> Long bibliography of Spanish-American books.

MOTT, ALBERT J. On the literature of Expeditions to the Nile. Proceedings of the Literary and Philosophical Society of Liverpool. 56th Session, 1866-67, No. XXI, pp. 145-184. London and Liverpool, 1867.

> An historical account of Nile literature, commencing with the French map of Africa, 1671, and the journey of Herodotus; and ending with Petherick's Egypt, 1861.—Ibrahim-Hilmy.

MURPHY, HENRY C. The Voyage of Verrazano. A chapter in the Early History of Maritime Discovery in America. 8vo. London, 1875.

MURRAY, HUGH. Account of Discoveries and Travels in Asia from the Earliest Ages to the present time. 3 vols. Edinburgh, 1820.

—— Historical Account of Discoveries and Travels in Africa, from the Earliest Ages to the Present Time, including the substance of the late Dr. Leyden's work on that subject. Folding map. 8vo. Edinburgh, 1818.

—— Historical Account of Discoveries and Travels in North America including the shores of the Polar Sea and the voyage in search of a North-West Passage. 2 vols. Maps and bibliography. London, 1829.

The Naval Chronicle; or Voyages, Travels, Expeditions, Remarkable Exploits and Achievements, Of the most Celebrated English Navigators, Travellers, and Sea-Commanders, From the Earliest Accounts to . . . 1759; . . . thro Asia, Africa, and America; The many Conquests they obtained over the Spaniards, French and other Nations; . . . Including the Lives of the most Eminent British Admirals and seamen, who have distinguished themselves by their Bravery and love of Liberty. . . . Adorned with Cuts. 30 plates. 3 vols. 8vo. London, 1760.

> Contains accounts of the voyages of Sir Walter Raleigh, Sir Francis Drake, the Cabots, the first attempts for the discovery of New England, etc.

NAVARRETE, MARTIN FERNANDEZ DE. Coleccion de los Viages y Descubrimientos, que hicieron por mar los Españoles desde fines del Siglo XV. Con varios documentos ineditos concernientes a la historia de la Marina Castellana y de los extablecimentos Españoles en Indias. Maps and plates. 5 vols. 4to. 2nd edit.,   Madrid, 1837-1880.

> This contains the text of many historical and unpublished documents relating to the discovery of America.—Quaritch, No. 449.

NAVY RECORDS SOCIETY'S PUBLICATIONS, complete set to 1932, Vols. 1-69. 69 vols. and 1 vol. of plates. 8vo.   London, 1894-1932.

> Contents:—State papers relating to the Spanish Armada.—Letters of Lord Hood, 1781-82.—Index to James's Naval History.—Life of Capt. S. Martin.—Journal of Admiral B. James, 1752-1828.—Holland's Discourses of the Navy, 1638-58.—Naval Accounts, etc., of Henry VII.—Journal of Sir Geo. Rooke.—Letters, etc., relating to the War with France, 1512-13.—Papers relating to the Spanish War, 1585-87.—Journals, etc., of Admiral Sir Th. B. Martin.—Papers relating to the Dutch War, 1652-54.—The same, Blockade of Brest.—History of the Russian Fleet, temp., Peter the Great.—Logs of the Great Sea Fights, 1794-1805.—Naval Miscellany.—Naval Tracts of Sir Wm. Monson, Nelson and the Neapolitan Jacobins.—Descriptive Catalogue of the Naval MSS. in the Pepysian Library.—Correspondence of Admiral John Markham.—Fighting instructions, 1530-1816.—Recollections of Commander J. A. Gardner, 1775-1814.—Letters, etc., of Charles, Lord Barham, 1758-1813.—Naval Ballads and Songs: Views of the Battles of the Third Dutch War.—Signals and Instructions, 1776-94.—Papers relating to the Loss of Minorca in 1756.—The Old Scots Navy, 1689-1710.—Private Papers of George, Second Earl Spencer.—Law and Custom of the Sea.—Autobiography of Phineas Pett—Life of Sir John Leake—Life and Works of Sir Henry Mainwaring.—Letters of Lord St. Vincent, 1801-04.—Samuel Pepys' Naval Minutes—Letters and Papers of Admiral Viscount Keith.—Journal of the First Earl of Sandwich.—Boteler's Dialogues, etc.

NEVINS, ALLAN. American Social History as Recorded by British Travellers. Bibliography. 8vo.   New York, 1923.

> With critical and explanatory chapter introductions. Contains the texts of the travellers. Deals mainly with early 19th century.

NEWTON, ARTHUR PERCIVAL. The European Nations in the West Indies. 1493-1688.   London, 1933.

> This is the first work to deal with the broad lines of development of national policies in Caribbean and the repercussion of world events, etc., etc.—From the Prospectus.

—— (Editor). The Great Age of Discovery. 31 illus. 8vo.   London, 1932.

> A collection of Essays by various authors forming a supplement to *Travels and Travellers of the Middle Ages,* a similar collection published in 1926 which dealt with earlier travels.—Bookseller's Note. Especially useful for travels in the Far East and Central Asia.

—— (Editor).  Travel and Travellers in the Middle Ages.  7 illus.  8vo. London, 1926.

Contents:

The Conception of the World in the Middle Ages.  By A. P. Newton.

The Decay of Geographical Knowledge and the Decline of Exploration, A. D. 300-500.  By M. L. W. Laistner.

Christian Pilgrimages, A. D. 500-800.  By Rev. Claude Jenkins.

The Viking Age.  By Prof. Alan Mawer.

Arab Travellers and Merchants, A. D. 1000-1500.  By Sir T. W. Arnold.

Trade and Communication in Eastern Europe, A. D. 800-1200.  By Baron A. F. Meyendorff.

The Opening of the Land Routes to Cathay.  By Eileen Power.

"Travellers' Tales" of Wonder and Imagination; and European Travellers in Africa in the Middle Ages.  By A. P. Newton.

Prester John and the Empire of Ethiopia.  By Sir E. Denison Ross.

The Search of the Sea Route to India.  By Prof. Edgar Prestage.


NEWTON, C. T.  Travels and Discoveries in the Levant.  Illus. and maps.  2 vols.  8vo.  London, 1865.


NICHOLS, JOHN.  Literary Anecdotes of the 18th Century; comprising Biographical Memoirs of William Bowyer, and many of his learned Friends; an incidental View of the Progress and Advancement of Literature in this Kingdom during the last Century; and Biographical Anecdotes of a considerable Number of eminent Writers and ingenious Artists, with a very copious Index.  9 vols., 1812-15.—Illustrations of the Literary History of the 18th Century.  8 vols., 1817-58.  Together 17 vols.  Numerous portraits.  8vo.  London, 1812-1858.

Besides lists of books printed, this valuable work contains lengthy notes, biographical, critical, and historical, of authors and their works.  Frequently cited in this bibliography.


NORDENSKIÖLD, A. E.  Periplus.  An Essay on the early History of Charts and Sailing-Directions, translated from the Swedish Original by Francis A. Bather, with numerous Reproductions of old Charts and Maps.  160 maps.  Fol.  Stockholm, 1897.

This volume deals with the earlier and mainly unprinted portion of the subject of Cartography, and gives for the first time in literature a comprehensive view of the early MS. maps and Portulani, carried through the Middle Ages and ending, as a rule, with the sixteenth century.—Bookseller's Note.

—— Voyage of the "Vega" round Asia and Europe, with historical view of previous journeys. Portraits, maps, illus. 8vo. London, 1881.

> This voyage is cited here because it is the first one to accomplish the North-east Passage since the earliest attempt of Chancellor and Willoughby. The voyage lasted from June, 1878, to April, 1880.

NUNN, GEORGE E. The Columbus and Magellan Concepts of South American Geography. 2 plates. 7 figures. 8vo. Glenside, Penn., 1923.

> Only 95 copies have been printed. Dr. Nunn has worked out the figures on the Columbus longitudes, traced the changes in ideas due to the failure of the fourth voyage, explained the conversion of eastern Asia into a peninsula designated as South America and finally, has found the "Dragon Map."—Bookseller's Note. It shows that both Columbus and Magellan adhered to the belief that South America was part of Asia. Columbus first thought that America was a huge island until by a voyage he failed to find any passage between Central and South America.

OATEN, E. F. European Travellers in India during the 15th, 16th, and 17th Centuries; the evidence afforded by them with respect to Indian Social Institutions, and the Nature and Influence of Indian Governments. 8vo. London, 1899.

> Frequently cited in this bibliography.

ORIGINAL NARRATIVES OF EARLY AMERICAN HISTORY SERIES. Edited by Franklin Jameson. Each 8vo. New York, 1906-1930.

> Andrews, C. M. Narratives of the Insurrections, 1675-1690. 1915.
>
> Bolton, H. E. Spanish Exploration in the Southwest, 1542-1706. 1930.
>
> Bradford, Wm. History of the Plymouth Plantation. 1908.
>
> Burr, G. L. Narratives of the Witchcraft Cases, 1648-1706. 1914.
>
> Burrage, H. S. Early English and French Voyages. 1909.
>
> Champlain, Samuel de. Voyages of, 1604-1619. 1907.
>
> Danckaerts, Jasper. Journal, 1679-1680. 1913.
>
> Hall, C. C. Narratives of early Maryland, 1633-1684. 1925.
>
> Hodge, F. W., and Lewis, T. H. Spanish Explorers in the Southern United States. 1907.
>
> Jameson, J. F. Narratives of New Netherland, 1609-1664. 1909.
>
> Johnson, Edward. Johnson's Wonder-Working Providence, 1628-1651. 1910.
>
> Kellogg, L. P. Early Narratives of the Northwest, 1634-1699. 1917.
>
> Lincoln, C. H. Narratives of the Indian Wars, 1675-1699. 1913.
>
> Myers, A. C. Narratives of early Pennsylvania, West New Jersey, and Delaware, 1630-1707. 1912.
>
> Olson, J. E., and Bourne, E. G. The Northmen, Columbus and Cabot. 1906.

Salley, A. S. Narratives of early Carolina, 1650-1708. 1911.

Tyler, L. G. Narratives of early Virginia. 1907.

Winthrop, John. Journal. "History of England," 1636-1649. 2 vols. 1908.

PARKMAN, FRANCIS. Complete Works, revised edition. 12 vols. 8vo. Boston, 1893.

  Comprising: The Oregon Trail; Conspiracy of Pontiac, 2 vols.; Pioneers of France in the New World; Jesuits in North America; La Salle and the Discovery of the Great West; Old Regime in Canada under Louis XIV; Count Frontenac and New France under Louis XIV; Half Century of Conflict, 2 vols.; Montcalm and Wolfe, 2 vols.

PARKS, GEORGE BRUNER. Richard Hakluyt and the English Voyages. American Geographical Society, Special Publication No. 10. New York, 1928.

  This scholarly research into the contribution made by Hakluyt in expanding and synthesizing the knowledge of Elizabethan history, geography, and colonization is a necessary complement to the study of the life and literature of the period. This present bibliography owes to it a generous obligation for data on Tudor explorations and geographies.

PAULITSCHKE, PHILLIP. Die Afrika-Literatur in der Zeit von 1500 bis 1750 nach Christ. Ein Beitrag zur geograph. Quellenkunde. 8vo. Vienna, 1882.

PENROSE, B. (Editor). Sea Fights in the East Indies in the years 1602-39. With Introduction by B. Penrose. 7 plates. 8vo. London, 1931.

  A collection of contemporary accounts of the principal naval engagements between the Portuguese, Dutch, and English in the Indian Ocean and adjacent waters, from the beginnings of the seventeenth century until 1640, some reprinted for the first time. There is a sketch of Eastern colonial expansion from the days of Vasco da Gama.—Bookseller's Note.

PIERIS, P. E., and FITZLER, M. A. H. Ceylon and Portugal. Part I, Kings and Christians 1539-1552, from the original documents at Lisbon. 8vo. Leipzig, 1927.

  The first of an important series dealing with Ceylon and Portugal. Sixty-two documents are translated *in extenso* from the originals: they include letters from the kings and princes of Ceylon, the king of Portugal, the Governor of Goa, Franciscan missionaries, Portuguese Captains, Adventurers, Residents, Councillors and St. Francis Xavier.—Bookseller's Note.

PINCON, VINCENTE AÑES. By J. R. McClymont. 4to. London.

  This memoir treats of the most famous of the four Pincon brothers, Vincente, who accompanied Columbus as pilot on his first voyage.

PINKERTON, R. E.  Hudson Bay Company.  The Charter, Prosperous Early Days, Samuel Hearne—Arctic Explorer, The Rival Company, The Verge of Ruin, Red River Colony. 8vo.  London, 1932.

PRESCOTT, W. H.  History of the Conquest of Peru.  Plates. 2 vols.  New York, 1847.

PRESTAGE, E.  The Portuguese Pioneers.  Maps.  8vo.  London, 1933.

> The expeditions comprise those which revealed Madeira, the Azores and Cape Verde Islands, the coasts of Africa and Brazil, the Sea Passages to India, Malaya, the Spice Islands, China and Japan.  The leaders include such pioneers as Prince Henry the Navigator, Diogo Cao, Cadamosto, Bartholomew Dias and Vasco da Gama.—Heffer and Sons.

PROWSE, D. W.  A History of Newfoundland, from the English, Colonial, and foreign records.  Maps and illus.  London, 1896.

PURVIS, DAVID L., and COCKRANE, R. (Editors).  The English Circumnavigators.  The most remarkable voyages round the world by English sailors (Drake, Dampier, Anson and Cook), with a sketch of their lives, etc. Portraits.  Maps.  8vo.  Edinburgh, c. 1870.

QUAIFE, M. M. (Editor).  The Lakeside Press Classics of Western Exploration and Travel.  Each 12mo.  Chicago (recent).

RALEIGH, SIR WALTER.  The English Voyages of the Sixteenth Century: The Voyagers, Influence on Poetry and Imagination, etc. 8vo.  Glasgow and London, 1910.

RAMSAY, W. M.  The Historical Geography of Asia Minor. *Roy. Geog. Soc. Suppl. Papers.*  Maps.  London, 1890.

RENNELL, JAMES (Major).  Dissertations on Ancient Circumnavigation of Africa.  In his *Geographical System of Herodotus.*  See under 1800, AFRICA.

Reisebeschreibungen von deutschen Beamten und Kriegsleuten im Dienst der Niederländischen West-und Ostindischen Kompagnien, 1602-1797.  Eine Reihe von etwa 25 Kleineren und Grosseren mehr oder weniger wichtigen Journalen.  Martinus Nijhoff.  The Hague. (In progress.)

REYNOLDS, MYRA.   The Treatment of Nature in English Poetry between Pope and Wordsworth.   Chicago, 1909.

> See ch. iv for material relating to travels.

RICE, WARNER G.   Early English Travellers to Greece and the Levant. In *Univ. of Michigan Publications in Lang. and Lit.*, vol. X.   Ann Arbor, Mich., 1933.

ROBERTSON, JOHN W.   Francis Drake and other early Explorers along the Pacific Coast.   Several early maps reproduced in colors.   8vo. San Francisco, 1927.

> Five sections relate to Cortes, the Discoverer; Indians of the Californias; Jesuit survey of Baja California; Drake's Voyage in the South Sea; The Harbor of St. Francis.—Maggs, No. 534.

ROSEDALE, H. G. (Rev.).   Queen Elizabeth and the Levant Company. A Diplomatic Episode of the Establishment of our Trade with Turkey. 26 facsimile illus. of MSS., portraits, etc.   Fol.   London, 1904.

> This work throws much light on the early days of our Turkish trade, the difficulties of the Levant Company's agents, etc.—Bookseller's Note.

ROYAL GEOGRAPHIC SOCIETY.   Journal.   From 1831 to 1933: comprising Original Series, 50 vols. (1831-1880), Proceedings and Monthly Record, 14 vols. (1879-1892); New Series, *The Geographical Journal,* vols. 1-81 (1893-1933).   With General Indexes to Original Series 1-50, and New Series 1-20, and Supplementary Papers, 4 vols. Together 151 vols.   London, 1831-1933.

RUGE, S.   Geschichte des Zeitalters der Entdeckungen.   Berlin, 1881.

> This is the best work dealing with this period.—Baker, *Geographical Discovery.*

RUSSELL, W. CLARK.   Life of William Dampier.   Men of Action Series.   London, 1889.

> This contains a number of references to voyages.

SANS, CONWAY W.   The Conquest of Virginia.   The Forest Primeval. An Account based on original documents of the Indians in that portion of the continent in which was established the first English colony in America.   Maps and illus.   8vo.   New York, 1916.

SAVAGE, HENRY (Editor). The Harleian Miscellany. An entertaining Selection, commented upon and generally edited by Henry Savage. 2 portraits. 8vo. London, 1924.

> This is a selection from the 16th and 17th century tracts, pamphlets, and other records collected by Robert Harley, the first Earl of Oxford, and Edward Harley, the second Earl. See *The Harleian Miscellany* above.

SCHOFF, W. H. (Editor). Parthian Stations by Isidore of Charax. An Account of the Overland Trade Route between the Levant and India in the First Century B.C. The Greek text, with a translation and commentary. Illus. and Maps. 8vo. London, 1914.

—— The Periplus of Hanno, A Voyage of Discovery down the West Coast of Africa by a Carthaginian Admiral of the Fifth Century B.C. The Greek text with a translation. 8vo. London, 1914.

SCHOOLING, SIR WILLIAM. The Governors and Company of Adventurers of England trading into Hudson's Bay during 250 years, 1670-1920. London, 1920.

THE SEAFARERS LIBRARY. Edited by G. E. Manwaring. Illus. Each 8vo. London, 1928—.

> Fryke, C., and Schweitzer, C. Voyages to the East Indies. 1929.
>
> Raigersfeld, Baron de. The Life of a Sea Officer. 1929.
>
> Rogers, Woodes (Captain). A Cruising Voyage round the World. 1928.
>
> Shelvocke, George (Captain). A Voyage Round the World. 1928.
>
> Uring, Nathaniel (Captain). Voyage and Travels of. 1928.
>
> Walker, George (Commodore). The Voyage and Cruises of. 1928.

SEATON, ETHEL. Literary Relations of England and Scandinavia in the Seventeenth Century. Oxford, 1935.

> This work is thoroughly documented with references and quotations to memoirs, travels, diaries, letters, state papers, etc. It also contains a generous bibliography.

SHILLINGLAW, J. J. A Narrative of Arctic Discovery from the earliest to the present Time. With the details from measures adopted for the Relief of the Expedition under J. Franklin. London, 1850.

SKEEL, C. A. J. Travel in the First Century after Christ, with special reference to Asia Minor. Map. 8vo. London, 1901.

SMITH, EDWARD.  The Life of Sir Joseph Banks, with some Notices of his Friends and Contemporaries. 16 plates. 8vo.  London, 1911.

> This contains much information on the South Sea voyages of Cook and others both to the South and to the North.

SOMERS, JOHN (Lord).  A Collection of Scarce and Valuable Tracts, on the most interesting and entertaining Subjects, but chiefly such as relate to the History and Constitutions of these Kingdoms. 2nd edit. revised, augmented and arranged by Sir Walter Scott. 13 vols. in 14. 4to.  London, 1809-1815.

> This valuable collection includes the most interesting and important tracts in print and manuscripts, in the Royal, Cotton, Sion, and other public as well as private libraries. From the Holford Collection.—Bookseller's Note.

SPEARS, JOHN R.  Master Mariners. Short Bibliography. 12mo. Home University Library.  London, 1912.

SPILHAUS, M. WHITING.  The Background of Geography. Illus. and maps. 8vo.  London, 1912.

> This work contains many references to navigators.

STEENSBY, H. P.  Norsemen's Route Greenland to Wineland. 8vo. Copenhagen, 1917.

STEPHEN, LESLIE (Editor).  Dictionary of National Biography. Edited by Leslie Stephens. Supplements to 1930. 63 vols.  New York, 1885-1921.

STEVENS, BENJAMIN FRANKLIN.  B. F. Stevens' facsimiles of manuscripts in European archives relating to America, 1773-1783; with descriptions, editorial notes, collations, references and translations. 25 vols. Fol.  London, 1889-98.

> This extraordinary work is of the first importance for Franco-American relations during the decade 1773-1783. It is elaborately indexed and cross-indexed. For the following French travellers in the United States it is of very considerable interest and value: du Buysson, d'Estaing, Gerard, Holker, Kalb, Lafayette, Mauroy, Rochambeau, de Rousroy, and de Ternay.

ST. JOHN, PERCY B.  The North Pole and what has been done to reach it. A narrative of the various arctic explorations undertaken by all nations from the earliest period to the present time and the expedition preparing to be sent out on the "Discovery" and "Alert" under the command of Captain Nares. Map.  London, 1875.

STUCK, GOTTLIEB HEINRICH (K.P.). Verzeichnis von älteren, und neueren Reisebeschreibungen. Versuch eines Hauptstücks der geographischen Litteratur mit einen vollständigen Real Register, und einer Vorrede von M.I.E. Fabri, Inspector der Königlichen Freytische und Secretaire der Hallischen Naturforschenden Gesellschaft. II Theile. Halle, 1784, 1785, 1787.

SYKES, SIR PERCY. A History of Exploration from the earliest times to the present day. 8vo. London, 1934.

—— The Quest for Cathay. London, 1936.

> From earliest European explorers in Asia to the Portuguese discovery of the Ocean Route to China.

TAYLOR, E. G. R. Tudor Geography 1485-1583. With bibliography of early Tudor works on Geography. 16 plates. 8vo. London, 1930.

> A most informative work for the study of early English and continental interest in geography. Frequently cited in this bibliography.

THACHER, JOHN BOYD. Christopher Columbus, His Life, His Work, His Remains as revealed by Original Printed and Manuscript Records. With an Essay on Peter Martyr and Bartolome de las Casas. Maps, portraits, plates. 6 vols. bound in 3 vols. 4to. New York, 1903.

——— COLLECTION. For Early Americana see U. S. Library of Congress—John Boyd Thacher Collection. Washington, 1931.

THOMSON, JOSEPH. Mungo Park and the Niger. Portraits. Illus. The World's Great Explorers Series. London, 1890.

T'IEN-TSE CHANG. Sino-Portuguese Trade from 1514 to 1644. A synthesis of Portuguese and Chinese Sources. 8vo. London, 1933.

> The trade between the Chinese and the Portuguese in history is a subject which, in spite of its importance, has been thus far neglected. The reason is evident. Although important material exists, it has lain hidden in languages such as Chinese, Portuguese and to some extent, Dutch, which are either not much studied by Western historians, or are unfamiliar to Chinese scholars. The earliest period going back to the beginning of the Christian era is sketched by vivid quotations from the oldest Chinese historians, the later periods extending far into the XVIIth century, by the co-ordination of the principal and decisive facts, taken from Chinese, Portuguese, Arab sources and for the later period, also from Dutch sources. The author calls special attention to the way merchants were received in China, and how piracy grew when governments were disturbed.—From Bookseller's Note.

TILLOTSON, J. Adventures in the Ice. A comprehensive summary of arctic exploration, discovery and adventure, including unpublished experiences of a veteran whaler. London, 1869.

TYLER, MOSES COIT. A History of American Literature during the Colonial Period 1607-1765. 2 vols. in 1. New York, 1904.

Literary History of the American Revolution. 1763-1783. 2 vols. New York, 1895-1900.

> This work serves as a guide through the jungle of revolutionary writings. It selects, describes and appraises with splendid critical judgment all of the important papers, public and private, which contribute to our knowledge of this epoch. —From Waldman. Bibliography, vol. 2, pp. 429-483.

TYTLER, PATRICK FRASER. Historical View of the Progress of Discovery on the more northern Coasts of America from the earliest period to the present time. With descriptive sketches of the natural history of the North American regions, etc. 9 engravings. Map. 12mo. Edinburgh, 1832.

VAN LOON, HENDRIK WILLEM. The Golden Book of the Dutch Navigators. 70 illus. 8vo. New York, 1916.

WAGNER, HENRY R. Spanish Explorations in the Strait of Juan de Fuca. 13 maps. 8vo. Santa Ana, Calif., 1933.

—— Spanish Voyages to the Northwest coast of America in the 16th century. 20 maps and numerous facsimiles. 4to. San Francisco, 1929.

> This fully illustrated monograph contains translation with notes and facsimiles of the original narratives of Ulloa, Bolanes, Cabrillo, Gali, Juan de la Isla, Pedro de Unamuno, Cermeño, and Vizcaino.—Hiersemann.

WALDMAN, MILTON. Americana, the Literature of American History. 8vo. London, 1926.

> Chapters on the early Spanish, French and British explorers in America. Many references to early published works on America with critical evaluation of works mentioned. Frequently cited in this bibliography.

WEISE, ARTHUR J. The Discoveries of America to the year 1525. 8vo. London, 1884.

WESSELS, C. Early Jesuit travellers in Central Asia 1603-1721. 5 plates. Map. The Hague, 1924.

> Das wertvolle Werk legt die Geschichte der dogen., alten Jesuiten dar, die im XVII. u. XVIII. jh. die Erforschung Tibets, insbesondere die von Lhassa abstrebten, u. umfasst gleichzeitig ihre Missionsreisen durch Afghanistan, Turkestan, Hindustan u. die Himalaya-Bergkette.—Bookseller's Note.

WILLIAMS, JOHN. South Seas. A Narrative of Missionary Enterprises in the South Sea Islands. With remarks upon the Natural History of the Islands, Origin, Languages, Traditions, and Usages of the Inhabitants. . . . Frontispiece. 8vo. Baxter prints. London, 1838.

WINSOR, JUSTIN. Cartier to Frontenac. Geographical Discovery in the Interior of North America in its Historical Relations. 1534-1700. With Full Cartographical Illustrations from Contemporary Sources. 8vo. Boston, 1894.

—— The Narrative and Critical History of America. 8 vols. Boston, 1884-89.

> For its wealth of documented detail and critical evaluation this History is to be heartily recommended. See especially vols. III and VIII.

WOOD, S. A. The Disovery of Australia. London, 1922.

WOOLACOTT, A. P. Mackenzie and his Voyageurs. London, 1927.

WRIGHT, A. The Rise of Portuguese Power in India, 1497-1550. London, 1899.

WRIGHT, JOHN KIRTLAND. Geographical Lore at the Time of the Crusades. Amer. Geog. Soc., vol. I, No. 15. New York, 1925.

WRIGHT, LOUIS B. Middle Class Culture in Elizabethan England. University of North Carolina Press. Chapel Hill, N. Car., 1935.

> A closely documented study of the reading provided for the middle class population of that period.

WYCHERLEY, GEORGE. Buccaneers of the Pacific. Indianapolis, 1928.

> Of the bold English Buccaneers, pirates, privateers and gentlemen adventurers, who sailed in peril through the stormy straits or pierced the Isthmus jungle, to

vex the King of Spain in the South Seas and the Western Pacific, plundering his cities and coasts, and preying on his silver fleets and his golden galleons.—Bookseller's Note.

WYNDHAM, MAUD. Chronicles of the Eighteenth Century. 2 vols. London, 1924.

See vol. II, chs. iv-vii, for life in the British navy in peace times: Admiral Smith and his naval friends.

# XXI

## Bibliographies

ADAMS, JOSEPH Q.  See Northup, Clark S., *A Register of Bibliographies of the English Language and Literature.*  1925.

ALLEN, E. G.  Sale Catalogue of Books relating to America. 8vo. London, 1857.  (28 pp.)

—— Old Books relating to America prior to 1800. Also Since 1800. London, 1858-9.

AMERICAN HISTORICAL ASSOCIATION.  Writings on American History. A Bibliography of Books and Articles on United States History (published during a given year). 43 vols. Washington, 1904-1936.

> Beginning with vol. XVIII, the name of the series was changed to "Annual Report of the American Historical Association." The compilers of the first volume were A. C. McLaughlin, W. A. Slade, and D. L. Lewis; of the remaining volumes, Grace G. Griffin. The years covered run from 1902 to 1934, with the exception of 1903 and 1904. The work lists many books and tracts and reprints pertinent to this present bibliography.

ANGUS & ROBERTSON, Ltd.  Catalogue of books . . . etc., relating to Australia, New Zealand, etc. 8vo.  Sydney, 1927.

ARBER, EDWARD.  Term Catalogues, 1668-1709, with a Number for Easter Term 1711. A Contemporary Bibliography of English Literature in the Reigns of Charles II, James II, William and Mary, and Anne, edited from the very rare Quarterly Lists of New Books and Reprints of Divinity, History, Science, Law, Medicine, Music, Trade, Finance, Poetry, Plays, etc., with Maps, Engravings, Playing Cards, etc., issued by the Booksellers, etc., of London, by Edward Arber. 3 vols. 4to.  London, 1903-06.

> The kinds of books most popular during these forty-two years: (1) "Clearly Religious Books: especially works on the Lord's Supper; of which there were endless Editions. (2) Most popular secular works: Voyages and Travels, and Geographical Works generally: to which taste we were indebted, later on, for Robinson Crusoe and Gulliver's Travels. James Knapton set the fashion in this, with Dampier's Voyages. That led the way to the Collections of Voyages by Hacke, Churchill, Harris, and others; and even to a monthly Geographical Journal, the "Atlas Geographus."—From the Editor's introduction to Vol. III

—— Transcript of the Registers of the Company of Stationers of London, 1554-1640 A.D., complete, with Copious Indexes. 5 vols. 1875-94.

> A complete transcript of (1) All entries relating to books; (2) All other entries relating to the careers of individual printers, binders, publishers, and other members of the Company; (3) The dinner bills, 1557-1560, and other similar items, affording data for the history of wages, prices of food, etc. Together with a large mass of illustrative matter of contemporary date, and only inserted when its origin is as authoritative as the text itself, relating to the history of the Stationers' Company and the production of books.—Bookseller's Note.

ASHER, A. A Bibliographical Essay on the collection of voyages and travels, edit. and publ. by Levinus Hulsius and his successors, 1598-1660. London and Berlin, 1839.

BAKER, MARCUS. See Dall, W. H., *Pacific Coast Pilot. Alaska*. 1879.

BARBIER, ANTOINE ALEXANDRE. Dictionnaire des Ouvrages Anonymes et Pseudonymes composés, traduits ou publiés en français, avec les noms d'Auteurs, Traducteurs et Editeurs accompagné de Notes Historiques et critiques. 3 vols. 8vo. Paris, 1806-08.

BARTLETT, JOHN RUSSELL. Bibliography of Rhode Island. A Catalogue of Books and other Publications relating to the State of Rhode Island with Notes, Historical and Bibliographical. 8vo. Providence, 1864.

—— Bibliotheca Americana. 4 vols. 1865-67.

> This is a catalogue of books relating to America in the John Carter Brown Library at Providence. See under John Carter Brown below.

BERISTAIN Y SOUZA, D. J. M. (Dr.). Bibliotheca Hispano-Americana Septentrional. 4 vols. 8vo. Amecameca and Santiago, 1883-1897.

> This includes a supplementary volume by José Toribio Medina It consists of a catalogue of the authors who were born, educated, or flourished in Spanish North America. An important reference work.—Maggs, No. 526.

BERWICK, LORD. Catalogue of a Portion of the Library of the Right Hon. the Lord Berwick, consisting of a valuable collection of antiquities, history, voyages, travels, classics and miscellanies. 8vo. London, 1817.

BIBLIOGRAPHICAL SOCIETY OF AMERICA. Papers of. Chicago, 1899-1934.

> This society started out as the Bibliographical Society of Chicago, but in 1904 it became the Chicago Branch of the Bibliographical Society of America. The titles of the publications changed with the passage of the years: The Year Book, 1899/1900-1902-3, published by the Bibliographical Society of Chicago; Bulletins, I-IV, 1907/09-1912, The Bibliographical Society of America; Proceedings and Papers, I-III, 1904-06 and 1908; The Papers, IV-XXVII, 1909-1934.

BIBLIOGRAPHICAL SOCIETY. Transactions, 15 vols., London, 1892-1920. New Series, 11 vols. London, 1920-1931.

BIBLIOTHECA AMERICANA. Catalogue of a Valuable Collection of Books, Pamphlets, Manuscripts, Maps, Engravings, and Engraved Portraits, illustrating the History and Geography of North and South America, and the West Indies, forming the most extensive Collection ever Offered for Sale, by John Russell Smith. 8vo. London, 1865.

BIBLIOTHECA GEOGRAPHICA ET HISTORICA. A Catalogue of a Nine Days' Sale of Rare and Valuable Books, Maps, Charts, etc., of historical Geography and geographical History, etc., collected, used and described, with an Introduction by Henry Stevens. London, 1872.

BIBLIOTHECA STANLEIANA. A Splendid Selection of Rare and Fine Books, from the Distinguished Library of Colonel Stanley. The Selection contains all His Rare Italian and Spanish Poetry, Novels and Romances, Extraordinary Collection of Voyages and Travels, all the Old Chronicles, Books of Natural History, Very Fine Classics, Collection of Facetiae; The Books will be sold by Auction by R. H. Evans. 8vo. London, 1813.

BIBLIOTHEQUE NATIONALE DE PARIS. Catalogue de l'histoire de l'Amérique par Georges A. Barringer. Dept. des imprimés. 5 vols. 4to. Paris, 1903-1911.

> Issued for administrative purposes only, 50 copies.

Bibliothèque des Voyages Imaginaires, romanesques, merveilleux, allégoriques, amusans, comiques et critiques; suivie des Songes et Visions, et des Romans Cabalistiques. Illus. 39 vols. 8vo. Amsterdam, 1787-89.

BLAKE, A. V. A. S. Diccionario Bibliographico Brazileiro. 7 vols. 8vo. Rio de Janeiro, 1883.

BOHN, HENRY G.   Catalogue of Books, vol. I.  Natural History, Bibliography, Early Voyages, etc. 8vo.  London,  1847.

BOLTON, HERBERT EUGENE.  Guide to Materials for the History of the United States in the principal Archives of Mexico. 8vo.  Washington,  1913.

BOTSFORD, J. B.   For a selected bibliography of travel see his *English Society in the Eighteenth Century,*  London, 1924.

BOTURINI, BERNADUCI LORENZO.   Idea de una nueva Historia General de la America Septentrional.  Frontispiece. 4to.  Madrid, 1746.

> The curious and learned author arrived in Mexico in 1750; during the eight years he remained there he made most diligent researches into its antiquity, entered into friendship with the Indians and procured many valuable manuscripts from them. The appendix is of the highest bibliographical interest. It contains a catalogue of a rich collection of books, MSS. and maps relating to the early history of Mexico.—Bookseller's Note.

BOUCHER DE LA RICHARDERIE, G.   Bibliothèque Universelle des Voyages, ou Notice complète et raisonnée de tous les Voyages anciens et moderns dans les différentes parties du monde, classés par ordre de pays dans leur série chronologique; avec des extraits plus ou moins rapides des Voyages les plus estimés de chaque pays, et des jugemens motivés sur les Relations anciennes qui ont le plus de célébrité. 6 vols. 8vo.  Paris, 1808.

> "A work of considerable interest executed with care and minuteness. Boucher has deserved well of the book world by this truly, valuable, and almost indispensable performance."—Dibdin.

BOURGEOIS, EMILE and ANDRE, LOUIS. Les Sources de l'Histoire de France, XVII siècle (1610-1715), Géographie et Histoires générales.  Paris, 1913.

> "C'est la meillure bibliographie des Voyages du XVII siècle. Lacunes considerables, Biard, Bouton, et les deux Boyer, parmi les 'B' ici n'y figurent pas."— Atkinson, *Relations des Voyages.*

BRADFORD, T. L. (Dr.).  The Bibliographers' Manual of American History. Containing an account of all State, Territory, Town and County Histories relating to the United States of America, with an Exhaustive Index by Titles and States. 5 vols. 4to.  Philadelphia, 1907.

> Frequently cited in this bibliography.

BRASSEUR DE BOURBOURG. Bibliothèque Mexico-Guatemalienne précédée d'un coup d'oeil sur les études américaines dans leurs rapports avec les études classiques et suivie du tableau par ordre alphabétique des ouvrages de linguistique américaines contenus dans le même volume, redigée et mis en ordre d'après les documents de sa collection américaine. 8vo. Paris, 1871.

> Sous ce titre l'auteur a publié une bibliographie des ouvrages imprimés et manuscrits qu'il possédait (près de 500 articles) relatifs à l'histoire et à la linguistique de l'Amérique. Chaque ouvrage est décrit avec le plus grand soin et suivi d'une biographie de l'auteur.—Bookseller's Note.

BREYDENBACH, BERNARD VON. Bernard von Breydenbach and his Journey to the Holy Land, 1483-84. A Bibliography. Compiled by Hugh Wm. Davies. 60 plates. 4to. London, 1911.

> See under 1911, NEAR EAST.

BRITISH MUSEUM. Among the numerous catalogues of books in the British Museum the following are pertinent to this bibliography:

> Catalogue of Books in the Library of the British Museum, printed in England, Scotland and Ireland, and of Books in English printed abroad to the year 1640. With the extensive cross reference index. 3 vols. 8vo. London, 1884.
>
> Catalogue of Maps, Prints, Drawings, etc., forming the Geographical and Topographical Collection . . . Presented by H. M. King George IV to the British Museum. 2 vols. 8vo. London, 1829.
>
> Catalogue of the Printed Maps, Plans and Charts in the British Museum. 2 vols. 4to. London, 1885.
>
> General Catalogue of Printed Books in the Library of the British Museum. London, 1881-1905. With 10 Supplements. New edition, 1931-36 to Beow. 13 vols. Totals some 65 vols.
>
> > The introduction gives the history of the general catalogues, which begin in the year 1787 with two folio volumes entitled "Librorum impressorum qui in Museo Britannico Adservantur Catalogus."
>
> Subject Index of the modern Works added to the Library of the British Museum in the years 1901-1930. Edited by G. K. Fortesque. London, 1906. 6 vols.
>
> PROCTOR, ROBERT. An Index to the Early Printed Books in the British Museum: from the Invention of Printing to the year MD., with Notes on those in the Bodleian Library. (Part I). 4 parts. 4to. London, 1898-99.
>
> > Section I. Germany; II. Italy; III. Switzerland to Montenegro; IV. Registers.
>
> —— Supplement. I-IV. 8vo. London, 1899-1902. Index to the Supplements. By K. Burger. 8vo. London, 1906.
>
> —— Part II of the Index. MDI-MDXX. Section I. Germany. 4to. London, 1903.

BRITWELL LIBRARY.  Catalogue of the Library of S. Christie-Miller, Esq., Britwell, Bucks. Voyages and Travels. 8vo.  London.

BROWN, JOHN CARTER.  Bibliotheca Americana: Catalogue of the John Carter Brown Library in Brown University, Providence, Rhode Island. 4 vols.  Providence, 1919-1931.

> "The John Carter Brown Library is the only important library in the United States devoted to collecting Americana before the nineteenth century: its rival, the Lenox collection, has been absorbed in the New York Public Library, and the later collection of Mr. E. D. Church has been drawn into the general library of Mr. Henry E. Huntington. . . . (This catalogue) is planned to include all the printed books, pamphlets, maps, and manuscripts in the Library, with due emphasis upon the Americana, which will always constitute its strength."—From the Prefatory Note. Frequently cited in this bibliography.

BRUNET, JACQUES CHARLES.  Manuel du Libraire et de l'Amateur de Livres. Fifth and last edition complete with the Table and Supplement, by Deschamps and Brunet. Numerous facsimiles of colophons and printers' marks. 6 vols.  Paris, 1860-1880.

> The Supplement is almost the most useful part of Brunet's Manual.—Maggs, No. 553.

BRUSHFIELD, T. N.  Bibliography of Sir Walter Raleigh.  2nd edit., with notes revised and enlarged.  Exeter, 1908.

BUCK, SOLON J.  The Bibliography of American Travel: a Project. In the Papers of the Bibliographical Society of America XXII (1928), 52-59.  Period covered is from 1600 to 1900.

——  Travel and Description, 1765-1865. List of County Histories, biographies, etc.  Springfield, 1914.

CAMPBELL, F.  Index-Catalogue of Bibliographical Works (chiefly in the English Language), relating to India. A Study in Bibliography. 8vo.  London, 1897.

——  Index-Catalogue of Indian Official Publications in the British Museum Library Arranged in three parts. With a short Introduction. Together with Part IV (Accessions No. I, 30th November, 1899). In one vol. 4to.  London, 1900.

CAMBRIDGE HISTORY OF AMERICAN LITERATURE. Edited by W. P. Trent (and others). 4 vols. New York, 1917-1921. See for bibliographies to chs. 1, bk. I, and 1, bk. II, of vol. I. The first covers the period 1583-1763 and the second the period 1763-1846. Both lists are of generous proportions and testify to painstaking scholarly research in the field of Americana.

CAMBRIDGE HISTORY OF ENGLISH LITERATURE. Edited by A. W. Ward and A. R. Waller. 14 vols. New York, 1907-1917. See for bibliographies to chs. III, IV, and V of vol. IV.

Catalogue Général des Livres imprimés de la Bibliothèque Nationale. 137 vols. Paris, 1897-1936. (In progress.)

Catalogue of the Library of the Honourable East India Company. 2 vols. 8vo. London, 1845-1851.

Catalogue of the Printed Books in the Library of the University of Edinburgh. 3 vols. Fol. Edinburgh, 1918-1923.

CHARTON, E. For bibliographies of travels see his *Tour du Monde* under ·1861-1883, COLLECTIONS, App. II.

CHAVANNE, JOSEF (Dr.), KARPF, ALOIS (Dr.), and RITTER, FRANZ. Die Literatur über die Polar-Regionem der Erde. Published by the Royal Geographical Society of Vienna. Vienna, 1878.

> A topical and geographic bibliography of the vast stores of Polar Literature. This attempt at a complete compilation contains 6,617 titles. It includes circumnavigations and general works of travel. However, it is full of inaccuracies and needs to be used with caution.

CHURCH, E. DWIGHT. Catalogue of Books relating to the Discovery and Early History of North and South America. Compiled and Annotated by George Watson Cole. 5 vols. New York, 1907-09.

CHURCH, LESLIE F. Oglethorpe: A Study of Philanthropy in England and Georgia. London, 1932.

> This work contains a good list of authorities, original and secondary, on the founding of the colony of Georgia

CLAVEL, ROBERT (Bookseller). The General Catalogue of Books printed in England since the Dreadful Fire of London, 1666, to the End of Trinity Term, 1674. Together with the Titles of all Publick and Private Acts of Parliament: . . . With a General Account of the Names of all the Books of Law, Navigation, Musick, etc. . . . Fol. London, 1675.

This catalogue is arranged according to subjects under twenty headings, with indexes of authors.—Sotheran.

CLEMENTS, W. L. .Library of Americana at the University of Michigan, Ann Arbor, The University. 1923.

COLLIER, J. PAYNE. A Bibliographical and Critical Account of the Rarest Books in the English Language, alphabetically arranged, which during the last fifty years have come under the observation of J. P. Collier. 2 vols. 8vo. London, 1865.

COLLINS, ANTONY. Bibliotheca Antony Collins; or, a Complete Catalogue of the Library of Antony Collins: Containing a Collection of Several Thousand Volumes in Greek, Latin, English, French and Spanish in Divinity, History, Antiquity, Philology, Literature, Voyages, etc., which will be sold. By Thomas Ballard. 8vo. London, 1736-1807.

COOK, JAMES (Captain). Bibliography of Captain James Cook, R.N., F.R.S., Navigator. Comprising the Collections in the Mitchell Library and General Reference Library; the private Collections of William Dixson, Esq., and J. A. Ferguson, Esq., and Items of Special interest in the National Library, Canberra: the Australasian Pioneers' Club, Sydney; and in the Collection of the Kurnell Trust. Published by the Public Library of New South Wales, Sydney, Australia. 8vo. 1928.

This most comprehensive bibliography includes the various accounts of Cook's voyages, translations, articles in periodical literature, portraits, etc., in fact, every conceivable kind of reference to this navigator and his associates. It has been of inestimable service to this present bibliography.

CORDIER, HENRI. Bibliotheca Indosinica. Dictionnaire Bibliographique des Ouvrages relatifs à la Peninsule Indochinoise. 4 vols. 8vo. Paris, 1912-15.

—— Bibliotheca Japonica: Dictionnaire bibliographique des ouvrages relatifs à l'Empire Japonais rangés par ordre chronologique jusqu'à 1870 suivi d'un appendice renfermant la liste alphabétique des principaux ouvrages parus de 1870 à 1912. Paris, 1912.

—— Bibliotheca Sinica: Dictionnaire bibliographique des ouvrages relatifs à l'Empire Chinois. 4 vols. 2nd edit. Paris, 1904-08.

> This has also been printed with Supplements I-IV, making 12 parts altogether. 8vo. Paris, 1904-1912.

—— L'Imprimerie Sino-Européenne en Chine. Bibliographie des Ouvrages publiés en Chine par les Européens au XVII et au XVIII Siècle. 8vo. Paris, 1901.

COURTNEY, W. P. A Register of National Bibliography, with a Selection of the Chief Bibliographical Books and Articles printed in other Countries. 2 vols. 8vo. London, 1905.

COWAN, ROBERT ERNEST, and GRANNISS, ROBERT. A Bibliography of the History of California 1510-1930. 2 vols. 4to. Revised edition. San Francisco, 1933.

> The first edition of this bibliography, published in 1914, was immediately recognized as a standard reference book for collectors and students in the field of Pacific Coast history. The text of this edition has been completely revised, and many hundreds of new titles are now included. The greatest care has been exercised by the compilers to ensure not only the accuracy of the descriptions of the more than four thousand items included, but to render the information quickly and easily accessible.—Bookseller's Note. Despite the care exercised omissions have been found as has been pointed out by Philip Brooks in the *New York Times Book Review*, Sept. 2, 1935.

CUNDALL, F. (Editor). Bibliography of the West Indies (excluding Jamaica). 8vo. Kingston, Jamaica, 1909.

> Later editions in 1915 and 1919. While noncritical this work is very useful.— Davies, *Bibliography of British History*.

DALL, W. H., and BAKER, MARCUS. Pacific Coast Pilot, Alaska, vol. I. U.S. Coast and Geodetic Survey. Washington, D.C., 1879.

> This comprises 3,832 titles and sub-titles in eleven languages.

DAVIES, GODFREY. Bibliography of the Stuart Period. Edited by Professor Godfrey Davies. Under Auspices of the American Historical Association and the Royal Historical Society. Oxford, 1928.

> See Conyers Read below.

DUNBAR, SEYMOUR. For a bibliography of American items see his *A History of Travel in America,* under GENERAL REFERENCE.

EDDY, WILLIAM A. For a bibliography of fictitious voyages and related matter see his *Gulliver's Travels,* under GENERAL REFERENCE.

EINSTEIN, LEWIS. For a bibliography of travellers in the Renaissance period see his *Italian Renaissance in England,* under GENERAL REFERENCE.

EVANS, C. American Bibliography. A chronological Dictionary of all Books, Pamphlets, and periodical publications printed in the United States of America from . . . 1639 to 1820. 12 vols. 4to. Chicago, 1903-1934. (In progress.)

FARINELLI, ARTURO. Viages por España y Portugal desde la edad media hasta el siglo XX, divagaciones bibliograficas. Madrid, 1920-21.

> "Cette riche collection de notes accroît largement surtout pour le moyen âge, la 'Bibliographie des voyages en Espagne et Portugal' le M. Foulché-Delbosc; les pp. 29-80 sont consacrées au moyen âge, et surtout au xv siècle, elles contiennant le nombreuses indications sur les pêlerinages à Saint-Jacques-de-Compostelle et sur les voyages, souvent incertains, des troubadours en Espagne." *Romania,* vol. 47, p. 464. Paris, 1921.

FIELD, THOMAS W. Catalogue of the Library belonging to Mr. Thomas W. Field, including an unrivalled Collection of Books, relating to the American Indians, Collections of Historical Societies and American History and Biography. 2 parts. 4to. New York, 1875.

—— An Essay towards an Indian Bibliography. A Catalogue of Books relating to the American Indians with bibliographical and historical notes. 8vo. New York, 1873.

> For the collector of works on the American Indians this is a valuable reference book.

FORBES, HARRIETTE M. For a descriptive catalogue of New England diaries, etc., see under GENERAL REFERENCE.

FORD, P. L. Check-list of the Bibliographies, Catalogues, Reference-lists, and Lists of Authorities of American Books and Subjects. 4to. Brooklyn, 1889.

FORDHAM, SIR HERBERT G. Studies in Carto-Bibliography, British and French, and in the Bibliography of Itineraries and Road Books. 8vo. Oxford, 1914.

FOSBROKE, T. D. Encyclopedia of Antiquities, 2 vols. Foreign Topography, 3 vols. Plates. London, 1825-28.

FOULCHE-DELBOSC, R. Bibliographie des voyages en Espagne et Portugal. 8vo. Paris, 1896.

> This is a strictly descriptive bibliography of original voyages and descriptions, with the various editions and translations into other languages, ranging from the third century to date. 858 different items are listed. This work has been freely drawn upon by the present editor.

GAGNON, PHILEAS. Essai de Bibliographie Canadienne, Inventaire d'une Bibliothèque comprenant Imprimés, Manuscripts, Estampes, etc., relatifs à l'Histoire du Canada et des pays adjacens, avec des Notes Bibliographiques. Numerous facsimiles of rare title-pages, etc. 8vo. Quebec, 1895.

GARRAUX, A. L. Bibliographie Brésilienne. Catalogue des Ouvrages Français & Latins Relatifs au Brésil 1500-1898. 8vo. Paris, 1898.

GAY, RENE. Bibliographie des ouvrages relatifs à l'Afrique et à l'Arabie. Catalogue méthodique de tous les ouvrages français, et des principaux en langues étrangeres de la Géographie, du Commerce, des Lettres et des Arts de l'Afrique et de l'Arabie. 8vo. San Remo, 1875.

A General Catalogue of Books, printed in Britain and Published in London, from 1700 to 1778. 8vo. London, 1779.

GORDON-DUFF, E. Fifteenth Century English Books: a Bibliography of Books and Documents printed in England, and of Books for the English Market printed Abroad, with 53 facsimiles. 4to. Oxford, 1917.

GOSSE, PHILIP. My Pirate Library. London, 1926.

> A bibliographical list (selected) of books by and of pirates. It contains a number of references to voyages and expeditions.

GREELY, A. W. (Major-General). For bibliographies of Arctic voyages see his *Handbook of Polar Discoveries,* under GENERAL REFERENCE.

GRIFFIN, APPLETON P. C. A Bibliography of American Historical Societies (United States and Canada to 1905). 8vo. Amer. Hist. Assoc. Reprints. 2nd edit. Washington, 1907.

—— A List of Books relating to Hawaii. U. S. Library of Congress, Washington. 1898.

—— A List of Books (with references to periodicals) on the Philippine Islands in the Library of Congress. . . . With chronological list of maps in the Library of Congress by P. Lee Phillips. Washington, 1903.

HAKLUYT SOCIETY PUBLICATIONS. For a description of this series see under GENERAL REFERENCE. To each volume is usually appended a bibliography relating to its subject matter. For some more comprehensive lists see below:

> Ser. I., vol. 10, 1851: Bibliographical account of early travels to Russia beginning with Ohthere.
>
> Ser. I, vol. 59, 1878: Enumeration of works on the art of navigation.
>
> Ser. II, vol. 22, 1907: Bibliography of Peru, 1526-1907.
>
> Ser. II, vol. 23, 1908: Bibliography of Mexico.
>
> Reproductions of many famous old maps are bound up with various volumes. For a list see the "Prospectus," 1934.

HALKETT, SAMUEL, and LAING, JOHN. See their *Dictionary of the Anonymous and Pseudonymous Literature of Great Britain,* under GENERAL REFERENCE, for lists of books arranged alphabetically.

HARRISSE, HENRY. Bibliotheca Americana vetistussima. A description of works relating to America published between the years 1492 and 1551. 2 vols. 8vo. New York, 1866-1872.

> This important bibliography is indispensable to every collector of Americana. It gives a precise and detailed description of all the works in all languages printed before 1551, which treat of America. See also Harrisse under GENERAL REFERENCE.

HAWKINS, SIR JOHN. For a good bibliography of Hawkins see Williamson, J. A., *Sir John Hawkins, the Times and the Man.* Oxford, 1927.

HERMANNSSON, HALLDOR. Catalogue of the Icelandic Collection bequeathed by Willard Fiske to Cornell University Library. 2 vols. 4to. Ithaca, N. Y., 1914-1927.

> This collection comprises, as Mr. Fiske expressed it, "all the annals, travels, natural histories, government documents, ecclesiastical writings, biographies, and bibliographies, which can, in any way, throw light on the history, topography, indigenous products, commerce, language, and letters of Iceland," quoted by Mr. Hermannsson. Vol. I contains all the editions and translations of Old Icelandic and Old Norse texts so far as these were obtainable, with histories, commentaries, on literature, manners, customs, of Scandinavian peoples in early times, etc., together with modern Icelandic literature down to 1912. Vol. II is given up in the main to literature, etc., from 1912 on.

—— The Northmen in America (928 c. to 1500). A Contribution to Bibliography of the subject. Vol. II of *Islandica.* 8vo. Ithaca, N. Y., 1909.

HISPANIQUE AMERICAN BIBLIOGRAPHY. Including collective Biographies, Histories of Literature and Selected General Works. Compiled by Cecil K. Jones, with critical Notes of Sources by José Toribio Medina, translated by the Compiler. *Hispanic American Historical Review.* Baltimore, 1922.

HOARE, SIR R. C. A Catalogue of Books (in Stourhead Library) relating to the History and Topography of Italy, collected during the years 1786, 1787, 1788, 1789, 1790. 8vo. London, 1812.

HOCKEN, T. M. A Bibliography of the Literature Relating to New Zealand. Wellington, N. Z., 1909.

HOMER, A. Bibliotheca Americana; or, a Chronological Catalogue of the most curious and interesting Books, Pamphlets, State Papers, etc., upon the subject of North and South America, from the earliest period to the present, in print and manuscript. 4to. London, 1789.

> Compiled as the result of research in public and private libraries, such as the British Museum, the White Kennett Collection, etc. Reviews, such as the *Monthly Review,* were also consulted for material.—Quaritch.

HOWARD, CLARE. For a selected bibliography of travel in the Renaissance period see his *English Travellers of the Renaissance,* under GENERAL REFERENCE.

IBRAHIM-HILMY (H. H. Prince).   The Literature of Egypt and the
Soudan, from the earliest Times to the Year 1885 Inclusive. A Bibliography. 2 vols. 4to.   London.   1886.

> Cited in this present bibliography.

JACKSON, JAMES.   Cartographie et bibliographie relatives à Cook.
Société de Géographie.   Paris, 1879.

—— Liste provisoire de bibliographies géographiques speciales. Société
de Géographie.   Paris, 1881.

> This work and Stein's are the two principal bibliographies of geographical
> bibliographies.—Quoted.

KENNETT, WHITE (Bishop of Peterborough).   For an early bibliography of Americana see his *Bibliothecae Americanae Primordia,* under
1713, NORTH AMERICA.

> It is devoted particularly to the English colonies and especially to New
> England.—From Maggs, No. 465.

LA MARTINIERE, H. D.   Essai de bibliographie marocaine, suivi d'une
cartographie générale du même pays (1884-1886). 8vo.   Paris, 1889.

LANSON, GUSTAVE.   Manuel Bibliographique de la Littérature Française Modern. XVI, XVII, XVIII et XIX Siècles.   Nouvelle édition
revue et augmentée. 2 vols. 8vo.   Paris.

LASOR A VAREA, ALPHONSUS.   Universus Terrarum Orbis scriptor-
um calamo delineatus, hoc est auctorum fere omnium, qui de Europae,
Asiae, Africae et Americae Regnis, Provinciis, Populis, Civitatibus . . .
quovis tempore et qualibet lingua scripserunt, cum anno, loco, et forma
editionis eorum uberrimus elenchus.   Several hundred copperplate engravings and woodcuts of cities, fortresses, maps, temples, costumes,
etc. 2 vols. Fol.   Patavii, 1713.

> This very curious and laborious work contains, under the heading of the dif-
> ferent countries, a list of books relating to them, and we thus find under America
> the earliest attempt at an American bibliography, which, imperfect as it is, is
> nevertheless of great curiosity and interest. A great number of titles of old Eng-
> lish topographical tracts are also included, which one might look long for else-
> where. It is altogether a most remarkable book to have been printed at Padua
> at the beginning of the 18th century.—Thorp.

LECLERC, C. Bibliotheca Americana. Catalogue raisonné d'une très-précieuse collection de livres anciens et modernes sur l'Amérique et les Philippines, classés par ordre alphabétique de noms d'auteurs. Bibliographical and critical notes. Paris, 1867.

A second such "catalogue raisonné" and supplements appeared, Paris, 1878-1887. See below.
This work has been displaced by the *Bibliotheca Americana et Philippina*, nine parts, published by Maggs Bros., London.

—— Bibliotheca Americana. Histoire, géographie, voyages, archéologie et linguistique des deux Amériques, et des îles Philippines. Paris, 1878.

1st Supplement, Paris, 1881; 2nd Supplement, Paris, 1887.

LIMA FELNER, JOSE DE (and Others). Collecao de Monumentos ineditos para a historia das Conquista dos Portuguezes en Africa, Asia e America, publicados pela Academia Real das Sciencias de Lisboa, sobra direcao de Rodrigo Jose de Lima Felner, Raymundo Antonio de Bulhao Pato e Henrique Lopes de Mondonca. 21 vols. 4to. Lisbon, 1858-1915.

An important publication of the Lisbon Royal Academy of Sciences.

LORIN, HENRI (General Editor). Bibliographie Géographique de l'Egypte. Publiée sous la Direction de M. Henri Lorin. Tome I. Géographie Physique et Géographie Humaine. Par Mlle. Henriette Agrel, MM. Georges Hug, Jean Lozach et Réné Morin. Tome II. Géographie Historique. 8vo. Paris, 1928-29.

LOWERY, WOODURY. The Lowery Collection: a Descriptive List of the Maps of the Spanish Possessions within the Present Limits of the United States, 1502-1820, edited, with Notes, by P. L. Phillips. Portrait. 8vo. Washington, D. C., 1912.

See Lowery under GENERAL REFERENCE.

LOWNDES, WILLIAM THOMAS. Bibliographer's Manual of English Literature, containing an account of Rare, Curious and Useful Books, published in or relating to Great Britain and Ireland, from the Invention of Printing, with Bibliographical and Critical Notices, Collations, etc. New edition, revised, corrected and enlarged, by Henry G. Bohn. 11 vols. 8vo. London, 1857-1865.

The first edition of this much-quoted bibliography appeared in 1834.

LUKACH, H. C.   A Bibliography of Sierra Leone, with an Introductory Essay on the Origin, Character and Peoples of the Colony.   8vo.   Oxford, 1910.

> Another edition, London, 1916.  The name also appears as Luke.

MANWARING, G. E.   A Bibliography of British Naval History: a Biographical and Historical Guide to printed and manuscript sources.   8vo. London, 1929.

MAUNSELL, ANDREW.   The first part of the Catalogue of English printed Bookes: which concerneth such matters of diuinitie as haue ben either written in our owne Tongue, etc.   The seconde parte, which concerneth the sciences Mathematicall, as Arithmetick, . . . and Nauigation.   London, 1595.

> Cited in Hearne III, 112, 113.  See Hearne under GENERAL REFERENCE.

MAXWELL, CONSTANTIA.   For a selected bibliography of English travellers in France see her *The English Traveller in France,* under GENERAL REFERENCE.

McCOY, JAMES.   Jesuit Relations of Canada, 1632-1673.   A Bibliography.   With an Introduction by L. C. Wroth.   Portrait and facsimiles of 65 title-pages.   8vo.   Paris, 1936.

> In this work, which is announced as being published shortly, the 41 separate Relations are fully described, each one consisting of several editions and variants, to make a total of 132 different items. . . . At the end of the book is a complete synoptic table, summing up the editions and variants. The edition consists of 350 copies, . . .—Bookseller's Note.

MEAD, WILLIAM E.   For a bibliography of travels in France, Italy and Germany, see his *The Grand Tour in the Eighteenth Century,* under GENERAL REFERENCE.

MEDINA, J. T.   Bibliografia Española de las Islas Filipinas (1523-1810). 8vo.   Santiago de Chile, 1898.

> An indispensable bibliography of Spanish books on the Philippines.—Quoted.

—— Biblioteca Hispano-Americana (1493-1810).   7 vols. 8vo.   Santiago de Chile, 1898-1907.

> This forms an indispensable adjunct to Sabin, as it contains full collations and most important historical and bibliographical notes to the items described. It contains no less than 8,481 bibliographical descriptions of America.—From Maggs, No. 442.

—— Biblioteca Hispano-Chilena. 1523-1817. With illus. 3 vols. 8vo. Santiago de Chile, 1897.

MENDELSSOHN, S. South African Bibliography, being the Catalogue Raisonné of the Mendelssohn Library of Works relating to South Africa, including the full Titles of the Books, with synoptical, biographical, critical and bibliographical notes on the Volumes and their Authors, also a complete list of the British Parliamentary Blue-Books on South Africa, a Cartography of South Africa, etc., with a descriptive introduction by I. D. Colvin. 26 full-page illus. 2 vols. 8vo. London, 1910.

MORGAN, WILLIAM THOMAS. Bibliography of British History (1700-1715) with special Reference to the Reign of Queen Anne. Vol. I, 1700-1707. Indiana University Press. Bloomington, Ind., 1935.

MORRISON COLLECTION. Catalogue of the Asiatic Library of Dr. G. E. Morrison (now a part of the Oriental Library, Tokyo, Japan). 2 vols. 4to. London, 1924.

> The above catalogue records the result of an effort, sustained during more than twenty years, to form a comprehensive collection of books, papers, pamphlets, prints, and engravings dealing with the Chinese at home and abroad and with China and her Dependencies past and present in every subject and in every European language.—Bookseller's Note.

MOSES, BERNARD. For a long bibliography of Spanish-American books see his *Spanish Colonial Literature in South America,* under GENERAL REFERENCE.

MULLER, FREDERICK. Catalogue of books, maps, plates on America, and of a remarkable collection of early voyages. Essay of a Dutch-American Bibliography. 3 facsimiles. 8vo. Amsterdam, 1872.

MONOGHAN, FRANK. French Travellers in the United States, 1765-1932. Reprinted by New York Public Library with additions and revisions from several numbers of 1932 Bulletin. New York, 1933.

> Utilized for this bibliography.

NACHOD, O. Bibliography of Japan. 1906-1926. 2 vols. 8vo. London, 1928.

> This important work contains full descriptions of all Books, Pamphlets, Articles and Maps, dealing with Japan, in European Languages, published since Wenckstern's Bibliography of Japan.—Heffer and Sons.

—— Bibliographie von Japan, 1927-29. 8vo. London, 1931.

> This volume is a continuation of Nachod's Bibliography of Japan 1906-1926. Only a German edition of this volume is being published. The former two volumes can be had in English and German.—Heffer and Sons.

NAVARRETE, MARTIN FERNANDEZ DE. Biblioteca Maritima Española. 2 vols. 8vo. Madrid, 1851.

> A valuable and important bibliography, giving all Spanish works dealing with the sea, and with voyages and sea commerce of Spain, arranged under their various authors, and containing important biographical details concerning their authors. A work of especial importance with regard to America, the Philippines, and the East.—Maggs, No. 521.

NEVINS, ALLAN. For a bibliography of English travels in the United States see his *American Social History as Recorded by British Travellers,* under GENERAL REFERENCE.

NEW YORK PUBLIC LIBRARY. Catalogue of the De Bry Collection of Voyages. New York, 1904.

—— List of Works in the New York Public Library Relating to Arabia and the Arabs, Arabic Philosophy, Science and Literature, in Bulletin, vol. 15. Also published separately. New York, 1911.

—— List of Works in the New York Public Library Relating to Persia, in Bulletin, vol. 19. New York, 1915.

—— List of Works in the New York Public Library Relating to the Philippine Islands, in Bulletin, vol. 4, no. 1. New York, 1900.

—— List of Works in the New York Public Library relating to the West Indies, in Bulletin, vol. 16. New York, 1912.

NORTHUP, CLARK SUTHERLAND (Professor). A Register of Bibliographies of the English Language and Literature. With Contributions by Joseph Q. Adams and Andrew Keogh. 8vo. Cornell Studies in English. New Haven, 1925.

> See the section on Travel, pp. 392-395.

NOUVION, VICTOR DE. Extraits des auteurs et voyageurs qui ont écrits sur la Guyane, suivis du Catalogue bibliographique de la Guynae (Guyane?). 8vo. Paris, 1844.

PAGES, LEON.  Bibliographie Japonaise ou Catalogue des Ouvrages relatifs au Japon qui ont été publiés depuis le XVe siècle jusqu'à nos jours.  4to.  Paris, 1859.

> Reprinted, Paris, 1927.

PARKS, GEORGE BRUNER.  For a bibliography of Hakluyt's publications, and Tudor works on travel and geography see his *Richard Hakluyt and the English Voyages,* under GENERAL REFERENCE.

> This present bibliography has drawn freely upon these lists.

PENN, WILLIAM.  Sale Catalogue of an Important Collection of Books, MSS., Maps, Charts, and Engravings, including many articles of the highest historical interest . . . from the Libraries of Wm. Penn, founder of Pennsylvania, and of his descendants; to which are added, from other collections, rare early voyages and travels, books on America, East and West Indies, etc., sold by Puttick and Simpson, 29th Feb., 1872.  8vo.  London, 1872.

PETHERICK, EDWARD A.  Bibliography of Australia.  In "The Torch and Colonial Book Seller."  3 vols.  8vo.  London, 1887-1892.

—— Catalogue of the York Gate Library.  An Index to the Literature of Geography.  London, 1881.

PFANDI, LUDWIG.  Ein Beitrag zur Reiseliteratur über Spanien, aus einer Handschrift der Münschener Hof- und Staats, Bibliothek.  An Extract from the *Revue Hispanique,* vol. XXIII, 1910.  New York.

PHILLIPS, P. L.  List of Maps of America in the Library of Congress, preceded by a list of works relating to Cartography.  Washington, D.C., 1901.

PINKERTON, JOHN.  Collection of Voyages and Travels.  See vol. XVII for a very extensive bibliography of voyages and travels, one of the completest ever compiled, but unfortunately so full of mistakes that it needs to be constantly checked.  For this work see under 1808-1813, COLLECTIONS, ADD. I.

PLYMPTON, C. W.  Select Bibliography on Travel in North America.  In New York State Library Bulletin, May, 1897.  Pp. 35-60.  New York, 1897.

POLLARD, A. W., and REDGRAVE, G. R. (and Others). A Short-Title Catalogue of Books printed in England, Scotland, and Ireland, and of English Books printed abroad, 1475-1640, compiled by A. W. Pollard and G. R. Redgrave (and many others). 4to. Bibliographical Society. London, 1926.

    This work, along with the Bible and the Family Physician, should be on every library table. Few are the students that have escaped the necessity of consulting it for the period it covers.—It contains entries of over 26,000 different books in their various editions, each of which is numbered and arranged in alphabetical order of Author's name or heading as in the British Museum Catalogue; but with some modifications which make for greater clarity, and a chronological order of editions. Anonymous books which are entered under the Author's name when known are given a cross-reference. It must be remembered that the catalogue is not a bibliography of books known or believed to have been produced; it is a register of books of which copies have been traced in stated libraries and collections. So far as it can be tested by comparison with the Stationers' Register, however, it shows that the books, other than ballads and broadsides, which have totally disappeared, are surprisingly few.—Quoted from Bookseller's Note.

PONTON, THOMAS. Catalogue of the very choice and Valuable Library formed by the late Thomas Ponton, Esq., F.S.A., Comprising a very valuable Collection of Works on English Topography, History, Biography, Voyages and Travels, Sold by Auction by Farebrother, Clarke and Co. . . . April 2, 1873. 4to. London, 1873.

PUTTICK and SIMPSON. Catalogue of a Valuable Collection of Books Wholly Relating to the History and Literature of America and the Indies. In two parts. To be sold by Auction on Wednesday, March 20, 1861, and Three Following Days. London, 1860.

    An abridgement of the titles published in Henry Stevens' *American Nuggets*, together with the collations made by Stevens and with some corrections and additions. Frequently cited in this bibliography.

READ, CONYERS. Bibliography of British History. Tudor Period. Edited by Conyers Read. A Companion volume to the one of the Stuart Period. Oxford, 1933.

    This covers the period beginning with 1483. This volume, like that of the Stuart period, contains bibliographies of voyages, etc. See Davies above.

RICH, OBIDIAH. Bibliotheca Americana Nova. A Catalogue of Books relating to America, in various languages, including Voyages to the Pacific and round the World, and Collections of Voyages and Travels. 2 vols. 8vo. London, 1835-1846.

    Vol. I. 1701-1800 and supplement; vol. II. 1801-1844 and Catalogue of Duplicates for sale.

—— Catalogue of Books relating principally to America. 8vo. London, 1832.

> This contains Pigafetta and Magellan material.—Robinson.

ROBERTSON, JAMES ALEXANDER. Bibliography of the Philippine Islands printed and manuscript. Preceded by a Descriptive Account of the most important Archives and Collections containing Philippina. Cleveland, 1908.

> See Blair and Robertson, under GENERAL REFERENCE.

RODRIGUES, J. C. Catalogo Annotado dos livros sobre o Brasil e de alguna Autographos e Manuscrits pertencientes a J. C. Rodrigues, Socio Correspondent da Academia Real das Sciencias de Lisboa. 8vo. Rio de Janeiro, 1907.

> This volume is Part I (all published) of a famous collection of books on Brazil, and comprises works on the Discovery of America, from 1492 to 1822. There are full and interesting annotations, with valuable references to other bibliographies on the subject.—Maggs, No. 546.

RÖHRICHT, REINHOLD. Bibliotheca geographica Palaestinae. From 333 A.D. to 1878. Berlin, 1890.

RUSSIA. Correcturbogen des Katalog der Russica in der Kaiserlichen öffentlichen Bibliothek zu St. Petersburg (Feuilles d'épreuve du Catalogue des Russica de la Bibliothèque de St. Petersburg). 4to. St. Petersburg, 1860.

> Title page and preface in Russian, German and French. This important work contains more than 16,000 titles of books not written in Russian but relating to the country. It was lithographed at the expense of the Imperial Library and only a few copies printed for presents.—Booksellers' Note.

SABIN, JOSEPH. A Dictionary of Books relating to America from its Discovery to the Present Time. 28 vols. New York, 1868-1936.

> This work was begun by Sabin, continued by Wilberforce Eames, and completed by R. W. G. Vail, for the Bibliographical Society of America. It is the most comprehensive collection of American items in existence. It lists the various editions; notes their differences, and describes the contents of works cited. Needless to say, the sections of this present bibliography dealing with the Americas are under great obligation to it.

SALES CATALOGUES. Second-hand Book Catalogues have naturally furnished a very large number of titles, often accompanied with useful annotations. Care needs to be exercised, however, against misprints

in names and dates. Special acknowledgment for such assistance is
made to the following firms:

B. H. Blackwell, Ltd.  Oxford.

Henry Cork.  London.

P. C. Cuttelle.  London.

Dauber & Pine Bookshop, Inc.  New York.

P. J. & A. E. Dobell.  London.

William Dunlop.  Edinburgh.

Francis Edwards.  London.

William Elly.  Liverpool.

Charles P. Everitt.  New York.

Galloway & Porter.  Cambridge.

J. Gamber, Librairie Universitaire.  Paris.

William George's Sons.  Bristol.

John Grant.  Edinburgh.

Bernard Halliday.  Leicester.

George Harding's Bookshop.  London.

W. Heffer & Sons, Ltd.  Cambridge.

> These catalogues have been particularly rich in oriental travel lit-
> erature.

Karl W. Hiersemann.  Leipzig.

E. M. Lawson & Co.  Birmingham.

Lowe Bros., Ltd.  Birmingham.

Maggs Bros.  London.

> The editor's most grateful thanks are due to this firm, which so
> generously supplied back numbers of their catalogues as well as current
> publications relating to voyages and travels. The courtesy of this firm
> is as princely as is the format of the publications which continuously
> issue from their press, bearing evidence of the most scholarly research.
> Fortunate indeed is the possessor of these volumes, without whose help
> this bibliography would have been but a shadow of itself.

Museum Bookstore.  London.

Martinus Nijhoff.  Amsterdam.

Bernard Quaritch, Ltd.  London.

> This firm may be classed among the aristocrats of book publishers
> and sellers, for the quality of its output, its painstaking scholarship,
> and its range of interest. This bibliography has helped itself generously
> to its researches.

William H. Robinson.  London.

> For beauty of typography and wealth of material, for helpful an-
> notations and rare finds, these catalogues are a joy to read and to
> possess.

Chas. J. Sawyer.  London.

Henry Sotheran. London.

The annotations in these catalogues have been freely utilized.

Surrey Bookshop. London.

Albert Sutton. Manchester.

Thomas Thorp. London.

SAWYER, C. J., and DARTON, J. H. English Books, 1475-1900: A Signpost for Collectors. 100 illus. Vol. I, Caxton to Johnson; vol. II, Gray to Kipling. 2 vols. 8vo. London, 1927.

SCHERMAN, L. VON (Editor). Oriental Bibliography. Comprising Bibliotheca Orientalis, a complete list of Books, Papers, Serials and Essays on the East, 8 vols., 1876-1883; Literatur-Blatt für Orientalische Philologie, 4 vols., 1883-1888; Orientalische Bibliographie (Begrundet von A. Muller), bearbeitet und herausgegeben von L. Scherman. 25 vols. 1888-1911. Together 37 vols. 8vo. Berlin (?), 1876-1911.

SCOTT, JOHN. A Bibliography of printed Documents and Books relating to the Darien Company. Revised by George P. Johnston. Edinburgh, 1904.

SEATON, ETHEL. For a bibliography of works referring to Scandinavia, both continental and English, see her *Literary Relations of England and Scandinavia in the Seventeenth Century*, under GENERAL REFERENCE.

SHAW, N. (Dr.). In the text prefixed to the *Royal Illustrated Atlas of Modern Geography* are comprehensive classified lists of 1. Collections and History of Voyages and Travels; 2. Voyages and Travels in Asia and in India. See Introduction to the Hakluyt Society volume, ser. I, vol. 65, 1881.

SILVA, INNOCENCIO F. DA. Diccionario Bibliographico Portuguez. With Supplement. 22 vols. 8vo. Lisbon, 1858-1914.

This is the only bibliography of all Portuguese books printed before 1914.—Quoted.

SMITH, CHARLES W. Pacific Northwest Americana. A Checklist of Books and Pamphlets relating to the History of the Pacific Northwest. 8vo. 2nd edit., revised and enlarged. New York, 1921.

SMITH, J. R.   Catalogue of a Valuable Collection of Books, Pamphlets, MSS., Maps, Engravings, etc., illustrating the History and Geography of North and South America and the West Indies. 8vo. London, 1865.

SPEARS, JOHN R.   For a short bibliography of general voyages see his *Master Mariners,* under GENERAL REFERENCE.

STEIN, HENRI.   Manuel de bibliographie générale.   Paris, 1897.

A critical selection of bibliographies on all subjects printed down to 1896.

STEINER, B. C.   A Bibliography of American Travel. In *Proceedings American Library Institute,* 84-85, 1916.   Chicago.

This is merely a prospectus.

STEVENS, HENRY.   Bibliotheca Americana, (1860).   See Puttick and Simpson above.

—— Bibliotheca Americana, or a Descriptive Account of my Collection of Rare Books Relating to America. 2 vols. 12mo. London, 1862.

This also bears the title *Historical Nuggets.* It appeared first in 1859.

—— Facsimiles of Manuscripts in European Archives relating to America, 1773-1783. With Descriptions, Editorial Notes, Collations, References, and Translations. 25 vols. Fol. London, 1889-1898.

The facsimiles include secret and confidential correspondence of the British Government with its political agents and spies, intercepted intelligence and other papers of the highest interest.—Quoted.

STILLWELL, MARGARET BINGHAM.   Incunabula and Americana, 1450-1800.   A Key to Bibliographical Study. 8vo. New York, 1931.

Contains Incunabula: the Printed Books of the Fifteenth Century; Identification and Collation; Bibliography of Reference Material; Americana: Preliminary Survey of Sources and Methods; The Century of Maritime Discovery, 1492-1600; Two Centuries of Colonial Growth, 1500-1700; Later Americana and the Revolutionary Period; Early Printing in America. Followed by eight chapters of Reference Sections.—Bookseller's Note.

STONEHILL, CHARLES A. (Jr.), BLACK, ANDREW, and STONEHILL, H. WINTHROP.   Anonyma and Pseudonyma. 4 vols. London, 1926-27.

STREATFIELD, J. FREMLYN. A Catalogue of Valuable Books and MSS.: comprising a portion of the library of J. Fremlyn Streatfield; a very choice collection of Americana; several most interesting autograph MSS. of Alfred Lord Tennyson, etc. Sold by Sotheby, 12th June, 1889. 8vo. London, 1889.

SYDNEY FREE PUBLIC LIBRARY. Australasian Bibliography: Catalogue of Books in the Free Public Library, Sydney, Relating to or Published in Australia. Sydney, 1893.

Australian exploration and geography are well illustrated here.

TAYLOR, E. G. H. For a bibliography of Tudor geographical works printed and in MS. see his *Tudor Geography,* under GENERAL REFERENCE.

TAYLOR, L. M. Catalogue of Books on China in the Essex Institute (Salem, Mass.). 8vo. London, 1926.

TERNAUX-COMPANS, HENRI. Bibliothèque Américain. Paris, 1837.

Its sole merit is that of having arranged in chronological order books in this field published in all languages up to 1700.—Medina, *Hispanic American Review.*

—— Bibliothèque Asiatique et Africaine, ou Catalogue des ouvrages relatifs à l'Asie et à l'Afrique qui ont paru depuis la découverte de l'imprimérie jusqu'en 1700. 8vo. Paris, 1841.

THOMAS, HENRY. English Translations of Portuguese Books before 1640. In *The Library,* 4th series, vol. VII, No. 1, June, 1926, pp. 1-30. London, 1927.

TYLER, MOSES COIT. For a bibliography of American Revolutionary writings see his *Literary History of the American Revolution,* under GENERAL REFERENCE.

WAGNER, HENRY. The Plains and Rockies: a Bibliography of Original Narratives of Travel and Adventure, 1800-1865. San Francisco, 1921.

—— The Spanish Southwest, 1542-1794. An Annotated Bibliography. 100 full size reproductions of title pages, etc. Berkeley, 1924.

> Only 100 copies printed. In it are described 177 separate works (apart from hundreds of different editions) relating to those parts of the United States which formerly formed part of the province of New Spain, such as Texas, New Mexico, and California, up to the year 1794.—Maggs, No. 465.

WARDENS, D. B. Bibliotheca Americo-Septentrionalis: being a choice selection of Books in various languages relating to the history, climate, geography, produce, population, agriculture, commerce, etc., of North America, from its first discovery to its present existing government; among which are many valuable and rare articles, together with all the important Official Documents published by the Authority of Congress. 8vo. Paris, 1820.

WATT, R. Bibliotheca Britannica; or a general Index to British and Foreign Literature. 4 vols. Edinburgh, 1824.

WEBB, ——. For Travels Lists see *Bulletin of the British Library of Political Science,* November 1921.

WEEKS, STEPHEN B. A Bibliography of the Historical Literature of North Carolina. 8vo. Cambridge, Mass., 1895.

WEGELIN, OSCAR. Books Relating to the History of Georgia in the Library of Wymberley Jones de Renne, of Wormslow, Isle of Hope, Chatham County, Georgia. Compiled and annotated by Oscar Wegelin. Wormslow, 1911.

WENCKSTERN, F. VON. Bibliography of the Japanese Empire, 1457-1906. A Classified List of all Books, Essays and Maps in European Languages, relating to Dai Nipon (Great Japan), published in Europe, America, and in the East, from 1859-1893 A.D. (VIth year of Ansei-XXVth of Meiji), to which is added a facsimile reprint of Leon Pages' Bibliographie Japonaise depuis le XVe siècle jusqu'à 1859. With the supplementary volume completing the entries to 1906, with a list of Swedish Literature on Japan by V. Palmgren. 2 vols. 8vo. London, 1895-1907.

> This work has been severely criticized (Cordier, *Bibliotheca Japonica,* p. v) and should be used with care. It is, none the less, the only large, topically arranged bibliography of Japan and for this reason may occasionally be more serviceable if less scholarly than Cordier.—J. K. Wright, *Aids to Geographical Research.*

WHEELER, HENRY ALBERT. A Short Catalogue of Books printed in England and English Books printed abroad before 1641 in the Library of Wadham College, Oxford, with Biographical Introduction by J. C. Squire. 8vo. London, 1920.

WICKERSHAM, JAMES. A Bibliography of Alaskan Literature, 1724-1924. Vol. I. Miscellaneous Publications of the Alaska Agricultural College and School of Mines. Containing the titles of all Histories, Travels, Voyages, Newspapers, Periodicals, etc., printed in English, Russian, German, French, Spanish, etc., Relating to, Descriptive of, or published in Russian America and Alaska. From 1724 to and including 1924. Cordova, Alaska, 1924.

WILSON, SIR ARNOLD T. A Bibliography of Persia. 8vo. London, 1930.

"In scope, this bibliography is general rather than specialised, and is concerned, firstly and mainly, with original works in European tongues having a direct bearing on Persia, its history, geography, archaeology, its people, and with the principal branches of knowledge so far as they deal with or refer to Persia; secondly, with standard translations in European languages, of original Persian books and writings; thirdly, and in a more limited degree, with bibliographies and writings on Persian literature, religions, etc. Beyond this last, Persian literature and works in the Persian language find no place or receive only incidental mention." —Preface.

WINSHIP, G. P. Cabot Bibliography, with an introductory Essay on the Careers of the Cabots. 8vo. New York, 1900.

This is based upon an independent examination of the Sources of Information. —Quoted.

WINSOR, JUSTIN. For bibliographies of American Travels, Voyages, and documents see his *The Narrative and Critical History of America,* under GENERAL REFERENCE.

WRIGHT, JOHN KIRTLAND. Aids to Geographical Research. Bibliographies and Periodicals. American Research Series No. 10. New York, 1923.

The author is Librarian of the American Geographical Society. "Neither a geographical bibliography nor a bibliography of geographical bibliographies, these notes are intended to furnish a clue to various bibliographical aids through the use of which the geographer may quickly and systematically gain access to printed materials. The first part of the book is devoted to the discussion of the means of finding geographical material in publications not avowedly and specifically geographical: general literature, government documents, yearbooks and doctoral dissertations, the publications of academies and learned societies, and the literature of sciences related to geography. The second part is devoted to the bibliographies of specifically geographical publications: general geographical bibliographies, both retrospective and current, and the bibliography of special geographical topics and regions. The third is devoted to the bibliography of maps, only the outstanding aids to the finding of maps being mentioned. . . . In conclusion there is a list of selected geographical periodicals and regional bibliographies."—From the Introduction. Of special service is the critical valuation liberally scattered throughout the work, which, together with the thoroughness of the lists, will save the student many hours of searching for himself.

—— For a bibliography of medieval travels see his *Geographical Lore at the Time of the Crusades,* under GENERAL REFERENCE.

# CORRIGENDA

Page 8, *for* SWINDRAGE, THEODORE, *read* SWAINE, CHARLES; likewise same name page 9.

Page 119, *for* HASKE *read* HUSKE.

Page 165 (under BRISSOT DE WARVILLE), *for* MONOGHAN *read* MONAGHAN; likewise in other instances.

Page 175 (under SCOTT), *place of printing* London.

Page 185 (under SEWELL), *for* 1878-1882 *read* 1876-1882.

Page 188 (under GLOVER), *for* Phi. Trans. *read* Phil. Trans.

Page 205, *to* ROCHEFORT *add* CHARLES DE.

Page 209, *for* MOQUET *read* MOCQUET.

Page 219 (under POOLE), *delete phrase* under West Europe.

Page 260, *to* PAGAN *add* BLAISE FRANCOIS DE.

Page 379 (under LOCKE), *add* 1st edit. 1722.

Page 410, *to* BOWLES *add* CARRINGTON.

Page 428, *to* DIROM *add* ALEXANDER.

Page 432, *for* 1601 *read* 1621.

Page 462, *to* ANDERSON *add* THOMAS.

Page 463, *to* INGLEFIELD *add* J. N.

Page 471, *delete item* HERBERT, THOMAS.

Page 479 (under QUARLL), *delete* This is the 7th edition.

Page 527, *for* WOOLACOTT *read* WOOLLACOTT.

Page 553 (under TAYLOR, E. G. H.), *for* his *read* her.

# INDEX OF PERSONAL NAMES

(Personal names when cited in the text in lieu of titles of collections are omitted in this index; when cited as authorities they are listed. As aids to identification names have frequently been expanded and the spelling normalized. Otherwise vagaries and variations in spelling are passed over in silence.)